T0248811

Computational Neuroscience: Modeling and Applications

Computational Neuroscience: Modeling and Applications

Edited by
Scott Carter

www.willfordpress.com

Published by Willford Press,
118-35 Queens Blvd., Suite 400,
Forest Hills, NY 11375, USA

ISBN: 978-1-68285-617-8

Cataloging-in-Publication Data

Computational neuroscience : modeling and applications / edited by Scott Carter.
    p. cm.
Includes bibliographical references and index.
ISBN 978-1-68285-617-8
1. Computational neuroscience. 2. Nervous system--Computer simulation.
3. Neurogenetics--Computer simulation. 4. Neural networks (Neurobiology).
5. Neural computers. 6. Computational biology. I. Carter, Scott.
QP357.5 .C66 2019
612.8--dc23

For information on all Willford Press publications
visit our website at www.willfordpress.com

Contents

Preface

Computational neuroscience is the branch of neuroscience that uses mathematical models, theoretical analysis and abstractions, to understand the development, structure and information-processing of the nervous system. It also attempts to understand the principles that govern the physiology and cognitive abilities of the nervous system. Computational neuroscience models help in the understanding of biological phenomena at different spatial-temporal scales. It covers all aspects of membrane currents, proteins, network oscillations, learning, memory, etc. Research in computational neuroscience delves into the concepts of consciousness and the processes of cognition, sensory processing, memory and axonal patterning and development. This book discusses the fundamentals as well as modern approaches of computational neuroscience. It covers all the important aspects of modeling and their applications. Different approaches, evaluations, methodologies and advanced studies have been included in this book. With state-of-the-art inputs by acclaimed experts of this field, this book targets students and researchers alike.

After months of intensive research and writing, this book is the end result of all who devoted their time and efforts in the initiation and progress of this book. It will surely be a source of reference in enhancing the required knowledge of the new developments in the area. During the course of developing this book, certain measures such as accuracy, authenticity and research focused analytical studies were given preference in order to produce a comprehensive book in the area of study.

This book would not have been possible without the efforts of the authors and the publisher. I extend my sincere thanks to them. Secondly, I express my gratitude to my family and well-wishers. And most importantly, I thank my students for constantly expressing their willingness and curiosity in enhancing their knowledge in the field, which encourages me to take up further research projects for the advancement of the area.

Editor

Epileptic Seizure Prediction Using CSP and LDA for Scalp EEG Signals

Turky N. Alotaiby,[1] Saleh A. Alshebeili,[2] Faisal M. Alotaibi,[1] and Saud R. Alrshoud[1]

[1]KACST, Riyadh, Saudi Arabia
[2]KACST-TIC in Radio Frequency and Photonics for the e-Society (RFTONICS), Electrical Engineering Department, King Saud University, Riyadh, Saudi Arabia

Correspondence should be addressed to Turky N. Alotaiby; totaiby@kacst.edu.sa

Academic Editor: Pedro Antonio Gutierrez

This paper presents a patient-specific epileptic seizure predication method relying on the common spatial pattern- (CSP-) based feature extraction of scalp electroencephalogram (sEEG) signals. Multichannel EEG signals are traced and segmented into overlapping segments for both preictal and interictal intervals. The features extracted using CSP are used for training a linear discriminant analysis classifier, which is then employed in the testing phase. A leave-one-out cross-validation strategy is adopted in the experiments. The experimental results for seizure prediction obtained from the records of 24 patients from the CHB-MIT database reveal that the proposed predictor can achieve an average sensitivity of 0.89, an average false prediction rate of 0.39, and an average prediction time of 68.71 minutes using a 120-minute prediction horizon.

1. Introduction

Epilepsy is a brain disorder characterized by excessive, infrequent, and synchronous discharge of a large number of neurons [1] and affects 1% of the world's population [2]. Epileptic seizure can be managed in two-thirds of the patients using prescription drugs, while another 8% can be cured using resected surgery. Seizures of about 25% of patients with epilepsy cannot be managed sufficiently by any available therapy [2, 3]. Therefore, the early anticipation of seizures could be very valuable for those patients, caregivers, or family members to save patients and others from possible hazards [4, 5]. An effective seizure prediction approach would improve the quality of patients' daily lives. Electroencephalogram (EEG) is the most often used brain disorders' diagnostic tool, specifically for epilepsy [6]. It is measuring the voltage fluctuations resulting from ionic current within the neurons of the brain through electrodes [7]. There are two types of EEGs: intracranial EEG (iEEG) and scalp EEG (sEEG). In iEEG, electrodes are placed directly on the exposed surface of

the brain to record the electrical signals. However, in sEEG, the electrical signals are collected with electrodes placed on the scalp area according to certain placement specifications, such as the International 10-20 System.

Seizure prediction is based on the hypothesis that there exists a transition state (preictal) between the interictal (normal state) and the ictal state (seizure). There are numbers of clinical evidences that support this hypothesis. These evidences include increases in cerebral blood flow [8, 9], cerebral oxygenation [10], cortical excitability [11], highly significant blood-oxygen-level-dependent signal on fMRI studies [12], and variations in heart rate [13, 14]. Accordingly, researchers have invested a great deal of effort over the last decades on attempting to predict epileptic seizures based on iEEG and sEEG signals, where the latter are more convenient to apply clinically. Around forty years ago, Viglione and his colleagues presented the first attempt for seizure prediction [15, 16]. After that, many researchers published their attempts to predict epileptic seizures suing different methods.

Several time-domain techniques have been reported in the literature for seizure prediction [17–22, 22–24, 24–39]. Transform methods [40–54], attractor state analysis [55], and neural mass models [56] have been used for EEG seizure prediction. A comprehensive review of the most recently developed seizure prediction methods can be found in [2, 57–59].

Common spatial pattern (CSP) is a feature extraction algorithm used in different applications, such as electromyography (EMG) signal separation [60], EEG signal analysis for motor imagery purposes [61, 62], and, more recently, seizure detection [63–65]. The objective of this paper is to develop a patient-specific CSP-based seizure prediction algorithm for sEEG signals. The extracted feature using the CSP will be fed to a linear classifier to classify the epoch as either a preictal or interictal segment. Note that the data segment preceding the seizure onset is called the preictal interval and ranges from a few seconds to several hours long [38, 47, 54]. The performance of the proposed predictor is compared with the random and Poisson predictors and with existing sEEG-based prediction methods [17, 18, 28, 41, 45, 47, 48, 54, 55]. The results show that the proposed prediction method could be of potential value for early warnings for epileptic patients and/or their caregivers.

The remainder of the paper is organized as follows. The CSP mathematical formulation is discussed in Section 2. The data collection and seizure prediction approach are presented in Section 3. Section 4 presents the prediction performance metrics. The experimental results and comparisons with other existing seizure prediction algorithms are provided in Section 5. Finally, Section 6 offers concluding remarks.

2. Common Spatial Pattern (CSP)

CSP is a statistical method that was introduced to the field of EEG analysis by Koles et al. [66, 67] and is used to extract spatial filters for discriminating between two classes of EEG signals. In this work, the CSP method is used to distinguish between two classes, preictal and interictal EEG activities, by constructing a projection matrix, W, that minimizes the variance for preictal activity and maximizes it for the other class. The following steps describe the mathematical formulation of the CSP approach [66, 67]:

(1) Calculate the normalized covariance matrix C for each data segment $D \in R^{N \times L}$

$$C = \frac{DD^T}{\text{trace}(DD^T)}, \tag{1}$$

where N is the number of channels, L is the number of samples, and T is the transpose operation.

(2) Perform an averaging process on the covariance matrices of each class ($i = 1, 2$) to find two discriminated covariance matrices, C_1 (preictal state) and C_2 (interictal state), and then find the composed covariance matrix C_c:

$$C_c = C_1 + C_2. \tag{2}$$

(3) Decompose the composed matrix C_c using singular value decomposition (SVD) to find the Eigenvalue matrix ψ and normalized Eigenvector matrix F_c:

$$C_c = F_c \psi F_c^T. \tag{3}$$

(4) Form a new matrix P:

$$P = \psi^{-1} F_c^T \tag{4}$$

to obtain the following two matrices:

$$\begin{aligned} S_1 &= P C_c P^T, \\ S_2 &= P C_c P^T. \end{aligned} \tag{5}$$

S_1 and S_2 share common eigenvectors. Hence, the sum of the corresponding Eigenvalues of the two matrices is always 1.

(5) Apply the SVD to the matrices S_1 and S_2 as follows:

$$\begin{aligned} S_1 &= U \Lambda_1 U^T, \\ S_2 &= U \Lambda_2 U^T. \end{aligned} \tag{6}$$

Note that $\Lambda_1 + \Lambda_2 = I$, where I is the identity matrix, U, and Λ represent the matrix of eigenvectors and the diagonal matrix of Eigenvalues, respectively. The Eigenvalues are then sorted in descending order; thus, the CSP projection matrix is formulated as $W = U^T P \in R^{N \times N}$.

3. Materials and Methods

3.1. Clinical Data. In this work, long-term continuous multichannel sEEG recordings of 24 patients from a publicly available dataset (Children's Hospital Boston [CHB-MIT] database [68]), which consists of sEEG recordings from pediatric subjects with intractable seizures, were used. Subjects were monitored for up to several days following withdrawal of antiseizure medication in order to characterize their seizures and assess their candidacy for surgical intervention. This data contains 987.85 hours, with 170 seizures. Each seizure onset is marked by an experienced electroencephalographer and corresponds to the onset of a rhythmic activity that is associated with a clinical seizure [11, 22, 26–32]. The data is multichannel in nature, with 23 or 18 channels for each patient obtained by sampling at a rate of 256 Hz. The International 10-20 System of EEG electrode positions and nomenclature was used for these recordings. A summary of this dataset is presented in Table 1. The data is segmented into one-hour-long records. Records that do not contain seizure activity are referred to as nonseizure records, and those that contain one or more seizures are referred to as seizure records.

3.2. Seizure Prediction Approach. The block diagram of the proposed seizure prediction methodology is depicted in Figure 1. It is comprised of two main stages: feature extraction and classification. In the feature extraction stage, the multichannel signal is segmented and the CSP is used to extract the training and testing features. In the classification stage, a trained classifier is used to classify the incoming segment as a preictal or interictal segment.

TABLE 1: Summary of utilized EEG data.

Patient number	Sex	Age	Number of hours	Number of Seizures	Number of channels	Average interictal interval
(1)	F	11	40.55	7	23	6.00
(2)	M	11	35.3	3	23	12.00
(3)	F	14	38	6 (7)*	23	6.33
(4)	M	22	155.9	4	23	39.50
(5)	F	7	39	5	23	7.80
(6)	F	1.5	66.7	10	23	6.80
(7)	F	14.5	68.1	3	23	23.33
(8)	M	3.5	20	5	23	4.00
(9)	F	10	67.8	4	23	17.50
(10)	M	3	50	7	23	7.14
(11)	F	12	34.8	2 (3)**	23	17.50
(12)	F	2	23.7	21 (40)**	23	1.09
(13)	F	3	33	11 (12)**	18	2.75
(14)	F	9	26	8	23	3.25
(15)	M	16	40	17 (20)**	23	2.00
(16)	F	7	19	9 (10)**	18	1.90
(17)	F	12	21	3	23	7.00
(18)	F	18	36	6	23	6.00
(19)	F	19	30	3	18	10.00
(20)	F	6	29	8	23	3.63
(21)	F	13	33	4	23	8.25
(22)	F	9	31	3	23	10.33
(23)	F	6	28	7	23	1.29
(24)	—	—	22	14 (16)**	23	0.75
Total			987.85	170 (198)		

*First seizure is not used since it is in the first hour and does not have enough preictal time. **Two seizures are combined when the second one is in the postseizure interval of the first one.

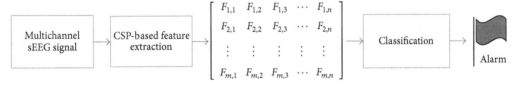

FIGURE 1: CSP-based patient-specific seizure predictor.

3.2.1. CSP-Based Features Extraction Stage.

First, the multichannel signal was segmented into overlapping epochs of length $L = 3$ seconds (this value for L was selected based on several trials). A sliding window was used for signal framing with an overlap of $L - 1$ seconds between two successive segments. In this work, we extracted preictal training features from data intervals of 3, 5, and 10 minutes. Similar intervals have been considered in [38, 51, 52]. Based on literature, it has been reported that there are electrophysiological changes, which might develop minutes to hours before the actual seizure onset [38, 47, 54]. Therefore, the preictal training data could be selected from any of the following options:

(i) Preictal-0: the preictal training interval ends right at the beginning of seizure onset.

(ii) Preictal-60: the preictal training interval ends 60 minutes before seizure onset.

(iii) Preictal-120: the preictal training interval ends 120 minutes before seizure onset.

Therefore, we used a sliding window of length 3 seconds to extract preictal features from four different preictal training intervals (3, 5, and 10 minutes), each of which could be located at three different distances with respect to seizure onset. Nonseizure hours were used for interictal training data.

The CSP algorithm was applied to each segment of size 23×768 (number of channels × number of samples) by computing $\mathbf{X}^T\mathbf{W}$, where $\mathbf{W}$ is a projection matrix of size 23×23. Following the approach of [69], the log of variance of each row of the resulting matrix was taken as a feature.

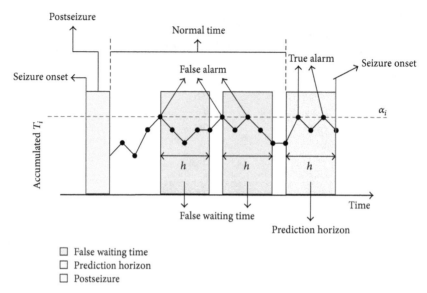

FIGURE 2: Example of sensitivity and specificity estimation.

3.2.2. Classification Stage.

3.2.2. Classification Stage. In the classification stage, a linear discriminant analysis (LDA) classifier [70] was trained with preictal and interictal feature vectors. We used random undersampling strategy to balance the number of preictal and interictal segments in the training set [71, 72]. In the testing phase, the trained classifier was tasked to classify any incoming epoch as a preictal or interictal state. The classifier results were binary "1" for the preictal state and zero otherwise. A seventh-order median filter was used to smooth the results. The prediction alarm was raised if $\sum T_i = \alpha_i$, where T_i is consecutive "1s" with a moving window of 1 second, α_i is a patient-dependent threshold, and $i = 1 \cdots 24$. The value of α_i is obtained from the training dataset. The alarm is positive if it is within the prediction horizon; otherwise, it is a false alarm. In this study, three different prediction horizons were used: 60, 90, and 120 minutes, which are within the ranges used by other authors [18, 43, 47, 55]. We adopt a postictal interval of 10 minutes as in [43, 54]. Moreover, the alarms in the 10 minutes before or after a missing hour (when the patient's data is not continuous) are not considered.

4. Performance Evaluation

The proposed predictor performance is evaluated by estimating the sensitivity, specificity, false prediction rate (FPR), and prediction time. In our development, the FPR is computed such that a patient has to wait until the end of prediction horizon to determine if a warning is false. The prediction time is defined as the time from the positive alarm to seizure onset. The sensitivity is the percentage of predicted seizures. A seizure is considered to have been predicted if there is at least one alarm before it within the prediction horizon. For estimating the specificity, we adopted the method of Wang et al. [43, 73], which considers the effect of the prediction horizon on prediction performance. The authors estimated the specificity (spec) by quantifying the portion of time

during the normal interval that was not considered to be false waiting time (see (7) below). A normal interval starts from the end of the posthorizon of a seizure and ends at the beginning of the prediction horizon of the next seizure. The false waiting time is the time from a false alarm to the end of its horizon or the end of the current normal interval. A positive or false alarm occurring within another alarm horizon of the same type is considered to be one.

$$\text{spec} = 1 - \frac{\text{fwt}}{np}, \tag{7}$$

where fwt is the length of the false waiting time and np is the length of the normal interval. Figure 2 presents an example of estimating the sensitivity and specificity of six continuous hours using a prediction horizon of 60 minutes. The seizure has at least one alarm within the prediction horizon, so the sensitivity is 100%. The fwt = 2 hours and np = 4 hours yield a specificity of 50%.

We evaluate the performance of the proposed predictor with two random predictors: periodic predictor which raises an alarm at a fixed time period T and Poisson predictor which gives an alarm according to an exponential distributed random time period with fixed mean M. The two parameters T and M were determined to be the average length of interictal intervals for each patient, as presented in Table 1.

5. Experimental Results and Comparison

This section shows the results of the proposed seizure predictor's and compares the predictor's results with those of other sEEG-based algorithms. The proposed predictor was tested on the sEEG recordings of 24 epilepsy patients from the CHB-MIT database with a total of 987.85 hours containing 170 seizures (Table 1) and using three prediction horizons (60, 90, and 120 minutes). We adopted a leave-one-out strategy for evaluating the performance of the proposed approach

TABLE 2: CSP-based patient-specific predictor performance (preictal-0 with a length of 3 minutes and 60-minute horizon).

Patients	60-minute horizon									
	Sens	Spec	Pred time	FPR	SensP1	SpecP1	FPR1	SensP2	SpecP2	FPR2
(1)	1	0.74	39.77	0.33	0.29	0.9	0.10	0	0.82	0.20
(2)	0.67	0.61	39.78	0.42	0.33	0.93	0.07	0	0.93	0.16
(3)	0.5	0.89	34.38	0.13	0.33	0.87	0.13	0	0.85	0.30
(4)	1	0.18	36.22	0.85	0	0.98	0.02	0	0.98	0.55
(5)	0.8	0.5	38.48	0.56	0.2	0.91	0.09	0.2	0.91	0.38
(6)	0.1	0.89	9.97	0.11	0.3	0.87	0.13	0.1	0.87	0.52
(7)	1	0.56	59.72	0.45	0	0.97	0.05	0.33	0.97	0.06
(8)	1	0.7	48.35	0.46	0.6	0.92	0.08	0	0.83	0.25
(9)	1	0.44	59.38	0.6	0.25	0.95	0.05	0	0.95	0.15
(10)	1	0.6	47.9	0.47	0.29	0.89	0.11	0.14	0.87	0.40
(11)	1	0.61	27.88	0.41	0	0.98	0.04	0	0.99	0.08
(12)	0.73	0.58	24.45	0.57	0.41	0.51	0.65	0.36	0.36	0.13
(13)	1	0.51	33.56	0.59	0.33	0.7	0.34	0.33	0.71	0.22
(14)	1	0.3	33.48	0.84	0.25	1	0.10	0.38	0.9	0.51
(15)	0.65	0.36	40.54	0.77	0.35	0.61	0.49	0.35	0.68	0.35
(16)	0.89	0.45	23.6	0.61	0.4	0.56	0.44	0.4	0.56	0.35
(17)	0.33	0.63	27.75	0.48	0.33	0.91	0.09	0	0.83	0.17
(18)	0.17	0.97	30.57	0.03	0.33	0.87	0.13	0.17	0.87	0.03
(19)	1	0.72	50.23	0.34	0.33	0.92	0.08	0.33	0.92	0.26
(20)	1	0.87	39.38	0.23	0.25	0.84	0.19	0.13	0.87	0.06
(21)	1	0.63	44.54	0.44	0.25	0.89	0.11	0	0.9	0.22
(22)	1	0.49	46.15	0.57	0.33	0.96	0.04	0	1	0.36
(23)	1	0.55	52.31	0.67	0.71	1	0.00	0.43	0.8	0.18
(24)	0.5	0.77	32.02	0.37	0.56	1	0.00	0.63	1	0.37
Average	0.81	0.61	38.35	0.47	0.31	0.87	0.15	0.18	0.85	0.26

in terms of each patient's data. There were N rounds for each patient with N recordings. In each round, the data were divided into two sets: training segments obtained from $N - 1$ recordings and testing segments obtained from the remaining one recordings. That is, we performed N runs where in each run a new recording is used for testing and the remaining $N - 1$ recordings are used for training. The $N - 1$ dataset used for training is divided into 5 folds in the implementation of the leave-one-out cross-validation procedure. The best model parameters obtained from training are then applied to the initially excluded recording for testing. So, all the parameters estimated from the $N - 1$ recordings during training remained unchanged during the evaluation on the remaining one recording. Then, the average of the N results was computed.

5.1. Results. Tables 2, 3, and 4 present the results of the proposed seizure predictor for the 24 patients with the three horizons (60, 90, and 120 minutes) and preictal-0 with a preictal interval of 3 minutes and compares it against periodic and Poisson random predictors. The proposed predictor achieved a 1.00 prediction rate in most of the patients in all three prediction horizons. It achieved an average sensitivity of 0.89 and average FPR of 0.39 and an average prediction time of 68.71 minutes in the 120-minute horizon.

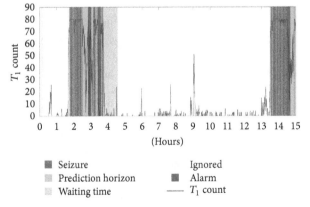

FIGURE 3: The results of patient 1 (hours 1–15) with prediction horizon of 60 min.

An example of predictor outcomes is shown in Figure 3, which represents the results of Patient 1 (hours 1–15) with a 60-minute prediction horizon (sliding one second) for preictal-0 and preictal intervals of 5 minutes. The seizure and postseizure are shown as the red area. The green area is the prediction horizon. The yellow area covers the unconsidered

TABLE 3: CSP-based patient-specific predictor performance (preictal-0 with a length of 3 minutes and 90-minute horizon).

Patient	90-minute horizon									
	Sens	Spec	Pred time	FPR	SensP1	SpecP1	FPR1	SensP2	SpecP2	FPR2
(1)	1	0.71	52.02	0.26	0.29	0.85	0.19	0.14	0.78	0.19
(2)	0.67	0.55	39.78	0.34	0.33	0.9	0.07	0	0.9	0.07
(3)	0.5	0.92	45.42	0.07	0.33	0.79	0.14	0	0.79	0.17
(4)	1	0.15	50.4	0.6	0	0.97	0.02	0	0.97	0.02
(5)	1	0.55	56.65	0.34	0.4	0.88	0.10	0.2	0.85	0.10
(6)	1	0.19	64.83	0.57	0.3	0.79	0.14	0.2	0.81	0.14
(7)	1	0.51	75.16	0.34	0.33	0.96	0.03	0.33	0.95	0.03
(8)	1	0.69	57.55	0.37	0.6	0.84	0.11	0	0.68	0.21
(9)	1	0.59	85.78	0.29	0.25	0.93	0.05	0	0.93	0.05
(10)	0.86	0.56	61.35	0.35	0.29	0.84	0.12	0.14	0.83	0.15
(11)	1	0.51	40.04	0.33	0	1	0.00	0	1	0.00
(12)	0.73	0.61	30.43	0.69	0.41	0.57	0.64	0.36	0.41	0.85
(13)	1	0.49	48.86	0.46	0.33	0.52	0.32	0.33	0.53	0.32
(14)	1	0.16	49.94	0.72	0.38	1	0.00	0.38	0.91	0.16
(15)	0.71	0.26	63.68	0.85	0.45	0.66	0.44	0.5	0.52	0.37
(16)	0.89	0.38	24.26	0.41	0.5	0.38	0.41	0.4	0.43	0.52
(17)	0.67	0.52	44.08	0.32	0.33	0.84	0.11	0	0.79	0.21
(18)	0	0	*	0	0.33	0.79	0.14	0.17	0.79	0.14
(19)	1	0.71	59.8	0.2	0.33	0.88	0.08	0.33	0.88	0.08
(20)	1	0.87	45.4	0.1	0.25	0.77	0.15	0.13	0.77	0.15
(21)	1	0.62	50.72	0.27	0.25	0.83	0.11	0	0.88	0.11
(22)	1	0.44	58.36	0.41	0.33	1	0.00	0.33	1	0.00
(23)	1	0.71	61.2	0.23	0.71	1	0.00	0.43	1	0.00
(24)	0.86	0.53	46.46	1.07	0.69	*	*	0.63	*	*
Average	0.87	0.51	52.7	0.4	0.35	0.83	0.15	0.21	0.8	0.18

*: not applicable.

interval. The alarms are the magenta lines. The false alarms create false waiting times that are shown as light-blue areas.

For selecting the proper preictal interval length, we investigated four different sizes, 3, 5, and 10 minutes, with all prediction horizons. These intervals are segmented into 3 seconds with an overlap of 2 seconds in the training phase. Table 5 presents the overall average results of the different preictal sizes of the 24 patients with the three horizons. It shows that the best results in all three horizons were achieved when the preictal length was 3 minutes with an average sensitivity of 0.89, average prediction time of 68.71 minutes, and average FPR of 0.39. The FAR with a 10-minute preictal length was the highest while the FAR with a 5-minute preictal length was the lowest.

As stated previously, the preictal interval ranges from a few seconds to several hours preceding the seizure onset. In this work, we studied a selection of preictal intervals immediately preceding (preictal-0), 60 minutes before (preictal-60), and 120 minutes before (preictal-120) onset with an interval of 3 minutes. Table 6 shows that selecting the preictal intervals exactly before the onset (preictal-0) was the most suitable. Preictal-0/-60/-120 achieved average sensitivity of 0.81, 0.87, and 0.89, respectively, with the prediction horizon of 120

minutes. This is intuitively unsurprising, as going back from the seizure onset is most likely to have a smaller seizure activity signature.

5.2. Comparison with Existing sEEG-Based Method. A comparison of our method with previously published sEEG-based seizure prediction methods shows the effectiveness of the proposed method. However, the comparison must be interpreted correctly, as it is based on different datasets and prediction horizons. Table 7 shows a comparison of some of the previously published works with the proposed method. Zandi et al. [17] presented zero-crossing intervals-based seizure prediction algorithm that was tested on sEEG recordings of three patients provided by the EEG Department of Vancouver General Hospital (VGH) with a total of 15.5 hours, including 14 seizures and a prediction horizon of 30 minutes. Using three channels, their method yielded an average sensitivity of 85.71%, average false prediction rate of 0.12/h, and average prediction time of 20.8 minutes. However, when they used five channels, they obtained an average sensitivity of 71.43%, average false prediction rate of 0.06/h, and average prediction time of 18.9 minutes. In [18], Zandi et al. used the sEEG recordings of 20 patients with a total of 561.3 hours, including 86 seizures from two

TABLE 4: CSP-based patient-specific predictor performance (preictal-0 with a length of 3 minutes and 120-minute horizon).

Patient	120-minute horizon									
	Sens	Spec	Pred time	FPR	SensP1	SpecP1	FPR1	SensP2	SpecP2	FPR2
(1)	1	0.55	61.89	0.33	0.57	0.82	0.13	0.14	0.77	0.22
(2)	1	0.39	103.08	0.33	0.33	0.86	0.07	0	0.89	0.07
(3)	0.33	1	46.3	0	0.33	0.72	0.14	0.17	0.72	0.14
(4)	1	0.13	65.68	0.48	0	0.96	0.02	0	0.96	0.02
(5)	1	0.44	99.15	0.37	0.4	0.86	0.11	0.2	0.78	0.11
(6)	0.8	0.45	60.89	0.29	0.4	0.78	0.11	0.3	0.76	0.13
(7)	1	0.25	97.91	0.4	0.33	0.96	0.03	0.33	0.94	0.03
(8)	1	0.7	65.38	0.23	0.6	0.74	0.13	0	0.63	0.26
(9)	1	0.32	111.73	0.36	0.25	0.9	0.05	0	0.9	0.05
(10)	0.86	0.47	87.66	0.32	0.29	0.79	0.13	0.14	0.79	0.13
(11)	1	0.28	53.53	0.37	0	1	0.00	0	1	0.00
(12)	0.77	0.14	37.43	0.88	0.36	0.76	0.78	0.36	0.62	0.78
(13)	1	0.5	65.49	0.3	0.33	0.38	0.34	0.33	0.4	0.34
(14)	0.88	0.25	66.09	0.54	0.38	1	0.00	0.38	0.98	0.26
(15)	0.88	0.22	77.62	0.72	0.55	0.68	0.30	0.5	0.5	0.50
(16)	0.89	0.41	27.62	0.35	0.5	0.53	0.47	0.4	0.54	0.59
(17)	1	0.2	45.35	0.41	0.33	0.8	0.13	0	0.73	0.13
(18)	0	0	*	0	0.33	0.71	0.14	0.17	0.71	0.14
(19)	1	0.48	79.16	0.28	0.33	0.84	0.08	0.33	0.84	0.08
(20)	1	0.56	49.23	0.26	0.25	0.66	0.17	0.13	0.72	0.17
(21)	1	0.37	69.11	0.36	0.25	0.84	0.08	0.25	0.84	0.08
(22)	1	0.3	86.53	0.45	0.33	1	0.00	0.33	1	0.00
(23)	1	0.26	64.96	0.43	0.71	*	*	0.43	*	*
(24)	0.93	0.15	58.57	0.89	0.69	*	*	0.63	*	*
Average	**0.89**	0.37	68.71	0.39	0.37	0.8	0.16	0.23	0.77	0.19

SensP1, SpecP1, and FPR1: sensitivity, specificity, and false prediction rate of periodic predictor. SensP2, SpecP2: sensitivity, specificity, and false prediction rate of Poisson predictor; *: not applicable. Bold values highlight the best Sen results.

TABLE 5: Average performance for preictal-0 with different preictal interval lengths.

Pred horizon	60-minute horizon				90-minute horizon				120-minute horizon			
Preictal interval length	Sen	Spec	Pred time	FAR	Sen	Spec	Pred time	FAR	Sen	Spec	Pred time	FAR
3 minutes	0.81	0.61	38.35	0.47	0.87	0.51	52.7	0.4	0.89	0.37	68.71	0.39
5 minutes	0.78	0.62	40.32	0.46	0.8	0.56	51.62	0.37	0.82	0.51	64.05	0.32
10 minutes	0.8	0.43	36.53	0.57	0.82	0.39	49.17	0.46	0.83	0.32	59.55	0.4

TABLE 6: Average performance with preictal-0/-60/-120 and length of 5 minutes.

Pred horizon	60-minute horizon				90-minute horizon				120-minute horizon			
Preictal	Sen	Spec	Pred time	FAR	Sen	Spec	Pred time	FAR	Sen	Spec	Pred time	FAR
Preictal-0	0.81	0.61	38.35	0.47	0.87	0.51	52.7	0.4	0.89	0.37	68.71	0.39
Preictal-60	0.46	0.78	28.61	0.28	0.44	0.77	32.52	0.23	0.49	0.74	51.53	0.21
Preictal-120	0.36	0.79	32.64	0.26	0.37	0.76	50.19	0.21	0.38	0.74	60.75	0.18

databases (Vancouver General Hospital [VGH] and CHB-MIT [Patients 4, 6, and 10]). They reported an average sensitivity of 88.34%, average false prediction rate of 0.155/h, and average prediction time of 22.5 minutes with a prediction horizon of 40 minutes. Chiang et al. [41] applied their method to the sEEG recordings of eight patients, seven of which were from the CHB-MIT database (Patients 1, 3, 6, 7, 9, 10, and 22) and one of which was from the National Taiwan University Hospital (NTUH) database, resulting in an average sensitivity of 52.2%. However, the specificity and prediction time were not reported. Bandarabadi et al. [45] presented a spectral-based seizure prediction algorithm for tracking

TABLE 7: sEEG-based seizure prediction methods in comparison with the proposed method.

Method	EEG data source	Number of used seizures	Sen	FPR/h	Spec	Pred time (min)
Zandi et al. [17]	3 patients from VGH	14	85.71	0.12		
Zandi et al. [18]	17 patients from VGH 3 patients from CHB-MIT	60	88.34	0.155	—	22.5
Chiang et al. [41]	7 patients from CHB-MIT 1 patient from NTUH	23	52.2	—	—	—
Myers et al. [47]	10 patients from CHB-MIT	31	77	0.17		—
Consul et al. [48]	10 patients from CHB-MIT	51	88.2	—	—	51 s–188 min
Chu et al. [55] 86-minute horizon	13 patients from CHB-MIT 3 patients from SNUH	45	86.67	0.367	—	45.3
Bandarabadi et al. [45]	16 patients from the European Epilepsy Database	97	73.98	0.06		—
Zhu et al. [28]	17 patients from ECXH	18	67.4		0.78	
Direito et al. [54]	185 patients from the European Epilepsy Database		38.47	0.2		
Proposed method						
60-minute horizon			0.81	0.47	0.61	38.35
90-minute horizon	24 patients from CHB-MIT	170	0.87	0.4	0.51	52.7
120-minute horizon			0.89	0.39	0.37	68.71

gradual changes preceding seizures and applied their method on sEEG signals of 16 patients (from the European Epilepsy Database) and reported an average sensitivity of 73.98% and average false prediction rate of 0.06/h, but they did not report the prediction time. Myers et al. [47] used the Phase Lock Values as the seizure prediction marker and applied their method to 10 sEEG recordings of patients from CHB-MIT database (Patients 1, 2, 3, 5, 6, 11, 18, 20, 22, and 24) with three seizure events of each patient. They achieved an average sensitivity of 77% and an average false prediction rate of 0.17/h with 60-minute prediction horizon, but they did not report the prediction time. Consul et al. [48] presented a hardware prediction algorithm based on phase difference and applied their method to the first 10 patients of CHB-MIT database with 51 seizure events, resulting in an average sensitivity of 88.2% and a prediction latency between 51 s and 188 minutes, but without reporting the false prediction time. Chu et al. [55] presented a seizure prediction method based on attractor state analysis and applied it to 16 sEEG recordings, 13 of which were from the CHB-MIT database (Patients 1, 3, 5, 6, 8, 10, 12, 13, 14, 15, 18, 20, and 23) and three of which were from the Soul National University Hospital database with 45 testing seizure events. They reported an average sensitivity of 86.67%, an average false prediction rate of 0.367/h, and an average prediction time of 45.3 minutes with a prediction horizon of 86 minutes. Zhu et al. [28] developed a seizure prediction method based on empirical mode decomposition and applied their method to 17 sEEG recordings of patients provided by Epilepsy Center of Xijing Hospital (ECXH) and reported an average sensitivity of 67.4% and average specificity of 78% of eight channels, but they did not report the prediction time. Direito et al. [54] used multiclass support vector machine with multichannel high-dimensional feature sets for epileptic seizure prediction. They evaluated their method on 216 patients (185 sEEG and 31 iEEG) from European Epilepsy Database and reported an average sensitivity of 38.47% and false positive rate of 0.20/h.

6. Conclusion

In this paper, we have presented a patient-specific seizure predictor based on CSP and a linear classifier using three prediction horizons: 60, 90, and 120 minutes. The CSP was used as a feature extractor to find the best discriminative features and reduce the amount of data used for each segment of dimensions 23×768 (number of channels × number of samples) to a feature vector of size 23×1 containing the log of variances computed from the rows of the resulting matrix after projection. This data reduction process enabled a linear classifier capable of labeling an incoming segment as either the preictal or interictal state to be built. Three alternatives for the proper selection of the preictal interval location were investigated: preictal-0, preictal-60, and preictal-120. Furthermore, three preictal interval lengths (3, 5, and 10 minutes) were studied. Using sEEG recordings from 24 epileptic patients, the best prediction performance was achieved using preictal-0 with a 3-minute preictal size and the prediction horizon of 120 minutes, in which the average sensitivity was 0.89, average specificity was 0.37, average FPR was 0.39, and average prediction time was 68.71 minutes.

Acknowledgments

The authors would like to acknowledge the support received from College of Engineering Research Center, King Saud University.

References

[1] T. Browne and G. Holmes, *Handbook of Epilepsy*, Lippincott Williams and Wilkins, 2000.

[2] B. Litt and J. Echauz, "Prediction of epileptic seizures," *The Lancet Neurology*, vol. 1, no. 1, pp. 22–30, 2002.

[3] T. Lehnert, F. Mormann, T. Kreuz et al., "Seizure prediction by nonlinear EEG analysis," *IEEE Engineering in Medicine and Biology Magazine*, vol. 22, pp. 57–63, 2003.

[4] A. Schulze-Bonhage, F. Sales, K. Wagner et al., "Views of patients with epilepsy on seizure prediction devices," *Epilepsy & Behavior*, vol. 18, no. 4, pp. 388–396, 2010.

[5] R. S. Fisher, B. G. Vickrey, P. Gibson et al., "The impact of epilepsy from the patient's perspective I. Descriptions and subjective perceptions," *Epilepsy Research*, vol. 41, no. 1, pp. 39–51, 2000.

[6] E. Niedermeyer and F. L. da Silva, *Electroencephalography: Basic Principles, Clinical Applications, and Related Fields*, Lippincott Williams & Wilkins, 2004.

[7] W. O. Tatum, *Handbook of EEG Interpretation*, Demos Medical Publishing, 2014.

[8] C. Baumgartner, W. Series, F. Leutmezer et al., "Preictal SPECT in temporal lobe epilepsy: Regional cerebral blood flow is increased prior to electroencephalography-seizure onset," *Journal of Nuclear Medicine*, vol. 39, no. 6, pp. 978–982, 1998.

[9] M. E. Weinand, L. P. Carter, W. F. El-Saadany, P. J. Sioutos, D. M. Labiner, and K. J. Oommen, "Cerebral blood flow and temporal lobe epileptogenicity," *Journal of Neurosurgery*, vol. 86, no. 2, pp. 226–232, 1997.

[10] P. D. Adelson, E. Nemoto, M. Scheuer, M. Painter, J. Morgan, and H. Yonas, "Noninvasive continuous monitoring of cerebral oxygenation periictally using near-infrared spectroscopy: A preliminary report," *Epilepsia*, vol. 40, no. 11, pp. 1484–1489, 1999.

[11] R. Badawy, R. MacDonell, G. Jackson, and S. Berkovic, "The peri-ictal state: Cortical excitability changes within 24 h of a seizure," *Brain*, vol. 132, no. 4, pp. 1013–1021, 2009.

[12] P. Federico, D. F. Abbott, R. S. Briellmann, A. S. Harvey, and G. D. Jackson, "Functional MRI of the pre-ictal state," *Brain*, vol. 128, no. 8, pp. 1811–1817, 2005.

[13] D. H. Kerem and A. B. Geva, "Forecasting epilepsy from the heart rate signal," *Medical & Biological Engineering & Computing*, vol. 43, no. 2, pp. 230–239, 2005.

[14] V. Novak, A. L. Reeves, P. Novak, P. A. Low, and F. W. Sharbrough, "Time-frequency mapping of R-R interval during complex partial seizures of temporal lobe origin," *Autonomic Neuroscience: Basic and Clinical*, vol. 77, no. 2-3, pp. 195–202, 1999.

[15] S. S. Viglione, V. A. Ordon, and F. Risch, "A methodology for detecting ongoing changes in the EEG prior to clinical seizures," in *Proceedings of the 21st Western Institute on Epilepsy*, McDonnell Douglas Astronautics Co paper WD1399(A), West Huntington Beach, Calif, USA, February 1970.

[16] S. S. Viglione and G. O. Walsh, "Proceedings: epileptic seizure prediction," *Electroencephalography and Clinical Neurophysiology*, vol. 39, pp. 435–436, 1975.

[17] A. S. Zandi, R. Tafreshi, M. Javidan, and G. A. Dumont, "Predicting temporal lobe epileptic seizures based on zero-crossing interval analysis in scalp EEG," in *Proceedings of the 32nd Annual International Conference of the IEEE Engineering in Medicine and Biology Society (EMBC '10)*, pp. 5537–5540, September 2010.

[18] A. S. Zandi, R. Tafreshi, M. Javidan, and G. A. Dumont, "Predicting epileptic seizures in scalp EEG based on a variational bayesian gaussian mixture model of zero-crossing intervals," *IEEE Transactions on Biomedical Engineering*, vol. 60, no. 5, pp. 1401–1413, 2013.

[19] A. Aarabi and B. He, "A rule-based seizure prediction method for focal neocortical epilepsy," *Clinical Neurophysiology*, vol. 123, no. 6, pp. 1111–1122, 2012.

[20] B. Schelter, H. Feldwisch-Drentrup, M. Ihle, A. Schulze-Bonhage, and J. Timmer, "Seizure prediction in epilepsy: From circadian concepts via probabilistic forecasting to statistical evaluation," in *Proceedings of the 33rd Annual International Conference of the IEEE Engineering in Medicine and Biology Society (EMBS '11)*, pp. 1624–1627, September 2011.

[21] S. Wang, W. A. Chaovalitwongse, and S. Wong, "A novel reinforcement learning framework for online adaptive seizure prediction," in *Proceedings of the IEEE International Conference on Bioinformatics and Biomedicine (BIBM '10)*, pp. 499–504, December 2010.

[22] S. Li, W. Zhou, Q. Yuan, and Y. Liu, "Seizure prediction using spike rate of intracranial EEG," *IEEE Transactions on Neural Systems and Rehabilitation Engineering*, vol. 21, no. 6, pp. 880–886, 2013.

[23] Y. Varatharajah, R. K. Iyer, B. M. Berry, G. A. Worrell, and B. H. Brinkmann, "Seizure Forecasting and the Preictal State in Canine Epilepsy," *International Journal of Neural Systems*, vol. 27, no. 1, Article ID 1650046, 2017.

[24] H. Niknazar and A. M. Nasrabadi, "Epileptic seizure prediction using a new similarity index for chaotic signals," *International Journal of Bifurcation and Chaos*, vol. 26, no. 11, Article ID 1650186, 2016.

[25] S. M. R. Miri and A. M. Nasrabadi, "A new seizure prediction method based on return map," in *Proceedings of the 18th Iranian Conference of Biomedical Engineering (ICBME '11)*, pp. 244–248, December 2011.

[26] Z. Rogowski, I. Gath, and E. Bental, "On the prediction of epileptic seizures," *Biological Cybernetics*, vol. 42, no. 1, pp. 9–15, 1981.

[27] Y. Salant, I. Gath, and O. Henriksen, "Prediction of epileptic seizures from two-channel EEG," *Medical & Biological Engineering & Computing*, vol. 36, no. 5, pp. 549–556, 1998.

[28] T. Zhu, L. Huang, and X. Tian, "Epileptic seizure prediction by using empirical mode decomposition and complexity analysis of single-channel scalp electroencephalogram," in *Proceedings of the 2nd International Conference on Biomedical Engineering and Informatics (BMEI '09)*, pp. 1–4, October 2009.

[29] Y. Zheng, G. Wang, K. Li, G. Bao, and J. Wang, "Epileptic seizure prediction using phase synchronization based on bivariate empirical mode decomposition," *Clinical Neurophysiology*, vol. 125, no. 6, pp. 1104–1111, 2014.

[30] J. R. Williamson, D. W. Bliss, D. W. Browne, and J. T. Narayanan, "Seizure prediction using EEG spatiotemporal correlation structure," *Epilepsy & Behavior*, vol. 25, no. 2, pp. 230–238, 2012.

[31] L. Kuhlmann, D. Freestone, A. Lai et al., "Patient-specific bivariate-synchrony-based seizure prediction for short prediction horizons," *Epilepsy Research*, vol. 91, no. 2-3, pp. 214–231, 2010.

[32] J. C. Sackellares, D.-S. Shiau, J. C. Principe et al., "Predictability analysis for an automated seizure prediction algorithm," *Journal of Clinical Neurophysiology*, vol. 23, no. 6, pp. 509–520, 2006.

[33] M. Bedeeuzzaman, T. Fathima, Y. U. Khan, and O. Farooq, "Seizure prediction using statistical dispersion measures of intracranial EEG," *Biomedical Signal Processing and Control*, vol. 10, no. 1, pp. 338–341, 2014.

[34] L. Iasemidis, D. Shiau, P. Pardalos, W. Chaovalitwongse, and K. Narayanan, "Long-term prospective on-line real-time seizure prediction," *Clinical Neurophysiology*, vol. 116, pp. 532–544, 2005.

[35] W. Chaovalitwongse, L. D. Iasemidis, P. M. Pardalos, P. R. Carney, D.-S. Shiau, and J. C. Sackellares, "Performance of a seizure warning algorithm based on the dynamics of intracranial EEG," *Epilepsy Research*, vol. 64, no. 3, pp. 93–113, 2005.

[36] P. M. Pardalos, C. Wanpracha, L. D. Iasemidis et al., "Seizure warning algorithm based on optimization and nonlinear dynamics," *Mathematical Programming*, vol. 101, pp. 365–385, 2004.

[37] C. E. Elger and K. Lehnertz, "Seizure prediction by non-linear time series analysis of brain electrical activity," *European Journal of Neuroscience*, vol. 10, no. 2, pp. 786–789, 1998.

[38] F. Mormann, T. Kreuz, C. Rieke et al., "On the predictability of epileptic seizures," *Clinical Neurophysiology*, vol. 116, no. 3, pp. 569–587, 2005.

[39] L. Chisci, A. Mavino, G. Perferi et al., "Real-time epileptic seizure prediction using AR models and support vector machines," *IEEE Transactions on Biomedical Engineering*, vol. 57, no. 5, pp. 1124–1132, 2010.

[40] S.-H. Hung, C.-F. Chao, S.-K. Wang, B.-S. Lin, and C.-T. Lin, "VLSI implementation for epileptic seizure prediction system based on wavelet and chaos theory," in *Proceedings of the IEEE TENCON*, pp. 364–368, November 2010.

[41] C.-Y. Chiang, N.-F. Chang, T.-C. Chen, H.-H. Chen, and L.-G. Chen, "Seizure prediction based on classification of EEG synchronization patterns with on-line retraining and post-processing scheme," in *Proceedings of the 33rd Annual International Conference of the IEEE Engineering in Medicine and Biology Society (EMBS '11)*, pp. 7564–7569, September 2011.

[42] K. Gadhoumi, J. Lina, and J. Gotman, "Seizure prediction in patients with mesial temporal lobe epilepsy using EEG measures of state similarity," *Clinical Neurophysiology*, vol. 124, no. 9, pp. 1745–1754, 2013.

[43] S. Wang, W. A. Chaovalitwongse, and S. Wong, "Online seizure prediction using an adaptive learning approach," *IEEE Transactions on Knowledge and Data Engineering*, vol. 25, no. 12, pp. 2854–2866, 2013.

[44] R. P. Costa, P. Oliveira, G. Rodrigues, B. Direito, and A. Dourado, "Epileptic seizure classification using neural networks with 14 features," in *Knowledge-Based Intelligent Information and Engineering Systems: 12th International Conference, KES 2008, Zagreb, Croatia, September 3–5, 2008, Proceedings, Part II*, pp. 281–288, 2008.

[45] M. Bandarabadi, C. A. Teixeira, J. Rasekhi, and A. Dourado, "Epileptic seizure prediction using relative spectral power features," *Clinical Neurophysiology*, vol. 126, no. 2, pp. 237–248, 2015.

[46] Z. Vahabi, R. Amirfattahi, F. Shayegh, and F. Ghassemi, "Online epileptic seizure prediction using wavelet-based Bi-phase correlation of electrical signals tomography," *International Journal of Neural Systems*, vol. 25, no. 6, Article ID 1550028, 2015.

[47] M. H. Myers, A. Padmanabha, G. Hossain, A. L. De Jongh Curry, and C. D. Blaha, "Seizure prediction and detection via phase and amplitude lock values," *Frontiers in Human Neuroscience*, vol. 10, article 80, 2016.

[48] S. Consul, B. I. Morshed, and R. Kozma, "Hardware efficient seizure prediction algorithm," in *Nanosensors, Biosensors, and Info-Tech Sensors and Systems*, vol. 8691 of *Proceedings of the SPIE*, San Diego, Calif, USA, March 2013.

[49] S. Xie and S. Krishnan, "Signal decomposition by multi-scale PCA and its applications to long-term EEG signal classification," in *Proceedings of the 5th IEEE/ICME International Conference on Complex Medical Engineering (CME '11)*, pp. 532–537, May 2011.

[50] Y. Park, L. Luo, K. K. Parhi, and T. Netoff, "Seizure prediction with spectral power of EEG using cost-sensitive support vector machines," *Epilepsia*, vol. 52, no. 10, pp. 1761–1770, 2011.

[51] N. Moghim and D. W. Corne, "Predicting epileptic seizures in advance," *PLoS ONE*, vol. 9, no. 6, Article ID e99334, 2014.

[52] P. Mirowski, D. Madhavan, Y. LeCun, and R. Kuzniecky, "Classification of patterns of EEG synchronization for seizure prediction," *Clinical Neurophysiology*, vol. 120, no. 11, pp. 1927–1940, 2009.

[53] P. Ghaderyan, A. Abbasi, and M. H. Sedaaghi, "An efficient seizure prediction method using KNN-based undersampling and linear frequency measures," *Journal of Neuroscience Methods*, vol. 232, pp. 134–142, 2014.

[54] B. Direito, C. A. Teixeira, F. Sales, M. Castelo-Branco, and A. Dourado, "A realistic seizure prediction study based on multiclass SVM," *International Journal of Neural Systems*, vol. 27, no. 3, Article ID 1750006, 2017.

[55] H. Chu, C. K. Chung, W. Jeong, and K.-H. Cho, "Predicting epileptic seizures from scalp EEG based on attractor state analysis," *Computer Methods and Programs in Biomedicine*, vol. 143, pp. 75–87, 2017.

[56] A. Aarabi and B. He, "Seizure prediction in hippocampal and neocortical epilepsy using a model-based approach," *Clinical Neurophysiology*, vol. 125, no. 5, pp. 930–940, 2014.

[57] T. N. Alotaiby, S. A. Alshebeili, T. Alshawi, I. Ahmad, and F. E. Abd El-Samie, "EEG seizure detection and prediction algorithms: a survey," *EURASIP Journal on Advances in Signal Processing*, vol. 2014, no. 1, article no. 183, pp. 1–21, 2014.

[58] K. Gadhoumi, J.-M. Lina, F. Mormann, and J. Gotman, "Seizure prediction for therapeutic devices: A review," *Journal of Neuroscience Methods*, vol. 260, pp. 270–282, 2016.

[59] E. Bou Assi, D. K. Nguyen, S. Rihana, and M. Sawan, "Towards accurate prediction of epileptic seizures: A review," *Biomedical Signal Processing and Control*, vol. 34, pp. 144–157, 2017.

[60] J. M. Hahne, B. Graimann, and K.-R. Muller, "Spatial filtering for robust myoelectric control," *IEEE Transactions on Biomedical Engineering*, vol. 59, no. 5, pp. 1436–1443, 2012.

[61] W. Wu, Z. Chen, X. Gao, Y. Li, E. N. Brown, and S. Gao, "Probabilistic common spatial patterns for multichannel EEG analysis," *IEEE Transactions on Pattern Analysis and Machine Intelligence*, vol. 37, no. 3, pp. 639–653, 2015.

[62] N. Tomida, T. Tanaka, S. Ono, M. Yamagishi, and H. Higashi, "Active data selection for motor imagery EEG classification," *IEEE Transactions on Biomedical Engineering*, vol. 62, no. 2, pp. 458–467, 2015.

[63] T. N. Alotaiby, F. E. A. El-Samie, S. A. Alshebeili, K. H. Aljibreen, and E. Alkhanen, "Seizure detection with common spatial pattern and Support Vector Machines," in *Proceedings of the 1st International Conference on Information and Communication Technology Research (ICTRC '15)*, pp. 152–155, May 2015.

[64] M. Qaraqe, M. Ismail, and E. Serpedin, "Band-sensitive seizure onset detection via CSP-enhanced EEG features," *Epilepsy & Behavior*, vol. 50, pp. 77–87, 2015.

[65] T. N. Alotaiby, F. E. El-Samie, S. A. Alshebeili et al., "A common spatial pattern approach for scalp EEG seizure detection," in *Proceedings of the 5th International Conference on Electronic*

Devices, Systems and Applications (ICEDSA '16), pp. 1–5, December 2016.

[66] Z. J. Koles, M. S. Lazar, and S. Z. Zhou, "Spatial patterns underlying population differences in the background EEG," *Brain Topography*, vol. 2, no. 4, pp. 275–284, 1990.

[67] Z. J. Koles, J. C. Lind, and P. Flor-Henry, "Spatial patterns in the background EEG underlying mental disease in man," *Electroencephalography and Clinical Neurophysiology*, vol. 91, no. 5, pp. 319–328, 1994.

[68] http://www.physionet.org/cgi-bin/atm/ATM.

[69] F. Lotte and C. Guan, "Regularizing common spatial patterns to improve BCI designs: unified theory and new algorithms," *IEEE Transactions on Biomedical Engineering*, vol. 58, no. 2, pp. 355–362, 2011.

[70] M. Welling, *Fisher Linear Discriminate Analysis*, vol. 3, Department of Computer Science, University of Toronto, 2005.

[71] H. He and E. A. Garcia, "Learning from imbalanced data," *IEEE Transactions on Knowledge and Data Engineering*, vol. 21, no. 9, pp. 1263–1284, 2009.

[72] N. V. Chawla, N. Japkowicz, and A. Kotcz, "Special issue on learning from imbalanced data sets," *ACM SIGKDD Explorations Newsletter*, vol. 6, no. 1, pp. 1–6, 2004.

[73] F. Mormann, R. G. Andrzejak, C. E. Elger, and K. Lehnertz, "Seizure prediction: the long and winding road," *Brain*, vol. 130, no. 2, pp. 314–333, 2007.

2

A Grey Wolf Optimizer for Modular Granular Neural Networks for Human Recognition

Daniela Sánchez, Patricia Melin, and Oscar Castillo

Tijuana Institute of Technology, Tijuana, BC, Mexico

Correspondence should be addressed to Oscar Castillo; ocastillo@tectijuana.mx

Academic Editor: José Alfredo Hernández-Pérez

A grey wolf optimizer for modular neural network (MNN) with a granular approach is proposed. The proposed method performs optimal granulation of data and design of modular neural networks architectures to perform human recognition, and to prove its effectiveness benchmark databases of ear, iris, and face biometric measures are used to perform tests and comparisons against other works. The design of a modular granular neural network (MGNN) consists in finding optimal parameters of its architecture; these parameters are the number of subgranules, percentage of data for the training phase, learning algorithm, goal error, number of hidden layers, and their number of neurons. Nowadays, there is a great variety of approaches and new techniques within the evolutionary computing area, and these approaches and techniques have emerged to help find optimal solutions to problems or models and bioinspired algorithms are part of this area. In this work a grey wolf optimizer is proposed for the design of modular granular neural networks, and the results are compared against a genetic algorithm and a firefly algorithm in order to know which of these techniques provides better results when applied to human recognition.

1. Introduction

In this paper, a grey wolf optimizer for modular granular neural networks (MGNN) is proposed. The main goal of this optimizer is the design of modular neural networks architectures using a granular approach and to evaluate its effectiveness, these modular granular neural networks are applied to one of the most important pattern recognition problems, human recognition. For a long time human recognition has been a widely studied area, where its study mainly lies in finding those techniques and biometric measures that allow having a trustworthy identification of persons to protect information or areas [1, 2]. Some of the most used biometric measures are face [3, 4], iris [5], ear [6, 7], voice [8], vein pattern [9], hand geometry [10], signature [11], and gait [12], among others.

On the other hand, within the most used techniques are those that belong to the soft computing category such as artificial neural networks [13, 14], fuzzy logic [15], computational vision [16], granular computing [17, 18], data mining [19], and evolutionary computation [20, 21]. Within the evolutionary computation area, bioinspired algorithms are found to be one of type of method. The already well-known genetic algorithm (GA) [22, 23], ant colony system (ACO) [24], particle swarm optimization (PSO) [25], bat algorithm (BA) [26], grey wolf optimizer (GWO) [27], harmony search (HS) [28], gravitational search algorithm (GSA) [29], and firefly algorithm (FA) [30, 31], just to mention a few, belong to this category.

It is important to mention that some soft computing techniques such as neural networks and fuzzy logic combined with a bioinspired algorithm can allow achieving better performance when they are individually used. When two or more techniques are combined the resulting system is called hybrid intelligent system [7, 32]. In this paper a hybrid intelligent system is proposed using modular neural networks (MNN), granular computing (GrC), and a grey wolf optimizer (GWO). The optimization of artificial neural network (ANN) using a grey wolf optimizer was already proposed in [33–36]. These works applied their methods to classification and function-approximation, where optimal initials weights of a neural network are sought using the grey wolf optimizer.

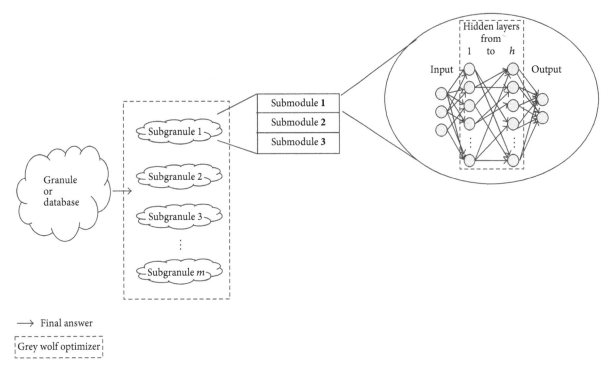

FIGURE 1: The general architecture of proposed method.

A modular neural network is an improvement of the conventional artificial neural network, where a task is divided into subtasks and an expert module learns some of these subtasks without communication with other modules; this technique allows having systems resistant to failures and works with a large amount of information. Usually this kind of networks has been used for human recognition based on biometric measures, classification problems, and time series prediction [40]. On the other hand, granular computing defines granules as classes or subsets used for complex applications to build computational models where a large amounts of data and information are used [19, 41, 42]. In this work granular computing is applied to perform granulation of information into subsets that also define number of modules of a modular neural network; the combination of modular neural networks and granular computing was already proposed in [7, 37, 38], where the advantages of modular granular neural networks over conventional neural networks and modular neural networks were widely demonstrated. In [7], the modular granular neural network architectures were designed using an improvement of a genetic algorithm, a hierarchical genetic algorithm (HGA), where the main differences between them are the control genes in the HGA that allow activating and deactivating genes allowing solving complex problems. That design consisted in optimization of number of modules (subgranules), percentage of data for the training phase, learning algorithm, goal error, and number of hidden layers with their respective number of neurons. In [38], a firefly algorithm was proposed for MGNN optimization using an experts submodules for each division of image. In [37], also modular granular neural network architectures were designed but using a firefly algorithm and

without an expert submodule for each division of image. In this work, the design of MGNN architecture is performed and applied to human recognition based on ear, face, and iris, but using a grey wolf optimizer, statistical comparisons are performed to define which of these optimization techniques is better to perform optimization of MGNNs.

This paper is organized as follows. In Section 2, the proposed method is described. The results achieved by the proposed method are explained in Section 3. In Section 4, statistical comparisons of results are presented. Finally, conclusions are given in Section 5.

2. Proposed Method

The proposed hybrid intelligence method is described in this section; this method uses modular neural networks with a granular approach and their architectures are designed by a grey wolf optimizer.

2.1. General Architecture of the Proposed Method. The proposed method uses modular granular neural networks, this kind of artificial neural network was proposed in [7] and [37], and their optimization were performed using, respectively, a hierarchical genetic algorithm and a firefly algorithm. In this work, the optimization is performed using a grey wolf optimizer and a comparison among HGA, FA, and GWO is performed to know which of these techniques is better for MGNN optimization. As a main task, the optimization techniques have to find the number of subgranules (modules), and as a preprocessing process each image is divided into 3 regions of interest; these regions will be described later. In Figure 1, the granulation process used in this work and

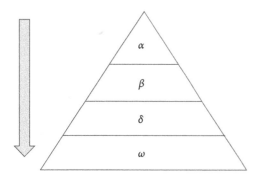

FIGURE 2: Hierarchy of grey wolf.

proposed in [7] is illustrated, where a database represents a whole granule. This granule can be divided into "m" subgranules (modules), this parameter (m) can have up to a certain limit set depending on the application, each of these subgranules can have different size for example, when this granulation is applied to human recognition, and each granule can have different number of persons that the corresponding submodules will learn. The grey wolf optimizer in this work performs optimization of the granulation and hidden layers and other parameters described later.

2.1.1. Description of the Grey Wolf Optimizer. This algorithm is based on the hunting behavior of grey wolf and was proposed in [27]. A group of wolves has been between 5 and 12 wolves, and each wolf pack has a dominant hierarchy where the leaders are called alphas, and this type of wolves makes the most important decisions of the pack. The complete social dominant hierarchy is illustrated in Figure 2.

This algorithm is based on 5 points: social hierarchy, encircling prey, hunting, attacking prey, and search for prey. These points are explained as follows.

Social Hierarchy. The best solution is alpha (α), the second best solution is beta (β), the third best solution is delta (δ), and the rest of the population are considered as omega (ω), where the omega solutions follow alpha, beta, and delta wolves.

Encircling Prey. During the hunt process grey wolves encircle their prey. Mathematically model encircling behavior can be represented using the equations

$$\vec{D} = \left| \vec{C} \cdot \vec{X_p}(t) - \vec{X}(t) \right|,$$
$$\vec{X}(t+1) = \vec{X_p}(t) - \vec{A} \cdot \vec{D}, \tag{1}$$

where $\vec{A}$ and $\vec{C}$ are coefficient vectors, $\vec{X_p}$ is the prey position vector, $\vec{X}$ is the position vector of a grey wolf, and t is the current iteration. Vectors $\vec{A}$ and $\vec{C}$ are calculate by

$$\vec{A} = 2\vec{a} \cdot \vec{r_1} - \vec{a},$$
$$\vec{C} = 2 \cdot \vec{r_2}, \tag{2}$$

where $\vec{r_1}$ and $\vec{r_2}$ are random vectors with values in 0 and 1 and $\vec{a}$ is a vector with components that linearly decreased from 2 to 0 during iterations.

Hunting. It is assumed that alpha, beta, and delta are the best solutions; therefore, they have knowledge about location of prey, as these solutions are saved; the position of the other search agents is updated according to the position of the best search agent. This part is mathematically represented by

$$\vec{D_\alpha} = \left| \vec{C_1} \cdot \vec{X_\alpha} - \vec{X} \right|,$$
$$\vec{D_\beta} = \left| \vec{C_2} \cdot \vec{X_\beta} - \vec{X} \right|,$$
$$\vec{D_\delta} = \left| \vec{C_3} \cdot \vec{X_\delta} - \vec{X} \right|,$$
$$\vec{X_1} = \vec{X_\alpha} - \vec{A_1} \cdot \left(\vec{D_\alpha} \right), \tag{3}$$
$$\vec{X_2} = \vec{X_\beta} - \vec{A_2} \cdot \left(\vec{D_\beta} \right),$$
$$\vec{X_3} = \vec{X_\delta} - \vec{A_3} \cdot \left(\vec{D_\delta} \right),$$
$$\vec{X}(t+1) = \frac{\vec{X_1} + \vec{X_2} + \vec{X_3}}{3}.$$

Attacking Prey (Exploitation). $\vec{a}$ decreases from 2 to 0 during iterations and $\vec{A}$ has random numbers in an interval $[-a, a]$ so the next position of a search agent will be any position between its current position and the prey.

Search for Prey (Exploration). There are different components that allow having divergence and a good exploration. The divergence is mathematically modeled using $\vec{A}$, this part obliges solutions to diverge and to have a global search; meanwhile $\vec{C}$ contains values in an interval $[0, 2]$ and provides to the prey random weights to favor exploration and avoid a local optima problem. In Pseudocode 1, the pseudo code of the grey wolf optimizer is shown.

2.1.2. Description of the Grey Wolf Optimizer for MGNN. The grey wolf optimizer seeks to optimize modular granular neural networks architectures. The optimized parameters are as follows:

(1) Number of subgranules (modules).

(2) Percentage of data for the training phase.

(3) Learning algorithm (backpropagation algorithm for training the MGNN).

(4) Goal error.

(5) Number of hidden layers.

(6) Number of neurons of each hidden layer.

Each parameter is represented by a dimension in each solution (search agent), and to determine the total number of dimensions for each solution the next equation is used:

$$\text{Dimensions} = 2 + (3 * m) + (m * h), \tag{4}$$

```
Initialize the grey wolf population $X_i$ $(i = 1, 2, \ldots, n)$
Initialize $a$, $A$, and $C$
Calculate the fitness of each search agent
$X_\alpha$ = the best search agent
$X_\beta$ = the second best search agent
$X_\delta$ = the third best search agent
        while ($t$ < Max number of iterations)
                for each search agent
                        Update the position of the current search agent by above equations
                end for
                Update $a$, $A$, and $C$
                Calculate the fitness of all search agents
                Update $X_\alpha$, $X_\beta$, and $X_\delta$
                $t = t + 1$
        end while
return $X_\alpha$
```

PSEUDOCODE 1: Pseudocode of the grey wolf optimizer.

where m is the maximum number of subgranules that the grey wolf optimizer can use and h is maximum of number of hidden layers per module that the optimizer can use to perform the optimization. The variables mentioned above can be established depending of the application or the database, and the values used for this work are mentioned in the next section. In Figure 3, the structure of each search agent is shown.

This optimizer aims to minimize the recognition error and the objective function is given by the equation:

$$f = \sum_{i=1}^{m} \left(\frac{\left(\sum_{j=1}^{n_m} X_j \right)}{n_m} \right), \qquad (5)$$

where m is the total number of subgranules (modules), X_j is 0 if the module provides the correct result and 1 if not, and n_m is total number of data/images used for testing phase in the corresponding module.

2.2. Proposed Method Applied to Human Recognition. One of the most important parameters of the architecture is its learning algorithm, backpropagation algorithms are used in the training phase to perform the learning, and 3 variations of this algorithm can be selected by the proposed optimizer: gradient descent with scaled conjugate gradient (SCG), gradient descent with adaptive learning and momentum (GDX), and gradient descent with adaptive learning (GDA). These 3 algorithms were selected because they have between demonstrated to be the fastest algorithms and with them better performances and results have been obtained [6, 7, 37–39].

The main comparisons with the proposed method are the optimizations proposed in [7, 37, 38]. In the first one a hierarchical genetic algorithm is developed, in the second and third work a firefly algorithm is developed to perform the MGNN optimization, and to have a fair comparison the number of individuals/fireflies and number of generations/iterations used in [7, 37, 38] are the same used by the proposed method

in this work; obviously for the GWO these values are number of search agents and iterations. In Table 1, the values of the parameters used for each optimization algorithm are presented.

As it was mentioned, the number of dimensions is established using (4), where values such as h and m are established depending on the application. For this work as in [7, 37, 38], the minimum and maximum values used for the search space of each optimizer are shown in Table 2. The optimization techniques also have two stopping conditions: when the maximum number of iterations/generations is achieved and when the best solution has error value equal to zero. In Figure 4, the diagram of the proposed method is shown.

2.3. Data Selection, Databases, and Preprocessing. The description of the databases, data selection for each phase (training and testing), and the applied preprocessing are presented below.

2.3.1. Data Selection. To understand the data selection, it is important to mention that the MGNNs as the MNNs and the conventional ANNs have two important phases:

(i) *First phase*: neural network learns information or patterns.

(ii) *Second phase*: neural network simulates other pieces of information not given for learning.

As it was observed, data selection is an important part of the neural network and for this reason in [7], a new method to select information or images was proposed. In the proposed data selection, depending of a percentage of data (a value between 20% and 80%) for the training phase, this percentage is converted to a number of images (depending of the number of images per person in the database), and randomly images for each phase are selected. In Figure 5, an example is illustrated, when a person has 4 images (as ear database) and 2 of them are for training phase.

TABLE 1: Table of parameters.

HGA [7]		FA [37, 38]		GWO	
Parameter	Value	Parameter	Value	Parameter	Value
Individuals (n)	10	Fireflies	10	Search agents (n)	10
Maximum number of generations (t)	30	Maximum number of iterations (t)	30	Maximum number of iterations (t)	30

Number of modules	Percentage of data for training

Error goal module 1	Learning algorithms module 1	Number of hidden layers module 1	Neurons (hidden layer 1)	Neurons (hidden layer 2)	Neurons (hidden layer 3)	...	Neurons (hidden layer H_1)

...

Error goal module 2	Learning algorithms module 2	Number of hidden layers module 2	Neurons (hidden layer 1)	Neurons (hidden layer 2)	Neurons (hidden layer 3)	...	Neurons (hidden layer H_2)

...

Error goal module 3	Learning algorithms module 3	Number of hidden layers module 3	Neurons (hidden layer 1)	Neurons (hidden layer 2)	Neurons (hidden layer 3)	...	Neurons (hidden layer H_3)

...

Error goal module m	Learning algorithms module m	Number of hidden layers module m	Neurons (hidden layer 1)	Neurons (hidden layer 2)	Neurons (hidden layer 3)	...	Neurons (hidden layer H_m)

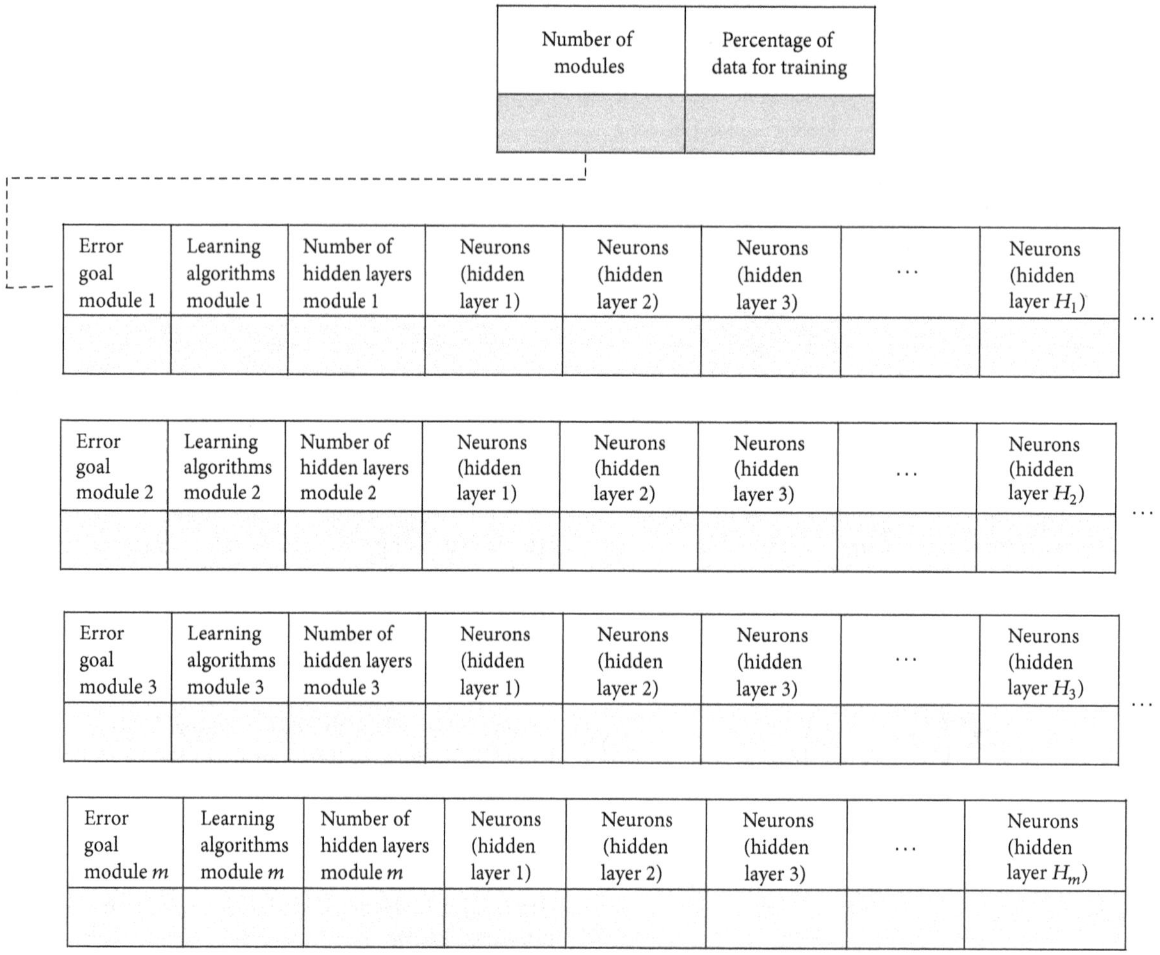

FIGURE 3: Structure of each search agent.

TABLE 2: Table of values for search space.

Parameters of MNNs	Minimum	Maximum
Modules (m)	1	10
Percentage of data for training	20	80
Error goal	0.000001	0.001
Learning algorithm	1	3
Hidden layers (h)	1	10
Neurons for each hidden layers	20	400

2.3.2. Database of Ear. The ear database is from the Ear Recognition Laboratory of the University of Science & Technology Beijing (USTB). The database contains 77 persons, where each person has 4 images of one ear. The image dimensions are 300×400, with BMP format [47]. A sample of the images is shown in Figure 6.

2.3.3. Database of Face (ORL). The ORL database contains 40 persons, and each person has 10 images. This database is from the AT&T Laboratories Cambridge, where each image has a dimension of 92×112 pixels, with PGM format. Figure 7 shows a sample of the images of this database [48].

2.3.4. Database of Face (FERET). The FERET database [49] contains 11338 images from 994 persons, and each image has a dimension of 512×768, pixels, with PGM format. Figure 8 shows a sample of the images of this database.

2.3.5. Database of Iris. The iris database [50] contains 77 persons, each person has 14 images. The image dimensions

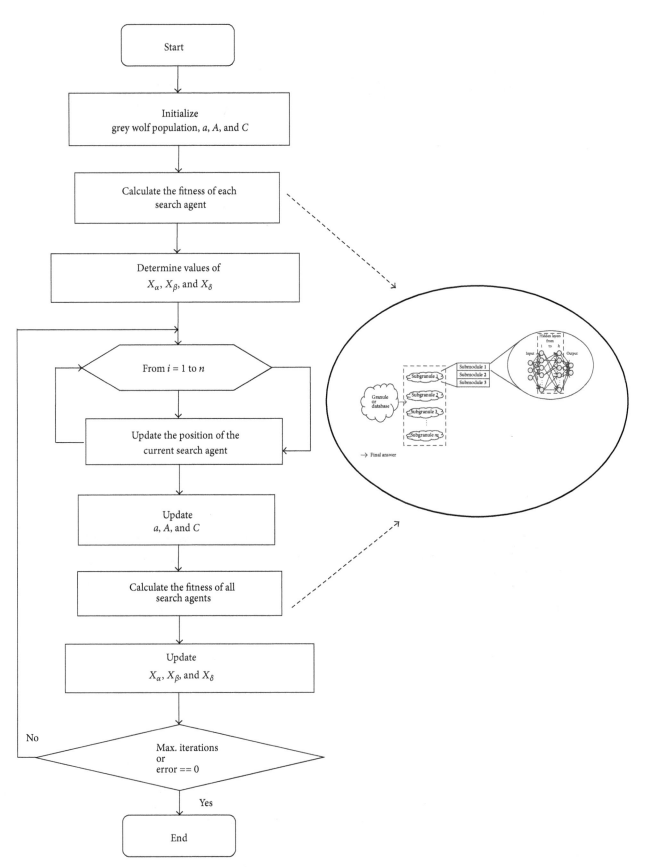

FIGURE 4: Diagram of the proposed method.

Images per person: 4

Percentage for training phase: 55% = 2.20 images = 2 images

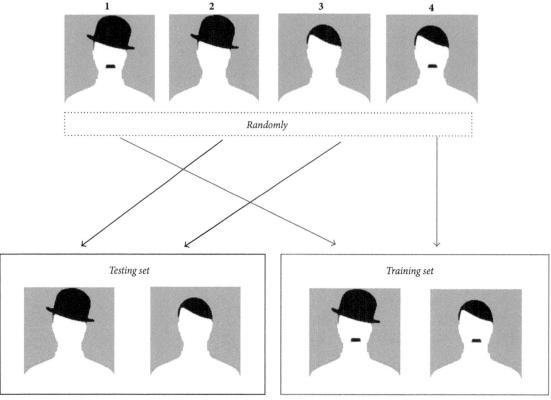

FIGURE 5: Example of selection of data for training and testing phase.

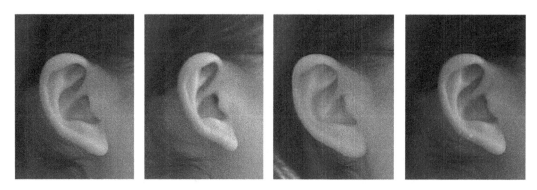

FIGURE 6: Sample of the Ear Recognition Laboratory database from the University of Science & Technology Beijing (USTB).

are 320×280 pixels, with JPEG format. Figure 9 shows a sample of the images of this database.

2.3.6. Preprocessing. The preprocessing applied to these databases is simple because the focus of the proposed method is the optimization of the granulation. For the ear database, the ear image is manually cut, a resizing of the new image to 132×91 pixels is performed, and automatically the image is divided into three regions of interest (helix, shell, and lobe); this preprocessing was already performed in [7]. For the

FERET database, the Viola-Jones algorithm [51, 52] was used to detect the face in each image, and a resizing of 100×100 pixels is performed to each image, converted to grayscale, and automatically the image is divided into three regions (front, eyes, and mouth). For iris database the method developed by Masek and Kovesi [53] is used to obtain the coordinates and radius of the iris and pupil to perform a cut in the iris, a resizing of 21×21 pixels is performed to each image, and finally, each image is automatically divided into three parts. For the ORL database, each image is automatically

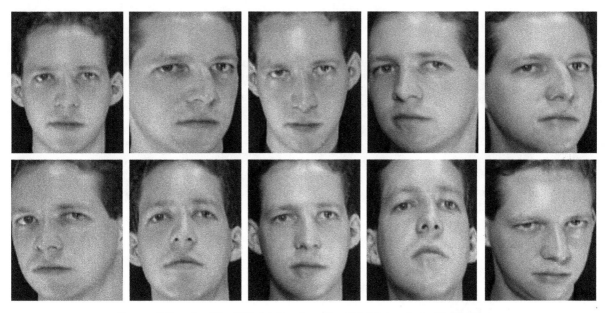

FIGURE 7: Sample of the ORL database from the AT&T Laboratories Cambridge.

FIGURE 8: Sample of the FERET database.

divided into three regions of interest (front, eyes, and mouth). The preprocessing process for these databases is shown in Figure 10.

3. Experimental Results

The proposed method is applied to human recognition and the results achieved are shown in this section. The main comparisons of the proposed method are against a hierarchical genetic algorithm proposed in [7] and a firefly algorithm proposed in [37, 38], where in [7, 38] the ear database is used; meanwhile in [37] the iris database is used and architectures of MGNNs are optimized. In [7, 38], two optimized tests for the MGNNs were performed, these tests in this work are replicated (30 trials/runs for each test), and to summarize only the 5 best results are shown. In [37], two optimized tests for the MGNNs were performed, the second test in this work is replicated (20 trials/runs), and to summarize also only the

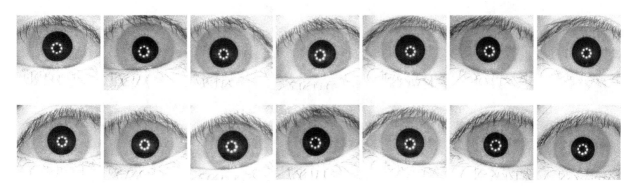

FIGURE 9: Sample of the iris database.

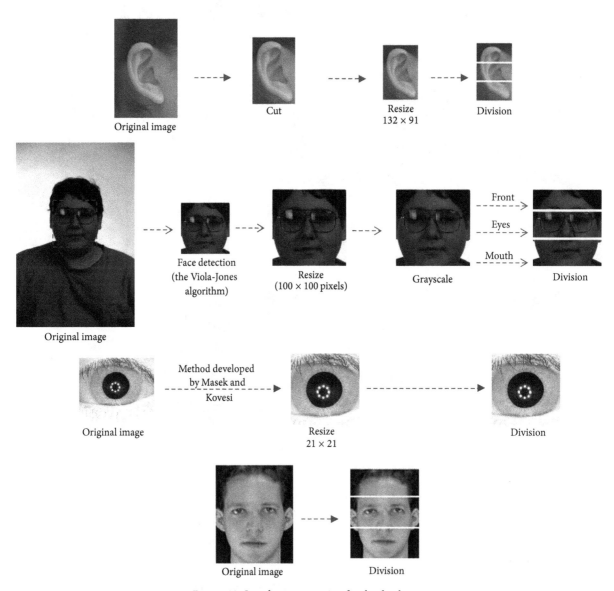

FIGURE 10: Sample preprocessing for the databases.

TABLE 3: The best 10 results (test #1, ear).

Trial	Images		Number of hidden layers and number of neurons	Persons per module	Rec. rate	Error
	Training	Testing				
1	80% (1, 2, and 3)	20% (4)	5 (126, 96, 179, 239, 37) 4 (188, 196, 93, 171) 5 (109, 107, 110, 168, 29)	Module #1 (1 to 12) Module #2 (13 to 40) Module #3 (41 to 77)	100% (77/77)	0
2	69% (2, 3 and 4)	31% (1)	5 (222, 238, 113, 27, 75) 4 (151, 53, 99, 79) 2 (209, 31) 2 (144, 71) 4 (30, 218, 194, 199) 4 (25, 81, 239, 20) 5 (237, 43, 83, 102, 128)	Module #1 (1 to 5) Module #2 (6 to 21) Module #3 (22 to 31) Module #4 (32 to 46) Module #5 (47 to 63) Module #6 (64 to 73) Module #7 (74 to 77)	100% (77/77)	0
3	66% (2, 3, and 4)	34% (1)	5 (141, 70, 120, 158, 242) 4 (124, 55, 23, 243) 3 (96, 186, 213) 4 (28, 62, 51, 42) 1 (223)	Module #1 (1 to 34) Module #2 (35 to 40) Module #3 (41 to 44) Module #4 (45 to 75) Module #5 (76 to 77)	100% (77/77)	0
4	74% (2, 3, and 4)	26% (1)	5 (139, 97, 200, 121, 231) 5 (204, 114, 164, 216, 138) 5 (195, 137, 124, 71, 86) 5 (144, 70, 92, 220, 63) 5 (119, 176, 154, 167, 161) 4 (199, 162, 96, 65)	Module #1 (1 to 6) Module #2 (7 to 29) Module #3 (30 to 50) Module #4 (51 to 58) Module #5 (59 to 71) Module #6 (72 to 77)	100% (77/77)	0
5	63% (2, 3, and 4)	37% (1)	5 (136, 183, 149, 193, 161) 5 (181, 132, 175, 140, 155)	Module #1 (1 to 68) Module #2 (69 to 77)	100% (77/77)	0

5 best results are shown. For the ORL and FERET databases, 5 and 4 trials/runs were, respectively, performed to compare with other works.

3.1. Ear Results. The results achieved, using the ear database, are presented in this section. Each test is described as follows:

(i) *Test #1*: the search space for the percentage of data for the training phase is limited up to 80%; that is, the optimization technique can select up to this percentage of images of the total number of images per person.

(ii) *Test #2*: in this test the search space for the percentage of data for the training phase is limited up to 50%.

3.1.1. Test #1 Results for the Ear. In this test, the proposed grey wolf optimizer can use up to 80% of data for the training phase to design the MGNN architectures. In Table 3, the best 5 results using the proposed method in this work are shown.

The behavior of trial #4 is shown in Figure 11, where the best, the average, and the worst results of each iteration are shown. In Figure 12, alpha (first best solution), beta (second best solution), and delta (third best solution) behavior of trial #4 are shown. This trial was one of the fastest trials to obtain an error value equal to zero.

In Figure 13, the recognition errors obtained by the proposed grey wolf optimizer, the HGA proposed in [7], and the FA proposed in [38] are shown.

In all the trials performed by the grey wolf optimizer an error equal to zero is obtained. In Table 4, a comparison of

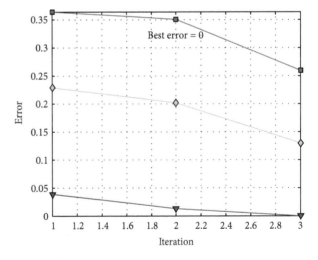

FIGURE 11: Convergence of trial #4.

results between the proposed method and the work in [7, 38] is shown.

An average of convergence of the 30 trials/runs of each optimization technique is shown in Figure 14, where it can be observed that the GWO always found an error equal to zero in the first 5 iterations; meanwhile the HGA and the FA in some runs did not obtain this value.

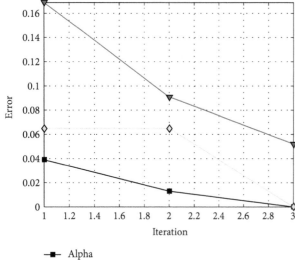

FIGURE 12: Alpha, beta, and delta behavior of trial #4.

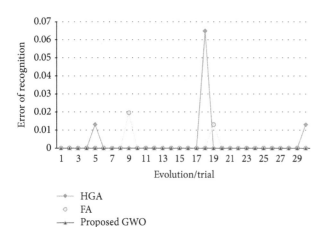

FIGURE 13: Obtained errors of recognition (up to 80%, ear).

TABLE 4: Comparison of results (test #1, ear).

Method	Best	Average	Worst
HGA [7]	100%	99.70%	93.50%
	0	0.00303	0.0649
FA [38]	100%	99.89%	98.05%
	0	0.0011	0.0195
Proposed GWO	100%	100%	100%
	0	0	0

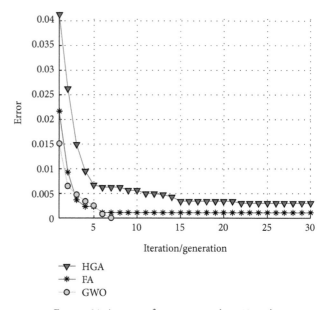

FIGURE 14: Average of convergence (test #1, ear).

algorithm; meanwhile the worst errors are improved by the proposed method and the firefly algorithm.

An average of convergence of the 30 trials/runs of each optimization technique is shown in Figure 18, where the HGA tends in a general behavior to stagnate more than the GWO and the FA.

3.2. Face Results (ORL). The results achieved, using the ORL database, are presented in this section. For this database 2 tests were also performed, but to compare with other works the percentage of data for the training phase is set fixed. Each test is described as follows:

(i) *Test #1:* the percentage of data for the training phase is set to 80%.

(ii) *Test #2:* the percentage of data for the training phase is set to 50%.

3.2.1. Test #1 Results for Face. In this test, the proposed grey wolf optimizer uses 80% of data for the training phase to design the MGNNs architectures. In Table 7, five architectures with the best results are shown.

The behavior of trial #5 is shown in Figure 19, where the best, the average, and the worst results of each iteration

3.1.2. Test #2 Results for Ear. In this test, the proposed grey wolf optimizer can use up to 50% of data for the training phase to design the MGNNs architectures. In Table 5, five architectures with the best results are shown.

The behavior of trial #2 is shown in Figure 15, where the best, the average, and the worst results of each iteration are shown. In Figure 16, the alpha (first best solution), beta (second best solution), and delta (third best solution) behaviors of trial #2 are shown. This trial was one of the best trials, where an error of recognition equal to 0.325 is obtained.

In Figure 17, the errors of recognition obtained by the proposed grey wolf optimizer, the HGA proposed in [7] and the FA proposed in [38] for test #2, are shown. It can be visually seen that the results obtained by grey wolf optimizer and firefly algorithm are more stable than the HGA.

In Table 6, a comparison of results between the proposed method and [7, 38] is shown. The best result is obtained by the HGA, but the average is slightly improved by the firefly

TABLE 5: The best 10 results (test #2, ear).

| Trial | Images | | Number of hidden layers and number of neurons | Persons per module | Rec. rate | Error |
	Training	Testing				
2	43% (2 and 3)	57% (1 and 4)	5 (115, 49, 187, 122, 194) 5 (182, 139, 50, 217, 54) 5 (132, 182, 56, 187, 159) 5 (167, 132, 121, 123, 219) 4 (116, 195, 54, 174) 5 (157, 108, 166, 95, 88) 5 (116, 119, 76, 121, 94) 5 (102, 58, 69, 111, 42)	Module #1 (1 to 9) Module #2 (10 to 22) Module #3 (23 to 33) Module #4 (34 to 36) Module #5 (37 to 51) Module #6 (52 to 63) Module #7 (64 to 75) Module #8 (76 to 77)	96.75% (149/154)	0.0325
4	48% (2 and 3)	52% (1 and 4)	4 (98, 136, 165, 141) 3 (176, 104, 215) 4 (142, 222, 65, 28) 5 (97, 139, 129, 99, 28) 4 (225, 83, 188, 34)	Module #1 (1 to 26) Module #2 (27 to 39) Module #3 (40 to 55) Module #4 (56 to 65) Module #5 (66 to 77)	96.75% (149/154)	0.0325
7	49% (2 and 3)	51% (1 and 4)	5 (201, 84, 169, 113, 131) 5 (199, 189, 62, 159, 151) 5 (104, 129, 88, 166, 66) 5 (123, 96, 52, 26, 67) 5 (125, 141, 86, 77, 105) 5 (121, 145, 87, 122, 31) 5 (36, 126, 146, 143, 145) 5 (126, 140, 88, 173, 206)	Module #1 (1 to 5) Module #2 (6 to 17) Module #3 (18 to 32) Module #4 (33 to 34) Module #5 (35 to 40) Module #6 (41 to 51) Module #7 (52 to 63) Module #8 (64 to 77)	96.75% (149/154)	0.0325
8	39% (2 and 3)	61% (1 and 4)	5 (125, 75, 69, 114, 140) 5 (138, 157, 101, 164, 98) 5 (76, 78, 86, 135, 70) 4 (74, 53, 57, 73) 5 (123, 55, 75, 125, 143) 5 (99, 118, 149, 224, 67) 5 (130, 184, 156, 180, 153)	Module #1 (1 to 11) Module #2 (12 to 14) Module #3 (15 to 27) Module #4 (28 to 33) Module #5 (34 to 43) Module #6 (44 to 57) Module #7 (58 to 77)	96.75% (149/154)	0.0325
14	40% (2 and 3)	60% (1 and 4)	5 (58, 26, 159, 123, 106) 5 (157, 156, 197, 22, 112) 4 (215, 78, 97, 220) 5 (120, 68, 219, 194, 58) 5 (142, 185, 141, 33, 187) 5 (108, 160, 61, 100, 54)	Module #1 (1 to 12) Module #2 (13 to 20) Module #3 (21 to 40) Module #4 (41 to 52) Module #5 (53 to 66) Module #6 (67 to 77)	96.75% (149/154)	0.0325

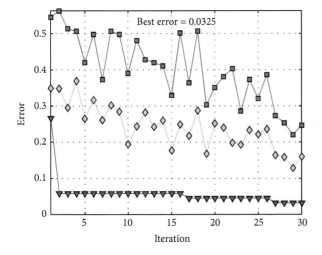

FIGURE 15: Convergence of trial #2.

TABLE 6: Comparison of results (test #2, ear).

Method	Best	Average	Worst
HGA [7]	98.05%	94.82%	79.65%
	0.01948	0.0518	0.20346
FA [38]	97.40%	96.82%	95.45%
	0.0260	0.0318	0.04545
Proposed GWO	96.75%	96.15%	95.45%
	0.03247	0.03853	0.04545

are shown. In Figure 20, the alpha (first best solution), beta (second best solution), and delta (third best solution) behaviors of trial #5 are shown. This trial was one of the fastest trials to obtain an error value equal to zero.

In Figure 21, the recognition rates obtained by [4, 38, 39] and the proposed grey wolf optimizer are shown. The proposed method and the firefly proposed in [38] allow obtaining a recognition rate of 100%.

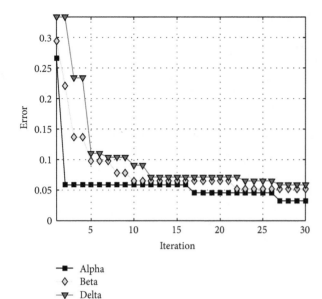

FIGURE 16: Convergence of trial #2.

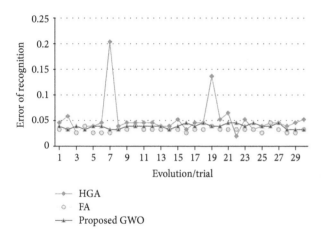

FIGURE 17: Obtained errors of recognition (up to 50%, ear).

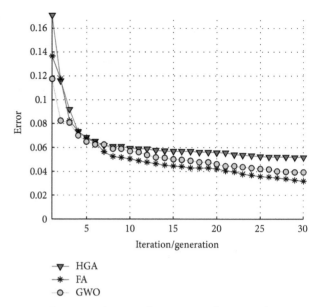

FIGURE 18: Average of convergence (test #2, ear).

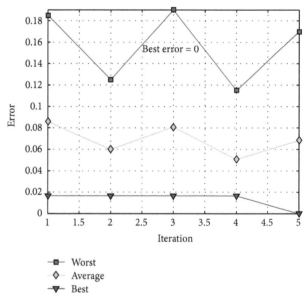

FIGURE 19: Convergence of trial #5.

In Table 8, a comparison of results is presented. The best result is obtained by the work in [38, 39] and the proposed method, but the average and the worst error are improved by the proposed method and the firefly algorithm.

3.2.2. Test #2 Results for Face.

In this test, the proposed grey wolf optimizer uses 50% of data for the training phase to design the MGNNs architectures. In Table 9, the best 5 results using the proposed method in this work are shown.

The behavior of trial #1 is shown in Figure 22, where the best, the average, and the worst results of each iteration are shown. In Figure 23, the alpha (first best solution), beta (second best solution), and delta (third best solution) behaviors of trial #1 are shown. This trial was one of the best trials, where an error of recognition equal to 0.0100 is obtained.

In Figure 24, the recognition rates obtained by [3, 38, 39, 43] and the proposed method are shown.

In Table 10, a comparison of results between the proposed method and the other works is shown. The best and the worst error are improved by the proposed method and the firefly algorithm, but the average of recognition is slightly improved by the proposed method.

3.3. Iris Results.

In this test, the proposed grey wolf optimizer uses up to 80% of data for the training phase to design the MGNNs architectures as in [37, 44]. In Table 11, five architectures with the best results are shown.

The behavior of trial #2 is shown in Figure 25, where the best, the average, and the worst results of each iteration are shown. In Figure 26, the alpha (first best solution), beta (second best solution), and delta (third best solution)

TABLE 7: The results for face database (test #1, ORL).

Trial	Images		Number of hidden layers and number of neurons	Persons per module	Rec. rate	Error
	Training	Testing				
1	80% (1, 2, 3, 4, 7, 8, 9, and 10)	20% (5 and 6)	5 (109, 109, 69, 74, 210) 5 (175, 32, 170, 214, 86) 4 (117, 52, 134, 197) 4 (190, 162, 99, 81) 5 (111, 130, 247, 160, 64) 4 (111, 250, 116, 127)	Module #1 (1 to 4) Module #2 (5 to 12) Module #3 (13 to 15) Module #4 (16 to 24) Module #5 (25 to 33) Module #6 (34 to 40)	100% (80/80)	0
2	80% (1, 3, 4, 5, 6, 7, 8, and 10)	20% (2 and 9)	5 (52, 188, 138, 154, 71) 5 (216, 183, 74, 142, 112) 5 (73, 204, 139, 94, 114) 5 (101, 124, 144, 207, 133) 4 (96, 205, 157, 238) 5 (46, 160, 86, 119, 105) 5 (138, 169, 152, 146, 48) 5 (32, 65, 173, 156, 56)	Module #1 (1 to 5) Module #2 (6 to 15) Module #3 (16 to 17) Module #4 (18 to 19) Module #5 (20 to 29) Module #6 (30 to 32) Module #7 (33 to 38) Module #8 (39 to 40)	100% (80/80)	0
3	80% (1, 2, 4, 5, 7, 8, 9, and 10)	20% (3 and 6)	5 (158, 67, 80, 49, 124) 5 (138, 72, 51, 87, 218) 5 (138, 176, 108, 21, 139) 5 (136, 46, 66, 41, 68) 5 (182, 40, 246, 104, 45) 5 (126, 202, 171, 45, 228) 5 (228, 153, 133, 199, 85) 4 (98, 140, 72, 188)	Module #1 (1 to 3) Module #2 (4 to 5) Module #3 (6 to 13) Module #4 (14 to 18) Module #5 (19 to 23) Module #6 (24 to 25) Module #7 (26 to 30) Module #8 (31 to 40)	100% (80/80)	0
4	80% (1, 3, 4, 5, 7, 8, 9, and 10)	20% (2 and 6)	5 (39, 55, 21, 84, 210) 1 (224) 3 (98, 204, 243) 5 (61, 86, 237, 49) 2 (199, 62) 1 (180) 5 (206, 29, 240, 215, 105)	Module #1 (1 to 7) Module #2 (8 to 9) Module #3 (10 to 12) Module #4 (13 to 17) Module #5 (18 to 26) Module #6 (27 to 34) Module #7 (35 to 40)	100% (80/80)	0
5	80% (1, 2, 3, 5, 6, 7, 8, and 10)	20% (4 and 9)	5 (75, 156, 197, 128, 233) 5 (225, 87, 193, 58, 182) 5 (161, 240, 36, 157, 151) 5 (228, 222, 64, 102, 132) 5 (161, 50, 80, 175, 105) 5 (150, 105, 194, 122, 80) 5 (121, 116, 122, 88, 42) 5 (66, 210, 92, 48, 179)	Module #1 (1 to 4) Module #2 (5 to 13) Module #3 (14 to 16) Module #4 (17 to 23) Module #5 (24 to 26) Module #6 (27 to 29) Module #7 (30 to 31) Module #8 (32 to 40)	100% (80/80)	0

TABLE 8: Comparison of results (test #1, ORL).

Method	Best	Average	Worst
Mendoza et al. [4]	97.50%	94.69%	91.5%
Sánchez et al. [38]	100%	100%	100%
Sánchez et al. [39]	100%	99.27%	98.61%
Proposed GWO	100%	100%	100%

behaviors of trial #2 are shown. This trial was one of the best trials, where an error of recognition equal to 0 is obtained.

In Figure 27, the errors of recognition obtained by [37, 44] and the proposed method are presented.

In Table 12, a comparison of results is presented. The best, the average, and the worst errors are improved by the proposed method.

An average of convergence of the 20 trials/runs of each optimization technique is shown in Figure 28, where although these techniques does not tend to stagnate for a long time, the GWO tends to convergence faster with better results.

3.4. Summary Results. Summary of results and comparison with other works using the same databases and neural networks are shown in this section. The testing time of a set of images depends on the number of images and their size, but the training time also depends on the neural network architecture (number of hidden layers, neurons in each hidden layers, and number of modules) and learning factors (initial weights and error goal, among others). An approximation of the training and testing times for each search agent is, respectively, shown in Figures 29 and 30.

TABLE 9: The results for face database (test #2, ORL).

Trial	Images		Number of hidden layers and number of neurons	Persons per module	Rec. rate	Error
	Training	Testing				
1	50% (2, 3, 4, 7, and 9)	50% (1, 5, 6, 8 and, 10)	5 (139, 149, 64, 49, 69) 5 (112, 89, 137, 112, 203) 5 (109, 141, 115, 142, 206) 5 (69, 183, 84, 33, 233) 5 (43, 127, 176, 236, 39) 5 (124, 192, 92, 92, 193) 5 (70, 188, 227, 165, 98) 5 (75, 79, 128, 171, 159)	Module #1 (1 to 5) Module #2 (6 to 12) Module #3 (13 to 17) Module #4 (18 to 22) Module #5 (23 to 30) Module #6 (31 to 34) Module #7 (35 to 36) Module #8 (37 to 40)	99% (198/200)	0.0100
2	50% (1, 2, 4, 5, and 7)	50% (3, 6, 8, 9 and, 10)	5 (141, 99, 172, 88, 81) 4 (198, 101, 244, 148) 5 (159, 31, 175, 125, 168) 5 (31, 90, 125, 116, 111) 5 (102, 107, 110, 87, 21) 5 (113, 78, 55, 184, 209) 5 (248, 108, 150, 88, 40) 4 (119, 136, 90, 126) 3 (213, 71, 127) 4 (207, 131, 182, 48)	Module #1 (1 to 7) Module #2 (8 to 12) Module #3 (13 to 15) Module #4 (16 to 18) Module #5 (19 to 21) Module #6 (22 to 23) Module #7 (24 to 30) Module #8 (31 to 33) Module #9 (34 to 38) Module #10 (39 to 40)	98.50% (197/200)	0.0150
3	50% (3, 5, 7, 8, and 10)	50% (1, 2, 4, 6, and 9)	4 (60, 37, 220, 169) 5 (84, 106, 155, 187, 182) 5 (33, 222, 144, 23, 123) 5 (199, 85, 38, 78, 103) 5 (63, 143, 89, 191, 93) 5 (122, 189, 135, 95, 181) 5 (91, 194, 227, 119, 130) 3 (188, 124, 238) 5 (44, 105, 217, 102, 199) 5 (114, 129, 24, 140, 208)	Module #1 (1 to 2) Module #2 (3 to 7) Module #3 (8 to 10) Module #4 (11 to 16) Module #5 (17 to 21) Module #6 (22 to 23) Module #7 (24 to 27) Module #8 (28 to 31) Module #9 (32 to 35) Module #10 (36 to 40)	98% (196/200)	0.0200
4	50% (3, 4, 7, 9, and 10)	50% (1, 2, 5, 6 and 8)	5 (52, 173, 68, 176, 133) 5 (143, 202, 54, 67, 55) 5 (82, 142, 191, 47, 183) 5 (205, 115, 95, 143, 218) 5 (95, 142, 73, 47, 117) 5 (182, 86, 87, 113, 102) 5 (40, 115, 98, 95, 120) 5 (196, 181, 82, 69, 154) 5 (97, 117, 142, 216, 65) 5 (153, 155, 91, 48, 124)	Module #1 (1 to 3) Module #2 (4 to 6) Module #3 (7 to 9) Module #4 (10 to 13) Module #5 (14 to 15) Module #6 (16 to 22) Module #7 (23 to 27) Module #8 (28 to 31) Module #9 (32 to 35) Module #10 (36 to 40)	99% (198/200)	0.0100
5	50% (2, 3, 5, 8, and 9)	50% (1, 4, 6, 7, and 10)	5 (128, 150, 50, 26, 73) 5 (145, 149, 49, 69, 58) 5 (129, 58, 124, 86, 70) 5 (127, 69, 126, 139, 69) 5 (33, 174, 146, 137, 218) 5 (137, 95, 232, 187, 97) 5 (101, 104, 158, 66, 95) 5 (142, 207, 48, 140, 51) 5 (79, 157, 191, 129, 222) 5 (199, 102, 148, 103, 49)	Module #1 (1 to 2) Module #2 (3 to 4) Module #3 (5 to 13) Module #4 (14 to 18) Module #5 (19 to 20) Module #6 (21 to 25) Module #7 (26 to 30) Module #8 (31 to 33) Module #9 (34 to 35) Module #10 (36 to 40)	98% (196/200)	0.0200

In Table 13 a summary of each database setup is shown. It can be noticed that the Iris database has more images in each test, but images size is smaller than the other databases; for this reason the training and testing times for this database are the smallest ones. In the case of ear database the number of images is smaller than the other databases but the size of its images is bigger, so the training and testing times tend to increase.

In Table 14, the summary of results obtained using the GWO applied to the ear, face, and iris database is shown.

In [7], modular granular neural networks are proposed and are compared with conventional neural networks using a hierarchical genetic algorithm to design neural networks architectures. In [38], the design of modular granular neural networks architectures is proposed using a firefly algorithm. In [45], the architectures of modular neural networks are

TABLE 10: Comparison of results (test #2, ORL).

Method	Best	Average	Worst
Azami et al. [43]	96.50%	95.91%	95.37%
Ch'Ng et al. [3]	96.5%	94.75%	94%
Sánchez et al. [38]	99%	98.30%	98%
Sánchez et al. [39]	98.43%	97.59%	94.55%
Proposed GWO	99%	98.50%	98%

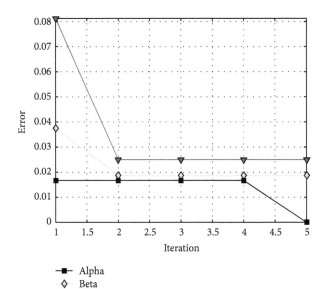

FIGURE 20: Convergence of trial #5.

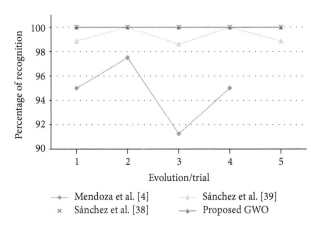

FIGURE 21: Obtained recognition rates (test #1, ORL database, comparison 1).

designed using a hierarchical genetic algorithm but without a granular approach; that is, the number of modules and the number of persons learned by each modules always were left fixed. In Table 15, the comparisons among the optimized results obtained using the proposed method and other optimized works are presented, where the average was improved for the ear database by the proposed method (test #1, using 3 images) and the firefly algorithm (test #2, using 2 images).

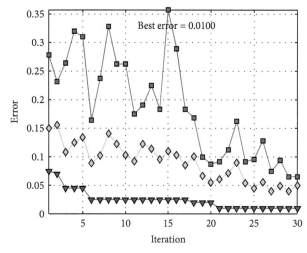

FIGURE 22: Convergence of trial #1.

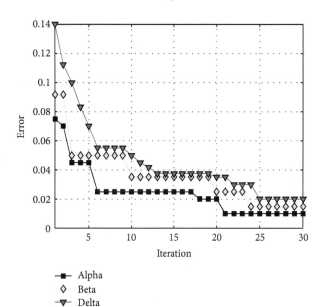

FIGURE 23: Convergence of trial #1.

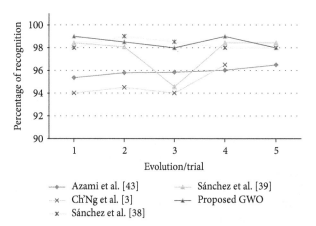

FIGURE 24: Obtained recognition rates (test #2, ORL database, comparison 2).

TABLE 11: The results for iris database.

Trial	Images		Number of hidden layers and number of neurons	Persons per module	Rec. rate	Error
	Training	Testing				
1	79% (1, 2, 3, 5, 6, 8, 10, 11, 12, 13, and 14)	21% (4, 7, and 9)	5 (133, 205, 93, 203, 184) 4 (112, 198, 134, 97) 5 (39, 159, 68, 76, 119) 2 (158, 148) 5 (183, 139, 135, 51, 72) 4 (224, 168, 148, 195) 5 (152, 170, 65, 47, 55) 5 (114, 218, 162, 85, 107) 3 (86, 205, 172)	Module #1 (1 to 15) Module #2 (16 to 22) Module #3 (23 to 34) Module #4 (35 to 45) Module #5 (46 to 47) Module #6 (48 to 49) Module #7 (50 to 64) Module #8 (65 to 74) Module #9 (75 to 77)	99.57% (230/231)	0.0043
2	75% (2, 3, 4, 5, 6, 8, 9, 10, 12, 13, and 14)	25% (1, 7, and 11)	5 (97, 66, 149, 117, 144) 5 (69, 210, 77, 70, 203) 4 (159, 102, 153, 152) 5 (35, 171, 134, 124, 101) 3 (167, 166, 169) 5 (198, 64, 80, 176, 131) 3 (81, 80, 227) 4 (106, 114, 89, 148)	Module #1 (1 to 4) Module #2 (5 to 15) Module #3 (16 to 23) Module #4 (24 to 31) Module #5 (32 to 46) Module #6 (47 to 58) Module #7 (59 to 62) Module #8 (63 to 77)	100% (231/231)	0
6	76% (1, 2, 3, 4, 5, 6, 8, 9, 12, 13 and, 14)	24% (7, 10, and 11)	4 (73, 210, 138, 49) 5 (119, 161, 63, 96, 112) 3 (180, 135, 77) 5 (124, 164, 177, 216, 94) 5 (129, 123, 215, 88, 100) 5 (65, 89, 69, 144, 80) 5 (67, 110, 112, 200, 134) 3 (86, 72, 160)	Module #1 (1 to 3) Module #2 (4 to 13) Module #3 (14 to 30) Module #4 (31 to 40) Module #5 (41 to 51) Module #6 (52 to 60) Module #7 (61 to 65) Module #8 (66 to 77)	99.57% (230/231)	0.0043
7	78% (1, 2, 3, 4, 5, 6, 7, 8, 10, 11, and 13)	22% (9, 12, and 14)	5 (168, 99, 94, 156, 175) 4 (90, 122, 124, 122) 5 (129, 32, 159, 174, 50) 4 (218, 93, 237, 71) 5 (117, 36, 167, 143, 52) 5 (135, 60, 226, 140, 112) 5 (169, 117, 95, 36, 96) 5 (97, 71, 225, 147, 176) 3 (162, 170, 139)	Module #1 (1 to 4) Module #2 (5 to 16) Module #3 (17 to 20) Module #4 (21 to 37) Module #5 (38 to 46) Module #6 (47 to 51) Module #7 (52 to 71) Module #8 (72 to 73) Module #9 (74 to 77)	99.57% (230/231)	0.0043
11	78% (1, 2, 3, 4, 5, 6, 7, 8, 10, 13, and 14)	22% (9, 11, and 12)	5 (86, 162, 217, 168, 168) 4 (167, 189, 62, 193) 5 (115, 53, 154, 105, 79) 3 (62, 89, 134, 87) 4 (119, 142, 105, 204) 3 (128, 115, 175, 127) 5 (147, 197, 61, 110, 217) 3 (142, 164, 96, 141) 5 (140, 104, 57, 108, 122)	Module #1 (1 to 4) Module #2 (5 to 8) Module #3 (9 to 16) Module #4 (17 to 32) Module #5 (33 to 39) Module #6 (40 to 46) Module #7 (47 to 57) Module #8 (58 to 68) Module #9 (69 to 77)	100% (231/231)	0

In Table 16, the 4-fold cross-validation results for the ear database are shown, where for each training set 3 images for each person were used.

In [43], a neural network is proposed based on a conjugate gradient algorithm (CGA) and a principal component analysis. In [3], the principal components analysis (PCA) and a linear discriminant analysis (LDA) are used. In [38], a firefly algorithm is developed to design modular granular neural networks architectures. In [39], modular neural network with a granular approach is used, but in that work, the granulation is performed using nonoptimized training to assign a complexity level to each person and to form subgranules with persons that have the same complexity level. That method was recommended for databases with a large numbers of people. In [4], a comparison of fuzzy edge detectors based on the image recognition rate as performance index calculated with neural networks is proposed. In Table 17, the comparisons among the optimized results obtained using the proposed method and other optimized works for the face database are presented, where the best, average, and worst values were improved for this database by the proposed method and the firefly algorithm for test #1 (using 8 images) and in test #2 (using 5 images); the average is only improved by the proposed method.

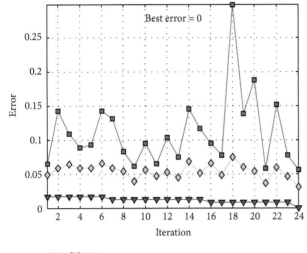

FIGURE 25: Convergence of trial #2.

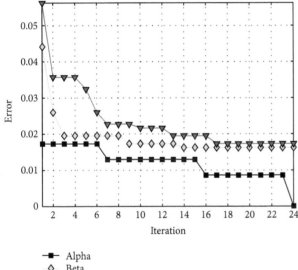

FIGURE 26: Convergence of trial #2.

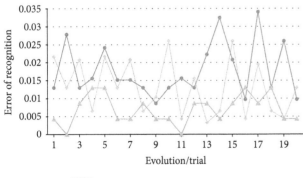

FIGURE 27: Obtained recognition rates (iris database).

TABLE 12: Comparison of results (iris).

Method	Best	Average	Worst
Sánchez and Melin [44]	99.68%	98.68%	97.40%
	0.0032	0.0132	0.0260
Sánchez et al. [37]	99.13%	98.22%	96.59%
	0.0087	0.0178	0.0341
Proposed GWO	100%	99.31%	98.70%
	0	0.0069	0.0130

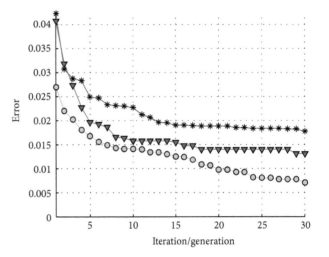

FIGURE 28: Average of convergence (iris).

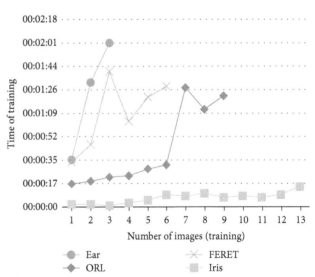

FIGURE 29: Average of training time.

In Table 18, the 5-fold cross-validation results are shown, where for each training set 4 images for each person were used.

In [46] a scale invariant feature transform (SIFT) is proposed. In Table 19, the comparisons among the results obtained using the proposed method and the other work for the FERET database are presented.

TABLE 13: Databases setup.

Database	Number of persons	Max. number of images per person		Image size (pixels)
		Training	Testing	
Ear	77	3	3	132×91
ORL	40	9	9	92×112
FERET	200	6	6	100×100
Iris	77	13	13	21×21

TABLE 14: The summary of results (proposed method).

Method	Number of images for training	Recognition rate		
		Best	Average	Worst
Proposed method (ear database)	3 (up to 80%)	100%	100%	100%
Proposed method (ear database)	2 (up to 50%)	96.75%	96.15%	95.45%
Proposed method (ORL database)	8 (up to 80%)	100%	100%	100%
Proposed method (ORL database)	5 (up to 50%)	99%	98.50%	98.50%
Proposed method (FERET database)	(up to 80%)	98%	92.63%	88.17%
Proposed method (iris database)	(up to 80%)	100%	99.31%	98.70%

TABLE 15: Table of comparison of optimized results (ear database).

Method	Number of images for training	Recognition rate		
		Best (%)	Average (%)	Worst (%)
Sánchez and Melin [7] (ANN)	3	100%	96.75%	—
Melin et al. [45] (MNN)	3	100%	93.82%	83.11%
Sánchez and Melin [7] (MGNN)	3	100%	99.69%	93.5%
Sánchez et al. [38] (FA)	3	100%	99.89%	98.05%
Proposed method (MGNN)	3	100%	100%	100%
Sánchez and Melin [7] (ANN)	2	96.10%	88.53%	—
Sánchez and Melin [7] (MGNN)	2	98.05%	94.81%	79.65%
Sánchez et al. [38] (FA)	2	97.40%	96.82%	95.45%
Proposed method (MGNN)	2	96.75%	96.15%	95.45%

TABLE 16: Table of cross-validation results (ear database).

Experiment 1	Experiment 2	Experiment 3	Experiment 4	Average
100%	100%	94.81%	93.51%	97.07%

TABLE 17: Table of comparison of optimized results (ORL database).

Method	Images for training	Recognition rate		
		Best (%)	Average (%)	Worst (%)
Mendoza et al. [4] (FIS)	8	97.50%	94.69%	91.50%
Sánchez et al. [38] (FA)	8	100%	100%	100%
Sánchez et al. [39] (MGNNs + complexity)	8	100%	99.27%	98.61%
Proposed method	8	100%	100%	100%
Azami et al. [43] (CGA + PCA)	5	96.5%	95.91%	95.37%
Ch'Ng et al. [3] (PCA + LDA)	5	96.5%	94.75%	94%
Sánchez et al. [38] (FA)	5	99%	98.30%	98%
Sánchez et al. [39] (MGNNs + complexity)	5	98.43%	97.59%	94.55%
Proposed method	5	99%	98.5%	98%

TABLE 18: Table of cross-validation results (ORL database).

Experiment 1	Experiment 2	Experiment 3	Experiment 4	Experiment 5	Average
95.42%	94.58%	96.67%	97.92%	97.92%	96.50%

TABLE 19: Table of comparison of optimized results (FERET database).

Method	Number of persons	Number of images	Recognition rate
Wang et al. [46] (SIFT)	50	7	86%
Proposed method	50	7	98%
Wang et al. [46] (SIFT)	100	7	79.7%
Proposed method	100	7	92.33%
Wang et al. [46] (SIFT)	150	7	79.1%
Proposed method	150	7	92%
Wang et al. [46] (SIFT)	200	7	75.7%
Proposed method	200	7	88.17%

TABLE 20: Table of cross-validation results (FERET database).

Number of persons	Experiment 1	Experiment 2	Experiment 3	Experiment 4	Experiment 5	Average
50	93.33%	95.33%	94.00%	94.67%	94.67%	94.40%
100	83.67%	88.33%	89.00%	91.33%	92.00%	88.87%
150	79.78%	86.44%	87.78%	90.22%	89.33%	86.71%
200	76.17%	83.00%	82.83%	84.50%	85.83%	82.47%

In Table 20, the 5-fold cross-validation results are shown, where for each training set 4 images for each person were used.

In [44] and [37], a hierarchical genetic algorithm and a firefly algorithm are, respectively, proposed to optimize modular granular neural networks using iris as biometric measure. The main difference between these works is that in the first and the second one there is no a subdivision of each image as in the proposed method where submodules are experts in parts of the image. In Table 21, the comparison between the optimized results obtained using the proposed method and the other optimized works is presented.

TABLE 21: Table of comparison of optimized results (iris database).

Method	Images for training	Recognition rate		
		Best (%)	Average (%)	Worst (%)
Sánchez and Melin [44] (HGA)	Up to 80%	99.68%	98.68%	97.40%
Sánchez et al. [37] (FA)	Up to 80%	99.13%	98.22%	96.59%
Proposed method	Up to 80%	100%	99.31%	98.70%

TABLE 22: Table of cross-validation results (iris database).

Experiment 1	Experiment 2	Experiment 3	Experiment 4	Experiment 5	Experiment 6	Average
98.27%	99.13%	98.27%	96.97%	97.84%	96.97%	97.91%

TABLE 23: Values of ear database *(test #1)*.

Method	N	Mean	Standard deviation	Error standard deviation of the mean	Estimated difference	t-value	P value	Degree of freedom
Sánchez and Melin [7] (MGNN)	30	0.0030	0.0121	0.0022	0.003	1.38	0.1769	29
Proposed method	30	0	0	0				
Sánchez et al. [38] (MGNN)	30	0.00108	0.00421	0.00077	0.001082	1.41	0.169	29
Proposed method	30	0	0	0				

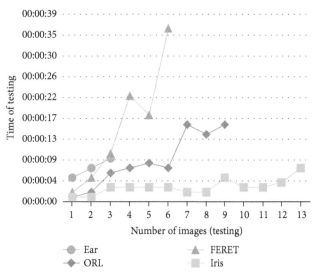

FIGURE 30: Average of training time.

In Table 22, the 5-fold cross-validation results are shown, where for each training set 11 images for each person were used.

4. Statistical Comparison of Results

The results obtained by the proposed method are visually better than the other works; now statistical t-tests are performed in order to verify if there is enough evidence to say that the results of the proposed method are better. In these t-tests, the recognition rates and errors previously presented were used.

4.1. Statistical Comparison for Test #1. In Table 23, the values obtained in the t-test between [7] and [38] and the proposed method are shown, where the t-values were, respectively, 1.38 and 1.41; this means that there is no sufficient evidence to say that ear results for test #1 were improved with the proposed method.

In Figure 31, the distribution of the samples is shown, where it can be observed that the samples are very close to each other.

For the ORL database in test #1, the different values obtained in the t-test between the proposed method and [4, 39] are shown in Table 24. The t-values were 4.12 and 2.42; this means that there is sufficient evidence to say that the results were improved using the proposed method. In Figure 32, the distribution of the samples is shown. It can be observed that samples of [39] are very separated from each other.

For the FERET database, the different values obtained in the t-test between the proposed method and [46] are shown in Table 25. The t-value was 4.24; this means that there is sufficient evidence to say that the results were improved using the proposed method. In Figure 33, the distribution of the samples is shown.

For the iris database, the different values obtained in the t-test between the proposed method and [44] and [37] are

TABLE 24: Values of ORL database *(test #1)*.

Method	N	Mean	Standard deviation	Error standard deviation of the mean	Estimated difference	t-value	P value	Degree of freedom
Mendoza et al. [4] (MG + FIS2)	4	94.69	2.58	1.3	−5.31	−4.12	0.026	3
Proposed method	4	100	0	0				
Sánchez et al. [39] (MGNNs + complexity)	5	99.27	0.676	0.30	−0.73	−2.42	0.072	4
Proposed method	5	100	0	0				

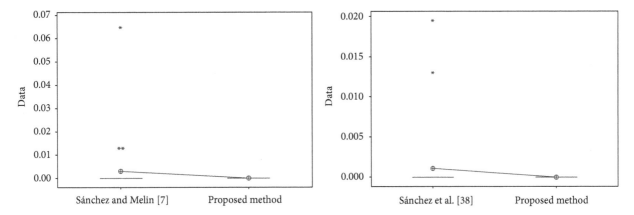

FIGURE 31: Sample distribution (test #1, ear database).

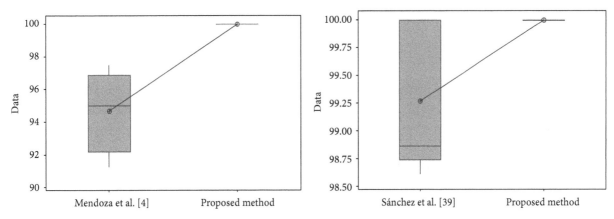

FIGURE 32: Sample distribution (test #1, ORL database).

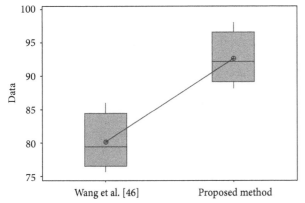

FIGURE 33: Sample distribution (FERET database).

shown in Table 26. The *t*-values were, respectively, 3.18 and 5.62; this means that there is sufficient evidence to say that the results were improved using the proposed method.

In Figure 34, the distribution of the samples is shown. It can be observed that samples of [44] are more separated from each other than in [37].

4.2. Statistical Comparison for Test #2. In Table 27, the values obtained in the *t*-test between [7] and [38] and the proposed method for ear database are shown, where the *t*-values were, respectively, 2.09 and −5.70; this means that there is sufficient evidence to say that face results were improved with the proposed method only versus [7].

TABLE 25: Values of FERET database.

Method	N	Mean	Standard deviation	Error standard deviation of the mean	Estimated difference	t-value	P value	Degree of freedom
Wang et al. [46] (SIFT)	4	80.13	4.29	2.1	−12.50	−4.24	0.00547	6
Proposed method	4	92.63	4.05	2.0				

TABLE 26: Values of iris database.

Method	N	Mean	Standard deviation	Error standard deviation of the mean	Estimated difference	t-value	P value	Degree of freedom
Sánchez and Melin [44]	20	98.68	0.779	0.17	−0.624	−3.18	0.0035	29
Proposed method	20	99.30	0.407	0.091				
Sánchez et al. [37]	20	98.22	0.758	0.17	−1.083	−5.62	$1.8623E − 06$	38
Proposed method	20	99.30	0.407	0.091				

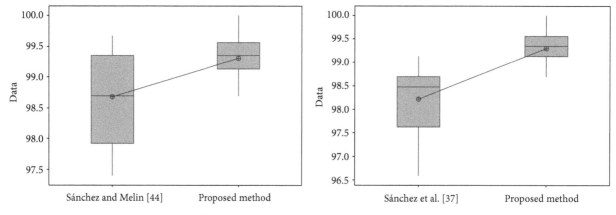

FIGURE 34: Sample distribution (iris database).

In Figure 35, the distribution of the samples is shown, where it can be observed that the samples for [7] and the proposed method are closer than the proposed method and [38]. The distribution of the proposed method and [38] seems to be uniform.

The different values obtained in the t-test for the face database between the proposed method and [43], [3], [38], and [39] are shown in Table 28. The t-values were, respectively, 8.96, 5.90, 0.67, and 1.15; this means that only compared with [3, 43] there is sufficient evidence to say that the face results were improved using the proposed method.

In Figure 36, the distribution of the samples is shown, where it can be observed that the samples are very close between the proposed method and [38, 39].

5. Conclusions

In this paper, the design of modular granular neural network architectures using a grey wolf optimizer is proposed. The design of these architectures consists in the number of modules, percentage of data for the training phase, error

goal, learning algorithm, number of hidden layers, and their respective number of neurons. As objective function this optimizer seeks to minimize the recognition error applying the proposed method to human recognition, where benchmark databases of ear and face biometric measures were used to prove the effectiveness of the proposed method. Statistical comparisons were performed to know if there is sufficient evidence of improvements using the proposed method, mainly with previous works, where a hierarchical genetic algorithm and a firefly algorithm were developed and also use MGNNs, but more comparisons with other works were also performed. As a conclusion, the proposed method has been shown which improves recognition rates in most of the comparisons, especially when the granular approach is not used. An improvement provided by the grey wolf optimizer over the genetic algorithm and the firefly algorithm lies in the fact that the first one allows having the first three best solutions (alpha, beta, and delta) and their others search agents will update their position based on them; otherwise, the genetic algorithm only has a best solution in each iteration, and the firefly algorithm updates

TABLE 27: Values of ear *database (test #2).*

Method	N	Mean	Standard deviation	Error standard deviation of the mean	Estimated difference	t-value	P value	Degrees of freedom
Sánchez and Melin [7] (MGNN)	30	0.0518	0.0345	0.0063	0.01328	2.09	0.045	29
Proposed method	30	0.03853	0.00449	0.00082				
Sánchez et al. [38] (FA)	30	0.03182	0.00462	0.00084	−0.00671	−5.70	4.1926E − 07	57
Proposed method	30	0.03853	0.00449	0.00082				

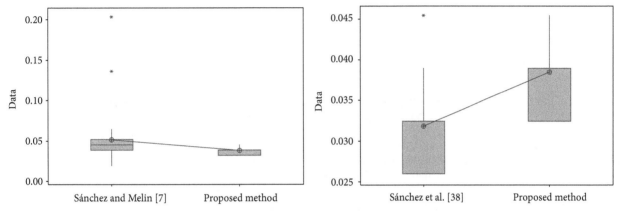

FIGURE 35: Sample distribution (test #2, ear database).

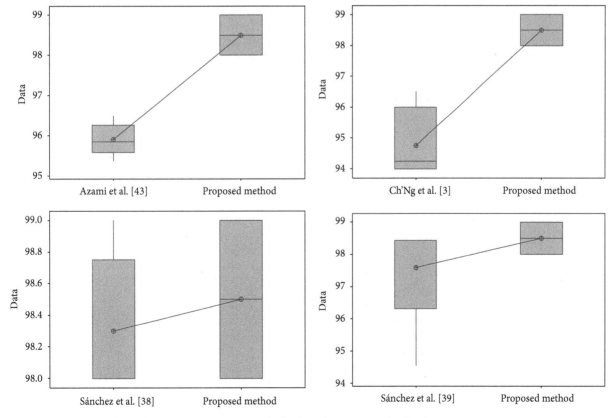

FIGURE 36: Sample database (test #2, ORL database).

TABLE 28: Values of *ORL database (test #2)*.

Method	N	Mean	Standard deviation	Error standard deviation of the mean	Estimated difference	t-value	P value	Degrees of freedom
Azami et al. [43] (CGA + PCA)	5	95.91	0.409	0.18	−2.590	−8.96	$1.9091E - 05$	8
Proposed method	5	98.50	0.500	0.22				
Ch'Ng et al. [3] (PCA + LDA)	4	94.75	1.19	0.60	−3.750	−5.90	0.004	3
Proposed method	5	98.50	0.500	0.22				
Sánchez et al. [38] (FA)	5	98.30	0.447	0.20	−0.20	−0.67	0.523	8
Proposed method	5	98.50	0.500	0.22				
Sánchez et al. [39] (MGNNs + complexity)	5	97.59	1.71	0.76	−0.94	−1.15	0.314	4
Proposed method	5	98.50	0.500	0.22				

the position of the fireflies by evaluating couples of fireflies, where if one firefly is not better than the other their move will be random. This allows the GWO to have greater stability in its trials and in its results. It is important to mention that the results shown in this work were performed using different databases; this prove that the proposed method was designed to be easily adaptable depending of the number of persons and the number of images independently of the biometric measure used. In future works, the proposed method will seek to reduce the complexity of the MGNNs architectures and to minimize the percentage of information and subgranules to design MGNNs.

References

[1] A. K. Jain, K. Nandakumar, and A. Ross, "50 years of biometric research: accomplishments, challenges, and opportunities," *Pattern Recognition Letters*, vol. 79, pp. 80–105, 2016.

[2] A. Ross and A. K. Jain, "Human recognition using biometrics: an overview," *Appeared in Annals of Telecommunications*, vol. 62, pp. 11–35, 2007.

[3] S. I. Ch'Ng, K. P. Seng, and L.-M. Ang, "Modular dynamic RBF neural network for face recognition," in *Proceedings of the 2012 IEEE Conference on Open Systems, ICOS 2012*, mys, October 2012.

[4] O. Mendoza, P. Melin, O. Castillo, and J. R. Castro, "Comparison of fuzzy edge detectors based on the image recognition rate as performance index calculated with neural networks," *Studies in Computational Intelligence*, vol. 312, pp. 389–399, 2010.

[5] A. M. Patil, D. S. Patil, and P. Patil, "Iris recognition using gray level co-occurrence matrix and hausdorff dimension," *International Journal of Computer Applications*, vol. 133, no. 8, pp. 29–34, 2016.

[6] L. Gutierrez, P. Melin, and M. Lopez, "Modular neural network integrator for human recognition from ear images," in *Proceedings of the International Joint Conference on Neural Networks, IJCNN 2010*, Barcelona, Spain, July 2010.

[7] D. Sánchez and P. Melin, "Optimization of modular granular neural networks using hierarchical genetic algorithms for human recognition using the ear biometric measure," *Engineering Applications of Artificial Intelligence*, vol. 27, pp. 41–56, 2014.

[8] M. Agrawal and T. Raikwar, "Speech recognition using signal processing techniques," *International Journal of Engineering and Innovative Technology*, vol. 5, no. 8, pp. 65–68, 2016.

[9] M. Soni, S. Gupta, M. S. Rao, and P. Gupta, "Vein pattern-based verification system," *International Journal of Computer Science and Information Security*, vol. 8, no. 1, pp. 58–63, 2010.

[10] R. C. Bakshe and A. M. Patil, "Hand geometry as a biometric for human identification," *International Journal of Science and Research*, vol. 4, no. 1, pp. 2744–2748, 2015.

[11] G. A. Khuwaja and M. S. Laghari, "Offline handwritten signature recognition," *World Academy of Science, Engineering and Technology*, vol. 59, pp. 1300–1303, 2011.

[12] M. Jhapate and M. Dixit, "An Efficient Human Identification on the Biometric Gait Recognition System using the Inner Angle of the Triangle," *International Journal of Computer Applications*, vol. 136, no. 13, pp. 19–22, 2016.

[13] J. Heaton, *Deep Learning and Neural Networks*, vol. 3, Deep Learning and Neural Networks, Create Space Independent Publishing Platform, 2015.

[14] J. Iovine, *Understanding Neural Networks The Experimenter's Guide*, Images, 2nd edition, 2012.

[15] L. A. Zadeh and J. Kacprzyk, *Fuzzy Logic for the Management of Uncertainty*, Wiley-Interscience, 1992.

[16] M. Pietikäinen, A. Hadid, G. Zhao, and T. Ahonen, *Computer Vision Using Local Binary Patterns*, vol. 40, Springer, 2011.

[17] W. Pedrycz and S.-M. Chen, "Granular computing and intelligent systems: Design with Information Granules of Higher Order and Higher Type," *Intelligent Systems Reference Library*, vol. 13, 2011.

[18] Y. Yao, "Perspectives of granular computing," in *Proceedings of the 2005 IEEE International Conference on Granular Computing*, pp. 85–90, Beijing, China, July 2005.

[19] T. Y. Lin, Y. Y. Yao, and L. A. Zadeh, "Data Mining, Rough Sets and Granular Computing," *Physica*, 2002.

[20] D. Ashlock, *Evolutionary Computation for Modeling and Optimization*, Springer, 2006.

[21] D. Simon, *Evolutionary Optimization Algorithms*, John Wiley & Sons, 2013.

[22] J. H. Holland, *Adaptation in Natural and Artificial Systems: An Introductory Analysis with Applications to Biology, Control, and Artificial Intelligence*, University of Michigan Press, Oxford, UK, 1975.

[23] K. F. Man, K. S. Tang, and S. Kwong, *Genetic Algorithms: Concepts and Designs*, Springer, London, UK, 1999.

[24] M. Dorigo, *Optimization, learning and natural algorithms*, Politecnico di [Ph.D. thesis], Milano, Italy, 1992.

[25] L. D. Mech, "Alpha status, dominance, and division of labor in wolf packs," *Canadian Journal of Zoology*, vol. 77, no. 8, pp. 1196–1203, 1999.

[26] Y. Xin-She and H. Xingshi, "Bat algorithm: literature review and applications," *International Journal of Bio-Inspired Computation*, vol. 5, no. 3, pp. 141–149, 2013.

[27] S. Mirjalili, S. M. Mirjalili, and A. Lewis, "Grey wolf optimizer," *Advances in Engineering Software*, vol. 69, pp. 46–61, 2014.

[28] Z. W. Geem, X.-S. Yang, and C.-L. Tseng, "Harmony search and nature-inspired algorithms for engineering optimization," *Journal of Applied Mathematics*, vol. 2013, Article ID 438158, 2 pages, 2013.

[29] E. Rashedi, H. Nezamabadi-pour, and S. Saryazdi, "GSA: a gravitational search algorithm," *Information Sciences*, vol. 213, pp. 267–289, 2010.

[30] X.-S. Yang, "Firefly algorithms for multimodal optimization," in *Proceedings of the 5th Symposium on Stochastic Algorithms, Foundations and Applications*, vol. 5792, pp. 169–178, 2009.

[31] X.-S. Yang and X. He, "Firefly algorithm: recent advances and applications," *International Journal of Swarm Intelligence*, vol. 1, no. 1, pp. 36–50, 2013.

[32] M. Farooq, "Genetic Algorithm Technique in Hybrid Intelligent Systems for Pattern Recognition," *International Journal of Innovative Research in Science, Engineering and Technology*, vol. 04, no. 04, pp. 1891–1898, 2015.

[33] M. F. Hassanin, A. M. Shoeb, and A. E. Hassanien, "Grey wolf optimizer-based back-propagation neural network algorithm," in *Proceedings of the 2016 12th International Computer Engineering Conference (ICENCO)*, pp. 213–218, Cairo, Egypt, December 2016.

[34] S. Mirjalili, "How effective is the Grey Wolf optimizer in training multi-layer perceptrons," *Applied Intelligence*, vol. 43, no. 1, pp. 150–161, 2015.

[35] M. Mosavi, M. Khishe, and A. Ghamgosar, "Classification of sonar data set using neural network trained by Gray Wolf Optimization," *Neural Network World*, vol. 26, no. 4, pp. 393–415, 2016.

[36] A. Parsian, M. Ramezani, and N. Ghadimi, "A hybrid neural network-gray wolf optimization algorithm for melanoma detection," *Biomedical Research*, vol. 28, no. 8, pp. 3408–3411, 2017.

[37] D. Sánchez, P. Melin, J. Carpio, and H. Puga, "A firefly algorithm for modular granular neural networks optimization applied to iris recognition," in *Proceedings of the 2016 International Joint Conference on Neural Networks, IJCNN 2016*, pp. 139–144, Vancouver, Canada, July 2016.

[38] D. Sánchez, P. Melin, and O. Castillo, "Optimization of modular granular neural networks using a firefly algorithm for human recognition," *Engineering Applications of Artificial Intelligence*, vol. 64, pp. 172–186, 2017.

[39] D. Sánchez, P. Melin, and O. Castillo, "Optimization of modular granular neural networks using a hierarchical genetic algorithm based on the database complexity applied to human recognition," *Information Sciences*, vol. 309, pp. 73–101, 2015.

[40] B. L. M. Happel and J. M. J. Murre, "Design and evolution of modular neural network architectures," *Neural Networks*, vol. 7, no. 6-7, pp. 985–1004, 1994.

[41] D. Li and Y. Du, *Artificial Intelligence with Uncertainty*, Chapman & Hall, Boca Raton, Fla, USA, 2007.

[42] L. A. Zadeh, "Some reflections on soft computing, granular computing and their roles in the conception, design and utilization of information/intelligent systems," *Soft Computing - A Fusion of Foundations, Methodologies and Applications*, vol. 2, no. 1, pp. 23–25, 1998.

[43] H. Azami, M. Malekzadeh, and S. Sanei, "A new neural network approach for face recognition based on conjugate gradient algorithms and principal component analysis," *Journal of mathematics and computer Science*, vol. 6, pp. 166–175, 2013.

[44] D. Sánchez and P. Melin, *Hierarchical modular granular neural networks with fuzzy aggregation*, Springer, 1st edition, 2016.

[45] P. Melin, D. Sánchez, and O. Castillo, "Genetic optimization of modular neural networks with fuzzy response integration for human recognition," *Information Sciences*, vol. 197, pp. 1–19, 2012.

[46] Y. Y. Wang, Z. M. Li, L. Wang, and M. Wang, "A scale invariant feature transform based method," *Journal of Information Hiding and Multimedia Signal Processing*, vol. 4, no. 2, pp. 73–89, 2013.

[47] Database Ear Recognition Laboratory from the University of Science Technology Beijing (USTB, http://www.ustb.edu.cn/resb/en/index.htm.

[48] AT&T Laboratories Cambridge, the ORL database of faces, Found on the Web page: https://www.cl.cam.ac.uk/research/dtg/attarchive/facedatabase.html.

[49] P. J. Phillips, H. Moon, S. A. Rizvi, and P. J. Rauss, "The FERET evaluation methodology for face-recognition algorithms," *IEEE Transactions on Pattern Analysis and Machine Intelligence*, vol. 22, no. 10, pp. 1090–1104, 2000.

[50] Database of Human Iris. Institute of Automation of Chinese Academy of Sciences (CASIA). Found on the Web page: http://www.cbsr.ia.ac.cn/english/IrisDatabase.asp.

[51] P. Viola and M. Jones, "Rapid object detection using a boosted cascade of simple features," in *Proceedings of the IEEE Computer Society Conference on Computer Vision and Pattern Recognition*, vol. 1, pp. I511–I518, December 2001.

[52] P. Viola and M. J. Jones, "Robust real-time face detection," *International Journal of Computer Vision*, vol. 57, no. 2, pp. 137–154, 2004.

[53] L. Masek and P. Kovesi, *MATLAB Source Code for a Biometric Identification System Based on Iris Patterns*, The School of Computer Science and Software Engineering, The University of Western Australia, 2003.

3

Pathological Brain Detection Using Weiner Filtering, 2D-Discrete Wavelet Transform, Probabilistic PCA, and Random Subspace Ensemble Classifier

Debesh Jha,[1] Ji-In Kim,[1] Moo-Rak Choi,[2] andGoo-RakKwon[1]

[1]Department of Information and Communication Engineering, Chosun University, 309 Pilmun-Daero, Dong-Gu, Gwangju 61452, Republic of Korea
[2]School of Electrical Engineering, Korea University, 145 Anam-ro, Sungbuk-gu, Seoul 02841, Republic of Korea

Correspondence should be addressed to Goo-Rak Kwon; grkwon@chosun.ac.kr

Academic Editor: George A. Papakostas

Accurate diagnosis of pathological brain images is important for patient care, particularly in the early phase of the disease. Although numerous studies have used machine-learning techniques for the computer-aided diagnosis (CAD) of pathological brain, previous methods encountered challenges in terms of the diagnostic efficiency owing to deficiencies in the choice of proper filtering techniques, neuroimaging biomarkers, and limited learning models. Magnetic resonance imaging (MRI) is capable of providing enhanced information regarding the soft tissues, and therefore MR images are included in the proposed approach. In this study, we propose a new model that includes Wiener filtering for noise reduction, 2D-discrete wavelet transform (2D-DWT) for feature extraction, probabilistic principal component analysis (PPCA) for dimensionality reduction, and a random subspace ensemble (RSE) classifier along with the K-nearest neighbors (KNN) algorithm as a base classifier to classify brain images as pathological or normal ones. The proposed methods provide a significant improvement in classification results when compared to other studies. Based on 5×5 cross-validation (CV), the proposed method outperforms 21 state-of-the-art algorithms in terms of classification accuracy, sensitivity, and specificity for all four datasets used in the study.

1. Introduction

Magnetic resonance imaging (MRI) of the brain provides comprehensive diagnostic information for diagnosis [1]. It is essential because it is noninvasive and safe and yields a higher resolution that cannot be obtained by other techniques. MRI is mainly utilized to diagnose different types of disorders such as strokes, tumors, bleeding, injury, blood-vessel diseases or infections, and multiple sclerosis (MS). The early diagnosis of pathological brain disease and its prodromal stage are critical and can decrease or halt the progression of the disease [2]. Therefore, the classification of normal/pathological brain status from MRIs is essential in clinical medicine as it focuses on soft tissue anatomy and generates a large and detailed dataset about the subject's brain. However, the use of a large database makes manual interpretation of the brain images

tedious, time consuming, and costly. The major drawback of the manual approach is its irreducibility. Therefore, there is a need for automated image analysis tools such as computer-aided diagnosis (CAD) systems [3].

Considerable research has been carried out to develop automatic tools for the classification of MR images to distinguish between normal and pathological brains. El-Dahshan et al. [4] utilized a three-level discrete wavelet transform, accompanied by principal component analysis (PCA), to decrease features. A good success rate was obtained by using feedforward backpropagation neural networks (BPNNs) and the K-nearest neighbor (KNN). Zhang and Wu [5] recommended the application of a kernel support vector machine (KSVM) and presented three new kernels: homogenous polynomial, inhomogeneous polynomial, and Gaussian radial basis for distinguishing between normal and abnormal images. Patnaik et al. [6] employed DWT to obtain the approximation coefficients. Later, a support vector machine (SVM) was utilized to perform the classification. Zhang et al. [7] recommended a training feedforward neural network (FNN) with a unique scaled conjugate gradient (SCG) technique. Kundu et al. [8] proposed combining the Ripplet transform (RT) for feature extraction, PCA for dimensionality reduction, and the least-square SVM (LS-SVM) for classification, and the 5 × 5 stratified cross-validation (SCV) offered high classification accuracies. El-Dahshan et al. [9] utilized the feedback pulse-coupled neural network for the preprocessing of MR images, the DWT for feature extraction, PCA for features reduction, and the FBPNN for the classification of pathological and normal brains. Damodharan and Raghavan [10] used wavelet entropy as the feature space, and they then used the traditional naïve-Bayes classifier classification method. Wang et al. [11] utilized the stationary wavelet transform (SWT) to substitute for DWT. Likewise, they proposed a hybridization of particle swarm optimization (PSO) and the artificial bee colony (HPA) method to obtain the optimal weights and biases of FNN. Nazir et al. [12] applied denoising at the beginning, and they achieved an overall classification accuracy of 91.8%. Harikumar and Vinoth Kumar [13] used wavelet-energy and SVM. Padma and Sukanesh [14] used the combined wavelet statistical feature to segment and classify Alzheimer's disease (AD) as well as benign and malignant tumor slices. Zhang et al. [15] utilized Hu moment invariants (HMI) and generalized eigenvalue proximal SVM (GEPSVM) for the detection of pathological brain in MRI scanning and obtained an accuracy of 98.89%, sensitivity of 99.29%, and specificity of 92.00%. Later on, Zhang et al. [16] used multilayer perceptron (MLP) for classification, where two pruning techniques like dynamic pruning (DP) and Bayesian detection boundaries (BDB were used to find the optimal hidden neurons and an adaptive real coded BBO (ARCBBO) method was implemented to determine the optimal weights and obtained an accuracy of 98.12% and 98.24%, respectively. Nayak et al. [17] used 2D-DWT, PCA, and Adaboost algorithm with random forest as its base classifier and obtained an accuracy of 98.44% for classification of pathological brain MR image with Dataset-255. Later on, Nayak et al. [18] utilized two-dimensional stationary wavelet transform (SWT), symmetric uncertainty ranking (SUR) filter, and Adaboost with SVM classifier for the detection of pathological brain MR images and obtained an accuracy of 98.43% with Dataset-255. Wang et al. [19] employed Pseudo Zernike moment and linear regression classifier for classification of Alzheimer's disease and yielded an accuracy of 97.51%, sensitivity of 96.71%, and specificity of 97.73%. Alam et al. [20] utilized dual-tree complex wavelet transform (DTCWT), principal component analysis (PCA), and twin support vector machine (TSVM) for the detection of Alzheimer's disease classification and obtained an accuracy of 95.46 ± 1.26.

Scholars have proposed different methods to extract features for the pathological brain disease [21]. After analyzing the above methods, we found that all of the methods achieved promising results which indicated that 2D-DWT is effective in feature extraction for pathological brain detection.

However, there are two problems. (1) Most of them utilize traditional PCA for feature extraction which is computational-intensive for large datasets with a higher dimensions. (2) The classification performance can be further improved, because the feature vector contains excessive features, which required more memory and increased computational complexity. Moreover, it required too much time to train the classifiers.

To address the above-mentioned problems, we proposed a new pathological brain detection system based on brain MR images which has the potential improvements over the other schemes. Weiner filter is used for the preprocessing of the images. The proposed method uses 2D DWT for the extraction of features because of its ability to analyze images at different scales. PPCA is used in place of PCA for the reduction of features which has the advantages of computing the efficient dimension reduction in terms of the distribution of latent variables, maximum-likelihood estimates, probability model, dealing with the missing data, and a combination of multiple PCA as probabilistic mixture. A relatively new classifier known as random subspace ensemble (RSE) classifier is employed which has the advantage of low computational burden over the traditional classifiers. Hence, the novelty of the proposed method lies in the application of PPCA features and RSE classifier.

The article is organized as follows: Section 2 presents details about the materials and methods. Section 3 describes the experimental results, evaluation procedure, and discussions. Finally, Section 4 presents the conclusion and future research.

2. Materials and Methods

2.1. Materials. At present, there are four benchmark datasets (DS) as DS-66, DS-90, DS-160, and DS-255, of different sizes of 66, 90, 160, and 255 images, respectively. All the datasets (DS) contain axial, T2-weighted, 256 × 256-pixel MR images downloaded from medical school of Harvard University (Boston, MA, USA) (URL: http://www.med.harvard.edu/aablib/home.html) website. T2-weighted images are selected as input image because T2-weighted (spin-spin) relaxation gives better image contrast that is helpful to show different anatomical structure clearly. Also, they are better in detecting lesions than T1 weighted images.

We selected five slices from each subject. The selection criterion is that, for healthy subjects, these slices were selected at random. For pathological subjects, the slices should contain the lesions by confirmation of these radiologists with ten years of experiences. A sample of diseased slices is shown in Figure 2. In this investigation, all diseases are treated as pathological, and our task is a binary classification problem, that is, to distinguish pathological brain from healthy brains. Here, the whole brain is considered as the input image. We did not select local characteristics like point and edge, and we extract global image characteristics that are further learned by the new cascade model. Let us keep in mind that our procedure is different from the way neuroradiologists do. They usually take the local features and compare with standard template to check whether focuses exist, such as shrink, expansion, bleeding, and inflammation. While our technique is like AlphaGO, the computer researcher gives the machine sufficient data, and then the machine can learn how to make classification naturally. Including patients' information (age, gender, handedness, memory test, education, etc.) can add additional information and thus may assist us to improve the classification performance. Nevertheless, this new model proposed in our research is only dependent on the imaging data. Besides, the imaging data from the website does not contain the subjects' information.

The cost of predicting pathological to normal types is severe, because the subjects may be told that she/he is normal and thus avoids the mild symptoms displayed. The treatments of patients may be postponed. Nevertheless, the cost of misclassification of healthy to pathological types is low, since correct treatment can be given by other diagnosis means. The cost-sensitivity (CS) problem was resolved by changing the class distribution at the beginning state, since original data was accessible. That means we purposely picked up more pathological brains than healthy ones into the dataset, with the goal of making the classifier biased to pathological brains, to solve the CS problem. The overfitting problem was supervised by cross-validation technique.

In our experiment, DS-66 and DS-160 are extensively employed for brain MR image classifications that consist of normal brain images as well as abnormal brain images from seven types of diseases, namely, glioma, meningioma, Alzheimer's disease, Alzheimer's disease plus visual agnosia, Pick's disease, sarcoma, and Huntington's disease. DS-90 contains MR brain images of a healthy brain, AIDS dementia, Alzheimer's disease plus visual agnosia, Alzheimer's disease, cerebral calcinosis, cerebral toxoplasmosis, Creutzfeldt-Jakob disease, glioma, herpes encephalitis, Huntington's disease, Lyme encephalopathy, meningioma, metastatic adenocarcinoma, metastatic bronchogenic carcinoma, motor neuron disease, MS, Pick's disease, and sarcoma.

The third dataset, DS-255, includes images of four new types of diseases embedded with the above seven types of diseased images and normal brain images. The four additional diseases are chronic subdural hematoma, cerebral toxoplasmosis, herpes encephalitis, and MS.

2.2. Proposed Methodology.

2.2. Proposed Methodology. The proposed method comprises four vital stages, namely, image preprocessing, feature extraction using 2D-DWT, feature reduction utilizing PPCA, and classification using the RSE classifier. In order to enhance the quality of the MR images, Wiener filter is employed, followed by the extraction of approximation coefficients from MR images utilizing a 2D-DWT with three-level decomposition. Then, we saved these obtained features as our primary features. Thereafter, then we employ PPCA for obtaining uncorrelated discriminant set of features. Finally, we classified the reduced features using the RSE classifier with KNN as a base classifier. The complete block diagram of the proposed system is shown in Figure 1. A brief description about all these four stages is shown below.

2.2.1. Preprocessing Using Wiener Filter. The gif images were downloaded individually from the website of the Harvard Medical School. Then, each of the gif images was converted into JPG format manually. The images were in RGB format, and they were then converted into grayscale intensity images. Next, the intensity image is converted to double precision. Acquired brain MR images require preprocessing to improve the quality, enabling us to obtain better features. In our study, we used the popular Wiener filter method.

The Wiener filter is used to replace the finite impulse response (FIR) filter in order to decrease noise in signals [22]. When an image is blurred by a familiar low-pass filter (LPF), we can recover the image by inverse filtering. However, inverse filtering is extremely sensitive to additive noise. Wiener filtering accomplishes an optimal trade-off between inverse filtering and noise smoothing in that it eliminates the additive noise and inverts the blurring simultaneously. In addition, it reduces the overall mean-square error during the course of inverse filtering plus noise smoothing. The Wiener filtering method generates a linear approximation of the original image and is based on the stochastic framework. The orthogonality principle indicates that the Wiener filter in the Fourier domain can be articulated as follows:

$$W(f_1, f_2) = \frac{H^*(f_1, f_2) S_{xx}(f_1, f_2)}{\|H(f_1, f_2)\|^2 S_{xx} + S_{nn}(f_1, f_2)}. \tag{1}$$

Here, $S_{xx}(f_1, f_2)$ is the power spectrum of the original image, $S_{nn}(f_1, f_2)$ is the adaptive noise, and $H(f_1, f_2)$ is the blurring filter.

2.3. 2D-DWT

2.3.1. Advantage of Wavelet Transform. The FT is the most commonly used tool for the analysis of signals, and it breaks down a time-domain signal into constituent sinusoids of various frequencies, thus changing the signal from the time domain to the frequency domain. Nevertheless, the FT has a serious disadvantage as it removes the time information from the signal. For instance, an investigator cannot determine when a specific event took place based on a Fourier spectrum. Therefore, the classification accuracy decreases as the time information is lost.

Gabor modified the FT to examine only a small part of the signal at a time. This approach is known as windowing or the short-time FT (STFT) [23]. It accumulates a window of appropriate shape to the signal. STFT can be considered as a compromise between the time information and frequency information. Nevertheless, the precision of the information is limited by the window size.

The wavelet transform (WT) constitutes the next logical step. It uses a windowing method with variable size, and the progress of the signal analysis is shown in Figure 3. Another benefit of the WT is that it selects a "scale" in place of the traditional "frequency"; that is, it does not generate a time-frequency view of a specific signal but a time-scale view. The time-scale view is another way of visualizing data and is more commonly used and effective.

2.3.2. DWT. This is an effective implementation of the WT, and it utilizes the dyadic scales and positions [24]. The

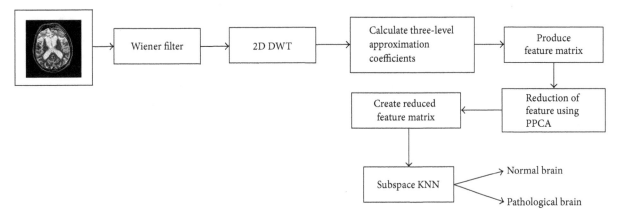

FIGURE 1: Block diagram of the proposed system.

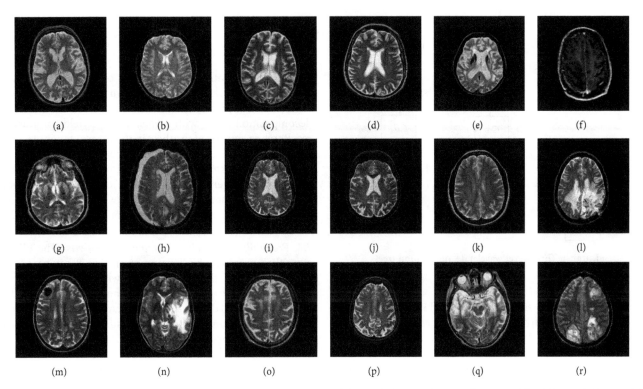

FIGURE 2: Brain MR images: (a) healthy brain; (b) AIDS dementia; (c) Alzheimer's disease plus visual agnosia; (d) Alzheimer's disease; (e) cerebral calcinosis; (f) cerebral toxoplasmosis; (g) Creutzfeldt-Jakob disease; (h) glioma, (i) herpes encephalitis; (j) Huntington's disease; (k) Lyme encephalopathy; (l) meningioma; (m) metastatic adenocarcinoma; (n) metastatic bronchogenic carcinoma; (o) motor neuron disease; (p) multiple sclerosis; (q) Pick's disease; and (r) sarcoma.

fundamentals of the DWT are as follows. Let $x(t)$ be a square-integral function. The continuous WT of the signal $x(t)$ relative to a real-valued wavelet $\psi(t)$ is defined as

$$W(a, \tau) = \int_{-\infty}^{\infty} x(t) \frac{1}{\sqrt{a}} \psi * \left(\frac{t - \tau}{a} \right) dt, \qquad (2)$$

where $W(a, \tau)$ is the WT, τ indicates the function across $x(t)$, and the variable a is the dilation factor (both real and positive numbers). Here, the asterisk ($*$) indicates the complex conjugate.

Equation (1) can be discretized by restraining a and τ to a discrete lattice ($a = 2^j$ and $\tau = 2^j k$) to provide the DWT, which is given as follows:

$$cA_{j,k}(n) = DS \left[\sum_n x(n) l_j^* \left(n - 2^j k \right) \right],$$

$$cD_{j,k}(n) = DS \left[\sum_n x(n) h_j^* \left(n - 2^j k \right) \right]. \qquad (3)$$

Here, $cA_{j,k}$ and $cD_{j,k}$ refer to the coefficients of the approximation components and detailed components,

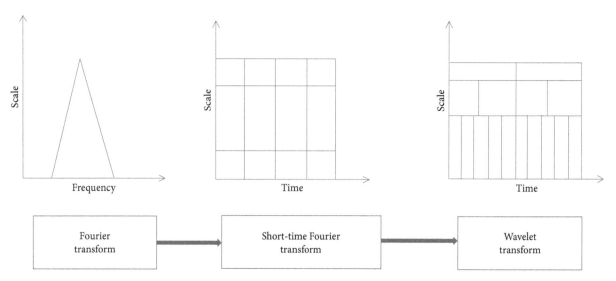

FIGURE 3: Progress of signal analysis.

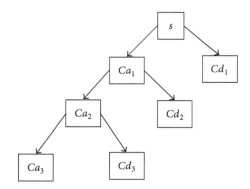

FIGURE 4: Three-level wavelet decomposition tree.

respectively. $l(n)$ and $h(n)$ represent the LPF and high-pass filter (HPF), respectively. j and k represent the wavelet scale and translation factors, respectively. The DS operator represents downsampling. The approximation component has low-frequency components of the image, whereas the detailed components contain high-frequency components. Figure 4 shows a three-level decomposition tree.

2.3.3. 2D-DWT. In a case involving 2D images, the DWT is employed in each dimension separately. A sample of a pathological brain MR image with its three-level wavelet decomposition is shown in Figure 5. Consequently, there are four subband images (LL, LH, HH, and HL) at each scale. The subband LL is utilized for the other 2D-DWT and can be considered as the approximation component of the image, whereas the LH, HL, and HH subbands can be considered as the detailed components of the image. As the level of the decomposition is increased, a more compact, but coarser approximation component is accessed. Thus, wavelets give a simple hierarchical foundation for clarifying the image information.

There are various types of wavelets, for example, Daubechies, symlets 1, coiflets 1, and biorthogonal wavelets and

reverse biorthogonal 1.1. We tested our result with each type of the wavelet family as shown in Table 2. In our research, the approximation coefficient of three-level wavelet decomposition along with a Haar wavelet yields promising results when compared to others in the wavelet family. Hence, Haar wavelet was selected in the experiment. It is also the simplest and most significant wavelet of the wavelet family. Moreover, it is very fast and can be used to extract basic structural information from an image. All the features are present for all the images, and a feature matrix is generated.

2.4. Probabilistic Principal Component Analysis. The PPCA algorithm proposed by Tipping et al. [36–38] is based on the estimation of the principal axes when any input vector has one or more missing values. The PPCA reduces the high-dimensional data to a lower-dimensional representation by relating a p-dimensional observation vector y to a k-dimensional latent (or unobserved) variable x that is regarded as normal with zero mean and covariance $I(k)$. Moreover, PPCA depends on an isotropic error model. The relationship can be established as

$$y^T = W * x^T + \mu + \varepsilon, \qquad (4)$$

where y denotes the row vector of the observed variable, ε denotes the isotropic error term, and x is the row vector of latent variables. The error term, ε, is Gaussian with zero mean and covariance $v * I(k)$, where v is the residual variance. To make the residual variance greater than 0, the value of k should be smaller than the rank. A standard principal component where v equals 0 is the limiting condition of PPCA. The observed variables, y, are conditionally independent for the given values of the latent variables x. Therefore, the correlation between the observation variables is explained by the latent variables, and the error justifies the variability unique to y_i. The dimension of the matrix W is $p \times k$, and it relates both latent and observation variables. The vector μ allows the model to acquire a nonzero mean. PPCA considers

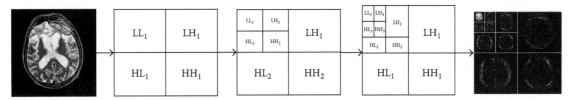

FIGURE 5: Pathological brain image and its wavelet coefficient at three-level decomposition.

the values to be missing and arbitrary over the dataset. From this model,

$$y \sim N\left(\mu, W * W^T + v * I\left(k\right)\right). \tag{5}$$

Given that the solution of W and v cannot be determined analytically, we used the expectation-maximization (EM) algorithm for the iterative maximization of the corresponding log-likelihood function. The EM algorithm considers missing values as additional latent variables. At convergence, the columns of W span the solution subspace. PPCA then yields the orthonormal coefficients.

With respect to our research, the size of the image is 256 × 256. After three-level decomposition, the vector feature becomes 32 × 32 = 1024. Here, all the features are not relevant for the classification. Because of the high computational cost, we utilized PPCA for the dimensionality reduction. The advantage of PPCA over PCA is its computational efficiency.

2.5. RSE Classifier. Ensemble classification includes combining multiple classifiers to obtain more accurate predictions than those obtained utilizing individual models. In addition, ensemble learning techniques are considered very useful for upgrading prediction accuracy. Nevertheless, base classifiers must be as precise and diverse as possible to increase the generalization capability of an ensemble model.

For the classification of normal and pathological brain MRI images, we used a random subspace classifier that uses KNN as a base classifier. The main idea behind the success of ensemble classification is the diversification in the classification that makes the ensemble classifier. With the ensemble classification approach, each classifier provides a different error for different instant. Therefore, we can develop a strong classifier that can decrease the error. The random subspace classifier is a machine-learning classifier that divides the entire feature space into subspaces. Each subspace randomly selects features from the original feature space. It must be guaranteed that the boundaries of the particular base classifier are significantly different. To realize this, an unstable or weaker classifier is utilized as base classifier because they create sufficiently varied decision boundaries, even for small disturbances in the training data parameters.

We used the majority voting method to obtain the final decision of the class membership. In the proposed algorithm, we used KNN as the base classifier owing to its simplicity. After selecting a random subspace, a new set of KNNs is estimated. The majority voting method was utilized to combine the output of each base classifier for the decision preparing test class.

TABLE 1: Confusion matrix for a binary classifier to discriminate between two classes (A_1 and A_2).

True class	Predicted class	
	A_1 (patients)	A_2 (controls)
A_1 (patients)	TP	FN
A_2 (controls)	FP	TN

Here, TP (true positive): correctly categorized as positive cases, TN (true negative): correctly categorized as negative cases, FP (false positive): incorrectly categorized as negative cases, FN (false negative): incorrectly categorized as positive cases.

TABLE 2: Comparison of different wavelet families.

Wavelet family	Accuracy
Haar	99.20%
Daubechies 2	98.60%
Coiflets 1	96.98%
Symlets 1	99.01%
Biorthogonal 1.1	98.64%

2.6. Pseudocode of Proposed System. Our proposed system can be outlined in four major stages. The steps involved are depicted in Pseudocode 1.

2.7. Performance Measures. Various techniques are used to evaluate the classifier's efficiency. The performance is determined based on the final confusion matrix. The confusion matrix holds correct and incorrect classification results. Table 1 illustrates a confusion matrix for binary classification, where TP, TN, FP, and FN depict true positive, true negative, false positive, and false negative, respectively.

Here, pathological brains are assumed to hold the value "true," and normal control (NC) ones are assumed to hold the value "false" following normal convention. Now, we calculate the performance of the proposed approach on the basis of sensitivity, specificity, accuracy, and precision as follows.

(i) Sensitivity (true positive rate): this is the tendency or ability to determine that the diagnostic test is positive when the person has the disease:

$$\text{Sensitivity} = \frac{\text{TP}}{\text{TP} + \text{FN}}. \tag{6}$$

(ii) Specificity (true negative rate): this is the tendency or ability to determine that the diagnostic test is negative when the person does not have the disease:

$$\text{Specificity} = \frac{\text{TN}}{\text{TN} + \text{FP}}. \tag{7}$$

```
Input: T2-weighted MR brain images.
Parameter: N, total number of images
Step 1 (weiner filter)
for i = 1 : N
Read the images and apply wiener filter
end
Step 2 (2D-DWT)
For i = 1 : N
Read in the image file
Apply the DWT using for the 3rd level using "Haar" wavelet to extract the wavelet coefficients.
A matrix X [M × N] is employed to store all the coefficients.
End
Step 3. Reduce the features from the coefficients using PPCA
for j = 1 : N
Apply PPCA transformation on the obtained wavelet coefficients.
Put the new dataset in a matrix Y.
End
Step 4 (RSE classification using 5 × 5 cross-validation)
Divide the input data I and target data T into 5 different groups randomly
For k = 1 : 5
Use the kth group for test, and other 4 groups to train the RSE algorithm.
Classify test image
End
Calculate average specificity, sensitivity, and accuracy.
```

PSEUDOCODE 1: Pseudocode of the proposed system.

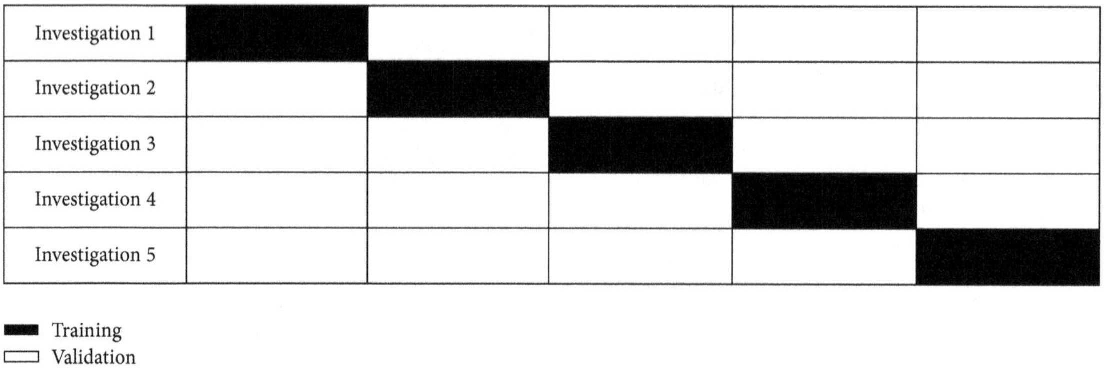

Investigation 1	■				
Investigation 2		■			
Investigation 3			■		
Investigation 4				■	
Investigation 5					■

■ Training
☐ Validation

FIGURE 6: Illustration of k-fold cross-validation.

(iii) Accuracy: this is a measure of how many diagnostic tests are correctly performed:

$$\text{Accuracy} = \frac{\text{TP} + \text{TN}}{\text{TP} + \text{TN} + \text{FP} + \text{FN}}. \qquad (8)$$

(iv) The precision and the recall are formulated by

$$\text{Precision} = \frac{\text{TP}}{\text{TP} + \text{FP}}. \qquad (9)$$

2.8. Cross-Validation. Cross-validation (CV) is a model-assessment method that is used to evaluate the performance of a machine-learning algorithm prediction on a new DS on which it has not been trained. It helps to solve the overfitting problems. Each cross-validation round involves randomly portioning the original DS into a training set and a validation set. The illustration of the k-fold CV is shown in Figure 6. The training set is used to train a supervised learning algorithm, while a test set is used to evaluate its performance.

To make the RSE classifier more reliable and generalize to independent datasets, a 5 × 6-fold stratified cross-validation (SCV) and 5 × 5-fold SCV are employed. A 5 × 6-fold SCV is employed for DS-66 and 5 × 5-fold SCV is used for DS-90, DS-160, and DS-255. For DS-66, 55 MR images are used for training whereas 75, 128, and 204 images are used for DS-90, DS-160, and DS-255 respectively. The validation images for DS-66, DS-90, DS-160, and DS-255 are 11, 15, 32, and 51, respectively.

TABLE 3: Comparison result of the proposed method.

Proposed method	Feature	DS-66	DS-90	DS-160	DS- 255
Logistic regression	13	100.00	100.00	100.00	92.50
QDA	13	100.00	98.90	98.90	96.50
KNN	13	100.00	100.00	100.00	97.30
RSE classifier	13	100.00	100.00	100.00	99.20

TABLE 4: Classification comparison with DS-90.

Existing methods	Success cases	Sensitivity (%)	Specificity (%)	Precision (%)	Accuracy (%)
DWT + PCA + BPNN [25]	388	88.00	56.00	97.14	86.22
DWT + PCA + RBF-NN [25]	411	92.47	72.00	98.25	91.33
DWT + PCA + PSO-KSVM [25]	440	98.12	92.00	99.52	97.78
WE + BPNN [26]	390	88.47	56.00	97.16	86.67
WE + KSVM [27]	413	93.18	68.00	98.02	91.78
DWT + PCA + GA-KSVM [28]	439	97.88	92.00	99.52	97.56
WE + PSO-KSVM [29]	437	97.65	88.00	99.28	97.11
WE + BBO-KSVM [29]	440	98.12	92.00	99.52	97.78
WE + QPSO-KSVM [30]	442	98.59	92.00	99.52	98.22
WFRFT + PCA + GEPSVM [31]	446	99.53	92.00	99.53	99.11
HMI + SEPSVM [15]	445	99.06	96.00		98.89
HMI + TSVM [15]	445	99.29	92.00		98.89
Proposed					
2D- DWT + PPCA + RSE (proposed)	450	100.00	100.00	100.00	100.00

3. Results and Discussion

In this study, we implemented a new machine-learning framework using MATLAB 2016a on an Intel computer with a Core-i5 processor and 16 GB RAM running under the Windows 7 operating system. This program can be tested or run on any computer platform where MATLAB is available.

3.1. Feature Extraction and Optimum Wavelet. In the proposed system, the three-level 2D-DWT of the Haar wavelet breaks down the input image into 10 subbands, as illustrated in Figure 5. The top left corner of the wavelet coefficient image (Figure 5) represents the approximation coefficients of the three-level decomposition of the image, whose size is only 32 × 32 = 1024. These obtained features are the initial features. The size of these features is still large, and the matrix size needs to be reduced. Now, these reduced features are sent as the input to the PPCA.

3.2. Feature Reduction. The use of PPCA as a dimension-reduction tool reduces the feature size to its desired size. Here, we can take the feature as desired. It is better that the desired number of features should at least preserve more than 90% of the variance. However, in this study, we did not take 95% of the variance because it may lead to a higher computational cost. Researchers have considered different numbers of features. In our case, we first used a small number of features, but the accuracy was poor. However, the result with 13 principal components was excellent. Hence,

the proposed method uses 13 principal components to earn higher classification accuracy.

3.3. Classification Results. The reduced features were sent to the classifier, and the results obtained with the different classifier are promising. From the experiment, it is seen that the proposed method works well for all four DSs using 13 principal components. The performances obtained with logistic regression, quadratic discriminant analysis, KNN, and RSE classifier with KNN as a base classifier are shown in Table 3. From the table, we see that the proposed method outperforms other methods. We utilized a 5-fold CV for DS-90, DS-160, and DS-255, whereas we utilized a 6-fold CV for DS-66. The RSE classifier obtained an accuracy of 100.00%, 100.00%, 100.00%, and 99.20%, with DS-66, DS-90, DS-160, and DS-255, respectively. The result obtained with the cubic SVM is the same as the RSE classifier for the dataset beside DS-66, where it could only achieve 98.50%.

3.4. Comparison with Existing Schemes. To further demonstrate the effectiveness of the proposed approach, we compared 21 existing algorithms. The algorithms and their corresponding results are listed in Tables 4 and 5. Table 4 shows the comparison result with DS-90. It is evident from Table 4 that our proposed method correctly matched all cases with 100% sensitivity, 100% specificity, 100% precision, and 100% accuracy. A comparison of the obtained results shows that our algorithm is superior to the others. This shows the effectiveness of the preprocessing technique combined with

TABLE 5: Classification comparison (DS-66, DS-160, and DS-255).

Approaches	Feature	Run	Accuracy (%)		
			DS-66	*DS-160*	*DS-255*
DWT + SVM + POLY [24]	4761				
DWT + SVM + RBF [24]	4761	5	98.00	97.15	96.37
DWT + PCA + *k*-NN [4]	7	5	98.00	97.33	96.18
DWT + PCA + FNN + ACPSO [32]	19	5	98.00	97.54	96.79
DWT + PCA + FNN + SCABC [33]	19	5	100.00	98.75	97.38
DWT + PCA + BPNN + SCG [7]	19	5	100.00	98.93	97.81
DWT + PCA + KSVM [5]	19	5	100.00	98.29	97.14
RT + PCA + LS-SVM [34]	9	5	100.00	99.38	98.82
SWT + PCA + IABAP-FNN [11]	7	10	100.00	98.88	98.43
WT + PCA + ABC-SPSO-FNN [11]	7	10	100.00	99.44	99.18
WE + NBC [35]	7	10	92.58	99.62	99.02
DWT + PCA + ADBRF [17]	13	5	100.00	99.30	98.44
DWT + SUR + ADBSVM [18]	7	5	100.00	99.22	98.43
FRFE + DP-MLP + ARCBBO [16]	12	10	100.00	99.19	98.24
FRFE + BDP-MLP + ARCBBO [16]	12	10	100.00	99.31	98.12
DWT + PCA + RSE	13	5	100.00	99.57	98.90
DWT + PPCA + RSE (proposed)	13	5	100.00	100.00	99.20

features extracted using the WT and PPCA. Table 4 shows the result of 5 runs of the proposed system. Table 5 demonstrates the comparison results over the three DSs in terms of the number of features, number of runs, and average accuracy. Here, some of the recent schemes were run 10 times, while others were run five times. From Tables 4 and 5, we see that most of the techniques achieved excellent classification when subjected to DS-66 as it is smaller in size. However, none of the algorithms achieved 100.00% with DS-90 and DS-160 because DS-255 is larger in size and includes more types of diseased brains; therefore, no current CAD system can earn a perfect classification.

Finally, this proposed "DWT + PPCA + RSE" achieved an accuracy of 100% for DS-66, DS-90, and DS-160 and an accuracy of 99.20% for DS-255, which is comparable with other recent studies and greater than the entire algorithm presented in Table 5. The improvement realized by the recommended scheme appears to be marginal compared with other schemes, but we obtained this result based on a careful statistical analysis (five repetitions of *k*-fold CV). Thus, this improvement is reliable and robust.

4. Conclusion

This paper proposed a new cascade model of "2D-DWT + PPCA + RSE" for the detection of pathological brains. The experiments validated its effectiveness as it achieved an accuracy of 99.20%. Our contributions lie in three points. First, we introduced the Wiener filter and showed its effectiveness. Besides this we introduced the PPCA and RSE classifier and proved it gives the better performance when compared with other state-of-the-art algorithms. In this work, we transformed the PBD problem to a binary classification task. We presented a novel method that replaced PCA and introduced RSE classifier. The experiment showed the superiority of our methods to existing approaches.

The proposed algorithm can also be employed in other fields, for example, face recognition, breast cancer detection, and fault detection. Moreover, this method has been validated on the publically available datasets which are limited in size. Also, in the selected dataset, the images are collected during the late and middle stage of diseases; however, the images with disease at early stages need to be considered.

In future research, we may consider images from other modalities like MRSI, PET, and CT to increase robustness to our scheme. The proposed method can be validated on a larger clinical dataset utilizing modern machine-learning techniques like deep learning, extreme learning, and so on, after collecting the enough brain images from the medical institutes. Internet of things can be another promising research field to embed this PBDS.

Nomenclature

MR(I):   Magnetic resonance (imaging)
DWT: Discrete wavelet transform
PPCA: Probabilistic principal component analysis
KNN: *k*-nearest neighbor
CV: Cross-validation
BPNN: Backpropagation neural network
KSVM: Kernel support vector machine
SCG: Scale conjugate gradient
LS-SVM: Least-square support vector machine
FBPNN: Feedforward backpropagation neural network
SWT: Stationary wavelet transform
PSO: Particle swarm optimization
CAD: Computer-aided diagnosis
STFT: Short-time Fourier transform
QDA: Quadratic discriminant analysis
SUR: Symmetric uncertainty ranking

PZM: Pseudo Zernike moment
SWT: Stationary wavelet transform
DTCWT: Dual-tree complex wavelet transform
RBFNN: Radial basis function neural network
CT: Computed tomography
TSVM: Twin support vector machine
HMI: Hu moment invariants
MLP: Multilayer perceptron
ARCBBO: Adaptive real coded biogeography-based
           optimization
DP: Dynamic pruning.

Acknowledgments

This research was supported by the Brain Research Program through the National Research Foundation of Korea funded by the Ministry of Science, ICT & Future Planning (NRF-2014M3C7A1046050). And this work was supported by the National Research Foundation of Korea Grant funded by the Korean Government (NRF-2017R1A2B4006533).

References

[1] D. Jha and G.-R. Kwon, "Alzheimers disease detection in MRI using curvelet transform with K-NN," *Journal of KIIT*, vol. 14, no. 8, 2016.

[2] S. Alam, M. Kang, J.-Y. Pyun, and G.-R. Kwon, "Performance of classification based on PCA, linear SVM, and Multi-kernel SVM," in *Proceedings of the 8th International Conference on Ubiquitous and Future Networks, ICUFN 2016*, pp. 987–989, Vienna, Austria, July 2016.

[3] F. Thorsen, B. Fite, L. M. Mahakian et al., "Multimodal imaging enables early detection and characterization of changes in tumor permeability of brain metastases," *Journal of Controlled Release*, vol. 172, no. 3, pp. 812–822, 2013.

[4] E.-S. A. El-Dahshan, T. Hosny, and A.-B. M. Salem, "Hybrid intelligent techniques for MRI brain images classification," *Digital Signal Processing*, vol. 20, no. 2, pp. 433–441, 2010.

[5] Y. Zhang and L. Wu, "An MR brain images classifier via principal component analysis and kernel support vector machine," *Progress in Electromagnetics Research*, vol. 130, pp. 369–388, 2012.

[6] L. M. Patnaik, S. Chaplot, and N. R. Jagannathan, "Classification of magnetic resonance brain images using wavelets as input to support vector machine and neural network," *Biomedical Signal Processing and Control*, vol. 1, no. 1, pp. 86–92, 2006.

[7] Y. Zhang, Z. Dong, L. Wu, and S. Wang, "A hybrid method for mri brain image classification," *Expert Systems with Applications*, vol. 38, no. 8, pp. 10049–10053, 2001.

[8] M. K. Kundu, M. Chowdhury, and S. Das, "Brain MR image classification using multi-scale geometric analysis of ripplet," *Progress in Electromagnetics Research*, vol. 137, pp. 1–17, 2013.

[9] E. A.-S. El-Dahshan, H. M. Mohsen, K. Revett, and A.-B. M. Salem, "Computer-aided diagnosis of human brain tumor through MRI: A survey and a new algorithm," *Expert Systems with Applications*, vol. 41, no. 11, pp. 5526–5545, 2014.

[10] S. Damodharan and D. Raghavan, "Combining tissue segementation and neural network for brain tumor detection," *The International Arab Journal of Information Technology*, vol. 12, no. 1, 2015.

[11] S. Wang, Y. Zhang, Z. Dong et al., "Feed-forward neural network optimized by hybridization of PSO and ABC for abnormal brain detection," *International Journal of Imaging Systems and Technology*, vol. 25, no. 2, pp. 153–164, 2015.

[12] M. Nazir, F. Wahid, and S. A. Khan, "A simple and intelligent approach for brain MRI classification," *Journal of Intelligent & Fuzzy Systems. Applications in Engineering and Technology*, vol. 28, no. 3, pp. 1127–1135, 2015.

[13] R. Harikumar and B. Vinoth Kumar, "Performance analysis of neural networks for classification of medical images with wavelets as a feature extractor," *International Journal of Imaging Systems and Technology*, vol. 25, no. 1, pp. 33–40, 2015.

[14] A. Padma and R. Sukanesh, "Segementation and classification of brain CT images using combined wavelet statistical texture features," *Arabian Journal for Science Engineering*, vol. 39, no. 2, 2014.

[15] Y. Zhang, J. Yang, S. Wang, Z. Dong, and P. Phillips, "Pathological brain detection in MRI scanning via Hu moment invariants and machine learning," *Journal of Experimental and Theoretical Artificial Intelligence*, vol. 29, no. 2, pp. 299–312, 2017.

[16] Y. Zhang, Y. Sun, P. Phillips, G. Liu, X. Zhou, and S. Wang, "A multilayer perceptron based smart pathological brain detection system by fractional fourier entropy," *Journal of Medical Systems*, vol. 40, no. 7, article 173, 2016.

[17] D. R. Nayak, R. Dash, and B. Majhi, "Brain MR image classification using two-dimensional discrete wavelet transform and AdaBoost with random forests," *Neurocomputing*, vol. 177, pp. 188–197, 2016.

[18] D. R. Nayak, R. Dash, and B. Majhi, "Stationary wavelet transform and AdaBoost with SVM based pathological brain detection in MRI scanning," *CNS and Neurological Disorders - Drug Targets*, vol. 16, no. 2, pp. 137–149, 2017.

[19] S.-H. Wang, S. Du, Y. Zhang et al., "Alzheimers disease detection by pseudo zernike moment and linear regression classifier," *CNS & Neurologicla Disorders*, vol. 16, no. 1, pp. 11–15, 2017.

[20] S. Alam, M. Kang, and G. Kwon, "Alzheimer disease classification based on TSVM and Kernel SVM," in *Proceedings of the 2017 Ninth International Conference on Ubiquitous and Future Networks (ICUFN)*, pp. 565–567, July 2017.

[21] D. Jha, J. Kim, and G. Kwon, "Diagnosis of Alzheimer's disease using dual-tree complex wavelet transform, PCA, and feed-forward neural network," *Journal of Healthcare Engineering*, vol. 2017, Article ID 9060124, 13 pages, 2017.

[22] H. Naimi, A. B. H. Adamou-Mitiche, and L. Mitiche, "Medical image denoising using dual tree complex thresholding wavelet transform and Wiener filter," *Journal of King Saud University - Computer and Information Sciences*, vol. 27, no. 1, pp. 40–45, 2015.

[23] L. Durak, "Shift-invariance of short-time FOUrier transform in fractional FOUrier domains," *Journal of the Franklin Institute. Engineering and Applied Mathematics*, vol. 346, no. 2, pp. 136–146, 2009.

[24] S. Chaplot, L. M. Patnaik, and N. R. Jagannathan, "Classification of magnetic resonance brain images using wavelets as input to support vector machine and neural network," *Biomedical Signal Processing and Control*, vol. 1, no. 1, pp. 86–92, 2006.

[25] Y. Zhang, S. Wang, G. Ji, and Z. Dong, "An MR brain images classifier system via particle swarm optimization and kernel support vector machine," *The Scientific World Journal*, vol. 2013, Article ID 130134, 9 pages, 2013.

[26] R. Choudhary, S. Mahesh, J. Paliwal, and D. S. Jayas, "Identification of wheat classes using wavelet features from near infrared hyperspectral images of bulk samples," *Biosystems Engineering*, vol. 102, no. 2, pp. 115–127, 2009.

[27] M. R. K. Mookiah, U. Rajendra Acharya, C. M. Lim, A. Petznick, and J. S. Suri, "Data mining technique for automated diagnosis of glaucoma using higher order spectra and wavelet energy features," *Knowledge-Based Systems*, vol. 33, pp. 73–82, 2012.

[28] S. Wang, G. Ji, P. Phillips, and Z. Dong, "Application of genetic algorithm and kernel support vector machine to pathological brain detection in MRI Scanning," in *Proceedings of the 2nd National Conference Information Technology Comp. Science*, pp. 450–456, Shanghai, China, 2015.

[29] G. Yang, Y. Zhang, J. Yang et al., "Automated classification of brain images using wavelet-energy and biogeography-based optimization," *Multimedia Tools and Applications*, vol. 75, no. 23, pp. 1–17, 2015.

[30] Y. Zhang, G. Ji, J. Yang et al., "Preliminary research on abnormal brain detection by wavelet-energy and quantum-behaved PSO," *Technology and Health Care*, vol. 24, pp. S641–S649, 2016.

[31] Y.-D. Zhang, S. Chen, S.-H. Wang, J.-F. Yang, and P. Phillips, "Magnetic resonance brain image classification based on weighted-type fractional Fourier transform and nonparallel support vector machine," *International Journal of Imaging Systems and Technology*, vol. 25, no. 4, pp. 317–327, 2015.

[32] Y. Zhang, S. Wang, and L. Wu, "A novel method for magnetic resonance brain image classification based on adaptive chaotic PSO," *Progress in Electromagnetics Research*, vol. 109, pp. 325–343, 2010.

[33] Y. Zhang, L. Wu, and S. Wang, "Magnetic resonance brain image classification by an improved artificial bee colony algorithm," *Progress In Electromagnetics Research*, vol. 130, pp. 369–388, 2012.

[34] S. Das, M. Chowdhury, and M. K. Kundu, "Brain MR image classification using multi-scale geometric analysis of ripplet," *Progress in Electromagnetics Research*, vol. 137, pp. 1–17, 2013.

[35] X. Zhou, S. Wang, W. Xu et al., "Detection of pathological brain in MRI scanning based wavelet-entropy and naïve Bayes classifier," in *Proceedings of the International Conference on Bioinformatics and Biomedical Engineering*, pp. 201–209, 2015.

[36] M. E. Tipping and C. M. Bishop, "Probabilistic principal component analysis," *Journal of the Royal Statistical Society. Series B. Statistical Methodology*, vol. 61, no. 3, pp. 611–622, 1999.

[37] S. Roweis, "EM algorithms for PCA and SPCA," in *Advance in Neural Information Proccessing System*, vol. 10, pp. 626–632, MIT Press, Cambridge, MA, USA, 1998.

[38] A. Ilin and T. Raiko, "Practical approaches to principal component analysis in the presence of missing values," *Journal of Machine Learning Research*, vol. 11, pp. 1957–2000, 2010.

4

Prototype Generation Using Self-Organizing Maps for Informativeness-Based Classifier

Leandro Juvêncio Moreira[1] and Leandro A. Silva[2]

[1]*Graduate Program in Electrical Engineering and Computing, Mackenzie Presbyterian University, Sao Paulo, SP, Brazil*
[2]*Computing and Informatics Faculty & Graduate Program in Electrical Engineering and Computing,*
 Mackenzie Presbyterian University, Sao Paulo, SP, Brazil

Correspondence should be addressed to Leandro A. Silva; leandroaugusto.silva@mackenzie.br

Academic Editor: Toshihisa Tanaka

The k nearest neighbor is one of the most important and simple procedures for data classification task. The kNN, as it is called, requires only two parameters: the number of k and a similarity measure. However, the algorithm has some weaknesses that make it impossible to be used in real problems. Since the algorithm has no model, an exhaustive comparison of the object in classification analysis and all training dataset is necessary. Another weakness is the optimal choice of k parameter when the object analyzed is in an overlap region. To mitigate theses negative aspects, in this work, a hybrid algorithm is proposed which uses the Self-Organizing Maps (SOM) artificial neural network and a classifier that uses similarity measure based on information. Since SOM has the properties of vector quantization, it is used as a Prototype Generation approach to select a reduced training dataset for the classification approach based on the nearest neighbor rule with informativeness measure, named iNN. The SOMiNN combination was exhaustively experimented and the results show that the proposed approach presents important accuracy in databases where the border region does not have the object classes well defined.

1. Introduction

The main task of a data classifier is to predict the class of an object that is under analysis. The simplest procedure for data classification tasks is the k nearest neighbor (kNN) algorithm. The algorithm strategy for classification comprises three operations: (i) an unlabeled sample is compared to dataset training through a similarity measure; (ii) the labeled objects are sorted in order of similarity to the unlabeled sample; and finally, (iii) the classification occurs giving the unlabeled sample the majority class of the nearest neighbors objects. Because of its simplified algorithm (three basic operations steps), and reduced number of parameters (similarity measure and the k number of nearest neighbor), this instance-based learning algorithm is widely used in the data mining community as a benchmarking algorithm [1–5].

Since the kNN algorithm has no model, an exhaustive comparison of the unlabeled sample with all the labeled and stored objects in the database is necessary, which increases the computational time of the process. In addition to this weakness of algorithm, the decision boundaries are defined by the instances stored in the training set and, for this, the algorithm has low tolerance to noise; that is, all training dataset objects are considered relevant patterns. Finally, the optimal choice of k depends upon the dataset mainly when the object analyzed is in a boundary region, making this parameter to be tuned according to the application [6–9].

To overcome the drawbacks above, there are in the literature different approaches such as similarity measure alternative to the Euclidean distance to minimize misclassification in boundaries region [10], methods to avoid searching the whole space of training set [11], and dataset summarization to find representative objects of training set [9]. For the dataset summarization approach, there are two main strategies to reduce the dataset volume: one of them based on instance selection and the other based on prototypes. For the approaches based on pattern (or instance) selection, the aim is to find a representative and reduced set of objects from the training dataset, which has the same or higher classification accuracy of a raw dataset [8, 12–15]. The strategies based on prototype, on the other hand, are defined in two approaches: Prototype Selection (PS) [16] and Prototype Generation (PG) [13, 17–19]. The approaches are equivalent; both can be used to identify an optimal subset of representative prototypes, discarding noise, and redundancy. The difference is that PG can also be used to generate and to replace the raw dataset by an artificial dataset. The use of prototypes or reduced training objects that are represented by prototypes minimizes some of kNN drawbacks previously mentioned as the exhaustive comparison of all training dataset.

Silva and Del-Moral-Hernandez [5] presented combination methods that use the winning neuron and topological maintain concepts of the Self-Organizing Maps (SOM) neural network to define a reduced subset of objects of the training set that are highly similar to the object that is under analysis for classification [5, 20]. This object subset is retrieved and then utilized by the kNN to execute the classification task. In other words, the SOM executes a preprocessing for the kNN classifier, recovering the similar objects from the winning neuron and from the adjacent neighbors of the SOM map [21].

With respect to drawback in the tuning of parameter k, Zhang et al. proposed a computation learning for this parameter [22]. Song et al., on the other hand, proposed a metric based on informativeness to perform the classification process in a boundaries region, where the choice of k is more sensible [10]. This algorithm was called iNN and the main idea is investigating the nearest objects more informative instead of the closest. This approach outperforms the use of kNN with Euclidean distance; however, it further increases the complexity of the comparison, consequently increasing process time [23].

Inspired by use of PG [5, 20, 21], we introduce a hybrid approach, where in a first step there is the SOM, which has the quantization vector and topological maintenance as important features for using it as a preprocessing in order to present to the classifier algorithm a reduced set of objects, highly similar to the unknown object that is being investigated. Next, the iNN algorithm will attribute a class to the unknown object based on the most informative objects of selected set. For the initial exploratory experiments, we observed important results of accuracy and time in classification process [23].

We here formally detail how SOMiNN works in hybrid architecture for classification problems. Besides that, here we introduced an experimental methodology to analyze qualitatively the SOMiNN classifier in three artificial datasets, experimenting different distribution in the region of class overlapping. In addition, we perform the experiments in 21 databases publicly (7 times more than in the previous study) available in the UCI repository and also sampling way by the 5-fold cross validation method in the complementary website to the paper published by Triguero et al. [9]. The results are analyzed using accuracy, kappa, prototype reduction, and time as performance indices.

The rest of the paper is organized as follows: in Section 2, a brief explanation of Prototype Generation and the taxonomy proposed by [9] are shown; Self-Organizing Maps and the methods to use them in classification with kNN are presented in Section 3. In Section 4, the experimental methodology is introduced. Experimental results, discussion, and comparative results are given in Section 5. In the last section, the conclusions are provided.

2. Theoretical Fundamental

2.1. A Brief Introduction to Prototype Generation. For a better understanding of the Prototype Generation idea, let us consider an object $\mathbf{x}_n$ of a dataset, defined as a set of descriptive attributes of m dimensional and with a class attribute y; that is, $\mathbf{x}_n = [x_{n1}, x_{n2}, \ldots, x_{nm}, x_{ny}]$. Then, let us assume that $\mathbf{X}_{\text{train}}$ is a training dataset with N_{train} samples of $\mathbf{x}_n$. The purpose of Prototype Generation (PG) is to obtain a reduced set, $\mathbf{X}_{\text{red}}$, with N_{red} instances selected or generated from $\mathbf{X}_{\text{train}}$, but with $N_{\text{red}} \ll N_{\text{train}}$. The cardinality of this reduced set must be sufficiently small to decrease the evaluation time taken by a classifier (kNN, for example), maintaining the classification accuracy. In fact, data reduction approaches aim mainly to summarize the raw dataset, without damaging the analytical properties, which implies performance accuracy.

For the PG methods, prototypes are used by classifiers instead of raw datasets, or they are used to generate an artificial dataset. Data generation can be interesting in some cases to eliminate data noise or to solve dataset with unbalanced class. Since the possibilities of usage are diversified, the literature presents different methods, approaches, and algorithms. This was the reason for Triguero et al. [9] to propose a PG taxonomy that is used to enhance kNN drawbacks, which was defined as a hierarchical way of three levels (generation mechanisms, resulting generation set, and type of reduction), and also review the all algorithms of the PG from the literature (see [9] for a detailed explanation).

In the next section, we introduce a brief of Self-Organizing Maps and the approach is proposed, the combination of SOM and kNN.

2.2. A Brief Summary for the Kohonen Self-Organizing Maps. Kohonen Self-Organizing Map (SOM) is a type of neural network that consists of neurons located on a regular low-dimensional grid, usually two-dimensional (2D). Typically, the lattice of the 2D grid is either hexagonal or rectangular [24]. The SOM learning or training process is an iterative algorithm which aims to represent a distribution of the input pattern objects in that regular grid of neurons. The similar input patterns are associated in the same neurons or in the adjacent neurons of the grid.

For the SOM training, a dataset is chosen and divided into two distinct sets. The training set is used to train the SOM which is here called $\mathbf{X}_{\text{train}}$. The other set is used to test the trained SOM ($\mathbf{X}_{\text{test}}$). After this dataset division, we start the training SOM. Formally, an object is randomly selected from $\mathbf{X}_{\text{train}}$ during a training, defined as $\mathbf{x}_n = [x_{n1}, x_{n2}, \ldots, x_{nm}]$, where the element x_{nm} is an attribute or feature of the object, which belongs to R^m. The object is similar to what was before defined, but without the class x_{ny} information. Additionally, each neuron j of the SOM grid has a weight vector $\mathbf{w}_j = [w_{j1}, w_{j2}, \ldots, w_{jm}]^T$, where $j = 1, 2, \ldots, l$; here l is the total number of neurons of the map.

During the learning process, the input pattern is randomly selected from the training set and it is compared with the weights vector of the map, initially initialized randomly. The comparison between $\mathbf{x}_n$ and $\mathbf{w}_j$ is usually made through Euclidean distance. The shortest distance indicates the closest neuron c, which will have its weight vector $\mathbf{w}_c$ updated to get close to the selected input pattern $\mathbf{x}_n$. Formally, neuron c is defined as follows:

$$c = \arg\min_j \left\| \mathbf{x}_n - \mathbf{w}_j \right\|. \tag{1}$$

The closest weights vector $\mathbf{w}_c$ and their neighbors are updated using the Kohonen algorithm [24]. However, the topological neighborhood is defined so that the farther away the neuron from $\mathbf{w}_c$, the lower the intensity for the neighborhood to be updated. The intensity of the neighborhood function is defined in relation to the training time. In other words, in initial times, the level has high value and, according to the next iterations, it is reduced at each iteration. See Kohonen [24] for a complete explanation of the training rule of the SOM map.

2.3. Building a Prototype Generation Based on SOM. Since the training phase has been completed, each input pattern object from the training set has to be grouped to the closest neuron. The idea in this approach of using SOM as a PG technique is that the index of each instance $\mathbf{x}_n$ is a part of the nearest neuron list. Thus, the list of each neuron j is here called the Best Matching Unit List (BMUL), formally defined as

$$\text{BMUL}_j = \left\{ n \mid d\left(\mathbf{x}_n, \mathbf{w}_j\right) \leq d\left(\mathbf{x}_n, \mathbf{w}_i\right) \vee i \neq j \right\}, \tag{2}$$

where j is assigned to the number of the map neuron and BMUL is a list with the indexes n of input patterns objects associated with the nearest neuron.

The relationship between the instance of training set $\mathbf{x}_n$ and the list of the best match unit BMUL_j is of many-to-one. That is, some units j, which we could call microclusters, must be associated with one or more instances and other units may have no associations; that is, the list can be empty $\{\emptyset\}$.

The classification method proposed herein explores two important characteristics of the SOM: vector quantization and topological ordering [24]. For better understanding these features, consider the representation of Figure 1 with input patterns objects (filled circles) used for training a SOM map and the weight vectors of each neuron (squares) after the training phase. In this figure, each weight vector represents a microcluster of input patterns, which is a quantization characteristic. The relationship between the weight vectors can be interpreted as a boundary, which can be understood as a Voronoi region, as exemplified by the shaded area in Figure 1. In operational aspects of use, this can be considered in a classification process in which the strategy, introduced and explored herein, means to establish a two-step process. In the first step, when a test sample $\mathbf{x}_t$ (see Figure 1, the unfilled

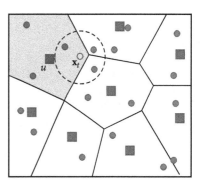

FIGURE 1: The border between the weight vectors (squares) can be interpreted as a Voronoi region (shaded area). Thus, the input patterns object (filled circles) belongs to a Voronoi region.

circle) is compared to the weight vectors of the trained SOM map (the squares of Figure 1), the algorithm defines the closest unit u according to the following equation:

$$u = \arg\min_j \left\| \mathbf{x}_t - \mathbf{w}_j \right\|. \tag{3}$$

Hence, as u is the nearest unit, we know the list with input patterns indices that should be queried, that is, BMUL_u. Illustratively, consider that weight vector u belongs to a Voronoi region; see Figure 1, the shaded area, which has a BMUL_u list with the indices of input patterns known (filled circle). Also in this figure, the unlabeled sample $\mathbf{x}_t$ (unfilled circle) belongs to the region covered by unit u (shaded area); that is, in the second step of the classification process, the kNN algorithm is performed with a reduced set of objects.

However, note that the input patterns object stored in the dataset (filled circles), which are the closest to the object being classified $\mathbf{x}_t$ (unfilled circle), belong to neighboring Voronoi regions and are consequently represented in other lists; see Figure 1, circle with a dotted line.

For that reason, in a classification task with kNN or (iNN as will be introduced in the next section) combined with SOM, the use of the objects represented only as BMUL_u list results in a substantially reduced classification process time but can reduce the accuracy rate. Thus, we explored the second important feature of SOM, the topological ordering of the training dataset objects. In other words, in addition to the BMUL_u list, the lists of adjacent neurons in the SOM map grid are also consulted.

The visit of adjacent units depends on the grid initially set at the SOM training phase. For the SOM trained with rectangular lattice topology, the units of the four adjacent units should be considered. Thus, the query list $\text{BMUL}_{\text{query}}$ for the unknown pattern $\mathbf{x}_t$ is defined as

$$\text{BMUL}_{\text{query}} = \left\{ \text{BMUL}_u, \text{BMUL}_u^{\text{top}}, \text{BMUL}_u^{\text{right}}, \right.$$
$$\left. \text{BMUL}_u^{\text{bottom}}, \text{BMUL}_u^{\text{left}} \right\}. \tag{4}$$

Otherwise, for a hexagonal lattice topology, we have to consider six adjacent units and so on. In previous studies using SOM with kNN [5, 20, 21], we compared the two

> **Input:** The weight vectors of SOM Map trained (**W**); training objects dataset ($\mathbf{X}_{\text{train}}$); and an unknown sample ($\mathbf{x}_t$)
> **Output:** the label of unknown sample (x_{ty})
>   Compare the unknown sample $\mathbf{x}_t$ with each weight vector $\mathbf{w}_j$ of **W** using Eq. (3)
>   The units to be visited are defined by Eq. (4) and the input patterns objects are retrieved by Eq. (5), recovering a reduced dataset training $X_{\text{BMUL}_{\text{query}}}$.
>   The reduced dataset and the unknown sample are used by a classifier (kNN or iNN) that return the object class.

ALGORITHM 1: Prototype Generation based on SOM briefly described in a pseudo-code.

neighborhood topologies (rectangular and hexagonal) and the results were equivalent. For this reason, the rectangular lattice topology was chosen in this work.

Finally, in the second step of the classification method proposed here, the reduced objects set belonging to $\text{BMUL}_{\text{query}}$ (4) is used to find the k nearest neighbors (kNN). Note that the set of objects extracted from the query lists, that is, $\mathbf{X}_{\text{BMUL}_{\text{query}}}$, is part of the set of input patterns objects used for the SOM training; that is, $\mathbf{X}_{\text{train}} = [\mathbf{x}_1, \mathbf{x}_2, \dots, \mathbf{x}_n]^T$ and $\mathbf{X}_{\text{BMUL}_{\text{query}}} \subset \mathbf{X}_{\text{train}}$. Formally, we have

$$\mathbf{X}_{\text{BMUL}_{\text{query}}} = \left\{\mathbf{x}_{\text{bmul}} \mid \text{bmul} \in \text{BMUL}_{\text{query}}\right\}. \qquad (5)$$

Thus, the class of the k nearest (or i informative instances as will be explained in the next section) is used to label the unknown sample $\mathbf{x}_t$. This framework combination was initially called SOMkNN (and here will be introduced the SOMiNN classifier).

In summary, the conventional algorithm NN (or kNN) compares the unknown sample with all the instances of the dataset; here, the comparison is limited to a selection of the objects; that is, the comparison is restricted to a small number of instances from the training dataset. The main implementation steps are described as a pseudo-code in Algorithm 1.

As verified in this section, we formalized a strategy to select input pattern objects to be used as references in a classification task and to speed the time of kNN algorithm. The next section introduces the iNN algorithm which is less sensible to k parameter and for this works better than kNN in datasets with overlapped classes (boundary not well defined).

2.4. Informative Nearest Neighbors. Some data classification approaches based on nearest neighbor, in addition to defining a given range of k values to find the nearest neighbors, also utilize new distance metrics, such as the informative nearest neighbor [10]. In other words, they utilize in the analysis of a new object of unknown class a measure that quantifies which training set object is most informative.

In order to find the informative nearest neighbor, the iNN algorithm, as it is called in the proposal by Song et al. [10], calculates the informativity through the following equation:

$$I\left(\mathbf{x}_i \mid \mathbf{x}_t\right) = -\log\left(1 - P\left(\mathbf{x}_i \mid \mathbf{x}_t\right)\right) \times P\left(\mathbf{x}_i \mid \mathbf{x}_t\right),$$
$$i = 1, \dots, N, \qquad (6)$$

where I is the value of the informativity between the neighbor $\mathbf{x}_i$ and the object under analysis of unknown class ($\mathbf{x}_t$), to the extent that $P(\mathbf{x}_i \mid \mathbf{x}_t)$ is the probability of the object $\mathbf{x}_i$ being the informative nearest neighbor. This probability is defined by the following equation:

$$P\left(\mathbf{x}_i \mid \mathbf{x}_t\right)$$
$$= \text{Pr}\left(\mathbf{x}_i \mid \mathbf{x}_t\right)^\eta \left(\prod_{n=1}^{N}\left(1 - \text{Pr}\left(\mathbf{x}_i \mid \mathbf{x}_t\right)\right) \times \left(\amalg_{[c_i \neg c_n]}\right)\right). \qquad (7)$$

The first term in (7) $\text{Pr}(\mathbf{x}_i \mid \mathbf{x}_t)^\eta$ is defined as the probability that the object $\mathbf{x}_i$ is close to the object $\mathbf{x}_t$ and η is defined as $N_{\mathbf{x}_i}/N$, where $N_{\mathbf{x}_i}$ is the number of objects that have the same class as $\mathbf{x}_i$. The second part in (7) indicates the probability that the object $\mathbf{x}_i$ is distant from the other objects of the training dataset $\mathbf{x}_n$. The indicator $\amalg[\cdot]$ will be 1 if the class attributes of the objects $\mathbf{x}_i$ and $\mathbf{x}_n$ are different; in other words, $c_i \neg c_n$. Therefore, it can be understood as a penalty factor.

The probability $\text{Pr}(\mathbf{x}_i \mid \mathbf{x}_t)$ in (7) can be defined as a function of distance between the objects; in other words,

$$\text{Pr}\left(\mathbf{x}_i \mid \mathbf{x}_t\right) = \exp\left(-\left\|\mathbf{x}_i - \mathbf{x}_t\right\|^2\right). \qquad (8)$$

To understand the iNN algorithm in practical terms, consider the dataset utilized in Figure 2(a), where it is represented by shaded circles, to the extent that the shades (dark and light) represent the two classes of the set. Now consider Figure 2(b), which has the same training objects with the addition of an object without class represented by a circle without shade. Now, consider in Figure 2(c) the contours in training objects and test object, representing the classification process executed utilizing the traditional kNN, with Euclidean distance and k value being equal to 5. In this process, the majority class of the nearest neighbors is the one that is represented by dark shading. And, therefore, the decision-making process is made by this class. However, the object under analysis has as its nearest neighbor an object of the training set that belongs to the class with light shading and this, on the other hand, also has as its neighbor another object of the same class. Therefore, utilizing the iNN algorithm, the informativity takes into consideration not only the majority class but also the nearest objects and the concordance that the other objects of the training set have with the nearest object. In conclusion, in the case of the iNN, the classification would be made by the class represented by the lightest shading Figure 2(d).

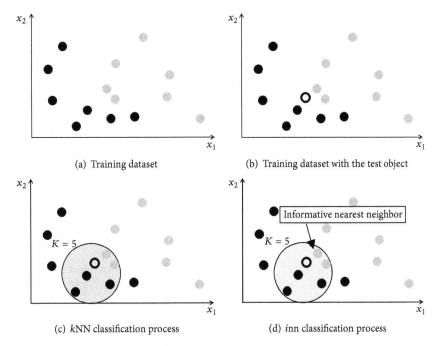

(a) Training dataset

(b) Training dataset with the test object

(c) kNN classification process

(d) $i$nn classification process

FIGURE 2: Illustration of the classification process made by the kNN and iNN algorithm.

Thus, the concept of informative nearest neighbor has the following definitions. Within the k nearest neighbors, the object that is nearest to the object that is being classified, which is distant from other objects of different classes, is considered the most informative object, such that its class is attributed to the unknown object. On the other hand, the object that has a different class from the most informative object is considered least informative. An object is also considered least informative within the k nearest neighbors when it has the same class as the most informative object and is nearest to other objects of different classes.

The informativity calculation has a high computational cost because, in addition to comparing the object under analysis with the objects of the training set (first part in (7)), the algorithm still requires a comparison between the training set objects (second part in (7)). In order to reduce the computational effort, Song et al. [10] suggest having the execution of the kNN algorithm before executing the iNN to define a reduced dataset with k most similar objects, according to the Euclidean metric. However, the kNN algorithm has the disadvantages presented in the Introduction (the need to store the training set, noise sensibility, etc.) and its use before the iNN can affect the performance in the classification of objects that are in a border region, as illustrated in Figure 2(c).

The following section presents a proposal that combines the SOM with the iNN algorithm to build a process that will be named SOMiNN. This section will also show the advantages of the SOMiNN over the iNN.

3. Methodology for Combining SOM and iNN: A Hybrid Classification SOMiNN

The approach utilized by the SOMiNN classifier explores the concept of quantization, topology maintenance, and informativity. As already mentioned, an informative object allows the correct prediction of an unknown object, even in boundary not well defined. When talking about information, we cannot have information quality without first significantly measuring this. Information quality is one of the determining keys for the quality of the decisions and actions that are made according to it [25]. It is exactly what the SOMiNN classifier proposes to do; in other words, before predicting the class of the unknown object, it measures the information of the training set objects before making the classification decision.

In order to understand the SOMiNN combination, consider a SOM trained with the objects from Figure 2(a) without using the class information (shaded color). The prototypes adjusted resulting in trained SOM map (weight vectors) are represented in Figure 3(a). The result of the SOM can be generally understood as being a summary of the training set, through a set of prototypes that have a Voronoi region, with the number of prototypes being smaller than that of the training set, in the following example: the twelve objects were summarized into four prototypes. The number of prototypes is a parameter that refers to the number of neurons of the SOM map.

Now consider the new object classification submitted to process that was presented in Figure 2(b). Also consider the prototype set being utilized in a first comparison, instead of the training set. In this case, for the classification process, in initial phase a comparison will be done between the object under analysis and the set of prototypes, as illustrated in Figure 3(a). Repeating the process that takes place in training the SOM for the selection of the winning neuron, made using the Euclidean distance, the nearest neuron is selected (winner or best match) to the object under analysis. From this process where the nearest prototype is known and that, on the other

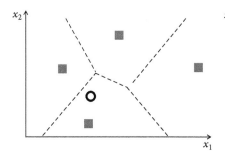 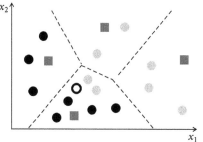 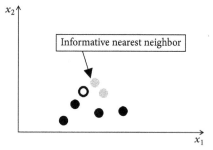

(a) Training set and prototypes generated after the training of the SOM

(b) SOM: The object to be classified is represented by the circle and the prototypes are represented by the squares

(c) iNN: The object under analysis will be compared with the objects represented by the nearest or best match prototype

FIGURE 3: Illustration of the classification process made by the SOM and iNN.

hand, it is possible to know which training set objects are represented by the prototype, see Figure 3(b) where each prototypes has a Voronoi region. Thus, the reduced training set objects are retrieved to start the classification phase with the iNN. Finally, the classification will be done with a reduced set, as shown in Figure 3(c).

In summary, the last step in Algorithm 1, the use of classifier algorithm, is executed with iNN. This process is called here as SOMiNN classifier.

Since the process will depend on the selection of the number of neurons of the SOM map, we will utilize the empirical proposal of Vesanto et al. [26] that defines the number of neurons as being the root of the number of objects of the training set. What happens is that, after training the SOM map, some prototypes can be empty; in other words, the prototype represents no object of the training set. In order to prevent this situation from happening, the proposal of Silva and Del-Moral-Hernandez [5] will be utilized. Thus, besides retrieving the objects of the winning prototype, it will also consider the retrieval of the adjacent prototypes.

The combination using the SOM neural networks approach with the iNN explores the main characteristics that define the potential of a data classifier, which are storage reduction, noise tolerance, generalization accuracy, and time requirements [9]. To the contrary of the iNN that preprocesses the data utilizing the kNN algorithm that has a high computational cost, the algorithm proposed in this work reduces the data representation through the SOM. In addition, with the use of the SOM, the classification time of the SOMiNN is expected to be shorter when compared with the iNN, which results in less memory use, maximizing the classifier's performance in terms of classification time.

The next section highlights all steps that were done to make the experiments with the SOMiNN classifier.

4. Experimental Methodology, Results, and Analysis

This section will present the dataset utilized in the experiments and the parameterization of the classifiers utilized for the comparison with our SOMiNN proposal. The experiments consist in using an artificial dataset for qualitative

and quantitative analysis and with public dataset used as benchmarking in the literature to evaluate the efficacy of the algorithm proposed.

4.1. Datasets. In order to provide a qualitative analysis with visualization of the border decision-making area and a quantitative analysis in terms of classifier accuracy, three datasets were generated with the following features: 300 objects, two attributes, two classes, and a balanced number of objects per class. For all datasets, the objects were distributed with the same mean but with difference in the standard deviation value, in order to force an overlapping of classes. Thus, each dataset represents distinct situations on the border of classes: no, low, and high confusion.

In order to evaluate the efficacy of the algorithm proposed and compare it with others from the literature, 21 public databases were chosen (Repository of the University of California, Irvine, UCI) that are used as benchmarking for Prototype Generation approaches. Table 1 summarizes the properties of each benchmarking dataset in number of objects (Obj), number of attributes (Att), and number of classes (Cla). For all databases, the attributes are numerical. The separation of these datasets in training and test set were done with the use of the 5-fold cross validation.

4.2. Parameterization of Algorithms. The SOMiNN approach will be compared with kNN, iNN, and SOMkNN. The classifiers parameterizations are represented in Table 2. The SOM parametrization is the same for SOMkNN and SOMiNN.

The experiments were implemented using the R language, version 3.1.2, with RStudio IDE version 0.98 and using a conventional computer with Windows 10, i7 with 8 GB RAM. The experimental results are presented in the following section.

4.3. Qualitative and Quantitative Analysis Using the Artificial Dataset. The objective of experiments using artificial dataset was to compare the performance of iNN, kNN, SOMiNN, and SOMkNN classifiers in situations where there are well-separated classes (Figure 4(a)), classes partially overlapped (Figure 4(b)), and a large number of classes overlapped (Figure 4(c)).

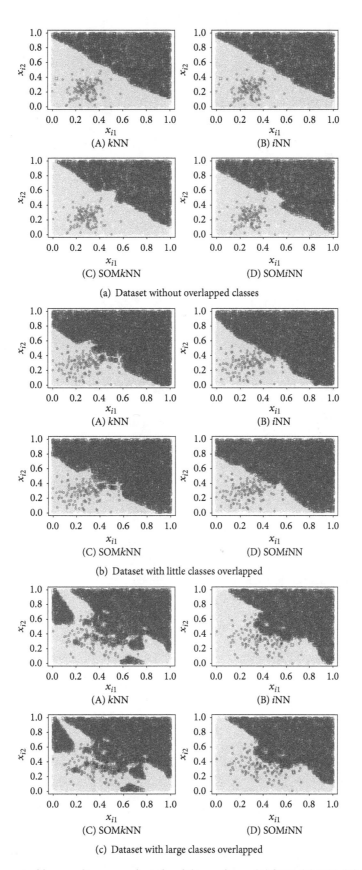

FIGURE 4: For each experiment, a set of four results was conducted and the results are (A) kNN; (B) iNN; (C) SOMkNN; and (D) SOMiNN.

TABLE 1: Properties of dataset used in experimental analysis of this work. These datasets are available in UCI webpage (https://archive.ics.uci.edu/ml/datasets.html) and also in webpage auxiliar of Triguero et al. publication [9].

#	Name	Properties		
		(#Obj)	(#Att)	(#Cla)
1	appendicitis	106	7	1
2	iris	150	4	2
3	australian	690	14	16
4	balance	625	4	15
5	dermatology	366	33	13
6	glass	214	9	7
7	haberman	306	3	11
8	heart	270	13	10
9	hepatitis	155	19	4
10	mammographic	961	5	20
11	monk-2	432	6	14
12	movement_libras	360	90	12
13	newthyroid	215	5	8
14	pima	768	8	18
15	sonar	208	60	6
16	spectfheart	267	44	9
17	tae	151	5	3
18	vehicle	846	18	19
19	vowel	990	13	21
20	wine	178	13	5
21	wisconsin	699	9	17

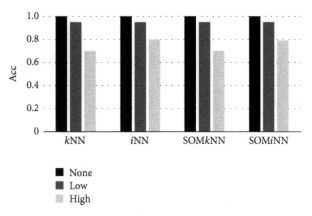

FIGURE 5: Accuracy results for classifiers using artificial dataset.

Analyzing qualitatively, starting by Figures 4(a)(A), 4(b)(A), and 4(c)(A), kNN results, we can note that the boundary separation degrades from the moment that the classes start the overlapping. In the worst case, we can observe that a high overlap (Figure 4(c)) is clearly one of the kNN disadvantages, because it makes the decision boundary considering all objects as having the same importance. For the iNN results (Figures 4(a)(B), 4(b)(B), and 4(c)(B)), it is clear that the border of separation is softer, even when the class overlap increases. This is because the separation was defined by informative representation of the objects from the same class. This fact is most evident in the last experiment (Figure 4(c)), where we can observe that the boundary separation is created to preserve the predominant class in the border region.

Figures 4(a)(C and D), 4(b)(C and D), and 4(c)(C and D) are the results using SOM as the Generation Prototype approach. That is, the decision boundary was generated without using all objects of the database but, instead, based on objects distributed in prototypes of the trained SOM map. In this qualitative analysis, the most important to note is that the preservation of the decision boundary was maintained in all experiments, without significant changes.

Finally, we analyzed quantitatively the experiments with artificial data, with an average classification accuracy defined by a dataset with 10^6 objects (which were used to generate the decision boundary of Figure 4). The results are shown in Figure 5. The conclusion for the experiments using artificial dataset is that the use of iNN is more effective than kNN when the separation class has high confusion and that for this, the performance accuracy has not been abruptly reduced. We also note in this qualitative analysis that the use of SOM as Prototype Generation method does not significantly degrade the accuracy performance.

The use of artificial datasets can make qualitative and quantitative analyses between the classifiers. The next experiment has the objective of expanding the previous study [23] through analysis with other performance measures, such as kappa, impact of dataset reduction on the accuracy, and performance of classification time. For these new experiments, 12 new public datasets were used that are benchmarking in Prototype Generation approach [9].

4.4. Experiments and Analysis Using the Benchmarking Dataset. This section shows the experiments and results for datasets introduced in Table 1. The results are analyzed using the following measures as performances: accuracy, kappa, hypothesis test, rate of dataset reduction, and classification time.

Table 3 shows all the classification results for the paper experiments. In this table, the accuracy and kappa measures are shown in terms of average and standard deviation. The other results are also discussed in this section.

In practical aspects, the accuracy and kappa measures are equivalent in terms of performance. For purposes of simplification, only the accuracy will be considered in the extended discussion of the result analysis.

The accuracy is analyzed by comparing the results of the classifiers in pairs. The average and the result deviation of each dataset are compared using the t-test with 95% of confidence interval. The comparison result is shown in Table 4. In this table, the datasets indices ("#," see Table 1) are separated according to the classifier results: higher results ($X > Y$), equal results ($X = Y$), and lower results ($X < Y$), with X and Y being a representation of classifiers compared in pairs. From this result, the same comparison structure will be used again for the count of the incidences percentage.

Table 2: Parametrization of algorithms.

Algorithm	Parameters
kNN	$k = 1$ and Euclidian distance
SOM	Euclidian distance, batch training, maximum training time equal to 1000, rectangular lattice, and Gaussian neighborhood function with maximum aperture of 1 with decay due to the number of iterations. The SOM map dimension has the square root of the number of dataset objects by two ($\sqrt{N}/2$)
iNN	Execution of the kNN algorithm with k value equal to 7 (best result from [10]) and informative neighbor number equal to 1

The general counting is shown in Table 5. This table has an additional column to represent the sum of the percentages of equal and lower results, in order to show when a classifier performance is really better than the other. This was the reason to compare $(X > Y)$ with $(X = Y)$ and $(X < Y)$ in Table 5.

Analyzing the results from Table 5 is possible to note in the first two lines of table that iNN showed to be better than kNN in most of cases (66.7% and 52.4%, combined with SOM). The use of SOM in the classification process (last two lines of the table) has been shown to be slightly better or worse in some cases. The SOM performance with iNN is improved (52.4%) and with kNN there is a little degradation (47.7%). However, an important result that should be emphasized (last row of the table) is that the use of SOM with iNN maintains or improves the performance in most databases (52.4%).

As a final analysis of the accuracy performance, in order to show that the degradation with the use of SOM has little impact on the final performance, the comparison of the same pair of classifier presented above is performed using a radar chart (Figure 6). In this graph, the external values (polar scale) indicate the dataset number of 1 to 21, and the internal values show the accuracy performance, starting from 0.6 to 1.0. The ideal result would be to have the graph contour in 1.0. In this study, the main results are obtained for the overlapped lines, representing an equivalent result for contrasted classifiers. Combining the results of the accuracy performance (statistical and chart), we can consider that iNN has, in the vast majority of studies, a superiority in the classification performance when compared to kNN. From this result, it is interesting to note that the iNN superiority occurs mainly in datasets with performance below 90% as follows: 7, 9, 11, 12, 14, 15, 16, 18, 19, and 20. On the other hand, the result is lower in experiments with datasets 2 and 21, that is, where the accuracy performance is close to 1 (100%). Therefore, the results also suggest that iNN has superior results in datasets in which the decision boundary is not well separated.

The next analysis consists in verifying the SOM efficiency in reducing input objects. For this, the reduction and accuracy percentage of each dataset performance is checked. The results are shown in Figure 7. Interestingly, in both results, SOMkNN and SOMiNN, there are three regions very well defined in the accuracy reduction experiment. The first datasets have an average of 150.5 objects, with the second averaging 215 and the last averaging 694.5 objects. That is, the reduction varies with the number of objects. Therefore, the

results of SOMkNN (Figure 7(a)) and SOMiNN (Figure 7(b)) show that the more objects in dataset, the higher the reduction rate.

The next results to be analyzed are the time consumed in the classification process. The results are shown in Figure 8, and, for interpretation purposes, the databases are arranged in the vertical axis and are organized in ascending order of number of objects. In vertical axis, each dataset is described by name, number of objects, and number of attributes (described in Table 3). The time shown on the horizontal axis is measured in seconds.

By analyzing in detail the result of the time classification algorithms iNN and kNN in Figure 8(a), it is observed that, to a certain number of objects, around 180 (datasets appendicitis to wine), the classification time is almost linear. From this point the tendency curve is not clear. The reason is that there are an increasing number of objects in these other databases and also a variation in the number of attributes. This means that the classification time depends not only on the number of objects but also on the number of attributes, for example, the balance database (625 objects) and dermatology (366 objects), whose last dataset has a smaller number of objects and consumes more time. Another interesting case to mention is observed between the base mov_libras and vowel. The former has almost half the number of objects and nearly ninefold more attributes than the latter but both consumed an equivalent time in the classification process. Another point to consider in the graph is that, for every experiment, the classification time of iNN is higher than kNN. This result was expected because, as mentioned earlier, iNN is computationally more costly due to the fact that kNN is run before it as a preprocessing step and, thus, it finds the closest informative object. Although it seems to be an obvious result, the experiments confirm their reliability. Finally, for a general idea of the time, a tendency line was added to the results and the best adjustment was an exponential trend, with Pearson coefficient above 0.7, which is considered a high value. As it is difficult to find a relationship between the numbers of objects and attributes to explain the process timing, the trend is more indicative about the number of objects. Thus, for this experiment, the classification time is more sensitive to the number of objects.

The same time experiment discussed above was repeated for SOMiNN and SOMkNN (Figure 8(b)). The behavior of the results in this experiment is similar to that discussed for Figure 8(a). This can be interpreted in two ways. The first is that the above analysis can be applied for these results and, more importantly, that the objects selected by the reduced

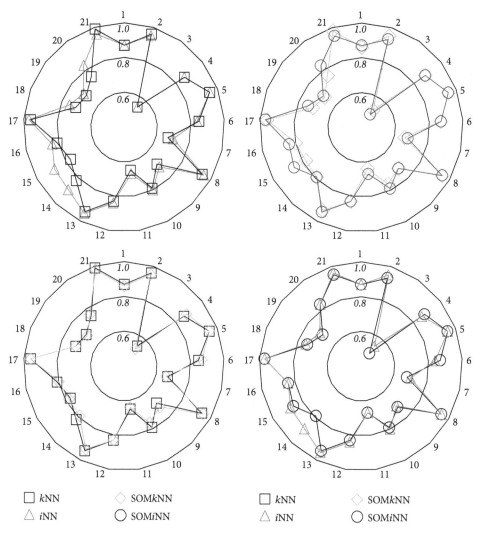

FIGURE 6: Radar graphic contrasting pairs of classifiers.

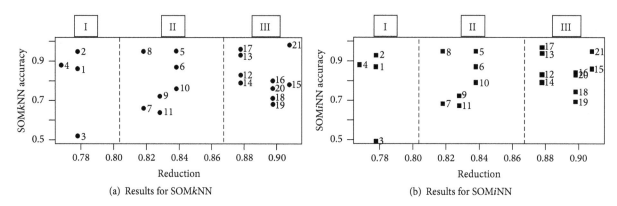

FIGURE 7: Results of reduction per accuracy.

set SOM prototypes can maintain the characteristics of the raw database. However, it should be noted in the result analysis that the time classification scale (horizontal axis) ranges from 0 to 100 seconds. In the earlier results, the scale ranged from 0 to 350 seconds. Nonetheless, the importance

of this result is that the trend remains exponential, R^2 with 0.7. It is noteworthy that, in the result time shown for SOM (SOMkNN and SOMiNN), the training time is included.

For a global analysis, in the Figure 9, there are all classification time results together: kNN, iNN, SOMkNN, and

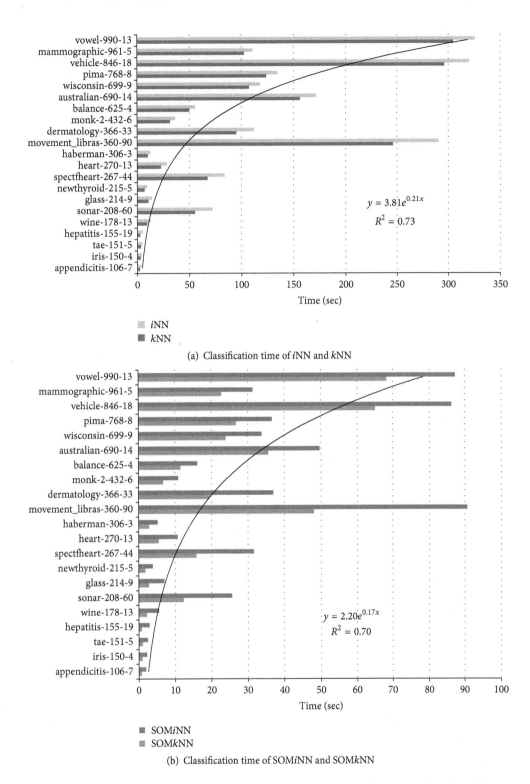

(a) Classification time of iNN and kNN

(b) Classification time of SOMiNN and SOMkNN

FIGURE 8: Classification time analysis. The datasets are organized in ascendant order of number of objects.

SOMiNN. The databases in the horizontal axis were arranged again in quantities of objects. By analyzing qualitatively the results shown in this figure, we can note that when the number is lower than about 180 (to the *wine* dataset), the use of SOM as a preprocessing to iNN and kNN algorithms in order to reduce the time classification does not have significant advantages. Thus, the use of SOM to decrease the classification time of iNN and kNN algorithms seems to be

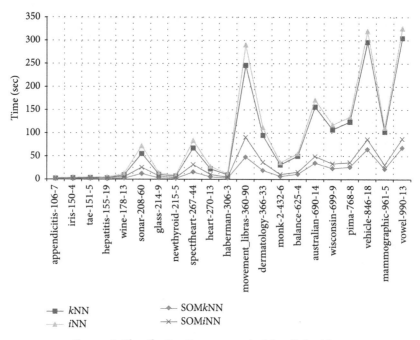

FIGURE 9: Classification time summarized for all classifiers.

more advantageous in database with more than 180 objects (from *sonar* dataset). This result can be observed at the upper end, where the consumption of classification time is high (*vowel* dataset), and the use of SOM can reduce by more than 3 times the *k*NN and *i*NN classification time.

4.5. Contrasting the Results of This Work with That in the Literature. For an idea about the importance of the results herein mainly using the *i*NN and the combination SOM*i*NN approach, the performance indexes obtained here was compared with the literature result [9]. The approach chosen for the comparative experiments, Chen algorithm, belongs to the same Prototype Generation category of SOM. The algorithm named Chen [9, 27] was executed using the datasets of Table 3 and the compiled results for this algorithm are shown in terms of average and standard deviation of accuracy, time, and reduction. The comparative results are summarized in Table 6.

Note from the comparative results of Table 6 that *i*NN is the algorithm that has the best performance accuracy. This is an important result because it is the algorithm introduced here as an alternative to *k*NN. In terms of time, the lowest result was obtained by the SOM*k*NN; therefore, it involves the SOM as the approach of Prototype Generation method introduced in this work and it is expected that *i*NN is more time consuming than the *k*NN, as discussed in Section 2. Finally, the Chen algorithm has the bigger reduction, which is to be expected too, since according to Triguero et al. [9], the prototypes parameter has to be configured as being 90% of the number of objects of the dataset.

5. Conclusion

This paper introduces a new classifier named SOM*i*NN, which is based on the combination of Self-Organizing Maps

(SOM) and *informative* nearest neighbors (*i*NN). The *i*NN classifier is costly in computational terms, because in a classification process the informativity is not calculated only by the object under classification analysis, but also considering the other objects of the training set. Song et al. [10] suggested the use of *k*NN algorithm (with the best *k* value experimentally found as being 7) before *i*NN to minimize the high computational cost, that is, using 7-NN to find a reduced subset for the classification process with the informative nearest neighbor algorithm.

In order to contribute to the Song et al. [10], in this paper, the *k*NN has been substituted by SOM because of quantization vector and maintenance topological of raw dataset. In other words, a SOM map is trained with the dataset and, after this, the objects of this set are associated with the nearest (or winning) neurons. And, thus, each neuron of the map or prototype represents an object subset. Now, in a classification process, the object is compared with the map prototypes, where the winner is elected. The objects mapped in this winning neuron and adjacent neurons are retrieved and presented to then have the execution of *i*NN.

Thus, due to the preprocessing made by the SOM to the *i*NN algorithm, the computational effort as a whole to find the informative nearest neighbor is much smaller, which results in a significant reduction in the classification time when compared to the classification time of the *i*NN without preprocessing.

Therefore, the primary objective of the classifier addressed in this paper was the maintenance of the accuracy of the *i*NN and the reduction of the classification time in a classification process, thus concluding that the use of the objects represented by the winning neuron and adjacent neurons was effective in the analytical aspects by not degrading the performance of *i*NN. The results presented in

TABLE 3: Classification results for all algorithms represented by mean and standard deviation of accuracy and kappa measures.

	Classifiers	Acc	Kappa
1	kNN	0.87 ± 0.1	0.6 ± 0.32
	iNN	0.87 ± 0.06	0.52 ± 0.24
	SOM-kNN	0.86 ± 0.09	0.57 ± 0.3
	SOM-iNN	0.87 ± 0.06	0.52 ± 0.24
2	kNN	0.96 ± 0.04	0.94 ± 0.07
	iNN	0.95 ± 0.05	0.93 ± 0.08
	SOM-kNN	0.95 ± 0.02	0.93 ± 0.03
	SOM-iNN	0.93 ± 0.05	0.90 ± 0.08
3	kNN	0.54 ± 0.1	0.30 ± 0.15
	iNN	0.54 ± 0.07	0.30 ± 0.10
	SOM-kNN	0.52 ± 0.07	0.28 ± 0.10
	SOM-iNN	0.49 ± 0.08	0.23 ± 0.11
4	kNN	0.86 ± 0.07	0.41 ± 0.32
	iNN	0.86 ± 0.07	0.41 ± 0.32
	SOM-kNN	0.88 ± 0.09	0.48 ± 0.41
	SOM-iNN	0.88 ± 0.09	0.48 ± 0.41
5	kNN	0.95 ± 0.03	0.92 ± 0.05
	iNN	0.95 ± 0.03	0.92 ± 0.05
	SOM-kNN	0.95 ± 0.03	0.93 ± 0.04
	SOM-iNN	0.95 ± 0.03	0.93 ± 0.04
6	kNN	0.85 ± 0.05	0.69 ± 0.10
	iNN	0.84 ± 0.04	0.68 ± 0.09
	SOM-kNN	0.87 ± 0.05	0.75 ± 0.11
	SOM-iNN	0.87 ± 0.05	0.75 ± 0.11
7	kNN	0.67 ± 0.05	0.55 ± 0.08
	iNN	0.7 ± 0.05	0.58 ± 0.07
	SOM-kNN	0.66 ± 0.04	0.54 ± 0.07
	SOM-iNN	0.68 ± 0.04	0.56 ± 0.05
8	kNN	0.94 ± 0.03	0.88 ± 0.05
	iNN	0.95 ± 0.02	0.9 ± 0.04
	SOM-kNN	0.95 ± 0.03	0.89 ± 0.06
	SOM-iNN	0.95 ± 0	0.9 ± 0
9	kNN	0.69 ± 0.03	0.16 ± 0.09
	iNN	0.71 ± 0.01	0.17 ± 0.07
	SOM-kNN	0.72 ± 0.05	0.2 ± 0.12
	SOM-iNN	0.72 ± 0.06	0.18 ± 0.12
10	kNN	0.79 ± 0.04	0.56 ± 0.09
	iNN	0.80 ± 0.03	0.59 ± 0.06
	SOM-kNN	0.76 ± 0.03	0.52 ± 0.06
	SOM-iNN	0.79 ± 0.04	0.56 ± 0.08
11	kNN	0.65 ± 0.05	0.11 ± 0.15
	iNN	0.67 ± 0.03	0.04 ± 0.02
	SOM-kNN	0.64 ± 0.05	0.07 ± 0.15
	SOM-iNN	0.67 ± 0.07	0.03 ± 0.17
12	kNN	0.83 ± 0.03	0.82 ± 0.03
	iNN	0.84 ± 0.03	0.82 ± 0.04
	SOM-kNN	0.83 ± 0.03	0.82 ± 0.04
	SOM-iNN	0.83 ± 0.03	0.82 ± 0.04

TABLE 3: Continued.

	Classifiers	Acc	Kappa
13	kNN	0.94 ± 0.02	0.92 ± 0.02
	iNN	0.95 ± 0.02	0.94 ± 0.02
	SOM-kNN	0.93 ± 0.02	0.92 ± 0.02
	SOM-iNN	0.94 ± 0.01	0.93 ± 0.01
14	kNN	0.82 ± 0.12	0.63 ± 0.25
	iNN	0.89 ± 0.04	0.78 ± 0.09
	SOM-kNN	0.79 ± 0.08	0.58 ± 0.15
	SOM-iNN	0.79 ± 0.03	0.58 ± 0.06
15	kNN	0.77 ± 0.02	0.6 ± 0.03
	iNN	0.88 ± 0.02	0.78 ± 0.03
	SOM-kNN	0.78 ± 0.03	0.62 ± 0.04
	SOM-iNN	0.86 ± 0.02	0.75 ± 0.05
16	kNN	0.81 ± 0.03	0.61 ± 0.06
	iNN	0.84 ± 0.04	0.68 ± 0.08
	SOM-kNN	0.8 ± 0.04	0.6 ± 0.08
	SOM-iNN	0.84 ± 0.04	0.68 ± 0.07
17	kNN	0.96 ± 0.02	0.90 ± 0.04
	iNN	0.97 ± 0.01	0.94 ± 0.02
	SOM-kNN	0.96 ± 0.02	0.92 ± 0.03
	SOM-iNN	0.97 ± 0.01	0.94 ± 0.02
18	kNN	0.71 ± 0.03	0.34 ± 0.05
	iNN	0.75 ± 0.02	0.42 ± 0.05
	SOM-kNN	0.71 ± 0.03	0.35 ± 0.06
	SOM-iNN	0.74 ± 0.04	0.42 ± 0.07
19	kNN	0.69 ± 0.02	0.58 ± 0.03
	iNN	0.71 ± 0.03	0.62 ± 0.04
	SOM-kNN	0.68 ± 0.03	0.57 ± 0.03
	SOM-iNN	0.69 ± 0.04	0.59 ± 0.05
20	kNN	0.75 ± 0.02	0.51 ± 0.04
	iNN	0.83 ± 0.02	0.66 ± 0.03
	SOM-kNN	0.76 ± 0.01	0.52 ± 0.03
	SOM-iNN	0.83 ± 0.02	0.65 ± 0.04
21	kNN	0.99 ± 0.01	0.99 ± 0.01
	iNN	0.96 ± 0.01	0.96 ± 0.01
	SOM-kNN	0.98 ± 0.01	0.98 ± 0.01
	SOM-iNN	0.95 ± 0.01	0.95 ± 0.01

Section 4 indicate this reduction of the time and, in addition, that the classification rates of the SOMiNN are statistically similar when compared to the iNN, that is, time reduction and accuracy preservation.

Another important conclusion in analysis of the classification experiments, mainly using artificial dataset, and also in benchmarking dataset where the accuracy performance was worst, the iNN approach presents more significant accuracy results when the objects of different classes are not well separated, with high mixture in the border region.

As a final conclusion, the iNN is an algorithm with accuracy performance better than kNN. But the classification time is a bottleneck for the algorithm, which is minimized using SOM as a Prototype Generation technique. Thus, the

TABLE 4: Classifiers compared in pairs and datasets index ("#") where the performance is significantly improved.

X	Y	$X > Y$	$X = Y$	$X < Y$
iNN	kNN	7, 8, 9, 10, 11, 12, 13, 14, 15, 16, 17, 18, 19, 20	1, 3, 4, 5	2, 6, 21
SOMiNN	SOMkNN	1, 7, 10, 11, 13, 15, 16, 17, 18, 19, 20	4, 5, 6, 8, 9, 12, 14	2, 3, 21
kNN	SOMkNN	1, 2, 3, 7, 10, 11, 13, 14, 16, 19, 21	5, 12, 17, 18	4, 6, 8, 9, 15, 20
iNN	SOMiNN	3, 7, 10, 12, 13, 14, 15, 18, 19, 21	1, 2, 5, 8, 11, 16, 17, 20	4, 6, 9

TABLE 5: Dataset percentage for performance analysis in terms of statistical significance.

X	Y	$X > Y$	$X = Y$	$X < Y$	$(X = Y) + (X < Y)$
iNN	kNN	66.7%	19.1%	14.2%	33.30%
SOMiNN	SOMkNN	52.4%	33.3%	14.3%	47.6%
kNN	SOMkNN	52.4%	19.1%	28.62%	47.7%
iNN	SOMiNN	47.6%	38.1%	14.3%	52.4%

TABLE 6: Comparing the results of this work with the Chen algorithm [27].

	Accuracy	Time	Reduction
kNN	0.81 ± 0.04	88.04 ± 0.05	0
iNN	$\mathbf{0.83 \pm 0.03}$	99.04 ± 107.81	0
SOMkNN	0.81 ± 0.04	$\mathbf{19.32 \pm 21.26}$	0.85 ± 0.05
SOMiNN	0.82 ± 0.04	29.76 ± 30.68	0.85 ± 0.05
Chen	0.79 ± 0.01	30.32 ± 31.83	$\mathbf{0.87 \pm 0.10}$

SOMiNN classifier is proposed here which is specialized to solve problems where the border region is not well defined in a tolerable time.

Acknowledgments

This work was partially supported by CNPq (Brazilian National Council for Scientific and Technological Development) Process 454363/2014-1.

References

[1] T. M. Cover and P. E. Hart, "Nearest neighbor pattern classification," *IEEE Transactions on Information Theory*, vol. 13, no. 1, pp. 21–27, 1967.

[2] S. B. Kotsiantis, B. Sotiris, I. Zaharakis, and P. Pintelas, *Supervised Machine Learning: A Review of Classification Techniques*, IOS Press, 2007.

[3] M. Sjöberg and J. Laaksonen, "Optimal combination of som search in best-matching units and map neighborhood," in *Proceedings of the 7th International Workshop on Advances in Self-Organizing Maps*, vol. 5629, pp. 281–289, Berlin, Germany, 2009.

[4] X. Wu and V. Kumar, *The Top Ten Algorithms in Data Mining*, CRC Press, 2009.

[5] L. A. Silva and E. Del-Moral-Hernandez, "A SOM combined with KNN for classification task," in *Proceedings of the 2011 International Joint Conference on Neural Network, IJCNN 2011*, pp. 2368–2373, San Jose, Calif, USA, August 2011.

[6] R. O. Duda, P. E. Hart, and D. G. Stork, *Pattern Classification*, Wiley-Interscience, New York, NY, USA, 2nd edition, 2001.

[7] A. Torralba, R. Fergus, and W. T. Freeman, "80 million tiny images: a large data set for nonparametric object and scene recognition," *IEEE Transactions on Pattern Analysis and Machine Intelligence*, vol. 30, no. 11, pp. 1958–1970, 2008.

[8] Z. Deng, X. Zhu, D. Cheng, M. Zong, and S. Zhang, "Efficient kNN classification algorithm for big data," *Neurocomputing*, vol. 195, pp. 143–148, 2016.

[9] I. Triguero, J. Derrac, S. García, and F. Herrera, "A taxonomy and experimental study on prototype generation for nearest neighbor classification," *IEEE Transactions on Systems, Man and Cybernetics Part C: Applications and Reviews*, vol. 42, no. 1, pp. 86–100, 2012.

[10] Y. Song, J. Huang, D. Zhou, H. Zha, and C. L. Giles, "IKNN: Informative K-Nearest Neighbor Pattern Classification," in *Proceedings of the European Conference on Principles of Data Mining and Knowledge Discovery*, pp. 248–264, Springer, Berlin, Germany, 2007.

[11] S. Zhang, X. Li, M. Zong, X. Zhu, and R. Wang, "Efficient kNN Classification With Different Numbers of Nearest Neighbors," *IEEE Transactions on Neural Networks and Learning Systems*, no. 99, pp. 1–12, 2017.

[12] D. Randall Wilson and T. R. Martinez, "Reduction techniques for instance-based learning algorithms," *Machine Learning*, vol. 38, no. 3, pp. 257–286, 2000.

[13] H. Brighton and C. Mellish, "Advances in instance selection for instance-based learning algorithms," *Data Mining and Knowledge Discovery*, vol. 6, no. 2, pp. 153–172, 2002.

[14] E. Marchiori, "Class conditional nearest neighbor for large margin instance selection," *IEEE Transactions on Pattern Analysis and Machine Intelligence*, vol. 32, no. 2, pp. 364–370, 2010.

[15] X. Zhao, W. Lin, J. Hao, X. Zuo, and J. Yuan, "Clustering and pattern search for enhancing particle swarm optimization with Euclidean spatial neighborhood search," *Neurocomputing*, vol. 171, pp. 966–981, 2016.

[16] E. Pękalska, R. P. W. Duin, and P. Paclík, "Prototype selection for dissimilarity-based classifiers," *Pattern Recognition*, vol. 39, no. 2, pp. 189–208, 2006.

[17] S.-W. Kim and B. J. Oommen, "A brief taxonomy and ranking

of creative prototype reduction schemes," *Pattern Analysis & Applications*, vol. 6, no. 3, pp. 232–244, 2003.

[18] M. Lozano, J. M. Sotoca, J. S. Sánchez, F. Pla, E. Pekalska, and R. P. W. Duin, "Experimental study on prototype optimisation algorithms for prototype-based classification in vector spaces," *Pattern Recognition*, vol. 39, no. 10, pp. 1827–1838, 2006.

[19] H. A. Fayed, S. R. Hashem, and A. F. Atiya, "Self-generating prototypes for pattern classification," *Pattern Recognition*, vol. 40, no. 5, pp. 1498–1509, 2007.

[20] L. A. Silva, E. Del-Moral-Hernandez, R. A. Moreno, and S. S. Furuie, "Combining wavelets transform and Hu moments with self-organizing maps for medical image categorization," *Journal of Electronic Imaging*, vol. 20, no. 4, Article ID 043002, 2011.

[21] L. A. Silva, E. C. Kitani, and E. Del-Moral-Hernandez, "Fine-tuning of the SOMkNN classifier," in *Proceedings of the 2013 International Joint Conference on Neural Networks, IJCNN 2013*, Dallas, TX, USA, August 2013.

[22] S. Zhang, X. Li, M. Zong, X. Zhu, R. Wang, and D. Cheng, "Learning *k* for knn classification," *ACM Transactions on Intelligent Systems and Technology*, vol. 8, no. 3, p. 43, 2017.

[23] L. J. Moreira and L. A. Silva, "Data classification combining Self-Organizing Maps and Informative Nearest Neighbor," in *Proceedings of the 2016 International Joint Conference on Neural Networks, IJCNN 2016*, pp. 706–713, Vancouver, BC, Canada, July 2016.

[24] T. Kohonen, "Essentials of the self-organizing map," *Neural Networks*, vol. 37, pp. 52–65, 2013.

[25] B. Stvilia, L. Gasser, M. B. Twidale, and L. C. Smith, "A framework for information quality assessment," *Journal of the American Society for Information Science and Technology*, vol. 58, no. 12, pp. 1720–1733, 2007.

[26] J. Vesanto, J. Himberg, E. Alhoniemi, and J. Parhankangas, "Som toolbox for matlab 5," Tech. Rep. A57, Helsinki University of Technology, Finland, 2000.

[27] C. H. Chen and A. Józwik, "A sample set condensation algorithm for the class sensitive artificial neural network," *Pattern Recognition Letters*, vol. 17, no. 8, pp. 819–823, 1996.

5

New Dandelion Algorithm Optimizes Extreme Learning Machine for Biomedical Classification Problems

Xiguang Li, Shoufei Han, Liang Zhao, Changqing Gong, and Xiaojing Liu

School of Computer, Shenyang Aerospace University, Shenyang 110136, China

Correspondence should be addressed to Shoufei Han; hanshoufei@gmail.com

Academic Editor: Luis Vergara

Inspired by the behavior of dandelion sowing, a new novel swarm intelligence algorithm, namely, dandelion algorithm (DA), is proposed for global optimization of complex functions in this paper. In DA, the dandelion population will be divided into two subpopulations, and different subpopulations will undergo different sowing behaviors. Moreover, another sowing method is designed to jump out of local optimum. In order to demonstrate the validation of DA, we compare the proposed algorithm with other existing algorithms, including bat algorithm, particle swarm optimization, and enhanced fireworks algorithm. Simulations show that the proposed algorithm seems much superior to other algorithms. At the same time, the proposed algorithm can be applied to optimize extreme learning machine (ELM) for biomedical classification problems, and the effect is considerable. At last, we use different fusion methods to form different fusion classifiers, and the fusion classifiers can achieve higher accuracy and better stability to some extent.

1. Introduction

Nature has evolved over hundreds of millions of years, showing the perfect efficiency and magic. People learn a lot from the study of natural systems and use them to develop new algorithms and models to solve complex problems. Therefore, imitation of biological intelligence behavior, drawing on its intelligent mechanism, making many new ways to solve complex problems continue to emerge. Through the modeling of natural intelligence, a number of intelligent algorithms have been proposed, including genetic algorithms [1], ant colony algorithm [2], particle swarm algorithm [3, 4], center gravity search algorithm [5, 6], and quantum computing [7]. Each intelligent algorithm corresponds to an actual source of inspiration. For example, DNA calculations are based on a double helix structure proposed by Watson and Crick who win the Nobel Prize in physiology or medicine and a polymerase linker response proposed by a Nobel Prize winner Mullis [8]. Artificial bee colony algorithm is based on the decoding of the bees dance behavior [9]. Artificial immune algorithm is based on immune network theory [10]. The bat algorithm is presented by simulating the bat echo positioning behavior [11]. Inspired by observing fireworks

explosion, enhanced fireworks algorithm is proposed for global optimization of complex functions [12]. In recent years, many intelligent algorithms have been applied in engineering problems successfully [13–20], which not only reduce the time consumed but also can guarantee better performance than manual adjustment.

The above-mentioned intelligent algorithms are all parallel to search for the optimal solution. However, the individuals in them are using the same mechanism in the process of searching. In this paper, inspired by the behavior of dandelion sowing, a novel swarm intelligence algorithm called dandelion algorithm (DA) is proposed for function optimization. Such an optimization algorithm has advantages such as a simple computational process and ease of understanding. In DA, dandelion populations are divided into two subpopulations, suitable for sowing and unsuitable for sowing, and then perform different sowing ways for different subpopulations. Meanwhile, another way of sowing is to carry out the subpopulation which is suitable for sowing, in order to avoid falling into the local optimum. To validate the performance of the proposed DA, in our simulation, we apply the twelve standard functions and compare the proposed algorithm (DA) with bat algorithm (BA), particle

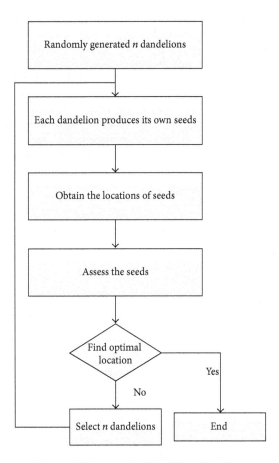

FIGURE 1: Framework of dandelion algorithm.

swarm optimization (PSO), and enhanced fireworks algorithm (EFWA). The results show that the proposed algorithm has better overall performance on the test functions.

Extreme learning machine is an advanced neural network [21]. The input weight and the hidden layer bias are randomly generated according to the number of input neurons and hidden layer nodes, and the output weight matrix is calculated according to the Moore-Penrose generalized inverse of the hidden layer output matrix. Although the extreme learning machine has many advantages over traditional neural networks, it causes its instability due to its random input weight and hidden layer bias. In order to obtain higher accuracy, this paper proposes a method to optimize the extreme learning machine with proposed algorithm (DA) for biomedical classification problems. Moreover, we combine multiple classifiers to form a fusion classifier with different fusion methods for biomedical classification, and the results show that it has better performance.

The paper is organized as follows. In Section 2, the dandelion algorithm is introduced. The simulation experiments and results analysis are given in detail in Section 3. Using DA to optimize ELM and combining multiple classifiers to form a fusion classifier with different fusion methods are presented in Section 4. Finally, the conclusion is summarized in final part.

2. Dandelion Algorithm

2.1. DA Framework. In DA, we assume that the earth is divided into two types: suitable for dandelion sowing and unsuitable for dandelion sowing, and the dandelion living in suitable environment is called core dandelion (CD); on the contrary, the dandelions except for the core dandelion are called assistant dandelions (AD).

Without loss of generality, consider the following minimization problem:

$$y = \min f(x); \tag{1}$$

the objective is to find an optimal x with minimal evaluation (fitness) value.

When a dandelion is sown, the seeds of dandelion will be scattered around the dandelion. In our view, the process of dandelion sowing can be seen to search an optimal in a particular space around a point. For example, now we need to find a point x to satisfy $y = f(x)$; then using the dandelion to sow the seeds in potential space until finding a point is infinitely close to the point x. Mimicking the process of dandelion sowing, a rough framework of the DA is depicted in Figure 1.

In DA, with each generation of sowing, firstly, we need to select n dandelions; that is to say, here we have n dandelions to sow. Then after sowing, the locations of seeds are obtained and assessed. The algorithm will stop when the optimal location is found. Otherwise, the algorithm needs to select other n dandelions from the all seeds and dandelions for the next generation of sowing.

From Figure 1, we can see that the process of sowing and selection strategy are important for DA, and they are, respectively, described in detail in the following.

2.2. Design of DA. In this section, we will introduce the design of the various operators of the dandelion algorithm and the mathematical model in detail. In the DA, we assume that there are only two types of dandelion: core dandelion (CD) and assistant dandelions (AD), and different types of dandelions perform different sowing ways. Meanwhile, another way of sowing, called mutation sowing, is designed to avoid falling into local optimum. Finally, the selection strategy is designed to select dandelions to enter the next generation.

To sum up, the dandelion algorithm consists of normal sowing, mutation sowing, and selection strategy.

2.2.1. Normal Sowing. In the DA, we stipulate that the core dandelion can produce more seeds, and the assistant dandelion produces less seeds, because the land with the core dandelion is suitable for the seeds to grow. The number of seeds produced by the sowing is calculated based on its relative dandelions fitness values in the dandelion population. Assume that the maximum number of seeds is *max* and the minimum number of seeds is *min*; the number of seeds M_i for each dandelion X_i is calculated as follows.

$$M_i = \begin{cases} max \times \dfrac{f_{max} - f(x_i) + \varepsilon}{f_{max} - f_{min} + \varepsilon} & M_i > min \\ min & M_i \le min, \end{cases} \tag{2}$$

where $f_{max} = \max(f(x_i))$, $f_{min} = \min(f(x_i))$, and ε is the machine epsilon to avoid the denominator which is equal to 0.

From (2), for the minimization problem, we can see that the dandelion with small fitness value will sow more seeds, and the dandelion with large fitness value will sow less seeds but can not be less than the minimum number of seeds.

In DA, dandelions are divided into two types: assistant dandelions and core dandelion; the core dandelion (CD) is the dandelion with the best fitness, and it is calculated by

$$X_{CD} = \min f(x_i). \tag{3}$$

The calculation of the radius of the assistant dandelions and the core dandelion is different. The assistant dandelions' sowing radius (except for CD) is calculated by

$$R_i(t)$$

$$= \begin{cases} UB - LB & t = 1 \\ w \times R_i(t-1) + (\|X_{CD}\|_\infty - \|x_i\|_\infty) & \text{otherwise,} \end{cases} \tag{4}$$

where t is the the number of iterations, UB is upper bound of the function, LB is lower bound of the function, and infinite norm is the maximum of all dimensions.

From (4), at the beginning of the algorithm, the sowing radius for the assistant dandelions is set to the diameter of the search space. After that, it is set to difference of distance between current assistant dandelion and core dandelion; here we use infinite norm to measure distance. Moreover, in order to slow down the convergence rate to improve the global search performance, on the basis of the above, we added the sowing radius of assistant dandelion in the previous generation, and the w is a weight factor, to adjust the impact of the sowing radius of previous generation on the current sowing radius dynamically. The weight factor w is designed as follows.

$$w = 1 - \dfrac{Fe}{Fe_{max}}, \tag{5}$$

where Fe is the current function evaluations and Fe_{max} is the maximum number of function evaluations. It can be seen that the value of w changed from large to small, it means that the sowing radius of the previous generation has less and less impact on the current sowing radius.

But for the CD, it is another way to calculate the sowing radius, which is adjusted based on the CD in the last generation; it is designed as follows.

$$R_{CD}(t) = \begin{cases} UB - LB & t = 1 \\ R_{CD}(t-1) \times r & a = 1 \\ R_{CD}(t-1) \times e & a \ne 1, \end{cases} \tag{6}$$

where $R_{CD}(t)$ is the sowing radius of the CD in generation t. At the beginning of the algorithm, the sowing radius for the CD is also set to the diameter of the search space. r and e are the withering factor and growth factor, respectively, and a reflects the growth trend, which is calculated by

$$a = \dfrac{f_{CD}(t) + \varepsilon}{f_{CD}(t-1) + \varepsilon}, \tag{7}$$

where ε is the machine epsilon to avoid the denominator which is equal to 0. When $a = 1$, it means that the algorithm does not find a better solution, and the place is not suitable for sowing; thus, we need to reduce the sowing radius, and the withering factor r is designed to describe this situation; of course r can not be too small; the value should be in [0.9, 1). On the contrary, when $a \ne 1$, it means that the algorithm finds a better solution than last generation, and the place is suitable for sowing, and the sowing radius should be enlarged, which can speed up the convergence rate; based on this, the growth factor e is proposed; of course e can not be too large; the value should be in (1, 1.1].

Algorithm 1 describes the process of the normal sowing in DA. $X_{min}{}^k$ and $X_{max}{}^k$ refer to the lower and upper bounds of the search space in dimension k.

2.2.2. Mutation Sowing for the Core Dandelion. In order to avoid falling into the local optimal and keep the diversity of

```
(1) Calculate the number of seeds $M_i$
(2) Calculate the ADs of sowing radius $R_i$
(3) Calculate the CD of sowing radius $R_{CD}$
(4) Set $z = \text{rand}(1, d)$
(5) For $k = 1 : d$ do
(6)     If $k \in z$ then
(7)         If $X_i^k$ is core dandelion then
(8)             $X_i^k = X_i^k + \text{rand}(0, R_{CD})$
(9)         Else
(10)            $X_i^k = X_i^k + \text{rand}(0, R_i)$
(11)        End
(12)        If $X_i^k$ out of bounds
(13)            $X_i^k = (2 \times \text{rand} - 1) \times (X_{max}^k - X_{min}^k)/2 + (X_{max}^k + X_{min}^k)/2$
(14)        End if
(15)    End if
(16) End for
```

ALGORITHM 1: Generating normal seeds.

```
(1) Find out the core dandelion $X_{CD}$ in current population
(2) Set $z = \text{rand}(1, d)$
(3) For $k = 1 : d$ do
(4)     If $k \in z$ then
(5)         Produce mutation seeds $X'_{CD}$ by Eq. (8)
(6)         If $X'_{CD}$ out of bounds
(7)             $X'_{CD} = (2 \times \text{rand} - 1) \times (X_{max}^k - X_{min}^k)/2 + (X_{max}^k + X_{min}^k)/2$
(8)         End if
(9)     End if
(10) End for
```

ALGORITHM 2: Generating mutation sparks.

the population, another way to sow, called mutation sowing, is proposed for the CD. It is defined as

$$X'_{CD} = X_{CD} \times (1 + \text{Levy}()), \tag{8}$$

where Levy( ) is a random number generated by the Levy distribution, and it can be calculated with parameter $\beta = 1.5$.

Algorithm 2 is performed for mutation sowing for CD to generate location of seeds. This algorithm is performed N_m times (N_m is a constant to control the number of mutation seeds).

2.2.3. Selection Strategy. In the DA, it requires that the current best location is always kept for the next iteration. In order to keep the diversity, the remaining locations are selected based on disruptive selection operator. For location X_i, the selection probability p_i is calculated as follows.

$$p_i = \frac{f_i}{\sum_{n=1}^{SN} f_n} \tag{9}$$

$$f_i = |f_i - f_{avg}|,$$

where f_i is the fitness value of the objective function, f_{avg} is the mean of all fitness values of the population in generation t,

and SN is the set of all dandelions (dandelions, normal seeds, and mutation seeds).

The selection probabilities determined by this method can give both good and poor individuals more chances to be selected for the next iteration, while individuals with mid-range fitness values will be eliminated. This method can not only keep the diversity of the population but also reflect the better global searching ability.

2.3. Summary. Assume that the number of dandelion populations is N. Algorithm 3 summarizes the framework of the DA. During each sowing, two types of seeds are generated, respectively, according to Algorithms 1 and 2. Firstly, the number of seeds and sowing radius are calculated based on the quality of the corresponding dandelion. Moreover, another type is designed with a Levy mutation, which can help to avoid falling into local optimum. After that, N locations are selected for the next generation. In the DA, we assume that the total number of normal seeds is N_s, and the number of mutation seeds is N_m. So approximate $N + N_s + N_m$ function evaluations are done in each generation. Suppose the optimum of a function can be found in t generations; then we can deduce that the complexity of the DA is $O(t \times (N + N_s + N_m))$.

(1) Randomly choosing N dandelions
(2) Assess their fitness
(3)   Repeat
(4)   Obtain R_i (except for R_{CD}) by Eq. (4)
(5)   Obtain R_{CD} by Eq. (5)
(6)   Obtain the number of seeds M_i by Eq. (2)
(7)   Produce normal seeds using Algorithm 1
(8)   Produce mutation seeds using Algorithm 2
(9)   Assess all seeds' fitness
(10)   Retain the best seed as a dandelion
(11)   Select other $N - 1$ dandelions randomly by Eq. (9)
(12)   Until termination condition is satisfied
(13) Return the best fitness and a dandelion location

ALGORITHM 3: Framework of DA.

TABLE 1: Parameter settings.

Algorithm	Parameters
BA	$n = 20, A = 1, r = 1, \alpha = \gamma = 0.9$
EFWA	$n = 50, m = 50, a = 0.8, b = 0.04, A_{max} = 40$
PSO	$n = 20, c1 = 2, c2 = 2, w = 0.7298$
DA	$n = 2, n_m = 2, \text{max} = 100, \text{min} = 10, r = 0.95, e = 1.05$

3. Experiments

To assess the performance of DA, it is compared with BA, EFWA, and PSO.

3.1. Experiment Settings. The parameters of DA, BA, EFWA, and PSO are setting as Table 1, and the settings are applied in all the comparison experiments.

In Table 1, n is population size, A is the loudness, r is the the rate of pulse emission, m is the total number of sparks, and a and b are fixed constant parameters that confine the range of the population size. A_{max} is the the maximum explosion amplitude and n_m is the number of mutation dandelions.

In the experiment, the function of each algorithm is repeated 51 times, and the final results after the 300,000 function evaluations are presented. In order to verify the performance of the algorithm proposed in this paper, we use the 12 different types of test functions, which are listed in Table 2 and their expressions are listed in the appendix.

Finally, we use Matlab R2014a software on a PC with a 3.2 GHz CPU (Intel Core i5-3470), and 4 GB RAM, and Windows 7 (64 bit).

*3.2. Comparison Experiments among the DA,
the BA, the EFWA, and the PSO*

3.2.1. Comparison of Optimization Accuracy. In this section, we compare the performance of the DA with the BA, the EFWA, and the PSO in terms of optimization accuracy.

Table 3 shows the optimization accuracy of the four algorithms on twelve benchmark functions, which are averaged over 51 independent runs. It can be seen that the proposed DA clearly outperforms among BA, EFWA, and PSO on most functions. In the function Six-Hump Camel-Back, the four algorithms almost achieve the same accuracy.

3.2.2. Comparison of Convergence Speed. Besides optimization accuracy, convergence speed is quite essential to an optimizer. To validate the convergence speed of the DA, we conducted more thorough experiments. Figure 2 shows the convergence curves of the DA, the BA, the EFWA, and the PSO on twelve benchmark functions averaged over 51 runs. From these results, in the function Six-Hump Camel-Back, the four algorithms have the same convergence speed, except for the fact that, in the other functions, we can arrive at a conclusion that the proposed DA has a much faster speed than the BA, the EFWA, and the PSO.

3.3. Discussion. As shown in the experiments, we can see that the proposed algorithm DA is a very promising algorithm. It is potentially more powerful than bat algorithm, particle swarm optimization, and enhanced fireworks algorithm. The primary reason lies in the following two aspects.

(1) In the DA, the dandelion population is divided into two separate populations: core dandelion and assistant dandelion, and these two types of dandelion are applied in different ways to sow seeds. The two dandelion populations complement each other and coevolve to fully extend the search range, which increases the probability of finding the optimal location.

(2) Two types of seeds are generated to avoid falling into local optimal and keep the diversity of seeds, and the selection strategy is a mechanism for keeping diversity. Therefore, the DA has the capability of avoiding premature convergence.

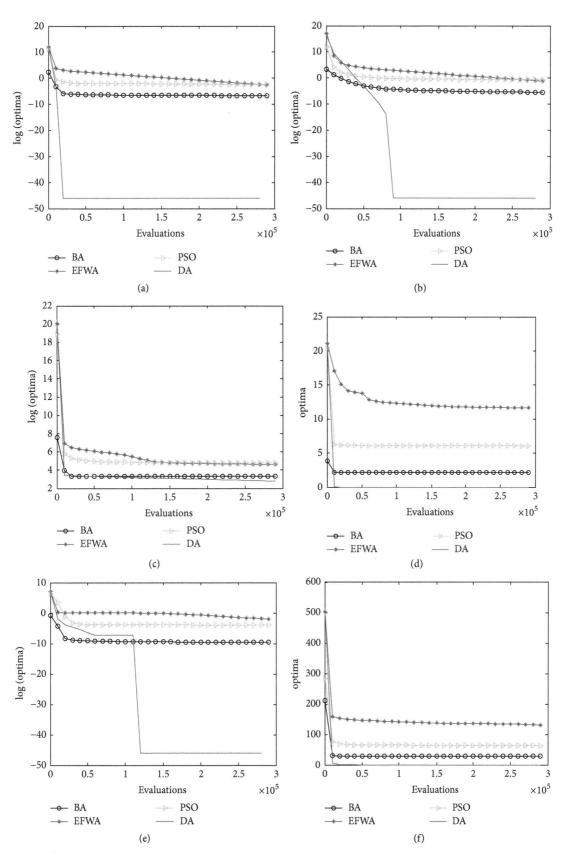

FIGURE 2: Continued.

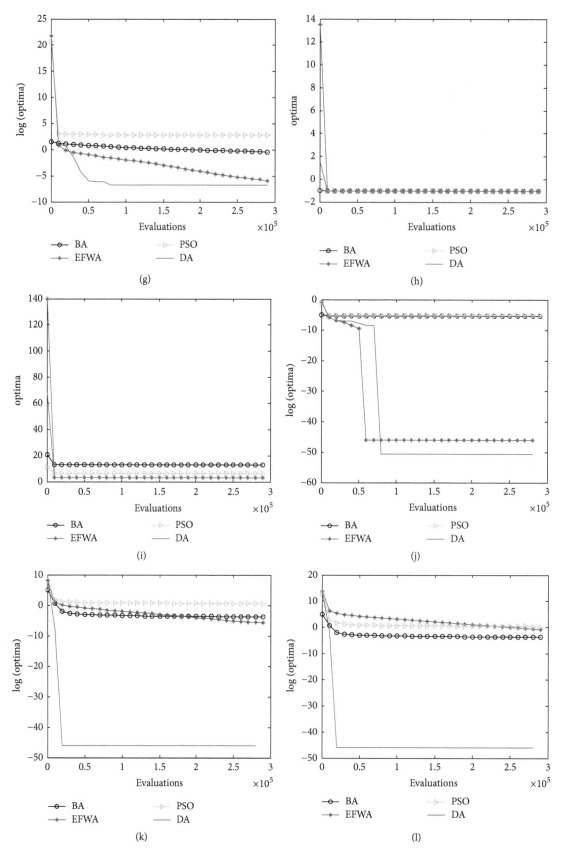

FIGURE 2: Convergence curves of the DA, the BA, the EFWA, and the PSO on twelve benchmark functions. (a) Sphere function; (b) Schwefel function; (c) Rosenbrock function; (d) Ackley function; (e) Griewank function; (f) Rastrigin function; (g) Penalized function; (h) Six-Hump Camel-Back function; (i) Goldstein-Price function; (j) Schaffer function; (k) Axis Parallel Hyper Ellipsoid function; (l) Rotated Hyper Ellipsoid function.

TABLE 2: Twelve benchmark functions utilized in our experiments.

Function	Range	Optimal value	Dimension
Sphere	$[-100, 100]$	0	30
Schwefel	$[-100, 100]$	0	30
Rosenbrock	$[-30, 30]$	0	30
Ackley	$[-32, 32]$	0	30
Griewank	$[-600, 600]$	0	30
Rastrigin	$[-5.12, 5.12]$	0	30
Penalized	$[-50, 50]$	0	30
Six-Hump Camel-Back	$[-5, 5]$	-1.032	2
Goldstein-Price	$[-2, 2]$	3	2
Schaffer	$[-100, 100]$	0	2
Axis Parallel Hyper Ellipsoid	$[-5.12, 5.12]$	0	30
Rotated Hyper Ellipsoid	$[-65.536, 65.536]$	0	30

TABLE 3: Mean value and standard deviation achieved by DA, BA, EFWA, and PSO (accurate to 10^{-6}).

Function	BA mean (Std)	EFWA mean (Std)	PSO mean (Std)	DA mean (Std)
Sphere	0.001277 (0.000144)	0.079038 (0.010276)	0.09323 (0.053308)	0.000000 (0.000000)
Schwefel	0.00417 (0.000856)	0.310208 (0.082243)	0.551331 (0.382977)	0.000000 (0.000000)
Rosenbrock	26.94766 (1.396553)	97.43135 (86.30464)	117.0419 (100.6725)	15.88892 (0.262501)
Ackley	2.175684 (0.386022)	11.67335 (9.79794)	6.062462 (1.350912)	0.000000 (0.000000)
Griewank	0.000069 (0.000009)	0.139219 (0.027736)	0.020483 (0.019879)	0.000000 (0.000000)
Rastrigin	29.47549 (7.795089)	130.8502 (22.96112)	63.04136 (15.74571)	0.000000 (0.000000)
Penalized	0.673172 (0.804593)	0.002687 (0.001646)	17.48197 (11.78603)	0.001939 (0.00423)
Six-Hump Camel-Back	-1.03163 (0.000000)	-1.03163 (0.000000)	-1.03163 (0.000000)	-1.03163 (0.000000)
Goldstein-Price	13.05883 (18.67556)	3.000000 (0.000000)	6.176471 (15.87918)	3.000000 (0.000000)
Schaffer	0.004731 (0.006673)	0.000000 (0.000000)	0.005302 (0.00666)	0.000000 (0.000000)
Axis Parallel Hyper Ellipsoid	0.023513 (0.004702)	0.00306 (0.000568)	1.743886 (1.521884)	0.000000 (0.000000)
Rotated Hyper Ellipsoid	0.024743 (0.005611)	0.490085 (0.073349)	1.30426 (2.23374)	0.000000 (0.000000)

4. Optimization for Extreme Learning Machine with DA

4.1. Brief Introduction of Extreme Learning Machine. Extreme learning machine (ELM) is a neural network algorithm, which is proposed by Huang [21]. The biggest feature of ELM

is faster and has better generalization performance than the traditional neural network learning algorithm (especially the single hidden layer feed-forward neural network).

For N arbitrary samples (x_i, y_i) and $x_i = [x_{i1}, x_{i2}, \dots, x_{in}]^T \in R^n$, $y_i = [y_{i1}, y_{i2}, \dots, y_{in}]^T \in R^n$. The output of the feed-forward neural network with L hidden layer nodes and the stimulus function $g(x)$ can be expressed as

$$\sum_{i=1}^{L} \beta_i \cdot g\left(w_i \cdot x_j + a_i\right) = O_j, \quad j = 1, \ldots, N, \qquad (10)$$

where w_i is the single hidden layer input weight, O_i is the single hidden layer output weight, and a_i is the single hidden layer bias.

The purpose of neural network training is to minimize the error of the output value:

$$\sum_{j=1}^{N} \left\| O_j - y_j \right\| = 0. \qquad (11)$$

From (11), we can see that there are β_i, w_i, a_i that make the following formula set up.

$$\sum_{i=1}^{L} \beta_i \cdot g\left(w_i \cdot x_j + a_i\right) = y_j, \quad j = 1, \ldots, N, \qquad (12)$$

expressed by the matrix as

$$H\beta = T. \qquad (13)$$

In the extreme learning machine, once the input weight w_i and the hidden layer bias a_i are randomly determined, the output matrix H of the hidden layer is uniquely determined. Then the training single hidden layer neural network is transformed into solving a linear equation $H\beta = T$, and the output weights can be determined, $\beta = H^{-1}T$.

4.2. Optimization for Extreme Learning Machine with DA. In ELM, the single hidden layer input weights and bias are randomly generated based on the number of hidden layer nodes and neurons and then calculate the output weight matrix. Randomly generated input weights and bias are only a few of which are superior. And even part of the input weight and bias is 0, which leads to the result that the hidden layer node is invalid directly.

In order to solve the above problems of ELM, a new dandelion algorithm is proposed to optimize the ELM (DA-ELM). DA is a new evolutionary algorithm with strong advantages in accuracy and convergence performance. The DA chooses the best input weight and bias matrix by the iteration. The most suitable input weight and bias form a new matrix, and then the output weight matrix is calculated.

The specific steps of the DA-ELM algorithm are as follows.

Step 1. Set the initial parameters of the ELM, including the number of hidden layer nodes L and the stimulus function $g(x)$.

Step 2. Initialize the parameters of the DA (refer to Table 1).

Step 3. Initialize the dandelion population and randomly generate the initial solution. The dimension of each solution is $L \times (n + 1)$ (n is the number of neurons). $L \times n$ dimension represents the input weight, and the remaining L dimension represents the hidden layer bias.

Step 4. Perform the dandelion algorithm to find the optimal solution, and the root mean square error (RMSE) calculated from the training sample is taken as the fitness function of the dandelion algorithm.

Step 5. Determine whether the DA has reached the maximum number of iterations, and if it is satisfied, go to Step 6; otherwise return to Step 4 to continue the algorithm.

Step 6. The optimal input weight and the hidden layer bias can be obtained by the returned optimal solution.

Step 7. Use the input weight value and the hidden layer bias to train the ELM.

4.3. Performance Evaluation

4.3.1. Parameter Settings. In order to measure the relative performance of the DA-ELM, a comparison among the DA-ELM, ELM, PSO-ELM, BA-ELM, and EFWA-ELM is conducted on the biomedical datasets. The algorithms compared here are described as follows.

(1) ELM: basic ELM with randomly generated hidden nodes and random neurons

(2) PSO-ELM: using PSO to optimize for extreme learning machine

(3) BA-ELM: using BA to optimize for extreme learning machine

(4) EFWA-ELM: using EFWA to optimize for extreme learning machine

In this simulation, the performance of DA-ELM is evaluated on 4 real biomedical datasets classification problems from the UCI database, namely, the EEG Eye State dataset (EEG), the Blood Transfusion Service Center dataset (Blood), the Statlog (Heart) dataset (Statlog), and the SPECT Heart dataset (SPECT). The following lists a detailed description of these 4 biomedical datasets.

(1) EEG: the dataset consists of 14 EEG values and a value indicating the eye state.

(2) Blood: the dataset is taken from the Blood Transfusion Service Center in Hsin-Chu City in Taiwan.

(3) Statlog: this dataset concerns the presence of heart disease in the patient by using 13 attributes.

(4) SPECT: data on cardiac Single Proton Emission Computed Tomography (SPECT) images, each patient classified into two categories: normal and abnormal.

The specification of these 4 datasets is shown in Table 4. All the attributes (inputs) have been normalized to the range of $[-1, 1]$ in our simulations and, for each trial of simulations, the training set and testing set are randomly generated from the whole dataset with the partition number shown in Table 4.

The parameters of the BA, the EFWA, the PSO, and the DA are setting as Table 1, and the algorithms all have 1000

TABLE 4: Biomedical datasets.

Datasets	Data		Type	Attributes	Classes
	Training	Testing			
EEG	7490	7490	Classification	14	2
Blood	374	374	Classification	4	2
Statlog	135	135	Classification	13	2
SPECT	133	134	Classification	44	2

TABLE 5: Results comparisons for biomedical classification.

Datasets	Algorithms	Training		Testing	
		Rate (%)	Dev	Rate (%)	Dev
EEG	DA-ELM	69.78	0.0052	**70.22**	0.0062
	ELM	63.51	0.0167	63.74	0.0139
	PSO-ELM	69.64	0.0069	70.06	0.0064
	BA-ELM	68.19	0.0098	68.79	0.0078
	EFWA-ELM	68.76	0.0068	68.82	0.0072
Blood	DA-ELM	79.81	0.0140	**81.68**	0.0133
	ELM	80.64	0.0162	78.64	0.0133
	PSO-ELM	80.83	0.0131	80.40	0.0141
	BA-ELM	79.97	0.0174	80.16	0.0159
	EFWA-ELM	80.70	0.0175	79.39	0.0154
Statlog	DA-ELM	86.22	0.0216	**88.15**	0.0175
	ELM	87.11	0.0286	80.52	0.0268
	PSO-ELM	86.74	0.0285	88.07	0.0228
	BA-ELM	84.96	0.0257	87.26	0.0167
	EFWA-ELM	87.11	0.0264	86.37	0.0177
SPECT	DA-ELM	81.35	0.0255	**85.22**	0.0243
	ELM	80.68	0.0313	80.75	0.0245
	PSO-ELM	81.95	0.0271	85.00	0.0370
	BA-ELM	80.00	0.0286	84.25	0.0250
	EFWA-ELM	80.98	0.0292	84.33	0.0354

function evaluations. In our experiments, we set the the number of hidden layer nodes $L = 20$ and set the stimulus function as "sigmoid," and the experimental results are the average of the algorithm running 10 times.

All these simulations are conducted in Matlab R2014a software on a PC with a 3.2 GHz CPU (Intel Core i5-3470), and 4 GB RAM, and Windows 7 (64 bit).

4.3.2. Optimization of ELM by Dandelion Algorithm for Biomedical Classification. In this section, we propose a new method to optimize the extreme learning machine by using the DA. The DA is used to optimize the input weight and the hidden layer bias of ELM. Combining the advantages of DA and ELM, the algorithm of DA-ELM is proposed.

The averaging classification results of multiple trials for all these four datasets are shown in Table 5. The one with the best testing rate or the best deviation is shown in boldface. We can easily find that the DA-ELM has higher classification accuracy and better stability among five algorithms in the biomedical classification problems.

4.3.3. Comparison between DA-ELM and Fusion Classifiers for Biomedical Classification. In order to further improve the accuracy and stability of the classification, we combine five classifiers to form a fusion classifier. There are some fusion methods available, such as majority voting method [22], maximum method [22], minimum method [22], median method [22], a new method for fusing scores corresponding to different detectors [23], and fusion of nonindependent detectors [24]. Here we select some simple and effective fusion methods to form fusion classifiers. The classifiers compared here are described as follows.

(1) Max-ELM: fusion of DA-ELM, PSO-ELM, ELM, EFWA-ELM, and BA-ELM to form a fusion classifier and the fusion classifier to make decisions with maximum method

(2) Min-ELM: fusion of DA-ELM, PSO-ELM, ELM, EFWA-ELM, and BA-ELM to form a fusion classifier and the fusion classifier to make decisions with minimum method

TABLE 6: Results comparisons between DA-ELM and fusion classifier for biomedical classification.

Datasets	Algorithms	Training		Testing	
		Rate (%)	Dev	Rate (%)	Dev
EEG	DA-ELM	69.78	0.0052	70.22	0.0062
	Max-ELM	70.13	0.005	**70.58**	**0.0053**
	Min-ELM	68.97	0.0087	69.72	0.0062
	Med-ELM	69.93	0.0063	70.42	0.0059
	MV-ELM	69.14	0.0091	69.13	0.0056
Blood	DA-ELM	79.81	0.0140	81.68	0.0133
	Max-ELM	81.63	0.0138	**81.96**	**0.0125**
	Min-ELM	80.56	0.0139	81.73	0.0142
	Med-ELM	80.79	0.0142	81.81	0.0131
	MV-ELM	79.06	0.0168	81.04	0.0125
Statlog	DA-ELM	86.22	0.0216	88.15	0.0175
	Max-ELM	87.16	0.0208	**89.95**	**0.0137**
	Min-ELM	86.56	0.0213	88.62	0.0142
	Med-ELM	86.75	0.0218	88.16	0.0151
	MV-ELM	88.74	0.0209	87.56	0.0143
SPECT	DA-ELM	81.35	0.0255	85.22	0.0243
	Max-ELM	81.56	0.0209	**86.83**	**0.0226**
	Min-ELM	81.73	0.0226	86.52	0.0235
	Med-ELM	81.25	0.0237	85.69	0.0239
	MV-ELM	80.68	0.0213	84.48	0.0232

(3) Med-ELM: fusion of DA-ELM, PSO-ELM, ELM, EFWA-ELM, and BA-ELM to form a fusion classifier and the fusion classifier to make decisions with median method

(4) MV-ELM: fusion of DA-ELM, PSO-ELM, ELM, EFWA-ELM, and BA-ELM to form a fusion classifier and the fusion classifier to make decisions with majority voting method

The averaging classification results for DA-ELM and the four fusion classifiers are shown in Table 6. The one with the best testing rate or the best deviation is shown in boldface. We can find that the Max-ELM (fusion classifier) has achieved the higher accuracy and the smallest deviation in these datasets, and the Max-ELM has better stability than other fusion methods and DA-ELM.

5. Conclusions

The major contribution of this article is to propose a new dandelion algorithm (DA) for function optimization and optimize the extreme learning machine for biomedical classification problems. From the test results, it is found that the DA can usually find solutions correctly and it clearly outperforms the BA, the EFWA, and the PSO on twelve benchmark functions in terms of both optimization accuracy and convergence speed. Moreover, we use DA to handle the ELM optimization; the results of the ELM optimization also showed that the DA has high performance in unknown,

challenging search spaces. At last, we combine five classifiers to form different fusion classifiers with different fusion methods, and the results show that the fusion classifier (Max-ELM) not only has a relatively high accuracy but also has better stability.

For future work, we will seek a deep theoretical analysis on the DA and try to apply the DA to more practical engineering applications. However, the DA is proposed by this article might not be thorough, and we hope that more researchers can participate in the promotion and test sincerely. Moreover, we will combine other neural networks with DA-ELM to achieve higher classification accuracy and better stability.

Appendix

The expression of the Sphere function is

$$f(x) = \sum_{i=0}^{D} x_i^2. \tag{A.1}$$

The expression of the Schwefel function is

$$f(x) = \sum_{i=1}^{D} \left(\sum_{j=1}^{i} x_j \right)^2. \tag{A.2}$$

The expression of the Rosenbrock function is

$$f(x) = \sum_{i=1}^{D-1} \left(100 \left(x_{i+1} - x_i^2 \right)^2 + \left(x_i - 1 \right)^2 \right). \tag{A.3}$$

The expression of the Ackley function is

$$f(x) = -20 \exp\left(-0.2\sqrt{\frac{1}{D}\sum_{i=1}^{D}x_i^2}\right)$$

$$- \exp\left(\frac{1}{D}\sum_{i=1}^{D}\cos\left(2\pi x_i\right)\right) + 20 + e. \tag{A.4}$$

The expression of the Griewank function is

$$f(x) = 1 + \sum_{i=1}^{D}\frac{x_i^2}{4000} + \prod_{i=1}^{D}\cos\left(\frac{x_i}{\sqrt{i}}\right). \tag{A.5}$$

The expression of the Rastrigin function is

$$f(x) = \sum_{i=1}^{D}\left(x_i^2 - 10\cos\left(2\pi x_i\right) + 10\right). \tag{A.6}$$

The expression of the Penalized function is

$$f(x) = 0.1\left(\sin^2\left(3\pi x_1\right)\right.$$

$$+ \sum_{i=1}^{D-1}\left(x_i - 1\right)^2\left(1 + \sin^2\left(3\pi x_{i+1}\right)\right)$$

$$+ \left(x_D - 1\right)^2\left(1 + \sin^2\left(2\pi x_D\right)\right)\Big) \tag{A.7}$$

$$+ \sum_{i=1}^{D}u\left(x_i, 5, 100, 4\right).$$

The expression of the Six-Hump Camel-Back function is

$$f(x) = 4x_1^2 - 2.1x_1^4 + \frac{x_1^6}{3} + x_1x_2 - 4x_2^2 + 4x_2^4. \tag{A.8}$$

The expression of the Goldstein-Price function is

$$f(x) = \left(1 + \left(x_1 + x_2 + 1\right)^2\left(19 - 14x_1 + 3x_1^2\right.\right.$$

$$- 14x_2 + 6x_1x_2 + 3x_2^2\Big)\Big) \cdot \left(30 + \left(2x_1 - 3x_2\right)^2\right.$$

$$\cdot \left(18 - 32x_1 + 12x_1^2 + 48x_2 - 36x_1x_2 \tag{A.9}\right.$$

$$+ 27x_2^2\Big)\Big).$$

The expression of the Schaffer function is

$$f(x) = \frac{\sin^2\sqrt{x_1^2 + x_2^2} - 0.5}{\left[1 + 0.001\left(x_1^2 + x_2^2\right)\right]^2}. \tag{A.10}$$

The expression of the Axis Parallel Hyper Ellipsoid function is

$$f(x) = \sum_{i=0}^{D}ix_i^2. \tag{A.11}$$

The expression of the Rotated Hyper Ellipsoid function is

$$f(x) = \sum_{i=1}^{D}\left(\sum_{j=1}^{i}x_j^2\right)^2. \tag{A.12}$$

Authors' Contributions

Xiguang Li participated in the draft writing. Shoufei Han participated in the concept and design and performed the experiments and commented on the manuscript. Liang Zhao, Changqing Gong, and Xiaojing Liu participated in the data collection and analyzed the data.

Acknowledgments

This paper is supported by the Liaoning Provincial Department of Education Science Foundation (Grant no. L2013064), AVIC Technology Innovation Fund (basic research) (Grant no. 2013S60109R), the Research Project of Education Department of Liaoning Province (Grant no. L201630), and the National Science Foundation for Young Scientists of China (Grant no. 61701322).

References

[1] D. Goldberg, *Genetic Algorithms in Search*, Addison-Wesley, Mass, USA, 1989.

[2] M. Dorigo, V. Maniezzo, and A. Colorni, "Ant system: optimization by a colony of cooperating agents," *IEEE Transactions on Systems, Man, and Cybernetics B: Cybernetics*, vol. 26, no. 1, pp. 29–41, 1996.

[3] J. Kennedy and R. Eberhart, "Particle swarm optimization," in *Proceedings of the IEEE International Conference on Neural Networks (ICNN '95)*, vol. 4, pp. 1942–1948, Perth, WA, Australia, November-December 1995.

[4] R. C. Eberhart and J. Kennedy, "A new optimizer using particle swarm theory," in *Proceedings of the 6th International Symposium on Micro Machine and Human Science (MHS '95)*, pp. 39–43, Nagoya, Japan, October 1995.

[5] R. A. Formato, "Central force optimization: a new metaheuristic with applications in applied electromagnetics," *Progress in Electromagnetics Research*, vol. 77, pp. 425–491, 2007.

[6] W. Y. Qian and T. T. Zhang, "Adaptive central force optimization algorithm," *Computer Science*, vol. 39, pp. 207–209, 2012.

[7] P. W. Shor, "Algorithms for quantum computation: discrete logarithms and factoring," in *Proceedings of the 35th Annual Symposium on Foundations of Computer Science (SFCS '94)*, pp. 124–134, IEEE, New York, USA, 1994.

[8] L. M. Adleman, "Molecular computation of solutions to combinatorial problems," *Science*, vol. 266, no. 5187, pp. 1021–1024, 1994.

[9] D. Teodorovic and M. Dell'Orco, "Bee colony optimization-a cooperative learning approach to complex transportation problems. advanced OR and AI methods in transportation," in

Proceedings of the In Proceedings of the 10th EWGT Meeting and 16th Mini-EURO Conference, pp. 51–60, Poznan, Poland, 2005.

[10] H. Bersini and F. Varela, "The immune recruitment mechanism: a selective evolutionary strategy," in *Proceedings of the Fourth International Conference on Genetic Algorithms*, pp. 520–526, University of California, San Diego, Calif, USA, July 1991.

[11] X.-S. Yang, "A new metaheuristic bat-inspired algorithm," in *Nature Inspired Cooperative Strategies for Optimization (NICSO '10)*, J. R. Gonzalez, D. A. Pelta, C. Cruz, G. Terrazas, and N. Krasnogor, Eds., vol. 284 of *Studies in Computational Intelligence*, pp. 65–74, Springer, Berlin, Germany, 2010.

[12] S. Zheng, A. Janecek, and Y. Tan, "Enhanced fireworks algorithm," in *Proceedings of the IEEE Congress on Evolutionary Computation*, vol. 62, pp. 2069–2077, Cancun, Mexico, June 2013.

[13] Q. He and L. Wang, "An effective co-evolutionary particle swarm optimization for constrained engineering design problems," *Engineering Applications of Artificial Intelligence*, vol. 20, no. 1, pp. 89–99, 2007.

[14] E. M. Montes and C. A. C. Coello, "An empirical study about the usefulness of evolution strategies to solve constrained optimization problems," *International Journal of General Systems*, vol. 37, no. 4, pp. 443–473, 2008.

[15] C. A. C. Coello, "Use of a self-adaptive penalty approach for engineering optimization problems," *Computers in Industry*, vol. 41, no. 2, pp. 113–127, 2000.

[16] M. Mahdavi, M. Fesanghary, and E. Damangir, "An improved harmony search algorithm for solving optimization problems," *Applied Mathematics and Computation*, vol. 188, no. 2, pp. 1567–1579, 2007.

[17] F. Huang, L. Wang, and Q. He, "An effective co-evolutionary differential evolution for constrained optimization," *Applied Mathematics and Computation*, vol. 186, no. 1, pp. 340–356, 2007.

[18] A. Carlos and C. Coello, "Constraint-handling using an evolutionary multiobjective optimization technique," *Civil Engineering and Environmental Systems*, vol. 17, pp. 319–346, 2000.

[19] K. Deb, "An efficient constraint handling method for genetic algorithms," *Computer Methods in Applied Mechanics and Engineering*, vol. 186, no. 2–4, pp. 311–338, 2000.

[20] K. S. Lee and Z. W. Geem, "A new meta-heuristic algorithm for continuous engineering optimization: harmony search theory and practice," *Computer Methods in Applied Mechanics and Engineering*, vol. 194, no. 36–38, pp. 3902–3933, 2005.

[21] G. B. Huang, Q. Y. Zhu, and C. K. Siew, "Extreme learning machine: a new learning scheme of feedforward neural networks," in *Proceedings of the IEEE International Joint Conference on Neural Networks*, vol. 2, pp. 985–990, Budapest, Hungary, July 2004.

[22] J. F. Chen, "Comparison of fusion methods for multi-neural network classifier," *Popular Technology*, vol. 9, pp. 30–32, 2011.

[23] A. Soriano, L. Vergara, B. Ahmed, and A. Salazar, "Fusion of scores in a detection context based on Alpha integration," *Neural Computation*, vol. 27, no. 9, pp. 1983–2010, 2015.

[24] L. Vergara, A. Soriano, G. Safont, and A. Salazar, "On the fusion of non-independent detectors," *Digital Signal Processing: a Review Journal*, vol. 50, pp. 24–33, 2016.

6

Decoding of Human Movements Based on Deep Brain Local Field Potentials Using Ensemble Neural Networks

Mohammad S. Islam,[1] **Khondaker A. Mamun,**[2] **and Hai Deng**[1,3]

[1]*Department of Electrical and Computer Engineering, Florida International University, Miami, FL 33174, USA*
[2]*AIMS Lab, Department of Computer Science and Engineering, United International University, Dhaka, Bangladesh*
[3]*Nanjing University of Aeronautics and Astronautics, Nanjing, China*

Correspondence should be addressed to Khondaker A. Mamun; mamun@cse.uiu.ac

Academic Editor: George A. Papakostas

Decoding neural activities related to voluntary and involuntary movements is fundamental to understanding human brain motor circuits and neuromotor disorders and can lead to the development of neuromotor prosthetic devices for neurorehabilitation. This study explores using recorded deep brain local field potentials (LFPs) for robust movement decoding of Parkinson's disease (PD) and Dystonia patients. The LFP data from voluntary movement activities such as left and right hand index finger clicking were recorded from patients who underwent surgeries for implantation of deep brain stimulation electrodes. Movement-related LFP signal features were extracted by computing instantaneous power related to motor response in different neural frequency bands. An innovative neural network ensemble classifier has been proposed and developed for accurate prediction of finger movement and its forthcoming laterality. The ensemble classifier contains three base neural network classifiers, namely, feedforward, radial basis, and probabilistic neural networks. The majority voting rule is used to fuse the decisions of the three base classifiers to generate the final decision of the ensemble classifier. The overall decoding performance reaches a level of agreement (kappa value) at about 0.729 ± 0.16 for decoding movement from the resting state and about 0.671 ± 0.14 for decoding left and right visually cued movements.

1. Introduction

A fundamental function of the brain-machine interfaces (BMI) is to decode and interpret the recorded neural potentials to classify the patient's intentions or intended behaviors. Such information allows for a better understanding of neuronal circuit mechanisms and enables possible development of treatment methods for neurodegenerative disorders [1].

Deep brain stimulation (DBS) [2–4] is a functional neurosurgical procedure of implanting a miniature medical device to send electronic signals to certain parts of the brain such as subthalamic nucleus (STN) or globus pallidus interna (GPi) in Basal Ganglia (BG) for treatment of movement disorders such as Parkinson's disease (PD) or Dystonia. At the same time, DBS devices can be considered for BMI design and they are able to record the neurosignals called local field potentials (LFPs) [5–7] for body movement prediction or interpretation. Deep brain LFPs represent the aggregation activities of a large population of local synchronous neurons [5] and can provide neuronal information with better quality (i.e., high SNR) and greater stability over time compared with single-unit activity (SUA). The acquired LFPs from implanted DBS macroelectrodes can be used by researchers and clinicians to investigate on functioning of the Basal Ganglia in motor control [8] for better understanding and more effective treatments of movement disorders [9]. Deep brain LFPs reflect synchronized, subthreshold currents generated in the somata and dendrites of local neuronal elements [10] and they can be subdivided into a number of frequency bands including delta (0–3 Hz), theta (4–7 Hz), alpha (8–12 Hz), beta (13–32 Hz), gamma (31–200 Hz), and high-frequency (>200 Hz) [9] bands. During human body movements, the frequency of the LFP signals can be as high as 300 Hz [7] and is likely to vary due to a varied degree of behavioral and disease correlation. For example, in case when self-paced (voluntary), externally cued movements or any specified action is intended to be performed, the frequency-dependent event-related synchronization (ERS) and event-related desynchronization (ERD) can be found in various LFP bands recorded in bilateral STNs and/or GPIs [5, 10], which suggests that these oscillations may be related to the preparations of motor response.

With the analysis of intra-operative LFP recordings, it has been found that the frequencies of the synchronized oscillatory activities generally belong to one of two different bands for PD patients withdrawn from dopaminergic therapy [10]. The first band contains activity frequencies (3–12 Hz) of Parkinsonian rest and action tremor, but the signal in this band is neither consistent nor a strong feature of LFPs. However, the second band, called beta band (13–32 Hz), is the frequency range representative of LFP oscillations. This band is antikinetic in nature and is manifested in single-unit activity [10]. Furthermore, for PD patients, the improvement in bradykinesia and rigidity with the subsequent dopaminergic therapy was shown to be correlated to the signal magnitude change in the beta band [9]. However, for PD patients, the oscillatory characteristics of beta frequency band are augmented to such an extent that they dominate over motor commands used for initializing voluntary movements, leading to movement disorders [13]. The most consistent of beta band activities can be found in the untreated, hypodopaminergic Parkinsonian state [14–16]. Recent study also substantiated that the strong signal components in beta frequency band were observed in LFPs recorded from the GPI of PD patients, whereas, for Dystonia patients, the signal in the same frequency band was much less salient [9]. For Essential Tremor (ET), the tremor signals are consistently in the frequency range of 8–27 Hz. For cervical Dystonia, the frequency ranges of 4–10, 11–30, and 65–85 Hz of LFPs are highly correlated to sternocleidomastoid muscle EMG signal frequencies [9]. In addition, ERD in beta band (10–24 Hz) was observed during human movement initiation process and ERS during cessation of movement [9]. At rest and during "OFF" medication Parkinsonian state, alpha (8–12) Hz and beta (13–32) Hz oscillatory activities dominate in the LFP frequency spectra, while they are drastically reduced during "ON" medication state [7]. Moreover, during "OFF" levodopa, the activity in gamma band increases bilaterally during active movement [9] and high-frequency oscillations (HFO) (300–350 Hz) may heighten. In addition, it was also reported that, during "ON" and "OFF' medication states in PD, the extent of power in the frequency band of 4–10 Hz is lower in contrast to Dystonia patients [9]. Although the oscillations in gamma band (>70 Hz) in LFPs that is correlated to human movement (prokinetic) were suppressed [13] or absent in PD patients, during the "ON" medication state, the synchronized oscillatory activity may occur in the STNs and GPIs. Although the evidence suggests that these frequency activities would increase when the body changes from rest to movement, the activities above 65 Hz appear to be an unreliable LFP feature for PD patients [10].

Basal Ganglia STNs activity can be modulated, while patient intends to perform a specified action or watches visual images of movements [17]. Such intended movements are responsible for generating ERS and ERD in Basal Ganglia which are similar in frequency and time to those during actual voluntary movement [1]. Although the differences in the midst of contra- and ipsi-lateral movement-related oscillatory changes in the STNs have been unknown, some studies suggest that there may not be substantial differences. However, it was also reported recently that, during wrist movement tasks, both contra- and ipsi-lateral ERS were observed in the gamma frequency band [7] but event-related desynchronization (ERD) was found in the low-beta frequency band (~10–24 Hz) [9].

Therefore, multiple frequency-dependent oscillations in motor cortex and BG are directly related to the process of action making, preparations, executions, and imaginations of movements [7]. Recent experimental results showed that, based on distinct oscillations of LFPs, self-paced hand movements can be predicted using a pattern recognition algorithm [18]. The result indicates that LFP activity is directly or indirectly involved in the process of motor preparation. In addition, it is found that the LFPs can be used to infer substantial information about specific types of arm movement parameters such as distance, speed, and directions for motor disorder patients [19, 20]. A recent study showed that movement in eight directions can be decoded with the best recognition rate of up to 92% using the spatial patterns of LFPs in premotor and primary motor areas [19].

Some studies have been conducted to find the coherence and causality between cortex and hand movement. In one study, it was found that noteworthy coherence only exists between the human sensorimotor cortex and contralateral hand and forearm muscles. However, no existence of coherence was found in sensorimotor cortices or any ipsi-lateral hand and forearm muscle [21]. In another study, it was shown that voluntary movement can be decoded up to $76.0 \pm 3.1\%$ using causal strength of LFP signal features computed on neural synchronization of bilateral STNs or GPIs and utilizing bivariate Granger Causality [1]. Additionally, it was found that left and right hand movements are associated with different spatiotemporal patterns of movement-related synchronization and de-synchronization [22]. Therefore, motor control or bilateral coordination can be predicted by decoding movement intention from Basal Ganglia neural activities for left and right hands [1, 7, 12]. These research findings have further demonstrated that LFPs during onset of movement contain supportive information that may advance our knowledge towards reliable movement decoding strategies for neuro-prosthetic device developments, diagnostic assessments, and possible treatment of some chronic neurological disorders. For instance, early prediction of onset of tremor of PD patients may provide the possibility of constructing an adaptive therapeutic intervention mechanism in using DBS for optimal neuromodulation effects [3].

Hence, the prediction and classification of human body movements can be achieved by decoding the recorded BG LFP signals using pattern recognition algorithms. In this paper, we have developed an innovative neural network (NN) based ensemble classifier for effectively decoding the LFP signals recorded from sequential occurrence of movements and identifying whether the movement is left- or right-sided visually cued in an automated and systematic fashion.

Artificial neural networks (ANNs) [23] are one of the most effective and commonly used machine learning algorithms. However, different types of ANN algorithms possess various advantages and disadvantages in classification. For instance, the FBANN, that is, multi-layer perceptron (MLP), is relatively efficient in optimization or classification with limited training data but tends to be stuck in the local minima and provides less satisfactory classification results [24]. On the other hand, RBFNN could find the global minimum [25] but requires much larger dataset to train. Alternatively, PNN, derived from the Bayes rule and kernel Fisher discriminant, is more accurate than MLP networks and insensitive to outliers in training data [26]. However, PNN needs more training data and is slower than MLP networks in classification. Therefore, it is highly preferable if we can design an ensemble classifier that uses all of the neural networks as the base classifiers for their collective advantages. The ensemble classifier would contain all the advantages of the above-mentioned networks for better activity decoding and classification using LFP dataset. Also, to get robust and consistent movement in decoding performance, we develop a decision fusion algorithm based on the majority voting strategy to combine the classification results from three individual neural networks. The majority voting is simple, intuitive, and effective ensemble approach for improving classification performance [27, 28]. Recently, it has been shown that when seven base classifiers were used in five different ensemble strategies, including majority voting, Bayesian, logistic regression, fuzzy integral, and neural network, the majority voting strategy proved to be as effective as any other algorithm in improving overall classification performance for the dataset provided [28]. We believe that identifying visually cued voluntary movements by decoding oscillatory characteristics of LFP activity may provide ways of developing more advanced neural interface systems such as BCIs and BMIs to enhance our understandings of the underlying process of movements and its important implications in STNs or GPIs for controlling movement activities.

2. Experimental Framework and Data Acquisition (DAQ) System

The LFP datasets used in training and testing for movement recognition were recorded through the DBS devices from the patients with Parkinson's diseases (PD) or Dystonia. The circumstances of the data acquisition are described in detail in this section.

2.1. Patient Details.
In this work, a total of twelve Parkinson's disease or Dystonia patients (7 males and 5 females) with their ages ranging between 23 and 72 years (49.6 ± 13.9, mean ± 1SD) were recruited. Each patient underwent bilateral implantation of deep brain stimulation (DBS) electrodes in the STN or GPI for therapeutic stimulation to provide the LFP signals for recording. Their disease-suffering durations were between 3 and 38 years (14.8 ± 10.3, mean ± 1SD). The

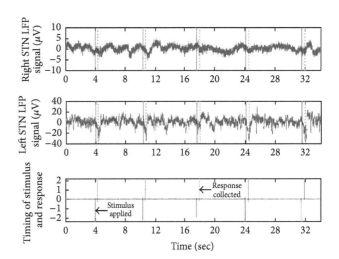

FIGURE 1: Recorded LFP signal from bilateral STNs with chronological visual stimulus applied to the patient. Time of stimulus is presented in solid lines and subsequent motor activity is presented in dotted lines.

corresponding demographics are summarized in Table 1. The LFP data collection was approved by the local research ethics board at Oxford University. All participants provided written consent prior to this study.

2.2. Deep Brain Stimulation (DBS) Electrode Setup.
The DBS macroelectrode (model: 3387, manufacturer: Medtronic Neurological Division, Minneapolis, USA) was implanted bilaterally in the left and right STNs or GPIs for treatment of the patients with Parkinson's disease or Dystonia. The macroelectrode consists of four platinum-iridium cylindrical surfaces (diameter: 1.27 mm, length: 1.5 mm, and center to center spacing: 2 mm; contact-0 is the most caudal and contact-3 is the most rostral). Macroelectrodes were inserted after STN and had been identified by using ventriculography and preoperative magnetic resonance imaging (MRI). Stimulation spots were chosen as the electrode positions, where lessening in Parkinsonian symptoms occurred during intra-operative electrical stimulation and the matching is confirmed by examining the post-operative MRI scan or the fused images of pre-implantation MRI with post-implantation CT.

2.3. Movement Activities of the Patients.
During LFP recording from STNs (Figure 1) or GPIs, all subjects were instructed to do a finger pressing task in a random order with a short resting period between tasks. Each subject was seated 60 cm (approx.) away from the experimental computer screen. After that, prior to each motor task, they were instructed to keep their left or right index fingers on the distinct keys on the left or right standard keyboard. In addition, all the patients were asked to look at a 10 mm cross that was repetitively displayed in the center of the screen and letter A (height: 8 mm; width: 7 mm) on the screen for the duration of 400 ms instantly to the left or right central cross. It was the indication signal to the patients to move the finger. The interval of cues and laterality were provided randomly in the experiment.

TABLE 1: Recording and clinical details of patients.

Patient #	Age	Sex	Years in disease	PD or Dystonia	Elec. placed	Electrode pair used
1	58	F	10	PD	STN	L23/R12
2	63	F	3	PD	STN	L12/R12
3	59	M	7	PD	STN	L01/R01
4	60	M	13	PD	STN	L12/R01
5	72	F	21	PD	GPI	L01/R01
6	55	M	10	PD	STN	L12/R01
7	36	M	14	Dystonia	GPI	L12/R12
8	53	M	5	Dystonia	GPI	L01/R01
9	23	M	7	Dystonia	GPI	L12/R01
10	54	F	38	Dystonia	GPI	L01/R01
11	40	M	25	Dystonia	GPI	L01/R01
12	32	F	24	Dystonia	GPI	L12/R23

2.4. LFP Signal Acquisition from Patients. The LFP signals of twelve patients were recorded at STNs and GPIs for 4–6 days via externalized electrode leads post-operatively after all the patients had been kept "OFF" medication overnight and high-frequency stimulation pulses were completely turned "OFF." Using MRI, the DBS lead contacts at STNs or GPIs to record LFP signals on both sides were confirmed. Three adjacent pairs consisting of 4 contacts named 0, 1, 2, and 3, respectively (pair positions are 0-1, 1-2, and 2-3), were used to record LFPs in the bipolar signal form and bilaterally. Usually, the bipolar configuration was used to provide "common mode rejection" to far-field activity signals against common mode noise contamination. If DBS stimulation and activity recording are conducted simultaneously, the LFP signal recording can be interfered by the DBS stimulation pulses, leading to inaccurate recording and decoding results. In this experimental setup, we recorded the LFP signals well before the stimulation started to avoid any possible interference of the simulation pulses to activity recording. DBS macroelectrode pairs were chosen for better therapeutic effects and anatomical structures. After that, the segments of the recorded signal containing erroneous, premature, or no responses were deliberately discarded from the datasets. The number of trials had to be kept at minimum to minimize the stress during the experiment imposed on the PD/Dystonia patients. In the experimental session, 114 ± 43.6 trials (mean $\pm$ 1SD) consisting of minimum 56 and maximum 202 trials across all subjects were employed in the movement decoding process. In addition, for most of the patients, the number of trials is unbalanced for each class. The average number of trials of each class is 58.2 ± 23.6 (mean $\pm$ 1SD) with a minimum of 25 trials and maximum of 113 trials and the average difference between the classes across all the subjects is $14.2\% \pm 19.0$ trials (with a minimum of 1.2% and a maximum of 57.6%). The DBS surgery was only warranted if the patient had exhibited motion-related dysfunction in postural control, gait, and locomotion in addition to usual motor symptoms such as tremor, rigidity, and bradykinesia. Under these circumstances, there will be always challenges with the amount of data with sufficient neuronal information to be collected; therefore to develop

an analysis method that does not rely on a large number of trials is of paramount importance. However, for avoiding rapid repetitive movements and obtaining valid ranges of inter-movement data, the LFP signals obtained outside the time range between 1s and 5s during a movement were excluded from the datasets. The contact pair (from bipolar mode: 0-1, 1-2, and 2-3) in the Basal Ganglia were chosen for analysis and showed greatest percentage of beta (β) band (13–32 Hz) modulation due to the movement in contrast to the amplitude of β modulation during the baseline activity period occurring 1-2 seconds before the onset of motor response. The LFP information obtained from the available contact pairs of each electrode would be highly correlated and therefore only one contact pair of each electrode was used for data recording and analysis. In the recording scheme, CED 1902 amplifiers ($\times 10{,}000$) were employed to amplify the initial signals recorded at the DBS contacts. With tripolar configurations (active-common-reference), surface EMGs were recorded using disposable adhesive Ag/AgCl electrodes (H27P, Kendall-LTP, MA, USA). Based on the recorded EMGs from the index finger, the onset of motor response and other voluntary and involuntary movements were determined by timing of the key presses as registration of motor response. The movement-related artifacts due to equipment lead were carefully identified and the recordings containing excessive noises were excluded from analysis. Contaminated trials with artifact were also removed. In addition, noise of the recorded data related to patients' movement were avoided as much as possible by instructing patients to stay in steady condition during each session of recordings. In the recorded EMGs, rest and movement conditions were defined as follows: "rest" is defined as no or little hypertonic bursts, "voluntary movements" are defined as regular pulses with a duration of tens of milliseconds, and "uncontrolled contractions" are defined as phasic spasm over seconds. The initial signals were amplified using isolated CED 1902 amplifiers ($\times 10{,}000$ for LFPs and $\times 1000$ for EMGs), low-pass filtered with a cut-off frequency of 500 Hz, and then digitized using 12-bit CED 1401 mark II with a sampling rate of 2000 Hz. Subsequently, a custom written program in SPIKE 2 (Cambridge Electronic Design (CED), Cambridge,

UK) software was used for recording, online monitoring, and storing the digitized data in the hard drive. Variations of instantaneous magnitude and frequency for both LFPs and EMGs were compared to find correlations between them during movement activities.

2.5. Preprocessing of STN's LFP Signals. For removing high-frequency noise and artifacts, a low-pass type-I Chebyshev filter (zero phase shifting and cut-off frequency 90 Hz) was applied to the STN's LFP signals. A notch filter at 50 Hz was further applied to the processed signals to remove the single-frequency noise associated with the power supplies. Then the LFP datasets were digitally resampled at 256 Hz prior to feature extraction and classification processing.

3. Methodology of Feature Extraction of LFP Signals Using Wavelet Packet Transform (WPT) and Hilbert Transform (HT)

To carry out the identification of finger movements from the LFP data, we used wavelet packet transform (WPT) and Hilbert Transform (HT) to extract the LFP signal features from different frequency bands in the frequency range from 0 to 90 Hz. For non-stationary biosignals such as LFPs, WPT is a better alternative as a data analysis tool than STFT or standard DWT in extracting relevant signal features for pattern recognition in the time-frequency domain [29].

WPT can decompose both approximation and detail spaces into further subbands with functionally distinct scales in a balanced binary tree and has ability to localize any specific information of interest as compared to DWT [30, 31]. In carrying out the WPT at decomposition scale of 5, the discrete Meyer wavelet (demy) was selected and applied to the LFP data to generate different multi-resolution coefficients. The WPT coefficients are obtained by recursively filtering out the coefficients generated in the previous stage with lower resolutions to compute the WPT coefficients at current scale.

After completion of the WPT processing, we segmented a 4-second time window from each frequency band for LFP's left and right clicking event tasks at each motor response registration (Figures 2(a) and 2(b)). Likewise, we can segment the resting activity into a total of 2-second time windows during each stimulus registration. The signal envelope in each frequency band of the reconstructed signal was computed by using the Hilbert Transform (HT) [32] and the signal features were extracted based on the power of each frequency band. From Figure 2(c), it can be seen that event-related synchronization and desynchronization happened in all frequency bands but visible amplitude decrement was found in β band at the left and right STNs or GPIs. However, at the event onset, the signal amplitude in the δ band was quite large compared to those in other bands.

For generating the classification features, instantaneous power was computed by averaging the amplitudes of the defined windows in each frequency band. The window length was either 100 ms or 50 ms and its center locations were varied from −500 ms to +500 ms. Ultimately, based on the left and right visually cued movements and the oscillatory characteristics of STN's or GPI's LFP signal due to mean energy increment (synchronization) or reduction (desynchronization), the average amplitudes of five consecutive windows (from −150 ms to 350 ms) of length of 100 ms were chosen as the desired period of interest for feature extraction (Figure 2(c)). Similarly, feature extractions were conducted for the resting state. The five windows with a window size of 100 ms from −750 ms to −250 ms were selected to extract features for resting condition (prior to the stimulus applied) of the patients.

Finally, for each patient in each frequency band, vectors of total seventy bilateral features (2 sides × 7 bands × 5 points in time) at contra- and ipsi-lateral STNs or GPIs were extracted for decoding voluntary movement and resting activity.

4. Design of the Neural Network Based Ensemble Classifiers for LFP Data Recognition

The objective of the work is firstly to detect if finger movement has happened by decoding deep brain-recorded LFP signals and, if so, subsequently to determine the laterality of that movement. The decoding process, which is actually a two-step three-class classification, consists of LFP data acquisition and preprocessing part, the signal feature extraction part using WPT and HT, and the ensemble classifier that includes three base neural network classifiers and a fusion decision system. The structure of the ensemble classifier for the decoding process is shown in Figure 3.

The proposed overall decoding process using the ensemble classifier in Figure 3 is illustrated in the state diagram in Figure 4. The three base neural network classifiers used in the ensemble classifier will be briefly reviewed and the decision fusion rules and the performance evaluation approaches will be introduced in the rest of the section.

4.1. Three Base Neural Network Classifiers. Three different neural networks that will be used as the base classifiers to form the proposed ensemble classifier will be discussed very briefly in this section.

4.2. Feedforward Backpropagation Artificial Neural Network (FBANN)/Radial Basis Function Neural Network (RBFNN)/ Probabilistic Neural Network (PNN). The FBANN [33, 34] was originally designed and trained based on the steepest descent training algorithm. The FBANN network's overall output, Ø, with an input vector Xq is computed based on the following equation:

$$\emptyset = f\left(\sum_{p=1}^{n} w_p^2 f\left(\sum_{q=1}^{m} W_{pq}^1 X_q + b_p^1\right) + b^2\right), \quad (1)$$

where W_{pq} $(q = 1, 2, \ldots, m; p = 1, 2, \ldots, n)$ are the connection weights, n is the total number of hidden nodes, and m is the total number of the input nodes used to fully connect with the hidden layers. Also, f is the nonlinear activation function. On the other hand, unlike FBANN, the RBFNN consists of an input layer, a hidden layer embedded with a nonlinear RBN activation function, and an output layer [35]. The PNN [26]

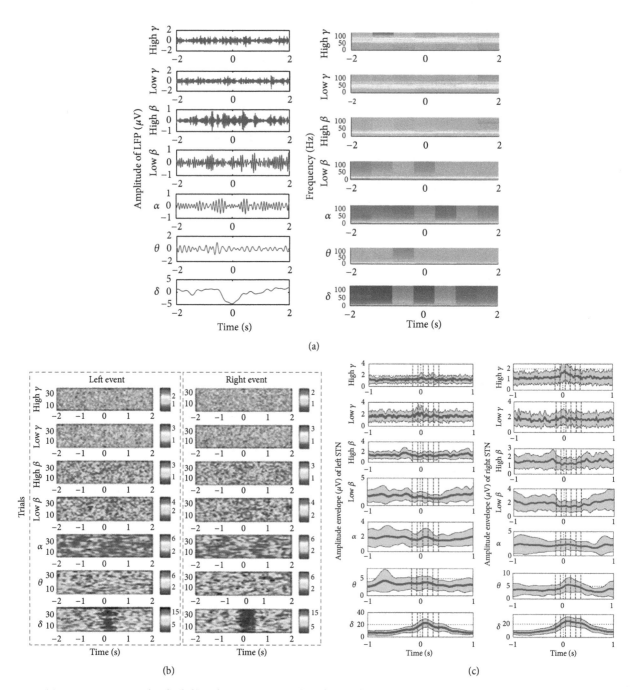

FIGURE 2: (a) Instantaneous amplitude (left) and spectrogram (right) of the right-sided STNs LFP for all frequency bands of patient #1 in a 4-second window centered at the time of response and visually cued left finger clicking events; the extracted frequency bands of LFP signal are delta (0–4 Hz), θ (4–8 Hz), α (8–12 Hz), low β (13–20 Hz), high β (20–32 Hz), low γ (32–60 HZ), and high γ (60–90 Hz), respectively, where high γ band [11] is not the same as the conventional high gamma band (80–200 Hz). (b) The instantaneous magnitude of different bands computed using Hilbert Transform (HT) for all trials of patient #1 during left and right finger visual cued clicking events obtained from deep brain's left STN LFPs (motor responses situated at the center of each time scale) [12]. (c) The average instantaneous magnitude (blue line) and standard deviation (SD) (green shadow area) acquired from STN LFPs of each component for patient #1 and visual cued left and right finger clicking events within 2 s time window. For each frequency band, LFP signal features were defined with average amplitude in five segments (area covered by dotted line.)

consisting of input, pattern, and decision layers is capable of performing classification tasks for multi-class problems. The decision layer classifies the patterns of the output of the summation layer according to Bayes optimal decision rule.

4.3. *Decision Fusion Rule.* To obtain an unbiased decision on movement identification, we will use the majority voting-based ensemble classifier for decision fusion processing. For ensemble classifier, the decisions of the base classifiers are

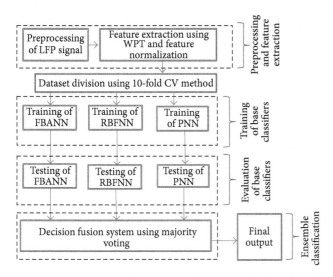

FIGURE 3: Proposed architecture of the ensemble classifier for training, testing, and evaluation.

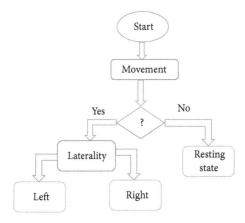

FIGURE 4: Movement detection and its subsequent laterality decoding process using bilateral deep brain's (STNs or GPIs) LFP signal.

TABLE 2: The distribution of trials used for each patient.

| Patient | Number of trials used | | |
	Left finger movement	Right finger movement	Total
1	52	41	93
2	31	37	68
3	71	84	155
4	31	82	113
5	56	54	110
6	25	31	56
7	61	62	123
8	73	72	145
9	34	28	62
10	59	48	107
11	113	89	202
12	80	76	156

assumed to be autonomous and the final decisions are derived from a mixture of all base system's decisions [36]. Inherently, in the plurality voting strategy, the ensemble decision picks class w_j, if there is

$$\sum_{t=1}^{T} d_{t,j} = \max_{j=1}^{C} \sum_{t=1}^{T} d_{t,j}, \tag{2}$$

where $d_{t,j}$ is the decision taken by tth base classifier ($t = 1, 2, \ldots, T$ and $j = 1, \ldots, C$); C is the number of classes and T is the total number of base classifiers used. For plurality voting, if tth classifier predicts class of w_j, then $d_{t,j} = 1$ or 0 for other cases.

In this work, because three base classifiers FBANN, RBFNN, and PNN are used, the majority rule dictates that any two or three base classifiers with the same decision would decide on the acceptance or rejection of the input data as the final decision.

4.4. Performance Evaluation. For classification purpose, a maximum of 28,280 data points from the patients were used for decoding movement versus rest activities. On the other hand, a maximum of 21,210 data points were employed to decode left- and right-sided visually cued movement activities. In our work, we used bootstrap resampling technique (i.e., random samples were chosen with replacement) in selecting movement and resting datasets of the patients. The corresponding number of trials for movement from each patient is shown in Table 2. Bootstrap is a useful statistical method widely used for classification performance assessment [37]. For a class w_j, if the training set is $X_{N_i}^j = \{x_1^j, x_2^j, x_3^j, \ldots, x_{N_i}^j\}$, one can construct the bootstrap samples as follows. Firstly, one sample, $x_{k_0}^j$ from $X_{N_i}^j$, is randomly selected, and the r nearest neighbor samples ($x_{k_1}^j, x_{k_2}^j, \ldots, x_{k_r}^j$) from $x_{k_0}^j$ are found based on the Euclidean distance. Then, the bootstrap samples are generated using $x_{k_0}^b = \sum_{i=0}^{r} w_i x_{k_i}^j$, where $w_i = c_i / \sum_{d=1}^{r} c_d$; $\sum_r w_i = 1$; and $r \geq c_d \geq 0$ [38]. Gaussian distribution (GD) used to choose c_d and the whole process is repeated until the whole N_i are selected.

To evaluate the overall classification performance of the proposed ensemble classifier, we used 10-fold cross-validation (CV) method to carry out the evaluation. For each design set, CV error was computed according to the following formula:

$$\text{CV error} = \frac{1}{N} \sum_{p=0}^{N} \left[d_p(n) - y_p(n) \right]^2, \tag{3}$$

where N denotes the total number of samples and $d_p(n)$ is the desired output; $y_p(n)$ is the classifier's output for each test set and n denotes the number of conducted epochs. The design sets with the lowest error were considered for the base classifier learning and training. The threshold selection methods for all three base classifiers and the ensemble classifier are summarized in Table 3. Also, the pseudocode for proposed decision fusion algorithm for classification of movement or resting and left or right finger movement activities are listed in Algorithm 1.

Threshold value = (FBANN = 1 and RBFNN = 1) or (FBANN = 1 and PNN = 1) or (RBFNN = 1
and PNN = 1);
for i = 1 to number of test vector sets do
if sum of sim(i) in (FBANN and RBFNN) or (FBANN and PNN) or (RBFNN and PNN)
≥ Threshold value
event activity or left finger movement = 1;
prediction(i) = event activity or left finger movement;
else if sum of sim(i) in (FBANN and RBFNN) or (FBANN and PNN) or (RBFNN and
PNN) < Threshold value
resting activity or right finger movement = 0;
Prediction(i) = resting activity or right finger movement;
if end
for end
{Find performance metrics of movement and its forthcoming laterality activity from
test data.}

ALGORITHM 1: Decision-based pseudocode for decoding event or resting and left or right finger movement activities.

TABLE 3: Threshold settings for individual classifier while detecting the movement and resting activity.

Class	Base classifier threshold setting	Classifier final output after threshold setting
Event condition	≥0.5	1
Resting condition	<0.5	0
Left movement	≥0.5	1
Right movement	<0.5	0

The performance of the proposed ensemble classifier for movement detection and classification was evaluated by using several standard metrics such as cross-validated classification accuracy (CVCA), detection rate (DR), specificity (Table 4), F-measure, TPR, FPR, FNR, kappa, and AUC values. These performance metrics are derived from the standard contingency table based on four commonly used measures (TP/FP/TN/FN) that are commonly adopted in evaluating medical decision systems.

In the contingency table, true positive (TP) is the correct classification rate of the LFP signal generated from the movement state or left movement. True negative (TN) is the correct classification rate of the LFP signal generated from the resting state or right movement. However, false positive (FP) represents the classification rate of the LFP signals as movement or left movement, while they are actually resting state or right movement, respectively. False negative (FN) is the classification rate of the LFP signals as the resting state or right movement when the actual state is movement or left movement.

To obtain highest degree of desirability among the base classifiers to detect movement and resting activity, we have computed unified desirability measures using the following:

$$\text{Desirability}_1 = \frac{\text{mean}_{\text{precision}}}{\text{std}_{\text{precision}}} \times \frac{\text{mean}_{\text{sensitivity}}}{\text{std}_{\text{sensitivity}}}$$
$$\times \frac{\text{mean}_{\text{specificity}}}{\text{std}_{\text{specificity}}},$$

$$\text{Desirability}_2 = \frac{\text{mean}_{\text{gmean-1}}}{\text{std}_{\text{gmean-1}}} \times \frac{\text{mean}_{\text{gmean-2}}}{\text{std}_{\text{gmean-2}}}$$
$$\times \frac{\text{mean}_{F\text{-measure}}}{\text{std}_{F\text{-Measure}}},$$

$$\text{Desirability} = \sqrt[6]{\text{Desirability}_1 \times \text{Desirability}_2}.$$
(4)

Furthermore, to gauge the correctness of the classifier, we computed Mathew's correlation coefficient (MCC), as shown in (5). MCC in essence is a correlation coefficient between the observed and the predicted binary classification outcomes.

$$\text{MCC}$$
$$= \frac{((\text{TP} \times \text{TN}) - (\text{FP} \times \text{FN}))}{\sqrt{(\text{TP} + \text{FP})(\text{TP} + \text{FN})(\text{TN} + \text{FP})(\text{TN} + \text{FN})}}.$$
(5)

A value of +1 in (5) represents a perfect prediction; a value of 0 represents no better than random prediction and −1 indicates a total disagreement between the prediction and the truth. AUC is the area under the receiver operating characteristic (ROC) curve which is a useful measure in evaluating the performances of binary classification methods [39]. The AUC is defined as follows:

$$\text{AUC} = \frac{1}{2}\left[\frac{\text{TP}}{\text{TP} + \text{FN}} + \frac{\text{TN}}{\text{TN} + \text{FP}}\right].$$
(6)

For the sake of convenience and simplicity in comparison, we can compute the AUC values only instead of generating ROC curves, since they would be relatively tedious with the large number of datasets.

Alternatively, to obtain the inflated and more intuitive measure of the performance from the unbalanced datasets of the PD and Dystonia patients, we can use the following balanced accuracy (BACC) [40]:

$$\text{BACC} = \frac{1}{2}(\text{TPR} + \text{TNR}).$$
(7)

TABLE 4: Statistical performance measures for decoding of movement and its laterality activity.

Overall accuracy	Sensitivity or DR	Specificity	Overall error rate (OER)
$\dfrac{\text{TP} + \text{TN}}{\text{TP} + \text{TN} + \text{FP} + \text{FN}}$	$\dfrac{\text{TP}}{\text{TP} + \text{FN}}$	$\dfrac{\text{TN}}{\text{TN} + \text{FP}}$	$\dfrac{\text{FP} + \text{FN}}{\text{TP} + \text{TN} + \text{FP} + \text{FN}}$

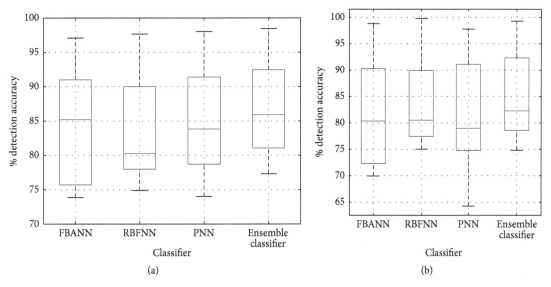

FIGURE 5: (a) Overall accuracy during detection of resting versus movement for all patients. (b) Classification accuracy while decoding left and right movement activity using base and ensemble classifiers.

To further measure the agreement between the predicted and desired classification results in the presence of unbalanced datasets, one can use Cohen's kappa coefficient as the agreement metric [41].

The kappa coefficient (κ) is estimated using the following equation:

$$\kappa = \frac{p_0 - p_e}{1 - p_e}, \tag{8}$$

where p_0 and p_e denote the classification accuracy and the expected agreement of chance, respectively, and these parameters can be calculated from the confusion matrix obtained from the proposed classifier.

If all values of κ within the 95% confidence interval (CI) around the mean are above 0 ($\kappa \pm 1.96 \times \varphi(\kappa) > 0$, where $\varphi(\kappa)$ is the standard error), then the average kappa value is above the chance value. The standard error function, $\varphi(\kappa)$, which is measuring the disagreement, is defined as

$$\varphi(\kappa) = \frac{\sqrt{P_e + P_e^2 - \sum_i \left[n_{i+}n_{+i}\left(n_{i+} + n_{+i}\right)\right]}}{(1 - p_e)\sqrt{N}}, \tag{9}$$

where n_{+i} and n_{i+} are the marginal column and rows sums, respectively, and N is the total number of trials.

5. Experimental Results

Comprehensive computations and simulations of the proposed ensemble classifier have been conducted using the extracted features for detection of finger movement and subsequent classification of the moving directions. The computer simulations were performed using MATLAB 2012b environment on a PC with 64-bit Intel Core i7-2600 CPU @ 3.40 GHz.

Figures 5(a), 6(a), and 6(b) show the average percentage accuracy, sensitivity, and specificity of the movement decoding for individual patients, respectively. The obtained performance parameters for three base neural networks (mean ± 1SD) are (a) 84.31% ± 8.56 in accuracy, 84.69% ± 8.60 in sensitivity, and 84.77% ± 8.11 in specificity with FBANN; (b) 83.94% ± 7.99 in accuracy, 84.77% ± 9.00 in sensitivity, and 86.25% ± 8.71 in specificity with RBFNN; and (c) 85.03% ± 8.30 (mean ± 1SD) in accuracy, 84.38% ± 8.59 in sensitivity, and 86.16% ± 8.65 in specificity with PNN. With the ensemble classifier, we achieved 87.07% ± 7.54 in accuracy, 87.19% ± 7.14 in sensitivity, and 87.54% ± 8.19 in specificity. These results are about 2–4% better compared to individual base classifier. In addition, from the results in Figures 5(b), 6(c), and 6(d), for laterality of movement decoding, FBANN achieved 82.20% ± 10.25 in overall accuracy, 82.19% ± 11.63 in sensitivity, and 82.80% ± 8.00 in specificity; RBFNN achieved 83.51% ± 7.84 in overall accuracy, 84.78% ± 8.93 in sensitivity, and 87.25% ± 9.41 in specificity; and PNN achieved 81.62% ± 11.45 in overall accuracy, 81.87% ± 11.82 in sensitivity, and 83.95% ± 9.70 in specificity.

The ensemble classifier fused the outputs of three base classifiers (i.e., accuracy in FBANN: 83.042%; in RBFNN: 83.658%; and in PNN: 82.98%) together and achieved 86.073% in detection accuracy, while patients were in resting

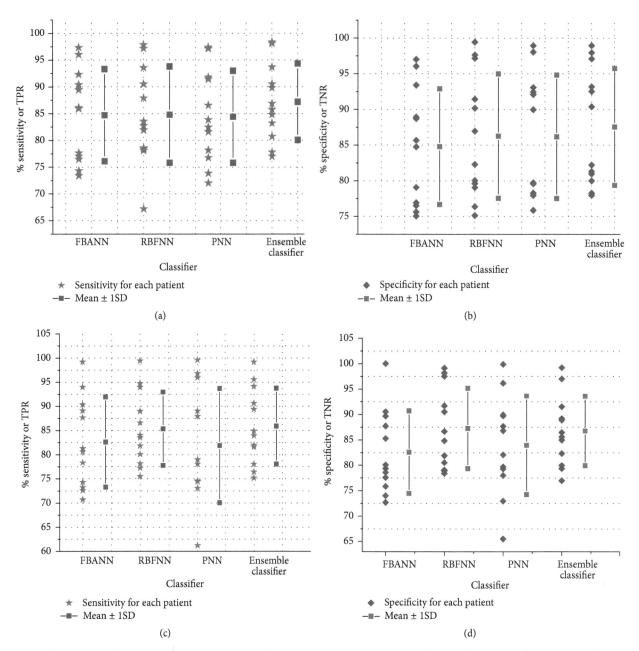

FIGURE 6: (a) Sensitivity during movement versus resting classification obtained from base and ensemble classifier. (b) Specificity of each base and ensemble classifier and detection of movement and resting activity. (c) Sensitivity during classification of left and right finger clicking events obtained from base and ensemble classifier. (d) Specificity obtained from both base and ensemble classifiers during decoding laterality of movement.

state and left or right finger movement activity. Therefore, the overall improvement in detection accuracy of resting from left/right finger movement reached about 3.0% (Figure 9(a)) and the overall error rate (OER) of the detection decreased notably. During movement decoding, RBFNN performed better than PNN and FBANN classifiers in terms of accuracy (83.94% ± 7.99 versus 87.07% ± 7.54 ($t(22) = -0.9866$, $p <$ 0.05)), sensitivity (84.77% ± 9.00 versus 87.19% ± 7.14 ($t(22) = -0.7300$, $p < 0.05$)), and specificity (86.25% ± 8.71 versus 87.54% ± 8.19 ($t(22) = -0.3728$, $p < 0.05$)). For laterality

decoding, RBFNN still managed to achieve better performance than the other two base classifiers in accuracy, sensitivity, and specificity.

Essentially, with various feature set sizes, all the classifiers managed high degree of classification accuracy. RBFNN achieved a lower false positive rate (FPR) but has lower detection rate than PNN classifier in decoding movement. On the other hand, in movement laterality decoding, RBFNN classifier maintained less intra-subject variability in performance than the other two base classifiers. Overall, RBFNN achieved

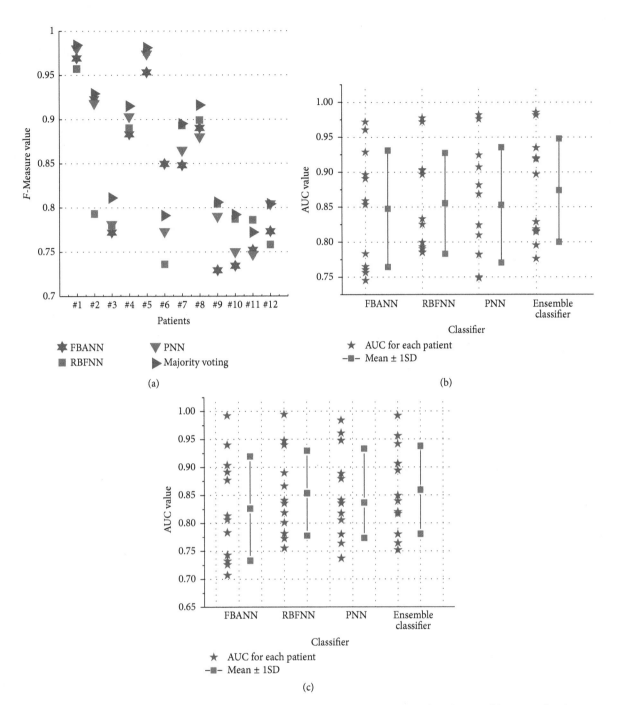

FIGURE 7: (a) *F*-Measure plot of base and ensemble classifier during movement versus resting classification. (b) Area under the ROC curve (AUC) for each patient with mean ± 1SD obtained from each base and ensemble classifier during movement versus resting classification. (c) Area under the ROC curve (AUC) for each patient with mean ± 1SD obtained from each base and ensemble classifier during left and right finger movement classification.

the highest classification rate as well as highest specificity among the three base classifiers. It also performs advantageously in comparison to PNN and FBANN in terms of balanced accuracy (Table 6). Although RBFNN classifier has achieved lowest FPR for both movement and laterality classifications compared to others, it did have higher value of FNR compared to FBANN; more importantly it achieved higher TPR and TNR values than PNN algorithm.

To show the impact of the imbalanced classes on the performance, we obtained the AUC values for each classifier in movement and laterality decoding as shown in Figures 7(b) and 7(c). It is found that the average value of AUC (0.873) with the ensemble classifier is greater than those with any individual classifier. Similarly, in laterality of movement decoding, the ensemble classifier achieved better AUC (0.859) values than any base classifier.

TABLE 5: Standardized 1st-order moment of evaluation measures.

Classifiers evaluated	F-Measure	gmean-1	gmean-2	Desirability value
During decoding movement and resting				
FBANN	9.77	9.92	10.17	9.13
RBFNN	10.41	11.52	11.74	10.25
PNN	10.08	10.57	10.32	10.02
Ensemble	11.08	11.78	11.82	11.22
For decoding left and right finger movement				
FBANN	7.27	8.09	8.62	8.25
RBFNN	8.37	11.30	11.90	9.39
PNN	6.88	7.96	8.15	7.58
Ensemble	8.46	9.58	10.98	9.67

Although all the base classifiers performed well in detecting movement and its forthcoming laterality, the ensemble classifier based on the majority voting algorithm performed better than the base classifiers in detection, especially in terms of FNR. The FNR rate of the ensemble classifier is improved by 2.98% compared with that of any of the base classifiers in decoding movement versus resting of the patients.

Moreover, we computed other distinctive performance indicators such as F-measure (Figure 7(a)), gmean-1, and gmean-2. Obviously, larger F-measure values indicate finer precision and higher sensitivity. g-mean value measures the balanced performance of the classifiers between sensitivity, specificity, and precision.

Standardized 1st-order moments of F-measure and g-mean values for this work are tabulated in Table 5. It is observed from Table 5 that RBFNN performs the best in terms of F-measures. In decoding resting versus movement and its forthcoming laterality, RBFNN also shows the highest degree of desirability, since it achieves the highest desirability value among other base classifiers.

From Table 6, it can be seen that PNN and RBFNN classifiers demonstrated better MCC results, showing better agreement between the prediction and actual results in detecting movement and classifying laterality of movement. RBFNN classifier achieves higher BACC value than other base classifiers. However, with the ensemble classifier, the BACC value is improved by at least 2.63% compared to any base classifier in movement and resting classification.

The data from all the patients demonstrated good kappa coefficient values using each classifier while classifying their LFP patterns of movement and laterality (overall values shown in Table 6). The experimental results also showed that the highest kappa value (0.692 ± 0.17) (mean ± 1SD) is obtained using PNN classifier in discriminating movement from resting activity. For movement laterality classification, it managed to have a value of 0.590 ± 0.28 (mean ± 1SD), which indicates a good agreement between actual and predicted identifications.

Figure 8 shows the kappa values using the ensemble classifier for the datasets generated from all twelve patients. Individual kappa value suitably exceeded 0.4, which is equivalent to an accuracy of >70%. An accuracy of 70% is considered necessary for meaningful communication with a 2-class

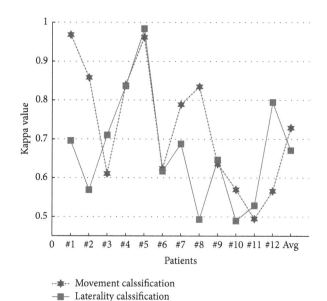

FIGURE 8: Plot of overall kappa value for movement and its laterality classifications using the ensemble classifier for all participating patients.

BCI [42]. Additionally, a very good agreement between the intended and predicted selections (kappa > 0.8 with the peak at 0.96 equivalent to decoding accuracy > 95%) was achieved for two participants while detecting movement and its forthcoming laterality.

Since we do not have enough information such as patient disease severity and handedness, it is difficult to do correlation analysis between movement decoding performance and disease situations. However, based on demographic data, as shown in Table 1, we have computed movement decoding performances, as shown in Table 7. It can be seen that, according to disease types, the patients with Parkinson's disease (PWP) exhibited much higher movement decoding rate than the Dystonia patients. Similarly, the decoding activity of LFP signals recorded through DBS electrodes from STNs achieved higher average accuracy than GPIs.

To show further robustness of three-class (resting and left or right hand finger movements) classification performance

TABLE 6: Statistical significance measures of the classifiers while decoding movement from the resting.

Classifiers evaluated	MCC value	Overall kappa value, $\bar{k} \pm \varphi(k)$	BACC
For decoding movement versus resting			
FBANN	0.691	0.607 ± 0.25	84.73
RBFNN	0.691	0.599 ± 0.27	85.51
PNN	0.701	0.692 ± 0.17	85.27
Ensemble	0.737	0.729 ± 0.16	87.36
For decoding left versus right finger movement			
FBANN	0.647	0.634 ± 0.20	82.49
RBFNN	0.665	0.563 ± 0.23	85.96
PNN	0.636	0.590 ± 0.28	82.91
Ensemble	0.712	0.671 ± 0.14	85.96

TABLE 7: Comparison of detection performances of the ensemble classifier for disease conditions and groups of patients.

Patient groups/LFP signal collection methods	Overall accuracy (%)	TPR (%)	TNR (%)
Patients with PD	88.79	88.17	92.33
Patients with Dystonia	82.03	81.55	81.81
LFPs from STNs	89.14	86.56	89.87
LFPs from GPIs	84.62	83.95	84.55

TABLE 8: Statistical performance measures of base and ensemble classifiers to classify resting and left or right finger movement.

Classifiers	F-Measure	AUC	Kappa	False positive rate (FPR)
FBANN	0.8277	83.67	0.6154	16.28
PNN	0.8433	85.29	0.6687	13.95
RBFNN	0.8365	85.42	0.5905	13.26
Ensemble	*0.8574*	*86.63*	*0.7067*	*12.88*

using the ensemble neural network (NN), we have computed numerical performance metrics based on available datasets from 12 PD and Dystonia patients. The results are presented in Figure 9. It can be seen that the ensemble classifier has better performances than any of the base classifiers (accuracy ~3% better than individual classifier). Furthermore, the majority voting also showed greater sensitivity and specificity (Figures 9(b) and 9(c)) as compared to the base classifiers. Other performance measures for both the ensemble and the base classifiers are shown in Table 8.

6. Further Discussions

This work investigated the potential advantages of neural network ensemble classifiers for decoding of human finger movements or resting activity using deep brain local potential signals. The aforementioned testing results show that the average decoding performance during movement and its laterality decoding process using the proposed ensemble classifier is very promising and this methodological framework may lead to the development of more effective BMI applications. With various feature set sizes, it was demonstrated that RBFNN has been proven to be better decoder

by managing impressive overall classification rate (CR) and PNN has shown the worst performance among the three weak learners. The RBFNN classifier performs advantageously over PNN and FBANN in terms of balanced accuracy with the lowest false detection rate. However, a few factors could have degraded the classifiers' performance; they are the unbalanced number of trials in the dataset, the unbalanced variability within the classes, the higher redundancy, and the unbalanced variation in the feature sets. Further additional factors need to be considered such as magnitude variation among the frequency bands as limited or less expertise of the participants to execute action according to stimulus applied, motivation and concentration to respond, and patient insensitiveness due to fatigue, age, and patient's depth of diseases.

(i) The total number of trials for the clicking events taken from each patient showed potential variation of decoding performance [43]. In the experimental session, obtained LFP datasets were limited in size. 114 ± 43.6 trials (mean $\pm$ 1SD) consisted of minimum 56 and maximum 202 trials across all subjects employed in the movement decoding process. For most of the patients, the number of trials is unbalanced for each class. The average number of trials of each class is 58.2 ± 23.6 (mean $\pm$ 1SD) with a minimum of 25 trials and maximum of 113 trials. This unbalancedness of the trials may contribute to the increase of the overall error rate (OER) for some participants in decoding. However, recent researches also suggest that a larger number of trials are needed to more accurately and robustly assess the predictive model [42].

(ii) It can be seen from Figures 6(c) and 6(d) that patients rapidly and efficiently responded during visually cued right hand finger clicking events compared to left finger clicking events for both STN's and GPI's LFP signal (overall specificity: $87.07\% \pm 7.21$; overall sensitivity: $84.86\% \pm 9.54$ (mean $\pm$ 1SD)). Although we had no abundant information

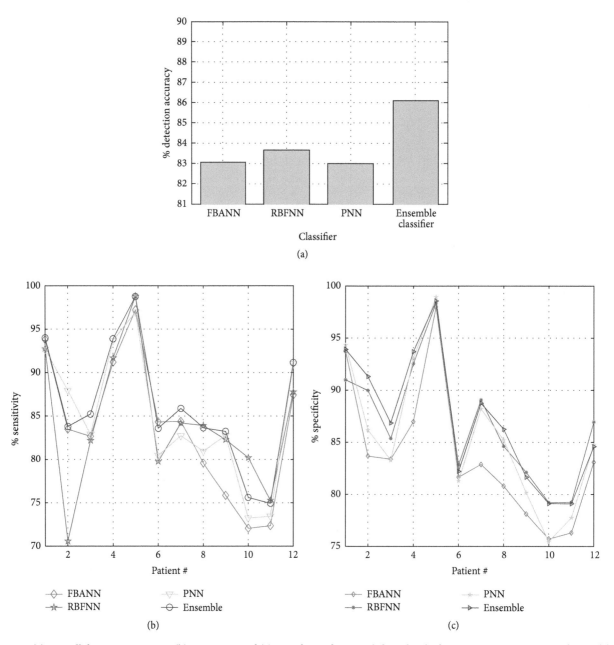

FIGURE 9: (a) Overall detection accuracy, (b) sensitivity, and (c) specificity of resting, left, and right finger movement activities obtained from base and ensemble classifiers.

about handedness of the patients, it can be considered that right handed patients were better trained than left handed patients due to generality of right handedness among human inhabitants.

(iii) LFPs obtained from the patients are more stable than single-neuron activity or noninvasive EEG; nonetheless it can contaminate with conspicuous motion artifact and patient insensitiveness due to fatigue, which ultimately deteriorates LFP signal momentarily during onset of movement event. The proposed decoder system has shown its effectiveness by addressing the aforementioned limitation to a greater extent by using different types and range of patients.

(iv) Although two-session recordings were obtained from four of the participants, LFP recordings from each patient used in this study are involved in a single session only. As a future work, several sessions will be recorded and single-session features will be enforced as a test set, while remaining sessions will be used to train the intelligent classifier to decide substantial, stable, and trustworthy decoding outcome. However, we will carry out further research on early prediction of movement conducted by normal and abnormal people in a controlled and distraction-free environment that is applicable in widespread neuro-interface scenario. With consideration of the above limitations, the performance of the proposed ensemble classifier in LFP movement detection and classification is very encouraging. To the best of our knowledge, these results achieved in this work are better than those reported previously in the literature in terms of detection rate and the number of patients [1]. Theoretically, the proposed two-layer two-class classifier could be replaced with a three-class classifier. However, our results showed that two-class classifiers are more robust for the datasets used in this work.

7. Conclusion

This study explores an innovative neural network ensemble classifier for effective identification of voluntary movements extracted from oscillatory activity of LFP signals recorded bilaterally in the STN or GPI of twelve Parkinson's disease and Dystonia patients. A majority voting algorithm is used in the ensemble classifier to fuse the results from three individual neural network classifiers. The experimental results demonstrate that decoding rate of clicking events is greater than its laterality of clicking (87.07% ± 7.54 versus 85.41% ± 8.68 (mean ± 1SD)) using the ensemble neural network classifier. The performances of movement decoding for each base classifier were investigated and evaluated and it is found that the ensemble classifier is consistently better than the base classifiers or other similar classifiers in terms of convergence rate as well as classification accuracy. The results also demonstrated that PNN achieves the best detection accuracy (DA) (85.03% ± 8.30 (mean ± 1SD)) among those three base classifiers in identifying event. In predicting sequential clicking events, RBFNN (83.51% ± 7.84 (mean ± 1SD)) outperforms FBANN and PNN. The proposed optimal classifying system may provide a channel for developing wearable and wireless smart stimulation devices that can predict involuntary movements (such as tremor) and adaptively respond to the onset of abnormal neurological events. With three different neural networks as the base classifiers, the classification performance improvement of the ensemble classifier appeared to be modest and yet noticeable. However, ensemble classifier was demonstrated to be an effective approach to improving human finger movement decoding and interpretation performance. It should be pointed out that the real-time convergence is a very important issue for any classification algorithm; however, the investigation of the proposed ensemble classifier is limited to offline analysis at this stage. Our future work in this area includes improvement of better feature extraction algorithms and the optimization of the base classifiers for the ensemble classifier.

Acknowledgments

The authors are very grateful to Oxford Functional Neurosurgery Group at University of Oxford in UK for providing the datasets necessary for the successful completion of this research work. The authors are also grateful to United International University (UIU), Bangladesh (UIU-RG-161010), for supporting this research work.

References

[1] K. A. Mamun, M. N. Huda, M. MacE et al., "Pattern classification of deep brain local field potentials for brain computer interfaces," in *Proceedings of the 15th International Conference on Computer and Information Technology, ICCIT 2012*, pp. 518–523, bgd, December 2012.

[2] C. O. Oluigbo, A. Salma, and A. R. Rezai, "Deep brain stimulation for neurological disorders," *IEEE Reviews in Biomedical Engineering*, vol. 5, pp. 88–99, 2012.

[3] M. L. Kringelbach, N. Jenkinson, S. L. F. Owen, and T. Z. Aziz, "Translational principles of deep brain stimulation," *Nature Reviews Neuroscience*, vol. 8, no. 8, pp. 623–635, 2007.

[4] B. Rosin, M. Slovik, R. Mitelman et al., "Closed-loop deep brain stimulation is superior in ameliorating parkinsonism," *Neuron*, vol. 72, no. 2, pp. 370–384, 2011.

[5] P. Brown and D. Williams, "Basal ganglia local field potential activity: Character and functional significance in the human," *Clinical Neurophysiology*, vol. 116, no. 11, pp. 2510–2519, 2005.

[6] A. Mazzoni, N. K. Logothetis, and S. Panzeri, *The Information Content of Local Field Potentials: Experiments and Models*, 2012.

[7] M. Alegre, F. Alonso-Frech, M. C. Rodríguez-Oroz et al., "Movement-related changes in oscillatory activity in the human subthalamic nucleus: Ipsilateral vs. contralateral movements," *European Journal of Neuroscience*, vol. 22, no. 9, pp. 2315–2324, 2005.

[8] N. F. Ince, R. Gupta, S. Arica, A. H. Tewfik, J. Ashe, and G. Pellizzer, "High accuracy decoding of movement target direction in non-human primates based on common spatial patterns of local field potentials," *PLoS ONE*, vol. 5, no. 12, Article ID e14384, 2010.

[9] J. A. Thompson, D. Lanctin, N. F. Ince, and A. Abosch, "Clinical implications of local field potentials for understanding and treating movement disorders," *Stereotactic and Functional Neurosurgery*, vol. 92, no. 4, pp. 251–263, 2014.

[10] T. Boraud, P. Brown, J. A. Goldberg, A. M. Graybiel, and P. J. Magill, "Oscillations in the Basal Ganglia: The good, the bad, and the unexpected," *Advances in Behavioral Biology*, vol. 56, p. 24, 2005.

[11] S. Ray and J. H. R. Maunsell, "Different origins of gamma rhythm and high-gamma activity in macaque visual cortex," *PLoS Biology*, vol. 9, no. 4, Article ID e1000610, 2011.

[12] K. A. Mamun, M. MacE, M. E. Lutman et al., "A robust strategy for decoding movements from deep brain local field potentials to facilitate brain machine interfaces," in *Proceedings of the 2012 4th IEEE RAS and EMBS International Conference on Biomedical Robotics and Biomechatronics, BioRob 2012*, pp. 320–325, ita, June 2012.

[13] W. D. Hutchison, J. O. Dostrovsky, J. R. Walters et al., "Neuronal oscillations in the basal ganglia and movement disorders: Evidence from whole animal and human recordings," *Journal of Neuroscience*, vol. 24, no. 42, pp. 9240–9243, 2004.

[14] P. Brown, A. Oliviero, P. Mazzone, A. Insola, P. Tonali, and V. Di Lazzaro, "Dopamine dependency of oscillations between subthalamic nucleus and pallidum in Parkinson's disease," *Journal of Neuroscience*, vol. 21, no. 3, pp. 1033–1038, 2001.

[15] M. Cassidy, P. Mazzone, A. Oliviero et al., "Movement-related changes in synchronization in the human basal ganglia," *Brain*, vol. 125, no. 6, pp. 1235–1246, 2002.

[16] A. Priori, G. Foffani, A. Pesenti et al., "Movement-related modulation of neural activity in human basal ganglia and its L-DOPA dependency: Recordings from deep brain stimulation

electrodes in patients with Parkinson's disease," *Neurological Sciences*, vol. 23, no. 2, pp. S101–S102, 2002.

[17] A. A. Kühn, L. Doyle, A. Pogosyan et al., "Modulation of beta oscillations in the subthalamic area during motor imagery in Parkinson's disease," *Brain*, vol. 129, no. 3, pp. 695–706, 2006.

[18] C. Loukas and P. Brown, "Online prediction of self-paced hand-movements from subthalamic activity using neural networks in Parkinson's disease," *Journal of Neuroscience Methods*, vol. 137, no. 2, pp. 193–205, 2004.

[19] N. F. Ince, R. Gupta, S. Arica, A. H. Tewfik, J. Ashe, and G. Pellizzer, "Movement direction decoding with spatial patterns of local field potentials," in *Proceedings of the 2009 4th International IEEE/EMBS Conference on Neural Engineering, NER '09*, pp. 291–294, tur, May 2009.

[20] C. Mehring, M. P. Nawrot, S. C. De Oliveira et al., "Comparing information about arm movement direction in single channels of local and epicortical field potentials from monkey and human motor cortex," *Journal of Physiology Paris*, vol. 98, no. 4-6, pp. 498–506, 2004.

[21] J. M. Kilner, S. Salenius, S. N. Baker, A. Jackson, R. Hari, and R. N. Lemon, "Task-dependent modulations of cortical oscillatory activity in human subjects during a bimanual precision grip task," *NeuroImage*, vol. 18, no. 1, pp. 67–73, 2003.

[22] O. Bai, Z. Mari, S. Vorbach, and M. Hallett, "Asymmetric spatio-temporal patterns of event-related desynchronization preceding voluntary sequential finger movements: A high-resolution EEG study," *Clinical Neurophysiology*, vol. 116, no. 5, pp. 1213–1221, 2005.

[23] T. Wu, B. Yang, and H. Sun, "EEG classification based on artificial neural network in brain computer interface," *Communications in Computer and Information Science*, vol. 97, no. 1, pp. 154–162, 2010.

[24] K. Fukumizu and S. Amari, "Local minima and plateaus in hierarchical structures of multilayer perceptrons," *Neural Networks*, vol. 13, no. 3, pp. 317–327, 2000.

[25] T. Xie, H. Yu, and B. Wilamowski, "Comparison between traditional neural networks and radial basis function networks," in *Proceedings of the 2011 IEEE International Symposium on Industrial Electronics, ISIE 2011*, pp. 1194–1199, pol, June 2011.

[26] D. F. Specht, "Probabilistic neural networks," *Neural Networks*, vol. 3, no. 1, pp. 109–118, 1990.

[27] R. Polikar, "Ensemble based systems in decision making," *IEEE Circuits and Systems Magazine*, vol. 6, no. 3, pp. 21–45, 2006.

[28] L. Lam and C. Y. Suen, "Application of majority voting to pattern recognition: an analysis of its behavior and performance," *IEEE Transactions on Systems, Man, and Cybernetics Part A:Systems and Humans*, vol. 27, no. 5, pp. 553–568, 1997.

[29] M. Mace, N. Yousif, M. Naushahi et al., "An automated approach towards detecting complex behaviours in deep brain oscillations," *Journal of Neuroscience Methods*, vol. 224, pp. 66–78, 2014.

[30] A. T. Walden, "Wavelet analysis of discrete time series," in *Proceedings of the 3rd European Congress of Mathematics*, vol. 202, pp. 627–641, 2001.

[31] V. J. Samar, A. Bopardikar, R. Rao, and K. Swartz, "Wavelet analysis of neuroelectric waveforms: a conceptual tutorial," *Brain and Language*, vol. 66, no. 1, pp. 7–60, 1999.

[32] S. Lawrence Marple Jr., "Computing the discrete-time analytic signal via fft," *IEEE Transactions on Signal Processing*, vol. 47, no. 9, pp. 2600–2603, 1999.

[33] S. O. Haykin et al., *Neural Networks and Learning Machines*, vol. 3, Upper Saddle River: Pearson Education, UpperSaddleRiver, 2009.

[34] S. Pan, K. Warwick, J. Burgess, M. N. Gasson, S. Y. Wang, and T. Z. Aziz, "Prediction of Parkinson's disease tremor onset with artificial neural networks," in *Proceedings of the International Conference on Biomedical Engineering*, pp. 341–345, 2007.

[35] J. Park and I. W. Sandberg, "Universal approximation using radial basis function networks," *Neural Computation*, vol. 3, no. 2, pp. 246–257, 1991.

[36] M. Mace, K. Abdullah-Al-Mamun, A. A. Naeem, L. Gupta, S. Wang, and R. Vaidyanathan, "A heterogeneous framework for real-time decoding of bioacoustic signals: Applications to assistive interfaces and prosthesis control," *Expert Systems with Applications*, vol. 40, no. 13, pp. 5049–5060, 2013.

[37] K. Cho, P. Meer, and J. Cabrera, "Performance assessment through bootstrap," *IEEE Transactions on Pattern Analysis and Machine Intelligence*, vol. 19, no. 11, pp. 1185–1198, 1997.

[38] F. Wang and B. Li, "A new method for modulation classification based on bootstrap technique," in *Proceedings of the 2008 International Symposium on Computer Science and Computational Technology*, pp. 11–14, Shanghai, China, December 2008.

[39] T. Fawcett, "An introduction to ROC analysis," *Pattern Recognition Letters*, vol. 27, no. 8, pp. 861–874, 2006.

[40] Q. Wei and R. L. Dunbrack Jr., "The role of balanced training and testing data sets for binary classifiers in bioinformatics," *PLoS ONE*, vol. 8, no. 7, Article ID e67863, 2013.

[41] M. Feuerman and A. R. Miller, "The kappa statistic as a function of sensitivity and specificity," *International Journal of Mathematical Education in Science and Technology*, vol. 36, no. 5, pp. 517–527, 2005.

[42] F. Nijboer, A. Furdea, I. Gunst et al., "An auditory brain–computer interface (BCI)," *Journal of Neuroscience Methods*, vol. 167, no. 1, pp. 43–50, 2008.

[43] K. A. Mamun, M. Mace, M. E. Lutman et al., "Movement decoding using neural synchronization and inter-hemispheric connectivity from deep brain local field potentials," *Journal of Neural Engineering*, vol. 12, no. 5, p. 056011, 2015.

7

Search for an Appropriate Behavior within the Emotional Regulation in Virtual Creatures Using a Learning Classifier System

Jonathan-Hernando Rosales,[1] Félix Ramos,[1] Marco Ramos,[2] and José-Antonio Cervantes[3]

[1]Department of Computer Science, Cinvestav-IPN, Unidad Guadalajara, Av. del Bosque No. 1145, 45019 Zapopán, JAL, Mexico
[2]Department of Computer Science, Universidad Autónoma del Estado de México, Instituto Literario, No. 100, 50000 Toluca, MEX, Mexico
[3]Department of Computer Science and Engineering, Los Valles University Center, University of Guadalajara, Carretera Guadalajara-Ameca Km. 45.5, Ameca, JAL, Mexico

Correspondence should be addressed to Marco Ramos; marco.corchado@gmail.com

Academic Editor: Jussi Tohka

Emotion regulation is a process by which human beings control emotional behaviors. From neuroscientific evidence, this mechanism is the product of conscious or unconscious processes. In particular, the mechanism generated by a conscious process needs a priori components to be computed. The behaviors generated by previous experiences are among these components. These behaviors need to be adapted to fulfill the objectives in a specific situation. The problem we address is how to endow virtual creatures with emotion regulation in order to compute an appropriate behavior in a specific emotional situation. This problem is clearly important and we have not identified ways to solve this problem in the current literature. In our proposal, we show a way to generate the appropriate behavior in an emotional situation using a learning classifier system (LCS). We illustrate the function of our proposal in unknown and known situations by means of two case studies. Our results demonstrate that it is possible to converge to the appropriate behavior even in the first case; that is, when the system does not have previous experiences and in situations where some previous information is available our proposal proves to be a very powerful tool.

1. Introduction

The need for virtual creatures with behaviors similar to human beings has been increasing in recent years in different areas, for instance, disaster simulation, serious games, and training, because of the need for increasing interaction between human beings and virtual environments. The creation of these virtual creatures is an open problem due to the complexity involved. It is evident that emotions play a key role in human behavior; current research uses different approaches to deal with the problem of computing behavior for virtual creatures while taking emotions into account.

A human being's emotion is the psychophysiological result of the process of perceiving stimuli. A stimulus is a set of objects, situations, or memories with which the human being interacts within the environment [1] (see Figure 1). The emotion is made up of an internal emotional state and an emotional behavior response to the environment. When it comes to the development of emotions, there are emotional theories about how human beings carry out an emotional assessment of the environment in order to generate emotions from a stimulus or a set of stimuli within a situation. In particular, we use the appraisal theory [2], because it presents a general process for emotions. Also, it is widely cited and used in research studies making up the state of the art. Appraisal theory is a psychological theory that considers emotions as appraisals of the environment. Gross's approach (an extension of appraisal theory) considers three appraisals to compute the emotion process.

(i) The first appraisal gives a certain emotional value to a perceived stimulus in order to differentiate it from

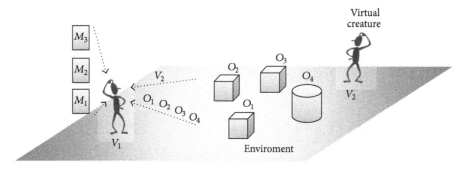

FIGURE 1: Environment. Environment example for virtual creatures, showing a possible environment for virtual creatures where $O_1, \ldots, O_n$ are possible objects perceived, $V_1, \ldots, V_n$ are other virtual creatures perceived, and $M_1, \ldots, M_n$ are possible memories recovered from previous situations.

the rest of the stimuli perceived in the environment. A stimulus can have different appraisals depending on the perceived situation.

(ii) The second appraisal helps to understand the individual involvement in the situation. At this step, the sum of stimuli perceived in the environment generates the emotional state. This emotional state generates an emotional behavior (fear, anger, joy, etc.) in response to the perceived stimulus. Humans generate multiple appraisals for a specific situation, due to the diversity of appraisals that each perceived stimulus has in that situation.

(iii) The third appraisal helps to choose what to do in response to the specific situation. In contrast to the previous appraisals, this appraisal computes multiple responses to a specific situation perceived in the environment. Thus, in this case, a process is needed to choose the most appropriate response to the current situation (a decision-making process).

However, in order to compute behavior for virtual creatures it is not enough to take emotions into account. For instance, there are situations where emotions must be regulated in order to reach an objective. In this case, the third appraisal must consider the emotion regulation needed to reach an objective. In other words, if the computed emotion does not contribute to reaching the objective, the emotion regulation process helps to modify the emotional behavior in order to reach the objective [3].

An emotion regulation mechanism is a bridge between emotion and cognition in the neurosciences. In human beings, it helps to achieve objectives through a cognitive change [1, 4, 5]. Appropriate behavior is defined in this paper as the behavior that best serves a virtual creature's objective to achieve the maximum possible reward in a given situation. Emotion regulation is achieved by modifying the virtual creature's body and facial expressions and/or by modifying the cognitive meaning of the objects within the setting in order to direct the behavior [4]. For instance, if the leader of a project in a company is angry with a key worker, his emotions might suggest to him firing the worker. However, the leader must regulate his emotions to keep him from firing the key resource, thus ensuring the successful completion

of the project; otherwise, the project will not be completed satisfactorily. This example shows the importance of the emotion regulation process.

Emotion regulation can be the result of conscious or unconscious processes. Unconscious emotion regulation is carried out by changing the stimulus perceived in the environment. By changing the perceived emotional stimulus, the emotion generation process restarts and the internal emotional state changes, thus generating a different response behavior to the situation. The conscious emotional regulation process, on the other hand, is carried out using emotional regulation techniques [4]. These techniques can be classified into two groups: emotional regulation achieved by changing the meaning of the perceived stimulus and emotional regulation achieved by suppressing the response behavior. These two techniques require a prior mechanism for their functioning. This prior mechanism is responsible for identifying what behavior would be appropriate to meet a specific objective, as in the previous example where the project leader needs to control his behavior to avoid aborting a project. The appropriate behavior is generated from previous experiences when they are available [3], the conclusion being that learning is the prior mechanism required to determine appropriate behavior for a given situation in the environment. Thus, information for emotional regulation is given by the fundamental process of memory.

In this article, we propose a mechanism for the automatic generation of appropriate behavior in a situation that requires emotion regulation. The structure of this article is as follows: Section 2 presents some work done in the field of cognitive architectures dealing with emotions and the search for appropriate behaviors. Section 3 presents the theoretical evidence of emotion regulation as well as neuroscientific evidence related to the search for appropriate behavior within the brain. Section 4 presents our proposal for a virtual creature finding an appropriate behavior for a specific situation. Section 5 presents a case study that showcases the functionality of the proposal. Finally, conclusions and a discussion of the results are presented.

2. Related Work

There are a number of studies that propose emotional models [7–10], among other cognitive processes that are inspired by biological evidence. Some of the most important proposals for this work deal with cognitive architectures that include multiple cognitive processes working together to compute a human-like behavior to be exhibited by virtual creatures. These cognitive architectures for virtual creatures are inspired mainly by psychological theories and/or neuroscientific evidence.

Some of the existing cognitive architectures that consider emotion in the computation of behavior are presented below. The selection is based on the theory of emotion assessment. We look at the implementation of all steps of the appraisal theory. In particular, we want to see the possibility of regulating emotion consciously in these processes.

2.1. SOAR. State Operator and Result, "SOAR" [7], is a cognitive architecture for artificial intelligence. It is used for the development of intelligent agents that solve problems ranging from simple to complex open problems. The design of SOAR is based on the assumption that all deliberative behavior-oriented goals can be formulated as the selection of operators and their application to the state.

Thus, if an agent has a particular goal in a specific situation, this goal can be achieved by different actions and in multiple ways. The state is a representation of the current situation. The possible actions in such specific situations are the possible operations for that state.

SOAR has not fully implemented the emotional process. However, it proposes implementing the generation of several hypotheses based on appraisal theory. This architecture uses the three steps of appraisal theory; however, it does not implement these steps and reduces deployment to a simple tool for improving the virtual creature's learning through a greater reward function when it selects a good action in a specific scene. SOAR does not contemplate different meanings of the perceived stimulus.

Given the absence of a full emotional evaluation process, the agent may not compute an appropriate emotional behavior if it does not consider multiple cognitive meanings of the same stimulus within the environment, or an emotional state of the virtual creature within their case studies.

2.2. iCub. Integrated Cognitive Universal Body, "iCub" [9], is a cognitive architecture designed for virtual creatures and humanoid robots. This architecture seeks to copy cognitive processes in humans and incorporate them into the humanoid robots. The approach is based on psychological and neuroscientific evidence. The architecture is implemented in the iCub Humanoid robot, which has the appearance of a 2.5-year-old child, and the objective is to provide it with the basic skills that a boy of that age possesses. The architecture is not yet complete; it is only a preliminary architecture.

Through three components, iCub generates an affective state. This affective state is equal to the emotional state in appraisal theory. These components are curiosity (dominated by external stimuli), experimentation (dominated by internal stimuli), and social commitment (based on a good balance between external and internal stimuli). These three components generate the affective state in conjunction with a process of selection of action that generates a small homeostatic process that regulates the iCub robot's behavior. iCub generates simple basic emotions such as joy, fear, anger, and sadness. It also generates behavior that is similar to a little child's. The emotional process is simple and focuses on the interaction with the environment, ignoring conscious emotional processes.

Emotions in iCub are regulated by the change of stimuli in the setting. That is, it does not have a process of conscious emotion regulation.

2.3. Kismet. Kismet [10–12], developed by MIT (Massachusetts Institute of Technology), is capable of expressing emotions; it was developed in the 1990s. The architecture developed for this robot began as a working framework made up of four subsystems:

(i) Motivation system, which consists of handlers and emotions

(ii) Behavior system, which consists of several types of behavior

(iii) System of perception and attention, which extracts the characteristics from the atmosphere

(iv) Motor system, which runs facial expressions.

There are seven emotions expressed in Kismet, based on the theory of basic emotions [6]. The emotions can be used for three purposes: first, to influence the behavior of the robot by giving preference to one behavior over others; second, to have an impact on the robot's emotional state, which in turn will be shown through the motor system; and third, to serve as a learning mechanism: after the completion of predetermined satisfactions, the robot can learn the way it accomplished the task or not. Facial expressions are predefined to produce a motor response commensurate to the emotions. As in iCub, Kismet regulates its emotions in response to changes in the environment. It does not have conscious emotion regulation.

3. Theoretical Evidence

In Section 2 we described some cognitive architectures. From their descriptions, it is possible to see why they are unable to compute an appropriate natural behavior in certain situations. This comes from not taking into account factors such as conscious emotion regulation that can influence the achievement of objectives within the environment.

There is biological evidence that shows how human beings seek an appropriate behavior when they face situations [3, 13–15]. In order to compute the appropriate behavior, humans take into account prior knowledge regarding similar situations and the association of known situations with the current situation (known or unknown). However, it is also true that emotions can make humans' behavior inappropriate in specific situations. In those cases, emotion regulation is needed. Emotion regulation consists of trying to ignore stimuli that cause emotional overflow or suppressing the emotional behavior, that is, pretending that we are not feeling

TABLE 1: Description of areas. General architecture structures for emotion regulation, inputs, and outputs.

Structure	Input	Output
AMYGDALA	Frame with preprocessed and processed information.	Frame with emotional information.
HIPPOCAMPUS	Requests.	Information retrieved from the emotional memory.
INSULA	Sensory information.	Affective information oriented towards pain.
VS	Sensory information.	Affective information oriented towards pleasure.
rACC	Frame with processed information and emotional state.	Possible actions.
OFC	Possible actions and emotional state.	The frame of selected action.
DMPFC	The frame of action and information from memory.	Emotional state and appropriate emotional behavior.
DLPFC	Requests.	Information retrieved from working memory.
VLPFC	Required emotional state.	The cognitive-emotional change closest to what is required.
sgACC	Emotional behavior and emotional state.	General behavior.
Sensory Cortex	Environmental information.	Sensory information.
Motor Cortex	General behavior.	Execution frame.

the emotion. But how do human beings do this? And where in the brain are these processes carried out?

Human beings associate old knowledge with new. This is done by identifying similar characteristics between known and unknown situations. This process is carried out within the brain in areas that retrieve information and high-level cognitive processes.

Table 1 summarizes neuroscientific evidence showing the areas involved in emotional regulation. Some of these are the Dorsomedial Prefrontal Cortex (DMPFC), the Dorsolateral Prefrontal Cortex (DLPFC), the Ventrolateral Prefrontal Cortex (VLPFC), the Orbitofrontal Cortex (OFC), the Amygdala (AMYGDALA), the Hippocampus (HIPPOCAMPUS), the Insula (INSULA), the Ventral Striatum (VS), the rostral Anterior Cingulate Cortex (rACC), and the subgenual Anterior Cingulate Cortex (sgACC) [16–21]. As described previously, our proposal is based on neuroscientific evidence. Thus, these areas are taken as the basis for the development of our model of emotion regulation for virtual creatures. Reference [3] defines a flow of information between these areas based on neuroscientific evidence and also on the model proposed by Gross for emotion regulation [22–25].

The elements of our proposed architecture are explained below, including a few elements to complete the information flow.

The Dorsomedial Prefrontal Cortex (DMPFC) is associated with the choice of behavior [15]. This area of the brain is active during the identification of situations. It associates small parts of the setting with some situation previously stored in the brain. Thus, it generates a behavior according to the information stored from previous similar lived situations. It is even possible to predict social consequences from stored information [13–15, 26]. Although this area ensures the generation of consistent behavior, it does not mean that the proposed behavior is the most appropriate. However, it is a good beginning for learning in an unknown situation.

In our model, this structure is responsible for choosing an appropriate emotional behavior from the available options. It is fed with recollections or memories, which are received from the DLPFC. If the appropriate behavior requires a different emotional state, it is sent to the VLPFC.

Finally, the computed behavior is sent to the sgACC, where a deletion process takes place [27, 28], if required.

The Dorsolateral Prefrontal Cortex (DLPFC) is believed to include participation in the working memory, the preparation of the response and the selection of the response [19, 29]. This structure is associated with the recovery of information and is one of the structures that allow access to the working memory within the frontal lobe [29]. It is associated with the selection of the response, probably due to its proximity to structures dedicated to executive planning.

We use this structure to access the working memory in order to generate a set of plans. The decision-making cognitive function will select one plan from this set in a given situation.

The Ventrolateral Prefrontal Cortex (VLPFC) is associated with the suppression of emotional responses in a changing situation [16, 17, 19]. This area decreases the emotional response through a cognitive process, which involves changing the meaning of the scene to reinterpret the situation [17, 18].

In our model, this structure reassesses the incoming stimuli, trying to give them another cognitive meaning in order to achieve a better fluidity of the desired emotional behavior. It receives the memories provided by the DLPFC and sends its results to the Amygdala in order to have a second emotional evaluation. If there is a different emotional evaluation, it is used to modify the emotional state from the current situation.

The Orbitofrontal Cortex (OFC) is associated with the decision-making process: it is responsible, along with the DLPFC, for seeking and choosing an action [30]. People with damage in this area lose the capacity to make decisions [30]. The DLPFC is associated in the same manner with memory, so the OFC feeds on it to make a decision in any specific situation [19, 30].

We use this area to perform a search and selection of actions from multiple plans generated in collaboration with the DLPFC and the rACC.

The Amygdala (AMYGDALA) is believed to collaborate with other structures within the limbic system in assessing the emotional environment [19, 25, 26, 31]. Its internal cores are responsible for the assessments. An entry core is responsible for generating a first emotional evaluation in conjunction with the thalamus. A second entry core receives this first evaluation and subsequently receives a second evaluation from the VLPFC. This second core modifies the emotional meaning of the environment if this is needed. A third core receives the emotional meaning computed in the entry cores and sends it to the rest of the cerebral areas. A fourth core receives the emotional state from the entry cores. It is responsible for maintaining the person's emotional state and sending it to the cerebral areas that require it. This behavior is according to our assumptions and the neuroscientific evidence [31].

The Amygdala in our model is responsible for processing the stimuli, meaning it has the job of emotional assessment within our architecture. It serves to generate an emotional state in collaboration with the motivation to the perceived situation.

The Insula (INSULA) has a strong involvement in pain processing [32–35], in addiction studies [36], appetite studies [37], and multimodal sensory integration [33]. Within the work of emotions, its participation is observed both in the generation of the negative affective values of the stimuli and in the generation of emotional behaviors, such as disgust and fear [38, 39]. Within our model, it collaborates on the construction of the emotional state in conjunction with the AMY and the VS, providing affective information.

The Ventral Striatum (VS) is involved in motor responses directly related to stimuli perceived with rewards [40]. It is part of the dopaminergic system of the brain, in conjunction with other structures [41]. It is activated during the processing of the reward in both sent signals and the output [40]. Within our model, it collaborates on building the emotional state in conjunction with AMY and INS, providing affective information.

The Hippocampus (HIPPOCAMPUS) is associated with the processes of memory. This structure works as an index for past experiences and the emotion felt at the moment they occurred. If there is no previous experience, the Hippocampus is responsible for storing the new experience and its appraisal-emotion is provided by other structures such as the Amygdala [31]. The Hippocampus is associated with the memory of emotions. Damage to this structure can produce memory loss, lack of expressiveness, and even inability to generate emotions [42].

Within the architecture, this structure provides the emotional memory of the perceived environment and is responsible for storing new emotional experiences and retrieving existing ones.

The rostral Anterior Cingulate Cortex (rACC) is activated during the exhibition of any emotional response to our behavior. It has no activity during the cognitive processes of the PFC. However, it is believed to be associated with the emotional process. This structure might regulate the emotional behavior on the basis of information provided by the PFC [28].

This structure, in collaboration with the OFC, seeks an appropriate reaction to the situation the environment presents.

The subgenual Anterior Cingulate Cortex (sgACC) is associated with emotional behavior. People with depressive or bipolar disorders present more activity in this area than the rest of the population does [27, 28].

In our proposal, this area controls emotional behavior by trying to ignore the current emotion. This objective of controlling emotional behavior depends on the internal emotional state.

The Sensory Cortex is the component responsible for encoding perceived environmental stimuli. It refers to the visual, tactile, gustatory, olfactory, and auditory sensory cortex.

The Motor Cortex is in charge of executive planning, which generates a frame of execution for the body's reaction to the perceived stimuli.

4. Proposal

As established in the introduction, the objective of this article is to endow a virtual creature with a mechanism to compute the appropriate behavior for a specific situation. Our proposal is based on biological requirements previously expressed and ensures that the best reward behavior is computed for the specific situation.

In order to attain our objective, we use neuroscientific evidence regarding emotional regulation. Our proposed model is presented in Figure 2. In this model we can see the neural structures, found at this moment, involved in the process of emotion regulation. In Table 2 we can see the type of information sent by each internal component of the proposed model. We focus on the module we believe is responsible for finding the appropriate behavior (see Involve module in Figure 2). First, we want to describe the functions involved in the proposed model of emotion regulation in order to obtain a global view.

Sensory Information. This is the first step, responsible for producing the input signals of the environment to the correct functions of the subsequent steps in the proposed model.

Emotional Response. This makes an emotional evaluation of the perceived environment. This step can be executed more than once. It has a direct connection to stimulus perception and to the cognitive region of the brain. We can see this process as a first unconscious response and as a second conscious response (i.e., we assume that the first was already executed) to the environment. As described previously, in this study we deal with the conscious emotional response.

Action Selection. In this step an action is selected to be executed in the environment, and it is determined whether an emotional regulation or a change in behavior is needed in order to improve the reward for the specific situation. This step is based on similar previous experiences of the current situation. That is exactly why this process is closely related to the working memory.

Appropriate Behavior. In this step, an appropriate behavior is selected for the current situation. To make this selection, a comparison is made between the reward of the action selected and the reward of behaviors selected in similar previous situations. If the process cannot find an appropriate behavior,

TABLE 2: Informal description of input and output of a proposed model.

Label	Meaning	Description
SI	Sensory input	Sensory values from the environment
AS	Affective signal	Affective values computed by the system
ES	Emotional signal	Emotional values associated with emotions
PA	Possible action	Possible action to run in the environment
EMS	Emotional mental state	Current emotional state of the virtual creature
AB	Appropriate behavior	Appropriate emotional behavior to be computed
SS	Stimulus signal	Sign of stimuli perceived in the environment
SEV	Stored emotional value	Emotional values stored from past experiences
NSEV	New stored emotional value	New emotional value to be stored for a stimulus
NM	New meaning	New emotional meaning of the situation
RB	Regulated behavior	Regulated behavior to be expressed

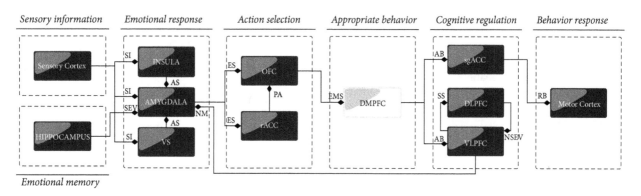

FIGURE 2: Emotion Regulation Model. A proposed model based on neural evidence and psychological theories (SI = sensory input, AS = affective signal, ES = emotional signal, PA = possible action, EMS = emotional mental state, AB = appropriate behavior, SS = stimulus signal, SEV = stored emotional value, NSEV = new stored emotional value, NM = new meaning, and RB = regulated behavior).

an option can be selected randomly. However, this is done only if the punishment is not very high. This analysis is achieved in the previous step.

Cognitive Regulation. In this step, the system has determined to change the behavior. Thus, different meanings are sought for perceived stimuli in order to try to provoke a change in the emotional response and, consequently, a change in the behavior in the environment. In parallel the suppression mechanism is activated together with the control of physiological behavior, to obtain the appropriate behavior.

Emotional Memory. This serves as a place to store and recover the emotional evaluation of the perceived stimulus.

Behavior Response (This Is the Final Step). A physiological behavior response is computed according to the emotional behavior given by the proposed model.

As we can see in the previous descriptions, after activating the emotional regulation mechanism it is necessary to obtain an appropriate behavior. This behavior is computed only if the actual behavior is not appropriate to obtain the specific goal in the environment.

TABLE 3: Variables used in our proposal and their meaning.

Variable	Meaning
S	Stimuli set
S_μ	Stimulus μ
S_M	Stimulus meaning
$E1, E2, \ldots, E6$	Six basic emotions described by Ekman 1994 [6]
Bz	Behavior z
μ, x, n, z	Integers used as indices

4.1. Formal Description of the Evidence. In this work, we propose an adaptive mechanism allowing the appropriate behavior to be computed for autonomous virtual creatures facing a specific situation. In our case (Figure 1), virtual creatures have sensors allowing them to perceive their environment continually and a memory mechanism where they store their experiences. Using these sensors, we want to formally describe the functions necessary for obtaining an appropriate behavior. We do not describe all of functions, because not all of them are necessary to compute the proposed mechanism. In Table 3 we describe the variables used for our proposal.

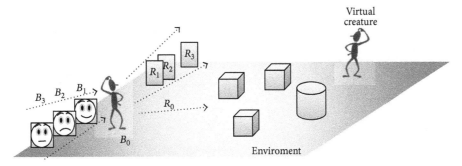

FIGURE 3: An example of internal emotional action from a virtual creature. Showing possible emotional behaviors from the environment where $B_1, \ldots, B_n$ are possible emotion behaviors and $R_1, \ldots, R_n$ are the possible responses from the environment.

Sensory Information gives the set of stimuli S for the subsequent functions in the proposed model. This set is made up of objects and virtual creatures in the environment.

Emotional response gives the initial behavior B_1, necessary for the computation of actions. Let S_μ and $S_M = \{S_{M_{\mu 1}}, S_{M_{\mu 2}}, \ldots, S_{M_{\mu \alpha}}\}$ be a stimulus and its meaning, respectively. Each entry of S_M is another vector of six elements $E = \{E_1, E_2, \ldots, E_6\}$, where E_x has a real value $0.0 \leq E_x \leq 1.0$ representing the evaluation of each of the six basic emotions described by Ekman [6]. Let $S_{\mu r} = S_{M_{\mu \beta}}$ be the most relevant evaluation of S_μ (Figure 3). Thus, the initial behavior is computed by $B_1 = \sum_{\mu=1}^{n} S_{\mu r}$.

Action selection determines whether the initial behavior B_1 is good for the actual objective in the situation. In the event it is not, it will be necessary to compute another behavior.

Appropriate behavior tries to generate an appropriate behavior taking into account the initial behavior B_1 and the actual situation ST (Figure 4). That is, we know that the computed behavior B_1 is not suitable to reach the final objective; however, we obtain useful information as the starting point to compute the appropriate behavior.

5. Implementation of the Appropriate Behavior Function

In order to compute the *appropriate behavior* function, we choose to work with a learning classifier system (LCS), because this sort of tool allows for the exhaustive search, with the possibility of stopping the search in order to explore local solutions while working to find global solutions. The learning classifier system or LCS was proposed initially by Holland [43, 44]. This LCS combines genetic algorithms and machine-learning techniques. In this article, we use the LCS called GXCS [45] (Figure 5). This LCS was developed by searching its applications specifically to solve problems in the area of virtual agents. However, it can be applied in different areas. The GXCS goes beyond the representation of binary rules and makes it possible to use any kind of data. In our case, it allows us to use the most natural and appropriate data to represent the environment.

The GXCS provides a way to assign a behavior to a virtual creature based on the characteristics of the current setting. That is, the GXCS uses the similarity between the current setting and previous experiences (settings) to compute the virtual creature's optimal behavior for the current setting. In order to use this GXCS, whose behavior is explained in [45], first we need to define the vector rule used for this purpose. The basic emotions proposed by Ekman [6] and the identification of a situation are embedded in the vector. That is, our vector rule has 7 entries, six for the basic emotion given by $E_1, E_2, \ldots, E_6$ and the last used to identify the situation corresponding to that emotional evaluation. Each of the entries has real values bounded by 0 and 1 (Figure 6).

The internal behavior of the six components of our GXCS for this study (see Figure 5) is described extensively below.

Sensors form an interface, fed by the previous action selection function, in which the aforementioned rule of 7 inputs is predefined $\{E_1, E_2, E_3, E_4, E_5, E_6, ST\}$ (Figure 6).

Classification database represents the knowledge base of the system. It consists of a population of n rules of the type condition : action, where the condition is provided by the sensors and the action is produced by the genetic algorithm.

Genetic algorithm is responsible for generating new actions based on the best evaluated rules existing within the knowledge base. If no rule exists, actions are randomly formulated.

Distribution of credits is the function in charge of evaluating the condition : action rules existing within the classification database. This function requires feedback from the environment, which helps determine the impact of the rule used in the current situation.

Message list is the set of condition : action rules retrieved from the classification database associated with the input rule provided by the sensors. See Figure 7.

Actuators are the output interface composed of effectors, responsible for expressing the action determined by the chosen rule of the message list. The actions consist of 6 exits $\{E_1, E_2, E_3, E_4, E_5, E_6\}$ associated again with Ekman's basic emotions [6]. Each of the exits has real values bounded by 0 and 1.

This implementation also uses unsupervised reinforcement learning. On the basis of the environment, a certain expected behavior of the virtual creature is defined; if the behavior that the virtual creature exhibits comes close to the environmentally predefined behavior, the rule formulator of this behavior receives a high reward. The way to provide such a reward is simple: first define an emotion (joy, fear,

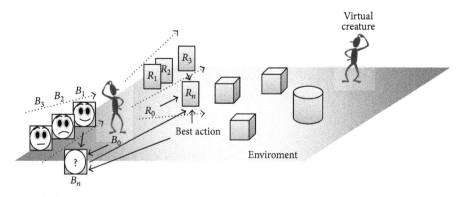

FIGURE 4: Selection of the rule that best satisfies the conditions of the environment. Showing possible emotional behaviors in response to the environment where B_n are possible emotional behaviors and R_n are the possible responses from the environment.

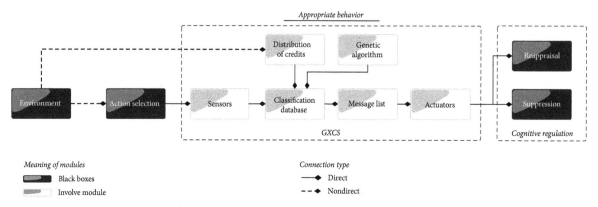

FIGURE 5: General process of GXCS. Showing a general process of GXCS with inputs and outputs.

E1	E2	E3	E4	E5	E6	ST
0.99	0.35	0.60	0.50	0.22	0.10	1.0

FIGURE 6: A sample of a rule's structure for LCS. Showing a syntax rule where $E1, E2, \ldots, E6$ are emotions and ST is the current situation.

sadness, disgust, or anger) on the basis of the environment, and then the virtual creature should seek to express that emotion. If it does, the intensity of the emotion will determine the recombination obtained, which will be provided to the GXCS in order to evaluate the generating rule; otherwise, the rule will be punished by being assigned values of 0. For example, let us say the expected behavior is predicted in the environment by the array {0.0, 0.0, 1.0, 0.0, 0.0, 0.0, 0.0}, the first 6 fields being expected emotional intensities and the last one, an identifier of the situation. On the other hand, the virtual creature expresses a behavior given by the array {0.2, 0.4, 0.6, 1.0, 0.8, 0.0}, where all fields are emotional intensities. The generating rule will be evaluated with 0.6 of reward, since it is approaching the emotional value specifically descaled in the emotion of field three. Initially, the rules are generated randomly and they feed the GXCS. The rules are graded from 0.0 to 1.0, where 0.0 is a very poor response and 1.0 is a high emotional intensity. The GXCS offers the possibility to

experiment or take the best option. This means that we can choose to use one existent rule or use this information to generate a new rule hoping it will be better suited to the environment's stimuli. The number of generated rules is given by the number of components of the action vector (Figure 8). We maintain the experimentation until we achieve a rating of 0.8 or higher on any rule within a new situation. A rule is associated with a behavior, and a highly evaluated rule is considered an appropriate behavior. This type of rule is functional and it is stored. The nonfunctional rules or rules with a low evaluation are also stored, because they may be useful in a similar situation in the future.

5.1. Case Study: Unfamiliar Situations. In unfamiliar situations, the GXCS at first does not have a specific number of rules to converge on a specific emotional valuation. The objective, within this case study, is to get the virtual creature to converge on a certain response behavior. We do this by defining a specific behavior in the environment and providing reward values, as explained above. The case study uses three different emotions in each simulation; that means that the virtual creature converges on three different emotional behaviors in a single situation. The GXCS is not stopped, so there are evaluated rules belonging to other emotional responses. The simulation runs 20 times to determine which number of rules converges on the appropriate behavior and its intensity.

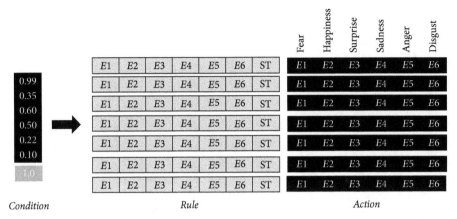

FIGURE 7: A sample of a rule's database for GXCS. Showing a syntax rule where $E1, E2, \ldots, E6$ are emotions and ST is the current situation.

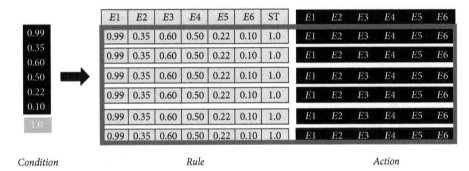

FIGURE 8: A sample of generated rules for GXCS. Showing rules generated by an action with 6 components.

5.1.1. Results. In this experiment, where the virtual creature does not have previous experiences, the results are shown in the graph of search behavior (Figure 9). In this case, the number of rules generated by the classifier ranges between 5 and 145. In 20 tries, the average was 50 rules. In all cases, the behavior that was sought was a specific emotion (as defined in the graph) with a rating of 0.8 or higher. In all the events a rule was generated containing the emotional value within the first 20 rules.

5.2. Case Study: Familiar Situations. In a familiar situation, the initial set of rules allows the GXCS to look for appropriate behaviors to respond to an unknown situation in the environment. The continuous environment evaluation enables the system to converge, if possible, towards an appropriate behavior. The GXCS associates the unknown situation with situations that are already partially known; that means there are a few differences in the situation and the emotional mental state of the creature (condition of GXCS) is slightly changed. The classifier relates the rules of the previous situations in order to propose an approximately appropriate behavior. This experiment consists of five simulations with five different settings each; each setting changes a little in order to show the number of rules generated in familiar situations.

5.2.1. Results. The graph (Figure 10) shows the number of rules that were required to generate the appropriate behavior for a specific setting. The number of rules generated for

appropriate behavior in each of the experiments varied in the range of 5–20, with an average of 7 rules over 5 experiments. The generation time of the new rules is between 1 and 4 seconds for an unknown but similar setting (modified setting). When the classifier receives a setting similar to one it has already learned, it proceeds as follows to compute appropriate behavior: it first calculates the similarity with the known setting and then calculates the appropriate behavior using the behavior associated with an initial behavior from the setting with the closest similarity.

6. Discussion

As we established previously, the objective of this research is to propose a mechanism whereby a virtual creature can autonomously calculate appropriate behavior for a specific situation (Figure 11). Our proposal is to create a mechanism for the virtual creature to be able to choose an appropriate behavior in a specific situation. The mechanism is based on neuroscientific and psychological evidence. From neuroscience, we obtain some of the cerebral regions involved in this process, the functions they achieve, and the flow of the information.

In the proposed model, not all of the brain structures described in the state of the art concerning emotion regulation are involved [13, 26]. This is because there is currently no consensus on which structures actually contribute. For this reason, in our proposed model we consider only structures

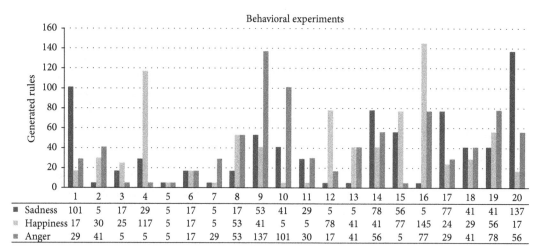

	1	2	3	4	5	6	7	8	9	10	11	12	13	14	15	16	17	18	19	20
■ Sadness	101	5	17	29	5	17	5	17	53	41	29	5	5	78	56	5	77	41	41	137
▨ Happiness	17	30	25	117	5	17	5	53	41	5	5	78	41	41	77	145	24	29	56	17
■ Anger	29	41	5	5	5	17	29	53	137	101	30	17	41	56	5	77	29	41	78	56

FIGURE 9: Graph of search behavior showing results from the first experiment in three columns. Each column is one emotion; the numbers are the rules generated in the experiment. The time taken for each experiment was less than one second.

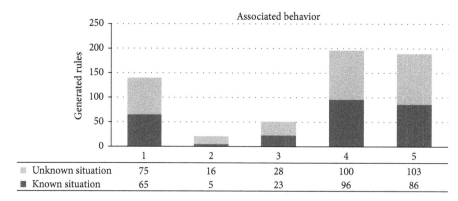

	1	2	3	4	5
▨ Unknown situation	75	16	28	100	103
■ Known situation	65	5	23	96	86

FIGURE 10: Graph of association of behavior. Showing a result of the second experiment, with two columns—unknown situations and known situations—for each experiment using the same LCS. The difference between the unknown and known situation was less than 15 new rules.

for which there is consensus. These structures are described in Section 4. In other words, on the basis of neuroscientific evidence we propose that the DMPC is the structure responsible for computing behavior that is appropriate to a specific situation (see Figure 2). In addition, there is also evidence that some brain structures are involved in different ways in the tasks of different cognitive functions. In this study, we focus on the functions of the brain structures that contribute to the calculation of a behavior for a situation that requires emotion regulation.

One might think that the search for appropriate behavior would only favor the so-called "social cognitive emotion regulation" [13]. However, there is evidence that, in specific cases, for example, survival situations where it is necessary to control emergent behavior (fear) to avoid a predator, emotion regulation is required in addition to appropriate behavior. This is why we propose in our model the activation of the DMPFC structure in both social regulation and self-regulation [13–15] in order to calculate appropriate behavior. Along the same lines, as mentioned previously in the introduction, having the appropriate behavior is necessary for the proper functioning of cognitive emotion regulation

techniques (suppression and reevaluation); a more detailed description of this is described in [3].

Regarding the implementation and results of the case studies presented, we can underline first the use of an LCS named GXCS proposed by M. A. Ramos and F. Ramos [45], which allowed us to use a structure that summarizes the six basic emotions defined by Ekman [6] as well as a field that associates the emotions with a specific situation (which provokes the emotional state, e.g., desert, sea, and field). This structure is simplistic and overlooks multiple aspects of emotion regulation, such as social interaction or risk situations, but it is a first approach to explore the functionality of an LCS in learning appropriate behaviors for creatures subjected to situations requiring emotion regulation.

Second, behaviors simply refer to Ekman's 6 basic emotions and are the virtual creature's calculated and displayed behavior in each experiment. This behavior receives a high evaluation if it approaches the appropriate behavior for the situation and a low evaluation in the opposite case.

Third, from the results we must emphasize that, in the unfamiliar case study, the system does not know the appropriate behavior and only has the creature's internal state

Environment

(a)

Appraisal

Reappraisal

(b)   (c)

FIGURE 11: Alfred sample. This picture shows how the model of emotional regulation works. Part (a) shows the environment with difference evaluations stored in the memory; part (b) shows Alfred with an expression of fear, which is the first emotion. Applying the LCS to obtain the appropriate behavior, we have a visible decrease of emotion seen in Alfred in part (c). This result is obtained from the appropriate behavior given by LCS and multiple evaluations of emotional objects in the setting using an emotion regulation architecture.

and a specific context. In this case, the first rules are randomly generated to initiate the evaluation of behaviors; each of these rules is evaluated within the system using the same situation, thus setting off an iteration using the rules that had better performance in the specific situation. The iteration runs until an appropriate behavior is obtained.

In Figure 9 we can see a summary of the results obtained: the number of rules formulated in each situation. Each situation is shown by means of 3 columns, which represent different emotions. We can also observe that there are considerably high numbers of generated rules, reaching 145 rules evaluated. This was expected since technically the answers given by the virtual creature are almost random, but in all situations it was possible to get to the behavior that was appropriate to the situation presented.

With respect to the family case study, the system already had a priori rules associated with the same context, but with different internal emotional states. In this case, the results

obtained are considerably better compared to the results of the unfamiliar case study, approximately 15 more rules to identify unknown situations but with similarities. This case shows the performance of the LCS when it has a priori knowledge about the situations presented to it.

In spite of the very good results we have obtained, there is still work to do, primarily the optimizations to improve the performance of our proposal in both time and quality. For example, in the implementation, we define explicit values for the emotions used for seeking an appropriate behavior. This knowledge can improve efficiency, making the GXCS discriminate useless elements during the process of seeking a behavior for a situation. Another possible area of improvement is the evaluation method, which can be improved by reducing the set of rules evaluated to those that approach the appropriate behavior. This is possible because we have sought the value of the rule. Another possible improvement we are currently working on is the selection of rules within the classifier to consider. We want the learning classifier system to consider the evaluation of a larger number of related rules in order to reduce the rule generation process, which is quite costly.

Finally, we have proposed an automatic way of calculating appropriate behavior in situations requiring emotion regulation. Our proposal is based on neuroscientific evidence. This proposal is novel, since it is not contemplated by proposals of the state of the art, which are oriented more towards the correct operation of the cognitive regulation techniques or towards the identification of the context and the current situation.

6.1. Conclusions. Although our proposed model of emotion regulation cannot be considered complete, it contains the necessary foundations for the search for appropriate behavior in a situation that requires emotion regulation. This behavior, as we have already mentioned, is the fundamental component to carry out emotional cognitive regulation. From the implementation presented we can observe that the proposal is appropriate, because the virtual creature is able to calculate an appropriate behavior from scratch for a situation that requires emotion regulation when the creature does not have previous experiences and in an efficient way when it does have previous experiences for the situation it is facing. In the same way, we can conclude that the use of a GXCS classifier to carry out the learning of the appropriate behavior is viable and favors us in similar situations by giving us quick answers. On the other hand, we can also conclude that it is possible to improve the efficiency of the system by making adjustments, for example, by improving the generation of GXCS rules to accelerate the calculation of appropriate behaviors.

Acknowledgments

The research is financed by CONACYT with Scholarship no. 263588.

References

[1] J. J. Gross, "The emerging field of emotion regulation: an integrative review," *Review of General Psychology*, vol. 2, no. 3, pp. 271–299, 1998.

[2] K. R. Scherer, A. Schorr, and T. Johnstone, *Appraisal Processes in Emotion: Theory, Methods, Research. Series in Affective Science*, O. U. Press, New York, NY, USA, 2001.

[3] J. H. Rosales, K. Jaime, and F. Ramos, *An Emotional Regulation Model with Memories for Virtual Agents*, 2013, ICCI*CC*2013.

[4] J. J. Gross, "Emotion regulation: affective, cognitive, and social consequences," *Psychophysiology*, vol. 39, no. 3, pp. 281–291, 2002.

[5] R. A. Thompson, "Emotion and self-regulation.," *Nebraska Symposium on Motivation*, vol. 36, pp. 367–467, 1988.

[6] P. A. Ekman, *The nature of emotion: fundamental questions*, O. U. Press, New York, NY, USA, 1st edition, 1994.

[7] J. E. Laird, "The Soar Cognitive Architecture," in *The Soar Cognitive Architecture. (M. I. of Technology*, M. I. of Technology, Ed., vol. 1, p. edition, 2012.

[8] L.-F. Rodríguez, F. Ramos, and Y. Wang, "Cognitive Computational Model of Emotions," in *Proceedings of the 10th IEEE I. C on Cognitive Informatics and Cognitive Computing (ICCI' CC' 11)*, 2011.

[9] D. A. Vernon, *A Roadmap for Cognitive Development in Humanoid Robots*, vol. 11, Springer, Berlin, Germany, 2011, COSMOS.

[10] C. Breazeal, "Emotion and sociable humanoid robots," *International Journal of Human-Computer Studies*, vol. 59, no. 1-2, pp. 119–155, 2003.

[11] C. Breazeal and B. Scassellati, "Infant-like social interactions between a robot and a human caregiver," *Adaptive Behavior*, vol. 8, no. 1, pp. 49–74, 2000.

[12] C. Breazeal, "Early experiments using motivations to regulate human-robot interaction," AAAI FS-98-03, 1998.

[13] X. Xie, S. Mulej Bratec, G. Schmid et al., "How do you make me feel better? Social cognitive emotion regulation and the default mode network," *NeuroImage*, vol. 134, pp. 270–280, 2016.

[14] J. C. Cooper and T. A. Furey, "Dorsomedial prefrontal cortex mediates rapid evaluations predicting the outcome of romantic interactions," *The Journal of Neuroscience*, vol. 32, no. 45, pp. 15647–15656, 2012.

[15] J. Grinband, J. Savitskaya, T. D. Wager, T. Teichert, V. P. Ferrera, and J. Hirsch, "The dorsal medial frontal cortex is sensitive to time on task, not response conflict or error likelihood," *NeuroImage*, vol. 57, no. 2, pp. 303–311, 2011.

[16] L. Campbell-Sills, A. N. Simmons, K. L. Lovero, A. A. Rochlin, M. P. Paulus, and M. B. Stein, "Functioning of neural systems supporting emotion regulation in anxiety-prone individuals," *NeuroImage*, vol. 54, no. 1, pp. 689–696, 2011.

[17] S. J. Banks, K. T. Eddy, M. Angstadt, P. J. Nathan, and K. Luan Phan, "Amygdala-frontal connectivity during emotion regulation," *Social Cognitive and Affective Neuroscience*, vol. 2, no. 4, pp. 303–312, 2007.

[18] K. L. Phan, D. A. Fitzgerald, P. J. Nathan, G. J. Moore, T. W. Uhde, and M. E. Tancer, "Neural substrates for voluntary suppression of negative affect: a functional magnetic resonance imaging study," *Biological Psychiatry*, vol. 57, no. 3, pp. 210–219, 2005.

[19] L. A. Miller, K. H. Taber, G. O. Gabbard, and R. A. Hurley, "Neural underpinnings of fear and its modulation: implications for anxiety disorders," *J Neuropsychiatry ClinNeurosci*, vol. 17, no. 1, pp. 1–6, 2005.

[20] A. R. Hariri, V. S. Mattay, A. Tessitore, F. Fera, and D. R. Weinberger, "Neocortical modulation of the amygdala response to fearful stimuli," *Biological Psychiatry*, vol. 53, no. 6, pp. 494–501, 2003.

[21] R. J. Davidson, K. M. Putnam, and C. L. Larson, "Dysfunction in the neural circuitry of emotion regulation—a possible prelude to violence," *Science*, vol. 289, no. 5479, pp. 591–594, 2000.

[22] M. R. Bennett, "The prefrontal-limbic network in depression: a core pathology of synapse regression," *Progress in Neurobiology*, vol. 93, no. 4, pp. 457–467, 2011.

[23] H. Barbas, "Prefrontal cortex: structure and anatomy," *Encyclopedia of Neuroscience*, vol. 7, pp. 909–918, 2009.

[24] J. M. Fuster, *The Prefrontal Cortex*, Elsevier, Amsterdam, Netherlands, 4th edition, 2008.

[25] E. R. Kandel, *Principles of Neural Science*, McGraw-Hill, New York, NY, USA, 4th edition, 2000.

[26] L. F. Barrett and A. Satpute, "Large-scale brain networks in affective and social neuroscience: Towards an integrative functional architecture of the brain," *Current Opinion in Neurobiology*, vol. 23, no. 3, pp. 361–372, 2013.

[27] W. C. Drevets, J. Savitz, and M. Trimble, "The subgenual anterior cingulate cortex in mood disorders," *CNS Spectrums*, vol. 13, no. 8, pp. 663–681, 2008.

[28] G. Bush, P. Luu, and M. I. Posner, "Cognitive and emotional influences in anterior cingulate cortex," *Trends in Cognitive Sciences*, vol. 4, no. 6, pp. 215–222, 2000.

[29] M. Petrides, "The role of the mid-dorsolateral prefrontal cortex in working memory," in *Executive Control and the Frontal Lobe: Current Issues*, pp. 44–54, 2000.

[30] J. D. Wallis, "Orbitofrontal cortex and its contribution to decision-making," *Annual Review of Neuroscience*, vol. 30, pp. 31–56, 2007.

[31] P. J. Whalen and E. A. Phelps, *The Human Amygdala*, T. G. Press, Texas, Tex, USA, 1st edition, 2009.

[32] J. A. Hashmi, M. N. Baliki, L. Huang et al., "Shape shifting pain: chronification of back pain shifts brain representation from nociceptive to emotional circuits," *Brain*, vol. 136, no. 9, pp. 2751–2768, 2013.

[33] R.-D. Treede and A. V. Apkarian, *5.45 - nociceptive processing in the cerebral cortex*, A. K. llan and I. Basbaum, Eds., The Senses: A Comprehensive Reference, 2008.

[34] A. V. Apkarian, M. C. Bushnell, R.-D. Treede, and J.-K. Zubieta, "Human brain mechanisms of pain perception and regulation in health and disease," *European Journal of Pain*, vol. 9, no. 4, pp. 463–484, 2005.

[35] V. Legrain, G. D. Iannetti, L. Plaghki, and A. Mouraux, "The pain matrix reloaded: a salience detection system for the body," *Progress in Neurobiology*, vol. 93, no. 1, pp. 111–124, 2011.

[36] N. H. Naqvi, D. Rudrauf, H. Damasio, and A. Bechara, "Damage to the insula disrupts addiction to cigarette smoking," *Science*, vol. 315, no. 5811, pp. 531–534, 2007.

[37] A. Dagher, "Functional brain imaging of appetite," *Trends in Endocrinology & Metabolism*, vol. 23, no. 5, pp. 250–260, 2012.

[38] E. Arce, A. N. Simmons, K. L. Lovero, M. B. Stein, and M. P. Paulus, "Escitalopram effects on insula and amygdala BOLD activation during emotional processing," *Psychopharmacology*, vol. 196, no. 4, pp. 661–672, 2008.

[39] M. B. Stein, A. N. Simmons, J. S. Feinstein, and M. P. Paulus, "Increased amygdala and insula activation during emotion processing in anxiety-prone subjects," *The American Journal of Psychiatry*, vol. 164, no. 2, pp. 318–327, 2007.

[40] S. Palminteri, D. Justo, C. Jauffret et al., "Critical Roles for Anterior Insula and Dorsal Striatum in Punishment-Based Avoidance Learning," *Neuron*, vol. 76, no. 5, pp. 998–1009, 2012.

[41] K. S. Smith, K. C. Berridge, and J. W. Aldridge, "Disentangling pleasure from incentive salience and learning signals in brain reward circuitry," *Proceedings of the National Acadamy of Sciences of the United States of America*, vol. 108, no. 27, pp. E255–E264, 2011.

[42] P. A. Andersen, *The Hippocampus Book*, O. U. Press, New York, NY, USA, 1st edition, 2007.

[43] J. H. Holland, "Properties of the bucket brigade," in *Proceedings of the International Conference on Genetic Algorithms*, 1985.

[44] J. H. Holland, "Adaptation," in *Progress in Theoretical Biology*, 1976.

[45] M. A. Ramos and F. Ramos, "Autonomous agents and anticipative systems," in *Proceedings of the 10th IEEE International Workshop on Object-Oriented Real-Time Dependable Systems, WORDS '05*, pp. 371–377, February 2005.

8

Enrichment of Human-Computer Interaction in Brain-Computer Interfaces via Virtual Environments

Alonso-Valerdi Luz María and Mercado-García Víctor Rodrigo

Escuela de Ingeniería y Ciencias, Tecnológico de Monterrey, Eugenio Garza Sada 2501, 64849 Monterrey, NL, Mexico

Correspondence should be addressed to Alonso-Valerdi Luz María; lm.aloval@itesm.mx

Academic Editor: Fabio Solari

Tridimensional representations stimulate cognitive processes that are the core and foundation of human-computer interaction (HCI). Those cognitive processes take place while a user navigates and explores a virtual environment (VE) and are mainly related to spatial memory storage, attention, and perception. VEs have many distinctive features (e.g., involvement, immersion, and presence) that can significantly improve HCI in highly demanding and interactive systems such as brain-computer interfaces (BCI). BCI is as a nonmuscular communication channel that attempts to reestablish the interaction between an individual and his/her environment. Although BCI research started in the sixties, this technology is not efficient or reliable yet for everyone at any time. Over the past few years, researchers have argued that main BCI flaws could be associated with HCI issues. The evidence presented thus far shows that VEs can (1) set out working environmental conditions, (2) maximize the efficiency of BCI control panels, (3) implement navigation systems based not only on user intentions but also on user emotions, and (4) regulate user mental state to increase the differentiation between control and noncontrol modalities.

1. Introduction

Brain-Computer Interfaces (BCI) are systems that attempt to establish communication between the human brain and a computer in order to replace the natural connection between central nervous system (CNS) and musculoskeletal system. The interest on BCI research has been greatly increased due to a wide variety of applications, including neurorehabilitation, robotic devices, exoskeletons, and domotic systems. Although BCI research started in the sixties, this technology is not efficient or reliable yet for everyone at any time. Over the past few years, some researchers such as Fabien Lotte and Camille Jeunet have argued that main BCI flaws could be associated with human-computer interaction (HCI) issues [1–4]. As can be seen in Figure 1, virtual environments (VEs) have many distinctive features that can significantly improve HCI in highly demanding and interactive systems such as BCI. The present paper moves on to describe in greater detail five key points:

(i) Main characteristics of VEs (Section 2)

(ii) How those characteristics can improve HCI (Section 3)

(iii) How the improvement of HCI via VE may help to overcome several drawbacks of BCI systems (Section 4)

(iv) Extensive revision of recent advances in the field (Section 4)

(v) Strong tendencies of this research area (Section 5).

2. Virtual Environments: System Requirements and User Concerns

People have an overall clear perception of their environment in spite of their limited sensory system. Owing to the extraordinary signal processing of the nervous system, which constantly updates human reactions, people can carry out complex activities. For example, a person is capable of recognizing and classifying a large number of sounds merged in a surrounding space. It is, therefore, a difficult task to

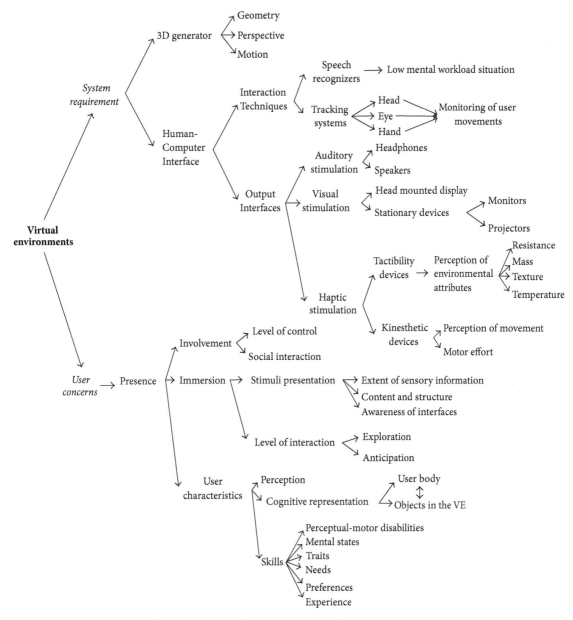

FIGURE 1: Structure of a virtual environment on the basis of two key elements: system requirements and user concerns.

develop VEs that generate synthetic visual, auditory, and haptic sensations, which could deceive human perception. A VE has two basic elements: system requirements and user concerns [5]. Figure 1 provides a summary of all the components encompassed under these two categories.

With respect to system requirements, a VE generally requires a 3D generator and a HCI. The 3D generator consists in modeling and animating 3D objects under the following criteria: (1) *geometry*, definition of the visual appearance, sound, odor, taste, and/or texture of each object in the VE; (2) *perspective*, spatial relationship between the geometry and the user; and (3) *motion*, geometrical changes in response to user actions and time progress. Regarding the HCI, there are *output interfaces* for stimulating the user senses and *interaction techniques* for decoding the user desires. The *output interfaces* are classified as auditory, visual, and haptic

devices. Auditory devices foster user awareness, and even the high quality sound can help in creating a more realistic and immersive experience. Headphones and speakers are the most commonly used auditory devices [6–9]. Visual devices allow users to see around, over, and under objects and also give users a stereoscopic vision of the VE [10–12]. They can be head-mounted devices or stationary devices such as monitors and projectors. Haptic systems are divided into tactibility and kinesthetic devices. Tactibility devices provide tactile feedback to perceive the attributes of the environment such as resistance, mass, texture, or temperature. Kinesthetic devices provide perception of movement or motor effort [13–15]. The *interaction techniques* refer to the mode of interacting with the VE. The common ones are graphical user interfaces, speech recognizers, and head/eye/hand tracking systems. Speech recognizers are suitable for low mental workload situations because humans tend to block their auditory channels under extreme workload situations. Tracking systems are position sensors that monitor the user movements in the VE. This allows the VE generator to render and display the VE from the user perspective, achieving the effect of physical immersion [13–15]. Some examples of tracking systems are as follows: (1) electromagnetic sensors to determine position and orientation, (2) mechanical sensors to simulate force effects, (3) optical sensors to determine 3D position, (4) ultrasonic sensors to calculate distances, and (5) inertial sensors to detect motion such as gyroscopic force, acceleration, or inclination.

In addition to the technological side, the human side of these cybersystems (or user concerns) must be also considered. User concerns are associated with the generation of a virtual world cognitively equivalent to the real one. The closest similarity between these two worlds takes place when users have the sense of being there. Users interact in and with the virtual space as if they were there; that is, they experience presence. Presence occurs when users feel immersed in the VE, feel capable of interacting with it, and have an interest in undertaking tasks. The three main aspects of presence are immersion, user characteristics, and involvement [16, 17]. Immersion is brought about when users perceive themselves to be enveloped by and included in the VE. The stimuli presentation and the level of interaction are the tools that a virtual system uses to have a good quality immersion. The stimuli presentation depends on three factors: (1) quality of immersion related to the extent of sensory information presented to VE users, (2) dramatic content and structure that are implemented in the VE, and (3) awareness of interfaces that distracts from the VE experience. The level of interaction is controlled by the possibility of exploring extensively the VE and the ability to predict and anticipate what will happen next [18, 19]. The virtual interaction is highly modified by individuals' characteristics, and because they cannot be controlled, they must be considered. User perception dynamically changes as users move through and interact with the VE, so this is the first psychological process to take into account. The cognitive representation of the VE is another important individual contribution, which captures the relation between the user body and the objects in the environment. Finally, user skills vary significantly across individuals, distorting the virtual interaction. Some instances of such skills are perceptual-motor abilities, mental states, traits, needs, preferences, and experience. Last but not least, the last element of VEs in terms of user concerns is involvement. The relation between the VE as a space and the individual body is called involvement. When the level of control that users have over the virtual sensor mechanisms is high, and their social interaction with the VE is good, users focus on the system suppressing possible constraints of the VE. As a result, users forget the real environment achieving a complete involvement [20].

3. Improvement of Human-Computer Interaction via Virtual Environments

As VEs rely on representing real-life traits, objects, and scenarios, 3D representations of objects and places augment user experience (UX), in comparison with 2D representations. Tridimensional representations stimulate cognitive processes that are the core and foundation of HCI. Those cognitive processes take place while the user navigates and explores the VE and are mainly related to spatial memory storage, attention, and perception. Even more important, such cognitive processes could be somehow modulated since VEs are designed according to both research goals and user needs [12]. In addition, VEs easily reach user engagement and UX, two desire factors in a proficient HCI. So far, VEs have been validated as an effective, safe, and motivating approach used to enhance the interaction between a user and a system [21].

VEs cannot, however, contribute to HCI by itself. User interaction in VEs could become sloppy, redundant, and frustrating. Along with a realistic and sophisticated design, VEs must be conceptualized and designed according to human factors and user characteristics.

4. Integration of Virtual Environments and Brain-Computer Interfaces

VEs have been widely used in BCI development to increase motivation and immersion, and a wide variety of scenarios have been proposed, from daily life situations to video games [12]. Several applications of VEs in BCI have included the control of virtual cars [22], navigations through virtual bars [21] or virtual flats [23], and walks through virtual streets [24]. One of the most common applications is in domotic systems. For example, a typical situation is to make an avatar to select and manipulate 3D virtual objects such as turning on/off lights, TVs, or lamps [25]. Other applications are wheelchair control, flying simulators [26], and virtual cities [27]. In sections that follow, BCI research is summarized, scientific relevance of BCI is discussed, current shortcomings of BCI are argued, the VE role in BCI research is justified, and a review of advances in the field is provided.

4.1. Brain-Computer Interfaces. BCI is as a nonmuscular communication channel that attempts to reestablish the interaction between an individual and his/her environment. A BCI system involves two stages: calibration (offline analysis) and control (online analysis). The former refers to training processes of a machine to recognize different brain patterns of the user, and the latter concerns the control of a device of interest via the trained machine. The essential function of a BCI is as follows. The user is who controls the device in the system by modifying his/her brain state through external (e.g., visual, auditory, or tactile stimuli) or internal stimulation (e.g., mental tasks). Such brain activity modulation is sensed, amplified, processed, displayed, and saved in two different ways, invasive and noninvasive. The most commonly used invasive recording method is electrocorticography, while some examples of noninvasive methods are electroencephalography (EEG), functional magnetic resonance imaging, and near-infrared spectroscopy. EEG has, however, become the widely used method in BCI community. Once brain signals have been acquired, a feature generator

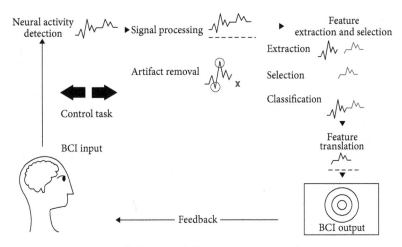

FIGURE 2: Block diagram of a brain-computer interface system.

emphasizes relevant neurophysiological features and generates feature vectors in time, frequency, or space domains, or even thereof. The feature translator then attempts to differentiate among control and noncontrol states and translates the classifier output into control commands. The control module and the device controller convert the control commands into semantic control signals for a particular device. Figure 2 illustrates the structure of BCI systems [28–34].

According to [35], BCI systems can be classified into active, reactive, and passive systems. *Active systems* produce their outputs from commands modulated directly by users in a conscious mental state. The most commonly used control task in active systems is motor imagery (MI), which relies primarily on the detection of slow cortical potentials, sensorimotor rhythms (SMR), and movement-related cortical potentials (MRCP). In particular, SMR can be estimated under two schemes: absolute and relative. In the former case, SMR are not referenced against a baseline state and the processing technique is known as band power. In the latter case, SMR are referenced against a baseline state, typically extracted in a couple of seconds before MI activity, and the processing technique is well-known as event-related (de)synchronization. In both cases, the signal power in μ (8–12 Hz) and β (16–24 Hz) frequency bands is being quantified. *Reactive BCIs* produce their outputs from reactions to external stimuli such as visual, auditory, and tactile. Most of reactive BCIs rely on the detection of event-related potentials (ERP) that are brain responses, appearing some hundreds of milliseconds after stimulus onset, with different polarities, and at different recording sites. The most widely used ERP is P300, which is a positive potential, appearing from 300 to 500 ms after stimulus onset and frequently over parieto-occipital area. P300 is a component associated with selective attention and memory mechanisms. Other types of reactive BCIs are those based on steady-state evoked potentials, which are much more responsive to sensory input decoding, rather than cognitive processes such as P300. Lastly, in *passive BCIs*, users' mind does not control the system directly as in active and reactive systems. These systems are applied to detect mental workload, working memory load, fatigue,

self-induced errors, and deception or anticipation errors (and many other states) when users interact with mobile devices, vehicles, robots, or any other systems.

4.2. Relevance of Brain-Computer Interfaces. Although BCI development has been encouraged over the past few years, there is a general lack of research in portable and reliable technology to detect brain activity; accurate and efficient algorithms; direct, relevant, and constructive feedback techniques; and instructive and intuitive interactive methods. According to [32], BCI research should be conducted on the basis of three factors: (1) recent appearance of powerful and inexpensive hardware and software that can perform complex high speed analysis of brain activity, (2) greater understanding of the CNS that has emerged from research, and (3) new recognition of needs and abilities of people suffering from disorders such as cerebral palsy, spinal cord injury, stroke, amyotrophic lateral sclerosis, multiple sclerosis, and muscular dystrophies. BCI progress has always been of particular interest for industrial and medical areas, and applications have been mainly considered in five areas [32]: (1) *replacement*, a BCI may replace CNS function in people with neurodegenerative diseases such as multiple sclerosis; (2) *restorage*, a BCI could restore mobility by reconnecting the peripheral nervous system and the musculoskeletal system in people with amputations; (3) *enhancement*, a BCI might enhance human reactions: for example, it can monitor levels of attention in order to raise alertness when necessary; (4) *supplementation*, a BCI system could supplement natural CNS output: for example, it can be used to control robotic arms as an aid in several tasks ranging from computing to industrial applications; and (5) *improvement*, a BCI can also improve the functionality of devices such as orthoses by monitoring natural CNS outputs and providing feedback that would lead to control properly and effectively the orthosis of interest.

4.3. Controversial Issues. Even when promises and expectations on BCIs have increased considerably, these systems are not a completely working prototype. In accordance with

[36], BCIs have four potentials pitfalls. Firstly, far too little attention has been paid to end-user requirements when designing BCI solutions, particularly those associated with human aspects, learning strategies, and interactive design. In this respect, it has been well documented that up to 40% of healthy users cannot control an active BCI system at all, while the remaining ones only reach a moderate performance. This phenomenon is called BCI illiteracy and indicates that the omission of end-user needs and their cognitive profiles may be playing a crucial role in BCI shortcomings [37]. Secondly, researchers in the field seem to neglect that user behavior and experience in BCI systems largely depend on coping with the control task, previous sensorimotor abilities, and motivation. As users must produce stable, clear, and detectable neural patterns, training procedures, and feedback methods should facilitate the acquisition of control skills based on modulation of EEG signals. Thirdly, real working environments are much noisier, more dynamic, and unforeseeable in contrast with well-controlled laboratory environments; therefore, signal processing and pattern recognition should be versatile and robust algorithms. Finally, there is a lack of clear metrics to assess the effective performance of a BCI system. It is not clear yet how to weight human and machine factors, such as detection and accuracy, respectively, on metrics that result from BCI outputs. Up to now, researchers in the field have reported metrics directly obtained from the performance of machine learning classifiers, specifically accuracy, and specificity. Nevertheless, the very own nature of classifier metrics cannot indicate whether the user has correctly modulated his/her brain signals or whether he/she is comfortable and concentrated on the control task in use.

4.4. How Can VE Improve BCI in Terms of HCI? Not only is a BCI related to the development of the system per se, but it is also associated with the design of a good quality HCI, considering that BCI users need to be trained exhaustively. The key aspects of user training are repetition, feedback, and motivation [38]. Users must repeat the control tasks over and over since human beings normally learn by trial and error practice. This learning process can be accelerated through feedback and motivation. Feedback provides information about the performance of the ongoing control task, which gradually improves the user performance in the forthcoming repetitions. Motivation creates an encouraging environment, where the growing fatigue caused by the repetitiveness of the control tasks can be reduced. The user training eventually leads to automatizing control tasks, allowing users to confine their attention on the control device, rather than on the function of the BCI system.

The assumption of isolating cognitive processes related to BCI control, along with the disregard of human factors and environment demands (as discussed above), has complicated HCI in BCI applications. In recent years, VEs have become an attractive alternative to enrich HCI in BCI systems. It has been considered that VEs facilitate the user-system adaptation in BCIs because they provide user senses with appropriate feedback. Furthermore, users can learn to control BCI systems under more realistic conditions because virtual simulations offer a more direct interaction with the environment. In general, it has been demonstrated that users are much more comfortable when they manipulate a BCI system in a VE. This is because VEs induce motivation and entertainment, and even more, offer an ample scope on how to achieve a goal [21, 39, 40].

VEs have become a promising alternative to enrich HCI in BCI systems since they lead to a higher user performance [41]; they test BCIs under more realistic situations; they improve attention, motivation, and learning; they facilitate prototyping; and they are feasible for diagnostic and therapeutic purposes [12]. A more detailed account of these points is given hereunder.

4.4.1. Higher BCI Performance. It has been considered that highly immersive VEs induce a high sense of presence, which in turn facilitates BCI performance because VEs provide the user senses with appropriate feedback. A better BCI performance results in a shorter user training and a higher user confidence. VEs could lead to greater performance due to their nature of accurately representing elements of real life in the virtual domain. These representations of environments and objects permit the elaboration of a virtual scenario which can map everyday tasks and routines. This mapping allows establishing a training protocol that can provide feedback associated with the tasks in use. The current interactive systems are not explicit enough to become congruent with the tasks in use. While implementing VEs demands effort and time, often not available, the payoff relies on the possibility of representing and contextualizing tasks for users, who see and become part of something beyond abstract symbols on the screen. In a VE, users can perceive the ongoing changing of their mental tasks. For example, if a mental task is to imagine "kicking a ball," and then, they see a virtual leg coming from themselves to kick a ball, they will have sense of proprioception and agency. VE offers the possibility of being explicit and accurate. Virtual representations encourage users to generate and maintain mental images by facilitating sensory information and providing feedback within a meaningful context for them [18, 41–45].

4.4.2. BCI Implementation under More Realistic Situations. Human interaction is a huge limitation in laboratories. As virtual simulations offer a more direct interaction with the environment, users can learn to control systems under more realistic situations. Furthermore, the influences of human factors (such as mental fatigue, frustration, or idleness) and distraction sources (such as other people's conversations, ambient noises, or household appliances working) on BCI usability can be studied simultaneously.

The term "realistic situation" does not only refer to high technological implementations, but it also concerns the VE relevance for the users [46]. This factor could even have a higher impact on the system performance. A good example of this is the work presented in [41]. In such work, the control task was to imagine the draw of different basic strokes of Chinese characters. Furthermore, the effectuation of the control task was as real as possible since users observed the explicit representation of the drawing process. Researchers considered that the graphical presentation of imaginary movements could promote MI generation. The research study was conducted as follows. Fourteen subjects (between 22 and 25 years) were divided into two groups: experimental and control. The experimental group used the proposed paradigm based on drawing basic strokes of Chinese characters. The control group used the traditional Graz approach. On average, the experimental group achieved 79.8% system accuracy, whereas the control group yielded around 65.1%. In addition, participants filled in a UX questionnaire, and results suggested that the proposed paradigm was easier to use and more understandable. Overall, this work strengthens the idea that VEs must be contextualized to provide a familiar working environment where users can make full use of their previous knowledge. In this work, it was shown that the modulation of EEG signals through MI activity could be significantly improved if appropriate environmental working conditions are provided.

4.4.3. Improvement of Attention, Motivation, and Learning.
Galliard and collaborators (whose work is cited in [47]) defined a human state as the psychophysiological regulation of the brain to reach an optimal condition. This process enables humans to meet environment demands. In this respect, the readiness to catch relevant stimuli (attention) and the desire to learn and to explore (motivation [48]) are essential in BCI applications. VEs have proved to be a potential tool for directing attention, increasing motivation, and accelerating learning of BCI users.

4.4.4. Laboratory for Prototyping BCI Systems.
Virtual experiments can facilitate the development of BCI systems, and exhaustive testing of BCI prototypes could be also undertaken. In fact, this might justify the huge expense of implementing physical devices such as robot arms and exoeskeletons.

4.4.5. Diagnostic and Therapeutic Purposes.
VEs are suitable for guiding severely paralyzed patients through how to adapt themselves to their new circumstances (e.g., how to control a wheelchair) or on how to regain their basic functions such as walking or talking.

4.5. Advances in the Field.
A large number of virtual applications in BCI systems have already been undertaken. Active BCIs have been mostly used for navigation purposes [49, 50], and to improve user performance by increasing user motivation [10, 51]. Reactive BCIs have been used to select and manipulate objects inside virtual dwelling places. For example, P300 evoked potentials have been applied to control the functionality of devices such as TV, lamps, or fans [52, 53]. Another example is the utilization of steady-state visual evoked potentials (SSVEPs) to control the behavior of virtual avatars [12, 54]. On simulations of daily applications, VEs and BCIs interactive system have represented scenarios ranging from holding a cup and pouring water [43] to identify and recognize subjects [55]. However, applications have also been focused on more engaging experiences such as playing tennis [39] or even an aesthetic experience provided by a virtual play

[56]. Despite the several directions presented on the advances on the intersection between BCI systems and VEs, in further sections trends on this field will be explained and detailed.

In this section, a review about the existing body of research on VE applications in BCIs is presented, excluding those related to gaming purposes. Video games are usually used for entertainment; however, the system contextualization regarding the user requirements is neither specified nor considered. The review presented in this section attempts to highlight the enrichment of BCI systems by means of VEs in terms of human behavior and learning, user adaptability, significance of virtual scenarios, and user concerns. Specifically, all those research studies carried out to facilitate the acquisition of MI skills by providing high quality of immersion and spatial cognition are of special interest. A great deal of research into this framework has focused on augmenting the level of interaction between the user and the system in order to evoke and maintain clearer EEG patterns (e.g., MRCPs and SSVEP), thus increasing the pattern recognition efficiency. Researchers in the field are aware of the importance of using VEs as interactive paradigms for HCI enrichment. Their work has shown that sensory-enriched interfaces, particularly in visual modality, do not only provide satisfactory system outcomes, but they also make users feel comfortable and attentive during the interaction.

It is considered that the user ability to modulate his/her EEG signals by MI can be much more gainful to enhance BCI performance, rather than the computational algorithm complexity. Users have been ignored so far, and possibly if now we pave the way for facilitating human learning and adaptation, they could finally establish a regular communication with the system. In the following sections, three main topics are discussed: (1) VEs as working environments and control panels, (2) VEs for navigation purposes in BCI systems, and (3) relevance of user mental state in sensory-enriched environments. The most purposeful and recent works on this matter are summarized in Table 1.

4.5.1. Working Environments and Control Panels.
Virtual reality (VR) and augmented reality (AR) have been widely used in reactive BCIs based on SSVEP since the level of user attention towards visual stimuli increases significantly. In a study conducted in [43], three male subjects aged between 25 and 27 years were asked to perform two types of tasks: VR-based and AR-based. The aim of this study was to assess AR as a means to emulate not controlled environments such as patients' home or hospital. The general task was to navigate across a virtual room and through an avatar. Three participants were recruited for the study and their performances revealed that they had greater difficulty in controlling the avatar in AR mode. Researchers suggested that distracting elements in AR scenarios hindered the avatar manipulation. AR forces users to interact with surroundings at any time, which definitely complicates the interaction between user and system. AR may be harnessed to analyze BCI systems under environments where users' attention, immersion, and performance are compromised by external factors [42].

TABLE 1: Comparison of recent applications of VEs in BCI systems.

Authors	Type of environment	BCI System	Type of potential searched	Algorithm for detection	Contribution/novelty
Faller et al. 2017 [42]	Avatar navigation with sound stimuli	g.tec biosignal amplifier	SSVEP	Harmonic sum detection (HSD)	Comparison of feedback provided by users using VR and AR
Chun et al. 2016 [57]	Object manipulation	Emotiv EPOC	SSVEP	Common spatial P patterns (CSP) 8–30 Hz and support vector machines (SVMs)	Using concentration as a way to interact with environment
Kryger et al. 2017 [26]	Flight simulation	NeuroPort Neural Signal Processor	SSVEP	—	Mapping of airplane movements (roll, pitch, yaw) to neural commands
Fan et al. 2017 [27]	Flight simulation	Emotiv EPOC	None	—	Measuring emotions with EEG signals along with a VE
Chen et al. 2016 [58]	Wheelchair control simulation	—	MRCP	k-nearest neighbors (kNN)	Detection of patterns in MRCP in four different navigational directions.
Shih et al. 2017 [59]	Car driving simulation	—	—	Double deep Q learning	Training of intelligent agent using emotion detection from EEG signals
Amores et al. 2016 [11]	Superpowers' simulation	Muse headband	—	—	Studying levels of concentration in EEG by stimulation with VEs based on mindfulness and hand movement
Yan et al. 2016 [56]	Virtual play and scenario	Emotiv EEG Headset	Amplitudes of α, β, and θ waves	—	Studying levels of concentration present in EEG signals by stimulation with VEs focused on aesthetic experiences
Kosunen et al. 2017 [60]	Meditation simulation with avatar	RelaWorld system	—	—	Studying levels of concentration in EEG by stimulation with VEs based on mindfulness
Yazmir & Reiner 2017 [39]	Tennis game simulation	Biosemi 64 channel EEG recording system	ERPs ERS/ERD	Blind source separation (BSS) 0–50 Hz	Measurement of correlation between success and error peaks presented on ERPs
Cecílio et al. 2016 [54]	Trash separation game	ActiCHamp amplifier	μ-rhythms	Independent component analysis (ICA), principal component analysis (PCA) and SVMs	Utilization of a virtual avatar as a representation of desired movement
Herweg et al. 2016 [61]	Wheelchair simulation	g.USBamp	P300	Step-wise linear discriminate analysis (SWLDA) 0.1–30 Hz	Combination of virtual navigation system along with P300 and tactile feedback
Cyrino & Viana 2016 [43]	Daily tasks simulation, filling a bowl with a cup, rotating levels	Emotiv EPOC	—	—	Virtual environments using daily tasks
Liu et al. 2016 [62]	Car driving simulation environment	NeuroScan NuAmps Express system	—	Fuzzy Neural Network (FNN) Delta, theta, beta and alpha channels.	Usage of FNN as a classifier for predicting driving fatigue
de Tommaso et al. 2016 [63]	Virtual home navigation	Micromed System Plus	P300b	ANOVA 0.5–80 Hz	Virtual environment could be personalized with different light/color options in order to look for different stimuli in simulation
Saproo et al. 2016 [64]	Flight simulator	Biosemi B.V. ActiveTwo	—	ICA 1–55 Hz	Generalization of similar control failures in other cases of tight man–machine coupling where gains and latencies in the control system must be inferred and compensated for by the human operators
Chen et al. 2017 [65]	Landscape navigation	BioSemi ActiveTwo	SSVEP	Canonical correlation analysis 1–80 Hz Multiclass LDA	Employment of SSVEP for navigation in virtual environments.
Gordon et al. 2017 [55]	Target recognition	BioSemi ActiveTwo	P300	Convolutional Neural Networks 0.1–50 Hz	Real-time application for performing BCI-based Human-Centric Scene Analysis.

On the other hand, VR can be applied to get the BCI system under control. By way of illustration, in [61], it was improved the performance of a hybrid BCI by employing VR technology based on Oculus Rift system. The aim of this study was to develop an efficient virtual control panel. The VE consisted of three spheres in different colors on which users must direct their attention. Once users had decided the one to be selected, they must imagine such sphere approaching to them. Attention on the spheres was detected via eye-trackers, but the sphere approximation was quantified by EEG processing. This control mechanism was very efficient because it was natural and intuitive. Users could understand clearly how to control a BCI system, even in a highly demanding situation. It is worth noting that BCI function relies on both user ability (imagination) and technology aspects (eyes' position). This lightened the workload regarding control tasks, and allowed users interact more easily [57].

4.5.2. Navigation Systems. Typically, VEs have been applied to navigate in virtual worlds. Researchers in the field have worked towards two major goals: transportation and effects of vehicular environmental stimuli on human reactions [61–64]. However, the application of navigation systems has recently gone beyond these two purposes. A notable example of this is the work presented in [65], who developed a VE using Oculus Rift system that was controlled through a BCI based on MRCPs. The key aim of this study was the pattern recognition of four different navigational directions (forward, backward, go right, and go left) decoded in MRCPs of the user. Authors demonstrated that VEs are quite efficient to train BCI users and make users generate different EEG patterns for different movements [58]. Another example of the usage of specific potentials include SSVEPs, where the authors have relied on the detection of these potentials in order to select a specific direction for navigating on a virtual environment; rather than using motor imagery, this work relied on eye fixation on four points on the environment representing possible directions of navigation (forward, backward, go right, and go left). They later took advantage of the graphic nature of VEs and the nature of SSVEP for the proposal of a paradigm for navigation using a BCI system which relies on attending key points of a graphic representation of a daily environment [65].

Vehicle control is another representative example of novel application of navigation systems. In [26], a flight simulation system with brain-computer interacting controls was implemented. A 53-year-old woman with quadriplegia was instructed to control a virtual airplane by correlating airplane movements in full flight with her arm movements. Researchers concluded that metaphorical interaction and practice did not lead to one-to-one relationship between arm and airplane movements. Nevertheless, user attention can be confined for longer periods of time, resulting in the mastery of MI based control tasks. The feminine user was able to control the airplane with no restriction after two training sessions. Authors argued that the feedback method in use was sufficiently efficient to instruct user how to modulate her brain signal using her arm movements [26]. In a similar case, in [58], a study based on the detection of pilot induced oscillations susceptibility was conducted. Researchers designed a

flight VE with a joystick based control mechanism. Control tasks were based on boundary avoidance task. That is, users required flying the plane on a specific trajectory, and whether they failed to follow the same trajectory, the flight simulation stopped automatically. Results showed that workload buildup in boundary avoidance tasks could be successfully decoded from EEG oscillations in δ, θ, α, β, and γ frequency bands.

Particularly, θ band over frontocentral recording sites and γ band over lateralized somatosensory areas were the major contributors in the EEG pattern recognition [64].

Apart from MI activity, other applications of navigation systems have played an important role in BCI research. This can be illustrated in [27], where a VE that rendered driving environments for children with autistic spectrum disorders (ASD) was designed. The virtual system consisted of a car to be driven in a city with full of details in the surroundings, including buildings, trees, pedestrians, and traffic lights. Authors claimed that realistic tasks might stimulate neural processes such as workload management, long-term memory access, visuospatial processing, regulation of emotions and attention, and decision-making, in children suffering from ASD. In this study, authors made use of EEG signals to detect emotions and cognitive states, including concentration, boredom, frustration, and mental load. As system performance was between 78% and 95%, this BCI based on virtual architecture seems to be promising to treat ASD [27]. In the same line of thinking, in [66], an emotion detection based on BCI technology to develop a decision-making system was proposed. Five subjects trained an intelligent agent by reinforcement learning to navigate through a virtual city where decision-making was based on user emotions, rather than user intentions as usual. The VE rendered a car cabin through which users could explore the virtual city. Instead of decoding user intentions, an intelligent agent received BCI outputs concerning human reactions such as surprise, anxiety, happiness, or concentration. All these human reactions were learned by the agent, which controlled the trajectory of the virtual vehicle [59].

Last but not least, navigation through virtual dwelling places has become one of the most examined applications. The work presented in [64] is a good exemplification of HCI enrichment in this type of navigation systems. Those researchers quantified levels of attention in VEs by detecting P3b components. The detection of P3b was based on color coding, and the user propose was to access different rooms in a virtual house. Authors demonstrated that color coding is a more proficient way to capture and hold user attention than the classical Donchin paradigm [63].

4.5.3. User Mental State. User mental state at the moment of the interaction is a key element to reach a stable performance system. According to [66], the modulation of EEG signals using MI activity greatly depends on the user mental balance since control tasks become much more differentiable. This can be seen in [11], where an interactive system based on mindfulness and meditation was designed. By using an Oculus Rift system to render the VE, a Leap Motion system to track hand movements, and a Muse headband to record EEG activity, researchers set up a stimulating environment to practice levitation, pyrokinesis, and telekinesis. Their setup induced great sense of immersion, which, in turn, promoted meditation and mindfulness, which facilitated MI training later [11]. Similarly, in [67], a VE where users controlled an avatar by their levels of concentration was proposed. By employing RelaWorld software and a ERP based BCI, authors significantly improved user-system interaction only prolonging lapse of concentration [60].

4.5.4. Applying VEs to BCI Paradigms.

To control a BCI system is a skill that must be acquired. The process of learning in current BCI paradigms generally stimulates only one sensory pathway, either visual or auditory. However, humans gather information from five sensory pathways (vision, hearing, touch, smell, and taste) and react accordingly. It has been shown that if environments are sensorially enriched, learning is much more effective. The effects of environmental enrichment are exemplified in the work reported in [67], where two groups of cortically injured rats were exposed to enriched and nonenriched environments. The enriched environment involved a variety of elements, including group housing, social stimulation, competition for food and water, stress, greater motor activity, manipulation of objects, and sensory stimulation augmentation. The nonenriched environment only involved food and water. The results showed that rats exposed to environmental enrichment made significantly fewer errors in their tasks than those in nonenriched conditions. Furthermore, three neurophysiological modifications were found. First, certain zones of the cerebral cortex, which are used in complex learning and problem solving processes, became heavier, deeper, and greater. Second, the neurons were larger, the synapse to neuron ratio was higher, the synapses were bigger, and there was more profuse dendritic branching in those zones. Third, there were clear effects of enrichment at the level of neurochemistry. An example of this is the considerable augmentation of the RNA/DNA ratio, which indicates an increased metabolic rate. In this work, it was demonstrated that the most important factor for stimulating brain changes was the enforced interaction with enriched environments. On the other hand, it has been found that sensory feedback plays a central role in the human learning process. The human brain makes use of sensory feedback to make predictions, thereby modifying human behaviors [68]. As learning is a process that involves changes in behavior that arise from interaction with the environment, it means that sensory feedback does not only influence behavioral patterns, but it also promotes perceptual learning. Recent neuroimaging evidence suggests that perceptual learning promotes neural plasticity over sensory-motor cortices and increases connectivity between such areas of the brain. Furthermore, the effect of perceptual learning is durable [69, 70]. This means that somatosensory function plays a vital role in human learning. It is hypothesized that if sensory feedback is properly given, perceptual learning will be gained, which in turn will achieve the acquisition of skills to control a BCI system.

In the light of the above information, it is encouraged to take advantage of VE features to provide sensorially enriched environments, which in turn may facilitate the acquisition of skills to control a BCI system. To work towards this goal, the adaptation of VEs via interactive methods for brain-computer communication sounds promising. This requires a process of conceptualization and design, which primarily depends on tasks or actions undertaken by users. The application and integration of VEs along with sensory stimulation in BCI paradigms rely on four stages: context, metaphor, design, and evaluation [71, 72].

Context. Considering a VE as an outcome that involves interactive design, earlier studies must be done to discover the correlation between the virtual proposal and a group of items that includes the user context (specifically everyday tasks), working environments, commonly used technology, devices, and navigation. These factors determine a metaphor, which integrates the user context with the set of tasks to be performed in the interactive system. Thereby, a contextualized scenario is constructed. Although HCI community has acknowledged the importance of human factors in the design and conceptualization of interactive systems for several years, the overlook of these factors has not only produced misleading interactive models but also inefficient VEs. The context of BCI systems is important for users since this helps to build awareness about the relevance of BCI training and control. So far, the classical example of contextualized applications is control tasks related to activities of daily living such as turning on and off lamps and switches [25] and wheelchair control [26]. A more recent and notorious example of contextualization is given in [41], where all participants were Chinese and the MI control task was directly associated with activities of their daily living, that is, drawing of basis strokes of Chinese characters.

Metaphor. Once the metaphor is established, the interactive design and layout of the VE can be proposed. Exploiting the metaphor leads to find optimal cues, feedback, and actions to be undertaken inside the VE. It is important to consider interactive design as a heuristic method to find solutions to a specific problem, rather than an ultimate solution. In particular, the metaphor based on concentration and mindfulness provides users with powerful tools to interact with the VE, including higher attention, clearer perception, and better conceptualization [11]. A good example of a movement metaphor was proposed by [39], where the task of hitting a tennis ball in a virtual court was used. In that environment, users could see an explicit outcome of their mental images. In this case, the metaphor was used to stimulate the imagination of a movement towards a specific direction. Another notable example is the metaphor used in [41], where the task of drawing basic strokes of Chinese characters was employed. Similar to [39], users observed the rendering of their imaginary writing.

Design. The overall layout, the model complexity, and the sensorial features depend on context, user profile, and available technological resources. Returning to aesthetic and functional features considered in the context stage, it is essential to design familiar, stimulating, and favorable environments for users. Particularly, details are critical when emulations of real-life situations are attempted. Lack of detail and/or emphasis in design might make users feel indifferent and disinterest. Flight simulators and car navigators are a good picture of interactive design applications, where details enrich beautifully the environment [26, 27, 62, 64]. Another case in point is the one shown in [41]. The black background, along with the animated image of a hand holding a chalk, was a close analogy of writing on a blackboard. This design illustrates the benefits and advantages of VEs in terms of graphic representation.

Testing. The first testing is an opportunity to gather information from potential users about the early version of a virtual implementation, including interaction flow between user and system and feedforward and feedback sources and models. This can come up with relevant interactive and aesthetic redesigns from users' perspective. Major changes based on further testing are advisable. It is essential to go through an iterative process of design, engaging users from the beginning and along the whole process. In each iteration, users' feedback must be taken in account, and, even more, it should be implemented properly. Although this iterative process demands resources and time [36], it could lead to an optimal and complete interaction between brains and machines.

5. Conclusion

The first applications of VEs in BCI research concerned the strength of user motivation, the maintenance of attention for longer periods, and the implementation of favorable feedback mechanism. However, virtual technology had been only seen as a tool to render illusory effects of realism by means of 3D graphics and electronically equipped helmets, headphones, goggles, and gloves. At present, tridimensional representations have become an attractive alternative to enrich HCI since they stimulate cognitive processes that take place while the user navigates and explores VEs, which are mainly associated with workload management, long-term memory access, visuospatial processing, regulation of emotions and attention, and decision-making. The evidence presented thus far shows that VEs can set out working environmental conditions, maximize the efficiency of BCI control panels, implement navigation systems based not only on user intentions but also on user emotions, and regulate user mental state to increase the differentiation between control and noncontrol modalities.

References

[1] F. Lotte and C. Jeunet, "Towards improved BCI based on human learning principles," in *Proceedings of the 2015 3rd International Winter Conference on Brain-Computer Interface, BCI 2015*, Republic of Korea, January 2015.

[2] F. Lotte, F. Larrue, and C. Mühl, "Flaws in current human training protocols for spontaneous brain-computer interfaces: lessons learned from instructional design," *Frontiers in Human Neuroscience*, Article ID A568, 2013.

[3] C. Jeunet, A. Cellard, S. Subramanian, M. Hachet, B. N'Kaoua, and F. Lotte, "How well can we learn with standard BCI training approaches? A pilot study," in *Proceedings of the 6th International Brain-Computer Interface Conference*, Graz, Austria, 2014.

[4] C. Jeunet, E. Jahanpour, and F. Lotte, "Why standard brain-computer interface (BCI) training protocols should be changed: an experimental study," *Journal of Neural Engineering*, vol. 13, no. 3, Article ID 036024, 2016.

[5] *Virtual Reality Systems*, Elsevier, 1993.

[6] N. Simon, I. Käthner, C. A. Ruf, E. Pasqualotto, A. Kübler, and S. Halder, "An auditory multiclass brain-computer interface with natural stimuli: usability evaluation with healthy participants and a motor impaired end user," *Frontiers in Human Neuroscience*, vol. 8, article no. 1039, 2015.

[7] S. Gao, Y. Wang, X. Gao, and B. Hong, "Visual and auditory brain-computer interfaces," *IEEE Transactions on Biomedical Engineering*, vol. 61, no. 5, pp. 1436–1447, 2014.

[8] D.-W. Kim, J.-C. Lee, Y.-M. Park, I.-Y. Kim, and C.-H. Im, "Auditory brain-computer interfaces (BCIs) and their practical applications," *Biomedical Engineering Letters*, vol. 2, no. 1, pp. 13–17, 2012.

[9] F. Nijboer, A. Furdea, I. Gunst et al., "An auditory brain–computer interface (BCI)," *Journal of Neuroscience Methods*, vol. 167, no. 1, pp. 43–50, 2008.

[10] R. Ron-Angevin and A. Díaz-Estrella, "Brain-computer interface: changes in performance using virtual reality techniques," *Neuroscience Letters*, vol. 449, no. 2, pp. 123–127, 2009.

[11] J. Amores, X. Benavides, and P. Maes, "PsychicVR: increasing mindfulness by using virtual reality and brain computer interfaces," in *Proceedings of the 2016 CHI Conference Extended Abstracts on Human Factors in Computing Systems*, Santa Clara, Calif, USA, 2016.

[12] A. Lécuyer, F. Lotte, R. B. Reilly, R. Leeb, M. Hirose, and M. Slater, "Brain-computer interfaces, virtual reality, and videogames," *The Computer Journal*, vol. 41, no. 10, pp. 66–72, 2008.

[13] M. Alcañiz and J. A. Lozano, "Technological background of virtual environment," in *Cybertherapy: Internet and Virtual Reality as Assessment and Rehabilitation Tools for Clinical Psychology and Neuroscience*, G. Riva, Ed., pp. 199–214, IOS Press, Amsterdam, Netherlands, 2004.

[14] N. I. Durlach and A. S. Mavor, Virtual Reality: Scientific and Technological Challenges, National Research Council: National Academic Press, 1994.

[15] K. M. Stanney, *Handbook of Virtual Environments: Design, Implementation, and Applications*, Lawrence Erlbaum Associates, London, England, 2002.

[16] G. Riva, F. Davide, and W. Ijsselsteijn, *Being There: The Experience of Presence in Mediated Environments*, IOS Press, Amsterdam, Netherlands, 2003.

[17] T. Schubert, F. Frank, and R. Holger, "Embodied presence in virtual environments," *Visual Representations and Interpretations*, vol. 20, no. 5687, pp. 269–278, 1999.

[18] S. Bangay and L. Preston, "An investigation into factors influencing immersion in interactive virtual reality environments," in *Studies in Health Technology and Informatics*, pp. 43–51, 1998.

[19] B. K. Wiederhold, D. Renee, and M. D. Wiederhold, "The effects of immersiveness on Physiology," in *Studies in Health Technology and Informatics*, pp. 52–62, 1998.

[20] A. Gaggioli and R. Breining, "Perception and cognition in immersive virtual reality," in *Communications through Virtual Technology: Identity Community and Technology in the Internet Age*, pp. 71–86, 2001.

[21] D. Friedman, R. Leeb, G. Pfurtscheller, and M. Slater, "Human-computer interface issues in controlling virtual reality with brain-computer interface," *Human–Computer Interaction*, vol. 25, no. 1, pp. 67–93, 2010.

[22] R. Ron-Angevin, A. Daz Estrella, and A. Reyes-Lecuona, "Development of a brain-computer interface (BCI) based on virtual reality to improve training techniques," *Cyberpsychology and Behavior*, vol. 8, no. 4, pp. 353-354, 2005.

[23] R. Leeb, F. Lee, C. Keinrath, R. Scherer, H. Bischof, and G. Pfurtscheller, "Brain-computer communication: Motivation, aim, and impact of exploring a virtual apartment," *IEEE Transactions on Neural Systems and Rehabilitation Engineering*, vol. 15, no. 4, pp. 473–482, 2007.

[24] R. Leeb, D. Friedman, G. R. Müller-Putz, R. Scherer, M. Slater, and G. Pfurtscheller, "Self-paced (asynchronous) BCI control of a wheelchair in virtual environments: a case study with a tetraplegic," *Computational Intelligence and Neuroscience*, vol. 2007, Article ID 79642, 8 pages, 2007.

[25] J. D. Bayliss, "Use of the evoked potential P3 component for control in a virtual apartment," *IEEE Transactions on Neural Systems and Rehabilitation Engineering*, vol. 11, no. 2, pp. 113–116, 2003.

[26] M. Kryger, B. Wester, E. A. Pohlmeyer et al., "Flight simulation using a Brain-Computer Interface: a pilot, pilot study," *Experimental Neurology*, vol. 287, pp. 473–478, 2017.

[27] J. Fan, J. W. Wade, A. P. Key, Z. Warren, and N. Sarkar, "EEG-based affect and workload recognition in a virtual driving environment for ASD intervention," *IEEE Transactions on Biomedical Engineering*, vol. PP, no. 99, 1 page, 2017.

[28] R. Boostani, B. Graimann, M. H. Moradi, and G. Pfurtscheller, "A comparison approach toward finding the best feature and classifier in cue-based BCI," *Medical & Biological Engineering & Computing*, vol. 45, no. 4, pp. 403–412, 2007.

[29] G. Pfurtscheller, R. Leeb, J. Faller, and C. Neuper, "Brain-computer interface systems used for virtual reality control," in *Virtual Reality*, pp. 4–20, 2011, http://www.intechopen.com/books/virtual-reality.

[30] G. Pfurtcheller, G. R. Müller-Putz, B. Graimann et al., "Graz-brain-computer inteface: Sate of research, in Toward Brain-Computer Interfacing," in *Graz-brain-computer inteface: Sate of research, in Toward Brain-Computer Interfacing*, G. Dornhege, J. D. R. Millán, T. Hinterberger, D. J. McFarland, and K. Müller, Eds., pp. 65–84, The MIT Press, 2007.

[31] G. Pfurtscheller and C. Neuper, "Motor imagery and direct brain-computer communication," *Proceedings of the IEEE*, vol. 89, no. 7, pp. 1123–1134, 2001.

[32] J. Wolpaw and E. Winter Wolpaw, *Brain-Computer Interfaces: Principles and Practice*, Oxford, New York, NY, USA, 2012.

[33] J. R. Wolpaw, "Brain-computer interfaces as new brain output pathways," *The Journal of Physiology*, vol. 579, no. 3, pp. 613–619, 2007.

[34] J. R. Wolpaw, N. Birbaumer, D. J. McFarland, G. Pfurtscheller, and T. M. Vaughan, "Brain-computer interfaces for communication and control," *Clinical Neurophysiology*, vol. 113, no. 6, pp. 767–791, 2002.

[35] T. O. Zander, J. Brönstrup, R. Lorenz, and L. R. Krol, "Towards BCI-based implicit control in human–computer interaction," in *Advances in Physiological Computing*, pp. 67–90, 2014.

[36] R. Chavarriaga, M. Fried-Oken, S. Kleih, and F. Lotte, "Heading for new shores! Overcoming pitfalls in BCI, Brain-Computer Interfaces," *Taylor Francis*, vol. IV, no. 1, pp. 60–73, 2016.

[37] C. Jeunet, B. N'Kaoua, R. N'Kambou, and F. Lotte, "Why and how to use intelligent tutoring systems to adapt mi-bci training to each user," in *Proceedings of the 6th International BCI Meeting*, Pacific Grove, Calif, USA, 2016.

[38] M. K. Holden, "Virtual environments for motor rehabilitation: review," *Cyberpsychology, Behavior, and Social Networking*, vol. 8, no. 3, pp. 187–211, 2005.

[39] B. Yazmir and M. Reiner, "I act, therefore I err: EEG correlates of success and failure in a virtual throwing game," *International Journal of Psychophysiology*, 2017.

[40] R. Scherer, F. Lee, A. Schlögl, R. Leeb, H. Bischof, and G. Pfurtscheller, "Toward self-paced brain-computer communication: navigation through virtual worlds," *IEEE Transactions on Biomedical Engineering*, vol. 55, no. 2, pp. 675–682, 2008.

[41] F. Lotte, Y. Renald, and A. Lécuyer, "Self-paced brain-computer interaction with virtual worlds: a quantitative and qualitative study out of the lab," in *Proceedings of the 4th International Brain Computer Interface Workshop and Training Course*, Graz, Austria, 2008.

[42] J. Faller, B. Z. Allison, C. Brunner et al., "A feasibility study on SSVEP-based interaction with motivating and immersive virtual and augmented reality," Human-Computer Interaction, 2017.

[43] G. F. Cyrino and J. C. Viana, "SBCI: 3D Simulator with Brain-Computer Interface and Virtual Reality," in *Proceedings of the 18th Symposium on Virtual and Augmented Reality, SVR 2016*, pp. 135–139, Brazil, June 2016.

[44] T. Ono, A. Kimura, and J. Ushiba, "Daily training with realistic visual feedback improves reproducibility of event-related desynchronisation following hand motor imagery," *Clinical Neurophysiology*, vol. 124, no. 9, pp. 1779–1786, 2013.

[45] S. Nagamine, Y. Hayashi, S. Yano, and T. Kondo, "An immersive virtual reality system for investigating human bodily self-consciousness," in *Proceedings of the 5th ICT International Student Project Conference, ICT-ISPC 2016*, pp. 97–100, Thailand, May 2016.

[46] F. Hoorn, E. A. Konijn, and G. C. Van der Veer, "Virtual reality: do not augment realism, augment relevance," *Upgrade-Human-Computer Interaction: Overcoming Barriers*, vol. 4, no. 1, pp. 18–26, 2003.

[47] D. Tan and A. Nijholt, "Brain-computer interfaces and human-computer interaction," in *Brain-Computer Interfaces*, pp. 3–19, Springer-Verlag, London, 1st edition edition, 2010.

[48] E. L. Deci and R. M. Ryan, "Self-determination theory and the facilitation of intrinsic motivation, social development, and well-being," *American Psychologist (Salma)*, vol. 55, no. 1, pp. 68–78, 2000.

[49] R. Leeb, R. Scherer, F. Lee, H. Bischof, and G. Pfurtscheller, "Navigation in virtual environments through motor imagery," in *Proceedings of the 9th Computer Vision Winter Workshop*, Piran, Slovenia.

[50] R. Scherer, F. Lee, A. Schlogl, R. Leeb, H. Bischof, and G. Pfurtscheller, "EEG-based interaction with virtual worlds: a self-paced three class brain-computer interface," in *BRAIN-PLAY 07 Brain-Computer Interfaces and Games Workshop at ACE (Advances in Computer Entertainment*, Graz, Austria, 2007.

[51] C. Neuper, R. Scherer, S. Wriessnegger, and G. Pfurtscheller, "Motor imagery and action observation: modulation of sensorimotor brain rhythms during mental control of a brain-computer interface," *Clinical Neurophysiology*, vol. 120, no. 2, pp. 239–247, 2009.

[52] J. D. Bayliss and D. H. Ballard, "A virtual reality testbed for brain-computer interface research," *IEEE Transactions on Neural Systems and Rehabilitation Engineering*, vol. 8, no. 2, pp. 188–190, 2000.

[53] C. Holzner, C. Guger, G. Edlinger, C. Grönegress, and M. Slater, "Virtual smart home controlled by thoughts," in *Proceedings of the 2009 18th IEEE International Workshops on Enabling Technologies: Infrastructures for Collaborative Enterprises, WETICE '09*, pp. 236–239, Netherlands, July 2009.

[54] J. Cecílio, J. Andrade, P. Martins, M. Castelo-Branco, and P. Furtado, "BCI framework based on games to teach people with cognitive and motor limitations," in *Proceedings of the 7th International Conference on Ambient Systems, Networks and Technologies, ANT 2016 and the 6th International Conference on Sustainable Energy Information Technology, SEIT 2016*, pp. 74–81, Spain, May 2016.

[55] S. M. Gordon, M. Jaswa, A. J. Solon, and V. J. Lawhern, "Real world BCI: cross-domain learning and practical applications," in *Proceedings of the 1st ACM Workshop on An Application-Oriented Approach to BCI Out of the Laboratory, BCIforReal 2017*, pp. 25–28, Cyprus.

[56] S. Yan, G. Ding, H. Li et al., "Enhancing audience engagement in performing arts through an adaptive virtual environment with a brain-computer interface," in *Proceedings of the 21st International Conference on Intelligent User Interfaces, IUI 2016*, pp. 306–316, USA, March 2016.

[57] J. Chun, B. Bae, and S. Jo, "BCI based hybrid interface for 3D object control in virtual reality," in *Proceedings of the 4th International Winter Conference on Brain-Computer Interface, BCI 2016*, Republic of Korea, February 2016.

[58] M. L. Chen, L. Yao, and N. Jiang, "Commanding wheelchair in virtual reality with thoughts by multiclass bci based on movement-related cortical potentials," *Journal of Computational Vision and Imaging Systems*, vol. 1, no. 2, 2016.

[59] V. Shih, D. Jangraw, S. Saproo, and P. Sajda, "Deep reinforcement learning using neurophysiological signatures of interest," in *Proceedings of the 12th Annual ACM/IEEE International Conference on Human-Robot Interaction, HRI 2017*, pp. 285-286, Austria, March 2017.

[60] I. Kosunen, A. Ruonala, M. Salminen, S. Järvelä, N. Ravaja, and G. Jacucci, "Neuroadaptive meditation in the real world," in *Proceedings of the 1st ACM Workshop on An Application-Oriented Approach to BCI Out of the Laboratory, BCIforReal 2017*, pp. 29–33, Cyprus.

[61] A. Herweg, J. Gutzeit, S. Kleih, and A. Kübler, "Wheelchair control by elderly participants in a virtual environment with a brain-computer interface (BCI) and tactile stimulation," *Biological Psychology*, vol. 121, pp. 117–124, 2016.

[62] Y.-T. Liu, S.-L. Wu, K.-P. Chou et al., "Driving fatigue prediction with pre-event electroencephalography (EEG) via a recurrent fuzzy neural network," in *Proceedings of the 2016 IEEE International Conference on Fuzzy Systems, FUZZ-IEEE 2016*, pp. 2488–2494, Canada, July 2016.

[63] M. de Tommaso, K. Ricci, M. Delussi et al., "Testing a novel method for improving wayfinding by means of a P3b Virtual Reality Visual Paradigm in normal aging," *SpringerPlus*, vol. 5, no. 1, article no. 1297, 2016.

[64] S. Saproo, V. Shih, D. C. Jangraw, and P. Sajda, "Neural mechanisms underlying catastrophic failure in human-machine interaction during aerial navigation," *Journal of Neural Engineering*, vol. 13, no. 6, Article ID 066005, 2016.

[65] J. Chen, D. Zhang, A. K. Engel, Q. Gong, and A. Maye, "Application of a single-flicker online SSVEP BCI," *PLoS ONE*, vol. 12, no. 5, 2017.

[66] J. Frey, C. Mühl, F. Lotte, and M. Hachet, Review of the use of electroencephalography as an evaluation method for human-computer interaction, 1311: 2222: arXiv, 2013.

[67] F. D. Rose, E. A. Attree, B. M. Brooks, and D. A. Johnson, "Virtual environments in brain damage rehabilitation: a rationale from basic Neuroscience," in *Virtual Environments in Clinical Psychology and Neuroscience*, G. Riva, B. K. Wiederhold, and E. Molinari, Eds., pp. 233–242, IOP Press, Amsterdam, Netherlands, 1998.

[68] D. M. Wolpert, Z. Ghahramani, and J. R. Flanagan, "Perspectives and problems in motor learning," *Trends in Cognitive Sciences*, vol. 5, no. 11, pp. 487–494, 2001.

[69] M. Darainy, S. Vahdat, and D. J. Ostry, "Plasticity in the human motor system induced by perceptual learning," in *Proceedings of the 2014 40th Annual Northeast Bioengineering Conference, NEBEC 2014*, Boston, Mass, USA, April 2014.

[70] D. J. Ostry and P. L. Gribble, "Sensory plasticity in human motor learning," *Trends in Neurosciences*, vol. 39, no. 2, pp. 114–123, 2016.

[71] F. Merienne, "Human factors consideration in the interaction process with virtual environment," *International Journal on Interactive Design and Manufacturing*, vol. 4, no. 2, pp. 83–86, 2010.

[72] K. M. Stanney, R. R. Mourant, and R. S. Kennedy, "Human factors issues in virtual environments: a review of the literature," *Presence: Teleoperators and Virtual Environments*, vol. 7, no. 4, pp. 327–351, 1998.

9

Research of Hubs Location Method for Weighted Brain Network Based on NoS-FA

Zhengkui Weng,[1,2] **Bin Wang,**[1] **Jie Xue,**[3] **Baojie Yang,**[1] **Hui Liu,**[1] **and Xin Xiong**[1]

[1]*Faculty of Information Engineering & Automation, Kunming University of Science and Technology, Kunming, China*
[2]*School of Communication and Information Engineering, Shanghai University, Shanghai, China*
[3]*College of Information and Network Security, Yunnan Police College, Kunming, China*

Correspondence should be addressed to Bin Wang; wangbin1@vip.sina.com

Academic Editor: Luis Vergara

As a complex network of many interlinked brain regions, there are some central hub regions which play key roles in the structural human brain network based on T1 and diffusion tensor imaging (DTI) technology. Since most studies about hubs location method in the whole human brain network are mainly concerned with the local properties of each single node but not the global properties of all the directly connected nodes, a novel hubs location method based on global importance contribution evaluation index is proposed in this study. The number of streamlines (NoS) is fused with normalized fractional anisotropy (FA) for more comprehensive brain bioinformation. The brain region importance contribution matrix and information transfer efficiency value are constructed, respectively, and then by combining these two factors together we can calculate the importance value of each node and locate the hubs. Profiting from both local and global features of the nodes and the multi-information fusion of human brain biosignals, the experiment results show that this method can detect the brain hubs more accurately and reasonably compared with other methods. Furthermore, the proposed location method is used in impaired brain hubs connectivity analysis of schizophrenia patients and the results are in agreement with previous studies.

1. Introduction

Human brain is one of the most complex systems in the world. The technology of human brain reconstruction based on nuclear magnetic resonance imaging (MRI) provides a powerful tool for the study of brain structure. The construction of human brain network may be realized in three levels: microscale (neuron), small-scale (neural cluster), and large-scale (brain region) [1]. Due to the physical particularity of the human brain and the limitation of magnetic resonance (MR) data collection technology, the large-scale brain region network is still the focus of current researches, which takes the different regions of the cerebral cortex as nodes and the specific connectivity between two brain regions as the edge of the network. Those researches based on large-scale human brain network can help people to study the overall structure and operation mechanism of human brain systematically because it can take advantage of graph theory and complex network theory [2]. The brain hubs refer to the phenomenon that there exist some central nodes in the structural human brain network, which have a large number of connections with other regions and play key roles in the topology of network [1, 3]. Recent studies have indicated the importance of these hubs in brain network. A small amount of hubs plays an important role in human brain's information transmission [4], and the damage of this kind of hubs will also cause a devastating impact on the whole human brain network [5]. Researches on hubs are helpful for diagnosis and treatment of common brain diseases such as Alzheimer's disease and schizophrenia [6]; furthermore, locating hub nodes in brain network and then mapping them onto the brain corresponding anatomical regions have an important clinical value in neurosurgical operation navigation for avoiding important brain functional region impairment [7].

In the studies for location method of brain hubs, a method using rich-club connectivity coefficient has been proposed to define the hub nodes [8] and it was verified in the comparison experiment between schizophrenic patients and healthy people [9]. The hubs definition methods based on degree centrality, betweenness centrality, and closeness centrality of nodes have been used to identify the hub nodes in the human brain network and the results were analyzed to compare the effects of these three different centrality indexes [10]. Another hub detecting method has been presented from the perspective of functional regions, which regarded the nodes involved in great number of subnetworks as potential hubs and then identified the real hubs from these potential hub nodes with spatial location information [11].

Currently in the researches of cognitive science and brain diseases, the most widely used brain hubs location methods are almost based on the betweenness centrality and degree centrality. On the basis of hubs identification method with betweenness centrality, the support vector machine algorithm was used to classify the patients with schizophrenia from normal people [12]. A rich-club connection coefficient with degree centrality was defined and the connections between core brains regions of the schizophrenic patients were found to be more sparse than the normal ones because the value is obviously decreased [13]. By comparing the hubs located with betweenness centrality value, those major depression disorder patients have shown abnormal changes in structural brain network compared with healthy people [14].

The aim of this study is to develop a framework for assessing the importance of regions in structural human brain network based on T1 and DTI data. Confined to the nodes local property, most hubs location methods only use one single index such as node degree centrality or betweenness centrality to define the importance of a region in the brain network, but as a part of complex system, the global performance of a node in the whole brain network is more important than its local performance. In this work, the number of white matter streamlines (NoS) between brain regions is taken as the weight to get a weighted adjacency matrix as the original human brain network. For more precise description of brain essential biological property, anisotropic fraction (FA) value is fused to correct the weight value deviation; then a new weighted brain adjacency matrix is built which is called NoS-FA matrix in this paper. Taking account of both local and global properties of a node, the brain region importance contribution matrix and information transmission efficiency value are constructed, respectively, based on NoS-FA matrix. Finally these two factors are used together to get an importance indicator for each node and then the hubs can be located according to the value.

Three experiments have been designed and finished to verify our proposed method. The results of hubs evaluation performance contrast experiment show that this method has better distinguishability and rationality. The results of vulnerability analysis experiment exhibit that hubs obtained with this method have more distinct influence on the overall density and efficiency of the human brain network when they are impaired. When applying this method for hubs locating in schizophrenia patients, siblings, and healthy people, the experiment results indicate that reasonable differences exist in these three groups which is in accordance with previous researches. The method proposed in this work could provide a new insight into systematic analysis of brain region and it is generalizable to the researches of how to find hub nodes in other similar networks.

2. Reconstruction of NoS-FA Weighted Brain Structural Network

2.1. Workflow for Reconstruction of Human Brain Structural Network. MR data was acquired on a 1.5 tesla GE scanner using the quadrature head coil and data acquisition included anatomical DTI and T1 weighted image. Acquisition parameters for the DTI-MR are as follows: high angular gradient set of 15 different weighted directions and 1 unweighted b0 scan; TR = 11000 ms, TE = 74.7 ms; b weighting of 1000 s/mm^2; matrix size = 128 × 128; field of view = 240 mm × 240 mm; slice thickness = 4 mm; slice gap = 0 mm; 35 slices covering the whole brain for each individual subject.

Several steps are necessary to construct the human brain structural network from T1 and diffusion MRI data as illustrated in Figure 1. Firstly T1 and DTI image data need to be acquired. Then the data need to be preprocessed, including format conversion of raw data, head realignment, eddy current distortions, and other necessary processing. Segmentation of the brain in white matter, grey matter, and Cerebrospinal Fluid (CSF) with T1 weighted image needs to be performed, and on this basis the brain cortical is divided into 83 brain regions by using Automated Anatomical Labeling (AAL) template in Cortical Parcellation with FreeSurfer [15], which will serve later on as 83 nodes of the brain structural network. With DTI image data the intravoxel reconstruction of diffusion information needs to be done to get the FA quantity and the fiber tracking needs to be performed with Tractography technique to get the number of streamlines between brain regions. These can be defined as the weight coefficients of the edges in the brain structural network [16]. The connectivity matrix is obtained by registering the two image spaces (morphological and diffusion). We can use the weighted human brain network adjacency matrix to represent the weighted human brain structural network. The color of each brain region changes from blue to red in the matrix, which represents the connectivity strengths that vary from the lowest to the highest. All the steps are processed with the Connectome Mapping Toolbox [17].

2.2. Fusing Method of NoS-FA Weighted Matrix. When using graph theory for the research, the weighted human brain network can be expressed with an undirected graph $G = \{V, E\}$, which consists of n nodes and m edges. Here $V = \{v_1, v_2, v_3, \ldots, v_n\}$ represents the collection of nodes and $E = \{e_1, e_2, e_3, \ldots, e_n\}$ represents the set of edges in the human brain network.

W is the weighted connective matrix of the network G and w_{ij} is used to represent the weight value between node i and node j. Since diffusion is a symmetric process and

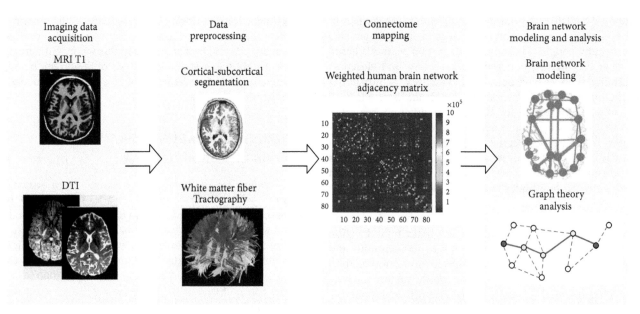

FIGURE 1: The workflow to create weighted human brain network.

the connection between two brain regions is regarded as undirected, W is a symmetric matrix; that is to say, $w_{ij} = w_{ji}$.

$$W = \begin{pmatrix} w_{11} & \cdots & w_{1j} \\ \vdots & \ddots & \vdots \\ w_{i1} & \cdots & w_{ij} \end{pmatrix}. \quad (1)$$

Taking the number of streamlines between brain regions M_{ij}^{NoS} as the strength of connection between adjacent nodes i and j, which is always a positive value [18], the edge weight value w_{ij} of the adjacency matrix should be

$$w_{ij}$$

$$= \begin{cases} \text{Inf}, & i = j, \\ M_{ij}, & i \neq j, \; i \text{ and } j \text{ are connected directly,} \\ 0, & i \neq j, \; i \text{ and } j \text{ are not connected directly.} \end{cases} \quad (2)$$

The number of streamlines connecting two regions is a simplistic and direct measure of connectivity, but in the process of Tractography, there exist a large number of white matter fibers crossing, convergence, and branching in a single voxel [19]. Because the size of each brain region is different, the region with larger area will access more fiber connections than the smaller ones. As a result, the numbers of streamlines between brain regions obtained by Tractography do have some deviations.

In order to reduce the influence of the deviations mentioned above, we propose a weighted adjacent matrix construction technique by fusing the fractional anisotropy index together with the number of streamlines. The fractional anisotropy value is based on the normalized variance of the eigenvalues and its range is between 0 and 1 (0 = isotropic diffusion, 1 = highly directional). As a physical characteristic of

different tissues in the brain, the FA value of the same object is comparability in different time, different objects, and different imaging equipment [20, 21]. FA can give information about the shape of the diffusion tensor at each voxel and it is a kind of diffusion properties of water molecules in the brain, so it can be used to characterize the connectivity strength among each pair of brain region.

Firstly, in order to eliminate the influence of different physical variables, the FA weighted adjacent matrix M^{FA} is normalized as follows:

$$M_{ij}^{\text{FA}} = \frac{M_{ij}^{\text{FA}} - \min M_{ij}^{\text{FA}}}{\max M_{ij}^{\text{FA}} - \min M_{ij}^{\text{FA}}}. \quad (3)$$

Then taking M_{ij}^{FA} as the correction parameters, each element in M_{ij}^{NoS} adjacency matrix is combined with this value so as to get a fused NoS-FA weighted adjacency matrix $M_{ij}^{\text{NoS-FA}}$ which is defined as

$$M_{ij}^{\text{NoS-FA}} = M_{ij}^{\text{NoS}} \times M_{ij}^{\text{FA}}. \quad (4)$$

This network has included not only the connection strength of fibers between two connected brain regions but also the inherent physical property of each region, so it can show more comprehensive bioinformation of the brain and we will take it as the foundation of our study in this work.

3. Human Brain Hubs Location Method Based on NoS-FA Matrix

3.1. Construction of Brain Region Importance Evaluation Matrix. Just like other complex networks, the human brain network is an integration of nodes and edges, and the importance of each node will be affected by all those connections which it has. That means when change happened with even one node, it will lead to the disorder or collapse of the entire network [22]. The relationships with other brain regions have very important influence on the performance of a node, and it is not enough to describe the complexity of topological relation only by the local characteristic of the brain region. On the basis of reference [23], in which a contribution matrix of the node importance degree in undirected and unweighted networks was presented, a hub evaluation method with weighted importance contribution matrix is proposed in our work. In this method, both the contribution of a single brain region for the other connected brain regions in the whole brain network and the information transfer ability of this brain region are considered together to find the hubs in the brain network effectively.

In a brain structural network with n brain regions, if the average connection degree of all brain regions is $\overline{k}$, which indicates the average number of all connections in the human brain, and the average brain connection strength is $\overline{S}$, which represents the average number of white matter fibers in all brain regions, then a single brain region v_i will have a contribution $D_i/\overline{Sk}^2$ to its connected brain regions. Because the NoS-FA adjacency matrix is weighted, the contribution of each brain region v_i to other connected brain regions should also consider the weight value w_{ij}, so the importance contribution matrix of brain regions in the human brain network H_{BRIM} is defined as

$$
H_{\mathrm{BRIM}} = \begin{bmatrix} 1 & \dfrac{D_2 w_{21}}{\overline{Sk}^2} & \cdots & \dfrac{D_n w_{n1}}{\overline{Sk}^2} \\ \dfrac{D_1 w_{12}}{\overline{Sk}^2} & 1 & \cdots & \dfrac{D_n w_{n2}}{\overline{Sk}^2} \\ \vdots & \vdots & \cdots & \vdots \\ \dfrac{D_1 w_{1n}}{\overline{Sk}^2} & \dfrac{D_2 w_{2n}}{\overline{Sk}^2} & \cdots & 1 \end{bmatrix}. \tag{5}
$$

Here the diagonal elements have a contribution value of 1.

On the other hand, in order to reflect the ability of a single brain region v_i in the information process, the information transmission efficiency E_i^w is defined as

$$
E_i^w = \frac{1}{n} \sum_{i \in n} \frac{\sum_{j,h \in n, j \neq i} a_{ij} a_{jh} \left(d_{ij}^w\right)^{-1}}{D_i \left(D_i - 1\right)}. \tag{6}
$$

Here a_{ij} is used to indicate whether there is a direct link between nodes i and j, if the connection exists, $a_{ij} = 1$; otherwise, $a_{ij} = 0$. d_{ij}^w represents the shortest weighted distance between two different brain regions, which is the harmonic mean weight of each brain region.

$$
d_{ij}^w = \min \left(\frac{1}{1/w_{ik} + \cdots + 1/w_{nj}}, \frac{1}{1/w_{iv} + \cdots + 1/w_{wj}}, \right.
$$
$$
\left. \cdots, \frac{1}{1/w_{il} + \cdots + 1/w_{kj}} \right). \tag{7}
$$

It can be seen from the definition of E_i^w that the transmission efficiency can reflect how important a brain region

is in the information transfer process in human brain. If E_i^w value of a brain region is very big that means it plays a more important role in information transmission; therefore, when this brain region is injured, the information transmission ability of the whole brain network will suffer a greater loss.

By now for each brain region we have a local contribution index $D_i \omega_{ij}/\overline{Sk}^2$ and a global importance property index E_i^w; then the values of these two index are integrated into an evaluation matrix H_{RC} as follows:

$$
H_{\mathrm{RC}} = \begin{bmatrix} E_1^w & \dfrac{D_2 w_{21}}{\overline{Sk}^2} E_2^w & \cdots & \dfrac{D_n w_{n1}}{\overline{Sk}^2} E_n^w \\ \dfrac{D_1 w_{12}}{\overline{Sk}^2} E_1^w & E_2^w & \cdots & \dfrac{D_n w_{n2}}{\overline{Sk}^2} E_n^w \\ \vdots & \vdots & \cdots & \vdots \\ \dfrac{D_1 w_{1n}}{\overline{Sk}^2} E_1^w & \dfrac{D_2 w_{2n}}{\overline{Sk}^2} E_2^w & \cdots & E_n^w \end{bmatrix}. \tag{8}
$$

Here $H_{\mathrm{RC}}(i, j)$ indicates the important influence of brain region i to brain region j, which depends not only on the quantity of white matter fibers between i and j but also on the important level of brain region i in the information transmission. Through the application of the hubs evaluation matrix H_{RC}, the important index of brain regions is expressed as follows:

$$
\mathrm{RC}_i = E_i^w \times \frac{\sum_{j=1, j \neq i}^{n} D_j w_{ji} E_j^w}{\overline{Sk}^2}. \tag{9}
$$

We can calculate all the RC_i values in the brain network and choose the 15 highest values of the brain regions as hubs in a human brain network [24].

3.2. Workflow of Hubs Location Based on Important Index RC_i. The brain hubs location algorithm based on important index considers both the global property of a brain region and the relationships with other connected regions in the brain; the overall workflow is as follows:

(1) The quantity of white matter fiber between regions is fused with anisotropic fraction value of this region to get $M^{\mathrm{NoS\text{-}FA}}$ according to (4), which is used as the input data of the algorithm.

(2) The importance matrix of all brain regions to the other connected brain regions is computed, respectively, according to (5).

(3) The information transfer efficiency values of each region are computed with (6) and integrated into the relative importance matrix.

(4) RC_i value is calculated according to (8) and (9), which represents the importance of each brain region.

Ranking the RC_i values in descending order, the nodes with the first 15 highest values are considered as hubs in brain structural network.

The algorithm flow diagram is shown as Figure 2.

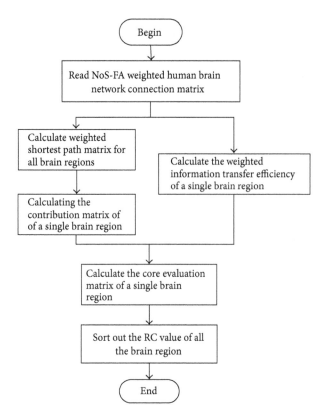

FIGURE 2: The workflow of weighted human brain network hubs location process.

4. Effect Analysis of Hubs Location Algorithm Based on NoS-FA Matrix

4.1. Effectiveness Analysis of the Algorithm. We use both the weighted betweenness hubs location method which is the most popular method in evaluating brain hubs and proposed hubs location method to calculate the importance value of each brain region for the same healthy people's brain network, and the results were shown in Figure 3.

There are three improvements when using the proposed method. Firstly, from the results, we can see when using the region evaluation method with weighted betweenness that there exist some nodes that have the same importance value. While in the results based on the proposed method every region has different value of importance, so our method is more accurate for evaluating the importance of brain regions. In addition, it can be seen clearly in the region evaluation results with weighted betweenness method that some brain regions have the same importance value of zero, but it is impossible for a region to have no importance in the network. While in the results of proposed method even the last one also has a no-zero importance value, so our method is more reasonable for evaluating the importance of brain regions. Finally in the region evaluation results with weighted betweenness method, the distribution of importance value is more even and the values in different regions are closed to each other. While in the results with proposed method the distribution looks sharper, the difference between the hubs and other noncore nodes in the brain network is more

apparent. For further analysis, the most important 15 brain regions located with two methods and some corresponding properties are listed in sort order in Table 1.

The location of hubs with the proposed method in brain space is shown in Figure 4; it can be seen that the human brain hubs are mainly located on the frontal lobe, parietal lobe, and the flat layer part of the organization, including the superior parietal gyrus, parietal gyrus, superior frontal gyrus, precentral gyrus, paracentral gyrus, thalamus, putamen, and brain stem. Benefitting from fusing two kinds of bioinformation, the NoS-FA weighted network involves more comprehensive information of brain, so it can distinguish the hub nodes from those noncore nodes more accurately; at the same time, the ranking of hubs importance value is more reasonable and highly recognizable.

4.2. Algorithm Vulnerability Analysis and Comparison. In order to verify the actual importance of the hubs, which are located by the proposed algorithm, the vulnerability analysis experiment is presented in our work. When a node in the network is removed, the global property of the network will be changed. Usually the ratio of the change of network property to the network property before the removal is defined as the vulnerability [25]. The greater vulnerability a node has, the higher damage will be put on the entire network, and the role of this node is more important. It needs to be emphasized that, in the experiment, when one node is removed, all the white matter fibers, which are connected with this brain regions, are invalid and the NoS weight of related edges in the network will be zero. Therefore, the vulnerability of brain region i is defined as

$$V_i = \frac{\text{PropValue} - \text{PropValue}'}{\text{PropValue}}. \tag{10}$$

Here PropValue represents one kind of network properties value before a node is removed, and PropValue$'$ represents this property value after the removal. In this research, the network properties of global efficiency and network density are taken as the vulnerability analysis parameters, respectively, which are shown as

$$\text{DensityValue} = \frac{\sum_{i=1,j=1}^{n} M_{ij} \left(w_{ij} \neq 0 \right)}{n \left(n - 1 \right)},$$

$$\text{EfficiencyRating} = \frac{1}{n} \sum_{i \in n} \frac{\sum_{j \in n, j \neq i} \left(d_{ij}^{w} \right)^{-1}}{n - 1}. \tag{11}$$

The network density reflects the ratio of the actual number of edges and the maximum number of edges the network may have, and it is an important attribute to test the network size. The global efficiency reflects the information transmission capability of a network.

To compare the influence that a hub may have on the entire brain network, three cases are considered in this experiment: brain hubs are computed and chosen with our proposed method, with weighted betweenness method or at random. The vulnerability change curves of three methods

TABLE 1: Comparison of the evaluation results under different methods.

Hub order number	Weighted betweenness method			Proposed method		
	Importance value	Region number	region name	Importance value	Region number	Region name
1	1234	12	R-RAC	15.515	8	R-SF
2	1162	56	L-ISTC	13.099	49	L-SF
3	748	32	R-ST	12.868	37	R-PUT
4	714	63	L-PCAL	8.070	78	L-PUT
5	644	62	L-CUN	7.987	83	BS
6	622	42	L-LOF	7.204	35	R-THA
7	616	15	R-ISTC	6.942	18	R-SP
8	598	37	R-PUT	5.972	10	R-PREC
9	568	59	L-SMAR	5.892	59	L-SP
10	498	36	R-CAU	5.315	76	L-THA
11	482	55	L-PC	4.693	51	L-PREC
12	472	35	R-THA	4.346	60	L-IP
13	448	25	R-FUS	2.961	19	R-IP
14	448	34	R-INS	2.942	20	R-PCUN
15	436	71	L-MT	2.509	34	R-INS

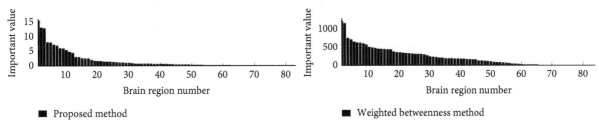

FIGURE 3: Comparison of the region evaluation results with different methods.

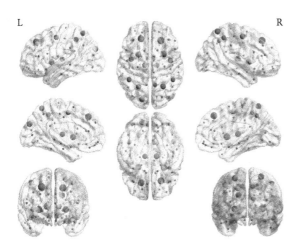

FIGURE 4: Location map of hubs in weighted human brain network based on NoS-FA.

are given and compared as shown in Figure 5. It can be seen that when one brain region is damaged, the properties of the whole brain network have also changed and the hubs obtained by proposed method have the greatest impact on the overall properties of the human brain network in both density and efficiency. Because both the local characteristic of

a single brain region and the global contribution that a brain region has to its connected regions are considered together, the evaluation process is based on more comprehensive bioinformation and so the hubs located with this method will have more important influence on the human brain network.

4.3. Hubs Property Analysis of Schizophrenia. The proposed method was applied to the MRI data of schizophrenia for the analysis of human brain structural network changing. Total of 205 people were divided into three groups: schizophrenia patients group (Patients) with 62 people, siblings of patients (Siblings) with 83 people, and healthy people group (healthy people) with 60 people. All the MRI data were processed according to the workflow in Figure 1.

Firstly three types of global brain network properties were calculated, respectively, to make the comparison. (1) Brain region connection strength $S = (1/N) \sum_{j \in N} a_{ij}$, which is the mean value of the weight values of all connections in the weighted brain network. The connection strength is the direct reflection of the numbers of white matter fibers in the human brain network. (2) The global efficiency $E = (1/N) \sum_{i=1, i \neq k}^{n} (1/d_{ki})$ of the brain network, which is the mean of all the reciprocals of the shortest path. Efficiency value reflects the transmission speed of information in the human brain network. (3) Clustering coefficient $C = (1/N) \sum_{i \in v} C_i$ of

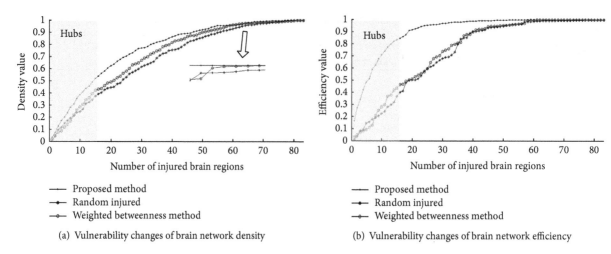

(a) Vulnerability changes of brain network density

(b) Vulnerability changes of brain network efficiency

FIGURE 5: Vulnerability change comparison of brain network vulnerability.

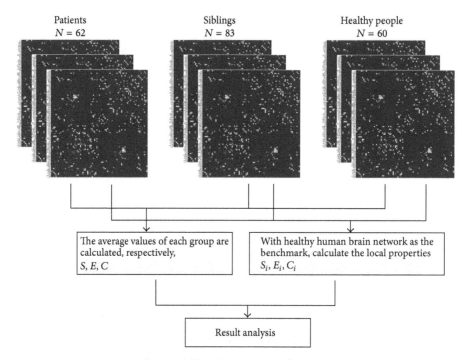

FIGURE 6: Experiment process diagram.

the brain network, which is the mean value of all clustering coefficients of all regions. Clustering coefficient is a measure of the degree of brain network group indicating the extent of the network clustering.

Taking the healthy human brain network as the benchmark, three local property values of each hub were calculated for each subject: connection strength $S_i = \sum_{j \in N} a_{ij}$, local efficiency $E_i = \sum_{i=1, i \neq k}^{n} (1/d_{ki})$, and clustering coefficient $C_i = 2E_i/k_i(k_i - 1)$; then the average values in each groups were calculated, respectively. The experiment is designed as the process shown in Figure 6 and all the computations are executed by the MATLAB brain connectivity toolbox [26].

The experiment results are shown in Table 2. The average global properties values of the brain network are presented in Table 2(a); the average local properties values with weighted betweenness method are presented in Table 2(b) and the average local properties values with proposed method are presented in Table 2(c). It can be seen from the results in Table 2 that both global and local properties in patients, siblings, and healthy people group have shown some interesting differences.

The global properties values are shown in Table 2(a), and compared with healthy group, the average values of connection strength, global efficiency, and clustering coefficient in patients group were decreased by 3.95%, 2.69%, and 3.55%, respectively. The significant ordered differences, such that healthy people > siblings > patients, were found in both connection strength and clustering coefficient, while for global efficiency patient group has a weak higher value than sibling group but still lower than healthy group.

TABLE 2: Experiment results comparison.

(a) Global properties values of the human brain network

Experimental group	Connection strength	Global efficiency	Clustering coefficient
Healthy people	9261.2	224.27	134.74
Siblings	9030.7	214.34	127.25
Patients	8895.3	218.24	122.49

(b) Local properties values of hubs based on weighted betweenness method

Experimental group	Connection strength	Local efficiency	Clustering coefficient
Healthy people	14491	231.57	102.92
Siblings	14188	221.82	99.95
Patients	14170	222.58	98.82

(c) Local properties values of hubs based on the proposed method

Experimental group	Connection strength	Local efficiency	Clustering coefficient
Healthy people	28097	410.74	189.37
Siblings	27142	392.82	181.56
Patients	25365	376.04	173.33

TABLE 3: Variance analysis results.

(a) Variance analysis result of connection strength S_i

	Sum of square	Degree of freedom	Mean of square	F	Sig.
Between-group	2.369E8	2	1.185E8	8.496	.000
Intragroup	2.817E9	202	13943176.62		
Total	3.053E9	204			

(b) Variance analysis result of clustering coefficient C_i

	Sum of square	Degree of freedom	Mean of square	F	Sig.
Between-group	7851.000	2	3925.500	5.325	.006
Intragroup	148924.522	202	737.250		
Total	156775.522	204			

(c) Variance analysis result of local efficiency E_i

	Sum of square	Degree of freedom	Mean of square	F	Sig.
Between-group	36705.578	2	18352.789	5.864	.003
Intragroup	632256.889	202	3129.985		
Total	668962.467	204			

The local properties values based on weighted betweenness method are shown in Table 2(b). The sequence that healthy people > siblings > patients still can be found but not so obvious in connection strength and clustering coefficient between three groups. The local efficiency of patient group is very close to that of sibling group, but the former was slightly higher than the latter.

For the local properties values based on the proposed method in Table 2(c), the significant ordered difference is that healthy people > siblings > patients were found clearly in connection strength, clustering coefficient, and local efficiency. The average values of hubs' local efficiency were the highest in healthy people, intermediate in siblings (4.36% reduced relative to healthy people), and lowest in patients (8.44% reduced compared with healthy people). Connection strength in patients hubs was decreased by 9.72% compared with healthy people and 6.55% compared with siblings.

Clustering coefficients in patients hubs were decreased by 8.47% compared with healthy people and 4.53% compared with siblings.

These results are consistent with the conclusion in [13]. More importantly, from the results of the above analysis, we can see that the difference between the hubs of healthy people, siblings, and patients in the proposed method is more apparent than in weighted betweenness method. These results indicate that hubs location with method proposed in this paper is more reasonable and accurate than the weighted betweenness method, which is most popular in finding hubs at present researches.

At the meantime, analysis of variance (ANOVA) was finished in our work to test the data difference and the results are shown in Table 3. The F value of connection strength S_i, clustering coefficient C_i, and local efficiency E_i was 8.496, 5.325, and 5.864, and the P value of each group was less than 0.05.

5. Conclusions

In this work, we presented a novel hub location method for the human brain structural network, which is based on MRI image reconstruction technique. One meaningful work is that the NoS weights matrix was fused with FA values to get more comprehensive bioinformation for brain region connections. The other valuable work is the construction of contribution matrix of the region's importance, which is an index including local contribution of a region to other correlative brain regions and the global transmission efficiency of this region in NoS-FA weighted human brain network. The experiment results testify that the proposed method can provide more precise and reasonable hubs location method compared with the most frequently used weighted betweenness evaluation index. The experiment results also emphasize the findings discovered by other researches; the hubs of human brain network in schizophrenia patients are impaired compared with healthy people.

Acknowledgments

This study was supported by the National Nature Science Foundation of China (Grant no. 61263017).

References

[1] M. Rubinov and O. Sporns, "Complex network measures of brain connectivity: Uses and interpretations," *NeuroImage*, vol. 52, no. 3, pp. 1059–1069, 2010.

[2] F. Jinqing, "Exploring progress on brain networks (I): research characteristics, methods and three major types," *Chinese Journal of Nature*, vol. 34, no. 6, pp. 344–349, 2012.

[3] S. Zhou and R. J. Mondragón, "The rich-club phenomenon in the internet topology," *IEEE Communications Letters*, vol. 8, no. 3, pp. 180–182, 2004.

[4] M. Daianu, N. Jahanshad, and T. M. Nir, "Rich club analysis in the Alzheimer's disease connectome reveals a relatively undisturbed structural core network," *Human Brain Mapping*, vol. 36, no. 8, p. 3087, 2015.

[5] M. Colombo and O. Sporns, "Discovering the human connectome," *Minds and Machines*, vol. 24, no. 2, pp. 217–220, 2014.

[6] M. Colombo and O. Sporns, "Networks of the brain," *Minds and Machines*, vol. 23, no. 2, pp. 259–262, 2013.

[7] L. Harriger, M. P. van den Heuvel, and O. Sporns, "Rich Club Organization of Macaque Cerebral Cortex and Its Role in Network Communication," *PLoS ONE*, vol. 7, no. 9, Article ID e46497, 2012.

[8] M. P. Van den Heuvel and O. Sporns, "Rich-club organization of the human connectome," *The Journal of Neuroscience*, vol. 31, no. 44, pp. 15775–15786, 2011.

[9] O. Sporns, C. J. Honey, and R. Kötter, "Identification and classification of hubs in brain networks," *PLoS ONE*, vol. 2, no. 10, pp. e10491–e104914, 2007.

[10] R. GeethaRamani and K. Sivaselvi, "Human brain hubs (provincial and connector) identification using centrality measures," in *Proceedings of the 4th International Conference on Recent Trends in Information Technology (ICRTIT '14)*, April 2014.

[11] J. Power, B. Schlaggar, C. Lessov-Schlaggar, and S. Petersen, "Evidence for hubs in human functional brain networks," *Neuron*, vol. 79, no. 4, pp. 798–813, 2013.

[12] H. Cheng, S. Newman, J. Goñi et al., "Nodal centrality of functional network in the differentiation of schizophrenia," *Schizophrenia Research*, vol. 168, no. 1-2, article 6499, pp. 345–352, 2015.

[13] G. Collin, R. S. Kahn, M. A. De Reus, W. Cahn, and M. P. Van Den Heuvel, "Impaired rich club connectivity in unaffected siblings of schizophrenia patients," *Schizophrenia Bulletin*, vol. 40, no. 2, pp. 438–448, 2014.

[14] M. S. Korgaonkar, A. Fornito, L. M. Williams, and S. M. Grieve, "Abnormal structural networks characterize major depressive disorder: a connectome analysis," *Biological Psychiatry*, vol. 76, no. 7, pp. 567–574, 2014.

[15] N. Tzourio-Mazoyer, B. Landeau, D. Papathanassiou et al., "Automated anatomical labeling of activations in SPM using a macroscopic anatomical parcellation of the MNI MRI single-subject brain," *NeuroImage*, vol. 15, no. 1, pp. 273–289, 2002.

[16] A. R. F. da Silva, "Generalized diffusion tractography based on directional data clustering," *Studies in Computational Intelligence*, vol. 577, pp. 311–320, 2014.

[17] A. Daducci, S. Gerhard, A. Griffa et al., "The connectome mapper: an open-source processing pipeline to map connectomes with MRI," *PLoS ONE*, vol. 7, no. 12, Article ID e48121, 2012.

[18] T. Liu, D. Zeng-Ru, and D. Hong, "Effect of distribution of weight on the efficiency of weighted networks," *Acta Physica Sinica*, vol. 60, no. 2, pp. 797–802, 2011.

[19] Y. Zhang and Z.-J. Song, "Advance in the study of white matter tractography," *Fudan University Journal of Medical Sciences*, vol. 1, no. 1, pp. 1–7, 2014.

[20] W. S. Feng, "Clinical outcome prediction of the DTI quantification of spinal cord with high intensity signal on 3.0T MRI in Cervical Spondylotic Myelopathy and corresponding pathological mechanism," Southern Medical University, 2013.

[21] H. Guang-wu, L. Yuan-xiang, and S. Tian-zhen, "Study development of MR diffusion tensor imaging on brain," *Chinese imaging journal of integrated traditional and western medicine*, vol. 4, no. 2, pp. 131–134, 2006.

[22] K. Zhang, P. Li, B. Zhu, and M. Hu, "Evaluation method for node importance in directed-weighted complex networks based on PageRank," *Journal of Nanjing University of Aeronautics and Astronautics*, vol. 45, no. 3, pp. 429–434, 2013.

[23] Z. Xuan, Z. Feng-ming, and L. Ke-wu, "Finding vital node by node importance evaluation matrix in complex networks," *Acta Physica Sinica*, vol. 61, no. 5, pp. 1–7, 2012.

[24] G. Ball, P. Aljabar, S. Zebari et al., "Rich-club organization of the newborn human brain," *Proceedings of the National Academy of Sciences of the United States of America*, vol. 111, no. 20, pp. 7456–7461, 2014.

[25] C. Pan, W. Xiao-feng, and L. Yi, "Attack strategy for uncertain topology of complex networks," *Application Research of Computers*, vol. 27, no. 12, pp. 4622-4623, 2010.

[26] M. Rubinov, R. Kötter, P. Hagmann, and O. Sporns, "Brain connectivity toolbox: a collection of complex network measurements and brain connectivity datasets," *NeuroImage*, vol. 47, Supplement 1, p. S169, 2009.

10

Classification of Hand Grasp Kinetics and Types Using Movement-Related Cortical Potentials and EEG Rhythms

Mads Jochumsen,[1] Cecilie Rovsing,[1] Helene Rovsing,[1] Imran Khan Niazi,[1,2,3] Kim Dremstrup,[1] and Ernest Nlandu Kamavuako[1]

[1]Centre for Sensory-Motor Interaction, Department of Health Science and Technology, Aalborg University, Aalborg, Denmark
[2]New Zealand College of Chiropractic, Auckland, New Zealand
[3]Rehabilitation Research Institute, Auckland University of Technology (AUT), Auckland, New Zealand

Correspondence should be addressed to Mads Jochumsen; mj@hst.aau.dk

Academic Editor: Saeid Sanei

Detection of single-trial movement intentions from EEG is paramount for brain-computer interfacing in neurorehabilitation. These movement intentions contain task-related information and if this is decoded, the neurorehabilitation could potentially be optimized. The aim of this study was to classify single-trial movement intentions associated with two levels of force and speed and three different grasp types using EEG rhythms and components of the movement-related cortical potential (MRCP) as features. The feature importance was used to estimate encoding of discriminative information. Two data sets were used. 29 healthy subjects executed and imagined different hand movements, while EEG was recorded over the contralateral sensorimotor cortex. The following features were extracted: delta, theta, mu/alpha, beta, and gamma rhythms, readiness potential, negative slope, and motor potential of the MRCP. Sequential forward selection was performed, and classification was performed using linear discriminant analysis and support vector machines. Limited classification accuracies were obtained from the EEG rhythms and MRCP-components: 0.48 ± 0.05 (grasp types), 0.41 ± 0.07 (kinetic profiles, motor execution), and 0.39 ± 0.08 (kinetic profiles, motor imagination). Delta activity contributed the most but all features provided discriminative information. These findings suggest that information from the entire EEG spectrum is needed to discriminate between task-related parameters from single-trial movement intentions.

1. Introduction

The detection of movement intentions is an essential part of a brain-computer interface (BCI) for motor rehabilitation after a stroke [1]. By detecting movement intentions from the ongoing EEG, it is possible to activate an electrical stimulator or rehabilitation robot [2, 3], so the elicited somatosensory feedback is paired with motor cortical activity. In this way, the requirement for Hebbian learning is fulfilled. The detection of movement intentions from EEG, specifically movement-related cortical potentials (MRCPs), has been thoroughly investigated and several techniques exist to detect executed and imaginary movements from healthy subjects and attempted movements from patients suffering from spinal cord injury or stroke [4–9]. Recent studies have

been published where the efficacy of BCI interventions for neurorehabilitation has shown promising results [1, 2]. To improve BCI interventions, task variability can be introduced into the rehabilitation which maximizes the retention of relearned movements [10]. Some studies have shown that it is possible to decode different task-related parameters from the same limb such as movement direction, movement type, force, and speed [7, 11–15]; by decoding such parameters, variability may be introduced in the training. In these studies, a wide variety of signal processing techniques and features have been used. The features, as for the movement intention detection, have primarily been extracted from the time and frequency domain. The features include mean amplitude in different time windows, either chosen systematically or based on the underlying physiology/signal morphology [7, 15], and spectral power in frequency bands that are systematically chosen with a width of, for example, 1–5 Hz or from the physiological EEG rhythms [7, 14, 16]. Other types of features have also been used such as time-frequency representations [17]. The features are often selected in an exhaustive systematic way to identify the features (and best channels) that fit the individual subject; in this way, it is possible to account for the great intersubject variability [7]. In summary, these studies show that task-related parameters can be decoded from single-trial analysis using different features extracted from premovement EEG. However, information is lacking regarding the importance of the features and where the discriminative information arise from in the physiologically established measures of EEG and MRCPs, that is, delta, theta, mu/alpha, beta, and gamma rhythms, readiness potential, negative slope, and motor potential, respectively. It has previously been shown that the components of the MRCP are modulated by variations in force and speed [18], but it is not known how variations in, for example, grasp types affect MRCPs. Moreover, it is not known how these task-related parameters modulate the different EEG rhythms. As outlined, many different kinds of features from the time and frequency domain have been used to classify single-trial EEG traces to discriminate between task-related parameters, but using only the established EEG rhythms (not to be mixed with the event-related synchronization/desynchronization) and MRCP components as features have not been evaluated. By testing this, it may be possible to explain the importance of the different features and give an indication of where the discriminative information is encoded.

In the current study, it was investigated if using the established EEG rhythms and MRCP components, extracted from the premovement EEG, can be used as features to discriminate between different task-related parameters for hand movements. Moreover, the importance of each feature type was investigated. For this investigation, two previously published data sets [6, 7] were used, which enables a direct comparison with previous results.

2. Methods

In the following sections, the data collection will be outlined as well as the analysis used in the current study.

2.1. Subjects.
29 healthy subjects participated; 14 subjects (7 women and 7 men: 24 ± 1 years old) performed different grasp types (motor execution, data set 1), while 15 subjects (12 women and 3 men: 27 ± 11 years old) performed the same grasp type but with variations in the level of force and speed (motor execution and imagination, data set 2). All subjects gave their written informed consent. All procedures were approved by the local ethical committee (number 20130081).

2.2. Experimental Setup.
The subjects were seated in a comfortable chair with their right hand resting on a table in front of them. The subjects held a handgrip dynamometer which was used to record the force that was produced. The right hand was dominant in all subjects except for one. At the beginning of the experiment, the maximum voluntary contraction (MVC) was determined. In data set 1 [7], the subjects were asked to perform three different hand grasps: palmar, lateral, and pinch grasps, where they had to reach ~5% MVC in 0.5 s (see (A2) in Figure 1). Each movement type was performed 4 × 25 times with a 1-minute break in-between each every 25th movement. Two consecutive movements were separated with 9 s. The movements were performed in blocks; the order was randomized. The subjects were visually cued (see (A2) in Figure 1) by a custom-made program (Aalborg University), and the produced force was recorded and used as input, so the subjects had continuous visual feedback. The subjects spent ~5 minutes practicing to become familiar with the setup.

In data set 2 [6], the subjects were asked to execute and imagine four isometric palmar grasps. The tasks were as follows: 0.5 s to reach 20% MVC, 0.5 s to reach 60% MVC, 3 s to reach 20% MVC, and 3 s to reach 60% MVC; each task was repeated 40 times. The subjects were visually cued (see (A1) in Figure 1), and they were provided with visual feedback in the same way as described above to ensure that the movements were performed with the correct level of speed and force. No force was produced for the imagined movements, but the subjects were still provided with the feedback, so they knew when to initiate the imagined movement. The tasks were randomized in blocks, and the subjects trained for two minutes before each task.

2.3. Recordings

2.3.1. EEG.
Continuous monopolar (Ag/AgCl ring electrodes) EEG (EEG Amplifiers, Nuamps Express, Neuroscan) was recorded from the following channels (according to the International 10–20 system): F5, F3, F1, Fz, FC5, FC3, FC1, FCz, C5, C3, C1, Cz, CP5, CP3, CP1, CPz, P5, P3, P1, and Pz; moreover, F7, FT7, T7, TP7, and P7 for the subjects performing three different hand grasps (data set 1). The signals were referenced to the right ear lobe and grounded at nasion. Electrooculography (EOG) was recorded from FP1. The EEG and EOG were sampled with 500 Hz and converted with 32-bit precision. The impedance of all electrodes was below 5 kΩ. During the recordings, the subjects were asked to minimize eye blinks and facial and body movements. Epochs were rejected if they were contaminated with EOG, peak-peak amplitude exceeding 125 μV. A digital trigger was sent from the visual cueing program to the EEG amplifier at the beginning of each trial (at $t = -3$ s in (A1) and (A2) in Figure 1).

2.3.2. Force and Maximum Voluntary Contraction.
A handgrip dynamometer (Noraxon USA, Scottsdale, AZ) was used to record the force, which was used as input to the visual cueing program. The force was sampled with 2000 Hz. The MVC was determined at the beginning of the experiment, where the subject performed three maximal contractions separated by one minute. The highest value of the three contractions was used as the MVC. For the tasks where the movements were executed, the force was used to determine the movement onset. This was defined as the instant where

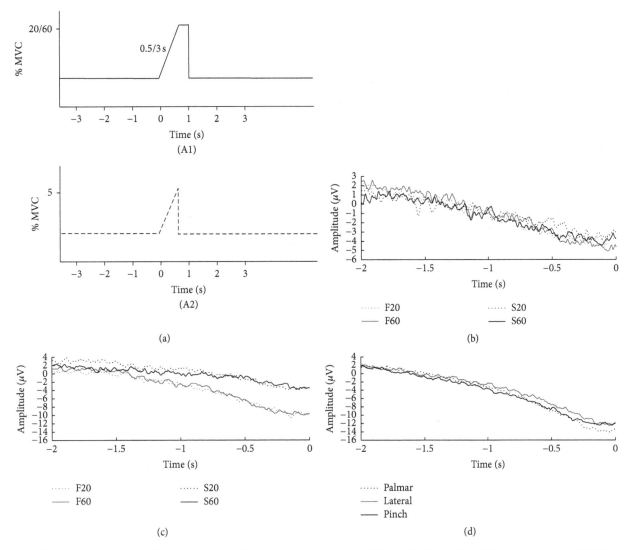

FIGURE 1: (a) Visual cues presented to the subjects performing movements with different kinetic profiles (A1) and grasp types (A2), (b) grand average across trials and subjects for imaginary movements with different kinetic profiles in channel C3, (c) grand average across trials and subjects for executed movements with different kinetic profiles in channel C3, and (d) grand average across trials and subjects for different executed grasp types in channel C3. F20: fast (0.5 s) 20% MVC, F60: fast (0.5 s) 60% MVC, S20: slow (3 s) 20% MVC, and S60: slow (3 s) 60% MVC. Note the difference in amplitude on the y-axis in (b). MVC: maximum voluntary contraction.

all values in a 200-ms wide moving time window were above the baseline. The baseline was calculated from the recordings during the rest phase. All onsets were visually inspected.

2.4. Signal Processing

2.4.1. Preprocessing. Initially, the signals were bandpass filtered from 0.05 to 45 Hz using a 2nd order zero-phase digital Butterworth filter. For dataset 2, a large Laplacian spatial filter was applied to be able to compare the findings in the current study with the ones reported previously [6]. F7, F3, Fz, T7, C3, Cz, P7, P3, and Pz were used to calculate a surrogate channel with C3 as the central channel [6]. The continuous EEG was divided into epochs from the movement onset (or task onset for motor imagery) and 2 s prior this point. Epochs containing EOG activity in FP1 were rejected if the peak-peak amplitude was above 125 μV.

2.4.2. Feature Extraction. Features were extracted from the time domain and the frequency domain from the MRCP and natural EEG rhythms, respectively. Three time domain features were extracted: (1) average amplitude from -2 s to -0.5 s with respect to the movement onset (early contingent negative variation (CNV), early Bereitschaftspotential (BP), or readiness potential (RP)), (2) average amplitude from -0.5 to -0.15 s with respect to the movement onset (late CNV, late BP, or negative slope), and (3) the peak of maximum negativity (the motor potential). Five spectral features were extracted from the movement onset and 2 s prior to this point; these were the average power in the delta (0–4 Hz), theta (4–7 Hz), alpha (7–15 Hz), beta (15–30 Hz), and gamma (30–45 Hz) frequency range. The average power was calculated using power spectral density with a Hamming window. The time and frequency domain features were extracted from each channel from data set 1 and from the surrogate channel from data set 2. These features were extracted from single-trial EEG traces.

2.5. Feature Selection and Classification. The data were randomly divided into ten parts, where nine parts were used for training and the last was used for evaluation. On the training set sequential forward selection was performed [7]. The features were ranked by the separability of a 2-class problem, for example, palmar grasp versus rest (lateral and pinch grasp), based on u-statistics from Mann–Whitney's test. The features were ranked with the highest u-statistics first and the features with the lowest u-statistics in the end. With leave-one-out cross-validation on the training set, the classification accuracy was obtained with linear discriminant analysis using the feature with the highest u-statistics value. Then the feature with the 2nd highest u-statistics was included and the classification accuracy was calculated; if the classification accuracy improved, the feature was added to the candidate feature set; otherwise, it was discarded. This procedure was repeated until all features were evaluated. Since a 3-class and two 4-class problems were considered, the optimal features were evaluated for all pairwise comparisons (e.g., palmar versus rest, lateral versus rest, and pinch versus rest) after which 3 (or 4) candidate feature sets were obtained. The 3 (or 4) candidate feature sets were merged and another round of feature selection was performed to obtain the final feature set that was used for the classification of the test set.

After the feature selection, the test data were classified in two different ways according to the two data sets. For data set 1, linear discriminant analysis was performed on a 3-class problem. For data set 2, a support vector machine with a linear kernel was used to classify the features for the two 4-class problems. The two different classifiers were chosen, so it would be possible to compare the findings with the previous publications on the data sets where linear discriminant analysis [7] and support vector machines [6] were used. The classification of features extracted from data set 2 was performed in three ways: (1) without feature selection to be able to compare the results with previous findings, (2) with sequential forward selection to estimate the importance of each feature type, and (3) with principal component analysis (PCA). The number of principal components used was equal to the number of features selected by sequential forward selection. The average classification accuracy was calculated across the ten testing folds. Moreover, to estimate if a global classifier can be used to classify new data, classification accuracies were calculated with leave-one-subject-out cross-validation; this was done on data set 2 to have a low dimensionality of the feature vector (eight features).

2.6. Feature Importance Evaluation. The importance of each feature type and channel location (for data set 1) was investigated. In this study, the feature importance is defined as how often each feature is selected in the training folds using sequential forward selection. The importance of each individual feature type (delta power, etc.) was merged across all channels for data set 1; this was done to investigate the effect of the feature type. The importance of each channel was evaluated by merging all feature types for the specific channel.

TABLE 1: Classification accuracies obtained for the three different grasps. Pal: palmar grasp, Lat: lateral grasp, and Pin: pinch grasp.

Grasp	Predicted		
	Pal	Lat	Pin
True			
Pal	0.43	0.28	0.29
Lat	0.25	0.47	0.28
Pin	0.23	0.24	0.52

The feature importance was averaged across the subjects for the two 4-class problems (executed and imaginary movement with different kinetic profiles) and the 3-class problem (different executed grasp types). The number of times the individual features were selected was divided by the total number of selected features to obtain the feature importance in percent. Moreover, the same analyses were performed for the best half of the subject ($n = 7$) based on classification accuracy.

2.7. Analysis Investigating the Effect of Gender, Age, and Motor Execution versus Imagination. To investigate if the gender and age imbalance in data set 2 was affecting the results, an analysis was performed on the resting EEG for motor execution and imagination. Epochs were extracted from -5 to -3 s prior to the movement onset from the preprocessed EEG. The variance in the interval was calculated and plotted (see Figure 2) as well as the mean $\pm$ the standard deviation of the single-trial EEG -5 s until the movement onset.

3. Results

From Figure 2(b), it can be seen that there is no trend for any differences related to gender or age, and the rest period for motor execution and imagination was similar. The classification accuracies are summarized in Tables 1–4 and in Figure 3, and the feature analysis is summarized in Figure 4. To investigate if there was an association between the ability to produce the specific force pattern and the classification accuracies, the root-mean-square error (RMSE) was calculated between the produced force and visual cue. The Spearman correlation (Rho: 0.25; $P = 0.38$) was calculated between the RMSE (0.25 $\pm$ 0.04) and the classification accuracies, but there was no association between the RMSE and the classification accuracies.

3.1. Classification of Movements. The results from the classification of the different grasp types (Table 1) show that the highest classification accuracies are on the diagonal; however, it should be noted that there is also a high number of misclassified samples. The overall classification accuracy for the 3-class problem was 0.48 $\pm$ 0.05 (mean $\pm$ standard deviation).

The results from the classification of the movements with different kinetics profiles (Tables 2 and 3) show that the highest classification accuracies are on the diagonal. Again, it should be noted that there is a high number of misclassified samples. The overall classification accuracies for

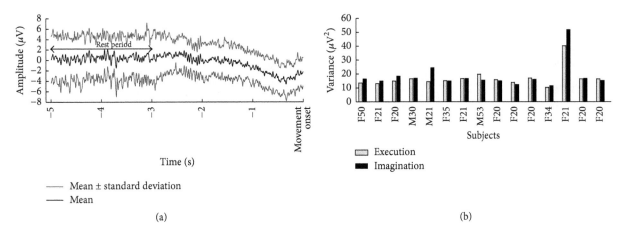

FIGURE 2: (a) Plot of the mean ± standard deviation of a representative subject ($n = 1$) performing motor execution to reach 60% MVC in 0.5 s. (b) The variance of the rest period is shown for each subject in data set 2. "M": male, "F": female, and the number is the age of the subject.

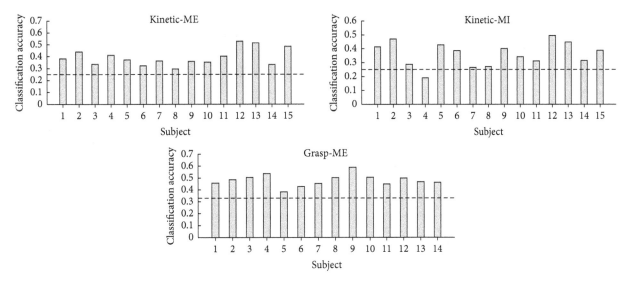

FIGURE 3: Individual classification accuracies across movement types for each subject. All classification accuracies are obtained after sequential forward selection. The theoretical chance levels have been added as horizontal dashed black lines.

the two 4-class problems were 0.41 ± 0.07 and 0.39 ± 0.08 (mean ± standard deviation) for motor execution and motor imagination, respectively, without using sequential forward selection. When the sequential forward selection was used, the classification accuracies were 0.39 ± 0.07 and 0.36 ± 0.09 for movement execution and motor imagination, respectively. For PCA, the classification accuracies were 0.38 ± 0.07 and 0.33 ± 0.09 for movement execution and motor imagination, respectively. In Figure 3, the intersubject variability in the classification accuracies is indicated.

In Table 4, the results are presented when using the leave-one-subject-out approach for estimating a global classifier where no training data are needed for the individual subject. With this approach, the average classification accuracies were 0.32 ± 0.04 and 0.31 ± 0.06 for movement execution and motor imagination, respectively. However, it should be noted that the highest values were only on the diagonal for fast 20% MVC and slow 60% MVC for motor execution and fast 20% MVC for motor imagination.

3.2. Feature and Channel Importance. The importance of each channel and feature type is outlined in Figure 4. No clear trend can be seen from the importance of each channel. The most important (most selected) feature type was the average power in the delta frequency range. The EEG rhythms were most important when discriminating between the movements with different kinetic profiles, but in general all of the eight feature types contain discriminative information. From Figure 4(a), it can be seen that the standard deviation of the feature importance across subjects is great. The patterns do not change much when only looking at the seven best subjects. There is a slight reduction in the importance of the delta activity and an increase in the importance of RP for the different grasp types.

4. Discussion

The results indicate that it is possible to discriminate between different grasp types and movements with different kinetic

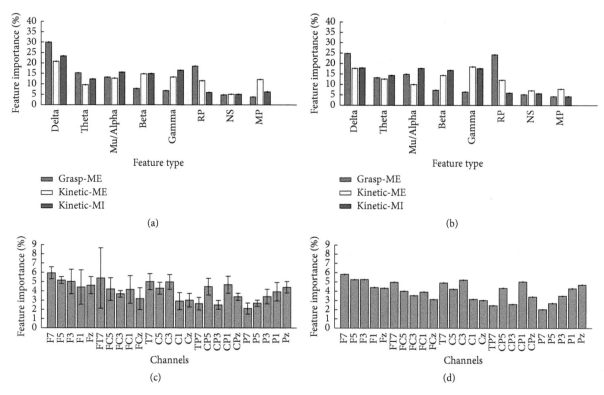

FIGURE 4: (a) Importance of each feature type for all subjects, (b) importance of each feature type for the seven best subjects (in terms of classification accuracy), (c) importance of each of the 25 channels in data set 1 for all subjects, and (d) importance of each of the 25 channels in data set 1 for the seven best subjects (in terms of classification accuracy). RP: readiness potential or early CNV/BP, NS: negative slope or late CNV/BP, and PN: peak negativity. The bars indicate ±1 × standard deviation.

profiles, although the classification performance is limited. The most discriminative feature type was the power in the delta frequency range, but all of the features contributed discriminative information.

The classification accuracies obtained using the EEG rhythms and the MRCP segments were higher than chance level calculated with a significance level of 5% [19] when using the subject's own training data. The classification accuracies associated with the leave-one-subject-out approach were at chance level, which suggests that the classifier should be trained on the subject's own data. The classification accuracies were slightly higher for motor execution compared to motor imagination, which was also expected based on the signal morphology in Figure 1. This is also consistent with previous studies using temporal and spectral features [6, 16, 20]. The classification accuracies associated with the different grasp types were lower compared to previous findings [7]; however, it should be noted that the features were different, since the aim of the current study was to investigate where the discriminative information is encoded in the established EEG rhythms and MRCP components. The classification accuracies associated with the movements with different kinetic profiles were ~10 percentage points higher than in the reference study on data set 1 [6]. In the current study, extra features were added in terms of the average power of the EEG rhythms, and based on the analysis of the feature importance, the increase in classification accuracies is possibly due to the inclusion of those features.

The feature analysis revealed that task-related discriminative information can be extracted from the frequency range of all the different EEG rhythms with the main contribution from the delta band, which is also the frequency area where the MRCP is located. These findings are consistent with previous studies where it has been found that the entire EEG spectrum is used for discriminating between task-related parameters and that it is possible to decode the MRCP for different levels of force and speed [7, 15, 20]. It was, however, expected that the late BP/CNV and peak negativity would contribute more to the classification since they, according to the signal morphology, contain more discriminative information around the movement onset, at least for motor execution with different kinetic profiles (Figure 1(c)). Also, it has been shown that these segments were different for movements with different kinetic profiles [18, 21]. The single-trial variability (Figure 2(a)) may be an explanation for the fact that peak negativity is not so important for the classification or the relatively high cut-off frequency of the low pass filter when performing MRCP analysis; this should be around 5–10 Hz instead of 45 Hz if looking at the MRCP frequency range instead of the entire EEG spectrum. It should be noted that the RP and NS were extracted in fixed time intervals with respect to the movement onset to account for the single-trial variability; this has been done in several other studies [18, 22]. However, the different phases of the MRCP are affected by variations in, for example, attention [23], and the peak of maximum negativity may not always occur at

TABLE 2: Classification accuracies obtained for different motor execution kinetic profiles. F20: fast 20% MVC, F60: fast 60% MVC, S20: slow 20% MVC, and S60: slow 60% MVC. SFS: sequential forward selection, and PCA: principal component analysis. The classification accuracies obtained without and with SFS and PCA are presented in the top and bottom part, respectively.

	Predicted			
	F20	F60	S20	S60
Kinetic-ME without SFS				
True				
F20	0.45	0.20	0.22	0.14
F60	0.23	0.41	0.18	0.18
S20	0.22	0.20	0.38	0.20
S60	0.26	0.22	0.11	0.41
Kinetic-ME with SFS				
True				
F20	0.39	0.23	0.22	0.17
F60	0.26	0.35	0.20	0.19
S20	0.20	0.18	0.37	0.24
S60	0.25	0.21	0.09	0.45
Kinetic-ME with PCA				
True				
F20	0.39	0.27	0.19	0.15
F60	0.26	0.40	0.19	0.15
S20	0.25	0.18	0.34	0.23
S60	0.31	0.19	0.12	0.38

TABLE 3: Classification accuracies obtained for different motor imagination kinetic profiles. F20: fast 20% MVC, F60: fast 60% MVC, S20: slow 20% MVC, and S60: slow 60% MVC. SFS: sequential forward selection, and PCA: principal component analysis. The classification accuracies obtained without and with SFS and PCA are presented in the top and bottom part, respectively.

	Predicted			
	F20	F60	S20	S60
Kinetic-MI without SFS				
True				
F20	0.48	0.19	0.19	0.15
F60	0.23	0.33	0.27	0.17
S20	0.20	0.22	0.38	0.19
S60	0.30	0.22	0.11	0.37
Kinetic-MI with SFS				
True				
F20	0.42	0.21	0.18	0.20
F60	0.24	0.33	0.25	0.18
S20	0.22	0.22	0.35	0.22
S60	0.34	0.22	0.10	0.35
Kinetic-MI with PCA				
True				
F20	0.40	0.21	0.17	0.22
F60	0.25	0.31	0.25	0.19
S20	0.22	0.24	0.35	0.19
S60	0.32	0.30	0.10	0.28

the movement onset; therefore, the different phases could have been calculated with respect to the peak of maximum negativity instead of the movement onset. However, it may be difficult to identify the onset of the different phases (e.g., by changes in the slopes) in single-trial MRCPs in an automated way to avoid bias.

As well as the feature types, the importance of each channel was evaluated on data set 1. The analysis showed that all channels contributed discriminative information, which may be due to the size of the cortical representation of the hand and the effect of volume conduction. On average, the frontal channels contributed slightly more discriminative information which can be explained by the neural generation of the initial negative phase of the MRCP that is produced more frontally and then propagates more posteriorly. From a BCI control perspective, decoding of movement intentions is highly relevant; however, the performance is limited. It is not known what the lower limit of a BCI for rehabilitation is [24], but it is expected that the rehabilitative outcome is related to the BCI performance [2]. The performance could be increased by reducing the number of classes and focusing on two classes instead of four or by calibrating the BCI to the individual subject from a larger number of features (e.g., power from 1 Hz bins or wavelet analysis from each channel). This leads to a larger feature vector than what was reported in this study, whose focus was on established physiological features of the EEG and MRCP. The dimensionality of the large feature vector should therefore be reduced. Sequential

TABLE 4: Classification accuracies obtained for different motor execution (top) and imagination (bottom) kinetic profiles using leave-one-subject-out classification (global classifier). F20: fast 20% MVC, F60: fast 60% MVC, S20: slow 20% MVC, and S60: slow 60% MVC. MVC: maximum voluntary contraction.

	Predicted			
	F20	F60	S20	S60
Kinetic-ME				
True				
F20	0.50	0.08	0.17	0.25
F60	0.49	0.09	0.21	0.21
S20	0.34	0.07	0.29	0.30
S60	0.35	0.06	0.17	0.41
Kinetic-MI				
True				
F20	0.55	0.05	0.22	0.18
F60	0.50	0.08	0.20	0.23
S20	0.44	0.05	0.28	0.22
S60	0.54	0.04	0.08	0.34

forward selection and PCA showed similar performance; however, it is expected that PCA will perform worse when a larger number of features are included than the nine that were used in this study, but it will be much faster to compute the PCA [7].

5. Conclusion

It was shown that the task-related parameters, force, speed, and grasp type, can be decoded using the established EEG rhythms and MRCP components; although the performance was limited, it was above chance level. The delta rhythm contributed the most, but all EEG rhythms and MRCP components contained discriminative information regarding different levels of force and speed and about the type of hand grasp.

References

[1] K. K. Ang, K. S. G. Chua, K. S. Phua et al., "A randomized controlled trial of EEG-based motor imagery brain-computer interface robotic rehabilitation for stroke," *Clinical EEG and Neuroscience*, 2014.

[2] I. K. Niazi, N. Mrachacz-Kersting, N. Jiang, K. Dremstrup, and D. Farina, "Peripheral electrical stimulation triggered by self-paced detection of motor intention enhances motor evoked potentials," *IEEE Transactions on Neural Systems and Rehabilitation Engineering*, vol. 20, no. 4, pp. 595–604, 2012.

[3] R. Xu, N. Jiang, N. Mrachacz-Kersting et al., "A closed-loop brain-computer interface triggering an active ankle-foot orthosis for inducing cortical neural plasticity," *IEEE Transactions On Biomedical Engineering*, vol. 61, no. 7, pp. 2092–2101, 2014.

[4] R. Xu, N. Jiang, C. Lin, N. Mrachacz-Kersting, K. Dremstrup, and D. Farina, "Enhanced low-latency detection of motor intention from EEG for closed-loop brain-computer interface applications," *IEEE Transactions on Biomedical Engineering*, vol. 61, no. 2, pp. 288–296, 2014.

[5] I. K. Niazi, N. Jiang, O. Tiberghien, J. F. Nielsen, K. Dremstrup, and D. Farina, "Detection of movement intention from single-trial movement-related cortical potentials," *Journal of Neural Engineering*, vol. 8, no. 6, Article ID 066009, 2011.

[6] M. Jochumsen, I. K. H. Niazi, D. Taylor, D. Farina, and K. Dremstrup, "Detecting and classifying movement-related cortical potentials associated with hand movements in healthy subjects and stroke patients from single-electrode, single-trial EEG," *Journal of neural engineering*, vol. 12, no. 5, p. 056013, 2015.

[7] M. Jochumsen, I. K. Niazi, K. Dremstrup, and E. N. Kamavuako, "Detecting and classifying three different hand movement types through electroencephalography recordings for neurorehabilitation," *Medical and Biological Engineering and Computing*, vol. 54, no. 10, pp. 1491–1501, 2016.

[8] A. Bashashati, S. Mason, R. K. Ward, and G. E. Birch, "An improved asynchronous brain interface: Making use of the temporal history of the LF-ASD feature vectors," *Journal of Neural Engineering*, vol. 3, no. 2, article no. 002, pp. 87–94, 2006.

[9] J. Ibáñez, J. I. Serrano, M. D. Del Castillo et al., "Detection of the onset of upper-limb movements based on the combined analysis of changes in the sensorimotor rhythms and slow cortical potentials," *Journal of Neural Engineering*, vol. 11, no. 5, Article ID 056009, 2014.

[10] J. W. Krakauer, "Motor learning: its relevance to stroke recovery and neurorehabilitation," *Current Opinion in Neurology*, vol. 19, no. 1, pp. 84–90, 2006.

[11] N. Robinson, A. P. Vinod, C. Guan, K. K. Ang, and T. K. Peng, "A Wavelet-CSP method to classify hand movement directions in EEG based BCI system," in *Proceedings of theInformation, Communications and Signal Processing (ICICS) 2011 8th International Conference*, pp. 1–5, Singapore, Singapore, 2011.

[12] E. Demandt, C. Mehring, K. Vogt, A. Schulze-Bonhage, A. Aertsen, and T. Ball, "Reaching movement onset- and end-related characteristics of EEG spectral power modulations," *Frontiers in Neuroscience*, no. MAY, Article ID Article 65, 2012.

[13] J. Deng, J. Yao, and J. P. A. Dewald, "Classification of the intention to generate a shoulder versus elbow torque by means of a time-frequency synthesized spatial patterns BCI algorithm," *Journal of Neural Engineering*, vol. 2, no. 4, pp. 131–138, 2005.

[14] J. Ibáñez, J. I. Serrano, M. D. del Castillo, J. Minguez, and J. L. Pons, "Predictive classification of self-paced upper-limb analytical movements with EEG," *Medical and Biological Engineering & Computing*, vol. 53, no. 11, pp. 1201–1210, 2015.

[15] M. Jochumsen, I. K. Niazi, N. Mrachacz-Kersting, D. Farina, and K. Dremstrup, "Detection and Classification of Movement-Related Cortical Potentials Associated with Task Force and Speed," *Journal of Neural Engineering*, vol. 10, Article ID 056015, 2013.

[16] E. N. Kamavuako, M. Jochumsen, I. K. Niazi, and K. Dremstrup, "Comparison of features for movement prediction from single-trial movement-related cortical potentials in healthy subjects and stroke patients," *Computational Intelligence and Neuroscience*, vol. 71, Article ID 858015, pp. 1–8, 2015.

[17] D. Farina, O. F. do Nascimento, M.-F. Lucas, and C. Doncarli, "Optimization of wavelets for classification of movement-related cortical potentials generated by variation of force-related parameters," *Journal of Neuroscience Methods*, vol. 162, no. 1-2, pp. 357–363, 2007.

[18] O. F. Nascimento, K. D. Nielsen, and M. Voigt, "Movement-related parameters modulate cortical activity during imaginary isometric plantar-flexions," *Experimental Brain Research*, vol. 171, no. 1, pp. 78–90, 2006.

[19] GR. Müller-Putz, R. Scherer, and C. Brunner, "Better than random? a closer look on BCI results," *International Journal of Bioelectromagnetism*, vol. 10, pp. 52–55, 2008.

[20] M. Jochumsen, I. K. H. Niazi, N. Mrachacz-Kersting, N. Jiang, D. Farina, and K. Dremstrup, "Comparison of spatial filters and features for the detection and classification of movement-related cortical potentials in healthy individuals and stroke patients," *Journal of Neural Engineering*, vol. 12, no. 5, p. 056003, 2015.

[21] O. F. Do Nascimento, K. D. Nielsen, and M. Voigt, "Relationship between plantar-flexor torque generation and the magnitude of the movement-related potentials," *Experimental Brain Research*, vol. 160, no. 2, pp. 154–165, 2005.

[22] A. Hatta, Y. Nishihira, T. Higashiura, S. R. Kim, and T. Kaneda, "Long-term motor practice induces practice-dependent modulation of movement-related cortical potentials (MRCP) preceding a self-paced non-dominant handgrip movement in kendo players," *Neuroscience Letters*, vol. 459, no. 3, pp. 105–108, 2009.

[23] H. Shibasaki and M. Hallett, "What is the bereitschaftspotential?" *Clinical Neurophysiology*, vol. 117, no. 11, pp. 2341–2356, 2006.

[24] M. Grosse-Wentrup, D. Mattia, and K. Oweiss, "Using brain-computer interfaces to induce neural plasticity and restore function," *Journal of Neural Engineering*, vol. 8, no. 2, Article ID 025004, 2011.

11

Convolutional Neural Networks with 3D Input for P300 Identification in Auditory Brain-Computer Interfaces

Eduardo Carabez, Miho Sugi, Isao Nambu, and Yasuhiro Wada

Department of Electrical Engineering, Nagaoka University of Technology, 1603-1 Kamitomioka, Nagaoka, Niigata 940-2188, Japan

Correspondence should be addressed to Eduardo Carabez; eduardo@stn.nagaokaut.ac.jp

Academic Editor: Athanasios Voulodimos

From allowing basic communication to move through an environment, several attempts are being made in the field of brain-computer interfaces (BCI) to assist people that somehow find it difficult or impossible to perform certain activities. Focusing on these people as potential users of BCI, we obtained electroencephalogram (EEG) readings from nine healthy subjects who were presented with auditory stimuli via earphones from six different virtual directions. We presented the stimuli following the oddball paradigm to elicit P300 waves within the subject's brain activity for later identification and classification using convolutional neural networks (CNN). The CNN models are given a novel single trial three-dimensional (3D) representation of the EEG data as an input, maintaining temporal and spatial information as close to the experimental setup as possible, a relevant characteristic as eliciting P300 has been shown to cause stronger activity in certain brain regions. Here, we present the results of CNN models using the proposed 3D input for three different stimuli presentation time intervals (500, 400, and 300 ms) and compare them to previous studies and other common classifiers. Our results show >80% accuracy for all the CNN models using the proposed 3D input in single trial P300 classification.

1. Introduction

Brain-computer interfaces (BCI) offer a way for people to communicate with devices using their brain. Although the applications and environments in which BCI have been explored are numerous, here we focus on their potential supporting role for people with muscle movement limitations.

Some BCI use event-related potentials (ERP) to link a person's brain to the actuator or device the person intends to interact with. ERP are brain activity patterns that can be measured by electroencephalography (EEG). Among the many ERP, we used P300 for this study. P300 is the positive deflection expected between 250 and 700 ms after the BCI user identifies an irregular (expected) cue among regular ones in an experimental setup. This way of presenting stimuli to the BCI user is known as the oddball paradigm. P300 can be elicited through the oddball paradigm using different stimuli (e.g., sound or image). BCI applications and experiments involving EEG, P300, and image stimuli that focus on people with motor disadvantages have been widely explored and successfully developed in the past [1–3].

For this study, we used sound stimuli to elicit P300 through the oddball paradigm. Although images have been successfully used for such tasks, their use requires that the subjects (who might have physical disabilities) retain control of their eyes and some face and head muscles as well. However, that is not the case for blind people who have lost their ability to see or were never sighted, or for patients with complete locked-in syndrome, who are not in control of their eye movements. By using sound stimuli, we believe that a more portable BCI can be developed, which is suitable for those who cannot receive visual stimuli or simply prefer to dedicate their vision to other tasks.

Once P300 is elicited, the BCI should be able to recognize it and classify it as such. For this purpose, we used several convolutional neural network (CNN) structures. CNN represent a specific topology of a multilayer perceptron (part of the artificial neural network (ANN) family). Like many other machine learning models, CNN have been used for classification purposes with satisfactory results in different applications [4–7].

Unlike many types of ANN, CNN can handle two- or three-dimensional (2D or 3D) inputs without mapping data onto a one-dimensional (1D) vector, which can be a cause of information loss depending on the nature of the data. Data mapping is common in BCI applications, but as studies show that eliciting P300 causes stronger brain activity in certain brain regions, maintaining both spatial and temporal EEG information when making the CNN input might be key to achieving higher accuracy in P300 classification. With this in mind, we propose a novel 3D input for the CNN. Our approach avoids the information loss that comes with data mapping and allows main CNN operations (convolution and pooling) to take place without the limitations described in other studies [8].

We use our proposed 3D input to test 30 different CNN structures for P300 classification. The CNN structures varied from each other by the kernels (patches) used during the convolution or pooling processes. We also used different pool strides to cause or avoid overlapping, depending on the case, as this has been reported to improve the CNN performance in some applications [9].

The following sections of this work are organized as follows: in Section 2, we explain in detail the experimental setup used to produce and process the dataset used. Further, the general CNN structure and details regarding the shape of the proposed 3D input are presented in Section 3. Finally, in Sections 4 and 5, we discuss our results, comparing them to those obtained in other similar studies and also presenting the performance of other common classifiers used in this context.

2. Dataset

2.1. Experimental Setup. The dataset used for this study corresponds to evoked P300 waves from nine healthy subjects (8 men, 1 women) obtained using an auditory BCI paradigm. A digital electroencephalogram system (Active Two, BioSemi, Amsterdam, Netherlands) was used to record brain activity at 256 Hz. The device consists of 64 electrodes distributed over the head of the subjects by a cap, using the configuration shown in Figure 1(a). This study was approved by the ethics boards of the Nagaoka University of Technology. All subjects signed consent forms that contained detailed information about the experiment and all methods complied with the Declaration of Helsinki.

The subjects were presented with auditory stimuli (100 ms of white noise), similar to that performed in [10], using the out-of-head sound localization method presented in [11], so that subjects could hear the stimuli coming from one of six virtual directions via earphones (see Figure 2(a)). Stimuli were followed by a silent interval of time. One stimulus and one corresponding silent interval were referred to as a trial. Three different trial lengths (500, 400, and 300 ms) were used to analyze the impact of the speed of stimuli presentation on the identification of the P300 wave. Each subject completed 12 experimental sessions, each consisting of around 180 trials

for a given trial length. On each session, the subjects were asked to focus on only the sound perceived to be coming from one of the six virtual directions, which was called the target direction. The subjects counted in silence with their eyes closed every time they perceived sound being produced from the target direction and ignored the rest. Ideally, this should elicit P300. The target direction rotated from directions 1 to 6, one by one, for sessions 1 to 6 and then repeated in the same order for sessions 7 to 12. The direction in which stimuli were presented was pseudorandomized; therefore for every six trials, sound from each direction was produced at least once and stimuli coming from the target direction were never produced sequentially to avoid overlapping of P300.

2.2. Preprocessing and Data Accommodation. Before sorting into training and test sets, EEG data were baseline corrected using a Savitzky-Golay filter from −100 ms before stimulus onset until the end of the trial (i.e., end of the silent period after stimulus offset).

A filtering process was also conducted along all EEG channels using Butterworth coefficients for a bandpass filter with cutoff frequencies of 0.1 and 8 Hz. Next data were downsampled to 25 Hz (approximately a tenth of the original size). Data were downsampled as the original size would result in longer processing and training/testing times. Similar downsampling can be found in [10]. Nonaveraged trials were used for this study.

As each subject performed 12 experimental sessions (see Figure 2(b)), with around 180 trials in each of them, data collection for each subject consists of approximately 2160 trials for a given trial length for each subject. Given the pseudorandomized nature of the stimuli production, for each six produced stimuli, one was from the target direction. That stimuli were labeled as the target trial and the rest as nontarget trials. Consequently, of nearly 2160 trials, each subject was expected to produce around 360 target trials as a result of 12 sessions (i.e., a sixth of them), while the remaining are nontarget trials. In this case, the target direction is not particularly relevant, as independently of where the target direction is located, perceiving stimuli correctly from that direction should elicit P300. What is important is to determine is whether the user can differentiate among the six virtual directions and that focusing on one of them and perceiving sound from it are possible with the proposed experimental setup.

Training and test sets were generated for each subject on a given trial length using only that subject's data. To generate the training and test sets for each subject, first we shuffled the target trials with the same happening to the nontarget trials. Next, we distributed half of the target trials in each set with the same applying for nontarget trials. This resulted in training and test sets for each subject containing around 1100 trials each, with approximately 180 target trials and 900 nontarget trials in each set.

As can be seen in Figure 3(c), regardless of the trial length, the proposed input consisted of 1100 ms of recorded brain activity after stimulus onset. We consider the same amount of information to fairly evaluate all trial lengths and compare our results to previous work in Section 4.

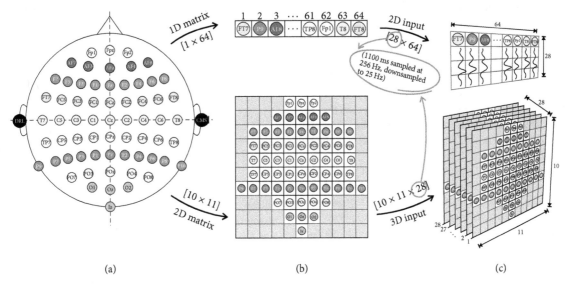

(a)

(b)

(c)

FIGURE 1: The different steps of input construction: (a) The experimental EEG channel layout. (b) EEG channel matrix disposition to form 2D and 3D inputs (upper and lower images, resp.). Gray cells contain no information. (c) Usual 2D input shape and proposed 3D input shape following our considerations (upper and lower images, resp.).

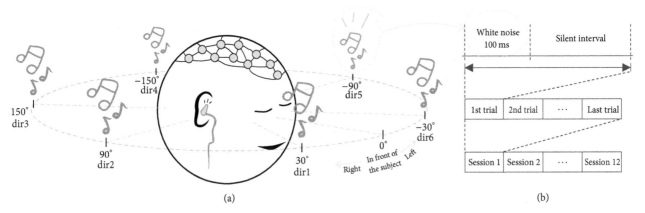

(a)

(b)

FIGURE 2: (a) Position representation for the six virtual directions with respect to the subject. (b) Conformation of the 12 sessions all 9 subjects took part of.

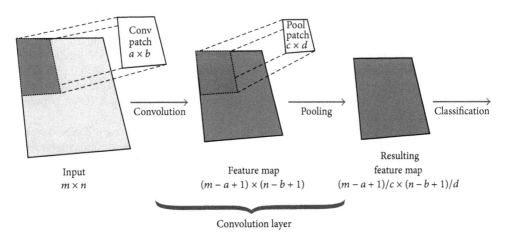

FIGURE 3: General structure of a CNN. Overlapping is not shown in this figure. Default pooling stride is being applied.

3. Input Shape and CNN Model

3.1. 3D Input. For the detection of P300 using EEG, the electrode position is relevant as there are areas where the potential is experienced more strongly [10]. This, however, has not been addressed in previous research, instead mapping the 3D data (position of electrodes and time) into a 2D vector that contains all EEG channel activity during the experiment. This not only causes information loss, but also prevents classifiers such as CNN to be used without special consideration (as observed in [8]).

To avoid information loss and limitations of CNN operations, positions of the 64 electrodes were mapped onto a 10 × 11 matrix (see Figure 1(b)), maintaining their position as close as possible to their real arrangement in the experimental setup. Time information is presented through an extra axis, so the 3D input has the shape shown in Figure 1(c). Cells that do not correspond to an electrode (gray ones) are set to zero in all instances.

In Section 4, we presented a 2D input for performance comparison purposes. In that case, the input has the shape depicted in Figure 1 (upper flow). The preprocessing, data accommodation (train and test set size), and any other considerations made for the 3D input in Section 2.2 also apply for the 2D one.

3.2. CNN Model. This particular neural network architecture is a type of multilayer perceptron with feature-generation and a dimension-reduction oriented layer, which together compose a convolutional layer. Unlike other layered-based neural networks, CNN can receive a multidimensional input in its original form, process it, and successfully classify it without a previous feature extraction step. The general structure of the CNN is presented in Figure 3. For our study, we used a 3D input and produce 28 feature maps (one for each time sample). While CNN with layers lacking the pooling process are also possible, the pooling process offers scale invariance for the resulting feature maps. It also helps preventing overfitting and allows reduction of computational complexity of the model by reducing the size of the resulting feature maps, thereby shortening training/test times.

Here, we proposed 30 different CNN models to investigate the impact that different convolution and pool patches have on model performance. The proposed models varied from each other in terms of convolution or pool patch size. The CNN models were implemented using a GeForce GTX TITAN X GPU by NVIDIA in Python 2.7 using the work developed by [12].

Additionally, fixed pooling strides were used as an alternative to the default value, which had the same size as the pool patch, with the purpose of forcing pool patches to overlap (or not) during the pooling process, as this has been reported to improve the CNN performance [9]. For this purpose, we applied fixed pooling strides with the values [1 × 1], [1 × 2], [1 × 3], [2 × 2], and [2 × 3]. While normally the pooling stride is given as an integer value, in the work of [12], used in this study, the pooling stride must be defined as an array of two values, with the first one corresponding to the step(s) taken along the x-axis and the second one of

TABLE 1: Proposed convolution, pool patches, and pool stride for the current study.

Patch number	Convolution patch	Pool patch	Pool stride
(0)	[3 × 3]	[2 × 2]	Default
(1)	[2 × 2]	[3 × 3]	[1 × 1]
(2)	[3 × 2]	[1 × 2]	[1 × 2]
(3)	[2 × 3]	[1 × 3]	[1 × 3]
(4)	[2 × 4]	[2 × 3]	[2 × 2]
(5)	[1 × 4]		[2 × 3]

those taken along the y-axis. The whole input is spanned using this approach, with only the pooling process affected. For the convolution process, the stride is 1. When a pooling stride different than the default one is used, areas where the pooling patch is applied to the feature map can overlap from one application to another, or contrarily certain areas can be skipped depending on the size of the stride and the pool patch. With our proposed pooling strides, we intended to cause overlapping in the application areas to show whether this impacts the CNN performance (as in [9]). We believe this approach could benefit CNN models as spanning the same area more than once with the max pooling approach could pick up the features corresponding to the P300 production as this wave causes stronger activity in specific brain areas. This should create a resulting feature map containing multiple times this part of the feature map, making classification easier.

For a given trial length and pool stride value, 30 CNN models were trained for each subject. As there are nine subjects, three trial lengths, and six pool stride values, a total of 4860 CNN were trained for this research. However, only results showing the average performance of the nine subjects will be presented. Tested convolution and pool patches are summarized in Table 1, as well as their patch number, which will be used to present results in the next section.

Each patch is referenced by a number, starting from 0. All possible patch combinations were tested with the resulting model using particular convolution and pool patches, with a patch code consisting of two digits being presented. The first digit corresponds to the convolution patch and the second one to the pool patch. Therefore, for patch code 24, we are referring to the CNN model that used the [3 × 2] convolution patch and the [2 × 3] pool patch. Given that the tested CNN are numerous, we present a statistical analysis in Section 4.1 implementing ANOVA between the models and the proposed pool strides.

As for the learning rate of CNN, it was set at 0.008 based on preliminary tests. The optimization method we used is the stochastic gradient descent as it has been demonstrated [13] to be beneficial for training neural networks on datasets with large examples, using the mini batch approach (batch size of 100). Classification at the output layer is performed using the softmax function, which produces a label based on the probability of a given example to belong to one dataset class.

To calculate classification accuracy we have to consider that the proportion of target and nontarget trials in the

	00	01	02	03	04	10	11	12	13	14
D	0.863	0.858	0.862	0.860	0.859	0.859	0.858	0.862	0.862	0.861
1 × 2	**0.865**	0.861	0.862	0.862	0.862	0.862	0.861	0.862	0.861	0.862
2 × 2	0.863	0.861	0.841	0.860	0.859	0.858	0.858	0.861	0.862	0.860
1 × 3	0.861	0.860	0.862	0.860	0.862	0.862	0.862	0.863	0.862	0.860
2 × 3	0.860	0.859	0.856	0.858	0.859	0.862	0.859	0.864	0.860	0.861
1 × 1	0.865	0.858	0.862	0.864	0.862	0.860	0.859	0.863	0.861	0.861
	20	21	22	23	24	30	31	32	33	34
D	0.863	0.859	0.862	0.863	0.861	0.862	0.857	0.862	0.861	0.857
1 × 2	0.862	0.862	0.862	0.860	0.862	0.862	0.861	0.862	0.862	0.865
2 × 2	0.863	0.859	0.859	0.836	0.860	0.862	0.860	0.864	0.862	0.862
1 × 3	0.861	0.859	0.861	0.863	0.861	0.861	0.862	0.859	0.861	0.863
2 × 3	0.862	0.857	0.840	0.845	0.856	0.838	0.862	0.861	0.860	0.859
1 × 1	0.863	0.854	0.863	0.861	0.862	0.863	0.858	0.863	0.862	0.864
	40	41	42	43	44	50	51	52	53	54
D	0.862	0.860	0.863	0.861	0.862	0.864	0.861	0.865	0.862	0.861
1 × 2	0.863	0.861	0.863	0.861	0.862	0.863	0.859	0.865	0.865	0.862
2 × 2	0.862	0.863	0.862	0.863	0.862	0.864	0.861	0.861	0.837	0.862
1 × 3	0.863	0.862	0.860	0.845	0.864	0.862	0.862	0.863	0.862	0.863
2 × 3	0.863	0.862	0.861	0.861	0.862	0.862	0.860	0.859	0.837	0.860
1 × 1	0.863	0.859	0.862	0.862	0.861	0.862	0.854	0.863	0.863	0.862

FIGURE 4: Summary of results from nine subjects in the 500 ms trial interval.

	00	01	02	03	04	10	11	12	13	14
D	0.861	0.856	0.861	0.858	0.856	0.859	0.856	0.861	0.860	0.857
1 × 2	0.861	0.859	0.861	0.860	0.859	0.861	0.858	0.861	0.860	0.859
2 × 2	0.861	0.856	0.837	0.857	0.858	0.859	0.857	0.859	0.860	0.857
1 × 3	0.861	0.858	0.861	0.857	0.858	0.858	0.855	0.861	0.860	0.857
2 × 3	0.858	0.857	0.861	0.856	0.856	0.858	0.858	0.858	0.858	0.857
1 × 1	0.859	0.855	0.862	0.861	0.858	0.859	0.853	0.860	0.861	0.856
	20	21	22	23	24	30	31	32	33	34
D	0.861	0.857	0.862	0.859	0.856	0.860	0.856	0.860	0.860	0.858
1 × 2	0.860	0.858	0.862	0.861	0.859	0.861	0.855	0.861	0.861	0.859
2 × 2	0.861	0.855	0.861	0.837	0.856	0.860	0.859	0.860	0.860	0.857
1 × 3	0.859	0.859	0.863	0.859	0.860	0.859	0.858	0.858	0.860	0.860
2 × 3	0.858	0.857	0.838	0.839	0.856	0.833	0.857	0.859	0.858	0.857
1 × 1	0.859	0.854	0.862	0.858	0.857	0.858	0.853	0.862	0.858	0.855
	40	41	42	43	44	50	51	52	53	54
D	0.862	0.856	0.863	0.859	0.859	0.856	0.853	0.861	0.860	0.858
1 × 2	0.862	0.855	0.863	0.863	0.861	0.859	0.856	**0.863**	0.860	0.858
2 × 2	0.862	0.858	0.861	0.860	0.859	0.856	0.858	0.859	0.834	0.857
1 × 3	0.859	0.857	0.860	0.859	0.859	0.857	0.859	0.860	0.860	0.857
2 × 3	0.859	0.857	0.860	0.859	0.859	0.856	0.855	0.858	0.835	0.858
1 × 1	0.857	0.856	0.860	0.862	0.857	0.857	0.854	0.860	0.859	0.857

FIGURE 5: Summary of results from nine subjects in the 400 ms trial interval.

training and test sets was not even. Thus, we used the expression

$$\text{accuracy} = \sqrt{\frac{TP}{P} \times \frac{TN}{N}}, \qquad (1)$$

where TP stands for true positives and reflects the number of correctly classified target examples, and TN stands for true negatives and reflects the number of correctly classified nontarget examples. P and N represent the total number of examples of target and nontarget classes, respectively, for this case. This expression heavily penalizes poor individual classification in binary classification tasks.

4. P300 Identification: Results and Discussion

The results presented next correspond to the average accuracy obtained for the nine subjects in testing of CNN models. The highest and lowest accuracy rates are highlighted in bold and red fonts, respectively. By analyzing the performance obtained using different pooling strategies in the form of different fixed pooling strides (presented in the first column from left to right), it is often observed that some pooling strategies do not offer relevant differences at first glance.

By analyzing the summarized results for the three trial intervals, we found no clear tendency for which model and pool stride offer the highest or lowest accuracies. For instance, in the 500 ms trial interval models (Figure 4), the lowest accuracy was obtained from the model with patch code 23 and [2 × 2] pool stride, while in both the 400 and 300 ms cases, these results were obtained using the model with patch code 30 and [2 × 3] pool stride, which is similar to the 500 ms case.

As for the highest accuracy results, there are some similarities in the 400 and 300 ms trial intervals (Figures 5 and 6, resp.). In these cases, the implemented models used

	00	01	02	03	04	10	11	12	13	14
D	0.848	0.847	0.851	0.850	0.849	0.847	0.845	0.850	0.850	0.848
1 × 2	0.848	0.849	0.851	0.851	0.849	0.849	0.849	0.850	0.850	0.849
2 × 2	0.848	0.848	0.835	0.848	0.849	0.847	0.847	0.851	0.850	0.846
1 × 3	0.849	0.848	**0.852**	0.850	0.849	0.848	0.846	0.851	0.850	0.848
2 × 3	0.850	0.847	0.850	0.850	0.849	0.849	0.848	0.848	0.848	0.848
1 × 1	0.848	0.848	0.851	0.850	0.849	0.847	0.847	0.849	0.850	0.849
	20	21	22	23	24	30	31	32	33	34
D	0.848	0.846	0.851	0.849	0.847	0.850	0.844	0.850	0.850	0.845
1 × 2	0.849	0.849	0.851	0.848	0.849	0.850	0.847	0.850	0.850	0.848
2 × 2	0.848	0.847	0.851	0.833	0.849	0.850	0.848	0.850	0.848	0.847
1 × 3	0.849	0.847	0.851	0.849	0.849	0.848	0.848	0.849	0.850	0.847
2 × 3	0.849	0.846	0.835	0.836	0.847	0.832	0.846	0.848	0.847	0.845
1 × 1	0.848	0.847	0.849	0.848	0.849	0.850	0.848	0.850	0.850	0.848
	40	41	42	43	44	50	51	52	53	54
D	0.849	0.846	0.848	0.850	0.848	0.847	0.844	0.848	0.850	0.845
1 × 2	0.849	0.848	0.848	0.848	0.848	0.851	0.845	0.848	0.848	0.845
2 × 2	0.848	0.847	0.847	0.850	0.848	0.847	0.845	0.846	0.833	0.846
1 × 3	0.849	0.848	0.851	0.850	0.850	0.846	0.846	0.849	0.850	0.848
2 × 3	0.847	0.848	0.850	0.848	0.848	0.847	0.845	0.847	0.834	0.845
1 × 1	0.849	0.846	0.850	0.849	0.848	0.846	0.843	0.851	0.846	0.847

FIGURE 6: Summary of results from nine subjects in the 300 ms trial interval.

pool patch (2) under the [1 × 3] or [1 × 2] pooling strides, which prevent the models from overlapping and are very similar one to each other. For the 500 ms case, pooling stride was also [1 × 2], the same as in the 400 ms trial interval, while the pool patch was different. If we look back at Table 1, we can see that these convolution patches are quite different from each other.

By analyzing Figure 8, it can be noted that even if the results do not vary strongly one from another, there is a clear pattern of improved performance using data from the 500 ms trial length, followed by the 400 and 300 ms ones. This behavior is expected, as faster production of stimuli can cause subjects to fail to identify stimuli coming from the target direction and therefore incorrectly produce the P300 wave.

TABLE 2: Summary of the highest, lowest, and average accuracies obtained for the CNN models using the 3D input.

	Highest	Lowest	Average
500 ms	0.865	0.836	0.86
400 ms	0.863	0.833	0.858
300 ms	0.852	0.832	0.848

By summarizing the results in this way, we also observed that the [1 × 2] pooling stride offers the best results, at least in the 500 and 400 ms trial length, while the [1 × 3] pool stride is optimal on the 300 ms trial length.

On the other hand, the [2 × 3] pool stride produces the lowest results, without being detrimental. Differences between the highest and lowest pool strides rely on how much overlapping the strides provide. While the [2 × 3] pooling stride prevents some pool patches from overlapping at all or even skipping some areas of the input, the [1 × 3] pooling stride forces most pool patches to overlap. In the study by [13], no differences were reported between performance for approaches with or without overlapping, contrary to the report by [9], where better CNN model performance was achieved using overlapping pool strategies. In our case, we found little to no change between different pooling strategies tested. In the above cited research, it is mentioned that success in applying pooling strategies might depend completely on the nature, shape, and conditions of the used data.

In Table 2, the average values considering all models for each of the three trial lengths are presented next to their corresponding lowest and highest values.

By comparing these numbers, apparently there are no big differences between trial lengths and their highest/lowest values. We believe this lack of variation between the many tested models is the result of the implementation of the 3D input, which, regardless of the speed of the stimuli presentation used in this study, can present the necessary information for correct classification. To support this idea, we tested 4 additional CNN models using the commonly 2D input approach with convolution patches [1 × 4] and [3 × 3]. As for the pool patches, we also tested two, with sizes [1 × 2] and [2 × 2], both with a default pooling stride as our results so far indicate the pooling strategies do not offer significant CNN performance differences. The patches were chosen as they are the same as those used by the CNN models with the best results using the 3D input. Besides the input shape and the convolution and pool patches, the parameters of the CNN models using the 2D input do not differ from the ones presented so far in Section 3.2. The results from the models using the 2D input can be seen in Table 3.

In the case of the results for the models using the 2D input, the difference between models and trial lengths is more easily noticed. While in the results involving the 3D input the difference of the overall highest and lowest accuracy is of about 3%; in the case of the 2D input results, the difference is around 10%. Also, we can see that the convolution and pool patches that consider information from only one channel at a time offer better results than those in which information from multiple channels is considered.

TABLE 3: Proposed convolution and pool patches for the CNN models in which a 2D input was implemented. CP and PP stand for *convolution patch* and *pool patch*, respectively.

CP	PP	Accuracy		
		500 ms	400 ms	300 ms
[1 × 4]	[1 × 2]	**0.781**	**0.768**	**0.734**
	[2 × 2]	0.753	0.716	0.727
[3 × 3]	[1 × 2]	0.766	0.725	0.732
	[2 × 2]	0.724	0.707	0.698
Average		0.756	0.729	0.722

TABLE 4: Results for each subject in those models with the highest accuracy for each trial length considering the CNN models with both the 3D and 2D input approach. The subject's number appears on the first column to the left.

	500 ms		400 ms		300 ms	
	3D	2D	3D	2D	3D	2D
(1)	0.880	0.72	0.877	0.736	0.859	0.685
(2)	0.873	0.823	0.866	0.78	0.878	0.744
(3)	**0.896**	**0.774**	**0.908**	**0.794**	0.859	0.774
(4)	0.828	0.812	0.83	0.766	0.831	0.785
(5)	0.864	0.78	0.851	0.792	0.826	0.697
(6)	0.828	0.808	0.828	0.763	0.825	0.685
(7)	0.881	0.788	0.858	0.752	**0.886**	**0.796**
(8)	0.879	0.792	0.904	0.77	0.847	0.721
(9)	0.863	0.736	0.847	0.76	0.853	0.722

In Table 4 the individual results for each subject considering the models with the highest accuracy for each trial length using both 3D and 2D approaches are shown. The models with highest accuracy are those presented with bold font in Figures 4–6 and Table 3.

The results obtained show individual performance patterns appearing in both approaches in a similar way. For a given trial length, the subject with the highest individual accuracy is the same regardless of the approach (3D or 2D). Although in some cases the accuracy difference between both approaches for a single subject is minimal, all the results from the CNN models using 3D input offered better accuracies.

Besides the difference in the obtained accuracies, the train/test of the 3D input models was also faster than that of the models using the 2D input. The average time of the 3D input models for training/testing a single subject was around 8 minutes, while for the case of the models using the 2D input, around 18 minutes were necessary.

4.1. Statistical Analysis. Given that the results obtained so far do not show big differences of the performance of the CNN models whether we consider the models themselves or the trial length in which they were tested, we conducted an analysis of variance (ANOVA) to further examine the results.

First, we checked if applying the different tested models (variation of convolution and pool patch sizes) had a significant impact on the performance of the CNN models. The

TABLE 5: Results for the ANOVA between the 30 tested models. The critical F value is 1.54.

	F	p	Significant differences
500 ms	1.29	0.159	No
400 ms	1.44	0.08	No
300 ms	1.55	0.047	Yes

TABLE 6: Results for the ANOVA between the 6 implemented pool strides. The critical F value is 2.26.

	F	p	Significant differences
500 ms	4.21	0.001	Yes
400 ms	4.72	0.0004	Yes
300 ms	5.015	0.0002	Yes

results are shown in Table 5 for the three trial lengths that were considered for this study.

We found that, for the models using examples from the 500 and 400 ms trial lengths, there were no significant differences, but there were ones for the case of the 300 ms trial length. As the trial length becomes shorter, it becomes harder for users to correctly identify the sound coming from the target direction and in this case the differences between models become clearer.

Next, we present the results for the ANOVA between the tested pool strides in Table 6. In this case, there are significant differences among the implemented pool strides regardless of the trial length. We proposed applying several pooling strides to explore whether by causing or avoiding overlapping during the pooling process the performance of the models improved. In Figure 5 we have the average accuracy for all the models under each pool stride displayed, but the small differences between the results made it difficult to state if they were different enough to make an assessment. Now, the results in Table 6 show that varying the pooling stride to cause overlapping or avoid it significantly impacts the performance of the tested CNN models.

4.2. Comparison with Previous Work and Other Classifiers. The current results show an improvement of around 15% over the work of [10], from where the experimental setup for this research was borrowed (see Figure 7). The EEG data was obtained also in a similar fashion, enabling the current comparison. Also, this study shares some similarities with that done by [14] which is why we also include it in the comparison. In most cases, it is difficult to make an appropriate comparison due to the differences in the nature of the experiments, subjects, and technologies used and for such reasons, the comparison is only demonstrative. All the results used for comparison in Figure 7 are the ones corresponding to the single trial (also noted as nonaveraged) case. The highest results obtained for the implementation of the 2D input are also included.

We now compare the results from the models using the proposed 3D input with those obtained by using support vector machines (SVM) and Fisher's discriminant analysis (FDA). We chose to use these two classifiers as they are

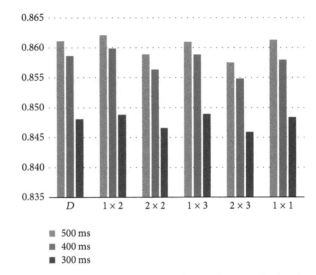

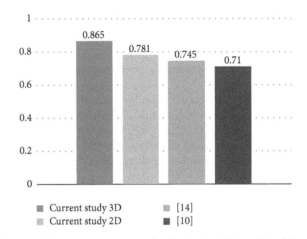

FIGURE 7: Averaged accuracy rate by pooling stride for three proposed trial intervals.

FIGURE 8: Average accuracy rate for the single trial case. Conditions of experiment and subjects might differ between the studies.

TABLE 7: Comparison between the highest accuracies obtained using the proposed 3D input for CNN models, a SVM, and a FDA.

	CNN 3D	SVM	FDA
500 ms	0.865	0.709	0.745
400 ms	0.863	0.711	0.731
300 ms	0.852	0.691	0.707

common in this context and the SVM was used in [10]. Table 7 shows the results for comparison of the highest accuracies obtained in the different trial lengths. Details about the SVM and FDA can be found in the appendix.

Both the FDA and the SVM offer accuracies below those from the model using the proposed input.

5. Final Comments and Future Work

Through this research we found that it is possible to implement a 3D input shape using EEG data with success for different CNN models that exhibit different pooling strategies based on proposed fixed pooling strides that might cause the models to overlap during the pooling process or avoid it. We hypothesize that using this approach might yield better results compared to the most common approaches which use 2D mapped version of the data. The basis of such thinking lies in the nature of the convolution and pooling processes, which highly depend on the relation between a data point and its surroundings. This lack of variation might point to a better representation of the information given by the proposed 3D input. Also, we found that, for the current study, causing overlapping with fixed pooling stride significantly impacts the performance of the tested CNN models.

The obtained results showed improvement over others seen in similar studies using nonaveraged data. Also, when compared to other classifiers commonly used in this context, the CNN models using the proposed input performed better.

While we believe this was a successful application of a novel input structure, we consider that such construction will perform particularly well when the nature of the data is such that mapping it to simpler representations comes with information loss. For other BCI approaches as well as for other kinds of brain activity readings, this approach might not be the best fit and its application might require a case by case analysis.

With the proposed 3D input we were able to find also a faster way to train/test, as this approach showed taking less time for such tasks than the models using a 2D input. We expect to keep using this input representation to test its limitations and possible new applications in future studies.

Appendix

SVM. Analysis was performed using LIBSVM software [15] and implemented in MATLAB (Mathworks, Natick, USA). We used a weighted linear SVM [16] to compensate for imbalance in the target and nontarget examples. Thus, we used a penalty parameter of C+ for the target and C− for the nontarget examples. The penalty parameter for each class was searched in the range of 10^{-6} to 10^{-1} ($10^{-6} \leq 10^m \leq 10^{-1}$; m: $-6 : 0.5 : -1$) within the training. We determined the best parameters as those obtaining the highest accuracy using 10-fold cross-validation for the training. Using the best penalty parameters, we constructed the SVM classifier using all training data and applied it to the test data.

FDA. We used a variant of the regularized Fisher discriminant analysis (FDA) as the classification algorithm [14]. In this algorithm, a regularized parameter for FDA is searched for by particle swarm optimization (for details, see [14]) within the training. In this study, we used all EEG channels without selection.

Acknowledgments

This work was partly supported by JSPS Kakenhi Grant nos. 2430051 and 16K00182 and Nagaoka University of Technology Presidential Research Grant.

References

[1] B. Rebsamen, E. Burdet, C. Guan et al., "Controlling a wheelchair indoors using thought," *IEEE Intelligent Systems*, vol. 22, no. 2, pp. 18–24, March 2007.

[2] E. W. Sellers and E. Donchin, "A P300-based brain-computer interface: initial tests by ALS patients," *Clinical Neurophysiology*, vol. 117, no. 3, pp. 538–548, 2006.

[3] M. Chang, N. Nishikawa, Z. R. Struzik et al., Comparison of P300 Responses in Auditory, Visual and Audiovisual Spatial Speller BCI Paradigms, ArXiv e-prints, Jan. 2013.

[4] H. Cecotti and A. Gräser, "Time Delay Neural Network with Fourier transform for multiple channel detection of Steady-State Visual Evoked Potentials for Brain-Computer Interfaces," in *Proceedings of the 16th European Signal Processing Conference (EUSIPCO '08)*, pp. 1–5, August 2008.

[5] I. Güler and E. D. Übeyli, "Multiclass support vector machines for EEG-signals classification," *IEEE Transactions on Information Technology in Biomedicine*, vol. 11, no. 2, pp. 117–126, 2007.

[6] O. Abdel-Hamid, L. Deng, and D. Yu, "Exploring convolutional neural network structures and optimization techniques for speech recognition," in *Proceedings of the 14th Annual Conference of the International Speech Communication Association, INTERSPEECH 2013*, pp. 3366–3370, fra, August 2013.

[7] K. Simonyan and A. Zisserman, Very deep convolutional networks for large-scale image recognition, CoRR, vol. abs/1409.1556, 2014, http://arxiv.org/abs/1409.1556.

[8] H. Cecotti and A. Gräser, "Convolutional neural networks for P300 detection with application to brain-computer interfaces," *IEEE Transactions on Pattern Analysis and Machine Intelligence*, vol. 33, no. 3, pp. 433–445, 2011.

[9] Y. LeCun, B. Boser, J. S. Denker et al., "Backpropagation applied to handwritten zip code recognition," *Neural Computation*, vol. 1, no. 4, pp. 541–551, 1989.

[10] I. Nambu, M. Ebisawa, M. Kogure, S. Yano, H. Hokari, and Y. Wada, "Estimating the Intended Sound Direction of the User: Toward an Auditory Brain-Computer Interface Using Out-of-Head Sound Localization," *PLoS ONE*, vol. 8, no. 2, Article ID e57174, 2013.

[11] S. Yano, H. Hokari, and S. Shimada, "A study on personal difference in the transfer functions of sound localization using stereo earphones," *IEICE TRANSACTIONS on Fundamentals of Electronics, Communications and Computer Sciences*, vol. 83, no. 5, pp. 877–887, 2000.

[12] I. J. Goodfellow, D. Warde-Farley, P. Lamblin et al., Pylearn2: a machine learning research library, ArXiv e-prints, Aug. 2013.

[13] T. N. Sainath, B. Kingsbury, G. Saon et al., "Deep Convolutional Neural Networks for Large-scale Speech Tasks," *Neural Networks*, vol. 64, pp. 39–48, 2015.

[14] A. Gonzalez, I. Nambu, H. Hokari, and Y. Wada, "EEG channel selection using particle swarm optimization for the classification of auditory event-related potentials," *The Scientific World Journal*, vol. 2014, Article ID 350270, 11 pages, 2014.

[15] C. Chang and C. Lin, "LIBSVM: a Library for support vector machines," *ACM Transactions on Intelligent Systems and Technology*, vol. 2, no. 3, article 27, 2011.

[16] E. Osuna, R. Freund, and F. Girosi, "An improved training algorithm for support vector machines," in *Proceedings of the 7th IEEE Workshop on Neural Networks for Signal Processing (NNSP '97)*, pp. 276–285, September 1997.

12

High Performance Implementation of 3D Convolutional Neural Networks on a GPU

Qiang Lan,[1,2] **Zelong Wang,**[1,2] **Mei Wen,**[1,2] **Chunyuan Zhang,**[1,2] **and Yijie Wang**[1,2]

[1]*College of Computer, National University of Defense Technology, Changsha 410073, China*
[2]*National Key Laboratory of Parallel and Distributed Processing, Changsha 410073, China*

Correspondence should be addressed to Qiang Lan; lanqiang_nudt@163.com

Academic Editor: Athanasios Voulodimos

Convolutional neural networks have proven to be highly successful in applications such as image classification, object tracking, and many other tasks based on 2D inputs. Recently, researchers have started to apply convolutional neural networks to video classification, which constitutes a 3D input and requires far larger amounts of memory and much more computation. FFT based methods can reduce the amount of computation, but this generally comes at the cost of an increased memory requirement. On the other hand, the Winograd Minimal Filtering Algorithm (WMFA) can reduce the number of operations required and thus can speed up the computation, without increasing the required memory. This strategy was shown to be successful for 2D neural networks. We implement the algorithm for 3D convolutional neural networks and apply it to a popular 3D convolutional neural network which is used to classify videos and compare it to cuDNN. For our highly optimized implementation of the algorithm, we observe a twofold speedup for most of the 3D convolution layers of our test network compared to the cuDNN version.

1. Introduction

Convolutional neural networks have proven advantages over traditional machine learning methods on applications such as image classification [1–4], tracking [5, 6], detection [7–11]. However, the primary downside of convolutional neural networks is the increased computational cost. This becomes especially challenging for 3D convolution where handling even the smallest instances requires substantial resources.

3D convolutional neural networks have recently come to the attention of the scientific community. In [12], a database for 3D object recognition named ObjectNet3D is presented. The database focuses on the problem of recognizing the 3D pose and the shape of objects from 2D images. Another repository of 3D CAD models of objects is ShapeNet [13]. In [14], the authors propose VoxNet, a 3D convolutional neural network, to solve the robust object recognition task with the help of 3D information, while the authors of [15] propose a 3D convolutional neural networks for human-action recognition.

In the light of these successful applications, it is worthwhile to explore new ways of speeding up the 3D convolution operation. In this paper we do so by deriving the 3D convolution forms of the minimal filtering algorithms invented by Toom and Cook [16] and generalized by Winograd [17]. Our experiments show this algorithm to be very efficient in accelerating 3D convolutional neural network in video classification applications.

2. Related Work

Many approaches aim to directly reduce the computational cost within CNN. In [18], the authors analyse the algebraic properties of CNNs and propose an algorithmic improvement to reduce the computational workload. They achieve a 47% reduction in computation without affecting the accuracy. In [19], convolution operations are replaced with pointwise products in the Fourier domain, which can reduce the amount of computation significantly. Reference [20] evaluates two fast Fourier transform (FFT) convolution implementations, one based on Nvidia cuFFT [21] and the other based on Facebook's FFT implementation. The FFT method can achieve an obvious speeding up of performance when the filter size is large, and the disadvantage of the FFT method is that it consumes much more memory than the standard method.

In [22], the authors use WMFA (Winograd Minimal Filter Algorithm) [17] to implement the convolution operation. In theory, fewer multiplications are needed in the WMFA, while not much extra memory is needed. WMFA is easy to parallelize; Lavin and Gray [22] implemented the algorithm on GPU, and they achieved better performance than the fastest cuDNN library. In [23], the authors show a novel architecture implemented in OpenCL on an FPGA platform; the algorithm they use to do the convolution is WMFA, which significantly boosts the performance of the FPGA. However, both works implemented 2D convolutional neural networks.

In this paper, we make four main contributions. Firstly, we derive the 3D forms of WMFA and design detailed algorithm to implement 3D convolution operation based on 3D WMFA. Secondly, we analyse the arithmetic complexity of 3D WMFA and prove 3D WMFA method can reduce computation in theory. Thirdly, we implement 3D WMFA for GPU platform and propose several optimization techniques to improve the performance of 3D WMFA. Finally, we evaluate the performance of 3D convolutional neural networks based on several implementations and prove the advantage of our proposed 3D WMFA method.

3. Fast 3D Convolution Algorithm

3.1. Preliminary: 3D Convolutional Neural Networks. For the 2D convolution, kernels have fixed width and height, and they are slid along the width and height of the input feature maps. For the 3D convolution, both feature maps and kernels have depth dimension, and the convolution also needs to slide along the depth direction. We can compute the output of a 3D convolutional layer using the following formula:

$$Y_{i,k,x,y,z} = \sum_{c=0}^{C-1} \sum_{t=0}^{T-1} \sum_{r=0}^{R-1} \sum_{s=0}^{S-1} I_{i,c,x+t,y+r,z+s} F_{k,t,r,s,c}, \quad (1)$$

where $Y_{i,k,x,y,z}$ represents the result of a convolution operation at the kth channel feature and $I_{i,c,x+t,y+r,z+s}$ is one of the input features, while $F_{k,t,r,s,c}$ is one of the filters. Equation (1) represents a direct convolution method, which requires intensive computability. The detailed arithmetic complexity of this method is shown in Section 3.3.

3.2. 3D WMFA. We introduce a new, fast algorithm to compute a 3D convolutional layer. The algorithm is based on WMFA. In order to introduce the 3D WMFA, firstly, we will give a simple introduction to the 1D WMFA. WMFA computes output with a tile size of m each time; we use $F(m, r)$ to represent the output tile and r is the filter size. According to the definition of convolution, $2 \times 3 = 6$ multiplications are required to compute $F(2, 3)$, but we can reduce the number of multiplications to do the convolution if we use the following WMFA:

$$F(2,3) = \begin{bmatrix} i_0 & i_1 & i_2 \\ i_1 & i_2 & i_3 \end{bmatrix} \begin{bmatrix} f_0 \\ f_1 \\ f_2 \end{bmatrix} = \begin{bmatrix} m_1 + m_2 + m_3 \\ m_2 - m_3 - m_4 \end{bmatrix}, \quad (2)$$

where

$$m_1 = (i_0 - i_2) f_0,$$

$$m_2 = (i_1 + i_2) \frac{f_0 + f_1 + f_2}{2},$$

$$m_4 = (i_1 - i_3) f_2,$$

$$m_3 = (i_2 - i_1) \frac{f_0 - f_1 + f_2}{2}.$$

$$(3)$$

The number of multiplications needed is $\mu(F(2, 3)) = 2 + 3 - 1 = 4$; however, four additions are needed to transform the input image, three additions to transform the filter, and four additions to transform the result of the dot product. We can use a matrix form to represent the computation:

$$Y = A^T \left[\left(B^T i \right) \odot \left(Gf \right) \right]. \quad (4)$$

We call the A^T, G, and B^T transform matrices, and the values of the transforming matrices are

$$B^T = \begin{bmatrix} 1 & 0 & -1 & 0 \\ 0 & 1 & 1 & 0 \\ 0 & -1 & 1 & 0 \\ 0 & 1 & 0 & -1 \end{bmatrix},$$

$$G = \begin{bmatrix} 1 & 0 & 0 \\ \frac{1}{2} & \frac{1}{2} & \frac{1}{2} \\ \frac{1}{2} & -\frac{1}{2} & \frac{1}{2} \\ 0 & 0 & 1 \end{bmatrix}, \quad (5)$$

$$A^T = \begin{bmatrix} 1 & 1 & 1 & 0 \\ 0 & 1 & -1 & -1 \end{bmatrix}.$$

In (4), $i = \begin{bmatrix} i_0 & i_1 & i_2 & i_3 \end{bmatrix}^T$ and $f = \begin{bmatrix} f_0 & f_1 & f_2 \end{bmatrix}^T$ represent the input tile and filter tile, respectively. As described in [22], the format of the 2D WMFA is as follows:

$$Y = A^T \left[\left[Gf G^T \right] \odot \left[B^T i B \right] \right] A, \quad (6)$$

where f is the filter with size $r \times r$ and i is the image with size $(m + r - 1) \times (m + r - 1)$. To compute $F(2 \times 2, 3 \times 3)$, we need $4 \times 4 = 16$ multiplications; however, $4 \times 9 = 36$ multiplications are needed according to the convolution definition. Therefore, 2D WMFA can reduce the number of multiplications by a factor of $36/16 = 2.25$ at the cost of increasing 32 additions in the data transformation stage, 28 floating point instructions at the filter transformation stage, and 24 additions at the inverse transformation stage. For a convolutional layer, the number of input channels and number of output channels are large, which means the input channels need to convolve different filters, so the transformed input tile can be reused as many times as the number of output channels. Each filter needs to be slid in x

```
Input: I₀[in_size][in_size][in_size]
Temp array: I₁[in_size][out_size][in_size], I₂[in_size][out_size][out_size]
Output: I₃[out_size][out_size][out_size]
for i = 0 to in_size do
    for j = 0 to in_size do
        I₁[i][0 : out_size][j] = Tₘ I₀[i][0 : in_size][j]
    end for
end for
for i = 0 to in_size do
    for j = 0 to out_size do
        I₂[i][j][0 : out_size] = Tₘ I₁[i][j][0 : in_size]
    end for
end for
for i = 0 to out_size do
    for j = 0 to out_size do
        I₃[0 : out_size][i][j] = Tₘ I₂[0 : in_size][i][j]
    end for
end for
```

ALGORITHM 1: 3D winograd transformation.

and y direction of input channel during convolution, so each transformed filter is reused as many times as the number of subtiles of input channel. And since the output tile is reduced along the input channels, the inverse transformation is done after reduction; then the number of inverse transformation is determined by the number of output channels. Therefore, the cost of data transformation stage, filter transformation stage, and the inverse transformation stage keep low in real convolutional layer implementation.

We can also apply the 3D WMFA to 3D convolution. To compute $F(2 \times 2 \times 2, 3 \times 3 \times 3)$, we apply the 3D Winograd transformation to the input tile and filter tile and apply 3D Winograd inverse transformation to the dot product of the transformed input image tile and the transformed filter tile. Algorithm 1 is a general form of the 3D Winograd transformation. In the algorithm, T_m is the transformation matrix; the transformation matrix can be G applied to transform the filter tile or B^T applied to transform the input image tile. The dot product of the transformed input image tile and transformed filter tile will be accumulated along the C channels, which can be converted to a matrix multiplication similar to the description in [22]

$$Y_{i,x,y,z,k} = \sum_{c=0}^{C-1} I_{i,c,x,y,z} * F_{k,c} = \sum_{c=0}^{C-1} A^T \left[U_{k,c} \odot V_{c,i,x,y,z} \right] A$$
$$= A^T \left[\sum_{c=0}^{C-1} U_{k,c} \odot V_{c,i,x,y,z} \right] A. \tag{7}$$

Consider the sum

$$M_{k,i,x,y,z} = \sum_{c=0}^{C-1} U_{k,c} \odot V_{c,i,x,y,z}. \tag{8}$$

The previous equation can be divided into several submatrix multiplications; assume the output tile size is (ε, η, ν), using new coordinates $(i, \tilde{x}, \tilde{y}, \tilde{z})$ to replace (i, x, y, z), yielding

$$M_{k,i,\tilde{x},\tilde{y},\tilde{z}}^{\varepsilon,\eta,\nu} = \sum_{c=0}^{C-1} U_{k,c}^{(\varepsilon,\eta,\nu)} V_{c,i,\tilde{x},\tilde{y},\tilde{z}}^{(\varepsilon,\eta,\nu)}. \tag{9}$$

This equation represents the matrix multiplication, and it can be simplified as follows:

$$M^{(\varepsilon,\eta,\nu)} = U^{(\varepsilon,\eta,\nu)} V^{(\varepsilon,\eta,\nu)}. \tag{10}$$

Algorithm 2 gives the overview of the 3D WMFA. The algorithm mainly consists of four stages, which are Winograd transformation of the input feature tile; Winograd transformation of the filter tile; the matrix multiplication, which is converted from the dot product of the transformed input tile and the transformed filter tile; and the inverse Winograd transformation of the result of the matrix multiplication.

3.3. Arithmetic Complexity Analysis. For input feature maps with size $N \times C \times D \times H \times W$, filters with size $K \times C \times k \times k \times k$, and the output features with size $N \times K \times M \times P \times Q$, the total number of float operations in the multiplication stage can be represented as follows:

$$L_1 = 2N \left\lceil \frac{M}{m} \right\rceil \left\lceil \frac{P}{m} \right\rceil \left\lceil \frac{Q}{m} \right\rceil CK (m + r - 1)^3, \tag{11}$$

where r is the filter size and m is the size of the output subtile. However, if we use the direct convolution method, which is computed according to the definition of convolution, the total number of float operations is computed as follows:

$$L_2 = 2NMPQCKr^3. \tag{12}$$

Dividing L_1 by L_2 yields

$$\frac{L_2}{L_1} = \frac{m^3 * r^3}{(m + r - 1)^3}. \tag{13}$$

$P = N\lceil M/m\rceil\lceil P/m\rceil\lceil Q/m\rceil$ is the number of image tiles.
$\alpha = m + r - 1$ is the input tile size.
Neighbouring tiles overlap by $r - 1$.
$d_{c,b} \in R^{\alpha\times\alpha\times\alpha}$ is input tile b in channel c.
$g_{k,c} \in R^{r\times r\times r}$ is filter k in channel c.
$Y_{k,b} \in R^{m\times m\times m}$ is output tile b in filter k.
for $k = 0$ to K **do**
    for $c = 0$ to C **do**
        $u = T_k(g_{k,c}) \in R^{\alpha\times\alpha\times\alpha}$
        Scatter u to matrices U: $U_{k,c}^{(i,j,k)} = u_{i,j,k}$
    end for
end for
for $b = 0$ to P **do**
    for $c = 0$ to C **do**
        $v = T_d(d_{c,b}) \in R^{\alpha\times\alpha\times\alpha}$
        Scatter v to matrices V: $V_{c,b}^{(i,j,k)} = v_{i,j,k}$
    end for
end for
for $i = 0$ to α **do**
    for $j = 0$ to α **do**
        for $k = 0$ to α **do**
            $M^{(i,j,k)} = U^{(i,j,k)}V^{(i,j,k)}$
        end for
    end for
end for
for $k = 0$ to K **do**
    for $b = 0$ to P **do**
        Gather m from matrices M: $m_{i,j,k} = M_{k,b}$
        $Y_{k,b} = T_m(m)$
    end for
end for

ALGORITHM 2: 3D Convolutional layer implemented with WMFA $F(m \times m \times m, r \times r \times r)$.

Assuming $m = 2$ and $r = 3$, there is an arithmetic complexity reduction of $(2 * 2 * 2 * 3 * 3 * 3)/(4 * 4 * 4) = 216/64 = 3.375$. However, there are some extra computations in Winograd transformation stage, so we cannot achieve so much complexity reduction in reality. The detailed performance improvements are shown in Section 5.2.

4. Implementation and Optimizations

4.1. Implementation. We have three implementation versions for the 3D WMFA on a GPU. In our implementations, cuBLAS is called to do the multiplication. Furthermore, we manually implement six kernels according to Algorithm 2. Figure 1 shows the flow of our baseline implementation. The *imageTransform* kernel transforms all the image subtiles, the *filterTransform* kernel transforms all the filter tiles, and *ouputTransform* kernel inversely transforms the result of the multiplication. For the baseline implementation, we also have two additional kernels to reorganize the transformed image data and transformed filter data and one kernel to reorganize the result of the multiplication before the results go to the *outputTransform* kernel.

Winograd transformation algorithm is suitable for parallelization on GPU. Taking the *imageTransform* kernel as an example, the input to the *imageTransform* kernel is the input

feature map. We assume the input feature maps have a size of $N \times C \times D \times H \times W$, where N is the batch size, C is the number of input channels, and $D \times H \times W$ is the size of a single channel. As is described in Algorithm 2, the number of image tiles for each channel is P, so the total number of image tiles is $P \times C$; all those image tiles can be transformed independently. For the baseline of the GPU implementation, the image data is stored in *NCDHW* order, and we set the number of threads in one block to be 32, each thread is responsible for processing Winograd transformation of one input subtile, and the number of blocks in the grid is set to $(\lceil N/32\rceil, \lceil M/m\rceil\lceil P/m\rceil\lceil Q/m\rceil, C)$. We can make full use of the large-scale parallel processing units of a GPU when the number of blocks is large.

For the *filterTransform* kernel, there are $K \times C$ filter tiles; we still set the number of threads of one block to be 32 and the number of blocks to $(\lceil K/32\rceil, C, 1)$. Before we call cuBLAS to implement the matrix multiplication, we need to reorganize the transformed filter and transformed image data. For transformed filter, there are $K \times C$ tiles in total, and each tile has size of $\alpha \times \alpha \times \alpha$, each time we gather one value from one tile to generate a submatrix of size $K \times C$. Figure 2 shows how the transformed data are reorganized in new layout on GPU; they are implemented by the kernels *reshapeTransformedImage* and *reshapeTransformedFilter* in

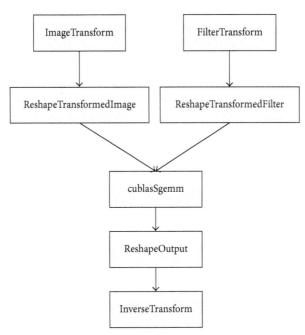

FIGURE 1: The computing flow of 3D WMFA.

our baseline implementation. They gather correlated and transformed filters and transformed image data to form two submatrices, and *SGEMM* from the cuBLAS library is called to do the multiplication. The result of the multiplication also needs to be reshaped before the inverse transformation.

4.2. Optimizations. We make two optimizations to achieve higher performance. The first optimization is to align memory access, which can make memory access more efficient and increase the cache hit rate. The second optimization is to combine the transformation kernel with the reshape kernel to reduce global memory access.

The storing order of data and how data is accessed by a thread can significantly affect the performance. For the baseline implementation, the image data is stored in *NCDHW* order, and threads in the same block access data along the *N*-dimension, which means data accessed by threads keeps long distances. However, the size of the cache on a GPU is limited; therefore, if the distance between the data items accessed by threads is larger than the size of the cache line, then each thread needs to access global memory separately, causing lots of memory accesses. In our first optimization version, we change the storage order of image data to *CDHWN*. Since the image data is stored starting from the N-dimension, data accessed by all threads in the same block is continually stored, and all data items loaded from the global memory are useful, which means the bandwidth is fully used. The same optimization method is applied to the filter transformation and inverse transformation kernel.

Based on the first optimization, we apply our second optimization to improve performance further. The second optimization is to reduce the number of global memory accesses. For the baseline implementation, after the filter transformation or image transformation kernel is executed,

TABLE 1: Properties of the GeForce GTX 1080.

Parameters	Values
CUDA capability major/minor version number	6.1
Total amount of global memory	8 GB
CUDA cores	2560
L2 cache Size	2 MB
Warp size	32
Total number of registers available per block	64 KB

the transformed filter or transformed image data need to be stored in a new layout using *reshapeTransformedFilter* and *reshapeTransformedImage* kernel and using the *ReshapeOutput* kernel before the inverse transformation, while on our second optimized version, we move the work of the reshape kernel to the transformation kernel, so in the optimized transform kernel, after the inputs are transformed, the result will be stored directly back in the expected layout. In the optimized inverse transformation, before inverse transformation, the required data is gathered directly from the global memory.

5. Experiments

5.1. Experimental Setup. All experiments are evaluated on a GeForce GTX 1080 GPU, which has a total amount of 8 GBytes global memory and has 20 multiprocessors. Detailed parameters of the GTX 1080 are shown in Table 1.

5.2. Performance Evaluation. We apply our 3D WMFA to a widely used 3D neural network called v3d [9], which is used to classify videos. The 3D neural network has five convolutional layers; Table 2 shows the information about these 3D convolutional layers.

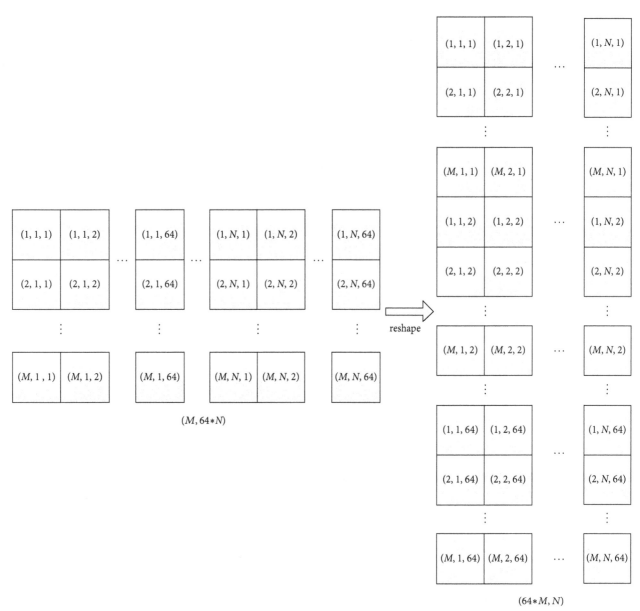

FIGURE 2: For an input matrix, its size is $(M, N * \alpha * \alpha * \alpha)$; α is the tile size, here equal to 4. After the reshape kernel is applied, lots of small submatrices with new layouts are generated.

TABLE 2: Convolution layers of a 3D network; the filter size in all layers is $3 \times 3 \times 3$, and the GFLOPS columns calculate the number of flops operations in each convolutional layer. Assume the batch size is 32.

Layer	$C \times D \times H \times W \times N$	K	GFLOPS
conv1	$3 \times 16 \times 112 \times 112 \times 32$	32	16.65
conv2	$32 \times 16 \times 56 \times 56 \times 32$	64	88.8
conv3	$64 \times 8 \times 28 \times 28 \times 32$	256	88.8
conv4	$256 \times 4 \times 14 \times 14 \times 32$	256	44.4
conv5	$256 \times 2 \times 7 \times 7 \times 32$	256	5.55

Firstly, we evaluate the performance of our three implementations on the 3D convolutional layers, except for the first convolutional layer, which has only three input channels and is not yet supported in the algorithm. Figure 3 shows the increase in speed we achieved after we used two optimizations. For the first optimization, we observe a 3 to 4 times speeding up for all these test convolution layers compared to the baseline implementation. However, for the second optimization, the maximum speeding up can be close to 42 for the third convolution; even the minimum speeding up is about 13 for the last convolution layer. The first optimization makes memory access more efficient, and the second optimization reduces lots of unnecessary global memory accesses. Since the latency of global memory access on a GPU is large, we achieve a good performance improvement in the second optimization.

We explore the detailed performance for one specific convolution layer to see how these two optimizations improve

TABLE 3: Performance of cuDNN SGEMM versus that of the 3D WMFA on 3D convolution layers. Performance is measured in effective TFLOPS.

| Layer | $C \times D \times H \times W \times N$ | K | TFLOPS | | Speedup |
			cuDNN SGEMM	3D WMFA	
conv2	$32 \times 16 \times 56 \times 56 \times 32$	64	1.21	1.28	1.05
conv3	$64 \times 8 \times 28 \times 28 \times 32$	256	2.38	3.31	1.39
conv4	$256 \times 4 \times 14 \times 14 \times 32$	256	2.4	4.72	1.96
conv5	$256 \times 2 \times 7 \times 7 \times 32$	256	1.46	2.1	1.44

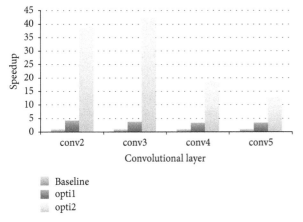

FIGURE 3: Speedup with different optimizations on 3D convolution layers.

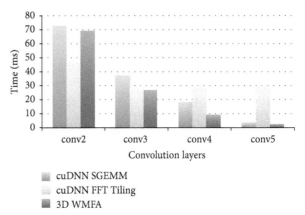

FIGURE 5: Execution time of different methods on 3D convolution layers.

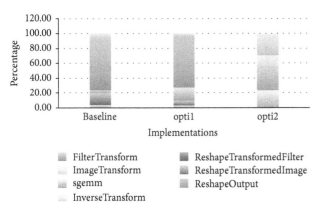

FIGURE 4: Time percentage distribution of each kernel in each implementation version for a specific convolution layer.

each kernel separately. We profile the time percentage of each kernel in each implementation version for conv3, which takes most of the computation time among all these convolution layers. Figure 4 shows the profiling results; the kernel *ReshapeOutput* in both baseline and the first optimization takes up the most time, since the kernel contains lots of global memory accesses. However, in the second optimization version, there are no *reshape* kernels and the kernel *sgemm* takes most of the execution time. In all three implementations, the kernel *filterTransform* takes only about 0.1% of the total time.

Finally, we compare our best optimized implementation with the cuDNN library. The cuDNN library is the fastest deep-learning library. There are two algorithms available to implement a 3D convolution layer: one converts the convolution to a matrix multiplication and the other exploits the FFT tiling method to implement the convolution. We use *cuDNN SGEMM* and *cuDNN FFT Tiling* to represent the two methods called in the cuDNN library, and we use *3D WMFA* to represent our algorithm. Figure 5 shows the execution time of these three methods on four convolution layers. The *3D WMFA* method is about 30% slower than the *cuDNN FFT Tiling* method on the conv2 layer; however, it is a bit faster than *cuDNN SGEMM* method. The *cuDNN FFT Tiling* method achieves a fast speed at the cost of consuming a large amount of memory. Since parameters C and K are not large in the conv2 layer, this makes the matrix multiplication in *3D WMFA* on small scale, which affects the performance. However, with parameters C and K increased on layers conv3, conv4, and conv5, the *3D WMFA* method achieves better performance than the other two methods. We added the execution time of each layer for each method, the total time of all layers is 132.6 ms for cuDNN SGEMM method, 135.4 ms for cuDNN FFT Tiling method, and 108.2 ms for 3D WMFA which is better than the other two methods.

We can also calculate the performance of these two methods in *TFLOPS*. Table 3 shows the effective *TFLOPS* of *cuDNN SGEMM* and 3D WMFA method. We achieve a maximum speedup of 1.96 compared to *cuDNN SGEMM*.

6. Conclusions

A 3D convolution layer requires a high computational cost and consumes lots of memory. We designed a 3D WMFA to implement 3D convolution operation. Compared to traditional convolution methods, such as SGEMM or FFT, the 3D WMFA can reduce computation, in theory. When we implemented the algorithm on a GPU, we observed the expected performance of the algorithm in the experiments. For some 3D convolution layers, we even achieve close to 2 times speedup compared to cuDNN library.

However, the computation and memory requirements of 3D convolution obviously increase with more complex 3D neural networks. In our future work, we will implement $F(4 \times 4 \times 4, 3 \times 3 \times 3)$ to reduce the computation further to ease the intensive computation problem and adopt a FP16 data type to compute, which can save half of the memory usage directly. It is also necessary to parallel the convolution computation among multi-GPUs or multinodes.

Acknowledgments

The authors gratefully acknowledge support from the National Key Research and Development Program under no. 2016YFB1000401; the National Nature Science Foundation of China under NSFC nos. 61502509, 61402504, and 61272145; the National High Technology Research and Development Program of China under no. 2012AA012706; and the Research Fund for the Doctoral Program of Higher Education of China under SRFDP no. 20124307130004.

References

[1] A. Krizhevsky, I. Sutskever, and G. E. Hinton, "Imagenet classification with deep convolutional neural networks," in *Proceedings of the 26th Annual Conference on Neural Information Processing Systems (NIPS '12)*, pp. 1097–1105, Lake Tahoe, Nev, USA, December 2012.

[2] M. Lin, Q. Chen, and S. Yan, Network in network, CoRR abs/1312.4400,.

[3] C. Szegedy, W. Liu, Y. Jia et al., "Going deeper with convolutions," in *Proceedings of the IEEE Conference on Computer Vision and Pattern Recognition (CVPR '15)*, pp. 1–9, Boston, Mass, USA, June 2015.

[4] K. Simonyan and A. Zisserman, *Very deep convolutional networks for large-scale image recognition*, abs/1409.1556, CoRR, 1409.

[5] J. Fan, W. Xu, Y. Wu, and Y. Gong, "Human tracking using convolutional neural networks," *IEEE Transactions on Neural Networks*, vol. 21, no. 10, pp. 1610–1623, 2010.

[6] S. J. Nowlan and J. C. Platt, "A convolutional neural network hand tracker," *Advances in Neural Information Processing Systems*, pp. 901–908, 1995.

[7] M. Szarvas, A. Yoshizawa, M. Yamamoto, and J. Ogata, "Pedestrian detection with convolutional neural networks," in *Proceedings of the 2005 IEEE Intelligent Vehicles Symposium*, pp. 224–229, Las Vegas, Nev, USA, June 2005.

[8] J. Redmon, S. Divvala, R. Girshick, and A. Farhadi, "You Only Look Once: Unified, Real-Time Object Detection," in *Proceedings of the 2016 IEEE Conference on Computer Vision and Pattern Recognition (CVPR)*, pp. 779–788, Las Vegas, Nev, USA, June 2016.

[9] A. Karpathy, G. Toderici, S. Shetty, T. Leung, R. Sukthankar, and F.-F. Li, "Large-scale video classification with convolutional neural networks," in *Proceedings of the 27th IEEE Conference on Computer Vision and Pattern Recognition, (CVPR '14)*, pp. 1725–1732, Columbus, Ohio, USA, June 2014.

[10] S. Lawrence, C. L. Giles, A. C. Tsoi, and A. D. Back, "Face recognition: a convolutional neural-network approach," *IEEE Transactions on Neural Networks*, vol. 8, no. 1, pp. 98–113, 1997.

[11] "Batch size for training convolutional neural networks for sentence classification," *Journal of Advances in Technology and Engineering Research*, vol. 2, no. 5, 2016.

[12] Y. Xiang, W. Kim, W. Chen et al., "Objectnet3D: A large scale database for 3D object recognition," *Lecture Notes in Computer Science (including subseries Lecture Notes in Artificial Intelligence and Lecture Notes in Bioinformatics)*, vol. 9912, pp. 160–176, 2016.

[13] A. X. Chang, T. A. Funkhouser, L. J. Guibas et al., *Shapenet: An information-rich 3d model repository., CoRR abs/1512.03012*, An information-rich 3d model repository, Shapenet.

[14] D. Maturana and S. Scherer, "VoxNet: A 3D Convolutional Neural Network for real-time object recognition," in *Proceedings of the IEEE/RSJ International Conference on Intelligent Robots and Systems, IROS 2015*, pp. 922–928, Hamburg, Germany, October 2015.

[15] S. Ji, W. Xu, M. Yang, and K. Yu, "3D Convolutional neural networks for human action recognition," *IEEE Transactions on Pattern Analysis and Machine Intelligence*, vol. 35, no. 1, pp. 221–231, 2013.

[16] D. E. Knuth, *The Art of Computer Programming*, vol. 2, Seminumerical Algorithms, Addison-Wesley Longman Publishing Co, Boston, Mass, USA, 3rd edition, 1997.

[17] S. Winograd, *Arithmetic complexity of computations*, vol. 33 of *CBMS-NSF Regional Conference Series in Applied Mathematics*, Society for Industrial and Applied Mathematics (SIAM), Philadelphia, Pa., 1980.

[18] J. Cong and B. Xiao, "Minimizing computation in convolutional neural networks," *Lecture Notes in Computer Science (including subseries Lecture Notes in Artificial Intelligence and Lecture Notes in Bioinformatics)*, vol. 8681, pp. 281–290, 2014.

[19] M. Mathieu, M. Henaff, and Y. LeCun, Fast training of convolutional networks through ffts, CoRR abs/1312.5851,.

[20] N. Vasilache, J. Johnson, M. Mathieu, S. Chintala, S. Piantino, and Y. LeCun, *Fast convolutional nets with fbfft: A GPU performance evaluation, CoRR abs/1412.7580*, Fast convolutional nets with fbfft, A GPU performance evaluation.

[21] J. W. Cooley and J. W. Tukey, "An algorithm for the machine calculation of complex Fourier series," *Mathematics of Computation*, vol. 19, pp. 297–301, 1965.

[22] A. Lavin and S. Gray, "Fast algorithms for convolutional neural networks," in *Proceedings of the 2016 IEEE Conference on Computer Vision and Pattern Recognition, CVPR 2016*, pp. 4013–4021, July 2016.

[23] U. Aydonat, S. O'Connell, D. Capalija, A. C. Ling, and G. R. Chiu, "An OpenCL™ deep learning accelerator on Arria 10," in *Proceedings of the 2017 ACM/SIGDA International Symposium on Field-Programmable Gate Arrays, FPGA 2017*, pp. 55–64, Monterey, Calif, USA, February 2017.

13

Underwater Inherent Optical Properties Estimation Using a Depth Aided Deep Neural Network

Zhibin Yu,[1] **Yubo Wang,**[2] **Bing Zheng,**[1] **Haiyong Zheng,**[1] **Nan Wang,**[1] **and Zhaorui Gu**[1]

[1]*Department of Electronic Engineering, College of Information Science and Engineering, Ocean University of China, Qingdao, China*
[2]*School of Life Science and Technology, Xidian University, Xi'an, China*

Correspondence should be addressed to Bing Zheng; bingzh@ouc.edu.cn

Academic Editor: Leonardo Franco

Underwater inherent optical properties (IOPs) are the fundamental clues to many research fields such as marine optics, marine biology, and underwater vision. Currently, beam transmissometers and optical sensors are considered as the ideal IOPs measuring methods. But these methods are inflexible and expensive to be deployed. To overcome this problem, we aim to develop a novel measuring method using only a single underwater image with the help of deep artificial neural network. The power of artificial neural network has been proved in image processing and computer vision fields with deep learning technology. However, image-based IOPs estimation is a quite different and challenging task. Unlike the traditional applications such as image classification or localization, IOP estimation looks at the transparency of the water between the camera and the target objects to estimate multiple optical properties simultaneously. In this paper, we propose a novel Depth Aided (DA) deep neural network structure for IOPs estimation based on a single RGB image that is even noisy. The imaging depth information is considered as an aided input to help our model make better decision.

1. Introduction

Light always plays an important role in physics, chemistry, and biology of oceans research. The process of the light transmission in the seawater is the foundation of ocean optical research. And the optical properties are the key to describe the light transmission process. The wavelength of the visible light is widely spread from 400 nm to 700 nm. The optical properties of the medium are crucial for the further research of underwater vision, marine organism, pollution detection, and other ocean research areas. The optical properties of ocean can be roughly classified as inherent optical properties (IOPs) and apparent optical properties (AOPs). Important IOPs contain spectral absorption coefficient, $a(\lambda)$, scattering coefficients, $b(\lambda)$, and attenuation coefficient, $c(\lambda)$. For a certain wavelength λ, these three properties can be simply described as

$$c(\lambda) = a(\lambda) + b(\lambda). \tag{1}$$

IOPs only correlate with medium itself and are irrelevant to the ambient light field or its geometric distribution.

Measuring these coefficients is fundamental and important to ocean optical research. Beam transmissometers, such as ac-spectra (AC-S) produced by Wetlabs, are the most commonly used devices for IOPs measurement [1–3]. However, its inconvenient to place such an equipment because of the high price and the limited volume of underwater IOPs measured by the device. Moreover, most of the researchers consider the water as homogeneous medium when measuring IOPs [4–7]. Actually, a slight turbulence caused by robots, marine pollution, or organisms may lead to an inhomogeneous medium. But the beam transmissometers can only detect the IOPs in the surrounding area. In such a case, an underwater camera with a real-time system will be more flexible to capture efficient information. Besides, there are some other ways to deduct IOPs based on AOPs [8, 9].

AOPs are those properties that depend both on the medium (the IOPs) and on the geometric structure of the radiation distribution. AOPs can be measured by remote sensing. And many researchers prefer to measure IOPs with transmissometers as the ground truth to verify their AOPs based deduction. But such deduction is not accurate enough.

On one hand, data based on remote sensing is obtained from satellites or airplane. The detailed information may be omitted. On the other hand, remote sensing cannot investigate the IOPs of undersea. AOPs based on remote sensing can only tell us the IOPs distribution of the surface water. Research also shows that the depth of water may bring difficulty when we want to calculate IOPs [10].

Underwater images are always with scattering and absorption. Because of these reasons, underwater images are always blurred because of different light field and IOPs, which may bring difficulty for us to build an accurate physical model [11]. However, there are many researchers showing that they can recover an underwater image with IOPs [12–14] and physical models [15]. That means an underwater image contains plenty of IOPs information. That is why we can restore images with correct IOPs and suitable physical models. If we can estimate IOPs with a single image, it would be much convenient to measure IOPs undersea. Unlike the most of underwater image restoration tasks which aim to reduce the noise caused by scattering and absorption effect [16], the image noisy information will help us to deduct IOPs.

Since Hinton and his colleges proposed the deep learning concept from 2006 [17], deep neural network becomes more and more popular these years. Neural network models are proven not only on computer vision, but also on symmetric recognition, image quality assessment, image restoration, and even optical flow processing [18–23]. Thus, we consider if it is possible to use deep neural network for analyzing underwater images to estimate IOPs in this study. Besides, if we want to build an end-to-end system with an image as inputs and IOPs as outputs, deep neural network is a suitable candidate to connect them together. In this paper, we used AC-S to provide 156 IOPs (78 attenuation coefficients and 78 absorption coefficients) as the ground truth for the neural network training.

2. Depth Aided Deep Neural Networks for IOPs Estimation

The framework of our system can be found in Figure 1. We used a color calibration board as the target underwater object and captured its RGB images with a video camera. We also measured the distance between the board and the camera as depth information. The depth information is used as an aided input to the deep convolutional neural network. Convolutional neural network (CNN), which is developed by Lecun and Bengio [24] in 1995, is a powerful model especially in computer vision research. CNN is improved by Krizhevsky and his colleges in 2012 as AlexNet [25]. We follow their idea to build our model for underwater image analysis. However, our inputs and outputs are different from their work.

Deep neural network can not only recognize what kind of the target object is, but also understand how much blur an image is. But the water quality is not the only factor which causes the image blur. In physical point of view, distance between the camera and the target is also an important factor. The underwater images would be blur if the water quality is low, and the images would also be unclear if the target object is far away from the camera. That is the reason why we

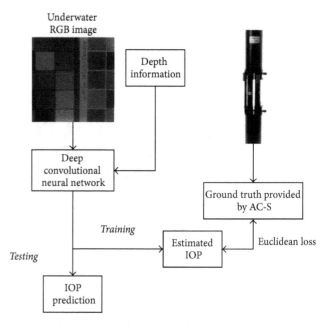

FIGURE 1: The framework of our experiment.

considered depth information of the target object as another useful feature.

Unlike some common neural network application tasks such as image classification, IOPs including multiple coefficients are not binary values. Thus, softmax activation function which is usually used for image classification tasks [26–28] in the last layer cannot be used for our goal. Instead, we applied min–max normalization and Euclidean loss function for IOPs regression:

$$E = \frac{1}{2N} \sum_{i=1}^{N} \left\| y_i - y_i^* \right\|^2, \tag{2}$$

$$y_i^* = \frac{y_{i,\text{original}}^* - y_{\min}}{y_{\max} - y_{\min}}, \tag{3}$$

where $y_{i,\text{original}}^*$ is the i_{th} desired IOP coefficient measured by AC-S, y_i^* is the IOP coefficient after min–max normalization, y_i is the i_{th} estimated IOPs by deep neural network, and N is the number of IOPs. The AC-S employed can provide 78 absorption and 78 attenuation coefficients. Hence, we have $N = 78 \times 2 = 156$. Equation (3) shows the detail of min–max normalization which is used for depth normalization. We also use this method to normalize the depth information.

We design the Depth Aided (DA) neural network model for IOPs estimation as shown in Figure 2. The AC-S can provide 78 attenuation coefficients and 78 absorption coefficients from 400 nm to 730 nm as network output labels when we capture RGB images. These IOPs are used as the targets of the AlexNet. Because our target object is a flat board, depth information is considered as a single number. Thus there is no need to put the depth information into convolution layer. So we set the depth information as an aided input in the feedforward layer 7. The weights between depth information and feedforward layer 7 are fully connected. Error backpropagation algorithm, stochastic gradient descendent (SGD), and

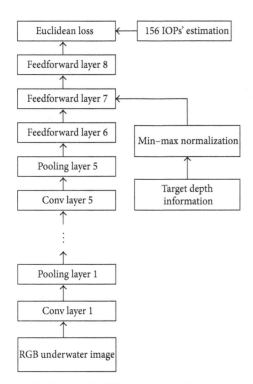

FIGURE 2: The Depth Aided (DA) deep neural network structure.

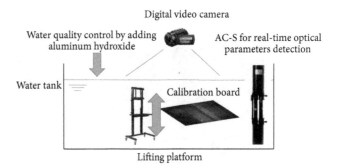

FIGURE 3: The framework of our experiment.

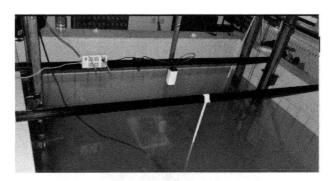

FIGURE 4: Experiment environment.

dropout algorithms [29] are used for evolving this network. The feedforward connections of each neurons in feedforward layer 7 can be described as

$$y_i = f\left(u_j\right) = f\left(w_f x_f + w_d x_d + b\right), \quad (4)$$

where y_j and u_j are the j_{th} neuron postsynaptic and presynaptic value of the feedforward layer 7, respectively; x_f is the neural inputs from the feedforward layer 6; w_f is the weights between layer 6 and layer 7, x_d is the depth information; w_d is the weight in depth information; b is the bias; and $f()$ is the activation function. The network weights updating can follow the error backpropagation rule as

$$\frac{\partial E}{\partial w_{ij}} = \frac{\partial E}{\partial u_j} y_i,$$

$$\Delta w \left(t + 1\right) = \mu \Delta w_t - \eta \frac{\partial E}{\partial w \left(t + 1\right)} - \xi w_t, \quad (5)$$

where w_{ij} represents the weight from the i_{th} neuron to the j_{th} neuron, E is the error function defined in (2), $\Delta w(t + 1)$ is the weight updating value in the $(t + 1)_{\text{th}}$ iteration, μ is the momentum, η is the learning rate, and ξ is the weight decay rate which can prevent overfitting.

Our datasets are collected in a large water tank as shown in Figures 3 and 4. We put a lifting platform inside the tank to hold the color calibration board. The digital camera is just above the water. The lifting platform can guarantee the board to always be inside the water and vertical to the camera. And it can also change the distance between the color board and the camera accurately. After we get enough data with

TABLE 1: Datasets description.

Datasets	Distance (mm)	Images	Image pack
Dataset A	500, 600, 700	2100	4–10
Dataset B	500, 600, 700	2100	4–10
Dataset C	460, 560, 660, 760	1200	1–3

different distances, we added the aluminium hydroxide into the water to change the water qualities and collect the data again. Meanwhile, we also use AC-S in the water to measure the real-time IOPs as ground truth. We did not use any additional light field in this experiment except indoor diffuse refection.

The data we collected are listed in Tables 1 and 2. Due to the size of the employed water tank (3.6 m (length) × 2.0 m (width) × 1.2 m (depth)), the precise concentration of aluminium hydroxide cannot be directly measured. However, we could estimate the concentration of aluminium hydroxide by using the volume of water filled in the tank and the weight of aluminium hydroxide added for each image collection. The results were given in Table 2. To ensure uniformity of aluminium hydroxide distribution, we used a circulating pump to stir the water before image collection started. Yet, it can be noticed that the average attenuation and absorption of image pack (4) look lower than the value obtained for image pack (3). The reason for that is the first 3 image packs and the remaining 6 image packs were taken on two consecutive days; some aluminium hydroxide settled at the bottom still standing after 10 hours.

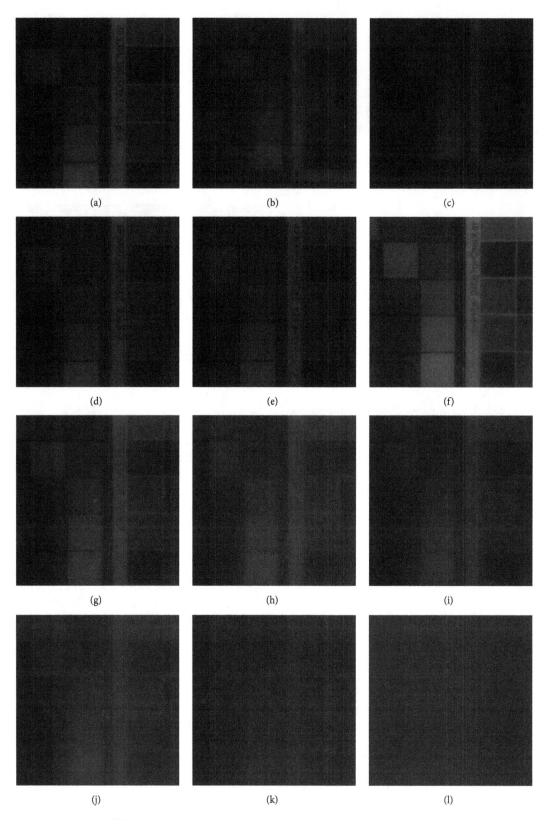

FIGURE 5: Images captured under different situations. (a)–(c) are captured without any aluminium hydroxide (image pack (1)) under 460 mm, 560 mm, and 660 mm. (d)–(l) are captured under 460 mm corresponding to image packs (2)–(10).

TABLE 2: IOPs description.

Image pack	Image number	Avg. attenuation (m^{-1})	Avg. absorption (m^{-1})	Aluminium hydroxide (g/m^3)
(1)	400	2.9380	0.6392	0
(2)	400	3.2664	0.6596	4.24
(3)	400	3.2725	0.6905	6.37
(4)	600	3.0048	0.6505	6.37
(5)	600	4.1257	0.8627	8.53
(6)	600	5.0092	1.0213	10.76
(7)	600	5.8371	1.1759	12.58
(8)	600	6.2485	1.2357	17.24
(9)	600	9.0333	1.7242	25.61
(10)	600	11.7797	2.0721	34.89

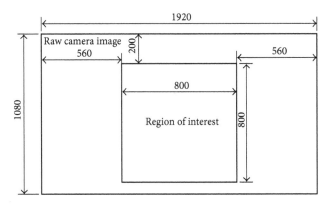

FIGURE 6: The ROI position.

We collected 3 groups of datasets. Please note that we do not add any aluminium hydroxide into the water when we take photos in image pack (1). Datasets A and B were taken under similar environments but at different time periods. Dataset C was taken with different distances and different IOPs. Each image pack was captured with a digital video camera during a short period. Lots of researchers used IOPs under 520 nm wavelength as reference properties [30, 31]. The average value of attenuation and absorption coefficients at 520 nm wavelength in each image pack can be found in Table 1. The frame rate of this camera is 25 frames per second. After we take enough images under a certain depth we can modify the distance between the camera and the board by adjusting the lifting platform. When we got enough photos in one pack, we modified the water IOPs by adding aluminium hydroxide and then started capturing the next image pack. The IOPs in one image pack are similar. But we still use the real-time results provided by AC-S as the training label of deep convolutional neural networks. Our camera type is Hikvision 2ZCN3007. It used a 1/2.8″ Progressive Scan CMOS sensor. The camera can provide videos with resolution of 1080 p. We used the raw RGB camera pictures (1920 ∗ 1080 pixels) and chose the center part as the region of interest (800 ∗ 800 pixels) as shown in Figure 6. And then we resized them into 200 ∗ 200 for network training. The input of the neural network used 3 channels for RGB format. We collected images in the daytime. The camera used

an automatic exposure system to record images. There is no other additional light source during our experiments except the diffuse reflection. No additional image preprocessing methods are used.

The sample images of 10 different image packs are displayed in Figure 5. Figures 5(a)–5(c) are captured in pack (1) under 460 mm, 560 mm, and 660 mm, respectively, and Figures 5(d)–5(l) are captured from pack (2) to pack (10) under the same distance (460 mm). The overview of IOPs estimation results can be found in Table 3. We use a single GTX1070 graphic card and Intel i7-6700 to train these networks. We set the learning rate as 0.0001. We use 3 kinds of deep neural network for IOPs estimation evaluation. We waited enough epochs until these networks converged. Cifar-Net, which is improved based on LeNet-5 [22], is used as benchmark for this experiment. Although we waited 100,000 epochs (about 1 hour), the results based on Cifar-Net are still poor even in training set. AlexNet, which costs us about 3 hours on training until we reach 30,000 epochs, performs better. And we get the minimum Euclidean loss if we consider the depth information. Lower loss means estimated IOPs are closer to the ground truth. That means depth information is helpful especially in clean medium. The DA Net costs about 3 and a half hours for 30,000 epochs. The training speed of our model is a little slower than AlexNet, but with better performance.

The detail of IOPs estimation results can be found in Figure 7. We choose 3 typical RGB images representing images captured in high, medium, and low turbidity, respectively. The performance of Cifar-Net is shown using blue lines; the regression curve of AlexNet is displayed with red dashed lines; the DA Net is shown with green asterisks and the ground truth provided by AC-S is represented using purple dot lines. In high turbidity case, both AlexNet and our method perform well on attenuation regression. A small amount error existed in blue-purple band (400–450 nm). Our method performs better than AlexNet in both absorption and attenuation coefficients regression task. In medium and low turbidity case, the curves of the DA Net get closer to the ground truth comparing with AlexNet. Although Cifar-Nets show a generally right regression result on three cases, its performance is much lower than the other two methods.

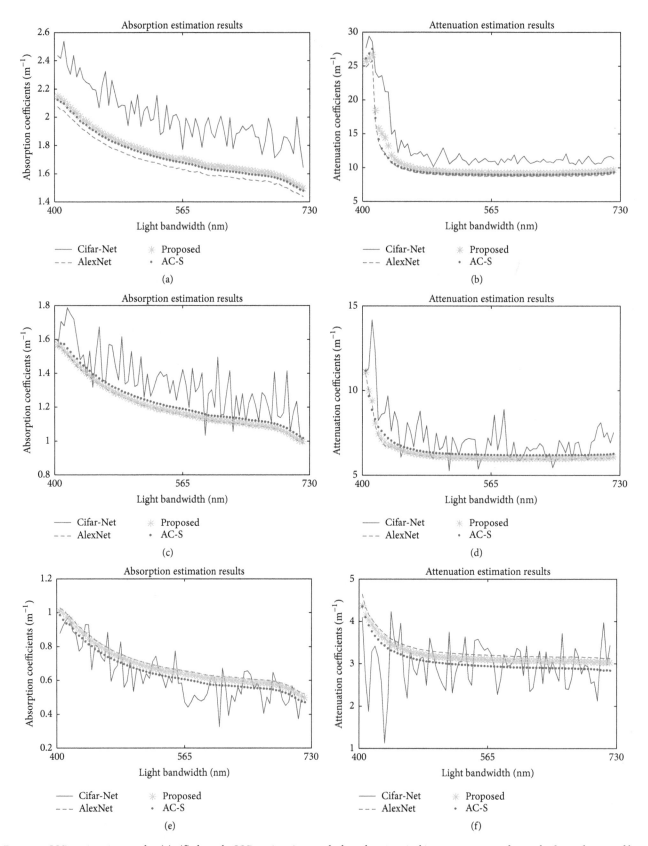

FIGURE 7: IOPs estimation results. (a)–(f) show the IOPs estimation results based on 3 typical images corresponding to high, medium, and low turbidity. (a) and (b) show the attenuation and absorption coefficients regression results based on Figure 5(i). (c) and (d) show the coefficients regression results based on Figure 5(f). (e) and (f) show the coefficients regression results based on Figure 5(d).

TABLE 3: IOPs estimation results.

Training set	Test set	Euclidean loss	Network
A	A	1.23	Cifar-Net
A	A	2.67	Cifar-Net
A	A	2.70	Cifar-Net
A	B	0.047	AlexNet
A	B	0.232	AlexNet
A	B	0.1532	AlexNet
A	C	0.032	DA Net
A	C	0.1996	DA Net
A	C	0.056	DA Net

3. Discussion and Conclusion

In summary, we propose a DA deep neural network for IOPs estimation method based on a single RGBD image with a DA deep neural network. We argue that an underwater image contains enough IOPs information that is even noisy. So we are able to deduct IOPs on a single RGBD image with a suitable system. Comparing with traditional methods based on transmissometers, our method can archive enough accuracy but cost-effectively and more flexibly than traditional devices. Our method is able to predict both attenuation and absorption coefficients of the medium simultaneously. The experimental results in Table 3 show that even a single RGB image seems enough for IOPs estimation with deep learning technologies. We can get better estimation results if we consider depth information as an aided input.

In our experiment, we did not consider any complex light field conditions and target objects with complex shape case. These factors may bring difficulty to measure IOPs when we want to put this system in an opening environment. Fortunately, research on deep neural network shows that it is possible to estimate a depth map on a complex target object and even under different light fields with a single RGB image [32, 33]. That may be a possible solution for us to improve our model. On the other hand, back-scattering coefficients, which cannot be measured by AC-S, are very important to build an underwater image recovering model. How to estimate back-scattering coefficients is another challenge. We wish to leave these two parts in our future work.

Authors' Contributions

Zhibin Yu and Yubo Wang contributed equally to this work.

Acknowledgments

This work was supported by the National Natural Science Foundation of China under Grant no. 61701463, Natural Science Foundation of Shandong Province of China under Grant no. ZR2017BF011, the Fundamental Research Funds for the Central Universities under Grant nos. 201713017 and 201713019, and the Qingdao Postdoctoral Science Foundation of China.

References

[1] J. H. Steele, S. A. Thorpe, and K. K. Turekian, *Measurement Techniques, Sensors and Platforms - A Derivative of Encyclopedia of Ocean Sciences*, vol. 272, 2009.

[2] H. Loisel, D. Stramski, B. G. Mitchell et al., "Comparison of the ocean inherent optical properties obtained from measurements and inverse modeling," *Applied Optics*, vol. 40, no. 15, pp. 2384–2397, 2001.

[3] E. Rehm and N. J. McCormick, "Inherent optical property estimation in deep waters," *Optics Express*, vol. 19, no. 25, pp. 24986–25005, 2011.

[4] H.-H. Lu, C.-Y. Li, H.-H. Lin et al., "An 8 m/9.6 Gbps underwater wireless optical communication system," *IEEE Photonics Journal*, vol. 8, no. 5, 2016.

[5] R. Schettini and S. Corchs, "Underwater image processing: State of the art of restoration and image enhancement methods," *EURASIP Journal on Advances in Signal Processing*, vol. 2010, Article ID 746052, 2010.

[6] W. Hou, D. J. Gray, A. D. Weidemann, G. R. Fournier, and J. L. Forand, "Automated underwater image restoration and retrieval of related optical properties," in *Proceedings of the 2007 IEEE International Geoscience and Remote Sensing Symposium, IGARSS 2007*, pp. 1889–1892, Spain, June 2007.

[7] J. S. Jaffe, "Underwater Optical Imaging: The Past, the Present, and the Prospects," *IEEE Journal of Oceanic Engineering*, vol. 40, no. 3, pp. 683–700, 2015.

[8] N. L. Swanson, B. D. Billard, V. M. Gehman, and T. L. Gennaro, "Application of the small-angle approximation to ocean water types," *Applied Optics*, vol. 40, no. 21, pp. 3608–3613, 2001.

[9] L. Sipelgas and U. Raudsepp, "Comparison of hyperspectral measurements of the attenuation and scattering coefficients spectra with modeling results in the north-eastern Baltic Sea," *Estuarine, Coastal and Shelf Science*, vol. 165, pp. 1–9, 2015.

[10] D. McKee, A. Cunningham, J. Slater, K. J. Jones, and C. R. Griffiths, "Inherent and apparent optical properties in coastal waters: A study of the Clyde Sea in early summer," *Estuarine, Coastal and Shelf Science*, vol. 56, no. 2, pp. 369–376, 2003.

[11] A. Cunningham, L. Ramage, and D. McKee, "Relationships between inherent optical properties and the depth of penetration of solar radiation in optically complex coastal waters," *Journal of Geophysical Research: Oceans*, vol. 118, no. 5, pp. 2310–2317, 2013.

[12] G. Wang, B. Zheng, and F. F. Sun, "Estimation-based approach for underwater image restoration," *Optics Expresss*, vol. 36, no. 13, pp. 2384–2386, 2011.

[13] B. Huang, T. Liu, H. Hu, J. Han, and M. Yu, "Underwater image recovery considering polarization effects of objects," *Optics Express*, vol. 24, no. 9, pp. 9826–9838, 2016.

[14] H. Mortazavi, J. P. Oakley, and B. Barkat, "Mitigating the effect of optical back-scatter in multispectral underwater imaging," *Measurement Science and Technology*, vol. 24, no. 7, Article ID 074025, 2013.

[15] J. S. Jaffe, "Computer modeling and the design of optimal underwater imaging systems," *IEEE Journal of Oceanic Engineering*, vol. 15, no. 2, pp. 101–111, 1990.

[16] R. Wang, Y. Wang, J. Zhang, and X. Fu, "Review on underwater image restoration and enhancement algorithms," in *Proceedings of the 7th International Conference on Internet Multimedia Computing and Service, ICIMCS 2015*, pp. 277–282, China, August 2015.

[17] G. E. Hinton, S. Osindero, and Y.-W. Teh, "A fast learning algorithm for deep belief nets," *Neural Computation*, vol. 18, no. 7, pp. 1527–1554, 2006.

[18] B. Cai, X. Xu, K. Jia, C. Qing, and D. Tao, "DehazeNet: an end-to-end system for single image haze removal," *IEEE Transactions on Image Processing*, vol. 25, no. 11, pp. 5187–5198, 2016.

[19] J. Long, E. Shelhamer, and T. Darrell, "Fully convolutional networks for semantic segmentation," in *Proceedings of the IEEE Conference on Computer Vision and Pattern Recognition (CVPR '15)*, pp. 3431–3440, IEEE, Boston, Mass, USA, June 2015.

[20] W. Hou, X. Gao, D. Tao, and X. Li, "Blind image quality assessment via deep learning," *IEEE Transactions on Neural Networks and Learning Systems*, vol. 26, no. 6, pp. 1275–1286, 2015.

[21] L. Kang, P. Ye, Y. Li, and D. Doermann, "Convolutional neural networks for no-reference image quality assessment," in *Proceedings of the 27th IEEE Conference on Computer Vision and Pattern Recognition, CVPR 2014*, pp. 1733–1740, USA, June 2014.

[22] S. Bianco, L. Celona, P. Napoletano, and R. Schettini, "On the use of deep learning for blind image quality assessment," *Signal, Image and Video Processing*, pp. 1–8, 2017.

[23] F. Weber, H. Eichner, H. Cuntz, and A. Borst, "Eigenanalysis of a neural network for optic flow processing," *New Journal of Physics*, vol. 10, Article ID 015013, 2008.

[24] Y. Lecun and Y. Bengio, *The Handbook of Brain Theory and Neural Networks*, vol. 255, 1995.

[25] A. Krizhevsky, I. Sutskever, and G. E. Hinton, "Imagenet classification with deep convolutional neural networks," in *Proceedings of the 26th Annual Conference on Neural Information Processing Systems (NIPS '12)*, pp. 1097–1105, Lake Tahoe, Nev, USA, December 2012.

[26] T. Mikolov, I. Sutskever, K. Chen, G. Corrado, and J. Dean, "Distributed representations of words and phrases and their compositionality," in *Proceedings of the 27th Annual Conference on Neural Information Processing Systems (NIPS '13)*, pp. 3111–3119, December 2013.

[27] R. Socher, C. C.-Y. Lin, C. D. Manning, and A. Y. Ng, "Parsing natural scenes and natural language with recursive neural networks," in *Proceedings of the 28th International Conference on Machine Learning (ICML '11)*, pp. 129–136, Bellevue, Wash, USA, June 2011.

[28] N. Kalchbrenner, E. Grefenstette, and P. Blunsom, "A Convolutional Neural Network for Modelling Sentences," in *Proceedings of the 52nd Annual Meeting of the Association for Computational Linguistics (Volume 1: Long Papers)*, pp. 655–665, Baltimore, Md, USA, June 2014.

[29] N. Kalchbrenner, E. Grefenstette, and P. Blunsom, "A convolutional neural network for modelling sentences," in *Proceedings of the 52nd Annual Meeting of the Association for Computational Linguistics, ACL 2014*, pp. 655–665, June 2014.

[30] D. C. English and K. L. Carder, "Determining bottom reflectance and water optical properties using unmanned underwater vehicles under clear or cloudy skies," *Journal of Atmospheric and Oceanic Technology*, vol. 23, no. 2, pp. 314–324, 2006.

[31] H. M. Oubei, C. Li, K. Park, T. K. Ng, M. Alouini, and B. S. Ooi, "2.3 Gbit/s underwater wireless optical communications using directly modulated 520 nm laser diode," *Optics Express*, vol. 23, no. 16, pp. 20743–20748, 2015.

[32] D. Eigen, C. Puhrsch, and R. Fergus, "Depth map prediction from a single image using a multi-scale deep network," in *Proceedings of the 28th Annual Conference on Neural Information Processing Systems 2014, NIPS 2014*, pp. 2366–2374, December 2014.

[33] F. Liu, C. Shen, and G. Lin, "Deep convolutional neural fields for depth estimation from a single image," in *Proceedings of the IEEE Conference on Computer Vision and Pattern Recognition, CVPR 2015*, pp. 5162–5170, USA, June 2015.

14

Robust and Adaptive Online Time Series Prediction with Long Short-Term Memory

Haimin Yang,[1] **Zhisong Pan,**[1] **and Qing Tao**[2]

[1]*College of Command and Information System, PLA University of Science and Technology, Nanjing, Jiangsu 210007, China*
[2]*1st Department, Army Officer Academy of PLA, Hefei, Anhui 230031, China*

Correspondence should be addressed to Zhisong Pan; hotpzs@hotmail.com

Academic Editor: Pedro Antonio Gutierrez

Online time series prediction is the mainstream method in a wide range of fields, ranging from speech analysis and noise cancelation to stock market analysis. However, the data often contains many outliers with the increasing length of time series in real world. These outliers can mislead the learned model if treated as normal points in the process of prediction. To address this issue, in this paper, we propose a robust and adaptive online gradient learning method, RoAdam (Robust Adam), for long short-term memory (LSTM) to predict time series with outliers. This method tunes the learning rate of the stochastic gradient algorithm adaptively in the process of prediction, which reduces the adverse effect of outliers. It tracks the relative prediction error of the loss function with a weighted average through modifying Adam, a popular stochastic gradient method algorithm for training deep neural networks. In our algorithm, the large value of the relative prediction error corresponds to a small learning rate, and vice versa. The experiments on both synthetic data and real time series show that our method achieves better performance compared to the existing methods based on LSTM.

1. Introduction

A time series is a sequence of real-valued signals that are measured at successive time intervals [1, 2]. Time series data occur naturally in many application areas such as economics, finance, environment, and medicine and often arrives in the form of streaming in many real-world systems. Time series prediction has been successfully used in a wide range of domains including speech analysis [3], noise cancelation [4], and stock market analysis [5, 6]. The traditional methods of time series prediction commonly use a potential model, for example, autoregressive moving average (ARMA) [7], autoregressive integrated moving average (ARIMA) [1], and vector autoregressive moving average (VARMA) [8], to mimic the data. However, these methods all need to deal with the whole dataset to identify the parameters of the model when facing new coming data, which is not suitable for large datasets and online time series prediction. To address this problem, online learning methods are explored to extract the underlying pattern representations from time series data in a sequential manner. Compared to traditional batch learning methods, online learning methods avoid expensive retraining cost when handling new coming data. Due to the efficiency and scalability, online learning methods including methods based on linear models [9], ensemble learning [10], and kernels [11] have been applied to time series prediction successfully.

Long short-term memory (LSTM) [12], a class of recurrent neural networks (RNNs) [13], is particularly designed for sequential data. LSTM has shown promising results for time series prediction. Its units consist of three gates: input gate, forget gate, and output gate. It is popular due to the ability of learning hidden long-term sequential dependencies, which actually helps in learning the underlying representations of time series. However, the time series data in real world often contains some outliers more or less especially in cyberattacks, which are commonly shown as anomalies in time series data monitoring some measurements of network traffic. Those outliers mislead the learning method in extracting the true representations of time series and reduce the performance of prediction.

In this paper, we propose an efficient online gradient learning method, which we call RoAdam (Robust Adam)

for LSTM to predict time series in the presence of outliers. The method modifies Adam (Adaptive Moment Estimation) [14], a popular algorithm for training deep neural networks through tracking the relative prediction error of the loss function with a weighted average. Adam is based on standard stochastic gradient descent (SGD) method without considering the adverse effect of outliers. The learning rate of RoAdam is tuned adaptively according to the relative prediction error of the loss function. The large relative prediction error leads to a smaller effective learning rate. Likewise, a small error leads to a larger effective learning rate. The experiments show that our algorithm achieves the state-of-the-art performance of prediction.

The rest of this paper is organized as follows. Section 2 reviews related work. In Section 3, we introduce some preliminaries. Section 4 presents our algorithm in detail. In Section 5, we evaluate the performance of our proposed algorithm on both synthetic data and real time series. Finally, Section 6 concludes our work and discusses some future work.

2. Related Work

In time series, a data point is identified as an outlier if it is significantly different from the behavior of the major points. Outlier detection for time series data has been studied for decades. The main work focuses on modeling time series in the presence of outliers. In statistics, several parametric models have been proposed for time series prediction. The point that deviated from the predicted value by the summary parametric model including ARMA [15], ARIMA [16, 17], and VARMA [18] is identified as an outlier. Vallis et al. [19] develop a novel statistical technique using robust statistical metrics including median, median absolute deviation, and piecewise approximation of the underlying long-term trend to detect outliers accurately. There also exist many machine learning models for time series prediction with outliers. The paper [20] proposes a generic and scalable framework for automated time series anomaly detection including two methods: plug-in method and decomposition-based method. The plug-in method applies a wide range of time series modeling and forecasting models to model the normal behavior of the time series. The decomposition-based method firstly decomposes a time series into three components: trend, seasonality, and noise and then captures the outliers through monitoring the noise component. The paper [21] gives a detailed survey on outlier detection.

LSTM has shown promising results for time series prediction. Lipton et al. uses LSTM to model varying length sequences and capture long range dependencies. The model can effectively recognize patterns in multivariate time series of clinical measurements [22]. Malhotra et al. use stacked LSTM networks for outliers detection in time series. A predictor is used to model the normal behavior and the resulting prediction errors are modeled as a multivariate Gaussian distribution, which is used to identify the abnormal behavior [23]. Chauhan and Vig also utilize the probability distribution of the prediction errors from the LSTM models to indicate the abnormal and normal behaviors in ECG time series [24].

These methods are not suitable for online time series prediction because they all need to train on time series without outliers to model the normal behavior in advance. In this paper, our online learning method for time series prediction is robust to outliers through adaptively tuning the learning rate of the stochastic gradient method to train LSTM.

3. Preliminaries and Model

In this section, we formulate our problem to be resolved and introduce some knowledge about Adam, a popular algorithm for training LSTM.

3.1. Online Time Series Prediction with LSTM. In the process of online time series prediction, the desirable model learns useful information from $\{x_1, x_2, \ldots, x_{t-1}\}$ to give a prediction $\tilde{x}_t$ and then compare $\tilde{x}_t$ with x_t to update itself, where $\{x_1, x_2, \ldots, x_{t-1}\}$ is a time series, $\tilde{x}_t$ is the time series data point forecasted at time t, and x_t is the real value. LSTM is suitable for discovering dependence relationships between the time series data by using specialized gating and memory mechanisms.

We give the formal definition of a neuron of a LSTM layer as follows. The jth neuron of a LSTM layer at time t, c_t^j consists of input gate i_t^j, forget gate f_t^j, and output gate o_t^j and is updated through forgetting the partially existing memory and adding a new memory content $\tilde{c}_t^j$. The expressions of i_t^j, f_t^j, o_t^j, and c_t^j are shown as follows:

$$i_t^j = \sigma \left(W_i x_t + U_i h_{t-1} + V_i c_{t-1} \right)^j,$$

$$f_t^j = \sigma \left(W_f x_t + U_f h_{t-1} + V_f c_{t-1} \right)^j,$$

$$o_t^j = \sigma \left(W_o x_t + U_o h_{t-1} + V_o c_{t-1} \right)^j, \qquad (1)$$

$$c_t^j = f_t^j c_{t-1}^j + i_t^j \tilde{c}_t^j.$$

Note that W_i, W_f, W_o, U_i, U_f, and U_o are the parameters of the jth neuron of a LSTM layer at time t. σ is a logistic sigmoid function. V_i, V_f, and V_o are diagonal matrices. h_{t-1} and c_{t-1} are the vectorization of h_{t-1}^j and c_{t-1}^j. The output h_t^j of this neuron at time t is expressed as

$$h_t^j = o_t^j \tanh \left(c_t^j \right). \qquad (2)$$

In our model of online time series prediction, we set a dense layer to map the outputs to the target prediction, which is formulated as

$$y = g \left(W_d h_t + b_d \right), \qquad (3)$$

where $g(\cdot)$ is the activation function of the dense layer, W_d is the weights, b_d is the bias, and h_t is the vectorization of h_t^j. The objection of our model at time t is to update the parameters $W_t = \{W_i, W_f, W_o, W_d, U_i, U_f, U_o, V_i, V_f, V_o, b_d\}$. The standard process is

$$W_{t+1} = W_t - \eta \nabla l \left(x_t, \tilde{x}_t \right), \qquad (4)$$

where η is the learning rate and $l(x_t, \tilde{x}_t)$ is the loss function.

RoAdam. Parameters carried over from Adam have the same default values: $\eta = 0.001$, $\beta_1 = 0.9$, $\beta_2 = 0.999$, $\epsilon = 10^{-8}$. For parameters specific to our method, we recommend default values $\beta_3 = 0.999$, $k = 0.1$, $K = 10$.

Require: η: learning rate
Require: $\beta_1, \beta_2 \in [0, 1)$: exponential decay rates for moment estimation in Adam
Require: $\beta_3 \in [0, 1)$: exponential decay rate for computing relative prediction error
Require: k, K: lower and upper threshold for relative prediction error
Require: ϵ: fuzz factor
Require: $l(W)$: loss function
Require: W_0: initial value for parameters

$\quad m_0 = v_0 = 0$
$\quad d_0 = 1$
$\quad l(W_0) = l(W_{-1}) = 1$
$\quad t = 0$
$\quad$**while** stopping condition is not reached **do**
$\quad\quad g_t = \nabla_W l(W_{t-1})$
$\quad\quad m_t = \beta_1 m_{t-1} + (1 - \beta_1)g_t$
$\quad\quad \widehat{m}_t = m_t/(1 - \beta_1^t)$
$\quad\quad v_t = \beta_2 v_{t-1} + (1 - \beta_2)g_t^2$
$\quad\quad \widehat{v}_t = v_t/(1 - \beta_2^t)$
$\quad\quad$**if** $\|l(W_{t-1})\| \geq \|l(W_{t-2})\|$ **then**
$\quad\quad\quad r_t = \min\{\max\{k, \|l(W_{t-1})/l(W_{t-2})\|\}, K\}$
$\quad\quad$**else**
$\quad\quad\quad r_t = \min\{\max\{1/K, \|l(W_{t-1})/l(W_{t-2})\|\}, 1/k\}$
$\quad\quad$**end if**
$\quad\quad d_t = \beta_3 d_{t-1} + (1 - \beta_3)r_t$
$\quad\quad W_{t+1} = W_t - \eta\widehat{m}_t/(d_t\sqrt{\widehat{v}_t} + \epsilon)$
$\quad\quad t = t + 1$
$\quad$**end while**
$\quad$**return** W_t

ALGORITHM 1

3.2. Adam.

Adam is a method for efficient stochastic optimization, which is often used to train LSTM. It computes adaptive learning rates for individual parameters from estimates of the first moment and the second moment of the gradients, only requiring first-order gradients. Adam keeps an exponentially decaying average of the gradient and the squared gradient:

$$m_t = \beta_1 m_{t-1} + (1 - \beta_1)g_t,$$
$$v_t = \beta_2 v_{t-1} + (1 - \beta_2)g_t^2, \tag{5}$$

where m_t and v_t initialized as zero are estimates of the first moment and the second moment and β_1 and β_2 are exponential decay rates for the moment estimates. We can find that m_t and v_t are biased towards zero, when β_1 and β_2 are close to 1. So Adam counteracts these biases through bias correction of m_t and v_t:

$$\widehat{m}_t = \frac{m_t}{1 - \beta_1^t},$$
$$\widehat{v}_t = \frac{v_t}{1 - \beta_2^t}. \tag{6}$$

The rule of updating parameters is

$$W_{t+1} = W_t - \frac{\eta}{\sqrt{\widehat{v}_t} + \epsilon}\widehat{m}_t, \tag{7}$$

where $\eta = 0.001$, $\beta_1 = 0.9$, $\beta_2 = 0.999$, and $\epsilon = 10^{-8}$ by default.

4. Method

In this section, we introduce our online gradient learning method, which is called RoAdam (Robust Adam) to train long short-term memory (LSTM) for time series prediction in the presence of outliers. Our method does not directly detect the outliers and adaptively tunes the learning rate when facing a suspicious outlier.

In Algorithm 1, we provide the details of the RoAdam algorithm. The main difference between our algorithm and Adam is r_t, a relative prediction error term of the loss function. The relative prediction error term indicates whether the point is an outlier. The larger value of r_t means the current point is more suspicious to be an outlier. It is computed as $r_t = \|l(W_{t-1})/l(W_{t-2})\|$, where $l(W_{t-1}) = l(x_t, \widetilde{x}_t)$ and $l(W_{t-2}) = l(x_{t-1}, \widetilde{x}_{t-1})$. $l(x_t, \widetilde{x}_t)$ and $l(x_{t-1}, \widetilde{x}_{t-1})$ are the absolute prediction errors of x_t and x_{t-1}. In practice, a threshold is used to scheme to ensure the stability of relative prediction error term. k and K denote the lower and upper thresholds for r_t. We let $r_t = \min\{\max\{k, \|l(W_{t-1})/l(W_{t-2})\|\}, K\}$ (1), if $\|l(W_{t-1})\| \geq \|l(W_{t-2})\|$ and $r_t = \min\{\max\{1/K, \|l(W_{t-1})/l(W_{t-2})\|\}, 1/k\}$ (2) otherwise, which captures both increase and decrease of relative prediction

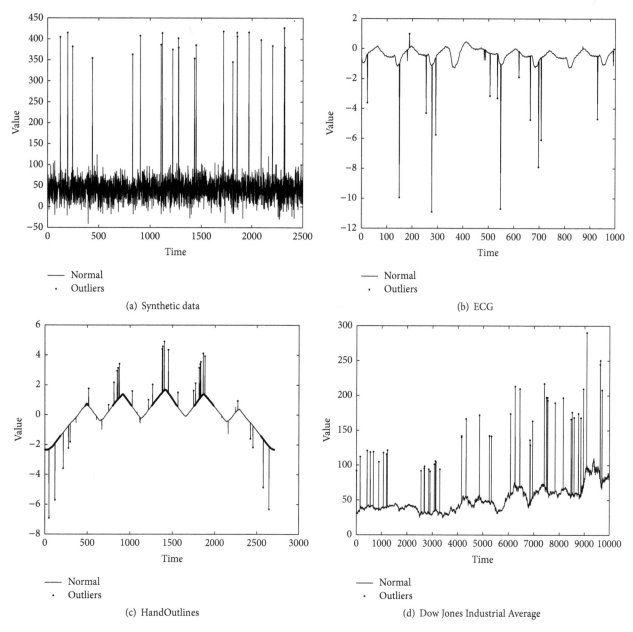

FIGURE 1: True value of data sets.

TABLE 1: Different values of r_t.

x_{t-1}	x_t	
	Outlier	Normal
Outlier	(1)	(2)
Normal	(2)	(1)

error. Our settings consider different situations when the preceding point x_{t-1} and current point x_t are at different status. The details are listed in Table 1.

To get a smoother estimate, we compute the relative prediction error with a weighted average. The final result d_t is $\beta_3 d_{t-1} + (1 - \beta_3)r_t$. Here the effect of β_3 is the same as β_1 and β_2 in Adam. In general, RoAdam is modified in the basis

of Adam through multiplying the denominator $\sqrt{\hat{v}_t}$ with d_t. The large value of d_t corresponds to a small learning rate, and vice versa.

5. Experiment

In this section, we illustrate the performance of our proposed algorithm RoAdam compared to RLSTM, SR-LSTM, and RN-LSTM on both synthetic data and real time series.

5.1. Experiment Setup. RLSTM means real time LSTM, which updates the model using the newly coming data without considering the effect of outliers. SR-LSTM stands for LSTM with suspicious point removal. The difference between SR-LSTM and RN-LSTM is that once a suspicious point is

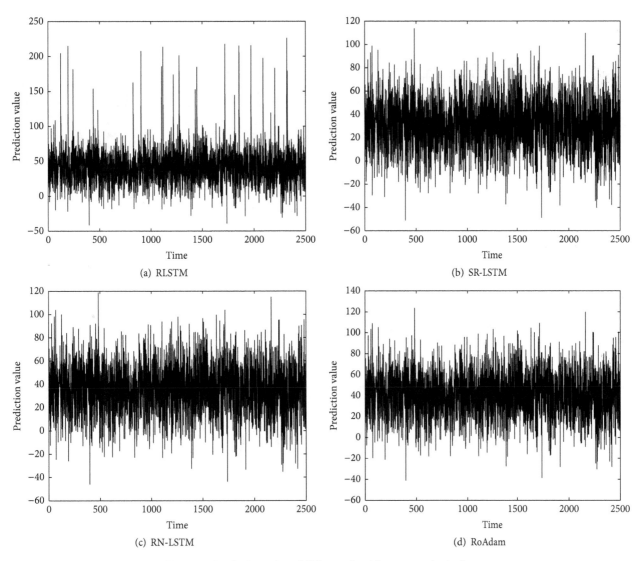

FIGURE 2: Prediction value of different algorithms on synthetic data.

detected as an outlier, SR-LSTM does not update on this point and RN-LSTM updates using a recent normal point. They both use the method proposed in [25] to detect the outlier. In addition, all the algorithms use the same LSTM model besides the optimizer. RLSTM, SR-LSTM, and RN-LSTM adopt the original Adam optimizer. The LSTM model has 3 layers and the number of neurons in each layer is 400. The mean squared error is chosen as the loss function and the L2 regularization with 0.0001 penalty is used. The parameters of RoAdam carried from Adam have the same default values: $\eta = 0.001$, $\beta_1 = 0.9$, $\beta_2 = 0.999$, and $\epsilon = 10^{-8}$. For parameters specific to our method, we try different values and recommend default values $\beta_3 = 0.999$, $k = 0.1$, and $K = 10$.

5.2. Data Sets. To examine the prediction performance, we evaluate all the previous algorithms on synthetic data and real time series.

5.2.1. Synthetic Data. The synthetic data is sampled from a Gaussian distribution with the corresponding mean $u \in [0, 100]$ and variance $\sigma \in [10, 30]$ plus the trend component $T \in [-0.5, 0.5]$. The length l is 2,500. The outliers are injected based on a Bernoulli distribution identified by $\alpha = 0.01$ and $l \cdot \alpha$ is the expected number of outliers. The values of outliers are also sampled from a Gaussian distribution with mean $u \in [0, 1000]$ and variance $\sigma \in [10, 30]$. The expression of x_t is

$$x_t = \begin{cases} x + T, x \sim N(u, \sigma), u \in [0, 100], \sigma \in [10, 30], T \in [-0.5, 0.5], & \text{when } x_t \text{ is a normal point;} \\ x, x \sim N(u, \sigma), u \in [0, 1000], \sigma \in [10, 30], & \text{when } x_t \text{ is an outlier.} \end{cases} \tag{8}$$

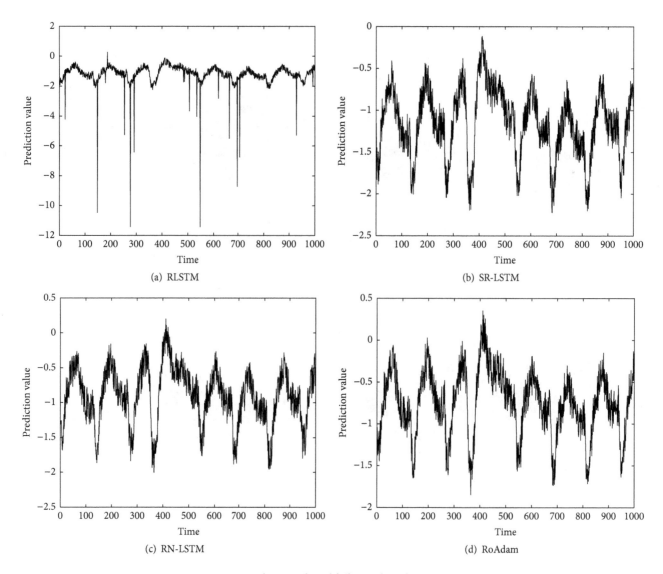

FIGURE 3: Prediction value of different algorithms on ECG.

5.2.2. Real Time Series. The first time series data is ECG data, which consists of 70 series of 1000 ECG measurements [26]. We choose 100 samples from ECG data set. The second one is HandOutlines, which is from the commonly used UCR (http://www.cs.ucr.edu/~eamonn/time_series_data/.). The last time series data is daily index of Dow Jones Industrial Average (DJIA) during years 1885–1962. We randomly select 1% of each real time series as outliers, whose values are 2 or 3 times bigger than the true ones. Figure 1 presents the true value of synthetic data and real time series. The *x*-axis is time (the number of samples) and the *y*-axis is true value.

5.3. Experimental Results. In this section, we test RMSE of the algorithms mentioned above to examine the effectiveness and efficiency.

$$\text{RMSE} = \frac{1}{T}\sum_{t=1}^{T}\left(X_t - \widetilde{X}_t\right)^2. \qquad (9)$$

RMSE allows us to compare errors with the number of samples increasing. In addition, we average the results over 100 runs for stability.

Table 2 shows the RMSE of different algorithms both on synthetic data and real time series. We can find that RoAdam outperforms all the other algorithms on RMSE. Figures 2–5 visualize the prediction value of all the algorithms on synthetic data and real time series. The *x*-axis is time (the number of samples) and the *y*-axis is prediction value. We can observe that the prediction value produced by RLSTM has oscillations around outliers. It indicates that the prediction performance of RLSTM is indeed affected by outliers. Although SR-LSTM, RN-LSTM, and RoAdam have almost the same shape of prediction value, RoAdam has the least RMSE. The reason may be that SR-LSTM and RN-LSTM may lose some information of the normal points when they are mistaken outliers.

TABLE 2: RMSE on synthetic data and real time series.

Algorithm	Data			
	Synthetic	ECG	HandOutlines	DJIA
RLSTM	0.7606	0.8505	0.9756	1.8454
SR-LSTM	0.7329	0.8323	0.9411	1.7574
RN-LSTM	0.7218	0.8217	0.9376	1.6218
RoAdam	**0.4946**	**0.5626**	**0.7633**	**1.3875**

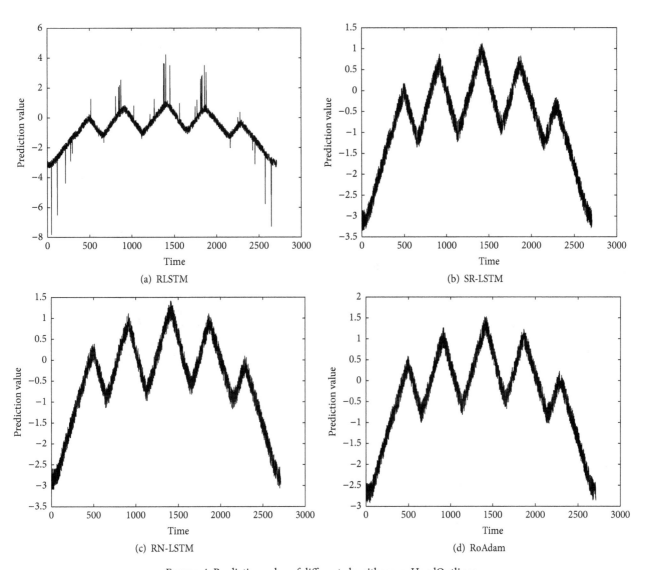

FIGURE 4: Prediction value of different algorithms on HandOutlines.

6. Conclusions

In this paper, we propose an efficient online gradient learning method, RoAdam for LSTM, to predict time series, which is robust to outliers. RoAdam is modified on the basis of Adam, a popular stochastic gradient algorithm for training deep neural networks. Through tracking the relative prediction error of the loss function with a weighted average, this method adaptively tunes the learning rate of the stochastic gradient method in the presence of outliers. In the process of prediction, the large value of the relative prediction error corresponds to a small learning rate, and vice versa. The experiments on both synthetic data and real time series show that our method achieves less prediction error compared to the existing methods based on LSTM.

It remains for future work to study whether our approach could be extended to time series prediction with missing data.

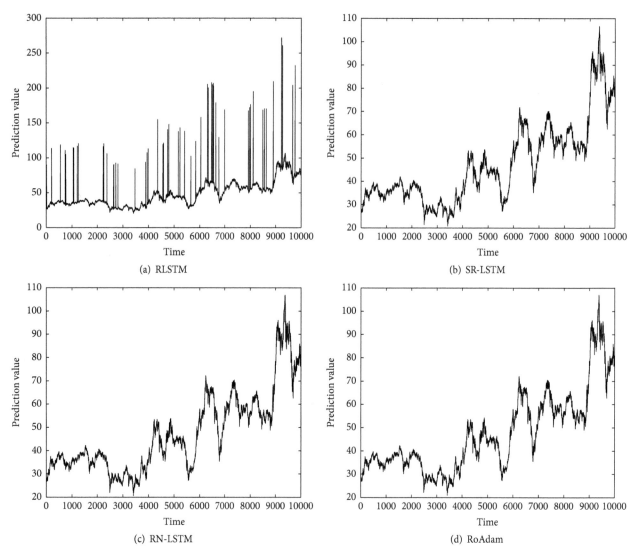

FIGURE 5: Prediction value of different algorithms on DJIA.

Authors' Contributions

Haimin Yang participated in the draft writing and experiments. Zhisong Pan and Qing Tao participated in the design of algorithms and commented on the manuscript.

Acknowledgments

Our work is supported by the National Natural Science Foundation of China (nos. 61473149 and 61673394).

References

[1] J. D. Hamilton, *Time Series Analysis*, Princeton University Press, New Jersey, NJ, USA, 1994.

[2] P. J. Brockwell and R. A. Davis, *Time Series: Theory and Methods*, Springer, New York, NY, USA, 2ND edition, 2006.

[3] L. R. Rabiner and R. W. Schafer, *Digital processing of speech signals*, Englewood Cliffs, N.J., Prentice-Hall, New Jersey, NJ, USA, 1978.

[4] J. Gao, H. Sultan, J. Hu, and W.-W. Tung, "Denoising nonlinear time series by adaptive filtering and wavelet shrinkage: a comparison," *IEEE Signal Processing Letters*, vol. 17, no. 3, pp. 237–240, 2010.

[5] C. W. J. Granger and P. Newbold, *Forecasting Economic Time Series*, Academic Press, New York, NY, USA, 1986.

[6] M. Nerlove, D. M. Grether, and J. L. Carvalho, *Analysis of Economic Time Series: A Synthesis*, Academic Press, New York, NY, USA, 1979.

[7] J. L. Rojo-Alvarez, M. Martınez-Ramon, M. de Prado-Cumplido et al., "Support vector method for robust ARMA system identification," *IEEE Transactions on Signal Processing*, vol. 52, no. 1, pp. 155–164, 2004.

[8] R. S. Tsay, *Multivariate Time Series Analysis: with R And Financial Applications*, John Wiley and Sons, New Jersey, NJ, USA, 2014.

[9] O. Anava, E. Hazan, S. Mannor et al., "Online learning for time series prediction," *Journal of Machine Learning Research*, vol. 30, pp. 172–184, 2013.

[10] L. L. Minku and X. Yao, "DDD: a new ensemble approach for dealing with concept drift," *IEEE Transactions on Knowledge and Data Engineering*, vol. 24, no. 4, pp. 619–633, 2012.

[11] C. Richard, J. C. Bermudez, and P. Honeine, "Online prediction of time serise data with kernels," *IEEE Transactions on Signal Processing*, vol. 57, no. 3, pp. 1058–1067, 2008.

[12] S. Hochreiter and J. Schmidhuber, "Long short-term memory," *Neural Computation*, vol. 9, no. 8, pp. 1735–1780, 1997.

[13] Y. LeCun, Y. Bengio, and G. Hinton, "Deep learning," *Nature*, vol. 521, no. 7553, pp. 436–444, 2015.

[14] D. P. Kingma and J. L. Ba, "Adam: a method for stochastic optimization," in *Proceedings of the in Proceedings of International Conference on Learning Representations (ICLR '15)*, 2015.

[15] V. Barnett and T. Lewis, *Outliers in Statistical Data*, John Wiley & Sons, New Jersey, NJ, USA, 1978.

[16] D. M. Hawkins, *Identification of Outliers*, Chapman and Hall, London, UK, 1980.

[17] P. J. Rousseeuw and A. M. Leroy, *Robust Regression and Outlier Detection*, John Wiley & Sons, New Jersey, NJ, USA, 1987.

[18] R. S. Tsay, "Time series model specification in the presence of outliers," *Journal of the American Statistical Association*, vol. 81, no. 393, pp. 132–141, 1986.

[19] O. Vallis, J. Hochenbaum, and A. Kejariwal, "A novel technique for long-term anomaly detection in the cloud," in *Proceedings of 2014 6thUSENIX Workshop on Hot Topics in Cloud Computing*, 2014.

[20] N. Laptev, S. Amizadeh, and I. Flint, "Generic and scalable framework for automated time-series anomaly detection," in *Proceedings of the 21st ACM SIGKDD Conference on Knowledge Discovery and Data Mining (KDD '15)*, pp. 1939–1947, Australia, August 2015.

[21] M. Gupta, J. Gao, C. C. Aggarwal, and J. Han, "Outlier detection for temporal data: a survey," *IEEE Transactions on Knowledge and Data Engineering*, vol. 26, no. 9, pp. 2250–2267, 2014.

[22] Z. C. Lipton, D. C. Kale, C. Elkan et al., Learning to diagnose with lstm recurrent neural networks, https://arxiv.org/pdf/1511.03677.pdf.

[23] P. Malhotra, L. Vig, G. Shroff, and P. Agarwal, "Long Short Term Memory networks for anomaly detection in time series," in *Proceedings of the 23rd European Symposium on Artificial Neural Networks, Computational Intelligence and Machine Learning (ESANN '15)*, pp. 89–94, April 2015.

[24] S. Chauhan and L. Vig, "Anomaly detection in ECG time signals via deep long short-term memory networks," in *Proceedings of the IEEE International Conference on Data Science and Advanced Analytics (DSAA '15)*, October 2015.

[25] J. T. Connor, R. D. Martin, and L. E. Atlas, "Recurrent neural networks and robust time series prediction," *IEEE Transactions on Neural Networks and Learning Systems*, vol. 5, no. 2, pp. 240–254, 1994.

[26] A. J. Bagnall and G. J. Janacek, "Clustering time series from ARMA models with clipped data," in *Proceedings of The 2004 ACM SIGKDD International Conference*, p. 49, August 2004.

Improving EEG-Based Motor Imagery Classification for Real-Time Applications Using the QSA Method

Patricia Batres-Mendoza,[1] **Mario A. Ibarra-Manzano,**[2,3] **Erick I. Guerra-Hernandez,**[1]
Dora L. Almanza-Ojeda,[2,3] **Carlos R. Montoro-Sanjose,**[3,4] **Rene J. Romero-Troncoso,**[3,5]
and Horacio Rostro-Gonzalez[1,3,6]

[1]*Laboratorio de Sistemas Bioinspirados, Departamento de Ingeniería Electrónica, DICIS,*
 Universidad de Guanajuato, Carr. Salamanca-Valle de Santiago Km. 3.5 + 1.8 Km., 36885 Salamanca, GTO, Mexico
[2]*Laboratorio de Procesamiento Digital de Señales, Departamento de Ingeniería Electrónica, DICIS,*
 Universidad de Guanajuato, Carr. Salamanca-Valle de Santiago Km. 3.5 + 1.8 Km., 36885 Salamanca, GTO, Mexico
[3]*Cuerpo Académico de Telemática, DICIS, Universidad de Guanajuato, Carr. Salamanca-Valle de Santiago Km. 3.5 + 1.8 Km.,*
 36885 Salamanca, GTO, Mexico
[4]*Departamento de Arte y Empresa, DICIS, Universidad de Guanajuato, Carr. Salamanca-Valle de Santiago Km. 3.5 + 1.8 Km.,*
 36885 Salamanca, GTO, Mexico
[5]*Departamento de Ingeniería Electrónica, DICIS, Universidad de Guanajuato, Carr. Salamanca-Valle de Santiago Km. 3.5 + 1.8 Km.,*
 36885 Salamanca, GTO, Mexico
[6]*Neuroscientific System Theory, Department of Electrical and Computer Engineering,*
 Technical University of Munich, Munich, Germany

Correspondence should be addressed to Horacio Rostro-Gonzalez; hrostrog@ugto.mx

Academic Editor: Pedro Antonio Gutierrez

We present an improvement to the quaternion-based signal analysis (QSA) technique to extract electroencephalography (EEG) signal features with a view to developing real-time applications, particularly in motor imagery (IM) cognitive processes. The proposed methodology (iQSA, *improved* QSA) extracts features such as the average, variance, homogeneity, and contrast of EEG signals related to motor imagery in a more efficient manner (i.e., by reducing the number of samples needed to classify the signal and improving the classification percentage) compared to the original QSA technique. Specifically, we can sample the signal in variable time periods (from 0.5 s to 3 s, in half-a-second intervals) to determine the relationship between the number of samples and their effectiveness in classifying signals. In addition, to strengthen the classification process a number of boosting-technique-based decision trees were implemented. The results show an 82.30% accuracy rate for 0.5 s samples and 73.16% for 3 s samples. This is a significant improvement compared to the original QSA technique that offered results from 33.31% to 40.82% without sampling window and from 33.44% to 41.07% with sampling window, respectively. We can thus conclude that iQSA is better suited to develop real-time applications.

1. Introduction

In the last few years, interest in inferring information from the human brain stemming from cognitive thoughts by means of electroencephalography (EEG) has expanded to various disciplines such as neuroscience, robotics, computational science, physics, and mathematics. Research in these areas tends to revolve around the development of new communication and control technologies based on brain-computer interface (BCI) devices to support people with severe neuromuscular conditions in ways that can enable them to express their wishes or use devices as neuroprosthetics [1], wheelchairs [2, 3], control a cursor on a computer screen [4], or even a robot [5, 6]. Wolpaw et al. [7] argue that BCIs "give their users communication and control channels that do not depend on the brain's normal output channels of peripheral nerves and muscles." In other words, BCI devices establish a communication channel between the individual and a component (electromechanical devices, robots, software applications, etc.) to control it by means of brain activity generated by the user to carry out some intended action [8]. To that effect, the user must call upon those actions by means of a brain strategy known as motor imagery.

Motor imagery (MI) is a conscious process defined as a mental simulation of a particular movement [9]. The motor imagery is endowed with the same functional relationship to the imagined or represented movement and the same causal role in the generation of the movement in question [10]. In other words, MI is related to the intention and preparation of movements, whereby the subject imagines carrying out a particular action without making any real movements. This has led to studies using motor imagery to decipher processes that precede the execution of an action. For instance, Bai et al. [11] claim that mental practice using motor imagery of limb movement may facilitate motor recovery in persons who have experienced cerebrovascular injuries. In addition, McFarland et al. [12] conducted a comparative analysis of EEG topographies associated with actual hand movements and imagined hand movements, concluding that motor imagery plays an important role in EEG-based communication and suggesting that mu and beta rhythms might provide independent control signals.

Similarly, there have been studies focusing on MI support and BCI systems, proposing algorithms for feature extraction and classification. For instance, Pfurtscheller et al. [13] studied the reactivity of mu rhythms associated with the imagination of hand, foot, and tongue movements with 60 EEG electrodes in nine able-bodied subjects (with a 66.16% performance rate). In turn, Aghaei et al. [14] argue for the use of the separable common spatiospectral patterns (SCSSP) method to extract discriminant spatiospectral EEG features and a Laplacian filter of data set V of BCI competition III with the following mental imagery tasks: left-hand movement, right-hand movement, and generation of words beginning with a random letter involving 3 subjects. As for Gao et al. [15], they conducted EEG signal analysis during left-hand movements, right-hand movements, and resting with 10 subjects using the Kolmogorov complexity to extract the features and an AdaBoost multiclass classifier, achieving a 79.5% accuracy rate. In a separate study, Schlögl et al. [16] conducted a comparative study involving four classifiers to determine the global separability of data in relation to four different MI tasks with 5 subjects, modelling the EEG signal by means of an adaptive autoregressive (AAR) process whose parameters were extracted through Kalman filtering. Trad et al. [17] used empirical mode decomposition (EMD) and band power (BP) to extract EEG signals and classify MI in experiments involving 10 subjects aged 22–35 as they imagined left-hand and right-hand movements. Choi and Cichocki [18] implemented a MI-based algorithm to control a wheelchair using spatial filters to extract the features by means of a common spatial pattern (CSP) method and the linear SVMs to classify feature vectors. Three healthy men participated in the experiments where they had to

imagine clenching the right hand, squeezing the left hand, and walking. In [19] results of tests conducted with a 74% accuracy rate to control a robot indoors on the basis of three mental states are presented. In particular, there are several studies focusing on the development of processing techniques, feature extraction, and classification to improve the BCI systems. In Tables 1 and 2, we present the most commonly used algorithms for these tasks from Lotte' et al. works [20]. However, we only extracted information related to our work, that is, motor imagery activities (imagined movement of the left hand, imagined movement of the right hand, imagined movement of the foot, imagined movement of the tongue, relaxation, and mental calculation). These works use different algorithms in the classification stages, such as SVM, KNN, LDA, MLP, HMM, Gaussian classifier, and Bayes quadratic, including combinations of these, which result in most studies in acceptable performance rates. However, most experiments are performed on a small number of subjects, which returns a low number of trials per session. In the feature extraction stage, most techniques used to analyze EEG signals extract information within the frequency or time-frequency domain, which may lead to information loss when information is transformed. In addition, they require noise-elimination filters and frequency band localization to identify the patterns of motor imagery.

On the other hand, in [21], the design of a motor imagery experiment was reported based on three mental processes: arrow moving to the left, arrow moving to the right, and waiting time, lasting 5 seconds per image. This study analyzed EEG signals with the implementation of the quaternion-based signal analysis (QSA). The quaternion-based signal analysis (QSA) method is a technique that uses EEG signals within the time domain because it is based on quaternion algebra. The use of quaternion algebra with the QSA technique makes it possible to describe signals within the time domain by means of rotations and orientations of 3D objects and represent multichannel EEG signals as a single entity, preventing data ambiguity and producing a more accurate representation doing fewer calculations than are needed with other techniques. The offline analysis was conducted in the feature extraction phase considering the total number of samples in each class, which produced an 84.92% accuracy rate. However, while the analysis of offline signals is convenient and efficient, offline analysis results may not generalize their performance to online applications. In the case of the QSA method, the online analysis obtained was just 33.31% considering window sizes of 0.5 seconds.

Thus, this paper presents an improvement to the QSA method that we shall call *improved quaternion-based signal analysis* (iQSA) for use in the feature extraction and classification phases, whose contribution consists in providing a technique for use in real-time applications, focusing on analyzing EEG signals online reducing the sample sizes needed to a tenth of the ones required by QSA, resulting in a faster response and fewer delays to improve execution times in real-time actions. The experiment involved using an Emotiv-Epoc device to acquire the brain signals from the motor and visual regions of the cerebral cortex. Similarly, during the training and validation phases, the EEG signal

TABLE 1: Accuracy of classifier in motor imagery based BCI: multiclass. The classes are (T1) left imagined hand movements, (T2) right imagined hand movements, (T3) imagined foot movements, (T4) imagined tongue movements, (T5) relax (baseline), (T6) word generation starting with a letter specific, and (T7) mental calculation.

Dataset	Activity	Subjects	Trials	Filter	Feature	Classifier	Accuracy	References
	T1, T2, T3, T4	5	240 to 360	Yes	AAR	Linear SVM	63%	
						KNN	41.74%	[16]
						LDA	54.46%	
						Mahalanobis distance	53.50%	
	T1, T2, T6	3		Yes		Neuro-fuzzy algorithm S-dFasArt	89.04%	[23]
BCI competition III	T1, T2, T3, T4	3	240	Yes	CSP	CSP + SVM	79%	
						CSP + SVM + KNN + LDA	69%	[24]
						PCA + ICA + SVM	63%	
						CBN + SVM	91%	
	T1, T2, T6	3	12	Yes	SCSSP/LDA	FBCSP-NBPW	52.42 ± 6.94	
						FBCSP-Lin	59.77 ± 9.97	[14]
						SCSSP-NBPW	53.21 ± 6.94	
						SCSSP-Lin	59.33 ± 8.71	
	T1, T2, T3	5	280	Yes	CSP/ERD-ERS	BSSFO, SVM	75.46%	[25]
BCI competition IV	T1, T2, T3, T4	9	288	Yes	CSP	CSP + SVM	31%	
						LDA + SVM	30%	[24]
						CSP + SVM	29%	
						CBN + SVM	66%	
	T1, T2, T3, T4	9	288	Yes	SCSSP/LDA	LDA	85%	[14]
	T1, T2, T3, T4	9	288	Yes	CSP/ERD-ERS	BSSFO, SVM	80.26%	[25]
	T1, T2, T3, T4	9	240	Yes	AAR, Kalman Filter	MDA	—	[13]
	T1, T2, T5	9	120	Yes		SMR, two-dimensional linear classifier	85%	[26]
Other data sets	T1, T2, T3, T4	8	288	Yes	ICA, CSP (SampEn)	FDA	33%–84%	[27]
	T1, T2, T3	3	480	Yes		SVM (RBF Kernel)	69.93%	[28]
	T1, T2, T5	33		Yes	AAR	PCA		[12]
Epoc	T1, T2, T3	3	100	Yes	ICA, CWT	SVM	66.16%	[29]
	T1, T2	5	75	Yes		Simple logistic, Meta, MLP	80.40%	[30]
	T1, T2, T4	1		Yes		Neural networks (PSO)	91%	[31]
	T1, T2, T3, T4, T7	3	40	Yes	BP	HMM	77.50%	[32]
	T1, T2, T3	3	30	Yes	BP	LDA	95%	[33]

TABLE 2: Accuracy of classifier in motor imagery based BCI: two classes. The classes are (T1) left imagined hand movements and (T2) right imagined hand movements.

Dataset	Activity	Subjects	Trials	Filter	Feature	Classifier	Accuracy	References
BCI competition III	T1, T2	5	280	Yes		LS-SVM (RBF kernel)	95.72%	[34]
	T1, T2	4	140	Yes		HMM	77.50% +	[35]
	T1, T2	4	200	Yes	CSP	SVM (Gaussian kernel)	77.50%	[36]
	T1, T2	7	100	Yes	CSP/EMD, PCA	KNN	85.8%	[37]
	T1, T2	4	100	Yes		SVM	81%	[29]
Other data sets	T1, T2	4	90	Yes	CSP	SVM (Gaussian kernel)	74.10%	[36]
	T1, T2	1	140	Yes	CSP/ERD-ERS	BSSFO-SVM	97.57%	[25]
	T1, T2		80	Yes	PLS Regression	Based on the decoding principle	64%	[1]
	T1, T2	109	90	Yes	CSP	SUTCCSP	90%	[38]
	T1, T2	4	480	Yes	CSP/ERD-ERS, FFT	LDA, SVM, BPNN	84%+	[39]
	T1, T2	3		Yes	BSS, CSP	SVM	92%	[40]
Epoc	T1, T2	5	120	Yes	CSP/EMD, MIDKRA	PSD, Hjort, CWT, DWT	97.79%	[41]
	T1, T2	8	100	Yes	ERS, ERD	LDA	70.37%	[42]
	T1, T2	2	140	Yes	CSP	Naive Bayes	79%	[43]
	T1, T2	15	40	Yes	Wavelet, PSD, EMD	KNN	91.80%	[44]

database was strengthened by adding a greater number of subjects and by combining decision trees in the classification phase based on use of the boosting technique.

2. Materials and Methods

2.1. Quaternions. Quaternions were proposed in 1843 by Hamilton [22], as a set of four constituents (a real and three imaginary components) as follows: $q = w + ix + jy + kz$, where $w, x, y, z \in \mathbb{R}$ and i, j, k are symbols of three imaginary quantities known as imaginary units. These units follow these rules:

$$i^2 = j^2 = k^2 = ijk = -1$$
$$ij = k,$$
$$jk = i,$$
$$ki = j$$
$$ji = -k,$$
$$kj = -i,$$
$$ik = -j. \tag{1}$$

A quaternion can be described as

$$q = (s + \mathbf{a}), \quad \mathbf{a} = (x, y, z), \tag{2}$$

where s and $\mathbf{a}$ are known as the quaternion's scalar and vector, respectively. When $s = 0$, q is known as pure quaternion.

Based on the expanded Euler's formula, the rotation for quaternion around the axis $n = [nx, ny, nz]$ by angle theta is defined as follows (see [21, 45] for further details).

A rotation of angle θ around a unit vector $\mathbf{a} = [a_x, a_y, a_x]$ is defined as follows:

$$q = \cos\left(\frac{\theta}{2}\right) + \left(\mathbf{a_x} \cdot \mathbf{i} + \mathbf{a_y} \cdot \mathbf{j} + \mathbf{a_z} \cdot \mathbf{k}\right) \sin\left(\frac{\theta}{2}\right). \tag{3}$$

Furthermore, the operation to be performed on a vector $\mathbf{r}$ to produce a rotated vector $\mathbf{r}'$ is

$$\mathbf{r}' = q\mathbf{r}q^{-1} = \left(\cos\left(\frac{\theta}{2}\right) + \mathbf{a}\sin\left(\frac{\theta}{2}\right)\right)$$
$$\cdot \mathbf{r}\left(\cos\left(\frac{\theta}{2}\right) - \mathbf{a}\sin\left(\frac{\theta}{2}\right)\right). \tag{4}$$

Equation (4) is a useful representation that makes the rotation of a vector easier. We can see that $\mathbf{r}$ is the original vector, $\mathbf{r}'$ is the rotated quaternion, and q is the quaternion that defines the rotation.

2.2. iQSA Algorithm. The iQSA is a method that improves the performance and precision of the QSA method, which is a technique to analyze EEG signals for extracting features based

TABLE 3: Statistical features extracted using quaternions.

Statistical features	Equation
Mean (μ)	$= \dfrac{\sum(q_{\mathrm{mod}})}{N_s}$
Variance (σ^2)	$= \dfrac{(\sum(q_{\mathrm{mod}})^2 - \mu)^2 + \sum(q_{\mathrm{mod}})^2}{2N_s}$
Contrast (con)	$= \dfrac{\sum(q_{\mathrm{mod}})^2}{N_s}$
Homogeneity (H)	$= \sum \dfrac{1}{1 + (q_{\mathrm{mod}})^2}$

on rotations and orientations by means of quaternion algebra. With iQSA, we can conduct real-time signal analysis as the signals are being acquired, to difference of QSA method who performs an offline analysis.

The iQSA approach consists of three modules: quaternion, classification, and learning, which are described as follows.

(1) Quaternion module: in this module a features matrix (M) is defined from the description of the quaternion q and a vector R, where each of them corresponds to an array of 4 and 3 EEG channels, respectively. This module is divided into three steps, which are described as follows:

    (a) Sampling window: here, we define the sample size (ns) to be analyzed and a displacement of the window in the signal (t_disp). That is, the iQSA method performs the sampling by means of superposing, producing a greater number of samples to reinforce the learning stage of the algorithm.

    (b) Calculate rotation and module: then, a rotated vector q_{rot} is calculated using the quaternion q and vector R, where q is a m-by-4 matrix containing m quaternions and R is an m-by-3 matrix containing m quaternions displaced on the basis of a dt value. Later, the modulus is applied to the quaternion q_{rot} resulting in the vector q_{mod}.

    (c) Building an array of features: finally, the array q_{mod} is used to form a matrix with $M_{i,j}$ features, where i corresponds to the analyzed segment and j is one of the 4 features to be analyzed using the equations included in Table 3, that is, *mean* (μ), *variance* (σ^2), *contrast* (con), and *homogeneity* (H).

Equation (5) shows matrix M with its features vector. In this matrix rows correspond to samples and columns to features.

$$M = \begin{bmatrix} \mu_1 & \sigma_1^2 & \mathrm{con}_1 & H_1 \\ \mu_2 & \sigma_2^2 & \mathrm{con}_2 & H_2 \\ \vdots & \vdots & \vdots & \vdots \\ \mu_i & \sigma_i^2 & \mathrm{con}_i & H_i \end{bmatrix}. \tag{5}$$

(2) Classification module: the aim of this module is to create a combination of models to predict the value of a class according to its characteristics; to do this we use the boosting method adapted to the QSA model. To be more specific, we combine ten decision trees and a weight is obtained for each of them, which will be used during the learning to obtain the prediction by a majority rule. Here, we take 70% of samples from M, of which the 80% are used for training and the rest for validation as follows:

    (a) Training: the subset of training data (80% samples) is assessed, using the models of decision trees to obtain a matrix with accurately classified samples (G) and a matrix with inaccurately classified samples (B). The learning of each tree is done by manipulating the training data set and partitioning the initial set in several subsets according to the classification results obtained; that is, a new subset is formed, generated, and created with the accurately classified samples, twice that number of inaccurately classified samples and the worst-classified samples from the original training data set. Later, when the trees of classification are created, these are used with the test data set to determine a weight in function of the accuracy of their predictions.

    (b) Validation: in this block we obtain a matrix with the reliability percentages given by the decision trees. The subset of validation data (20% samples) is assessed, using the decision trees to obtain an array with reliability values given by the processing of decision trees and the classes identified in the training process.

(3) Learning module: in this module, the subset of test data of M (30% samples) is assessed to obtain reliability values matrix (R) and the prediction by majority rule ($\widehat{C}$). That is, the learning process will be conducted assessing features matrix of test using the trees that have been generated in classification process. The final predictor comes from a weighted majority rule of the predictors from various decision trees. Equation (6) shows the recognition and error rates obtained in each of the prediction models. In this matrix RT corresponds to accuracy rate, ET corresponds to error rate, and α corresponds to reliability value of each decision tree.

$$R = \begin{bmatrix} \mathrm{RT}_1 & \mathrm{ET}_1 & \alpha_1 \\ \mathrm{RT}_2 & \mathrm{ET}_2 & \alpha_2 \\ \vdots & \vdots & \vdots \\ \mathrm{RT}_i & \mathrm{ET}_i & \alpha_i \end{bmatrix}. \tag{6}$$

In Algorithm 1, we present the pseudocode for the main elements of the iQSA algorithm towards real-time applications.

<table>
<tr><td>

Algorithm 1: iQSA method
Require: quat = $\{q_1, q_2, q_3, q_4\}$, dt, ns, t_disp, task
(1) $y(t) \leftarrow$ segments of signals
(2)   **for each** ns in $y_i(t)$ **do**
        $q(ns) \leftarrow$ quat(ns)
        $r(ns) \leftarrow$ quat$(ns - dt)$
        $q_{\text{rot}}(ns) \leftarrow$ nrot $(q(ns), r(ns))$
        $q_{\text{mod}}(ns) \leftarrow$ mod$(q_{\text{rot}}(ns))$
        $M_{i,j} \leftarrow f_j$ (qmod(ns)) $\{j = 1, \ldots, m\}$
        $c_i \leftarrow \{c = (1, 2, 3, \ldots, n) \mid y_i(t) \in c\}$
        $ns = ns + t$disp;
    end for
(3) $M_{k,j} \leftarrow \{M_{i,j} \mid \#k/\#i = \%t\}$
(4) $M_{l,j} \leftarrow \{M_{i,j} \mid \{l\} \notin \{k\}, \#l/\#i = 1 - \%t\}$
(5) $[\beta, \text{BTree}]$ = Classify_module$(M_{k,j}, c_k)$
(6) $[R, \widehat{C}, Vm]$ = Learning_module$(M_{l,j}, c_l, \beta_i)$
(7)   % $rt = \#\{\widehat{C}_k \mid \widehat{C}_k = C_k\}/\#\{C_k\}$
(8)   % $rv = \#\{\widehat{C}_l \mid \widehat{C}_l = C_l\}/\#\{C_l\}$
Function: Classify_module (M, c)
(1) $M_{a,j} \leftarrow \{M_{i,j} \mid \#a/\#i = \%s\}$
(2) $M_{b,j} \leftarrow \{M_{i,j} \mid \{b\} \notin \{a\}, \#b/\#i = 1 - \%t\}$
    /*Training process*/
(3)   **for** $k = 1$ **to** 10 **do**
        $[G_{m,j}, B_{n,j}, \text{BTree}] \leftarrow$ training$(M_{a,j}, c_a)$
        $M_{a,j} \leftarrow \{M_{a,j} + B_{n,j} - G_{m,j}\}$
    end for
    /*Validation process*/
(4)   **for each** BTree **do**
        $[\widehat{C}_i] \leftarrow$ validation(BTree, $M_{b,j}, c_b$)
        $\beta_i \leftarrow \#\{\widehat{C}_i \mid \widehat{C}_i = C_i\}/\#\{C_i\}$
    end for
(5)   return $\beta, \widehat{C}$, BTree
Function: Learning module (M, c, β, B, Tree)
(1)   **for each** BTree **do**
        $[R_i, Vm] \leftarrow$ classify(BTree, $M_{i,j}, \beta_i, c_i$)
    end for
(2)   return $R, \widehat{C}_i, Vm$

</td></tr>
</table>

ALGORITHM 1: iQSA algorithm.

TABLE 4: Main modules in QSA and iQSA.

Modules	QSA	iQSA
Sampling window	X	•
Quaternion module	•	•
Classification module	•	•
Boosting technique	X	•
Learning module	X	•
Superposition technique	X	•
Weight normalization	X	•
Majority voting	X	•
Processing type	Batch	Real-time

classification during feature extraction, strengthening the classification phase by means of the boosting technique.

In this way, the signals produced by the iQSA algorithm affect the posterior brain signals, which in turn will affect the subsequent outputs of the BCI. Figure 2 presents the time system diagram of iQSA, which indicates the timeline of events in the algorithm. It follows the process of three EEG data blocks (N_1, N_2, N_3) obtained from the Emotiv-Epoc device. The processing block covers the analysis and processing of the data with the iQSA method until obtaining an output (OP), in this case, the class to which each N_i block belongs.

It is also possible to observe the start and duration of the next two sets of data, where the start of block N_2 is displaced from the progress of block N_1 by a time represented as T_{disp} between t_{-1} and t_0; therefore, while the block N_1 reaches the output at t_2, the process of N_2 continues executing until reaching its respective output.

2.3. BCI System. A brain-computer interface is a system of communication based on neural activity generated by the brain. A BCI measures the activity of an EEG signal by processing it and extracting the relevant features to interact in the environment as required by the user. An example of this device is the Emotiv-Epoc headset (Figure 3(a)), a noninvasive mobile BCI device with a gyroscopic sensor, and 14 EEG channels (electrodes) and two reference channels (CMS/DRL) with a 128 Hz sample frequency. The distribution of sensors in the headset is based on the international 10–20-electrode placement system with two sensors as reference for proper placement on the head with channels labeled as AF3, F7, F3, FC5, T7, P7, O1, O2, P8, T8, FC6, F4, F8, and AF4 (Figure 3(b)).

An advantage of the Emotiv-Epoc device is its ability to handle missing values, very common and problematic when dealing with biomedical data.

2.4. Decision Trees and Boosting. Decision trees (DT) [46–48] are a widely used and easy-to-implement technique that offers high speed and accuracy rates. DT are used to analyze data for prediction purposes. In short, they work by setting conditions or rules organized in a hierarchical structure where the final decision can be determined following conditions established from the root to its leaves.

2.2.1. iQSA versus QSA Methods. In Figure 1, we show through block diagrams the main differences between the iQSA and QSA methods. It can be observed that QSA method considers quaternion and classification modules. On the other hand, iQSA method considers an improved classification module and one more for learning.

In Table 4, we present some of the main improvements made in the iQSA algorithm.

The QSA method, by its characteristics, is an excellent technique for the offline processing of EEG signals considering large samples of data and being inefficient when such data is small. This last becomes essential for online processing because the operations depend on the interaction in real time between the signals produced by the subject and the EEG signals translated with the aid of the algorithm. In this regard, the iQSA method considers small samples of data and creates a window with the superposition technique for a better data

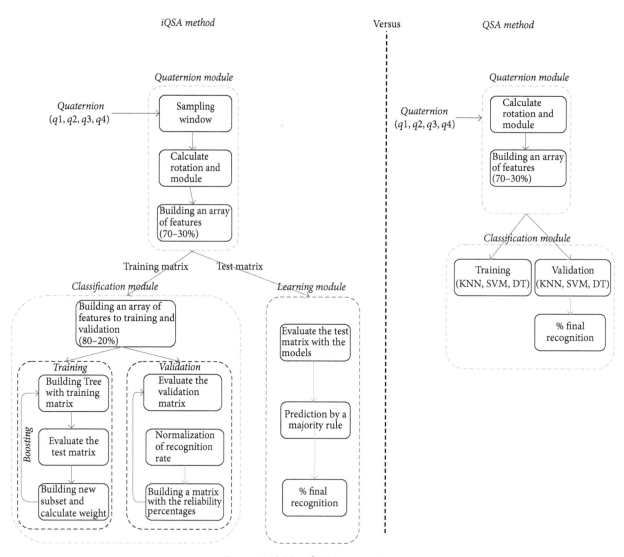

FIGURE 1: iQSA and QSA comparison.

Recently, several alternative techniques have been presented to construct sets of classifiers whose decisions are combined in order to solve a task and to improve the results obtained by the base classifier. There exist two popular techniques to build sets: bagging [49] and boosting [50]. Both methods operate under a base-learning algorithm that is invoked several times using various training sets. In our case, we implemented a new boosting method adapted to QSA method, whereby we trained a number of weak classifiers iteratively so that each new classifier *(weak learner)* focuses on finding weak hypothesis (inaccurately classified). In other words, boosting calls the weak learner w times thus determining, at each iteration, a random subset of training samples by adding the accurately classified samples, twice that number of inaccurately classified samples and the worst-classified samples from the original training data set to form a new weak learner w.

As a result, inaccurately classified samples of the previous iteration are given an (α) weight in the next iteration, forcing the classifying algorithm to focus on data that are harder to

classify in order to correct classification errors of the previous iteration. Finally, the reliability percentage of all the classifiers is added and a hypothesis is obtained by a majority vote, whose prediction tends to be the most accurate.

2.5. Channel Selection for iQSA. From the 14 electrodes that the Emotiv-Epoc device provides, we decided to perform an analysis on the electrodes located in three different regions of the cerebral cortex looking for those with better performance to form the quaternion: (1) electrodes located on the motor cortex, which generates neural impulses that control movements, (2) those on the posterior parietal cortex, where visual information is transformed into motor instructions [51], and (3) the ones on the prefrontal cortex, which appear as a marker of the anticipations that the body must make to adapt to what is going to happen immediately after [52].

In this regard, in Table 5 we present the performance for each of the sets of channels that were selected and further analyzed by the iQSA algorithm.

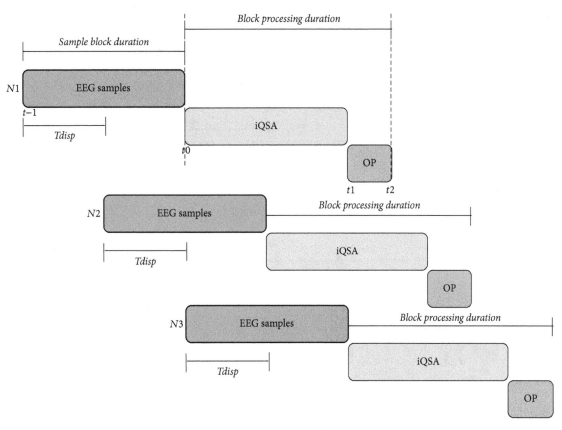

FIGURE 2: Timeline of events in the iQSA algorithm. Here, the iQSA performs the three aforementioned modules and OP represents the class obtained.

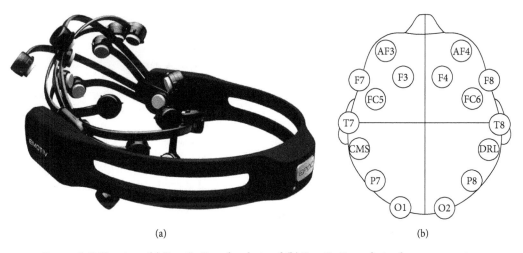

(a)   (b)

FIGURE 3: BCI system: (a) Emotiv-Epoc headset and (b) Emotiv-Epoc electrode arrangement.

Comparing the data sets shown in Figure 4, it is observed that all have a similar behavior in each sample size. For a 64-sample analysis, data sets 2 and 4 obtained 82.30% and 82.33%, respectively. The channels for data set 2 are related to the frontal and motor areas of the brain and the channels for data set 4 are related to the parietal and motor areas. From these results and due to the fact that we mainly focus on motor control tasks, set 2 (F3, F4, FC5, and FC6) has been chosen.

3. Experiment

As seen in earlier sections, one of the objectives of this paper is to analyze EEG signals towards real-time applications. Therefore, it is necessary to reduce the number of samples of EEG signals that have been acquired by subjecting them to a process based on the iQSA method to decode motor imagery activities, while keeping or improving

TABLE 5: Accuracy rate to several data sets of channel blocks.

Data sets	Samples					
	384	320	256	192	128	64
FC5, FC6, P7, P8	74.16	74.13	80.07	81.92	81.60	82.23
F3, F4, FC5, FC6	73.16	74.88	80.23	81.39	81.65	**82.30**
F3, F4, F7, F8	73.48	73.87	79.69	81.74	81.58	82.14
F3, F4, P7, P8	73.47	73.92	80.06	81.68	81.87	**82.33**
AF3, AF4, FC5, FC6	74.17	74.10	80.31	81.82	81.99	82.26

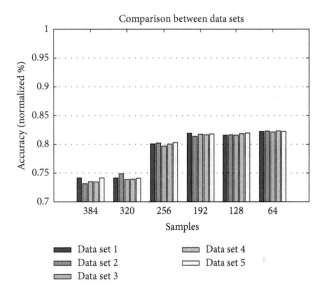

FIGURE 4: Comparison of data sets with different sample sizes. Data set 1: FC5, FC6, P7, P8; data set 2: F3, F4, FC5, FC6: data set 3, F3, F4, F7, F8; data set 4: F3, F4, P7, P8; data set 5: AF3, AF4, FC5, FC6.

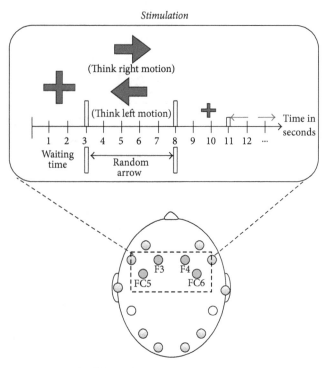

FIGURE 5: Methodology for activities in motor-cognitive experiments.

accuracy results achieved with this technique. In this way, the experiment was designed to register EEG signals from several individuals and to identify three motor-imagery-related mental states (think left motion, think right motion, and waiting time).

3.1. Description of the Experiment. The experiment was conducted in three sessions: Session 1 involved motor imagery with tagged visual support ($V+L$), that is to say, an arrow with the word LEFT or RIGHT written on it. Session 2 involved motor imagery with visual (V) support only. In Session 3 the subject only received a tactile stimulus (T) to evoke motor imagery while keeping his or her eyes closed. In each session, the aim was to identify three mental states (think left motion, think right motion, and waiting time). The visual V and VL stimuli were provided using a GUI interface developed in Python 2.7 to show the movement of a red arrow for 5 seconds for each of the motor brain actions and a fixed cross at the center of the GUI to indicate a rest period for 3 seconds (the third brain action). The tactile stimulus was provided by touching the left/right shoulder of the individual to indicate the brain action to be performed. Each session lasted for 5 minutes and was done on separate days.

To start with, the participant was asked to sit on a comfortable chair in front of a computer screen. As the

participant was given instructions regarding the test, an Emotiv-Epoc headset was placed on his or her head, making sure that each of the Emotiv device electrodes was making proper contact with the scalp (Figure 5). Once the participant was ready, he or she was asked not to make sudden body movements that could interfere with the signal acquisition results during the experiment.

The training paradigm consisted of a sequential repetition of cue-based trials (Figure 5). Each trial started with an empty blank screen; during the time $t = 0$ to $t = 3$ s a cross was displayed to indicate to the user that the experiment had started and that it was time to relax. Then at second 3 ($t = 3$ s) an arrow appearing for 5 s pointed either to the left or to the right. Each position indicated by the arrow instructed the subject to imagine left or right movement, respectively. The next trial started at $t = 8$ s with a cross. This process was repeated for 5 minutes, displaying the arrows 32 times and the cross 33 times within each run. Thus, the data set recorded for the three runs consisted of 96 trials.

3.2. iQSA Method Implementation. After data acquisition, the next stage consists in extracting EEG signal features in order to find the required classes, that is, think left motion, think right motion, and waiting time. To start with, the iQSA method was implemented to represent the four EEG signals within a quaternion and to carry out the feature extraction related to the stimuli presented. To that effect, data set 2 was prepared to assess their performance when time (and the number of samples) was reduced. Under these conditions, 3 seconds (384 samples), 2.5 seconds (320 samples), 2 seconds (256 samples), 1.5 seconds (192 samples), 1 second (128

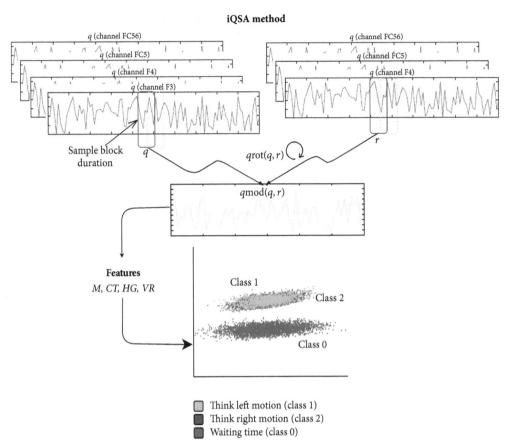

FIGURE 6: Graphic description of the iQSA method. q_{rot} represent the rotation of q with respect to r; q_{mod} is the module of q_{rot}; class 1, class 2, and class 0 represent the motor activities evaluated, in this case "think left motion," "think right motion," and "waiting time," respectively.

samples), and 0.5 seconds (64 samples) were considered. Values 0, 1, and 2 were used to refer to the three mental activities: waiting time (0), think left motion (1), and think right motion (2).

So, a segments matrix was obtained to detect sudden changes between classes for each data set. The segments matrix consisted of samples from 32 trials from left and right classes and samples from 33 trials for the waiting time class. In addition, the quaternion was created with the block signals proposed (F3, F4, FC5, and FC6), considering F3 as the scalar component and F4, FC5, and FC6 as the imaginary components (Figure 6). From the samples to be analyzed, several segments were created to generate the quaternion q and vector R with a displacement $dt = 4$ and thus obtain the rotation (q_{rot}) and modulus (q_{mod}).

Once the module was obtained, the *mean* (μ), *contrast* (con), *homogeneity* (H), and *variance* (σ^2) features were calculated to generate the matrix M and the vector c with the required classes. Later, we returned to the current segment, and a displacement of 64 samples for the signal was effected to obtain the next segment.

Later, M was used in the processing stage using 70% of data from training and 30% from test; here each class has the same sample size and was randomly chosen. In the classification module, we generate the matrix M_1 with the 80% from training data of M and M_2 with the remaining

20% of the training data, which will be used for training and validation, where 10 training trees were created to force the algorithm to focus on the inaccurately classified data. Here, for each iteration we generate new subsets of samples with the double of inaccurately classified samples and fewer accurately classified samples, along with a reliability rate for each tree. Later, with matrix M_2 the data were validated to obtain the percentage of reliability of each tree. Finally, with the remaining data of M, a prediction by majority rule is voted and a decision is reached based on the reliability rate of each classification tree.

4. Results

As said earlier, one of the aims of this study was to reduce the assessment time (sample size) without loss of the accuracy rate. Therefore, a comparison of the iQSA and QSA techniques was performed to show its behavior when the number of samples decreases.

4.1. Comparison between iQSA and QSA Methods. To evaluate and compare the performance of the iQSA online versus QSA offline algorithms, the same sets of data from the 39 participants were used, considering the different sample sizes (384, 320, 256, 192, 128, and 64 samples) as input for the algorithm.

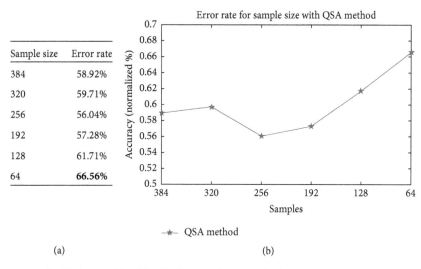

Sample size	Error rate
384	58.92%
320	59.71%
256	56.04%
192	57.28%
128	61.71%
64	**66.56%**

(a)   (b)

FIGURE 7: QSA method behavior. (a) Table of behavior of QSA method; (b) graphic of error rate for sample size.

TABLE 6: Table of accuracy rate for iQSA and QSA method with different number samples.

Sample size	QSA (1)	QSA (2)	iQSA (3)
384	40.82%	41.07%	73.16%
320	40.74%	40.29%	74.87%
256	43.56%	43.96%	80.23%
192	42.41%	42.71%	81.39%
128	37.45%	38.28%	81.65%
64	33.31%	33.44%	**82.30%**

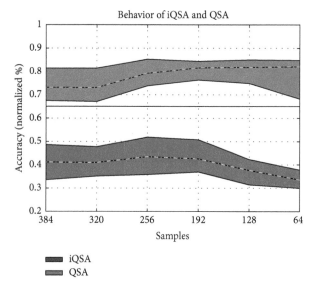

FIGURE 8: Behavior of the iQSA and QSA methods with different sample sizes.

In spite of the good performance rates reported with the QSA algorithm for offline data analysis, the classification results were not as good when the number of samples was reduced up to 64 samples as shown in Figure 7(a). Graphically, as can be seen, the error rate increases gradually when the sample size is reduced for analysis, reaching up to 66.56% error for a reading of 64 samples. In this way, it was necessary to make several adjustments to the algorithm, in such a way as to support an online analysis with small samples sizes, without losing information and sacrificing the good performance rates provided by the offline QSA algorithm.

Thus, the data of the 39 subjects were evaluated, considering three cases: (1) QSA method without window samples, (2) QSA method with window samples, and (3) iQSA proposed method. Comparing the results of Table 6, the precision percentages for the iQSA method range from 73.16% for 384 samples to 82.30%% for 64 samples, unlike the original QSA method whose percentage decreases to 33.31% for 64 samples in case 1 and 33.44% in case 2 although the sampling window has been implemented.

Figure 8 shows the behavior of the iQSA technique in blue and QSA technique in red, where the mean, maximum, and minimum of each technique are shown. Comparing both techniques, it is observed that the data analyzed with the original QSA method drastically loses precision as the number of samples selected decreases. This was not the

case for data sets using the iQSA technique whose precision did not vary too much when the number of samples for classification was reduced, improving even its performance.

4.2. iQSA Results. Figure 9 shows the behavior of 39 participants under both techniques (iQSA and QSA), considering all the sample sizes. The values obtained using the iQSA method are better than values obtained with QSA method whose values are below 50%. Numerical results show that the iQSA method provides a higher accuracy over the original QSA method for tests with a 64-sample size.

Given the above results, a data analysis was conducted using 64 samples to identify the motor imagery actions. The performances obtained with the set of classifiers were compared using various assessment metrics, such as recognition rate (RT) and error rate (ET), and sensitivity (S)

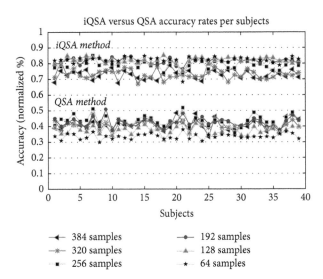

FIGURE 9: iQSA and QSA method performances per sample size and subjects.

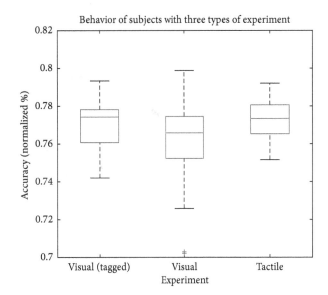

FIGURE 10: Graph of behavior of subjects with three types of experiments: tagged visual, visual, and tactile stimulation.

and specificity (Sp). The sensitivity metric shows that the classifier can recognize samples from the relevant class, and the specificity is also known as the real negative rate because it measures whether the classifier can recognize samples that do not belong to the relevant class.

$$RT = \frac{\#\{c \mid c = \widehat{c}\}}{\#\{c\}} \tag{7}$$

$$ET = \frac{\#\{c \mid c \neq \widehat{c}\}}{\#\{c\}} \tag{8}$$

$$S_d = \frac{\#\{c \mid c = d, c = \widehat{c}\}}{\#\{c \mid c = d\}} \tag{9}$$

$$Sp_d = \frac{\#\{c \mid c \neq d, c = \widehat{c}\}}{\#\{c \mid c \neq d\}}. \tag{10}$$

As Table 7 shows, the highest accuracy percentage was 84.50% and the lowest 68.75%. In addition, the sensitivity average for class 0 (S_0) associated with the waiting time mental state was 82.53%, and the sensitivity average for class 1 (S_1) and class 2 (S_2) associated with think left motion and think right motion was 81.07% and 81.65%, respectively, which indicates that the classifier had no problem classifying classes. In turn, the specificity rate for class 0 (Sp_0) shows that 81.36% of the samples classified as negative were actually negative, while class 1 (Sp_1) performed at 82.09% and class 2 (Sp_2) at 81.80%.

To evaluate the performance of our approach, we have carried out a comparison with other methods such as FDCSP [53], MEMD-SI-BCI [54], and SR-FBCSP [55] using data set 2a from BCI IV [56] and the results are shown in Table 8. Our method shows a slight improvement (1.09%) compared to the SR-FBCSP method, which presents the best results of the three.

To analyze our results, we performed a significant statistical test making use of the STAC (Statistical Tests for Algorithms Comparison) web platform [57]. Here, we chose the Friedman test with a significance level of 0.10 to get

a ranking of the algorithms and check if the differences between them are statistically significant.

Table 9 shows the Friedman test ranking results obtained with the p value approach. From such table, we can observe that our proposal gets the lowest ranking; that is, iQSA has the best results in accuracy among all the algorithms.

In order to compare whether the difference between iQSA and the other methods is significant, a Li post hoc procedure was performed (Table 10). The differences are statistically significant because the p values are below 0.10.

In addition, the classification shown in Table 8 is achieved by the iQSA in real time and compared to the other methods a prefiltering process is not required.

In Table 11, we show the time required for each of the tasks performed by the iQSA algorithm: (1) features extraction, (2) classification, and (3) learning. The EEG signal analysis in processes 1 and 2 was responsible for obtaining the quaternion from the EEG signals, learning trees, and training. Process 3 evaluates and classifies the signal based on the generated decision trees, as should be done in real-time analysis.

According to the experiment, for offline classification (processes 1 and 2), the processing time required was 0.3089 seconds. However, the time required to recognize the motor imagery activity generated by the subject was of 0.0095 seconds, considering that the learning trees were already generated, and even when the processing phase was done in real time, it would take 0.3184 seconds to recognize a pattern after the first reading. With this, our proposed method can be potentially used in several applications such as controlling a robot, manipulating a wheelchair, or controlling home appliances, to name a few.

As said earlier, the experiment consisted of 3 sessions with each participant (visual tagged, visual, and tactile). The average accuracy obtained from the 3 experiments is between 76% and 78%. Figure 10 shows results from the

TABLE 7: Comparison of performance measures for the decision tree classifier using 64 samples.

Subject	ER	RT	S_0	S_1	S_2	Sp_0	Sp_1	Sp_2
(1)	0.17667	0.82333	0.83000	0.81500	0.82500	0.82000	0.82750	0.82250
(2)	0.18625	0.81375	0.81375	0.79500	0.83250	0.81375	0.82312	0.80437
(3)	0.17542	0.82458	0.85125	0.79000	0.83250	0.81125	0.84188	0.82063
(4)	0.19145	0.80855	0.81923	0.81410	0.79231	0.80321	0.80577	0.81667
(5)	0.20875	0.79125	0.77750	0.79125	0.80500	0.79812	0.79125	0.78437
(6)	0.15792	0.84208	0.86500	0.81875	0.84250	0.83063	**0.85375**	0.84187
(7)	0.18417	0.81583	0.83500	0.79875	0.81375	0.80625	0.82438	0.81687
(8)	0.18333	0.81667	0.82125	0.80625	0.82250	0.81437	0.82188	0.81375
(9)	0.17125	0.82875	0.82875	0.83625	0.82125	0.82875	0.82500	0.83250
(10)	0.16458	0.83542	0.86375	0.84375	0.79875	0.82125	0.83125	**0.85375**
(11)	0.18803	0.81197	0.80641	0.81154	0.81795	0.81474	0.81218	0.80897
(12)	0.15500	**0.84500**	0.83125	0.84000	**0.86375**	**0.85187**	0.84750	0.83562
(13)	0.19542	0.80458	0.83125	0.78250	0.80000	0.79125	0.81563	0.80688
(14)	0.15792	0.84208	0.85000	0.82625	0.85000	0.83813	0.85000	0.83813
(15)	0.19167	0.80833	0.80625	0.79875	0.82000	0.80937	0.81312	0.80250
(16)	0.19458	0.80542	0.82500	0.76875	0.82250	0.79563	0.82375	0.79688
(17)	0.16292	0.83708	0.85000	0.83500	0.82625	0.83063	0.83813	0.84250
(18)	0.17137	0.82863	0.84615	0.81154	0.82821	0.81987	0.83718	0.82885
(19)	0.15875	0.84125	0.84000	0.83250	0.85125	0.84187	0.84562	0.83625
(20)	0.18250	0.81750	0.81500	0.80375	0.83375	0.81875	0.82438	0.80937
(21)	0.31250	0.68750	0.65625	0.68625	0.72000	0.70312	0.68812	0.67125
(22)	0.16708	0.83292	0.86250	0.82125	0.81500	0.81812	0.83875	0.84188
(23)	0.18917	0.81083	0.82375	0.81625	0.79250	0.80437	0.80813	0.82000
(24)	0.16958	0.83042	0.84250	0.81500	0.83375	0.82438	0.83813	0.82875
(25)	0.17500	0.82500	0.84079	0.83947	0.79474	0.81711	0.81776	0.84013
(26)	0.19583	0.80417	0.80750	0.80250	0.80250	0.80250	0.80500	0.80500
(27)	0.16500	0.83500	0.83000	0.82750	0.84750	0.83750	0.83875	0.82875
(28)	0.20083	0.79917	0.78500	0.79625	0.81625	0.80625	0.80063	0.79062
(29)	0.18947	0.81053	0.83421	0.79474	0.80263	0.79868	0.81842	0.81447
(30)	0.16083	0.83917	0.85875	0.83250	0.82625	0.82937	0.84250	0.84563
(31)	0.17875	0.82125	0.83375	0.80625	0.82375	0.81500	0.82875	0.82000
(32)	0.19083	0.80917	0.82125	0.81125	0.79500	0.80312	0.80812	0.81625
(33)	0.19333	0.80667	0.82125	0.79750	0.80125	0.79937	0.81125	0.80937
(34)	0.18917	0.81083	0.80250	0.82000	0.81000	0.81500	0.80625	0.81125
(35)	0.16333	0.83667	**0.86500**	0.82750	0.81750	0.82250	0.84125	0.84625
(36)	0.16833	0.83167	0.83250	0.82250	0.84000	0.83125	0.83625	0.82750
(37)	0.18833	0.81167	0.83125	0.81000	0.79375	0.80188	0.81250	0.82063
(38)	0.17000	0.83000	0.81125	**0.86750**	0.81125	0.83937	0.81125	0.83938
(39)	0.19083	0.80917	0.82125	0.80375	0.80250	0.80313	0.81187	0.81250
Mean	*0.18247*	*0.81753*	*0.82533*	*0.81071*	*0.81656*	*0.81363*	*0.82095*	*0.81802*
STD	0.02544	0.02544	0.03451	0.02796	0.02404	0.02315	0.02667	0.0291

visual stimulation session, which produced the lowest rate at 76.63%, followed by tagged visual session which reached 76.98% and the tactile session 77.28%.

In Figure 10, it is shown that the mental activity generated with the aid of a tactile stimulus is slightly more accurate than visual and visual tagged stimuli where recognition is more imprecise and slow with visual stimulus.

To summarize, the results of tests conducted with 39 participants using this new method to classify motor imagery brain signals, 20 times with each participant, considering 70%–30% of the data have been presented and creating several subsets of 80–20% for the classification process. The average performance accuracy rate was 81.75% when using 10 decision trees in combination with the boosting technique at 0.5-second sampling rates. The results show that this methodology for monitoring, representing, and classifying EEG signals can be used for the purposes of having individuals control external devices in real time.

Table 8: Comparison results.

Subject	iQSA	FDCSP	MEMD-SI-BCI	SR-FBCSP
(1)	0.8543	0.9166	0.9236	0.8924
(2)	0.8296	0.6805	0.5833	0.5936
(3)	0.8273	0.9722	0.9167	0.9581
(4)	0.8509	0.7222	0.6389	0.7073
(5)	0.7879	0.7222	0.5903	0.7810
(6)	0.8284	0.7153	0.6736	0.6998
(7)	0.8172	0.8125	0.6042	0.8824
(8)	0.8466	0.9861	0.9653	0.9532
(9)	0.8425	0.9375	0.6667	0.9192
Average	0.83164	0.8294	0.7292	0.8207
Std	0.02054	0.1238	0.1581	0.1302

Table 9: Friedman test ranking results.

Algorithm	Ranking
iQSA	15.3333
FDCSP	15.5556
SR-FBCSP	16.5556
MEMD-SI-BCI	26.5556

Table 10: Li post hoc adjusted p values for the test error ranking in Table 9.

Comparison	Adjusted p value
iQSA versus datasets	0.00118
iQSA versus SR-FBCSP	0.96717
iQSA versus FDCSP	0.97137
iQSA versus MEMD-SI-BCI	0.70942

Table 11: Execution time of iQSA method.

Process	Time in seconds
iQSA quaternion (1)	0.2054
iQSA classification (2)	0.1035
iQSA learning (3)	0.0095

5. Conclusions

Feature extraction is one of the most important phases in systems involving BCI devices. In particular, feature extraction applied to EEG signals for motor imagery activity discrimination has been the focus of several studies in recent times. This paper presents an improvement to the QSA method known as iQSA, for EEG signal feature extraction with a view to using it in real time with mental tasks involving motor imagery. With our new iQSA method, the raw signal is subsampled and analyzed on the basis of a QSA algorithm to extract features of brain activity within the time domain by means of quaternion algebra. The feature vector made up of mean, variance, homogeneity, and contrast is used in the classification phase to implement a set of decision-tree classifiers using the boosting technique. The performance achieved using the iQSA technique ranged from 73.16% to 82.30% accuracy rates with readings taken between 3 seconds

and half a second. This new method was compared to the original QSA technique, whose accuracy rates ranged from 40.82% to 33.31% without sampling window and from 41.07% to 33.34% with sampling window. We can thus conclude that iQSA is a promising technique with potential to be used in motor imagery recognition tasks in real-time applications.

Acknowledgments

This research has been partially supported by the CONACYT project "Neurociencia Computacional: de la teoría al desarrollo de sistemas neuromórficos" (no. 1961). Horacio Rostro-Gonzalez acknowledges the University of Guanajuato for the support provided through a sabbatical year.

References

[1] P. Ofner and G. R. Müller-Putz, "Using a noninvasive decoding method to classify rhythmic movement imaginations of the arm in two planes," *IEEE Transactions on Biomedical Engineering*, vol. 62, no. 3, pp. 972–981, 2015.

[2] R. Chai, S. H. Ling, G. P. Hunter, and H. T. Nguyen, "Toward fewer EEG channels and better feature extractor of non-motor imagery mental tasks classification for a wheelchair thought controller," in *Proceedings of the 34th Annual International Conference of the IEEE Engineering in Medicine and Biology Society (EMBC)*, pp. 5266–5269, San Diego, CA, USA, August 2012.

[3] H. S. Kim, M. H. Chang, H. J. Lee, and K. S. Park, "A comparison of classification performance among the various combinations of motor imagery tasks for brain-computer interface," in *Proceedings of the 2013 6th International IEEE EMBS Conference on Neural Engineering, NER 2013*, pp. 435–438, San Diego, CA, USA, November 2013.

[4] J. R. Wolpaw, D. J. McFarland, G. W. Neat, and C. A. Forneris, "An EEG-based brain-computer interface for cursor control," *Electroencephalography and Clinical Neurophysiology*, vol. 78, no. 3, pp. 252–259, 1991.

[5] A. Vourvopoulos and F. Liarokapis, "Robot navigation using brain-computer interfaces," in *Proceedings of the 11th IEEE International Conference on Trust, Security and Privacy in Computing and Communications, TrustCom-2012*, pp. 1785–1792, Liverpool, UK, June 2012.

[6] R. Upadhyay, P. K. Kankar, P. K. Padhy, and V. K. Gupta, "Robot motion control using Brain Computer Interface," in *Proceedings of the 2013 IEEE International Conference on Control, Automation, Robotics and Embedded Systems, CARE 2013*, 5, 1 pages, Jabalpur, India, December 2013.

[7] J. R. Wolpaw, N. Birbaumer, W. J. Heetderks et al., "Brain-computer interface technology: a review of the first international meeting," *IEEE Transactions on Neural Systems and Rehabilitation Engineering*, vol. 8, no. 2, pp. 164–173, 2000.

[8] J. R. Wolpaw, N. Birbaumer, D. J. McFarland, G. Pfurtscheller, and T. M. Vaughan, "Brain-computer interfaces for communication and control," *Clinical Neurophysiology*, vol. 113, no. 6, pp. 767–791, 2002.

[9] B. Graimann, A. Grendan, and G. Pfurtscheller, *Brain-Computer Interfaces, Revolutionizing Human-Computer Interaction,* Springer-Verlag, Berlin, Germany, 2010.

[10] M. Jeannerod, "Mental imagery in the motor context," *Neuropsychologia,* vol. 33, no. 11, pp. 1419–1432, 1995.

[11] O. Bai, D. Huang, D. Fei, and R. Kunz, "Effect of real-time cortical feedback in motor imagery-based mental practice training," *Neurorehabilitation,* vol. 34, pp. 355–363, 2014.

[12] D. J. McFarland, L. A. Miner, T. M. Vaughan, and J. R. Wolpaw, "Mu and beta rhythm topographies during motor imagery and actual movements," *Brain Topography,* vol. 12, no. 3, pp. 177–186, 2000.

[13] G. Pfurtscheller, C. Brunner, A. Schlögl, and F. H. Lopes da Silva, "Mu rhythm (de)synchronization and EEG single-trial classification of different motor imagery tasks," *NeuroImage,* vol. 31, no. 1, pp. 153–159, 2006.

[14] A. S. Aghaei, M. S. Mahanta, and K. N. Plataniotis, "Separable common spatio-spectral patterns for motor imagery BCI systems," *IEEE Transactions on Biomedical Engineering,* vol. 63, no. 1, pp. 15–29, 2016.

[15] L. Gao, W. Cheng, J. Zhang, and J. Wang, "EEG classification for motor imagery and resting state in BCI applications using multi-class Adaboost extreme learning machine," *Review of Scientific Instruments,* vol. 87, no. 8, Article ID 085110, 2016.

[16] A. Schlögl, F. Lee, H. Bischof, and G. Pfurtscheller, "Characterization of four-class motor imagery EEG data for the BCI-competition 2005," *Journal of Neural Engineering,* vol. 2, no. 4, pp. 14–22, 2005.

[17] D. Trad, T. Al-Ani, and M. Jemni, "Motor imagery signal classification for BCI system using empirical mode decomposition and bandpower feature extraction," *Broad Research in Artificial Intelligence and Neuroscience (BRAIN),* vol. 7, 2, pp. 5–16, 2016.

[18] K. Choi and A. Cichocki, *Control of a Wheelchair by Motor Imagery in Real Time,* vol. 5326, Springer-Verlag, 2008.

[19] J. D. R. Millán, F. Renkens, J. Mouriño, and W. Gerstner, "Noninvasive brain-actuated control of a mobile robot by human EEG," *IEEE Transactions on Biomedical Engineering,* vol. 51, no. 6, pp. 1026–1033, 2004.

[20] F. Lotte, M. Congedo, A. Lécuyer, F. Lamarche, and B. Arnaldi, "A review of classification algorithms for EEG-based brain–computer interfaces," *Journal of Neural Engineering,* vol. 4, no. 2, pp. R1–R13, 2007.

[21] P. Batres-Mendoza, C. R. Montoro-Sanjose, E. I. Guerra-Hernandez et al., "Quaternion-based signal analysis for motor imagery classification from electroencephalographic signals," *Sensors,* vol. 16, no. 3, article no. 336, 2016.

[22] W. R. Hamilton, "On quaternions," *Proceedings of the Royal Irish Academy,* vol. 3, pp. 1–16, 1847.

[23] M. Almonacid, J. Ibarrola, and J.-M. Cano-Izquierdo, "Voting Strategy to Enhance Multimodel EEG-Based Classifier Systems for Motor Imagery BCI," *IEEE Systems Journal,* vol. 10, no. 3, pp. 1082–1088, 2016.

[24] L. He, D. Hu, M. Wan, Y. Wen, K. M. Von Deneen, and M. Zhou, "Common Bayesian Network for Classification of EEG-Based Multiclass Motor Imagery BCI," *IEEE Transactions on Systems, Man, and Cybernetics: Systems,* vol. 46, no. 6, pp. 843–854, 2016.

[25] H.-I. Suk and S.-W. Lee, "A novel bayesian framework for discriminative feature extraction in brain-computer interfaces," *IEEE Transactions on Pattern Analysis and Machine Intelligence,* vol. 35, no. 2, pp. 286–299, 2013.

[26] S. Bermúdez I Badia, A. García Morgade, H. Samaha, and P. F. M. J. Verschure, "Using a hybrid brain computer interface and virtual reality system to monitor and promote cortical reorganization through motor activity and motor imagery training," *IEEE Transactions on Neural Systems and Rehabilitation Engineering,* vol. 21, no. 2, pp. 174–181, 2013.

[27] M. Naeem, C. Brunner, R. Leeb, B. Graimann, and G. Pfurtscheller, "Seperability of four-class motor imagery data using independent components analysis," *Journal of Neural Engineering,* vol. 3, no. 3, pp. 208–216, 2006.

[28] L. Wang, G. Xu, J. Wang, S. Yang, M. Guo, and W. Yan, "Motor imagery BCI research based on sample entropy and SVM," in *Proceedings of the 2012 6th International Conference on Electromagnetic Field Problems and Applications, ICEF'2012,* pp. 1–4, June 2012.

[29] L. Schiatti, L. Faes, J. Tessadori, G. Barresi, and L. Mattos, "Mutual information-based feature selection for low-cost BCIs based on motor imagery," in *Proceedings of the 38th Annual International Conference of the IEEE Engineering in Medicine and Biology Society, EMBC 2016,* pp. 2772–2775, Orlando, Fl, USA, August 2016.

[30] E. Abdalsalam M., M. Z. Yusoff, N. Kamel, A. Malik, and M. Meselhy, "Mental task motor imagery classifications for noninvasive brain computer interface," in *Proceedings of the 2014 5th International Conference on Intelligent and Advanced Systems, ICIAS 2014,* pp. 1–5, Kuala Lumpur, Malaysia, June 2014.

[31] N. Prakaksita, C.-Y. Kuo, and C.-H. Kuo, "Development of a motor imagery based brain-computer interface for humanoid robot control applications," in *Proceedings of the IEEE International Conference on Industrial Technology, ICIT 2016,* pp. 1607–1613, Taipei, Taiwan, March 2016.

[32] B. Obermaier, C. Neuper, C. Guger, and G. Pfurtscheller, "Information transfer rate in a five-classes brain-computer interface," *IEEE Transactions on Neural Systems and Rehabilitation Engineering,* vol. 9, no. 3, pp. 283–288, 2001.

[33] R. Scherer, G. R. Müller, C. Neuper, B. Graimann, and G. Pfurtscheller, "An asynchronously controlled EEG-based virtual keyboard: Improvement of the spelling rate," *IEEE Transactions on Biomedical Engineering,* vol. 51, no. 6, pp. 979–984, 2004.

[34] S. Siuly and Y. Li, "Improving the separability of motor imagery EEG signals using a cross correlation-based least square support vector machine for brain-computer interface," *IEEE Transactions on Neural Systems and Rehabilitation Engineering,* vol. 20, no. 4, pp. 526–538, 2012.

[35] S. Solhjoo, A. M. Nasrabadi, and M. R. H. Golpayegani, "Classification of chaotic signals using HMM classifiers: EEG-based mental task classification," in *Proceedings of the 13th European Signal Processing Conference, EUSIPCO 2005,* pp. 257–260, September 2005.

[36] C. Park, D. Looney, N. Ur Rehman, A. Ahrabian, and D. P. Mandic, "Classification of motor imagery BCI using multivariate empirical mode decomposition," *IEEE Transactions on Neural Systems and Rehabilitation Engineering,* vol. 21, no. 1, pp. 10–22, 2013.

[37] J. Hurtado-Rincon, S. Rojas-Jaramillo, Y. Ricardo-Cespedes, A. M. Alvarez-Meza, and G. Castellanos-Dominguez, "Motor imagery classification using feature relevance analysis: An Emotiv-based BCI system," in *Proceedings of the 2014 19th Symposium on Image, Signal Processing and Artificial Vision, STSIVA 2014,* September 2014.

[38] C. Park, C. C. Cheong-Took, and D. P. Mandic, "Augmented complex common spatial patterns for classification of noncircular EEG from motor imagery tasks," *IEEE Transactions on Neural Systems and Rehabilitation Engineering*, vol. 22, no. 1, pp. 1–10, 2014.

[39] Z. Tang, S. Sun, S. Zhang, Y. Chen, C. Li, and S. Chen, "A brain-machine interface based on ERD/ERS for an upper-limb exoskeleton control," *Sensors*, vol. 16, no. 12, article no. 2050, 2016.

[40] K. Choi and A. Cichocki, "Control of a Wheelchair by Motor Imagery in Real Time," in *Proceedings of the roceedings of the 9th International Conference on Intelligent Data Engineering and Automated Learning*, vol. 5326, pp. 330–337, Springer-Verlag, Daejeon, South Korea, 2008.

[41] L. Arias-Mora, L. López-Ríos, Y. Céspedes-Villar, L. F. Velasquez-Martinez, A. M. Alvarez-Meza, and G. Castellanos-Dominguez, "Kernel-based relevant feature extraction to support Motor Imagery classification," in *Proceedings of the 20th Symposium on Signal Processing, Images and Computer Vision, STSIVA 2015*, Bogota, Colombia, September 2015.

[42] S. Dharmasena, K. Lalitharathne, K. Dissanayake, A. Sampath, and A. Pasqual, "Online classification of imagined hand movement using a consumer grade EEG device," in *Proceedings of the 2013 IEEE 8th International Conference on Industrial and Information Systems, ICIIS 2013*, pp. 537–541, Peradeniya, Sri Lanka, December 2013.

[43] V. N. Stock and A. Balbinot, "Movement imagery classification in EMOTIV cap based system by Naïve Bayes," in *Proceedings of the 38th Annual International Conference of the IEEE Engineering in Medicine and Biology Society, EMBC 2016*, pp. 4435–4438, Orlando, Fl, USA, August 2016.

[44] D. M. Mann-Castrillon, S. Restrepo-Agudelo, H. J. Areiza-Laverde, A. E. Castro-Ospina, and L. Duque-Munoz, Exploratory analysis of motor imagery local database for BCI systems.

[45] A. Janota, V. Šimák, D. Nemec, and J. Hrbček, "Improving the precision and speed of Euler angles computation from low-cost rotation sensor data," *Sensors*, vol. 15, no. 3, pp. 7016–7039, 2015.

[46] S. Kotsiantis, "A hybrid decision tree classifier," *Journal of Intelligent & Fuzzy Systems: Applications in Engineering and Technology*, vol. 26, no. 1, pp. 327–336, 2014.

[47] R. L. White, "Astronomical applications of oblique decision trees," *AIP Conference Proceedings*, vol. 1082, pp. 37–43, 2008.

[48] A. A. Elnaggar and J. S. Noller, "Application of remote-sensing data and decision-tree analysis to mapping salt-affected soils over large areas," *Remote Sensing*, vol. 2, no. 1, pp. 151–165, 2010.

[49] L. Breiman, "Bagging predictors," *Machine Learning*, vol. 24, no. 2, pp. 123–140, 1996.

[50] Y. Freund and R. E. Schapire, "Experiments with a new boosting algorithm," in *Proceedings of the 13th International Conference on Machine learning (ICML)*, pp. 148–156, 1996.

[51] T. Jiralerspong, C. Liu, and J. Ishikawa, "Identification of three mental states using a motor imagery based brain machine interface," in *Proceedings of the 2014 IEEE Symposium on Computational Intelligence in Brain Computer Interfaces (CIBCI)*, pp. 49–56, Orlando, FL, USA, December 2014.

[52] J. M. Fuster, "Prefrontal neurons in networks of executive memory," *Brain Research Bulletin*, vol. 52, no. 5, pp. 331–336, 2000.

[53] J. Wang, Z. Feng, and N. Lu, "Feature extraction by common spatial pattern in frequency domain for motor imagery tasks classification," in *Proceedings of the 2017 29th Chinese Control And Decision Conference (CCDC)*, pp. 5883–5888, Chongqing, China, May 2017.

[54] P. Gaur, R. B. Pachori, H. Wang, and G. Prasad, "A multivariate empirical mode decomposition based filtering for subject independent BCI," in *Proceedings of the 27th Irish Signals and Systems Conference, ISSC 2016*, pp. 1–7, Londonderry, UK, June 2016.

[55] H. V. Shenoy, A. P. Vinod, and C. Guan, "Shrinkage estimator based regularization for EEG motor imagery classification," in *Proceedings of the 10th International Conference on Information, Communications and Signal Processing, ICICS 2015*, Singapore, December 2015.

[56] B. Blankertz, G. Dornhege, M. Krauledat, K.-R. Müller, and G. Curio, "The non-invasive Berlin brain-computer interface: fast acquisition of effective performance in untrained subjects," *NeuroImage*, vol. 37, no. 2, pp. 539–550, 2007.

[57] I. Rodríguez-Fdez, A. Canosa, M. Mucientes, and A. Bugarín, "STAC: a web platform for the comparison of algorithms using statistical tests," in *Proceedings of the IEEE International Conference on Fuzzy Systems*, pp. 1–8, Istanbul, Turkey, August 2015.

16

Mental Task Evaluation for Hybrid NIRS-EEG Brain-Computer Interfaces

Hubert Banville, Rishabh Gupta, and Tiago H. Falk

Energy, Materials, and Telecommunications, Institut National de la Recherche Scientifique, University of Quebec, Montreal, QC, Canada

Correspondence should be addressed to Hubert Banville; hubert.banville@emt.inrs.ca

Academic Editor: Manuel Rosa-Zurera

Based on recent electroencephalography (EEG) and near-infrared spectroscopy (NIRS) studies that showed that tasks such as motor imagery and mental arithmetic induce specific neural response patterns, we propose a hybrid brain-computer interface (hBCI) paradigm in which EEG and NIRS data are fused to improve binary classification performance. We recorded simultaneous NIRS-EEG data from nine participants performing seven mental tasks (word generation, mental rotation, subtraction, singing and navigation, and motor and face imagery). Classifiers were trained for each possible pair of tasks using (1) EEG features alone, (2) NIRS features alone, and (3) EEG and NIRS features combined, to identify the best task pairs and assess the usefulness of a multimodal approach. The NIRS-EEG approach led to an average increase in peak kappa of 0.03 when using features extracted from one-second windows (equivalent to an increase of 1.5% in classification accuracy for balanced classes). The increase was much stronger (0.20, corresponding to an 10% accuracy increase) when focusing on time windows of high NIRS performance. The EEG and NIRS analyses further unveiled relevant brain regions and important feature types. This work provides a basis for future NIRS-EEG hBCI studies aiming to improve classification performance toward more efficient and flexible BCIs.

1. Introduction

A brain-computer interface (BCI) is a communication system between a brain and a computer that bypasses the normal brain output pathways [1]. Such systems can be useful to replace, restore, enhance, supplement, or improve the natural output of the central nervous system [2], and have found applications in clinical as well as nonclinical contexts such as entertainment and education [3]. BCIs rely on the recording of brain activity using imaging modalities like electroencephalography (EEG), magnetoencephalography (MEG), near-infrared spectroscopy (NIRS), functional magnetic resonance imaging (fMRI), and others [4–10]. Although most of today's BCI designs use EEG alone to recognize user intent [11], other modalities offer different information about the underlying brain activity and can therefore complement the information obtained with EEG alone. The hybrid BCI (hBCI) approach thus consists of using more than one modality at a time, including at least one brain modality, but possibly including nonneurophysiological modalities as well [12, 13], to improve on the performance and usability of a unimodal system.

BCIs typically rely on the recognition of one or multiple distinguishable brain activity patterns. The most frequent patterns mentioned in the hBCI literature include event-related desynchronization/synchronization (ERD/ERS) elicited by motor imagery, the P300 event-related potential (ERP), and the steady-state visually evoked potential (SSVEP) [11]. Through their extensive use in the literature, these brain activity patterns have been shown to be highly recognizable when used in BCI designs; however, they may not be optimal for all BCI users. First of all, intersubject variability, a phenomenon that describes how neurophysiological signals can differ significantly from an individual to another, inevitably makes particular tasks better suited to some users than others [11]. Finding the optimal set of mental tasks for a user can thus significantly improve the performance and usability of a BCI. Moreover, users who have suffered a brain injury may lose normal functioning of regions of their brain associated with the above-mentioned patterns. For these users who are often the target of BCI systems, it is thus necessary to use different brain activity patterns that recruit other regions of the brain. Finally, BCI paradigms based on P300 and SSVEP, so-called *reactive BCIs*, rely on external visual stimuli to elicit the necessary brain activity patterns. These external stimuli can induce fatigue in the users when used for extended periods of time [14] and can necessitate additional hardware and software components. Internally triggered mental tasks are more attractive from this perspective as they do not require external stimuli.

To alleviate these problems, a promising approach aims at identifying and validating new brain activity patterns for use in BCI paradigms. Various mental tasks that recruit different parts of the brain, such as mental subtraction and mental rotation, were thus investigated in recent studies using EEG [15–25], NIRS [26–34], transcranial Doppler imaging (TCD) [35, 36], NIRS-TCD [37], and fMRI [38]. The most frequently used mental tasks in these articles were mental subtraction, mental object rotation, various verbal fluency tasks, motor imagery, and auditory imagery. These studies attempted either binary or multiclass classification of mental tasks, usually between tasks or against a resting state, and in most cases aimed at finding the combination of tasks that would yield the highest performance in a BCI context as measured by a classification metric.

Among studies that evaluated four or more different tasks in EEG, combinations of a brain teaser, that is, a task that involves mental work, and a dynamic imagery task were usually found to yield the highest performance. In Sepulveda et al., binary classification of mental singing and mental calculation (either addition or subtraction) was found to be in the top five of the best combinations in four of five subjects, with values above 93% in accuracy [17]. Although aiming to differentiate a mental task from resting state instead of from another mental task, Faradji et al. found that a mental multiplication task could produce a maximal true positive rate above 70% while maintaining a zero false negative rate [18]. Research by Friedrich and colleagues has supported the combination of a brain teaser and a dynamic imagery task as an optimal pair numerous times [21, 22, 25]. Pairs formed from a total of seven different mental tasks were evaluated on nine subjects [21]. Word association, mental subtraction, mental rotation, and motor imagery were identified as the most discriminative tasks, leading to Cohen's κ (an interrater agreement metric) values above 0.7. The ERD/ERS patterns evoked by brain teasers and dynamic imagery tasks were found to exhibit different characteristics which could explain why this type of combination is optimal [21]. In addition, in that study the authors characterized the subjective appreciation of each task, finding that while ratings were highly variable and no significant differences between tasks were found, word generation received the best rating and mental subtraction received the worst. Similarly, in a separate study, a combination of mental subtraction and motor imagery was found to produce consistent intersession performance in seven out of nine subjects (kappa higher than 0.6) [22]. Other work by Hortal et al. showed four-class classification of

right- and left-hand imagined movement, mental counting, and mental alphabet recitation in two subjects [39]. Although the study did not aim at identifying the best pair of tasks, the trained classifier was better at distinguishing different motor imagery tasks from one another than from other tasks, which could be explained by the centrally focused montage. Finally, in another study, eight subjects were trained to control a 4-class BCI in which mental tasks were selected based on an individual basis [25]. The most frequently selected task combinations included motor imagery, mental rotation, and additional brain teaser and dynamic imagery tasks, leading to average performances varying between 44 and 84% accuracy.

Only two studies were found to look at classifying more than two tasks at once using NIRS. In Herff et al. [31], using the hemodynamic information from the prefrontal cortex it was shown that binary classification accuracies around 60% could be obtained with pairs formed of mental subtraction, word generation, and mental rotation on 10 subjects. A more complete assessment of mental tasks using NIRS was reported in Hwang et al. [5], using a full head coverage. Classification accuracies around 71% were found for combinations of motor imagery, mental multiplication, and mental rotation tasks on seven subjects.

Some studies explored the effect of adding supplementary modalities to the classification of various mental tasks to either improve the number of classifiable tasks or improve the robustness of a precise task. Combinations of NIRS and EEG for recognizing motor imagery or execution tasks have been studied following three different approaches. Fazli et al. used a classifier fusion procedure based on the individual classification of EEG and NIRS data to distinguish left- from right-hand motor execution and imagery [40]. Using this approach, an average 5% increase in accuracy was obtained for 13 out of 14 subjects for the motor imagery task when EEG and NIRS were used simultaneously, yielding an average accuracy of 83.2%. The authors recognized the drawbacks of the long hemodynamic response delay that typically precludes the use of NIRS in practical BCIs. A different approach was explored by Khan et al. to increase the number of input commands in the context of four-direction movement control [41]. While the left and right movements were controlled with motor imagery as measured with EEG, the forward and backward movements were controlled with either counting or mental subtraction tasks measured in NIRS. A binary classification of each task against rest was used. Average classification accuracies of 94.7% and above 80% were obtained for EEG tasks and NIRS tasks, respectively. Finally, in another study, NIRS was used to detect the occurrence of a motor imagery task and trigger its classification as left or right imagery using EEG [42]. This approach led to a low false positive rate of 7% and a true positive rate of 88%.

NIRS has also been combined with peripheral physiological signals such as heart rate, respiration, blood pressure, skin temperature, and electrodermal activity measurements. For example, the impact of environment noise on music imagery detection was assessed using NIRS, physiological signals, and a combination of the two [29]. An average accuracy of 83% over eight participants was obtained when NIRS was used in conjunction with physiological signals, corresponding to a 12% gain from a NIRS-only system. Using a similar methodology, Zimmermann et al. explored the detection of a motor execution task [43]. The authors found that adding physiological signals to NIRS significantly improved classification accuracies by around 9% average in seven subjects. Joining the hemodynamic information obtained from NIRS with the ones obtained from TCD, a modality that measures blood flow velocity in the cerebral main arteries, was also shown to be beneficial in the classification of a mental task. Indeed, this approach helped improve unimodal classification of a verbal fluency task by around 7% average across nine subjects in a separate study in [37].

In light of these results, the purpose of the present article is to gain further ground in the investigation of new BCI control tasks, by adopting a hybrid BCI approach in which NIRS and EEG are simultaneously recorded. We seek to complement previous studies such as [21, 33] by carefully analyzing the functioning of such a hybrid system and assessing whether it can provide a gain in performance over standard unimodal approaches. The rest of this paper is structured as follows. Section 2 presents the methods used to collect and analyze the data. Section 3 shows the results of the analysis in terms of spatial patterns, selected features, and classification performance. Section 4 discusses the results in light of previous related studies. Finally, the conclusions drawn from this work are presented in Section 5. A more comprehensive description of the work can be found in [44].

2. Methods

2.1. Participants. Twelve participants (5 females, 3 left-handed, mean of 24.6 years old), fluent in English and/or French, took part in our NIRS-EEG study. Participants had to complete three separate recording sessions of two to three hours, inside a period of three to five weeks. Participants declared having no history of neurological disorders and had no previous experience with BCIs. A monetary compensation was given after each completed session. Each participant agreed with the terms and conditions of the study, which was approved by the university ethics committee. Two participants were rejected because their data contained a high number of artifacts; a third participant was rejected because they did not complete the three required sessions. Therefore, the data from a total of nine participants was used in this study.

2.2. Mental Tasks. Participants were asked to perform seven different types of mental tasks that are believed to elicit specific neural response patterns, based on previous studies using EEG and NIRS [21, 33].

Mental Rotation (ROT). Two 3-dimensional L-shaped figures, either identical or mirrored, but in each case in a different state of rotation, were presented to the participants. Participants had to imagine rotating one of the two figures in order to find if they were the same or if they were mirrored images.

Word Generation (WORD). Participants had to generate as many words as possible starting with a randomly chosen letter presented on the screen. Words in either English or French, depending on the participant's chosen language, were requested.

Mental Subtraction (SUB). Participants had to perform successive subtractions of two 1- or 2-digit numbers to a 3-digit number (e.g., $214 - 9 = 205$ and $205 - 13 = 192$).

Mental Singing (SING). Participants had to imagine singing a song that they chose beforehand, if possible with lyrics, while focusing on the emotional response it elicits.

Mental Navigation (NAV). Participants had to imagine walking from one point to another in their current or a previous home, while focusing on their spatial orientation (e.g., walking from their bedroom to the refrigerator).

Motor Imagery (MI). Participants had to imagine performing a finger tapping task with their right hand.

Face Imagery (FACE). Participants had to imagine the face of a friend, as recalled from a picture they were asked to bring to the recording session and memorize.

Following Friedrich et al.'s description of task types [21], we classify mental rotation, word generation, and mental subtraction as brain teasers, since they require problem-solving skills; mental singing, mental navigation, and motor imagery as dynamic imagery tasks; and face imagery as a static imagery task.

Before the recording started, participants were first guided through each task and asked to complete them in an overt manner. This step was used to make sure each participant performed the tasks appropriately and in the same manner. For example, for a mental rotation task, participants had to say aloud if the two figures were the "same" or "mirrored," for a mental subtraction task they had to give the experimenter their final answer, and so on. Participants were then asked to repeat the same tasks but in a covert manner, as they were then asked to during the experiment.

2.3. Experimental Paradigm. The experimental paradigm for a single session of our study is summarized in Figure 1. A session consisted of four subsessions in which each mental task type was randomly repeated four times, yielding a total of 28 task completions per subsession. Participants also had to complete a subjective evaluation questionnaire between the second and third subsession of each session. Each subsession started and finished with a 30 s baseline period in which participants were asked to remain in a neutral mental state and fixate the cross at the center of the screen. Before each trial, a 3 s countdown screen indicated the task to be performed next using the associated pictogram as shown in Figure 1. Once the countdown was over, participants had to execute the required mental task for a period of 15 seconds. Instructions were given to carry out the tasks as many times as possible and to start again tasks such as rotation, subtraction, and navigation if completed before the end of the 15 s period. Each trial was then followed by a rest period of random duration between 10 and 15 s, sampled

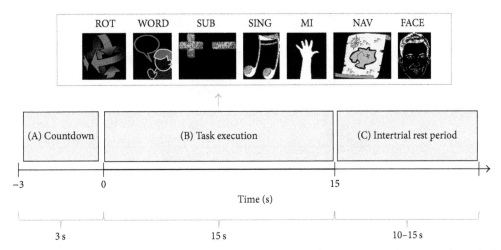

FIGURE 1: Diagram of a trial of the experimental paradigm. A trial is composed of (A) a 3 s countdown period in which participants are instructed about the coming mental task, (B) an imagery period where they execute the given task for 15 s, and (C) a randomized 10 to 15 s rest period.

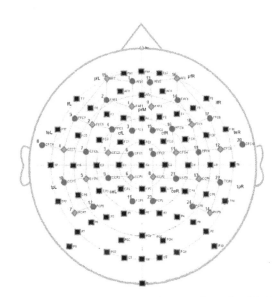

FIGURE 2: EEG and NIRS topology used in this study (adapted from [59]). EEG electrodes (black rectangles), NIRS detectors (red circles), and NIRS sources (green diamonds) were placed following the 10-5 system. NIRS channels are represented by dark straight lines connecting the sources to the detectors. Brain regions used to compute artificial NIRS channels are grouped in light blue.

from a uniform distribution. This randomization keeps the participants from expecting the exact start of the next trial and avoids the synchronization of systemic processes in NIRS with the paradigm. Once a subsession was over, participants were allowed to take as much time as desired to lightly stretch, drink, or eat a snack before resuming the experiment. The stimuli and questionnaire were both implemented using the Presentation software package (Neural Behavioral Systems, USA).

2.4. Data Collection

2.4.1. EEG and Physiological Signals. EEG data was recorded using an ActiveTwo system (Biosemi B.V., Amsterdam, The Netherlands) with 62 probes (plus two mastoids and CMS

and DRL electrodes) and four EOG electrodes, digitized at 512 Hz. No online filtering was applied. A standard 10-10 system was used for electrode placement, but without AF7 and AF8, whose holes were used for NIRS probes instead (see Figure 2).

2.4.2. NIRS. NIRS data was recorded using a NIRScout system (NIRx Medical Technologies, Los Angeles, USA), with 16 sources (wavelengths of 760 and 850 nm) and 24 detectors. Optodes were placed together with EEG electrodes on the same cap, as shown in Figure 2. The frontal, central, temporal, and parietal lobes were targeted by the used montage, following the extended 10-5 system. Coverage was not extended to the occipital lobe due to the low quality of NIRS signals in this region and because of the restricted

TABLE 1: Questionnaire items and description based on the NASA TLX test. The first five questions were given a rating between 1 and 10.

Dimension	Question
Mental demand	How mentally demanding was the task?
Temporal demand	How hurried or rushed was the pace of the task?
Performance	How successful were you in accomplishing what you were asked to do?
Effort	How hard did you have to work to accomplish your level of performance?
Frustration	How insecure, discouraged, irritated, stressed and annoyed were you?
Task ranking	Which are your preferred tasks, in order of importance?

number of available optodes. Source-detector pairs separated by approximately 3 cm were used as channels, giving a total of 60 NIRS channels, each sampled at 4.46 Hz. Amplifier gains were adjusted following an automatic calibration procedure handled by the NIRStar recording software.

2.4.3. Questionnaire and Subjective Ratings. At each recording session, participants were asked to fill out a questionnaire reporting their appreciation of the tasks. The questions were based on the first part of the widely used NASA Task Load Index (TLX) test [45], with the French version by Cegarra and Morgado [46]. Additionally, participants were asked to rank the mental tasks in order of preference. Table 1 shows the various items that were measured.

2.5. EEG Analysis

2.5.1. Preprocessing. The raw EEG data was preprocessed using EEGLAB [47]. The data was referenced to Cz and then downsampled to 256 Hz before filtering with a bandpass (0.5–100 Hz) and notch filters (60 Hz). Bad channels were visually assessed and removed if they were constantly bad across trials of the same session. Epochs of 25 seconds with 5 seconds of baseline before and after task execution were extracted for each trial, as well as for rests periods at the beginning and end of each subsession. Epochs contaminated by strong movement and physiological artifacts were visually identified and rejected. On average, 6.1% of the epochs were rejected, yielding an average of 315.4 valid epochs per subject (out of a possible 336). Further signal cleaning was performed by applying a semiautomatic method based on independent component analysis (ICA, with the Infomax algorithm [48]) to detect and subtract remaining artifacts and noise components [49]. Bad channels were reinterpolated and all channels were rereferenced to the average of all electrodes. Finally, baseline correction was applied to each epoch using the 300 ms period before the beginning of the tasks.

2.5.2. Descriptive Analysis. ERD is a phenomenon occurring when idle parts of the brain become active following some event or stimulus. A specific rhythmical activity can then be measured, such as μ and β waves over the primary motor cortex in motor execution and imagery tasks [50]. Similarly, ERS occurs when this activity ceases and the recruited brain regions return to an idle state. The intertrial variance method proposed in [51] was used to compute the ERD/ERS values for

each type of mental task and baseline over all three sessions of a participant.

2.5.3. Feature Extraction. Previous EEG studies mainly used band powers and Common Spatial Patterns-based (CSP) features to describe the neural activity patterns induced by mental tasks such as motor imagery [11]. In our case, since we are especially interested in the interpretation of the extracted features, and given the explicit link between band powers and measurements of ERD/ERS [52], we focused our classification analysis on classical power bands. Each trial was subdivided in nonoverlapping time windows of one second. Log-power features were then extracted in the following seven frequency bands with a Fast Fourier Transform: θ (4–8 Hz), α_{low} (8–10 Hz), α_{high} (10–12 Hz), β_{low} (12–21 Hz), β_{high} (21–30 Hz), θ to β (4–30 Hz), and total spectrum (0.1–100 Hz). Individual features for the δ (0–4 Hz) and γ (30–80 Hz) bands were not extracted in order to reduce the impact of ocular and muscle artifacts [20, 21, 24]. Moreover, the following ratios of band powers were computed: $\alpha_{total}/\beta_{total}$ and θ/β_{total}. This yielded a total of 620 features per window, which were finally log-transformed.

2.6. NIRS Analysis

2.6.1. Preprocessing. NIRS was preprocessed using the open source toolbox HOMER2 [53]. First, raw light intensities were converted to optical densities (OD) by computing the negative logarithm of the normalized intensities (using the average value of each channel over the entire recording). Second, channels with a low signal-to-noise ratio were identified by correlating the bandpass filtered OD (between 0.8 and 1.2 Hz) of channels S15-D1 and S15-D2 on the left and channels S16-D13 and S16-D14 on the right, with each left side or right side channel, respectively. These 4 frontal channels being the shortest in the used montage, and usually being clear of any hair, are expected to carry a clear cardiac pulse in the 45 to 100 BPM range, which corresponds to standard resting heart rate frequencies. Channels which significantly correlate with these short-distance channels in this frequency range (p value below 0.05) are thus expected to be of good quality, since they carry physiological information. Channels were rejected per session if the aggregate of their Pearson's correlation p value across all epochs was not significant. Third, the remaining channels' OD was bandpass-filtered between 0.01 and 0.30 Hz [10] and converted to the concentration changes of oxygenated, deoxygenated, and total hemoglobin (Δ[HbO], Δ[HbR], and Δ[HbT]) using the Modified Beer-Lambert Law

[54]. Finally, 13 artificial channels were computed by averaging the amplitude of neighboring channels in the prefrontal, lateral-frontal, centrofrontal, temporoparietal, and central regions (as shown in Figure 2). These steps produced 73 channels, each one measuring $\Delta[HbO]$, $\Delta[HbR]$, and $\Delta[HbT]$, giving a total of 219 measurement channels for NIRS.

2.6.2. Descriptive Analysis. The average $\Delta[HbO]$, $\Delta[HbR]$, and $\Delta[HbT]$ responses over sessions and participants were computed for each task to reveal spatiotemporal patterns of hemodynamic activation.

2.6.3. Feature Extraction. Classification of NIRS data is often based on simple features such as $\Delta[HbO]$, $\Delta[HbR]$, and $\Delta[HbT]$ averaged over time, their slope, or even the averaged raw light intensity values [11]. In this study, the average chromophore concentrations of each channel were extracted using the same windows as for EEG feature extraction. Features derived from NIRS channels that were rejected during preprocessing were set to 0. This yielded a maximum of 219 NIRS features.

2.7. Classification of EEG, NIRS, and EEG-NIRS. Each previously extracted feature set was then used to train a binary classification model over a pair of tasks. First, the training procedure was applied to the EEG and NIRS datasets separately to assess the individual performance of each modality. Then, the same procedure was applied on a merged dataset combining features from both EEG and NIRS to assess the impact of multimodal information on classification performance.

To avoid the overfitting problems linked to high-dimensional datasets, especially in cases where only a few training cases are available, feature selection procedures are required to select the most informative features prior to or during classifier training. In this study, we used a linear kernel Support Vector Machine (SVM) classifier combined with a sparsity-inducing l_1 penalty term to control the number of features used in the model. As opposed to filter feature selection methods, this embedded procedure allows the efficient discovery of interdependent features, while also making better use of the available data by avoiding an additional partitioning [55]. Combined with the robustness of SVMs in high-dimensional spaces [56], this embedded feature selection-classification procedure is designed to minimize the detrimental effects of our high-dimensional dataset with few examples.

A default value of 2.0 was used for the hyperparameter C that controls the balance between the data-dependent loss and the l_1 penalization of the weights. To account for the varying number of data points in each classification task, C was divided by the number of examples in the training set, yielding a maximal value of 0.023 when all 96 epochs were conserved.

A delay between the cue to execute a mental task and its actual execution is expected; moreover, participants are likely to get tired and stop executing the task before the end of the 15 s epoch. Therefore, to reveal the dynamics of mental task execution, each time window was analyzed independently;

that is, a new classifier was trained for each time window (e.g., 0-1 s and 1-2 s). This yields a series of performance estimates that show how classification evolves as the task is executed. The subject-specific classifiers were trained using a 10 times 10-fold stratified cross-validation procedure. Nine partitions were used for training, and the remaining one was used for validation. Partitions were created so that relative class frequencies were similar in each fold. The data was then randomly shuffled and the partitioning procedure repeated for another nine times. This yielded a total of 100 estimates per classification task. For each division of training and validation sets, each feature was then individually Z-score-normalized based on the mean and standard deviation of the training set. Finally, the classifier was retrained on all 10 folds to obtain the final weights w.

Since our study is targeted toward the eventual conception of a BCI, we focus the bulk of our analysis on models trained with features extracted on windows of one second. This allows a very short delay between the realization of the mental task and the output of the system. Moreover, using one-second windows allows a fine-grained analysis of the temporal evolution of selected features and of classification performance, which can uncover interesting physiological insights.

The performance of the classifiers was evaluated using Cohen's κ as in [21], which measures the agreement between two raters who classify N examples into mutually exclusive categories. This is useful here since an unequal number of repetitions were kept for each type of tasks, leading to an unbalanced number of examples in the dataset. In the case of a perfectly balanced problem, κ values of 0, 0.4, and 1 are equivalent to 50%, 70%, and 100% accuracy, respectively.

To identify the best pairs of tasks for each modality configuration, a procedure that takes into account both the average and the variance of the κ sample across participants was used. A two-tailed t-test was used to compare the κ values obtained with each pair of tasks to 0.4. Following this test, the resulting 21 t-statistics were ranked: the larger the t-statistic, the greater the performance of a pair. Additionally, to assess the impact of adding NIRS to EEG features, two-tailed paired t-tests were used to compare the κ values obtained for each pair of tasks of the EEG-only and NIRS-EEG cases. The Holm-Bonferroni method was used to correct for multiple comparisons [57].

The best features can also be analyzed using the SVM weights of these models as a feature ranking metric [58]. Since the features are normalized before training, the weights of the linear model effectively represent the importance of each feature. A feature with a high absolute weight can thus be thought of as being more important than one with a weight closer to 0. In the present study, the absolute values of the weights of a particular feature were averaged and then ranked against the other features.

3. Results

3.1. Descriptive Analysis

3.1.1. EEG. The ERD/ERS maps for each task in the low α, high α, low β, and high β bands are shown in Figure 3. In

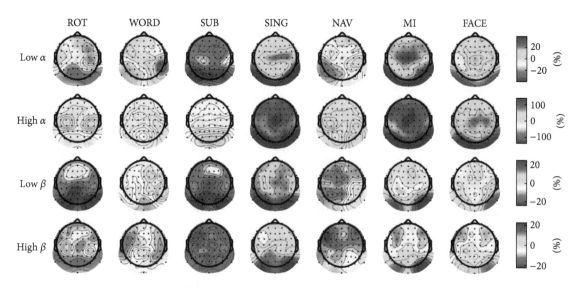

FIGURE 3: ERD/ERS maps for each task in the low α, high α, low β, and high β bands. ERD/ERS values are computed using the intertrial variance method [51] over the time window spanning 0.5 to two seconds after stimulus onset, using a baseline of −2 to 0 seconds before trial onset. Blue represents ERS while red represents ERD. Note that color ranges differ between power bands.

mental rotation, high amplitude ERD patterns were measured in the occipital region for all four bands. A pattern of weak ERS was observed over the two motor cortices in all bands except low β. Word generation produced ERS patterns over the left temporal lobe in the low α and high α bands. Patterns elicited by mental subtraction showed consistently high ERD in the occipital lobe, especially around PO7 and PO8 (both among the most important features identified in Table 3). In mental singing, ERD patterns over the left hemisphere in the low and high β bands were observed, as well as predominant all-band ERS in the occipital region. Mental navigation led to left hemispheric ERD in the low α and low β bands, as well as left and right prefrontal ERD in the high β band. In motor imagery, left hemispheric ERD patterns were dominant in the first three bands, except for a bilateral high α ERD pattern in the prefrontal lobe, similar to the one observed for NAV but of lower intensity. Finally, face imagery led to ERD patterns in the frontal (again, similar to the ones observed for NAV and MI in the high β band) and temporal lobes, as well as high α power in the occipital lobes.

3.1.2. NIRS. Figure 4 shows the average $\Delta[\text{HbO}]$, $\Delta[\text{HbR}]$, and $\Delta[\text{HbT}]$ topographical maps for each task during the time window spanning 10 to 15 seconds after stimulus onset. Mental rotation led to a decrease in $\Delta[\text{HbO}]$ and $\Delta[\text{HbT}]$ over the frontal lobe, as well as an increase in $\Delta[\text{HbR}]$ over the prefrontal lobe. In turn, word generation yielded an increase in $\Delta[\text{HbO}]$ over the left temporal lobe and a decrease in $\Delta[\text{HbR}]$ over the left and right temporal lobes. This was accompanied by a widespread increase in $\Delta[\text{HbT}]$ over the posterior left hemisphere. In mental subtraction, an increase in $\Delta[\text{HbO}]$ and $\Delta[\text{HbT}]$ over both the right and left temporal lobes, as well as a decrease in the prefrontal region, was observed. Oppositely, $\Delta[\text{HbR}]$ increased over the midline but decreased in both temporal lobes. Mental singing provoked a subtle decrease in $\Delta[\text{HbR}]$ over the temporal

lobes, similar to WORD and SUB. The mental navigation task led to decreased $\Delta[\text{HbR}]$ levels over both temporal lobes and increased $\Delta[\text{HbO}]$ levels in the same regions. A large increase in $\Delta[\text{HbO}]$ and $\Delta[\text{HbT}]$ was observed over the left hemisphere for the motor imagery task, without any patterns of similar amplitude in $\Delta[\text{HbR}]$. Finally, face imagery led to an increase in the levels of all chromophores on the midline. A consistently high $\Delta[\text{HbR}]$ pattern over the right centroparietal region can also be seen in most tasks.

3.2. Subject-Wise Mental Task Classification. In this section, the results of EEG-only and NIRS-only classification are described, followed by the results of NIRS-EEG fusion classification. Specifically, the peak classification performance across subjects and across task pairs, the evolution of kappa across time, and the feature selection results are described.

3.2.1. EEG Only. The peak classification performance of classifiers trained on one-second window EEG features, for each subject and pair of tasks, is shown in Table 2. The peak classification performance is defined as the highest *kappa* obtained across the 15 seconds of task execution. All subjects achieved satisfactory or high performance for most task pairs and with an average κ greater than 0.4. High performance was achieved for at least three different task pairs in all subjects but S04 and S09, and three subjects (S10, S03, and S06) showed an average peak κ greater than 0.7.

Twelve pairs of tasks yielded κ values significantly greater than 0.4. The seven best performing task pairs were combinations of a brain teaser and an imagery task: either ROT or SUB with SING, FACE, MI, or NAV. For instance, the ROT-MI pair had an average κ of 0.83. However, pairs of dynamic and static imagery tasks, including SING, FACE, NAV, and MI, showed a consistently lower κ; for example, SING-FACE led to the lowest average κ of 0.4.

Table 2: EEG-only peak κ for each subject and task pair, when using features extracted from one-second windows. Task pairs and participants are shown in descending order of average κ, from top to bottom and left to right, respectively. κ values between 0.4 and 0.7 (satisfactory performance) are highlighted in italic font, whereas kappa values greater than 0.7 (high performance) are highlighted in bold font. The average peak time with standard deviation is also included for each task pair. $^*p < 0.05$, $^{**}p < 0.01$, $^{***}p < 0.001$.

	S10	S03	S07	S06	S05	S11	S01	S09	S04	Average	Peak time (s)
ROT-MI	**0.93**	**0.89**	**0.87**	**0.95**	**0.84**	**0.80**	**0.77**	**0.77**	0.61	**0.83 ± 0.10*****	3.83 ± 3.3
ROT-FACE	**0.86**	**0.86**	**0.84**	**0.94**	**0.92**	0.68	**0.79**	0.66	0.51	**0.79 ± 0.14*****	2.61 ± 1.0
ROT-SING	**1.00**	**0.80**	**0.86**	**0.81**	**0.90**	**0.71**	**0.81**	0.56	0.53	**0.78 ± 0.15****	5.61 ± 4.4
ROT-NAV	**0.96**	**0.72**	**0.83**	*0.61*	0.68	0.58	**0.75**	0.58	0.63	**0.70 ± 0.13****	4.06 ± 1.0
SUB-MI	**0.91**	**0.89**	**0.82**	**0.91**	**0.81**	**0.74**	**0.70**	**0.85**	0.39	**0.78 ± 0.16****	4.28 ± 2.1
SING-SUB	**0.99**	**0.72**	**0.73**	**0.82**	**0.89**	0.65	**0.77**	0.68	0.42	**0.74 ± 0.16****	2.50 ± 1.6
SUB-FACE	0.65	**0.84**	**0.71**	**0.88**	**0.87**	0.62	**0.76**	0.68	0.37	**0.71 ± 0.16****	6.39 ± 5.0
ROT-WORD	**0.96**	*0.74*	*0.69*	*0.61*	**0.90**	0.62	0.56	0.50	0.53	*0.68 ± 0.16**	5.94 ± 5.3
NAV-MI	**0.78**	**0.86**	**0.78**	**0.81**	0.66	0.66	0.60	0.46	0.41	*0.67 ± 0.16**	5.61 ± 5.3
WORD-MI	**0.96**	*0.61*	*0.75*	**0.88**	0.57	0.64	0.58	0.63	0.44	*0.67 ± 0.16**	5.83 ± 3.8
WORD-FACE	**0.75**	*0.73*	*0.67*	**0.87**	*0.73*	0.64	0.65	0.44	0.36	*0.65 ± 0.16**	6.06 ± 3.9
SING-NAV	**0.83**	*0.69*	*0.72*	*0.69*	*0.72*	0.64	*0.74*	0.27	0.43	*0.64 ± 0.17**	3.39 ± 2.1
SUB-NAV	**0.88**	*0.59*	*0.71*	0.46	*0.69*	0.46	0.55	0.66	0.33	*0.59 ± 0.16*	3.61 ± 5.8
WORD-SING	**0.88**	*0.66*	*0.73*	**0.84**	0.53	0.53	*0.73*	0.36	0.35	*0.62 ± 0.19*	5.61 ± 6.6
ROT-SUB	*0.72*	*0.60*	*0.66*	0.39	0.38	0.53	*0.66*	0.50	0.43	*0.54 ± 0.13*	4.06 ± 5.2
WORD-SUB	**0.88**	*0.69*	0.42	*0.63*	*0.75*	0.37	0.40	0.68	0.44	*0.58 ± 0.18*	3.94 ± 2.9
NAV-FACE	*0.53*	*0.79*	*0.54*	**0.80**	**0.82**	0.49	0.44	0.28	0.28	*0.55 ± 0.21*	5.39 ± 4.8
WORD-NAV	**0.79**	*0.55*	*0.63*	0.41	0.46	0.50	0.48	0.35	0.30	*0.50 ± 0.15*	3.17 ± 2.8
SING-MI	**0.78**	*0.56*	0.39	0.47	0.36	0.41	0.25	0.38	0.40	*0.44 ± 0.15*	2.39 ± 2.4
FACE-MI	*0.62*	*0.60*	0.37	0.42	0.35	0.49	0.21	0.35	0.51	*0.44 ± 0.13*	1.61 ± 2.2
SING-FACE	*0.63*	*0.47*	0.30	0.50	0.39	0.28	0.25	0.27	0.22	*0.37 ± 0.14*	5.06 ± 5.5
Average	**0.82**	**0.71**	*0.67*	**0.70**	*0.68*	0.57	0.59	0.52	0.42	*0.63 ± 0.16*	4.33 ± 3.7

TABLE 3: Top five features for the five best task pairs of each modality combination, using the average absolute values of the SVM weights as ranking metric. The models trained on the best performing one-second window were used (three to four seconds after stimulus onset for EEG-only and 11 to 12 seconds for NIRS-only and fusion of signals).

(a) EEG only

	ROT-MI	ROT-FACE	ROT-SING	SUB-MI	SING-SUB
(1)	pwr_high_alpha_O2	pwr_high_alpha_O2	pwr_t4_30_P8	pwr_high_alpha_PO7	pwr_alpha/beta_PO8
(2)	pwr_low_alpha_CP6	pwr_t4_30_P10	pwr_t4_30_O2	pwr_alpha/beta_Iz	pwr_total_PO7
(3)	pwr_high_alpha_CP6	pwr_alpha/beta_O1	pwr_high_alpha_PO8	pwr_total_PO8	pwr_high_alpha_Iz
(4)	pwr_high_alpha_O1	pwr_high_alpha_PO7	pwr_t4_30_P10	pwr_theta/beta_O2	pwr_total_PO8
(5)	pwr_t4_30_P8	pwr_low_beta_P7	pwr_alpha/beta_PO8	pwr_theta/beta_P9	pwr_total_P7

(b) NIRS only

	ROT-MI	ROT-SING	ROT-FACE	SUB-MI	ROT-WORD
(1)	mean_S15-D1_HbO	mean_S15-D1_HbO	mean_S15-D1_HbO	mean_S14-D22_HbR	mean_S15-D5_HbO
(2)	mean_S10-D17_HbR	mean_S1-D2_HbT	mean_S10-D14_HbO	mean_S15-D1_HbR	mean_S13-D24_HbR
(3)	mean_S1-D2_HbT	mean_S6-D9_HbR	mean_S3-D6_HbR	mean_S15-D5_HbT	mean_S16-D17_HbR
(4)	mean_S13-D24_HbR	mean_S13-D22_HbR	mean_S10-D17_HbO	mean_S15-D1_HbO	mean_S13-D22_HbO
(5)	mean_S14-D24_HbR	mean_S14-D24_HbR	mean_S10-D17_HbR	mean_S1-D1_HbO	mean_S13-D24_HbO

(c) EEG-NIRS fusion

	ROT-FACE	ROT-MI	ROT-SING	SUB-MI	SING-SUB
(1)	mean_S15-D1_HbO	pwr_theta/beta_O2	mean_S15-D1_HbO	mean_S14-D22_HbR	pwr_high_alpha_O2
(2)	pwr_t4_30_O2	pwr_high_alpha_O1	pwr_high_alpha_O2	pwr_high_alpha_PO7	pwr_t4_30_P9
(3)	pwr_theta/beta_O2	pwr_t4_30_O2	pwr_t4_30_P9	pwr_t4_30_O2	pwr_high_alpha_P10
(4)	pwr_theta/beta_PO7	pwr_t4_30_PO8	pwr_t4_30_O2	pwr_high_alpha_O2	mean_S15-D1_HbO
(5)	pwr_high_alpha_PO8	mean_S14-D24_HbR	pwr_theta/beta_O1	pwr_high_alpha_PO8	pwr_low_alpha_P9

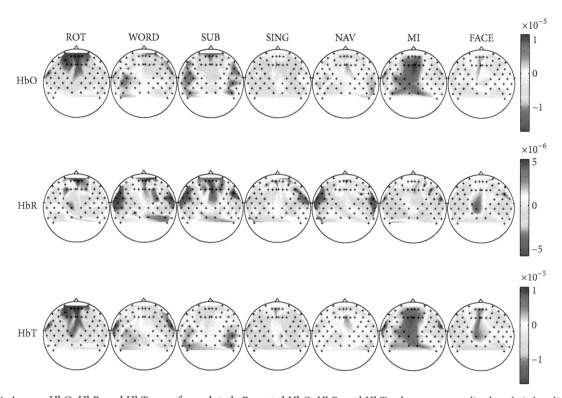

FIGURE 4: Average HbO, HbR, and HbT maps for each task. Reported HbO, HbR, and HbT values are normalized to their baseline values and averaged across the time window spanning 10 to 15 seconds after stimulus onset. Red represents an increase in concentration of the chromophore, while blue represents a decrease (in mmol/L).

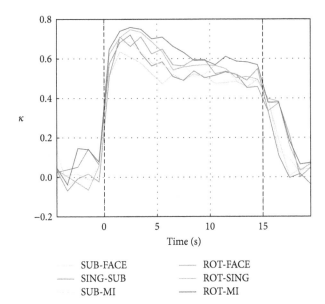

FIGURE 5: EEG-only classification κ over nonoverlapping one-second windows for the six best task pairs. The classification κ obtained with one-second windows was averaged over participants for each task pair. Each point is aligned with the middle of the window from which the features were extracted. Baseline κ values were not significantly greater than 0 (one-tailed t-tests).

The average classification κ over subjects, computed across one-second windows, is shown in Figure 5 for the six best task pairs. κ values increase quickly after stimulus onset and reach a peak around four seconds later, as seen also in Table 2. The performance then decreases gradually over the remaining 11 seconds of the trial and returns to chance level three seconds after the end of the task.

The l_1-SVM algorithm selected a minimum of zero and a maximum of 12 EEG features, with a median of seven features. The case where zero features are selected simply means that all the SVM weights are zero, so that the classifier always outputs the same decision, dependent on its bias. During the pre- and postepoch baseline, only around one or two features are selected. This number increases quickly after stimulus onset and remains stable across the 15 seconds of the epoch. It is interesting to note that S04, who obtained the lowest average peak κ, also consistently had the lowest number of selected features.

The five most important features following the approach described in Section 2.7 are listed in Table 3 for the five task pairs that produced the highest performance. Note that α- and β-related features showed strong importance, while θ and wide-band features were typically not highly ranked. Most of these features were extracted from electrodes located in the parietal and occipital regions. To support this observation, the average absolute values of the SVM weights are visualized on a topographical map of the head to show the importance of each channel according to the trained classifier (see Figure 6). In almost every case, channels in the occipital and parietal regions showed the highest feature importance. High performance pairs (first three rows in Figure 6) all displayed maximum feature importance for channels at the

back of the head. A pattern of high importance for channels PO7 and PO8 can be noticed in many pairs (i.e., ROT-FACE, SUB-FACE, ROT-NAV, SING-SUB, and WORD-NAV).

3.2.2. NIRS Only. The peak classification performance of classifiers trained on one-second window NIRS features, for each subject and pair of tasks, is shown in Table 4. The best overall κ is again obtained by S10, with 13 different pairs of tasks reaching high performance. S07, S04, and S11, respectively, ranked fifth, last, and seventh in the EEG-only analysis; all achieved an average κ above 0.50. On the other hand, S03, who ranked second in the EEG-only analysis, was ranked second to last in the NIRS-only case. The average peak time across task pairs is 11.5 seconds and again shows high variability.

Fifteen pairs of tasks were classified with average κ above 0.4, but only three yielded values significantly greater than 0.4. The best performing pairs were mostly a combination of a brain teaser and an imagery task (ROT-MI, ROT-SING, ROT-FACE, and SUB-MI), with the exception of ROT-WORD. Pairs combining two imagery tasks, such as SING-MI, NAV-FACE, FACE-MI, and SING-FACE, were constantly classified with the lowest average κ. Similar to the EEG-only case, ROT-MI achieved top-3 performance, while FACE-MI and SING-FACE achieved the lowest. ROT and SUB tasks were the most useful overall when paired with passive imagery tasks, whereas pairs of imagery tasks were all under the 0.4 κ threshold.

The average classification κ over subjects, computed across one-second windows, is shown in Figure 7 for the six best task pairs. The κ values of the best task pairs oscillated around $\kappa = 0$ during the baseline and the first five seconds of the trial. κ values then started rising approximately five seconds after stimulus onset and reached a plateau around six seconds later, which is consistent with the expected hemodynamic response delay [8]. As shown in Table 4, this leads to an average peak time of 11.5 s. Performance decreased after approximately eight seconds and did not return to preepoch baseline levels in the five seconds after the end of the trial.

When applied to NIRS features, the l_1-SVM algorithm selected a minimum of zero and a maximum of 11 features, with a median of three features. Only around one feature was selected during the preepoch baseline and up to five seconds after stimulus onset, after which this number increased and remained more stable until the end of the task and the postepoch baseline. Subject 10, who obtained the highest average peak κ, also consistently had the highest number of selected NIRS features.

The five most important features are listed in Table 3 for the five best task pairs. Sources 13 (CCP6) and 14 (PCP8) over the right parietal cortex and sources 15 (AF7) and 16 (AF8) over the right and left prefrontal cortex led to the highest ranking scores. $\Delta[\text{HbR}]$ and $\Delta[\text{HbO}]$ features generally showed more importance than $\Delta[\text{HbT}]$ features. To further identify regions of interest, the average absolute values of the SVM weights are visualized on a topographical map of the head in Figure 8. Channels in the prefrontal region showed consistently high importance for pairs including

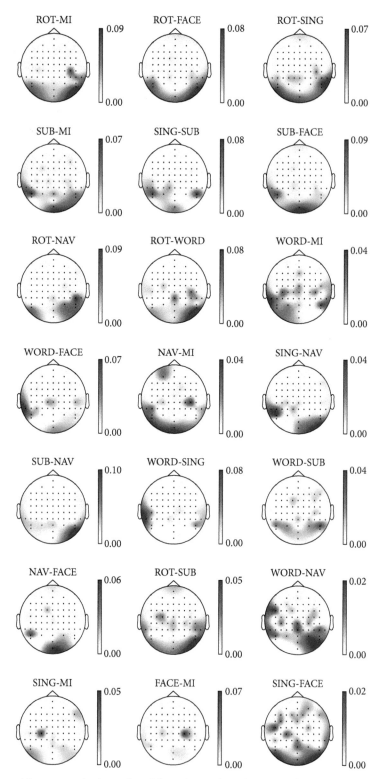

FIGURE 6: Topographical maps of the average absolute value of the SVM weights, when trained on EEG features only. Darker regions are those that are more important when classifying each task pair. Note that distinct color ranges are used for each map. This figure uses the models trained on the one-second window occurring three to four seconds after stimulus onset, which corresponds to the average peak time for EEG classification (see Table 2). The pairs are plotted in descending order of average κ (left to right and top to bottom) as presented in Table 2.

TABLE 4: NIRS-only peak κ values for each subject and task pair, when using features extracted from one-second windows. Task pairs and participants are shown in descending order of average κ, from top to bottom and left to right, respectively. κ values between 0.4 and 0.7 (satisfactory performance) are highlighted in italic font, whereas κ values greater than 0.7 (high performance) are shown in bold font. The average peak time with standard deviation is also included for each task pair. $^*p < 0.05$

	S10	S07	S04	S11	S09	S06	S01	S05	S03	Average	Peak time (s)
ROT-SING	**0.80**	*0.66*	**0.73**	*0.61*	*0.59*	*0.55*	*0.64*	*0.42*	*0.52*	*0.61 ± 0.11**	13.28 ± 3.6
SING-SUB	0.69	*0.60*	*0.59*	*0.60*	*0.68*	*0.46*	*0.50*	*0.42*	*0.53*	*0.56 ± 0.09**	12.39 ± 2.6
ROT-MI	**0.81**	**0.74**	**0.72**	*0.60*	*0.57*	*0.68*	*0.62*	*0.32*	*0.53*	*0.62 ± 0.14**	12.61 ± 4.7
SUB-MI	**0.83**	*0.60*	*0.57*	**0.72**	**0.77**	*0.57*	*0.57*	*0.33*	*0.42*	*0.60 ± 0.16*	12.06 ± 2.5
ROT-NAV	**0.80**	**0.74**	**0.73**	*0.53*	*0.50*	*0.68*	*0.49*	*0.40*	*0.38*	*0.58 ± 0.16*	12.72 ± 3.0
ROT-WORD	**0.89**	*0.66*	**0.76**	*0.63*	*0.62*	*0.55*	*0.58*	*0.42*	*0.28*	*0.60 ± 0.18*	12.72 ± 2.7
SUB-FACE	**0.78**	*0.60*	**0.76**	*0.66*	*0.62*	*0.48*	*0.53*	*0.33*	*0.33*	*0.57 ± 0.16*	13.39 ± 4.2
ROT-FACE	**0.80**	*0.51*	**0.84**	*0.53*	*0.48*	*0.66*	*0.70*	*0.48*	0.18	*0.58 ± 0.20*	14.72 ± 3.2
WORD-SUB	*0.67*	*0.53*	*0.63*	*0.60*	*0.53*	*0.36*	*0.41*	*0.43*	*0.24*	*0.49 ± 0.14*	14.61 ± 4.9
WORD-SING	**0.75**	**0.76**	*0.50*	*0.60*	*0.24*	*0.39*	*0.52*	*0.36*	*0.44*	*0.51 ± 0.18*	13.94 ± 2.8
SUB-NAV	**0.87**	*0.42*	*0.45*	*0.64*	*0.66*	*0.33*	*0.44*	*0.37*	*0.39*	*0.51 ± 0.18*	9.94 ± 3.8
ROT-SUB	*0.53*	*0.43*	*0.43*	*0.58*	*0.35*	*0.56*	*0.27*	*0.56*	*0.36*	*0.45 ± 0.11*	13.39 ± 3.7
WORD-FACE	**0.78**	*0.61*	*0.53*	**0.72**	0.12	*0.41*	*0.25*	*0.66*	*0.29*	*0.48 ± 0.23*	10.50 ± 6.0
WORD-MI	**0.74**	**0.72**	*0.54*	*0.66*	*0.40*	*0.39*	*0.28*	*0.32*	0.16	*0.47 ± 0.21*	8.94 ± 6.7
WORD-NAV	**0.84**	**0.74**	*0.44*	*0.53*	*0.34*	*0.33*	*0.31*	*0.28*	*0.28*	*0.45 ± 0.21*	7.83 ± 5.8
SING-NAV	*0.32*	*0.52*	*0.35*	*0.28*	*0.32*	*0.27*	*0.32*	*0.28*	*0.48*	*0.35 ± 0.09*	12.94 ± 3.1
NAV-MI	*0.66*	0.13	*0.31*	*0.33*	*0.34*	*0.28*	*0.30*	*0.20*	*0.29*	*0.32 ± 0.15*	11.83 ± 3.2
SING-MI	*0.39*	*0.42*	*0.29*	*0.33*	*0.25*	*0.32*	*0.30*	0.03	*0.41*	*0.30 ± 0.12*	12.50 ± 3.2
SING-FACE	*0.43*	*0.46*	0.16	0.02	*0.20*	*0.33*	0.05	0.09	*0.41*	*0.24 ± 0.17*	6.17 ± 7.4
NAV-FACE	*0.57*	*0.20*	*0.36*	*0.30*	*0.29*	*0.21*	0.17	*0.25*	0.17	*0.28 ± 0.13*	7.39 ± 6.8
FACE-MI	*0.40*	*0.30*	*0.43*	*0.28*	0.19	0.13	*0.26*	0.10	0.01	*0.23 ± 0.14*	8.06 ± 5.2
Average	**0.82**	*0.67*	*0.42*	*0.57*	*0.52*	**0.70**	*0.59*	*0.68*	**0.71**	*0.47 ± 0.15*	11.52 ± 4.2

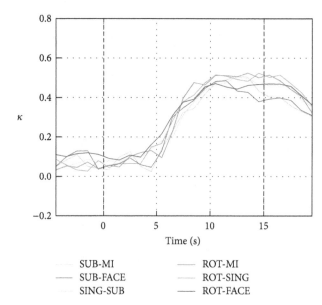

FIGURE 7: NIRS-only classification κ over nonoverlapping one-second windows for the six best task pairs. The classification κ obtained with one-second windows was averaged over participants for each task pair. Each point is aligned with the middle of the window from which the features were extracted. Baseline κ values were not significantly greater than 0 (one-tailed t-tests).

ROT and SUB tasks, whereas channels in the left prefrontal region showed consistent high feature importance in pairs that include the WORD task.

3.2.3. Fusion of Signals.

The peak classification κ values obtained for models trained on concatenated EEG and NIRS features are shown in Table 5. The three best pairs of tasks remained the same as for EEG-only classification (ROT-FACE, ROT-MI, and ROT-SING), as did the three worst pairs (SING-MI, FACE-MI, and SING-FACE). Again, most of the highest ranked task pairs were a combination of a brain teaser and an imagery task. Moreover, the task-wise κ values exhibited the same top-7 ranking as for EEG-only classification. Subject-wise, the four best participants (S10, S03, S07, and S06) were the same as for EEG-only classification. The other five subjects saw their ranking change by one or two positions. On the other hand, the peak time increased to an average of 6.4 seconds.

The average classification κ over subjects, computed across one-second windows, is shown in Figure 9 for the six best task pairs. Two peaks can be observed: first, at three seconds after trial onset, corresponding to the peak κ obtained with EEG features alone; and second, at around 11 seconds after trial onset, corresponding to the peak κ obtained with NIRS features alone. More specifically, when comparing these values to the ones obtained with EEG alone, we see that the improvement seems small in the first eight seconds of the task (as reported in Table 5) but is more noticeable in the last five seconds of the task, where more than one NIRS feature was originally selected.

To get a better idea of how feature fusion of EEG and NIRS impacted classification performance, Table 6 shows the increase in peak κ obtained by adding NIRS to EEG features, evaluated at the time windows where NIRS classification yielded the highest performance (as reported in Table 4). The

average increase was of 0.20, while the highest increase was of 0.84, achieved by S10 on task pair SING-SUB. Average performance gains were the highest for S04 ($\Delta\kappa = 0.40$), S11 ($\Delta\kappa = 0.30$), and S07 ($\Delta\kappa = 0.28$).

The seven best task pairs included either WORD or NAV (or both), while task pairs that included FACE or MI benefited less from fusion on average.

The l_1-SVM algorithm selected a minimum of zero and a maximum of 15 features with a median of seven features when trained on the concatenated EEG-NIRS dataset. The behavior is almost identical to that exhibited by EEG-only models, until around 11 seconds after stimulus onset, where a slight increase in the number of selected features is observed. This effect is particularly apparent for S04, who benefited the most from the fusion.

The five most important features per task are listed in Table 3 for the five best task pairs. Most of the previously chosen features are selected again. Figure 10 shows the relative importance of each subtype of feature (band power and chromophore type) for the same six task pairs. We see that α-related features were generally the most important, followed by β-related features. On the other hand, the θ, 4–30 Hz, and 0.1–100 Hz bands were usually less important. In NIRS, HbR-related features showed the strongest importance (while still inferior to α-related features), followed closely by HbO-related features. HbT did not show much importance. In some participants (S03, S07, and S11), HbR-related features were consistently more important than HbO-related ones, while it was the opposite for S04 and S09 (results not shown).

3.3. Questionnaire.

The average ratings, as well as the task rankings, are shown in Figure 11. Overall, the SUB task induced the most mental and temporal load, effort, and frustration, led to the poorest perceived performance, and was the least preferred. Other brain teasers (WORD and

TABLE 5: EEG-NIRS fusion peak κ values for each subject and task pair, when using features extracted from one-second windows. Task pairs and participants are shown in descending order of average κ, from top to bottom and left to right, respectively. κ values between 0.4 and 0.7 (satisfactory performance) are highlighted in italic font, whereas κ values greater than 0.7 (high performance) are shown in bold font. average peak time with standard deviation are also included for each task pair. $^* p < 0.05$, $^{**} p < 0.01$, $^{***} p < 0.001$.

	S10	S03	S07	S06	S11	S05	S01	S04	S09	Average	Peak time (s)
ROT-MI	**0.93**	**0.88**	**0.88**	**0.95**	**0.78**	**0.83**	0.77	0.75	0.77	**0.84 ± 0.08*****	9.83 ± 5.8
SUB-FACE	**0.78**	**0.83**	0.69	**0.87**	**0.74**	**0.90**	0.77	0.76	0.68	**0.78 ± 0.07*****	4.61 ± 3.5
ROT-FACE	**0.85**	**0.86**	**0.85**	**0.95**	0.69	**0.92**	**0.78**	**0.86**	0.69	**0.83 ± 0.09*****	9.39 ± 5.0
ROT-SING	**1.00**	**0.80**	**0.86**	**0.81**	**0.70**	**0.90**	**0.81**	**0.83**	0.59	**0.81 ± 0.11*****	6.39 ± 4.4
SUB-MI	**0.92**	**0.90**	**0.82**	**0.91**	**0.78**	**0.83**	**0.71**	0.55	**0.85**	**0.81 ± 0.12*****	5.17 ± 3.5
SING-SUB	**0.99**	**0.81**	**0.75**	**0.83**	0.67	**0.88**	**0.76**	0.59	**0.74**	**0.78 ± 0.12*****	5.28 ± 4.4
ROT-NAV	**0.96**	**0.73**	**0.85**	0.66	0.60	0.68	**0.74**	**0.72**	0.61	**0.73 ± 0.11*****	7.72 ± 5.3
ROT-WORD	**0.96**	**0.74**	**0.72**	0.65	0.66	**0.90**	0.61	**0.75**	0.61	**0.73 ± 0.12*****	9.17 ± 6.9
WORD-FACE	**0.78**	**0.74**	**0.71**	**0.87**	**0.78**	**0.76**	0.64	0.51	0.44	*0.69 ± 0.14***	8.72 ± 5.7
ROT-SUB	**0.74**	0.58	0.66	0.51	0.56	0.52	0.67	0.51	0.49	*0.58 ± 0.09***	7.61 ± 3.7
WORD-SUB	**0.89**	**0.71**	0.55	0.62	0.60	**0.75**	0.41	0.69	0.67	*0.66 ± 0.13***	7.28 ± 5.3
WORD-MI	**0.96**	0.60	**0.81**	**0.88**	**0.77**	0.53	0.56	0.53	0.63	*0.70 ± 0.16***	6.94 ± 4.7
NAV-MI	**0.82**	**0.86**	**0.75**	**0.81**	0.66	0.68	0.61	0.43	0.45	*0.67 ± 0.15***	1.50 ± 4.5
SUB-NAV	**0.89**	0.59	**0.73**	0.46	0.66	**0.70**	0.58	0.42	**0.72**	*0.64 ± 0.14***	6.06 ± 7.1
WORD-SING	**0.88**	0.66	**0.80**	**0.83**	0.60	0.52	**0.73**	0.57	0.31	*0.66 ± 0.18**	5.94 ± 4.0
SING-NAV	**0.80**	0.68	**0.73**	0.68	0.62	**0.74**	**0.71**	0.41	0.27	*0.63 ± 0.17**	5.06 ± 4.0
WORD-NAV	**0.80**	0.56	0.68	0.42	0.53	0.48	0.48	0.49	0.37	*0.53 ± 0.13*	6.39 ± 4.5
NAV-FACE	0.54	**0.77**	0.55	**0.79**	0.49	**0.82**	0.42	0.35	0.21	*0.55 ± 0.21*	4.50 ± 4.5
SING-MI	**0.78**	0.54	0.41	0.55	0.39	0.36	0.24	0.43	0.39	*0.46 ± 0.15*	4.39 ± 4.8
FACE-MI	0.61	0.56	0.37	0.39	0.46	0.30	0.18	0.51	0.38	*0.42 ± 0.13*	2.17 ± 2.7
SING-FACE	0.63	0.46	0.43	0.44	0.25	0.32	0.31	0.21	0.26	*0.37 ± 0.13*	2.39 ± 2.5
Average	**0.83**	**0.71**	0.70	**0.71**	0.62	0.68	0.60	0.56	0.53	*0.66 ± 0.13*	6.02 ± 4.6

Computational Neuroscience: Modeling and Applications

TABLE 6: Change in peak κ when adding NIRS features to EEG features, for the models trained on the windows that yielded the highest NIRS κ. Task pairs and participants are shown in descending order of average $\Delta\kappa$, from top to bottom and left to right, respectively. $\Delta\kappa$ values between 0.4 and 0.7 are highlighted in italic font, values greater than 0.7 are shown in bold font, and values below 0 are shown in underline font. * $p < 0.05$.

	S04	S11	S07	S09	S01	S10	S05	S03	S06	Average
SUB-NAV	0.36	0.35	0.02	0.32	0.07	0.33	0.35	0.10	0.11	0.22 ± 0.14*
ROT-WORD	0.40	0.56	0.42	0.41	0.48	-0.00	0.14	0.12	0.16	0.30 ± 0.20*
NAV-FACE	0.40	0.38	0.37	0.29	0.20	0.20	-0.00	0.23	0.00	0.23 ± 0.15*
ROT-NAV	0.53	0.16	0.21	0.28	0.20	0.09	0.27	-0.01	0.22	0.22 ± 0.15*
WORD-NAV	0.42	0.30	0.34	0.01	0.26	0.16	0.07	0.02	0.45	0.23 ± 0.17
WORD-SING	0.22	0.20	0.34	0.37	0.64	0.64	0.03	0.12	0.02	0.29 ± 0.23
WORD-SUB	0.79	0.58	0.13	0.27	0.11	0.24	0.32	-0.06	0.45	0.31 ± 0.26
ROT-SING	0.46	0.31	0.06	0.25	0.20	0.18	0.11	0.00	0.03	0.18 ± 0.15
SING-SUB	0.55	0.12	0.63	0.27	-0.01	0.84	0.47	0.07	-0.02	0.32 ± 0.31
NAV-MI	0.02	0.14	0.11	0.04	0.02	0.08	0.02	0.19	-0.00	0.07 ± 0.07
SING-NAV	0.17	0.14	0.59	0.20	0.46	0.16	0.01	0.08	-0.00	0.20 ± 0.20
ROT-SUB	0.18	0.46	-0.05	0.02	0.15	-0.01	0.61	0.21	0.47	0.23 ± 0.24
SING-MI	0.15	0.36	0.39	0.02	0.22	-0.02	0.09	0.53	-0.03	0.19 ± 0.20
ROT-MI	0.24	0.38	0.05	0.16	0.09	0.00	-0.01	0.01	0.22	0.13 ± 0.13
WORD-FACE	0.49	0.67	0.23	-0.07	0.05	0.32	0.18	0.13	-0.00	0.22 ± 0.24
SUB-FACE	0.74	0.16	0.63	0.09	0.17	0.11	0.04	0.13	0.00	0.23 ± 0.27
SING-FACE	0.17	-0.04	0.24	0.27	0.03	0.40	0.07	0.02	-0.03	0.13 ± 0.15
ROT-FACE	0.62	0.30	0.04	0.10	0.21	0.18	0.04	-0.02	-0.01	0.16 ± 0.20
SUB-MI	0.67	0.33	0.62	0.23	0.14	0.05	0.02	-0.11	-0.01	0.22 ± 0.28
WORD-MI	0.57	0.32	0.24	-0.07	0.04	0.00	0.03	0.03	-0.03	0.12 ± 0.21
FACE-MI	0.15	0.03	0.34	-0.00	0.15	0.01	0.03	-0.10	-0.00	0.07 ± 0.13
Average	0.40	0.30	0.28	0.17	0.18	0.19	0.14	0.08	0.09	0.20 ± 0.19

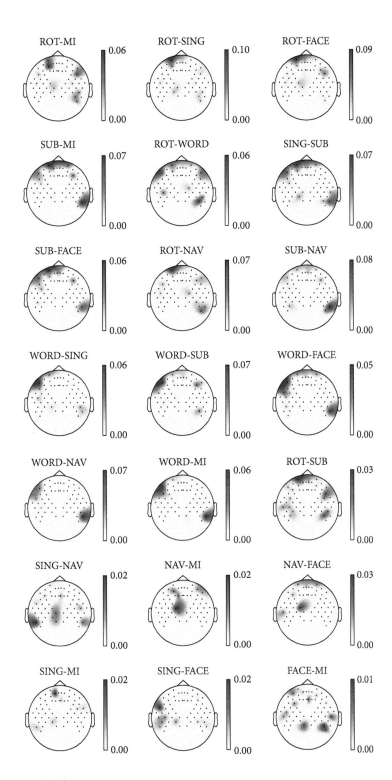

FIGURE 8: Topographical maps of the average absolute value of the SVM weights, when trained on NIRS features only. Darker regions are those that are more important when classifying each task pair. Note that distinct color ranges are used for each map. This figure uses the models trained on the one-second window occurring 11 to 12 seconds after stimulus onset, which corresponds to the average peak time for NIRS classification (see Table 4). The pairs are plotted in descending order of average κ (from left to right and top to bottom) as presented in Table 4.

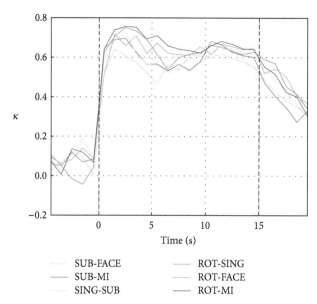

FIGURE 9: EEG and NIRS classification κ over nonoverlapping one-second windows for the six best task pairs. The classification κ obtained with one-second windows was averaged over participants for each task pair. Each point is aligned with the middle of the window from which the features were extracted. Baseline κ values were not significantly greater than 0 (one-tailed t-tests).

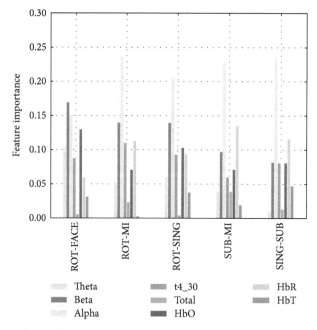

FIGURE 10: Importance of each EEG and NIRS feature subtype: EEG band powers (θ, α, β, 4–30 Hz, and total spectrum (0.1–100 Hz)) and chromophore types (HbO, HbR, and HbT). The histogram is based on the models trained on the one-second window occurring 11 to 12 seconds after stimulus onset, which corresponds to the average peak time for NIRS classification (see Table 4).

ROT) induced a medium load, effort, and frustration but were ranked high against other tasks in terms of preference. On the other hand, dynamic imagery tasks (SING, NAV, and MI) induced a relative low load, did not require much effort, and were the least frustrating, while leading to high perceived performance but mixed preference rankings. Finally, the only passive imagery task (FACE) required high mental load and effort but low temporal load and led to slightly lower performance and higher frustration levels, while being ranked among the least preferred tasks.

4. Discussion

4.1. Optimal Mental Task and Combinations. In this work, we studied seven different mental tasks (mental rotation, word generation, mental subtraction, mental singing, mental

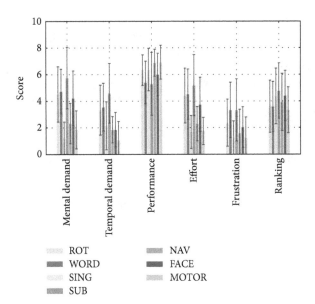

FIGURE 11: NASA TLX ratings and mental task ranking. Ratings and rankings are averaged over each subject and session. Error bars correspond to the standard deviation of each group of rating and mental task.

navigation, motor imagery, and face imagery) from an electrophysiological and neurohemodynamic perspective in order to uncover the most promising contenders. In the following sections, we discuss the results obtained with each mental task individually and highlight its potential usability in an online BCI.

4.1.1. Mental Rotation. Task pairs with mental rotation were always ranked among the best pairs, in all modality configurations. Pairs including ROT and any task other than SUB yielded peak κ higher than average. These results confirm the findings of previous studies [21, 33], in which ROT was also among the best tasks. However, in our study ROT was performed in a slightly different way: participants were shown two figures and had to rotate one to evaluate if it was the same as the other one or a mirrored version, instead of simply imagining a single figure rotating. The introduction of a clear goal puts this task in the brain teaser category with WORD and SUB, which were previously shown to yield high performance. However, the average increase in performance brought in by feature fusion was among the lowest of any tasks.

The features selected for the high performing pairs using ROT were consistently more important at the back of the head in EEG and in the left prefrontal region for NIRS. The ERD/ERS analysis supports this observation: high levels of ERD were observed in the occipital regions in all four plotted bands, suggesting that these regions were recruited during mental rotation. In another study [21], similar ERD patterns were found for the low β band between 0.5 and 2 seconds after the beginning of the task, with additional ERD in the prefrontal region. A distinct pattern over the two motor cortices can be seen in both α and β, suggesting motor imagery might have been used by some participants to help mentally rotate the L-shaped figures. The first findings are confirmed by a review looking at 32 fMRI and Positron

Emission Tomography (PET) neuroimaging studies that concluded that the posterior occipital cortex was consistently activated during mental rotation [60]. In this review, the author also notes the activation of focused prefrontal cortex regions and more precisely the left inferior frontal cortex for studies that encouraged motor simulation (i.e., when participants were asked to imagine manipulating the objects to be rotated). Although this was not precisely the case here, participants were not given specific instructions as to how they should perform the rotation, and so some might have used this approach, explaining the strong HbO decrease in the prefrontal regions.

Although ranked as third most demanding, frustrating, and effort-inducing task, ROT was often among the three user-preferred tasks. Therefore, even though ROT might induce fatigue more rapidly than other tasks, its high performance in both NIRS and EEG and its good preference ranking make it an excellent candidate for a BCI.

4.1.2. Word Generation. Word generation led to above average classification performance for all three modality configurations and usually ranked third or fourth among tasks. These results are similar to those observed in EEG for WORD pairs in another study [21]. The fusion proved to be particularly useful for WORD. Indeed, four task pairs with WORD yielded significant κ increases with EEG-NIRS fusion.

The selected features were predominantly in the left temporal region in EEG and in the left frontotemporal region in NIRS. In terms of ERD/ERS, this effect was mostly noticeable in the low α and high β bands, in which the left temporal region undergoes desynchronization. The low β pattern characterized by desynchronization in the occipital and central left regions is very similar to the one found in Friedrich et al. (2012) [21]. The temporal regions were also highlighted in NIRS, with strong HbO increase over the left temporal lobe and HbR decrease over both sides. Again, these findings are further confirmed by recent fMRI studies focused on anatomical regions supporting different aspects of language [61]. Indeed, Price found that the left middle frontal cortex and the left pars opercularis were consistently activated during word retrieval tasks. These brain areas overlap with the regions identified in our results.

Similarly to ROT, WORD ranked as the second most demanding, frustrating, and effort-inducing task but was still among the three user-preferred tasks. Contrary to ROT though, participants often rated their performance for the WORD task as low. This might be explained by the purely random selection of the first letter from which words had to be generated: some letters are rarely found at the beginning of a word (such as Z, X, or Q), and so participants who were given these letters probably performed worse. The difficulty of the WORD task would need to be adjusted in a future implementation by limiting the selection of some rarer letters. Overall, word generation is a good candidate for a BCI due to its high performance in both NIRS and EEG and its good subjective evaluation.

4.1.3. Mental Subtraction. Mental subtraction ranked second in terms of average classification performance for all three modality configurations. SUB is the task that benefited the most from the feature fusion, with two of the largest average increases in κ. These results confirm the findings of [21] in EEG, but not of [33] in NIRS. Indeed, Hwang et al. found mental subtraction to be on par with other imagery tasks (SING, MI) in terms of how often it led to classification accuracy above 70%. However, the authors defined their SUB task as the successive subtraction of two "simple numbers" (suggesting one-digit numbers) from a three-digit number, which is simpler than the task used in our study. Moreover, a mental multiplication task (of two two-digit numbers), which was not used here, led to the best performance in their work. Since some fMRI studies have found the two operations to be similarly encoded in the brain (although some studies found differences) [62], and since the difficulty level of Hwang et al.'s multiplication task might be closer to our subtraction task, we hypothesize that they could have achieved similar performance with harder subtractions.

The selected features revealed consistent importance at electrode positions PO7 and PO8 in EEG and in the prefrontal and right temporoparietal regions in NIRS. This is also seen in the ERD/ERS patterns as a strong desynchronization in low and high α as well as low β in the occipitoparietal regions and part of the prefrontal regions. FMRI studies identified the involvement of the precuneus, located in the midline portion of the centroparietal region, and of frontal regions as commonly activated during the execution of different arithmetic operations [63]. Interestingly, in the same study, Fehr et al. found a statistically significant increase in activity in the bilateral inferior parietal regions when comparing a complex subtraction task to a simple one, which could explain these clear patterns of importance for PO7 and PO8 features. As for the prefrontal patterns found in NIRS, they might be related to an increased working memory load, which would result in the activation of the dorsolateral prefrontal cortex [64]. The patterns of HbR decrease in both

temporal lobes being very similar to the ones observed in WORD; we hypothesize that participants might have used a speech-based strategy to perform the subtractions.

As a brain teaser, SUB ranked as the most demanding, frustrating, and effort-inducing task, making it the worst perceived for performance and the least preferred task. Before using SUB in a BCI, it might be useful therefore to further assess its optimal difficulty level to avoid tiring or frustrating the user. Additionally, alternative arithmetic operations such as mental multiplication might yield better results and should therefore be studied [33], again at optimal difficulty levels. In either case, SUB can definitely benefit from a EEG-NIRS fusion approach and is thus recommendable if such a system is already in use.

4.1.4. Mental Singing. Task pairs using mental singing led to below average performance for all three modality configurations. Analogous results were obtained for EEG [21] and for NIRS [33] in previous studies comparing many mental tasks. Similarly, in a prefrontal NIRS study, Power et al. (2011) compared the performances of rest-SING and rest-SUB pairs and found that mental singing led to poorer performance on average [28].

It is difficult to determine if consistent brain regions were recruited in the mental singing task based on the feature importance analysis, as in both EEG and NIRS the topographical maps show varying patterns for pairs using SING. Indeed, in EEG, the following regions all showed strong importance: parietooccipital (with ROT), bilateral parietal (with SUB), left parietal and right occipital (with NAV), left temporal (with SING), left motor cortex (with MI), and occipital (with FACE). Similar disparate patterns were found in NIRS. This high variability in importance of brain regions is most likely due to the low discriminability of the physiological processes behind mental singing, especially in the studied modalities, that are essentially limited to cortical structures. Indeed, if little information from singing could be decoded in EEG and NIRS, a classifier would focus on features provided by the second task to make its decision and thus would not choose consistent features across pairs containing SING.

Neuroimaging studies of covert singing identified activation in the frontoparietal regions (bilateral motor cortices and Broca's area) [65, 66]. This could explain the ERD patterns in the low and high β band located in the left hemisphere and the similar HbR patterns over the temporal and central lobes. These studies also provide insights into why mental singing did not produce distinguishable patterns: first, Gunji et al. (2007) used MEG to compare the oscillatory processes of humming, speaking, and overt and covert singing and found that covert singing consistently recruited the least cerebral area [66]. A very small area of activation will make it harder for modalities such as EEG and NIRS to pick up relevant activity when restricted to a small number of sensors. Second, in their study of opera singers, Kleber et al. (2007) found significant activation of emotion-related deep brain structures such as the insula, the amygdala, and the hippocampus [65]. Since in our study we specifically asked the participants to focus on the emotions produced by singing a song they personally chose, it is possible that these regions were activated but that the depth limitations of EEG and NIRS prevented these patterns from being measured. The strong α and β ERS visible in Figure 3 further supports this hypothesis. Indeed, the high increase in these oscillatory processes indicates that most cortical structures were not activated during singing. The strong ERS patterns in the occipital region thus suggest the cortical idling of visual processing centers during mental singing.

SING induced the lowest mental demand, effort, and frustration and was reasonably well ranked by participants. Since pairing SING with brain teasers led to high classification performance, it seems reasonable to use it in a BCI context. Nevertheless, because of the apparent low discriminability of mental singing in EEG and NIRS, it would be important to first assess how it compares to baseline data: if it is not different enough from the baseline, this task could eventually provoke false negatives in a BCI using a no-control state. It is to be noted that this analysis was not performed here due to baseline periods being used for normalization of the features, thus limiting the significance of such an analysis on our dataset.

4.1.5. Mental Navigation.

Task pairs using mental navigation led to below average performance for all three modality configurations, making them very similar in terms of performance to pairs including mental singing, and yielded the lowest average κ increase in fusion. Similar results were obtained in another study [21] for EEG-only classification, whereas no previous NIRS results were found in the literature.

ERD/ERS patterns for mental navigation showed mostly left hemispheric activation, particularly in the low α and low β bands. These results are consistent with the low β patterns found in Friedrich et al. (2012) above the left hemisphere [21] and are further supported by the results of an fMRI study looking at 16 subjects engaged in mental navigation of familiar places [67]. In their work, Ino et al. reported statistically significant activation in the left premotor area, the left angular gyrus (parietal lobe), and deeper brain structures such as the bilateral retrosplenial areas, parts of the hippocampus, and the cerebellum [67]. These patterns are not easily discerned in the feature importance topographical maps, where different brain regions seem informative for each pair in both EEG and NIRS, as was the case for SING. However, Ino et al. used a more complex navigation task in which participants were instructed to imagine walking through Kyoto while counting the number of turns they made. Since both our study and [21] obtained poor performance with this task, we hypothesize that increasing the difficulty level might have helped produce stronger and clearer activation.

NAV ranked as the third least demanding, frustrating, and effort-inducing task and led to high perceived performance. Ranked as fourth favorite task on average, NAV, like SING, should be considered for implementation in a BCI mostly because it led to good performance when paired with brain teasers. Increasing the difficulty level of the task might however lead to superior performance. Finally, its low κ increase in the multimodal case makes it less useful to use with a NIRS-EEG approach.

4.1.6. Motor Imagery.

Motor imagery is the most often used mental task in the hBCI literature [11], providing a wealth of previous articles to compare our results to. Whereas MI was the second worst task in NIRS, it achieved third and fourth best performance in EEG-only and EEG-NIRS configurations, respectively. MI was also the second worst task in terms of performance improvement when feature fusion was used. Although using a different processing and classification pipeline, Fazli et al. worked toward a similar hybrid EEG-NIRS-BCI as in our study but only evaluated the use of a left-hand versus right-hand MI paradigm [40]. The authors found that EEG-NIRS fusion could improve the classification accuracy by 5% on average in 90% of subjects, which is hard to compare to our study because of methodological differences. However, we also noted a marked improvement across participants ($\Delta\kappa = 0.13$), even though this improvement was among the lowest in our seven tasks.

Although patterns induced by MI are most likely obscured by those of brain teasers in most pairs (as was the case for SING and NAV), feature importance analysis shows the importance of left and right motor cortex features in NAV-MI, SING-MI, and FACE-MI in EEG. This phenomenon seems to occur only for the NAV-MI pair in NIRS, but this might reveal in fact a pattern proper to NAV, as the NAV-FACE map shows similar feature importance. The ERD/ERS patterns in the first three bands showed activation of the motor cortices, with the left hemisphere being predominant, as expected from the right-hand movement to be imagined. Classical BCI experiments have shown this pattern multiple times [68, 69], and the particular pattern in low β is very similar to the one reported in [21]. This is further supported by strong HbO and HbT increases over the left hemisphere. However, desynchronization of both the left and right frontal cortices is visible in the high β band, a phenomenon not reported in the aforementioned literature. Similar bilateral frontal ERD patterns were found for almost every task in high β, suggesting that there might have been an unexpected brain activity-inducing event affecting this band. As is the case for SING, strong ERS in the low and high α bands, predominantly in the occipital lobe, suggests that visual functions were not recruited during motor imagery.

MI induced either the lowest or second lowest demand, effort, and frustration, yielded the highest perceived performance, and was ranked as the most pleasant task on average. Pairing MI with brain teasers led to high classification performance in our case and was shown in the literature to yield good EEG and NIRS performance when paired with another imagery task (such as another MI task performed with the other hand) [40]. We thus conclude that MI is a useful task that deserves its predominant place in the BCI literature.

4.1.7. Face Imagery.

Face imagery was the worst task in all modality configurations. Fusion improved the classification performance of FACE, but not differently from most other tasks. These results are in line with those of Friedrich et al. for EEG [21], whereas no reference for NIRS-based classification of face imagery could be found.

The main brain structure known to be activated specifically in response to face stimuli is the fusiform gyrus, found in the posterior part of the cortex [70]. In addition, in reaction to famous faces, activation of subsets of the inferior occipital gyri, lateral fusiform gyri, superior temporal sulcus, and amygdala was identified in [70]. The fact that the main structure recruited (fusiform gyrus) is farther from the cortical layers accessible with EEG and NIRS could certainly account for the difficulty in classifying FACE tasks. This could also explain the disparate feature importance topographical patterns observed in both EEG and NIRS.

The ERD/ERS pattern observed in the low β band was similar to the one reported in [21]: desynchronization of the central and frontal lobes, with synchronization of the temporal lobes. Moreover, α bands showed distinctly high power in the occipital lobes, which could be explained by some low mental load-induced drowsiness. This is especially relevant since some of the brain structures mentioned above are located in the parietal and occipital brain regions.

Although inducing low temporal demand, the FACE task was almost on par with brain teasers for mental demand and effort, suggesting participants found it difficult to imagine the face of their closest friend. Falling among the three least preferred tasks, FACE is however not a good candidate for a BCI, as it produced consistently low unimodal and multimodal performance, and was generally not particularly appealing to users.

4.1.8. Best Task Pairs. Based on these results, we conclude that out of the 21 task pairs studied in our study combinations of a brain teaser (ROT, SUB, or WORD) and an imagery task (MI, FACE, NAV, and SING) are most likely to yield good performance. This confirms the previous results of previous studies [21, 33]. More specifically, the ROT-MI combination performed the best in our experiments. In the case where a NIRS-EEG system is available for the implementation of the BCI, our results show that pairs based on WORD and NAV might benefit the most from feature fusion.

4.2. Evaluation of Fusion Performance in a Realistic Context. A few methodological points would have to be approached differently in a realistic context application. First, the analysis of the effect of fusion on classification performance was done in two parts. The peak κ achieved by fusion was compared to the peak κ of EEG alone, leading to small increases on the order of $\Delta\kappa = 0.02$. By looking at the evolution of performance across time (Figures 5, 7, and 9), NIRS was found to provide additional information around 11 seconds into the task. We thus chose to report the performance increase for the one-second window between 11 and 12 seconds after stimulus onset to highlight the added value of a fusion approach. In contrast, many NIRS studies extracted the same feature over windows of many different sizes and combined them as different features of the same mental task instance [28–30, 33, 34]. While this approach can hamper classifier performance by increasing the dimensionality of the input, it also provides more information and thus can lead to better accuracy.

Another critical point highlighted in many of the aforementioned studies is the hemodynamic response delay in NIRS. Indeed, in our study, we found it took around 11 seconds for NIRS features to yield peak performance. This is a long time to wait when trying to operate an active BCI, making a unimodal NIRS-BCI poorly usable in most contexts. In turn, some participants saw their EEG performance decrease steadily across a trial, probably due to them being bored or tired, reducing the quality of their mental imagery and solving skills. However, by combining NIRS with EEG, we could reach satisfactory performance in the first seconds after stimulus onset, while still benefiting from increased performance later in the trial.

Despite these limitations, several applications could benefit from the peculiarities of our hBCI paradigm. For example, one could design a BCI where a decision has to be sustained over a few seconds before an output is given to ensure a certain level of certainty. Our system would be useful to recognize a specific mental task over longer periods of time, while also providing increased classification performance.

Another example of how the fusion of EEG and NIRS features might be useful was shown in our analysis for participant S04. Indeed, this participant had the lowest EEG-only performance and did not reach peak κ above 0.7 for a single task pair when using EEG features only. However, this participant's NIRS-only performance proved much better, and when EEG and NIRS were combined S04 benefited from the largest performance increase across participants and achieved high performance in seven task pairs. This pattern was observed for many participants: usually, one modality led to better performance than the other, and combining both EEG and NIRS allowed improvements in many task pairs. For example, this means a BCI user with poor EEG-only control would still be able to achieve high performance, thus potentially helping tackle the so-called BCI illiteracy problem.

5. Conclusion

In this work, we investigated the use of two noninvasive functional neuroimaging techniques, EEG and NIRS, for the binary classification of seven different mental tasks. We identified optimal mental task pairs across nine participants, for EEG-only, NIRS-only, and EEG-NIRS fusion classification schemes, and assessed the impact of a multimodal approach on the classification performance.

Pairs formed of a brain teaser, that is, a mental task that requires problem-solving skills (ROT, SUB, and WORD), and an imagery task (MI, FACE, and SING) consistently yielded the best classification performance for unimodal EEG and NIRS schemes, as well as for a multimodal fusion scheme. In contrast to unimodal performance results on par with those of previous reports, the multimodal approach led to an average increase of 0.03 in peak Cohen's κ when using features extracted from one-second windows (equivalent to a 1.5% accuracy increase in balanced settings). Similarly, a 0.20 increase in κ (10% accuracy increase) was obtained when focusing on the optimal NIRS windows.

The analysis of the trained classification models unveiled interesting spatial patterns of brain activity and the importance of feature subtypes in modality fusion. Particularly, α- and β-related EEG features proved to be the most useful, followed by HbO or HbR amplitude NIRS features, depending on the individual. The occipital and parietal regions yielded the most important EEG features, whereas NIRS features extracted from the prefrontal and frontal regions were the most informative. Our proposed feature analysis approach made it possible to delve deeper into the classification results, and shed light on the role of different neurophysiological modalities toward more efficient and flexible BCIs.

An important future research direction should be the implementation of online BCIs based on the optimal mental task pairs we identified. The restrictions induced by a real-time implementation (setup time, computing efficacy, robustness to noise, etc.) will all have to be overcome to yield a truly usable brain-computer interface.

Acknowledgments

The authors thank R. Cassani and A. Clerico for help with data acquisition. This work was supported by the Fonds de Recherche du Québec-Nature et Technologies (FRQNT) and the Natural Sciences and Engineering Research Council of Canada (NSERC).

References

[1] J. R. Wolpaw, N. Birbaumer, D. J. McFarland, G. Pfurtscheller, and T. M. Vaughan, "Brain-computer interfaces for communication and control," *Clinical Neurophysiology*, vol. 113, no. 6, pp. 767–791, 2002.

[2] J. R. Wolpaw and E. W. Wolpaw, "Brain-computer interfaces: something new under the sun," in *Brain-Computer Interfaces: Principles and Practice*, pp. 3–12, Oxford University Press, 2012.

[3] J. B. F. Van Erp, F. Lotte, and M. Tangermann, "Brain-computer interfaces: beyond medical applications," *Computer*, vol. 45, no. 4, pp. 26–34, 2012.

[4] S. M. Coyle, T. E. Ward, C. M. Markham, and G. McDarby, "On the suitability of near-infrared (NIR) systems for next-generation brain-computer interfaces," *Physiological Measurement*, vol. 25, no. 4, article 815, 2004.

[5] H.-J. Hwang, S. Kim, S. Choi, and C.-H. Im, "EEG-based brain-computer interfaces: a thorough literature survey," *International Journal of Human-Computer Interaction*, vol. 29, no. 12, pp. 814–826, 2013.

[6] E. C. Leuthardt, G. Schalk, J. R. Wolpaw, J. G. Ojemann, and D. W. Moran, "A brain-computer interface using electrocorticographic signals in humans," *Journal of Neural Engineering*, vol. 1, no. 2, pp. 63–71, 2004.

[7] J. Mellinger, G. Schalk, C. Braun et al., "An MEG-based brain-computer interface (BCI)," *NeuroImage*, vol. 36, no. 3, pp. 581–593, 2007.

[8] R. Sitaram, A. Caria, and N. Birbaumer, "Hemodynamic brain-computer interfaces for communication and rehabilitation," *Neural Networks*, vol. 22, no. 9, pp. 1320–1328, 2009.

[9] R. Sitaram, A. Caria, R. Veit et al., "FMRI brain-computer interface: A tool for neuroscientific research and treatment," *Computational Intelligence and Neuroscience*, vol. 2007, Article ID 25487, 2007.

[10] N. Naseer and K. Hong, "fNIRS-based brain-computer interfaces: a review," *Frontiers in Human Neuroscience*, vol. 9, article 3, 2015.

[11] H. Banville and T. Falk, "Recent advances and open challenges in hybrid brain-computer interfacing: a technological review of non-invasive human research," *Brain-Computer Interfaces*, vol. 3, no. 1, pp. 9–46, 2016.

[12] G. Pfurtscheller, B. Z. Allison, G. Bauernfeind et al., "The hybrid BCI," *Frontiers in Neuroscience*, vol. 4, no. 3, 3 pages, 2010.

[13] G. R. Müller-Putz, R. Leeb, J. d. Millán et al., "Principles of hybrid brain–computer interfaces," in *Towards Practical Brain-Computer Interfaces*, Biological and Medical Physics, Biomedical Engineering, pp. 355–373, Springer, Berlin, Germany, 2013.

[14] T. Cao, F. Wan, C. M. Wong, J. N. da Cruz, and Y. Hu, "Objective evaluation of fatigue by EEG spectral analysis in steady-state visual evoked potential-based brain-computer interfaces," *BioMedical Engineering Online*, vol. 13, no. 1, article no. 28, 2014.

[15] B. Obermaier, C. Neuper, C. Guger, and G. Pfurtscheller, "Information transfer rate in a five-classes brain-computer interface," *IEEE Transactions on Neural Systems and Rehabilitation Engineering*, vol. 9, no. 3, pp. 283–288, 2001.

[16] E. Curran, P. Sykacek, M. Stokes et al., "Cognitive Tasks for Driving a Brain-Computer Interfacing System: A Pilot Study," *IEEE Transactions on Neural Systems and Rehabilitation Engineering*, vol. 12, no. 1, pp. 48–54, 2004.

[17] F. Sepulveda, M. Dyson, J. Q. Gan, and C. L. Tsui, "A comparison of mental task combinations for asynchronous EEG-based BCIs," in *Proceedings of the 29th Annual International Conference of the IEEE*, pp. 5055–5058, Engineering in Medicine and Biology Society, 2007.

[18] F. Faradji, R. K. Ward, and G. E. Birch, "A brain-computer interface based on mental tasks with a zero false activation rate," in *Proceedings of the 2009 4th International IEEE/EMBS Conference on Neural Engineering, NER '09*, pp. 355–358, May 2009.

[19] M.-C. Dobrea and D. M. Dobrea, "The selection of proper discriminative cognitive tasks - A necessary prerequisite in high-quality BCI applications," in *Proceedings of the 2nd International Symposium on Applied Sciences in Biomedical and Communication Technologies, ISABEL 2009*, November 2009.

[20] E. V. C. Friedrich, R. Scherer, K. Sonnleitner, and C. Neuper, "Impact of auditory distraction on user performance in a brain-computer interface driven by different mental tasks," *Clinical Neurophysiology*, vol. 122, no. 10, pp. 2003–2009, 2011.

[21] E. V. C. Friedrich, R. Scherer, and C. Neuper, "The effect of distinct mental strategies on classification performance for brain-computer interfaces," *International Journal of Psychophysiology*, vol. 84, no. 1, pp. 86–94, 2012.

[22] R. Scherer, J. Faller, D. Balderas et al., "Brain-computer interfacing: more than the sum of its parts," *Soft Computing*, vol. 17, no. 2, pp. 317–331, 2013.

[23] E. V. C. Friedrich, R. Scherer, and C. Neuper, "Long-term evaluation of a 4-class imagery-based brain-computer interface," *Clinical Neurophysiology*, vol. 124, no. 5, pp. 916–927, 2013.

[24] E. V. C. Friedrich, R. Scherer, and C. Neuper, "Stability of event-related (de-) synchronization during brain-computer interface-relevant mental tasks," *Clinical Neurophysiology*, vol. 124, no. 1, pp. 61–69, 2013.

[25] E. V. C. Friedrich, C. Neuper, and R. Scherer, "Whatever works: a systematic user-centered training protocol to optimize brain-computer interfacing individually," *PLoS ONE*, vol. 8, no. 9, Article ID e76214, 2013.

[26] Y. Hoshi and M. Tamura, "Near-infrared optical detection of sequential brain activation in the prefrontal cortex during mental tasks," *NeuroImage*, vol. 5, no. 4, pp. 292–297, 1997.

[27] B. Abibullaev, J. An, and J.-I. Moon, "Neural network classification of brain hemodynamic responses from four mental tasks," *International Journal of Optomechatronics*, vol. 5, no. 4, pp. 340–359, 2011.

[28] S. D. Power, A. Kushki, and T. Chau, "Towards a system-paced near-infrared spectroscopy brain-computer interface: differentiating prefrontal activity due to mental arithmetic and mental singing from the no-control state," *Journal of Neural Engineering*, vol. 8, no. 6, Article ID 066004, 2011.

[29] T. H. Falk, M. Guirgis, S. Power, and T. T. Chau, "Taking NIRS-BCIs outside the lab: towards achieving robustness against environment noise," *IEEE Transactions on Neural Systems and Rehabilitation Engineering*, vol. 19, no. 2, pp. 136–146, 2011.

[30] S. D. Power, A. Kushki, and T. Chau, "Intersession consistency of single-trial classification of the prefrontal response to mental arithmetic and the no-control state by NIRS," *PLoS ONE*, vol. 7, no. 7, Article ID e37791, 2012.

[31] C. Herff, D. Heger, F. Putze, J. Hennrich, O. Fortmann, and T. Schultz, "Classification of mental tasks in the prefrontal cortex using fNIRS," in *Proceedings of the 2013 35th Annual International Conference of the IEEE Engineering in Medicine and Biology Society, (EMBC '13)*, pp. 2160–2163, July 2013.

[32] L. C. Schudlo, S. D. Power, and T. Chau, "Dynamic topographical pattern classification of multichannel prefrontal NIRS signals," *Journal of Neural Engineering*, vol. 10, no. 4, Article ID 046018, 2013.

[33] H.-J. Hwang, J.-H. Lim, D.-W. Kim, and C.-H. Im, "Evaluation of various mental task combinations for near-infrared spectroscopy-based brain-computer interfaces," *Journal of Biomedical Optics*, vol. 19, no. 7, Article ID 077005, 2014.

[34] L. C. Schudlo and T. Chau, "Single-trial classification of near-infrared spectroscopy signals arising from multiple cortical regions," *Behavioural Brain Research*, vol. 290, pp. 131–142, 2015.

[35] A. Myrden, A. Kushki, E. Sejdić, and T. Chau, "Towards increased data transmission rate for a three-class metabolic brain-computer interface based on transcranial Doppler ultrasound," *Neuroscience Letters*, vol. 528, no. 2, pp. 99–103, 2012.

[36] I. Aleem and T. Chau, "Towards a hemodynamic BCI using transcranial Doppler without user-specific training data," *Journal of Neural Engineering*, vol. 10, no. 1, Article ID 016005, 2013.

[37] A. Faress and T. Chau, "Towards a multimodal brain-computer interface: combining fNIRS and fTCD measurements to enable higher classification accuracy," *NeuroImage*, vol. 77, pp. 186–194, 2013.

[38] N. E. Nawa and H. Ando, "Classification of self-driven mental tasks from whole-brain activity patterns," *PLoS ONE*, vol. 9, no. 5, Article ID e97296, 2014.

[39] E. Hortal, D. Planelles, A. Costa et al., "SVM-based brain-machine interface for controlling a robot arm through four mental tasks," *Neurocomputing*, vol. 151, no. 1, pp. 116–121, 2015.

[40] S. Fazli, J. Mehnert, J. Steinbrink et al., "Enhanced performance by a hybrid NIRS-EEG brain computer interface," *NeuroImage*, vol. 59, no. 1, pp. 519–529, 2012.

[41] M. J. Khan, M. J. Hong, and K.-S. Hong, "Decoding of four movement directions using hybrid NIRS-EEG brain-computer interface," *Frontiers in Human Neuroscience*, vol. 8, no. 1, article 244, 2014.

[42] B. Koo, H.-G. Lee, Y. Nam et al., "A hybrid NIRS-EEG system for self-paced brain computer interface with online motor imagery," *Journal of Neuroscience Methods*, vol. 244, no. 1, pp. 26–32, 2015.

[43] R. Zimmermann, L. Marchal-Crespo, J. Edelmann et al., "Detection of motor execution using a hybrid fNIRS-biosignal BCI: a feasibility study," *Journal of NeuroEngineering and Rehabilitation*, vol. 10, no. 1, article 4, 2013.

[44] H. Banville, *HyBrid Brain-Computer Interfaces: Improving Mental Task Classification Performance through Fusion of Neurophysiological Modalities [Master, thesis]*, Hybrid Brain-Computer Interfaces, 2015.

[45] S. G. Hart and L. E. Staveland, "Development of NASA-TLX (Task Load Index): results of empirical and theoretical research," *Advances in Psychology*, vol. 52, pp. 139–183, 1988.

[46] J. Cegarra and N. Morgado, "Étude des propriétés de la version francophone du NASATLX," Communication présentée à la cinquième édition du colloque de psychologie ergonomique (Epique) , 2009.

[47] A. Delorme and S. Makeig, "EEGLAB: an open source toolbox for analysis of single-trial EEG dynamics including independent component analysis," *Journal of Neuroscience Methods*, vol. 134, no. 1, pp. 9–21, 2004.

[48] A. J. Bell and T. J. Sejnowski, "An information-maximization approach to blind separation and blind deconvolution," *Neural Computation*, vol. 7, no. 6, pp. 1129–1159, 1995.

[49] A. Mognon, J. Jovicich, L. Bruzzone, and M. Buiatti, "ADJUST: an automatic EEG artifact detector based on the joint use of spatial and temporal features," *Psychophysiology*, vol. 48, no. 2, pp. 229–240, 2011.

[50] G. Pfurtscheller and F. H. L. da Silva, "Event-related EEG/MEG synchronization and desynchronization: basic principles," *Clinical Neurophysiology*, vol. 110, no. 11, pp. 1842–1857, 1999.

[51] J. Kalcher and G. Pfurtscheller, "Discrimination between phase-locked and non-phase-locked event-related EEG activity," *Electroencephalography and Clinical Neurophysiology*, vol. 94, no. 5, pp. 381–384, 1995.

[52] G. Pfurtscheller, "Functional brain imaging based on ERD/ERS," *Vision Research*, vol. 41, no. 10-11, pp. 1257–1260, 2001.

[53] T. J. Huppert, S. G. Diamond, M. A. Franceschini, and D. A. Boas, "HomER: a review of time-series analysis methods for near-infrared spectroscopy of the brain," *Applied Optics*, vol. 48, no. 10, pp. D280–D298, 2009.

[54] M. Cope, D. T. Delpy, E. O. Reynolds, S. Wray, J. Wyatt, and P. van der Zee, "Methods of Quantitating Cerebral Near Infrared Spectroscopy Data," in *Oxygen Transport to Tissue X*, vol. 215 of *Advances in Experimental Medicine and Biology*, pp. 183–189, Springer, 1988.

[55] I. Guyon and A. Elisseeff, "An introduction to variable and feature selection," *Journal of Machine Learning Research*, vol. 3, pp. 1157–1182, 2003.

[56] M. L. Braun, J. M. Buhmann, and K.-R. Müller, "On relevant dimensions in kernel feature spaces," *Journal of Machine Learning Research*, vol. 9, pp. 1875–1908, 2008.

[57] S. Holm, "A simple sequentially rejective multiple test procedure," *Scandinavian Journal of Statistics*, pp. 65–70, 1979.

[58] I. Guyon, J. Weston, S. Barnhill, and V. Vapnik, "Gene selection for cancer classification using support vector machines," *Machine Learning*, vol. 46, no. 1–3, pp. 389–422, 2002.

[59] R. Gupta, H. J. Banville, and T. H. Falk, "PhySyQX: a database for physiological evaluation of synthesised speech quality-of-experience," in *Proceedings of the IEEE Workshop on Applications of Signal Processing to Audio and Acoustics, WASPAA 2015*, October 2015.

[60] J. M. Zacks, "Neuroimaging studies of mental rotation: A meta-analysis and review," *Journal of Cognitive Neuroscience*, vol. 20, no. 1, pp. 1–19, 2008.

[61] C. J. Price, "The anatomy of language: a review of 100 fMRI studies published in 2009," *Annals of the New York Academy of Sciences*, vol. 1191, pp. 62–88, 2010.

[62] A. Ischebeck, L. Zamarian, C. Siedentopf et al., "How specifically do we learn? Imaging the learning of multiplication and subtraction," *NeuroImage*, vol. 30, no. 4, pp. 1365–1375, 2006.

[63] T. Fehr, C. Code, and M. Herrmann, "Common brain regions underlying different arithmetic operations as revealed by conjunct fMRI-BOLD activation," *Brain Research*, vol. 1172, no. 1, pp. 93–102, 2007.

[64] C. E. Curtis and M. D'Esposito, "Persistent activity in the prefrontal cortex during working memory," *Trends in Cognitive Sciences*, vol. 7, no. 9, pp. 415–423, 2003.

[65] B. Kleber, N. Birbaumer, R. Veit, T. Trevorrow, and M. Lotze, "Overt and imagined singing of an Italian aria," *NeuroImage*, vol. 36, no. 3, pp. 889–900, 2007.

[66] A. Gunji, R. Ishii, W. Chau, R. Kakigi, and C. Pantev, "Rhythmic brain activities related to singing in humans," *NeuroImage*, vol. 34, no. 1, pp. 426–434, 2007.

[67] T. Ino, Y. Inoue, M. Kage, S. Hirose, T. Kimura, and H. Fukuyama, "Mental navigation in humans is processed in the anterior bank of the parieto-occipital sulcus," *Neuroscience Letters*, vol. 322, no. 3, pp. 182–186, 2002.

[68] G. Pfurtscheller and C. Neuper, "Motor imagery activates primary sensorimotor area in humans," *Neuroscience Letters*, vol. 239, no. 2-3, pp. 65–68, 1997.

[69] G. Pfurtscheller, C. Brunner, A. Schlögl, and F. H. Lopes da Silva, "Mu rhythm (de)synchronization and EEG single-trial classification of different motor imagery tasks," *NeuroImage*, vol. 31, no. 1, pp. 153–159, 2006.

[70] A. Ishai, J. V. Haxby, and L. G. Ungerleider, "Visual imagery of famous faces: effects of memory and attention revealed by fMRI," *NeuroImage*, vol. 17, no. 4, pp. 1729–1741, 2002.

17

Complexity Analysis of Resting-State fMRI in Adult Patients with Attention Deficit Hyperactivity Disorder: Brain Entropy

Gülsüm Akdeniz

Faculty of Medicine, Department of Biophysics and Yenimahalle Training and Research Hospital,
Ankara Yıldırım Beyazıt University, Ankara, Turkey

Correspondence should be addressed to Gülsüm Akdeniz; gakdeniz@ybu.edu.tr

Academic Editor: Silvia Conforto

Objective. Complexity analysis of functional brain structure data represents a new multidisciplinary approach to examining complex, living structures. I aimed to construct a connectivity map of visual brain activities using resting-state functional magnetic resonance imaging (fMRI) data and to characterize the level of complexity of functional brain activity using these connectivity data. *Methods.* A total of 25 healthy controls and 20 patients with attention deficit hyperactivity disorder (ADHD) participated. fMRI preprocessing analysis was performed that included head motion correction, temporal filtering, and spatial smoothing process. Brain entropy (BEN) was calculated using the Shannon entropy equation. *Results.* My findings demonstrated that patients exhibited reduced brain complexity in visual brain areas compared to controls. The mean entropy value of the ADHD group was 0.56 ± 0.14, compared to 0.64 ± 0.11 in the control group. *Conclusion.* My study adds an important novel result to the growing literature pertaining to abnormal visual processing in ADHD that my ADHD patients had lower BEN values, indicating more-regular functional brain structure and abnormal visual information processing.

1. Introduction

Functional magnetic resonance imaging (fMRI) is among the most powerful tools for noninvasive assessment of behavior, cognition, and psychiatric disorders [1] and is used to obtain volumetric images, including time-resolution data pertaining to human brain function. In particular, the resting-state [2] fMRI technique is a preferred, alternative tool to assess brain function abnormalities in psychiatric disorders. Blood-oxygen-level-dependent signals of resting-state fMRI allow for the analysis of functional connectivity patterns within brain networks [3] and the temporal dynamics of activity fluctuations therein [4].

The most complex living structure known to man is the human brain. The reason that complexity is assessed using resting-state fMRI, with respect to psychiatric diseases, is that complex output patterns in a living system can indicate its health and robustness [5]. Complex living systems, such as the human brain, develop to possess maximum adaptive capacity [6]. The deterioration of, and reductions in, the essential functions of these complex systems, in accordance with aging and disease, is associated with a loss of complexity in the dynamics of complex physiological systems [7]. Chaotic and complex behaviors are indicative of a healthy system, whereas more predictable and regular behaviors can denote pathological states [8].

Attention deficit hyperactivity disorder (ADHD) is a common neurodevelopmental disorder that typically begins in childhood, often persists into adulthood, and is associated with consistent deficits in error processing and inhibition and regionally decreased grey matter volume [9, 10]. Although diagnosis is made on a behavioral basis, cognitive deficits may also be significant, especially in terms of executive function [11, 12] and attentional processes [13, 14]. Numerous neuroimaging studies have been conducted on ADHD; Bush [5, 15] reviewed several functional imaging studies and observed a consistent pattern of frontal dysfunction in ADHD patients. However, few studies have examined both frontal and other brain regions [16].

Entropy, a powerful indicator of irregularity in a system [17], is not associated with the value of a random variable, but depends only on the distribution of values. Entropy can characterize the level of chaos in, and complexity of, a system, within the context of information theory [18]. In medical image processing applications, entropy provides a measure of the heterogeneity of the distribution of data in the image matrix. When all data are identical, the entropy value is zero; this value increases commensurately with differences in the data and its distribution. Entropy is a useful tool in neuroscience research for obtaining meaningful results from the analysis of fMRI data [19–21]. In previous fMRI studies, entropy was considered first as an innovative, alterative indicator [22] and then as a means of detecting activation [1]; it is viewed currently as a potential marker of brain diseases [23, 24]. Measurements of brain entropy (BEN) may be used to make inferences regarding brain status and alterations due to disease [21].

The aim of the present study was (i) to determine the complexity of visual brain activity by calculating brain entropy and (ii) to assess differences between attention deficit hyperactivity disorder patients and healthy controls in terms of brain status.

2. Material and Methods

2.1. Resting-State fMRI Data Acquisition. The fMRI images used in this study were downloaded freely from the website of the 1000 Functional Connectomes Project [25]. The gender distribution in the ADHD group ($n = 25$) was as follows: 20 males and 5 females, ranging in age between 20 and 50 years. The following scanning parameters were used: TR = 2; # slices = 39; and # timepoints = 192. The second group, comprising healthy volunteers ($n = 20$), included 8 males and 12 females between 18 and 46 years of age; in this group, the following scanning parameters were applied: TR = 2; # slices = 33; and # timepoints = 175.

All research conducted by ADHD-200 contributing sites was conducted with local IRB (institutional review board) approval and contributed in compliance with local IRB protocols. All data distributed via the International Neuroimaging Data-Sharing Initiative is fully anonymized in compliance with HIPAA (The Health Insurance Portability and Accountability Act) Privacy Rules.

2.2. Image Analysis. FEAT fMRI preprocessing analysis of the downloaded 4D fMRI data sets was performed using the FSL [26] software package. Standard preprocessing analysis includes head motion correction, temporal filtering, and spatial smoothing process. All data were filtered according to a high-pass filter cut-off value of 100 s, motion-corrected, and smoothed with a Gaussian kernel using a full width at half maximum value of 5 mm. Independent component analysis (ICA) is a computational technique for revealing hidden factors that underlie fMRI raw data. In this study, the MELODIC (Multivariate Exploratory Linear Optimized Decomposition into Independent Components) independent component analysis (ICA) technique was used to separate single fMRI data sets into different spatial and temporal components in analyzing the fMRI data. Each subject's structural image was registered to standard Montreal Neurological Institute space (i.e., to the MNI152 template) for the purposes of spatial

normalization. As a result of the analysis, components 17–44 were produced for each patient.

2.3. Entropy Calculation. Various components for each participant, including one pertaining to the most meaningful pattern of visual activation, were selected to assess complexity (one participant was excluded from the study, because no meaningful visual activation could was detected). The brain entropy values of the two sequential images most closely matched and, with the minimum degree of noise, were calculated for each subject using a program written using the MATLAB GUI (Mathworks, Inc.) software package [27]. This program was used to evaluate the brain entropy mapping from fMRI data. Entropy was calculated using Shannon's entropy as follows:

$$BEN = -\sum_{i=1}^{256} p(i) \log_2 p(i), \tag{1}$$

where $p(i)$ is the normalized probability function of the pixel intensity i of the image.

Shannon entropy is a measure of how much information is required, on average in a given discrete probability distribution. The probability function of the pixel intensities was acquired and normalized by dividing by the total pixel number.

Directly calculating BEN from fMRI data is challenging and prone to inaccuracy due to the effects of the image pixels that represent the brain tissue and to their negative correlation with entropy values. To overcome this, I segmented the images selected for BEN analysis according to their color. Profiles of five important colors were given in color image segmentation process: the background color, white, grey, blue, and red (Figure 1(a)). A display of these segmentation techniques and their application to extract white, grey, and blue colors is shown in Figure 1(b). After extraction, the remaining red color signals which do not represent the activation of occipital lobe had to be considered as an artifact and removed from the images in Figure 1(c). Figure 1 provides a flowchart of the color image processing steps necessary to calculate BEN.

2.4. Statistical Analysis. Parametric statistical analysis was performed using the Statistical Package for Social Sciences (SPSS16.0; Chicago, IL, USA) software. *t*-test was conducted for differences between the mean entropy values in the ADHD group and control group. Mann–Whitney *U* test was performed to reveal the group differences between the patient and control groups in gender and age. The relationship between the BEN and group and between gender and group was determined by using Pearson's chi-squared test.

3. Results

I have achieved fMRI components and Figure 2 depicts two example fMRI components. It should be noted that I selected and used, during calculation of BEN, only components exhibiting meaningful visual activation, such as those shown below.

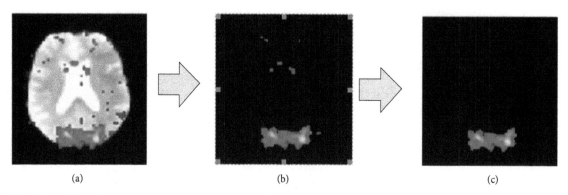

(a)   (b)   (c)

FIGURE 1: Flowchart of the color image segmentation process used to extract visual activation data: (a) fMRI image, (b) color segmentation process, and (c) a visual activation data.

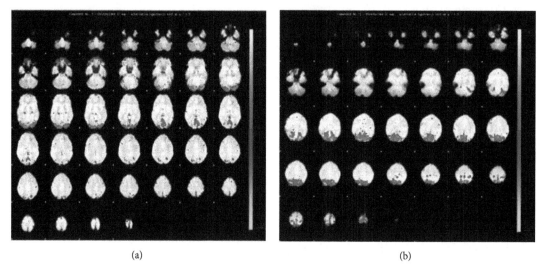

(a)   (b)

FIGURE 2: Images produced by fMRI analysis denoting visual activation in (a) an ADHD patient and (b) a control participant.

The BEN bars of the ADHD patients and controls are depicted in Figure 3. The mean entropy value of the ADHD group was 0.56 ± 0.14, compared to 0.64 ± 0.11 in the control group; this difference was significant ($p = 0.008$).

Table 1 lists the comparisons results between the patient and control groups. There were significant group differences in gender ($p = 0.010$) and age ($p = 0.045$). Data are provided as means $\pm$ SD.

On correlation analysis, there was a negative relationship between BEN and group ($r = -0.306$; $p = 0.043$) and between gender and group ($r = -0.390$; $p = 0.009$).

4. Discussion

Throughout the past decade, the majority of studies on psychiatric diseases have been fMRI-based investigations [10, 28, 29]. I studied ADHD using this technique due to the importance of functional connectivity in psychiatric diseases and because of the ability of fMRI to index this connectivity and activity within the brain. I employed BEN mapping, of functional brain connectivity, to better understand the disease.

Complexity analysis of functional brain structure [30] is a promising tool with which to examine functional brain connectivity at an organizational level [31]. The degree of complexity is associated with the number of brain connections; decreased connectivity indicates lower complexity, and increased connectivity reflects greater complexity. Numerous studies on brain activity in ADHD have been performed using functional neuroimaging techniques other than fMRI, such as electroencephalography and magnetoencephalography [32, 33]. Gómez et al. [32] demonstrated that MEG recordings of ADHD patients were more-regular compared to recordings obtained in a control group; furthermore, there were significant differences among these groups in five brain regions, that is, anterior, central, posterior, left lateral, and right lateral areas. Sokunbi et al. [34] used resting-state fMRI to demonstrate reduced complexity in the brain activity of adult ADHD patients compared to healthy, age-matched controls. van den Heuvel and Hulshoff Pol [3] suggested resting-state fMRI studies examining functional connectivity have provided a new and promising platform to examine hypothesized disconnectivity effects in psychiatric brain diseases. There has been a reawakening of interest in an alternative approach that focuses on the resting state [15]. I

TABLE 1: Comparison of group characteristics.

	ADHD ($n = 25$)	Control ($n = 20$)	Z/χ^2	p
Age	34.52 ± 9.54	29.32 ± 10.02	-2.007	0.045
Gender* (male/female)	20/5	8/11	6.699	0.010
Brain entropy (BEN)	0.56 ± 0.14	0.64 ± 0.11	-2.666	0.008
ADHD-RS				
Inattentive	16.79 ± 4.90	-	-	-
Hyperactive/impulsive	13.13 ± 5.17	-	-	-
Total	29.92 ± 8.75	-	-	-
ACDS				
Inattentive	6.59 ± 2.52	-	-	-
Hyperactive/impulsive	7.82 ± 1.33	-	-	-

Mann–Whitney U test, *Pearson's chi-squared test; ADHD-RS: ADHD-Rating Scale; ACDS: Adult ADHD Clinical Diagnostic Scale.

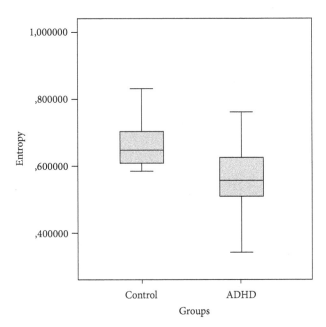

FIGURE 3: BEN bars of the ADHD patient and control groups.

investigated functional brain connectivity in occipital areas using resting-state fMRI; in contrast to previous studies, I observed a more-regular pattern of complexity, in the context of visual activities, in the patient group compared to the control group. A previous structural study reported decreased total brain and occipital lobe volume in ADHD patients [35, 36]. I suggested that this reduction in occipital lobe volume may account for the reduced functional brain connectivity, and more-regular pattern of complexity, observed in ADHD.

BEN can quantify the complexity of the functional architecture of the human brain [30], such that the BEN values I obtained during my complexity analysis provide a physiologically and functionally meaningful account of the brain activity of both ADHD patients and controls. My BEN results, obtained from fMRI image analyses, also show that individuals with ADHD exhibit lower entropy in particular brain regions compared to controls, thereby indicating a more-regular pattern of complexity. This is consistent with Goldberger and Lipsitz's model of robustness [5, 7, 37–39]

in which the complexity of a system's physiological output decreases commensurately with greater age and disease. Therefore, I proposed that entropy may represent a useful indicator for research on various brain states.

Several researchers have reported abnormal frontal-striatal brain function in patients with ADHD [40]. However, a growing number of studies also indicate abnormal posterior brain function, and associated abnormalities, in early-stage sensory information processing [41]. According to a recent meta-analysis of fMRI studies examining task-based cognition in ADHD, functional abnormalities in the visual cortex may represent a key finding in ADHD [41]. My study adds an important novel result to the growing literature pertaining to abnormal visual processing in ADHD; that is, my ADHD patients had lower BEN values, indicating more-regular functional brain structure and abnormal visual information processing. Furthermore, I demonstrated abnormalities in brain function in the occipital region using resting-state fMRI. Abnormal visual information processing in ADHD has been also identified by previous studies, consistent with my results [42, 43].

Numerous studies indicated that ADHD patients exhibit gender differences in clinical and sociodemographic characteristics [44–46]. Taken together, the results of these studies are in general agreement in terms of suggesting that young female ADHD patients exhibit lower ratings on hyperactivity, inattention, impulsivity, and externalizing problems, in addition to greater intellectual impairments and internalizing of problems, compared to young males with ADHD [37]. The prevalence of ADHD in the adult population is 4.4% in the US, of whom 38% are female and 62% are male (National Resource Center on ADHD). These data are generally supported by my study, with respect to gender differences between the study groups, but not in terms of BEN values. These results support Rubin and colleagues' study; they suggested that fMRI applications of complexity have dealt with both between the voxel and between-subject differences [30].

My BEN results indicate that excessive orderliness is not advantageous and in fact indicates abnormal function; greater complexity indicates a healthier system. I believe that using entropy analyses during fMRI may be of benefit to research in various pathologic and nonpathologic areas. Furthermore, I suggest that BEN can index brain activity and may help to determine abnormalities in brain activity, for example, in pilot studies of drug addiction [47].

In conclusion, the present study successfully demonstrated a reduction in BEN in ADHD patients compared to healthy controls, by calculating signal entropy (Shannon entropy) in accordance with the level of complexity of resting brain activity. This result supports the notion that the complexity of resting brain activity can be used as an indicator of ADHD.

References

[1] D. B. De Araujo, W. Tedeschi, A. C. Santos, J. Elias Jr., U. P. C. Neves, and O. Baffa, "Shannon entropy applied to the analysis of event-related fMRI time series," *NeuroImage*, vol. 20, no. 1, pp. 311–317, 2003.

[2] M. E. Raichle, A. M. MacLeod, A. Z. Snyder, W. J. Powers, D. A. Gusnard, and G. L. Shulman, "A default mode of brain function," *Proceedings of the National Acadamy of Sciences of the United States of America*, vol. 98, no. 2, pp. 676–682, 2001.

[3] M. P. van den Heuvel and H. E. Hulshoff Pol, "Exploring the brain network: a review on resting-state fMRI functional connectivity," *European Neuropsychopharmacology*, vol. 20, no. 8, pp. 519–534, 2010.

[4] A. Rotarska-Jagiela, V. Vande Ven, V. Oertel-Knöchel, P. J. Uhlhaas, K. Vogeley, and D. E. J. Linden, "Resting-state functional network correlates of psychotic symptoms in schizophrenia," *Schizophrenia Research*, vol. 117, no. 1, pp. 21–30, 2010.

[5] G. Bush, "Neuroimaging of attention deficit hyperactivity disorder: can new imaging findings be integrated in clinical practice?," *Child and Adolescent Psychiatric Clinics of North America*, vol. 17, no. 2, pp. 385–404, 2008.

[6] C. Wolf and D. E. J. Linden, "Biological pathways to adaptability - interactions between genome, epigenome, nervous system and environment for adaptive behavior," *Genes, Brain and Behavior*, vol. 11, no. 1, pp. 3–28, 2012.

[7] L. A. Lipsitz, "Physiological complexity, aging, and the path to frailty," *Science of aging knowledge environment: SAGE KE*, vol. 2004, no. 16, pe16 pages, 2004.

[8] R. Pool, "Is it healthy to be chaotic?" *Science (New York, NY)*, vol. 243, no. 4891, pp. 604–607, 1989.

[9] A. Mary, H. Slama, P. Mousty et al., "Executive and attentional contributions to Theory of Mind deficit in attention deficit/hyperactivity disorder (ADHD)," *Child Neuropsychology*, vol. 22, no. 3, pp. 345–365, 2016.

[10] R. Iannaccone, T. U. Hauser, J. Ball, D. Brandeis, S. Walitza, and S. Brem, "Classifying adolescent attention-deficit/hyperactivity disorder (ADHD) based on functional and structural imaging," *European Child and Adolescent Psychiatry*, vol. 24, no. 10, pp. 1279–1289, 2015.

[11] J. A. Sergeant, H. Geurts, and J. Oosterlaan, "How specific is a deficit of executive functioning for attention-deficit/hyperactivity disorder?" *Behavioural Brain Research*, vol. 130, no. 1-2, pp. 3–28, 2002.

[12] E. G. Willcutt, A. E. Doyle, J. T. Nigg, S. V. Faraone, and B. F. Pennington, "Validity of the executive function theory of attention-deficit/ hyperactivity disorder: a meta-analytic review," *Biological Psychiatry*, vol. 57, no. 11, pp. 1336–1346, 2005.

[13] O. Tucha, S. Walitza, L. Mecklinger et al., "Attentional functioning in children with ADHD - Predominantly hyperactive-impulsive type and children with ADHD - Combined type," *Journal of Neural Transmission*, vol. 113, no. 12, pp. 1943–1953, 2006.

[14] A. Pasini, C. Paloscia, R. Alessandrelli, M. C. Porfirio, and P. Curatolo, "Attention and executive functions profile in drug naive ADHD subtypes," *Brain & Development*, vol. 29, no. 7, pp. 400–408, 2007.

[15] Y. Paloyelis, M. A. Mehta, J. Kuntsi, and P. Asherson, "Functional MRI in ADHD: A systematic literature review," *Expert Review of Neurotherapeutics*, vol. 7, no. 10, pp. 1337–1356, 2007.

[16] J. R. Sato, D. Y. Takahashi, M. Q. Hoexter, K. B. Massirer, and A. Fujita, "Measuring network's entropy in ADHD: A new approach to investigate neuropsychiatric disorders," *NeuroImage*, vol. 77, pp. 44–51, 2013.

[17] S. I. Sandler, *Chemical, Biochemical, and Engineering Thermodynamics*, Wiely, New York, NY, USA, 2006.

[18] C. E. Shannon, "A mathematical theory of communication," *ACM SIGMOBILE Mobile Computing and Communications Review*, vol. 5, no. 1, pp. 3–55, 2001.

[19] E. Tavazzi, M. G. Dwyer, B. Weinstock-Guttman et al., "Quantitative diffusion weighted imaging measures in patients with multiple sclerosis," *NeuroImage*, vol. 36, no. 3, pp. 746–754, 2007.

[20] J.-L. Cui, C.-Y. Wen, Y. Hu, T.-H. Li, and K. D.-K. Luk, "Entropy-based analysis for diffusion anisotropy mapping of healthy and myelopathic spinal cord," *NeuroImage*, vol. 54, no. 3, pp. 2125–2131, 2011.

[21] G. Akdeniz, Z. Erdogan, İ. Atli, and M. İ. Atagün, "Complexity of the brain activity in the patients with schizophrenia using resting-state fMRI," in *Proceedings of the In 5th World Congress of Asian Psychiatry*, Fukuoka , Japan, 2015.

[22] R. Baumgartner, R. Somorjai, R. Summers, W. Richter, and L. Ryner, "Novelty indices: Identifiers of potentially interesting time-courses in functional MRI data," *Magnetic Resonance Imaging*, vol. 18, no. 7, pp. 845–850, 2000.

[23] D. S. Bassett, B. G. Nelson, B. A. Mueller, J. Camchong, and K. O. Lim, "Altered resting state complexity in schizophrenia," *NeuroImage*, vol. 59, no. 3, pp. 2196–2207, 2012.

[24] A. C. Yang, C.-C. Huang, H.-L. Yeh et al., "Complexity of spontaneous BOLD activity in default mode network is correlated with cognitive function in normal male elderly: A multiscale entropy analysis," *Neurobiology of Aging*, vol. 34, no. 2, pp. 428–438, 2013.

[25] NITRC, Functional Connectomes Project, 2015, http://www.nitrc.org/projects/fcon_1000/.

[26] Analysis Group FMRIB, Oxford, FMRIB Software Library, 2015, https://fsl.fmrib.ox.ac.uk/fsl/fslwiki/.

[27] The MathWorks, Inc. MathWorks, 2015, http://www.mathworks.com/.

[28] W. Gao, Q. Jiao, S. Lu et al., "Alterations of regional homogeneity in pediatric bipolar depression: A resting-state fMRI study," *BMC Psychiatry*, vol. 14, no. 1, article no. 222, 2014.

[29] J. M. Ford, V. A. Palzes, B. J. Roach et al., "Visual hallucinations are associated with hyperconnectivity between the amygdala and visual cortex in people with a diagnosis of schizophrenia," *Schizophrenia Bulletin*, vol. 41, no. 1, pp. 223–232, 2015.

[30] D. Rubin, T. Fekete, and L. R. Mujica-Parodi, "Optimizing complexity measures for FMRI data: algorithm, artifact, and sensitivity," *PLoS ONE*, vol. 8, no. 5, Article ID e63448, 2013.

[31] M. Rubinov and O. Sporns, "Complex network measures of brain connectivity: Uses and interpretations," *NeuroImage*, vol. 52, no. 3, pp. 1059–1069, 2010.

[32] C. Gómez, J. Poza, M. García, A. Fernandez, and R. Hornero, "Regularity analysis of spontaneous MEG activity in Attention-Deficit/ Hyperactivity Disorder," in *Proceedings of the 33rd Annual International Conference of the IEEE Engineering in Medicine and Biology Society, EMBS 2011*, pp. 1765–1768, USA, September 2011.

[33] A. Cerquera, M. Arns, E. Buitrago, R. Gutierrez, and J. Freund, "Nonlinear dynamics measures applied to EEG recordings of patients with Attention Deficit/Hyperactivity Disorder: Quantifying the effects of a neurofeedback treatment," in *Proceedings of the 34th Annual International Conference of the IEEE Engineering in Medicine and Biology Society, EMBS 2012*, pp. 1057–1060, USA, September 2012.

[34] M. O. Sokunbi, W. Fung, V. Sawlani, S. Choppin, D. E. J. Linden, and J. Thome, "Resting state fMRI entropy probes complexity of brain activity in adults with ADHD," *Psychiatry Research: Neuroimaging*, vol. 214, no. 3, pp. 341–348, 2013.

[35] F. X. Castellanos, J. N. Giedd, P. C. Berquin et al., "Quantitative brain magnetic resonance imaging in girls with attention-deficit/hyperactivity disorder," *Archives of General Psychiatry*, vol. 58, no. 3, pp. 289–295, 2001.

[36] F. Xavier Castellanos, P. P. Lee, W. Sharp et al., "Developmental trajectories of brain volume abnormalities in children and adolescents with attention-deficit/hyperactivity disorder," *Journal of the American Medical Association*, vol. 288, no. 14, pp. 1740–1748, 2002.

[37] A. L. Goldberger, "Non-linear dynamics for clinicians: chaos theory, fractals, and complexity at the bedside," *The Lancet*, vol. 347, no. 9011, pp. 1312–1314, 1996.

[38] A. L. Goldberger, "Fractal variability versus pathologic periodicity: Complexity loss and stereotypy in disease," *Perspectives in Biology and Medicine*, vol. 40, no. 4, pp. 543–561, 1997.

[39] A. L. Goldberger, L. A. N. Amaral, J. M. Hausdorff, P. C. Ivanov, C.-K. Peng, and H. E. Stanley, "Fractal dynamics in physiology: alterations with disease and aging," *Proceedings of the National Acadamy of Sciences of the United States of America*, vol. 99, no. 1, pp. 2466–2472, 2002.

[40] S. Durston, J. van Belle, and P. de Zeeuw, "Differentiating frontostriatal and fronto-cerebellar circuits in attention-deficit/hyperactivity disorder," *Biological Psychiatry*, vol. 69, no. 12, pp. 1178–1184, 2011.

[41] S. Cortese, C. Kelly, C. Chabernaud et al., "Toward systems neuroscience of ADHD: a meta-analysis of 55 fMRI studies," *The American Journal of Psychiatry*, vol. 169, no. 10, pp. 1038–1055, 2012.

[42] J. Wang, T. Jiang, Q. Cao, and Y. Wang, "Characterizing anatomic differences in boys with attention-deficit/hyperactivity disorder with the use of deformation-based morphometry," *American Journal of Neuroradiology*, vol. 28, no. 3, pp. 543–547, 2007.

[43] T. Sigi Hale, A. M. Kane, O. Kaminsky et al., "Visual network asymmetry and default mode network function in ADHD: An fMRI study," *Frontiers in Psychiatry*, vol. 5, article no. 81, 2014.

[44] J. Gershon, "A meta-analytic review of gender differences in ADHD," *Journal of Attention Disorders*, vol. 5, no. 3, pp. 143–154, 2002.

[45] F. Levy, D. A. Hay, K. S. Bennett, and M. McStephen, "Gender differences in ADHD subtype comorbidity," *Journal of the American Academy of Child and Adolescent Psychiatry*, vol. 44, no. 4, pp. 368–376, 2005.

[46] U. P. Ramtekkar, A. M. Reiersen, A. A. Todorov, and R. D. Todd, "Sex and age differences in attention-deficit/hyperactivity disorder symptoms and diagnoses: implications for DSM-V and ICD-11," *Journal of the American Academy of Child and Adolescent Psychiatry*, vol. 49, no. 3, pp. 217–228, 2010.

[47] J. S. ZW, Y. Li, Z. Singer, R. Ehrman, A. V. Hole, C. P. O'Brien et al., "Human brain entropy mapping using thousands of subjects and its application in a drug addiction study," in *Proceedings of the Annual Meeting of Society for Neuroscience*, 7491 pages, San Diego, Calif, USA, 2013.

18

Application of the Intuitionistic Fuzzy InterCriteria Analysis Method with Triples to a Neural Network Preprocessing Procedure

Sotir Sotirov,[1] **Vassia Atanassova,**[2] **Evdokia Sotirova,**[1] **Lyubka Doukovska,**[3] **Veselina Bureva,**[1] **Deyan Mavrov,**[1] **and Jivko Tomov**[1]

[1]*Laboratory of Intelligent Systems, University "Prof. Dr. Assen Zlatarov", 1 "Prof. Yakimov" Blvd., 8010 Burgas, Bulgaria*
[2]*Department of Bioinformatics and Mathematical Modelling, Institute of Biophysics and Biomedical Engineering, 105 "Acad. G. Bonchev" Str., 1113 Sofia, Bulgaria*
[3]*Department of Intelligent Systems, Institute of Information and Communication Technologies, 2 "Acad. G. Bonchev" Str., 1113 Sofia, Bulgaria*

Correspondence should be addressed to Sotir Sotirov; ssotirov@btu.bg

Academic Editor: George A. Papakostas

The approach of InterCriteria Analysis (ICA) was applied for the aim of reducing the set of variables on the input of a neural network, taking into account the fact that their large number increases the number of neurons in the network, thus making them unusable for hardware implementation. Here, for the first time, with the help of the ICA method, correlations between triples of the input parameters for training of the neural networks were obtained. In this case, we use the approach of ICA for data preprocessing, which may yield reduction of the total time for training the neural networks, hence, the time for the network's processing of data and images.

1. Introduction

Working with neural networks presents many difficulties; for example, the number of neurons in the perception of the individual values can be too large, and since a proportionally larger amount of memory and computing power is necessary to train the networks, this would lead to a longer periods for training. Therefore, researchers are forced to look for better methods for training neural networks. Backpropagation is the most applied such method—in it neural networks are trained with uplink (applied on a Multilayer Perceptron). There are, however, many other methods that accelerate the training of neural networks [1–3], by reducing memory usage, which in turn lowers the needed amount of computing power.

In the stage of preprocessing, the data at the input of the neural network can be used as a constant threshold value to distinguish static from dynamic activities, as it was done in [4]. This way, the amount of incidental values due to unforeseen circumstances is reduced.

Another approach is to use a wavelet-based neural network classifier to reduce the power interference in the training of the neural network or randomly stumbled measurements [5]. Here the discrete wavelet transform (DWT) technique is integrated with the neural network to build a classifier.

Particle Swarm Optimization (PSO) is an established method for parameter optimization. It represents a population-based adaptive optimization technique that is influenced by several "strategy parameters." Choosing reasonable parameter values for PSO is crucial for its convergence behavior and depends on the optimization task. In [6] a method is presented for parameter metaoptimization based on PSO and it is applied to neural network training. The idea of Optimized Particle Swarm Optimization (OPSO) is to optimize the free parameters of PSO by having swarms within a swarm.

When working with neural networks it is essential to reduce the amount of neurons in the hidden layer, which also reduces the number of weight coefficients of the neural network as a whole. This leads to a smaller dimension of the weight matrices, and hence the used amount of memory. An additional consequence from this is the decreased usage of computing power and the shortened training time [7].

Multilayer Perceptrons are often used to model complex relationships between sets of data. The removal of nonessential components of the data can lead to smaller sizes of the neural networks, and, respectively, to lower requirements for the input data. In [8] it is described that this can be achieved by analyzing the common interference of the network outputs, which is caused by distortions in the data that is passed to the neural network's inputs. The attempt to find superfluous data is based on the concept of sensitivity of linear neural networks. In [9] a neural network is developed, in which the outputs of the neurons of part of the layers are not connected to the next layer. The structure thus created is called a "Network in a Network." In this way part of the inputs of the neural network are reduced, which removes part of the information, and along with it part of the error accumulated during training and data transfer. The improved local connection method given in [9] produces a global collation by fundamental cards in the classification layer. This layer is easier to interpret and less prone to overloading than the traditional fully connected layers.

In this paper, we apply the intuitionistic fuzzy sets-based method of InterCriteria Analysis to reduce the number of input parameters of a Multilayer Perceptron. This will allow the reduction of the weight matrices, as well as the implementation of the neural network in limited hardware, and will save time and resources in training.

The neural network is tested after reducing the data (effectively the number of inputs), so as to obtain an acceptable relation between the input and output values, as well as the average deviation (or match) of the result.

2. Presentation of the InterCriteria Analysis

The InterCriteria Analysis (ICA) method is introduced in [10] by Atanassov et al. It can be applied to multiobject multicriteria problems, where measurements according to some of the criteria are slower or more expensive, which results in delaying or raising the cost of the overall process of decision-making. When solving such problems it may be necessary to adopt an approach for reasonable elimination of these criteria, in order to achieve economy and efficiency.

The ICA method is based on two fundamental concepts: intuitionistic fuzzy sets and index matrices. Intuitionistic fuzzy sets were first defined by Atanassov [11–13] as an extension of the concept of fuzzy sets defined by Zadeh [14]. The second concept on which the proposed method relies is the concept of index matrix, a matrix which features two index sets. The theory behind the index matrices is described in [15].

According to the ICA method, a set of objects is evaluated or measured against a set of criteria, and the table with these evaluations is the input for the method. The number of criteria can be reduced by calculating the correlations (differentiated in ICA to: positive consonance, negative

consonance, and dissonance) in each pair of criteria in the form of intuitionistic fuzzy pairs of values, that is, a pair of numbers in the interval $[0, 1]$, whose sum is also a number in this interval. If some (slow, expensive, etc.) criteria exhibit positive consonance with some of the rest of the criteria (that are faster, cheaper, etc.), and this degree of consonance is considered high enough with respect to some predefined thresholds, with this degree of precision the decision maker may decide to omit them in the further decision-making process. The higher the number of objects involved in the measurement, the more precise the evaluation of the intercriteria consonances (correlations). This makes the approach completely data-driven and ongoing approbations over various application problems and datasets are helping us better perceive its reliability and practical applicability.

Let us consider a number of C_q criteria, $q = 1, \ldots, n$, and a number of O_p objects, $p = 1, \ldots, m$; that is, we use the following sets: a set of criteria $C_q = \{C_1, \ldots, C_n\}$ and a set of objects $O_p = \{O_1, \ldots, O_m\}$.

We obtain an index matrix M that contains two sets of indices, one for rows and another for columns. For every p, q $(1 \leq p \leq m, 1 \leq q \leq n)$, O_p in an evaluated object, C_q is an evaluation criterion, and a_{O_p, C_q} is the evaluation of the pth object against the qth criterion, defined as a real number or another object that is comparable according to a relation R with all the other elements of the index matrix M.

$$
M = \begin{array}{c|ccccccc}
 & C_1 & \cdots & C_k & \cdots & C_l & \cdots & C_n \\
\hline
O_1 & a_{O_1,C_1} & \cdots & a_{O_1,C_k} & \cdots & a_{O_1,C_l} & \cdots & a_{O_1,C_n} \\
\cdots & \cdots & \cdots & \cdots & \cdots & \cdots & \cdots & \cdots \\
O_i & a_{O_i,C_1} & \cdots & a_{O_i,C_k} & \cdots & a_{O_i,C_l} & \cdots & a_{O_i,C_n} \\
\cdots & \cdots & \cdots & \cdots & \cdots & \cdots & \cdots & \cdots \\
O_j & a_{O_j,C_1} & \cdots & a_{O_j,C_k} & \cdots & a_{O_j,C_l} & \cdots & a_{O_j,C_n} \\
\cdots & \cdots & \cdots & \cdots & \cdots & \cdots & \cdots & \cdots \\
O_m & a_{O_m,C_1} & & a_{O_m,C_k} & & a_{O_m,C_l} & \cdots & a_{O_m,C_n}.
\end{array} \quad (1)
$$

The next step is to apply the InterCriteria Analysis for calculating the evaluations. The result is a new index matrix M^* with intuitionistic fuzzy pairs $\langle \mu_{C_k,C_l}, \nu_{C_k,C_l} \rangle$ that represents an intuitionistic fuzzy evaluation of the relations between every pair of criteria C_k and C_l. In this way the index matrix M that relates the evaluated objects with the evaluating criteria can be transformed to another index matrix M^* that gives the relations among the criteria:

$$
M^* = \begin{array}{c|ccc}
 & C_1 & \cdots & C_n \\
\hline
C_1 & \langle \mu_{C_1,C_1}, \nu_{C_1,C_1} \rangle & \cdots & \langle \mu_{C_1,C_n}, \nu_{C_1,C_n} \rangle \\
\cdots & \cdots & \cdots & \cdots \\
C_n & \langle \mu_{C_q,C_1}, \nu_{C_q,C_1} \rangle & \cdots & \langle \mu_{C_n,C_n}, \nu_{C_n,C_n} \rangle
\end{array} \quad (2)
$$

The last step of the algorithm is to determine the degrees of correlation between groups of indicators depending of the chosen thresholds for μ and ν from the user. The correlations between the criteria are called "positive consonance," "negative consonance," or "dissonance." Here we use one of the

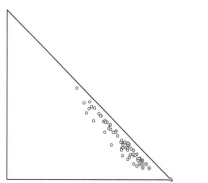 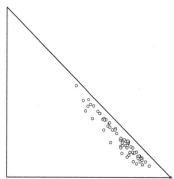 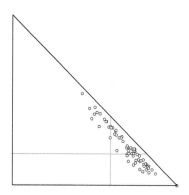

FIGURE 1: Three alternatives for constructing the subset Σ [17].

Type of correlations between the criteria
strong positive consonance [0,95; 1]
positive consonance [0,85; 0,95)
weak positive consonance [0,75; 0,85)
weak dissonance [0,67; 0,75)
dissonance [0,57; 0,67)
strong dissonance [0,43; 0,57)
dissonance [0,33; 0,43)
weak dissonance [0,25; 0,33)
weak negative consonance [0,15; 0,25)
negative consonance [0,15; 0,05)
strong negative consonance [0,05; 0]

Box 1: Type of correlations.

possible approaches to defining these thresholds, namely, the scale shown in Box 1 [16].

3. InterCriteria Analysis with Triples

The algorithm for identifying intercriteria triples is introduced in [17] by Atanassova et al.

Step 1. Starting from the input dataset of m objects measured against n criteria, we calculate the total number of $n(n-1)/2$ intuitionistic fuzzy pairs standing for the intercriteria consonances and plot these pairs as points onto the intuitionistic fuzzy triangle. Instead of maintaining a pair of two numbers for each pair of criteria C_i-C_j, namely, $\langle \mu_{ij}, \nu_{ij} \rangle$ we calculate (see [18]) for each pair the number d_{ij}:

$$d_{ij} = \sqrt{\left(1 - \mu_{ij}\right)^2 + \nu_{ij}^2} \qquad (3)$$

giving its distance from the $(1; 0)$ point, that is, the image of the complete Truth onto the intuitionistic fuzzy triangle. Our aim is to identify top-down all the $n(n-1)/2$ calculated values that are closest to the $(1; 0)$ and, at the same time, closest to each other; hence we sort them in ascending order by their distance to $(1; 0)$; see the example in Table 2.

Step 2. Let us denote with Σ the subset of the closest to $(1; 0)$ triples of criteria. The way we construct the subset Σ may

slightly differ per user preference or external requirement, with at least three possible alternatives, as listed below (see Figure 1):

(2.1) Select top p or top q% of the $n(n - 1)/2$ ICA pairs (predefined number of elements of the subset Σ).

(2.2) Select all ICA pairs whose corresponding points are within a given radius r from the $(1; 0)$ point.

(2.3) Select all ICA pairs whose corresponding points fall within the trapezoid formed between the abscissa, the hypotenuse, and the two lines corresponding to $y = \alpha$ and $x = \beta$ for two predefined numbers $\alpha, \beta \in [0; 1]$.

Step 3. Check if there are triples of criteria, each pair of which corresponds to a point, belonging to the subset Σ. If no, then no triples of criteria conform with the stipulated requirements. However, if triples are to be found, then we extend the subset Σ accordingly, by either taking a larger number p or q (Substep (2.1)), or a larger radius r (Substep (2.2)), or smaller α and/or larger β (Substep (2.3)). If now the subset Σ contains triples of criteria that simultaneously fulfil the requirements, then go to Step 4.

Step 4. We start top-down with the first pair of criteria, let it be C_i-C_j, that is, the pair with the smallest d_{ij}, thus ensuring maximal proximity of the corresponding point, say, P_{ij}, to $(1; 0)$ point. We may pick the third criterion in the triple either as C_k which is the next highest correlating criterion with C_i, that is, P_{ik} with d_{ik} ($>d_{ij}$), or as C_l which is the next highest correlating criterion with C_j, that is, P_{jl} with d_{jl} ($>d_{ij}$, noting that it is possible to have $d_{ik} = d_{jl}$). Then, we check the distances to $(1; 0)$ of the respective third points P_{jk} and P_{il}, taking that triple of criteria C_i-C_j-C_k or C_i-C_j-C_l that has the

$$\min \left(d_{ij} + d_{ik} + d_{jk}, d_{ij} + d_{il} + d_{jl} \right). \qquad (4)$$

Then for each triple of criteria C_i-C_j-C_x (where $x \in \{k, l\}$), we calculate the median point of the so formed triangle, which is a point plotted in the intuitionistic fuzzy triangle with coordinates:

$$\langle \tilde{\mu}, \tilde{\nu} \rangle = \left\langle \frac{\mu_{ij} + \mu_{jx} + \mu_{xi}}{3}, \frac{\nu_{ij} + \nu_{jx} + \nu_{xi}}{3} \right\rangle. \qquad (5)$$

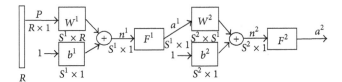

FIGURE 2: Abbreviated notation of a classical Multilayer Perceptron.

This pair gives us the level of $\langle \tilde{\mu}, \tilde{\nu} \rangle$-consonance of the whole triple. Repeat Step 4 until the number of the triples in the subset Σ is exhausted.

4. Artificial Neural Networks

The artificial neural networks [4, 19] are one of the tools that can be used for object recognition and identification. In the first step, it has to be learned and after that we can use for the recognitions and for predictions of the properties of the materials. Figure 2 shows in abbreviated notation of a classic two-layered neural network.

In the two-layered neural networks, one layer's exits become entries for the next one. The equations describing this operation are

$$a^2 = f^2 \left(w^2 f^1 \left(w^1 p + b^1 \right) + b^2 \right), \tag{6}$$

where

- (i) a^m is the exit of the mth layer of the neural network for $m = 1, 2$;
- (ii) w^m is a matrix of the weight coefficients of the each of the entries of the mth layer;
- (iii) b is the neuron's entry bias;
- (iv) f^1 is the transfer function of the 1st layer;
- (v) f^2 is the transfer function of the 2nd layer.

The neuron in the first layer receives p outside entries. The neurons' exits from the last layer determine the neural network's exits as a.

The "backpropagation" algorithm [20] is used for learning the neural networks. When the multilayer neural network is trained, usually the available data has to be divided into three subsets. The first subset, named "Training set," is used for computing the gradient and updating the network weights and biases. The second subset is named "Validation set." The error of the validation set is monitored during the training process. The validation error normally decreases during the initial phase of training, as does the training set error. Sometimes, when the network begins to overfit the data, the error of the validation set typically begins to rise. When the validation error increases for a specified number of iterations, the training stops and the weights and biases at the minimum of the validation error are returned [4]. The last subset is named "test set." The sum of these three sets has to be 100% of the learning couples.

For this investigation we use MATLAB and neural network structure 8:45:1 (8 inputs, 45 neurons in hidden layer,

and one output) (Figure 2). The numbers of the weight coefficients are $9 \times 45 = 405$.

The proposed method is focused on removing part of the number of neurons (and weight coefficients) and thus does not reduce the average deviation of the samples, used for the learning testing and validating the neural network.

5. Testing

We consider a number of C_q criteria, $q = 1, \ldots, n$, and a number of O_p measurements of cetane number of crude oil, $p = 1, \ldots, m$; that is, we use the following sets: a set of group of criteria $C_q = \{C_1, \ldots, C_n\}$ and a set of measurements of cetane number $O_p = \{O_1, \ldots, O_m\}$.

The ICA method was applied to the 140 crude oil probes, measured against 8 criteria as listed below:

- (I) density at $15°C$ g/cm^3;
- (II) 10% (v/v) ASTM D86 distillation, °C;
- (III) 50% (v/v) ASTM D86 distillation, °C;
- (IV) 90% (v/v) ASTM D86 distillation, °C;
- (V) refractive index at 20°C;
- (VI) H_2 content, % (m/m);
- (VII) aniline point, °C;
- (VIII) molecular weight g/mol.

So we work with a 140×8 table, and a software application that implements the ICA algorithm returns the results in the form of two index matrices (see Tables 1 and 2), containing, respectively, the membership and the nonmembership parts of the intuitionistic fuzzy correlations detected between each pair of criteria (28 pairs). The values in the matrix are colored in red-yellow-green color scale for the varying degrees of consonance and dissonance from green (highest values) to yellow. Naturally, each criterion best correlates with itself, which gives the respective intuitionistic fuzzy pairs $\langle 1; 0 \rangle$, or 1s and 0s, along the main diagonals of Tables 1 and 2.

In Table 3 the relations between the pairs of criteria obtained by applying the ICA method are shown.

The calculated distance d_{ij} for each pair of criteria C_i-C_j from the $(1; 0)$ point in the intuitionistic fuzzy triangle is shown in Table 4 (note that $d_{ij} \in [0, \sqrt{2}]$).

The next step is to choose the pair C_i-C_j with the smallest d_{ij}, thus ensuring maximal proximity of the corresponding point to $(1; 0)$ point. We pick the third criterion in the triple either as C_k that is the next highest correlating criterion with C_i, or as C_l that is the next highest correlating criterion with C_j, taking that triple of criteria C_i-C_j-C_k or C_i-C_j-C_l that has the $\min(d_{ij} + d_{ik} + d_{jk}, d_{ij} + d_{il} + d_{jl})$. In Table 5 the pairs of criteria C_i-C_j in "strong positive consonance," "positive consonance," and "weak positive consonance" are shown.

On the input of the neural network we put the experimental data for obtaining cetane number of crude oil. Testing is done as at the first step; all the measurements of the 140 crude oil probes against the 8 criteria are analyzed in order to make a comparison of the obtained results thereafter. For this comparison to be possible, the predefined weight coefficients

TABLE 1: Membership parts of the IF pairs, giving the InterCriteria correlations.

μ	(I)	(II)	(III)	(IV)	(V)	(VI)	(VII)	(VIII)
(I)	1	0.699	0.770	0.658	0.956	0.176	0.446	0.703
(II)	0.699	1	0.787	0.597	0.676	0.408	0.640	0.775
(III)	0.770	0.787	1	0.777	0.728	0.395	0.665	0.922
(IV)	0.658	0.597	0.777	1	0.627	0.468	0.674	0.771
(V)	0.956	0.676	0.728	0.627	1	0.134	0.404	0.661
(VI)	0.176	0.408	0.395	0.468	0.134	1	0.730	0.473
(VII)	0.446	0.640	0.665	0.674	0.404	0.730	1	0.743
(VIII)	0.703	0.775	0.922	0.771	0.661	0.473	0.743	1

TABLE 2: Nonmembership parts of the IF pairs, giving the InterCriteria relations.

ν	(I)	(II)	(III)	(IV)	(V)	(VI)	(VII)	(VIII)
(I)	0	0.288	0.217	0.326	0.042	0.822	0.552	0.295
(II)	0.288	0	0.204	0.391	0.312	0.580	0.348	0.213
(III)	0.217	0.204	0	0.212	0.261	0.595	0.325	0.068
(IV)	0.326	0.391	0.212	0	0.359	0.518	0.312	0.215
(V)	0.042	0.312	0.261	0.359	0	0.866	0.596	0.339
(VI)	0.822	0.580	0.595	0.518	0.866	0	0.270	0.527
(VII)	0.552	0.348	0.325	0.312	0.596	0.270	0	0.257
(VIII)	0.295	0.213	0.068	0.215	0.339	0.527	0.257	0

TABLE 3: Correlations between the pairs of criteria.

Type of InterCriteria Relation	Pairs of criteria
Strong positive consonance $[0.95; 1]$	(I-V)
Positive consonance $[0.85; 0.95)$	(III-VIII)
Weak positive consonance $[0.75; 0.85)$	(II-III, III-IV, II-VIII, IV-VIII, I-III)
Weak dissonance $[0.67; 0.75)$	(VII-VIII, III-V, VI-VII, I-II, I-VIII, II-V, IV-VII)
Dissonance $[0.57; 0.67)$	(III-VII, I-IV, V-VIII, II-VII, IV-V, II-IV)
Strong dissonance $[0.43; 0.57)$	(IV-VI, VI-VIII, I-VII)
Dissonance $[0.33; 0.43)$	(II-VI, V-VII, III-VI)
Weak dissonance $[0.25; 0.33)$	0
Weak negative consonance $[0.15; 0.25)$	(I-VI)
Negative consonance $[0.15; 0.05)$	(V-VI)
Strong negative consonance $[0.05; 0]$	0

and offsets that are normally random values between −1 and 1 are now established and are the same in all studies with coefficients 1.

For the learning process, we set the following parameters: performance (MSE) = 0.00001; validation check = 25. The input vector is divided into three different parts: training (70/100); validation (15/100); and testing (15/100). For target we use the cetane number ASTM D613.

At the first step of the testing process, we use all the 8 criteria listed above, in order to train the neural network.

After the training process all input values are simulated by the neural network.

The average deviation of the all 140 samples is 1,8134. The coefficient R (regression R values measure the correlation between outputs and targets) obtained from the MATLAB program is 0.97434 (see Table 6).

At the next step of the testing process, we make a fork and try independently to remove one of the columns and experiment with data from the remaining seven columns. We compare the results in the next section, "Discussion." First, we make a reduction of column 1 (based on Table 5) and put the data on the input of the neural network.

After the training process all input values are simulated. The average deviation of all the 140 samples is 1.63 and the coefficient R is 0.9772.

At the next step, we alternatively perform reduction of column 3 (according to Table 5), and put the data on the input of the neural network.

After the training process all input values are simulated. The average deviation of the all 140 samples is 1.8525 and the coefficient R is 0.97256. After that we can proceed with columns 5, 2, 8, and 4.

Now, at the next step, we proceed with feeding the neural network with 6 inputs, with the reduction of both columns, 3 and 5, according to the data from Table 5. The average deviation of all the 140 samples is 1.7644 and the coefficient R is 0.97089. In the same way we can reduce the inputs: 1 and 5, 1 and 3, 2 and 3, 3 and 8, 3 and 4, and 4 and 8, simultaneously.

At the next step, we reduce the number of inputs with one more, that is, we put on the input of the neural network experimental data from 5 inputs, with removed columns 1, 3, and 5. The average deviation of all the 140 samples is 1.857 and

TABLE 4: Distance d_{ij} for each pair of criteria C_i-C_j.

d	(I)	(II)	(III)	(IV)	(V)	(VI)	(VII)	(VIII)
(I)	0	0.416	0.316	0.473	0.061	1.165	0.783	0.419
(II)	0.416	0	0.295	0.561	0.450	0.829	0.501	0.310
(III)	0.316	0.295	0	0.307	0.377	0.849	0.467	0.104
(IV)	0.473	0.561	0.307	0	0.518	0.742	0.452	0.314
(V)	0.061	0.450	0.377	0.518	0	1.225	0.843	0.480
(VI)	1.165	0.829	0.849	0.742	1.225	0	0.382	0.745
(VII)	0.783	0.501	0.467	0.452	0.843	0.382	0	0.363
(VIII)	0.419	0.310	0.104	0.314	0.480	0.745	0.363	0

TABLE 5: Distance d_{ij} for pair of criteria C_i-C_j in positive consonance.

C_i	C_j	m_{ij}	d_{ij}	C_k	m_{ik}	d_{ik}	d_{jk}	C_l	m_{jl}	d_{il}	d_{jl}	$\min(d_{ij}+d_{ik}+d_{jk}, d_{ij}+d_{il}+d_{jl})$	Chosen triple of criteria	$\langle \tilde{\mu}, \tilde{v} \rangle$
(I)	(V)	0.956	0.061	(III)	0.770	0.319	0.377	(III)	0.728	0.319	0.377	0.756	$C_{(I)}$-$C_{(V)}$-$C_{(III)}$	$\langle 0.818; 0.173 \rangle$
(III)	(VIII)	0.922	0.104	(II)	0.787	0.295	0.310	(II)	0.775	0.295	0.310	0.709	$C_{(III)}$-$C_{(VIII)}$-$C_{(II)}$	$\langle 0.828; 0.162 \rangle$
(II)	(III)	0.787	0.295	(VIII)	0.775	0.310	0.104	(IV)	0.777	0.561	0.307	0.709	$C_{(II)}$-$C_{(III)}$-$C_{(VIII)}$	$\langle 0.828; 0.162 \rangle$
(III)	(IV)	0.777	0.307	(I)	0.770	0.319	0.473	(VIII)	0.771	0.104	0.314	0.725	$C_{(III)}$-$C_{(IV)}$-$C_{(VIII)}$	$\langle 0.823; 0.165 \rangle$
(II)	(VIII)	0.775	0.310	(I)	0.699	0.416	0.418	(IV)	0.771	0.561	0.314	1.144	$C_{(II)}$-$C_{(VIII)}$-$C_{(I)}$	$\langle 0.726; 0.265 \rangle$
(IV)	(VIII)	0.771	0.314	(VII)	0.674	0.452	0.363	(VII)	0.743	0.452	0.363	1.129	$C_{(IV)}$-$C_{(VIII)}$-$C_{(VII)}$	$\langle 0.729; 0.261 \rangle$
(I)	(III)	0.770	0.316	(VIII)	0.703	0.418	0.104	(V)	0.728	0.061	0.377	0.753	$C_{(I)}$-$C_{(III)}$-$C_{(V)}$	$\langle 0.818; 0.173 \rangle$

TABLE 6: Correlation coefficients for pair of criteria C_i-C_j according to Pearson.

C_i	C_j	Correlation coefficient C_i-C_j	C_k	Correlation coefficient C_i-C_k	C_l	Correlation coefficient C_j-C_l	max(correlation coefficient C_i-C_j+ correlation coefficient C_i-C_k; correlation coefficient C_i-C_j+ correlation coefficient C_j-C_l)	Chosen triple of criteria
(I)	(V)	0,989	(III)	0,616	(III)	0,495	1,605	(I-V-III)
(III)	(VIII)	0,971	(IV)	0,819	(II)	0,797	1,789	(III-VIII-IV)
(VI)	(VII)	0,831	(VIII)	0,024	(VIII)	0,576	1,406	(VI-VII-VIII)
(III)	(IV)	0,819	(VIII)	0,971	(VIII)	0,796	1,789	(III-IV-VIII)

the coefficient R is 0.97208 (see Table 6). In the same way are removed the parameters 2, 3, and 8 and 3, 4, and 8.

Finally, we experiment with the reduction of the fourth column, feeding the neural network with only 4 inputs. After the reduced columns 1, 2, and 4, the fourth reduced column is column 5. After the simulation the average deviation of the all 140 samples is 2.19 and the coefficient R obtained from the MATLAB program is 0.95927.

6. Discussion

In support of the method, Tables 6, 7, and 8 present the correlation coefficients between the different criteria. The tables also present the maximal values of the coefficient sums per criteria. In the last column, the triples of selected criteria are given, as sorted in the descending way by the *correlation coefficient C_i-C_j*.

In Table 9 compilations between ICA approach and correlation analysis according to Pearson, Kendall, and Spearman are shown.

The selected pairs, based on the four methods, are identical in the first row. In the second row three of the methods yield identical results (ICA, Kendall, and Spearman), and the only difference is in the selected criteria as calculated by the Pearson method. In the third row, the situation is the same. Here the triples are the same with precision of ordering. Only the triple of correlation criteria calculated by the *Pearson* method is different. In the fourth row, the triples are quite similar. The triples calculated by *ICA and Pearson* are identical. The triple determined by *Kendall* correlation coincides with the first row of the table. The last triple, defined by the *Spearman* correlation, coincides with the second and third row of the triples defined by the correlation analyses of *ICA, Pearson, and Spearman*.

So far, such a detailed comparison between the four methods has been conducted over medical [21, 22] and petrochemical [23] data. It was observed that considerable divergence of the ICA results from the results obtained by the rest of the methods is only found when the input data contain mistakes, as a result of misplacing the decimal point with at

TABLE 7: Correlation coefficients for pair of criteria C_i-C_j according to Kendall.

C_i	C_j	Correlation coefficient C_i-C_j	C_k	Correlation coefficient C_i-C_k	C_l	Correlation coefficient C_j-C_l	max(correlation coefficient C_i-C_j+ correlation coefficient C_i-C_k; correlation coefficient C_i-C_j+ correlation coefficient C_j-C_l)	Chosen triple of criteria
(I)	(V)	0,915	(III)	0,557	(III)	0,470	1,472	(I-V-III)
(III)	(VIII)	0,858	(II)	0,582	(II)	0,566	1,440	(III-VIII-II)
(II)	(III)	0,582	(VIII)	0,566	(VIII)	0,566	1,147	(II-III-VIII)
(I)	(III)	0,557	(V)	0,915	(VIII)	0,858	1,472	(I-III-V)

TABLE 8: Correlation coefficients for pair of criteria C_i-C_j according to Spearman.

C_i	C_j	Correlation coefficient C_i-C_j	C_k	Correlation coefficient C_i-C_k	C_l	Correlation coefficient C_j-C_l	max(correlation coefficient C_i-C_j+ correlation coefficient C_i-C_k; correlation coefficient C_i-C_j+ correlation coefficient C_j-C_l)	Chosen triple of criteria
(I)	(V)	0,988	(III)	0,728	(III)	0,641	1,716	(I-V-III)
(III)	(VIII)	0,962	(II)	0,762	(II)	0,753	1,724	(III-VIII-II)
(II)	(III)	0,762	(VIII)	0,753	(VIII)	0,962	1,724	(II-III-VIII)
(II)	(VIII)	0,753	(III)	0,762	(III)	0,962	1,715	(II-VIII-III)

TABLE 9

	ICA	Pearson	Kendall	Spearman
(1)	(I-V-III)	(I-V-III)	(I-V-III)	(I-V-III)
(2)	(III-VIII-II)	(III-VIII-IV)	(III-VIII-II)	(III-VIII-II)
(3)	(II-III-VIII)	(VI-VII-VIII)	(II-III-VIII)	(II-III-VIII)
(4)	(III-IV-VIII)	(III-IV-VIII)	(I-III-V)	(II-VIII-III)

least one position to the left or to the right. We anticipate in the future a theoretical research for checking the validity of this practical observation. If it proves to be true, then ICA, together with the rest three types of analysis, will turn into a criterion for data correctness.

As we stated above, reducing the number of input parameters of a classical neural network leads to reduction of the weight matrices, resulting in implementation of the neural network in limited hardware and saving time and resources in training. For this aim, we use the intuitionistic fuzzy sets-based approach of InterCriteria Analysis (ICA), which gives dependencies between the criteria and thus helps us reduce the number of highly correlating input parameters, yet keeping high enough the level of precision.

Table 10 summarizes the most significant parameters of the process of testing the neural network with different numbers of inputs, gradually reducing the number in order to discover optimal results. These process parameters are the NN-specific parameters "average deviation," "regression coefficient R," and "number of the weight coefficients."

The average deviation when we use 8 input vectors is 1.8134 with number of weight coefficients 405. By reducing the number of the inputs the number of weight coefficients is also decreased which theoretically is supposed to reduce the matching coefficient. In this case the removal of column 1 (and therefore one input is removed) causes further decreasing the average deviation of 1.6327. The additional information (without column 5) used for training the neural network is very little, and the total Mean Square Error is less. The result is better compared to the formerly used attempt by training the neural network with 8 data columns.

When we use 7 columns (and 7 inputs of neural networks) excluding some of the columns gives better result than the previous one. This shows that, while maintaining the number of weight coefficients and reducing the maximal membership in the intercriteria IF pairs, the neural network receives an additional small amount of information which it uses for further learning.

Best results (average deviation = 1.5716) are obtained by removing the two columns (6 inputs without inputs 1 and 3) with the greatest membership components of the respective d.

In this case, the effect of reducing the number of weight coefficients from 360 to 315 and the corresponding MSE is greater than the effect of the two columns.

The use of 5 columns (without columns 1, 3, and 5) leads to a result which is less than the previous, that is, 1.857. This shows that with reducing the number of weight coefficients (and the total MSE) and the information at the input of the neural network a small amount of information is lost with which the network is trained. As a result, the overall accuracy of the neural network is decreased.

TABLE 10: Table of comparison.

Number of inputs	Average deviation	Regression coefficient R	Number of the weight coefficients
8 inputs	1.8134	0.97434	405
7 inputs without input 1	1.6327	0.9772	360
7 inputs without input 3	1.8525	0.97256	360
7 inputs without input 5	1.6903	0.9734	360
7 inputs without input 2	2.1142	0.96511	360
7 inputs without input 8	1.7735	0.97511	360
7 inputs without input 4	1.9913	0.96932	360
6 inputs without inputs 3, 5	1.7644	0.97089	315
6 inputs without inputs 1, 5	1.8759	0.97289	315
6 inputs without inputs 1, 3	1.5716	0.97881	315
6 inputs without inputs 2, 3	2.0716	0.96581	315
6 inputs without inputs 3, 8	1.9767	0.97213	315
6 inputs without inputs 3, 4	1.9792	0.97163	315
6 inputs without inputs 4, 8	2.0174	0.96959	315
5 inputs without inputs 1, 3, 5	1.857	0.97209	270
5 inputs without inputs 2,3, 8	2.0399	0.96713	270
5 inputs without inputs 3, 4, 8	2.0283	0.96695	270
4 inputs without inputs 1, 2, 4, 5	2.217	0.95858	225
4 inputs without inputs 2, 3, 4, 8	2.1989	0.95927	225

The worst results (average deviation = 2.217) are obtained in the lowest number of columns—4. In this case, columns 1, 2, 4, and 5 are removed. Although the number of weight coefficients here is the smallest, the information that is used for training the neural network is less informative.

7. Conclusion

In the paper we apply the newest leg of theoretical research on InterCriteria Analysis to a dataset with the measurements of 140 probes of crude oil against 8 physicochemical criteria. On the first step we put all data from these measurements in the input of a classical neural network. After performing ICA analysis of the pairwise intercriteria correlations, we apply the recently developed method for identification of intercriteria triples in attempt to reduce the inputs of the neural network, without significant loss of precision. This leads to a reduction of the weight matrices, thus allowing implementation of the neural network on limited hardware and saving time and resources in training.

Very important aspect of the testing of the neural network after reducing some of the data (resp., the number of inputs) is to obtain an acceptable correlation between the input and output values, as well as the average deviation (or match) of the result.

Acknowledgments

The authors are thankful for the support provided by the Bulgarian National Science Fund under Grant Ref. no. DFNI-I-02-5 "InterCriteria Analysis: A New Approach to Decision Making."

References

[1] S. Bellis, K. M. Razeeb, C. Saha et al., "FPGA implementation of spiking neural networks - An initial step towards building tangible collaborative autonomous agents," in *Proceedings of the 2004 IEEE International Conference on Field-Programmable Technology, FPT '04*, pp. 449–452, December 2004.

[2] S. Himavathi, D. Anitha, and A. Muthuramalingam, "Feedforward neural network implementation in FPGA using layer multiplexing for effective resource utilization," *IEEE Transactions on Neural Networks*, vol. 18, no. 3, pp. 880–888, 2007.

[3] D. M. Karantonis, M. R. Narayanan, M. Mathie, N. H. Lovell, and B. G. Celler, "Implementation of a real-time human movement classifier using a triaxial accelerometer for ambulatory monitoring," *IEEE Transactions on Information Technology in Biomedicine*, vol. 10, no. 1, pp. 156–167, 2006.

[4] S. Haykin, *Neural Networks: A Comprehensive Foundation*, NY: Macmillan, 1994.

[5] Z.-L. Gaing, "Wavelet-based neural network for power disturbance recognition and classification," *IEEE Transactions on Power Delivery*, vol. 19, no. 4, pp. 1560–1568, 2004.

[6] M. Meissner, M. Schmuker, and G. Schneider, "Optimized Particle Swarm Optimization (OPSO) and its application to artificial neural network training," *BMC Bioinformatics*, vol. 7, article 125, 2006.

[7] S. Sotirov, V. Atanassova, E. Sotirova, V. Bureva, and D. Mavrov, "Application of the intuitionistic fuzzy InterCriteria analysis

method to a neural network preprocessing procedure," in *Proceedings of the 16th World Congress of the International Fuzzy Systems Association (IFSA) 9th Conference of the European Society for Fuzzy Logic and Technology (EUSFLAT)*, pp. 1559–1564.

[8] J. M. Zurada, A. Malinowski, and I. Cloete, "Sensitivity analysis for minimization of input data dimension for feedforward neural network," in *Proceedings of the 1994 IEEE International Symposium on Circuits and Systems. Part 3 (of 6)*, pp. 447–450, June 1994.

[9] M. Lin, Q. Chen, and S. Yan, "Network in network," arXiv preprint arXiv:1312.4400, 2013.

[10] K. Atanassov, D. Mavrov, and V. Atanassova, "InterCriteria decision making. A new approach for multicriteria decision making, based on index matrices and intuitionistic fuzzy sets," in *Issues in IFS and GN*, p. 11, 11, 1–7, 2014.

[11] K. T. Atanassov, "Intuitionistic fuzzy sets," *Fuzzy Sets and Systems*, vol. 20, no. 1, pp. 87–96, 1986.

[12] K. Atanassov, *Intuitionistic Fuzzy Sets: Theory and Applications*, Physica-Verlag, Heidelberg, Germany, 1999.

[13] K. T. Atanassov, "Intuitionistic Fuzzy Relations (IFRs)," in *On Intuitionistic Fuzzy Sets Theory*, vol. 283 of *Studies in Fuzziness and Soft Computing*, pp. 147–193, Springer Berlin Heidelberg, Berlin, Heidelberg, 2012.

[14] L. A. Zadeh, "Fuzzy sets," *Information and Control*, vol. 8, no. 3, pp. 338–353, 1965.

[15] K. T. Atanassov, *Index matrices: towards an augmented matrix calculus*, vol. 573 of *Studies in Computational Intelligence*, Springer, Cham, 2014.

[16] K. Atanassov, V. Atanassova, and G. Gluhchev, "InterCriteria analysis: ideas and problems," in *Notes on Intuitionistic Fuzzy Sets*, vol. 21, pp. 81–88, 1 edition, 2015.

[17] V. Atanassova, L. Doukovska, A. Michalíková, and I. Radeva, "Intercriteria analysis: from pairs to triples," *Notes on Intuitionistic Fuzzy Sets*, vol. 22, no. 5, pp. 98–110, 2016.

[18] V. Atanassova, D. Mavrov, L. Doukovska, and K. Atanassov, "Discussion on the threshold values in the InterCriteria decision making approach," *Notes on Intuitionistic Fuzzy Sets*, vol. 20, no. 2, pp. 94–99, 2014.

[19] M. Hagan, H. Demuth, and M. Beale, *Neural Network Design*, PWS Publishing, Boston, MA, USA, 1996.

[20] D. E. Rumelhart, G. E. Hinton, and R. J. Williams, "Learning representations by back-propagating errors," *Nature*, vol. 323, no. 6088, pp. 533–536, 1986.

[21] S. Krumova, S. Todinova, D. Mavrov et al., "Intercriteria analysis of calorimetric data of blood serum proteome," *Biochimica et Biophysica Acta (BBA) - General Subjects*, vol. 1861, no. 2, pp. 409–417, 2017.

[22] S. Todinova, D. Mavrov, S. Krumova et al., "Blood plasma thermograms dataset analysis by means of intercriteria and correlation analyses for the case of colorectal cancer," *International Journal Bioautomation*, vol. 20, no. 1, pp. 115–124, 2016.

[23] D. S. Stratiev, S. Sotirov, I. Shishkova et al., "Investigation of relationships between bulk properties and fraction properties of crude oils by application of the intercriteria analysis," *Petroleum Science and Technology*, vol. 34, no. 13, pp. 1113–1120, 2016.

Permissions

List of Contributors

Turky N. Alotaiby, Faisal M. Alotaibi and Saud R. Alrshoud
KACST, Riyadh, Saudi Arabia

Saleh A. Alshebeili
KACST-TIC in Radio Frequency and Photonics for the e-Society (RFTONICS), Electrical Engineering Department, King Saud University, Riyadh, Saudi Arabia

Daniela Sánchez, Patricia Melin and Oscar Castillo
Tijuana Institute of Technology, Tijuana, BC, Mexico

Debesh Jha, Ji-In Kim and Goo-Rak Kwon
Department of Information and Communication Engineering, Chosun University, 309 Pilmun-Daero, Dong-Gu, Gwangju 61452, Republic of Korea

Moo-Rak Choi
School of Electrical Engineering, Korea University, 145 Anam-ro, Sungbuk-gu, Seoul 02841, Republic of Korea

Leandro Juvêncio Moreira
Graduate Program in Electrical Engineering and Computing, Mackenzie Presbyterian University, Sao Paulo, SP, Brazil

Leandro A. Silva
Computing and Informatics Faculty & Graduate Program in Electrical Engineering and Computing, Mackenzie Presbyterian University, Sao Paulo, SP, Brazil

Xiguang Li, Shoufei Han, Liang Zhao, Changqing Gong and Xiaojing Liu
School of Computer, Shenyang Aerospace University, Shenyang 110136, China

Mohammad S. Islam
Department of Electrical and Computer Engineering, Florida International University, Miami, FL 33174, USA

Khondaker A. Mamun
AIMS Lab, Department of Computer Science and Engineering, United International University, Dhaka, Bangladesh

Hai Deng
Department of Electrical and Computer Engineering, Florida International University, Miami, FL 33174, USA

Nanjing University of Aeronautics and Astronautics, Nanjing, China

Jonathan-Hernando Rosales and Félix Ramos
Department of Computer Science, Cinvestav-IPN, Unidad Guadalajara, Av. del Bosque No. 1145, 45019 Zapopán, JAL, Mexico

Marco Ramos
Department of Computer Science, Universidad Autónoma del Estado de México, Instituto Literario, No. 100, 50000 Toluca, MEX, Mexico

José-Antonio Cervantes
Department of Computer Science and Engineering, Los Valles University Center, University of Guadalajara, Carretera Guadalajara-Ameca Km. 45.5, Ameca, JAL, Mexico

Alonso-Valerdi Luz María and Mercado-García Víctor Rodrigo
Escuela de Ingeniería y Ciencias, Tecnológico de Monterrey, Eugenio Garza Sada 2501, 64849 Monterrey, NL, Mexico

Bin Wang, Baojie Yang, Hui Liu and Xin Xiong
Faculty of Information Engineering & Automation, Kunming University of Science and Technology, Kunming, China

Zhengkui Weng
Faculty of Information Engineering & Automation, Kunming University of Science and Technology, Kunming, China
School of Communication and Information Engineering, Shanghai University, Shanghai, China

Jie Xue
College of Information and Network Security, Yunnan Police College, Kunming, China

Mads Jochumsen, Cecilie Rovsing, Helene Rovsing, Kim Dremstrup and Ernest Nlandu Kamavuako
Centre for Sensory-Motor Interaction, Department of Health Science and Technology, Aalborg University, Aalborg, Denmark

Imran Khan Niazi
Centre for Sensory-Motor Interaction, Department of Health Science and Technology, Aalborg University, Aalborg, Denmark

New Zealand College of Chiropractic, Auckland, New Zealand
Rehabilitation Research Institute, Auckland University of Technology (AUT), Auckland, New Zealand

Eduardo Carabez, Miho Sugi, Isao Nambu and Yasuhiro Wada
Department of Electrical Engineering, Nagaoka University of Technology, 1603-1 Kamitomioka, Nagaoka, Niigata 940-2188, Japan

Qiang Lan, Zelong Wang, Mei Wen, Chunyuan Zhang and Yijie Wang
College of Computer, National University of Defense Technology, Changsha 410073, China
National Key Laboratory of Parallel and Distributed Processing, Changsha 410073, China

Zhibin Yu, Bing Zheng, Haiyong Zheng, Nan Wang, and Zhaorui Gu
Department of Electronic Engineering, College of Information Science and Engineering, Ocean University of China, Qingdao, China

Yubo Wang
School of Life Science and Technology, Xidian University, Xián, China

Haimin Yang and Zhisong Pan
College of Command and Information System, PLA University of Science and Technology, Nanjing, Jiangsu 210007, China

Qing Tao
1st Department, Army Officer Academy of PLA, Hefei, Anhui 230031, China

Patricia Batres-Mendoza and Erick I. Guerra-Hernandez
Laboratorio de Sistemas Bioinspirados, Departamento de Ingeniería Electrónica, DICIS, Universidad de Guanajuato, Carr. Salamanca-Valle de Santiago Km. 3.5 + 1.8 Km., 36885 Salamanca, GTO, Mexico

Mario A. Ibarra-Manzano and Dora L. Almanza-Ojeda
Laboratorio de Procesamiento Digital de Señales, Departamento de Ingeniería Electrónica, DICIS, Universidad de Guanajuato, Carr. Salamanca-Valle de Santiago Km. 3.5 + 1.8 Km., 36885 Salamanca, GTO, Mexico
Cuerpo Académico de Telemática, DICIS, Universidad de Guanajuato, Carr. Salamanca-Valle de Santiago Km. 3.5 + 1.8 Km.,36885 Salamanca, GTO, Mexico

Carlos R. Montoro-Sanjose
Cuerpo Académico de Telemática, DICIS, Universidad de Guanajuato, Carr. Salamanca-Valle de Santiago Km. 3.5 + 1.8 Km.,36885 Salamanca, GTO, Mexico
Departamento de Arte y Empresa, DICIS, Universidad de Guanajuato, Carr. Salamanca-Valle de Santiago Km. 3.5 + 1.8 Km.,36885 Salamanca, GTO, Mexico

Rene J. Romero-Troncoso
Cuerpo Académico de Telemática, DICIS, Universidad de Guanajuato, Carr. Salamanca-Valle de Santiago Km. 3.5 + 1.8 Km., 36885 Salamanca, GTO, Mexico
Departamento de Ingeniería Electrónica, DICIS, Universidad de Guanajuato, Carr. Salamanca-Valle de Santiago Km. 3.5 + 1.8 Km.,36885 Salamanca, GTO, Mexico

Horacio Rostro-Gonzalez
Laboratorio de Sistemas Bioinspirados, Departamento de Ingeniería Electrónica, DICIS, Universidad de Guanajuato, Carr. Salamanca-Valle de Santiago Km. 3.5 + 1.8 Km., 36885 Salamanca, GTO, Mexico
Cuerpo Académico de Telemática, DICIS, Universidad de Guanajuato, Carr. Salamanca-Valle de Santiago Km. 3.5 + 1.8 Km.,36885 Salamanca, GTO, Mexico
Neuroscientific System Theory, Department of Electrical and Computer Engineering, Technical University of Munich, Munich, Germany

Hubert Banville, Rishabh Gupta and Tiago H. Falk
Energy, Materials, and Telecommunications, Institut National de la Recherche Scientifique, University of Quebec, Montreal, QC, Canada

Gülsüm Akdeniz
Faculty of Medicine, Department of Biophysics and Yenimahalle Training and Research Hospital, Ankara Yıldırım Beyazıt University, Ankara, Turkey

Sotir Sotirov, Evdokia Sotirova, Veselina Bureva, Deyan Mavrov and Jivko Tomov
Laboratory of Intelligent Systems, University "Prof. Dr. Assen Zlatarov", 1 "Prof. Yakimov" Blvd., 8010 Burgas, Bulgaria

Vassia Atanassova
Department of Bioinformatics and Mathematical Modelling, Institute of Biophysics and Biomedical Engineering,105 "Acad. G. Bonchev" Str., 1113 Sofia, Bulgaria

Lyubka Doukovska
Department of Intelligent Systems, Institute of Information and Communication Technologies, 2 "Acad. G. Bonchev" Str.,1113 Sofia, Bulgaria

Index

Printed in the USA
CPSIA information can be obtained
at www.ICGtesting.com
JSHW051433221024
72173JS00006B/1460